INDUSTRIAL RELATIONS
AND THE SOCIAL ORDER

◈ WILBERT E. MOORE, *Department of Economics and Social Institutions, and Office of Population Research, Princeton University*

Revised Edition   *New York*

THE MACMILLAN COMPANY

ₑ§ FOR MY PARENTS

SINCE THE PUBLICATION of the first edition of this book in 1946, industrial sociology has gained a secure place in many college curricula and in the company of professional sociologists. The intervening years have been marked not only by wide acceptance of the specialty but also by the correlative development of research and theory. If some of these developments may be traced more or less directly to the influence of the earlier edition of this book, the present edition in turn clearly owes much to them.

Purely for their possible historical interest, the following brief notes on the origin of the first edition may be recorded. During the academic year 1939–40 at the suggestion of Professor Kingsley Davis there was added to the curriculum in sociology at The Pennsylvania State College a course in "Industrial Sociology." The course was not actually offered until the following year, when it was given by the writer. As recounted in the preface to the previous edition, it was out of that course that the book developed. The manuscript was completed in the middle of 1944. Although composition and plates were completed at the beginning of 1945, wartime shortages of paper and printing facilities prevented publication until the early part of 1946.

In the most general sense, the present edition keeps the same focus as the first—the social organization of industry, and the relation of industry to society. However, major changes have been made in both organization and content. These changes have been based not only on the increased volume of research evidence now available and on the changed circumstances of industrial life, but also upon changes in the writer's views concerning the appropriate focus of sociological analysis.

Chapter I has been extensively rewritten, and Chapters XIII–XV, XVII, XXI, and XXV are entirely new with this edition. Only a small portion of Chapter XVI appeared previously. Chapters XVIII and XXIV each represent combinations of two chapters in the previous edition. Thus virtually the entire discussion of union organization and management-union relations is new, as are two chapters of Part Six. All other chapters have been rewritten in various degrees, and most of them have either substitute or additional sections.

The principal import of these changes organizationally has been to expand the coverage of Part Six, "Industry and Society," both by transfer and by addition. Aside from bringing all of the discussion "up to date" with reference to developing research and changing circumstances, the major substantive changes are three: (1) an attempt at a generalized and consistently sociological analysis of union organization and management-union relations, (2) a much greater attention to the common sociological features of industrialism in addition to the special features of American capitalism, and (3) a clearer sociological exposition of motivational problems, based in part on systematic comparative study of labor motivation in the industrialization of undeveloped areas.

References have been modernized, and many of the more "peripheral" references of the earlier edition have been discarded because of the expanding literature more closely relevant to the subject. On the other hand, the references still avoid a strict sociological parochialism with regard to professional affiliation of writers cited. For example, many of the studies on union organization and management-union relations have been made by professional labor economists. This provides no basis for ruling the studies out if they are sociologically relevant. By the same token, no apology is offered for sociological treatment of these subjects, which are certainly as near to the theoretical system of sociology as to that of economics.

My academic debts show a tendency to increase with time, without, I fear, corresponding credits. I am naturally indebted to the users and critics, whether friendly or otherwise, of the previous edition. And I should like to repeat my previous thanks to Kingsley Davis and William J. Goode. Charts were prepared by Daphne L. Notestein, and my wife, Dorothy M. Moore, again aided in preparing manuscript and indexes.

WILBERT E. MOORE

CONTENTS

ix

$\cdot \mathfrak{S}$ FIGURES

✒ TABLES

PART ONE

INTRODUCTION

ON THE NATURE OF
INDUSTRIAL SOCIOLOGY

WE LIVE in an industrial era. Nearly everything we buy and use or consume is directly or indirectly the product of the machine process. Not only our jobs but also our leisure activities are conditioned by the machine, by complex organizations of producers and distributors, by rapid communication and transportation. Most breadwinners have jobs or "positions," not trades or farms or businesses; they work for an employer, who may be an individual or a corporation or governmental agency. Even if the employer is an individual, the man who "meets the payroll" is very likely not the one who gives the worker his daily supervision; the supervisor is also an employee, and probably his supervisor in turn.

All this is commonplace and obvious. "Any fool" knows this. What merit is there in the elaboration of the obvious? None, unless obvious facts have subtle implications, unless the ordering of commonplaces yields principles of more fundamental validity because they help explain the confusing mass of things known, unless in short the effort yields greater knowledge and understanding of the nature of the modern industrial order.

This book aims at a comprehension of the peculiar features of industrial societies—the significance industry has for the state, the community, the voluntary association, the individual breadwinner. It attempts a systematic dissection and analysis of the industrial system as a social organization, and of the industrial way of life. This may be taken for the moment as the scope of *industrial sociology*.[1]

[1] There will be ample occasion in later chapters to deal with controversies over the proper aims of industrial sociology. They are largely matters of em-

A book about industrial life and industrial society must obviously limit itself somewhere. It is not possible, nor would it indeed be advisable, to range over the entire field of industrial production. This introductory chapter indicates where lines are drawn and the vantage points from which sorties are made into the sphere of industrial activity.

THE POINT OF VIEW

Goal of the Investigation. Our approach to the highly controversial field of industrial organization and relations is that of the scientific investigator and impartial observer. The discussion aims to be neither prolabor nor antilabor. No special brief is held for any one of the many interest groups which dot the American political scene. This point of view needs this early emphasis, for it may not always be apparent in the chapters that follow. The believer in any particular ethical system may view a host of scientific facts impartially, because they do not impinge upon his ethical outlook. But other facts tend to be viewed as obviously true or patently false as they seem to confirm or deny his beliefs. It may be confidently expected that the person who feels strongly about the rights of management or labor may find in any dispassionate treatment of industrial relations signs of prejudice against his particular views. Since the predominant legal and political morality in the United States, at least until fairly recent times, has strongly favored the position of the investor and manager, an objective appraisal of industrial relations is more likely to be thought prolabor than the contrary. Such is not, however, the intention.

Our guiding purpose is that of summarizing the scientific knowledge that is applicable in understanding the social aspects of industry. It will be useful from time to time to view the world from the standpoint of the laborer, the manager, or the public official, but it should be understood that fundamentally our approach coincides with no special interest save that of the impartial observer. In cases

phasis or of inferences drawn from particular studies, and can thus be most usefully discussed as the specific issue enters the organization of the materials adopted here.

of controversy over sentiments, ethics, and policies we shall act as reporters, not as combatants. For the application of science to social relationships it is important to remember that even if the participants insist on choosing up sides the observer is not playing the same game.

Applied Science in Industrial Relations. The approach here adopted for the study of industrial relations and the place of industry in society may be called that of "applied sociology." Sociologists have not generally shown much interest in industry as a field of observation and as a field of application of sociological principles; their interest has rather been turned to some of the social "problems" resulting from industrial labor and industrial dislocations. This has been in keeping with the common view that "applied sociology" is equivalent to social work or social reform. The term is used here in a quite different sense: it is the application of sociological (or social scientific) principles to the analysis of a concrete set of social relationships. To speak of this field as one of applied sociology has certain implications for general approach and specific subject matter. Thus, general principles are introduced only as they relate to specific aspects of employer-employee relations, the problems of managerial organization, or similar concrete and practical considerations. Although theory and observation must in any science proceed together, it is not proposed here to *develop* a body of scientific theory; the intention is rather to utilize available knowledge of social organization and social relationships for an understanding of industrial life and its relationship to the community. If it appears, in the course of examination of common situations in an industrial organization, that new principles may be formulated, so much the better.

"Industry" and "Industrial Relations." In the course of our investigation the terms *industry* and *industrial* will be frequently employed, often with slightly different connotations. In the most general sense, industry may be thought of as coextensive with the production of goods and services—practically synonymous with "economic organization." More specifically, industry is used to denote the orderly production of goods, as distinguished from financial and commercial activities. In a still more limited sense, industry refers to extractive and manufacturing activities, ordinarily involving the use of mechanical power. This use of the word will ordinarily exclude from the category "industry" various types of independent handicrafts and small-scale agricultural production. (Modern so-called commercial agriculture involves the extension of industrial principles into the production of food.) It is in this last sense that the term is most frequently employed in subsequent chapters of this book. It is important to note, however, that commercial, financial, and many other economic activities that are not strictly "industrial" in this narrow sense are likely to be organized along comparable lines and to present similar problems in the relation of the worker to his job. This similarity arises both from the intrinsic features of all complex rationalized work organizations and from the impact of industry as such on the rest of the economy.

In recent years industrial managers and many professional social scientists have increasingly emphasized "human relations" in industry. Incidentally, it is no mere coincidence that the growing interest in human relations in the factory parallels the rise of large and powerful independent labor unions. In previous thinking about industrial organization, it had been customary to consider the factory, shop, or mine as a big machine with human cogs. When something went wrong with these complicated social machines, it was often dismissed as being due to human irrationality or the variability (or invariability) of human nature. Only with the recognition that industrial relations are *social* relations, and that even departures from routine take place in definite directions and under definite circumstances, has it been recognized that the social scientist might be able to contribute to the understanding of industry. It is not meant to imply that only the social scientist need be consulted in order to step up the production of aluminum, or to keep the industrial peace. A large part of the facts with which this book deals are well known to industrial managers, to labor leaders, and to various specialists studying different aspects of modern economic life in general and industrial production in particular. Many of the basic materials of this book are the observations of such individuals. The literature concerning the various problems of industrial personnel, labor relations, governmental control, division of managerial labor, and so on is immense and growing. But facts gain their significance in relation to other facts. If the social scientist in industry has any virtue, it is chiefly that of "seeing industry whole": as a functioning organization made up of persons in various official and unofficial relationships, and as an organization which is in some way or other related to other organizations, to the community, and to society as a whole.

"Industrial Relations and the Social Order" accordingly has reference both to the *internal* relations within industrial organizations and to the *external* relations of industry to society. The former include not only what is ordinarily called *industrial relations* in the narrow sense—namely, the relations of management and labor—but also the whole network of organized activity that constitutes the productive system. Since the nature of the internal relationships is partly determined or modified by the character of the position of industry with respect to the larger society, both intensive and extensive examination are required for adequate appraisal of industrial relations.

Before introducing with more formality the particular subject matter with which the field of industrial sociology is concerned, a further preliminary caution may be issued. The industrial executive and the foreman, the labor leader and the labor economist, the industrial engineer and the industrial psychologist must all proceed upon the assumption that human behavior and social relationships are capable of being understood. It is dangerous if not disastrous to such understanding if the action or relationship which is not immediately understood by so-called "common" sense is dismissed by calling it a name or filing it in a well-worn pigeonhole. Such a nebulous catch-all as "human nature" covers a multitude of sins against scientific (and practical) thinking. Since in common speech it is used to explain almost everything, it follows that in fact it explains nothing. Only slightly less flagrant is the practice of evading troublesome questions by a sort of appeal to authority. The claim that the explanation of a particular social phenomenon or solution of a particular problem is "basically economic," "fundamentally psychological," "primarily a question of engineering," or "ultimately sociological" may or may not be true. Although there are real and appropriate differences of interest, emphasis, and point of view among these fields, a too-ready classification or an overzealous division of labor may defeat the practical purposes of knowledge, prediction, and control. Here at least it is improper to use the label that conceals rather than describes the product.

INDUSTRY AS A COMPLEX SOCIAL ORGANIZATION

It is a commonplace observation that the lone craftsman plying his trade is an anomaly, if he exists at all. In his place we have substituted the stereotype of a large industrial plant, with raw materials entering at one end and finished products coming out at the other. Between the raw material and the finished product, however, there is more than meets the casual eye.

Within a single mill or factory a number of persons have something to do with the operation of the organization. Nor are all these persons simply tenders of machines. There are laborers with various skills and diverse functions, and first-line supervisors who are the immediate directors of operations. There are managers, managerial assistants, and clerical workers. There are executives who formulate and direct the general policies of the organization, and perhaps a few or a host of technical specialists. It is only because of this differentiation of persons (or more properly, of positions) and activities that one may properly speak of organization at all.

The concept of organization implies an interrelationship among parts or elements—in this case, among persons. Thus one person's position places him in some definable relationship to all other persons in the organization. All this is not just much ado about nothing, nor can it be taken for granted in actual cases. The organization of an industrial plant is a *social* organization, and many concrete problems arise in reference to just these questions of position and activity. For example, the problems of authority and responsibility, of the division of labor with no gaps and no unnecessary duplication, of fitting the man to the job, of promotion and demotion, all require an understanding of the principles of cooperative activity.

It follows that every industrial plant has a "social structure": a network of reciprocal rights and obligations, supported by sentiment and formal rule. It is the general function of this structure to provide order and stability in the operation of the organization. This is chiefly accomplished by the more specific function of the structure, to provide *predictability* in the behavior and social relationships of individuals in various positions. Thus it is not only useful but necessary for continuity of production and for reasonably smooth operation of the plant for any individual to be able to predict the behavior of others with whom he is immediately or indirectly associated. This is as true of the machine operator who must depend upon those responsible for his supply of materials, the repair men who keep his machine in order, and the foreman who gives him any necessary directions—to name but a few—as for the higher executive who prides himself upon having his "finger on the pulse" of the entire unit. In considering the industrial plant as a social unit it is important to determine its fundamental structure: who does what, and why?

The industrial plant not only has a formal structure, but is, of course, a going concern. Organizational charts are dull and lifeless things unless they summarize with some degree of exactness the actual operation of the organization. In any case one must know many more things—the actual patterns of social relationships, whether formal and official (that is, in accordance with the formal division of labor and responsibility) or informal and unofficial; the prevalent sentiments and attitudes about the organization in general, or about particular rules and personalities. For example, a minor change in the interests of "efficiency" may accomplish the immediate aim and yet prove to be a net disadvantage in view of the uncertainty, dissatisfaction, or outright opposition which the change promotes. Moreover, it is not an adequate solution to such a problem to dismiss the unintended consequences as "unreasonable," however accurate that judgment may be. No matter how irrational the consequences may appear to be, they need not be completely unpredictable if one is armed with a knowledge of the interrelationships of the various parts of the system, as well as the social characteristics of the personnel. These problems will be dealt with in some detail in a subsequent section of the book, and are raised here only to illustrate the significance of the basic fact that industry is social as well as mechanical, an organized group of persons as well as an efficient grouping of machines. It is because the industrial plant is a complex social organization that the sociological viewpoint is especially useful for understanding the operation of the factory or mill.

INDUSTRIAL LIFE AND SOCIETY

For many purposes of scientific analysis as well as for many problems of practical industrial operation it is possible and proper to consider the industrial plant, the association of manufacturers, or the labor union as an isolated social unit. It is equally true that such a treatment is abstract, that is, overlooks other important aspects of industrial life and organization. The single organizational unit is related not only to the whole structure of economic production and distribution, but to the society and culture as a whole. A treatise on industrial relations which overlooked this range of social phenomena would do violence not only to logic, but to utility as well. A brief enumeration of the principal types of relationship between industry and the society of which it is a part may further clarify this general aspect of industrial relations.

1. *The Social Life of the Industrial Personnel.* Perhaps most obvious among the possible modes of relationship between industry and society is that of the social life of the industrial personnel and the bearing this has upon industrial organization, efficiency, and morale. The member of an industrial organization, whether he is an executive or an apprentice, not only has statuses and roles within the plant, but he is also a citizen, husband, father, Rotarian, Presbyterian, and so on. Nor can these other roles be completely disregarded, for they are played by the *same* concrete person and may seriously affect his strictly occupational activities. At numerous points in the subsequent chapters dealing with industrial organization it will be necessary to go outside the factory grounds to find the

sources of absenteeism, labor turnover, excessive fatigue, pressures for minimum or maximum effort, and other problems of industrial productivity. The industrial executive or personnel manager who overlooks these considerations does so at his own peril.

2. *Industry and Social Background.* One of the common errors of individuals lacking in historical or social perspective is to consider the present as the "natural" state of the social order for all times and all places. This error is often found in our times despite a rapidity of social change scarcely paralleled in human history. As an antidote for this mistaken conception it is appropriate to look at some of the social backgrounds which have made modern industrial developments possible, and have in turn undergone major transformations as the result of those developments. The tremendous increases in scientific and technological knowledge, together with the modern emphasis on efficiency, economic productivity, individual initiative, and similar basic tenets of our day, have all had a bearing on the social order as we know it. The norms of a society, whether deep-rooted in tradition or of comparatively modern invention, facilitate and restrict, modify and are modified by, industrial organization and activities.

3. *Industry and the Community.* Closely related to the first relationship noted is the place of industry in the community. This relationship is most clearly seen, and is perhaps most crucial, in the fairly small industrial center, often with but a single plant or with but a single type of manufacturing. While the diversified industries of some large cities make the interdependence of the community and its means of subsistence less obvious, the relationship is clear-cut in the "company town" or in the critical case of a community left stranded by migratory industry. Historically, one of the gravest charges made against the factory system has been the urban overcrowding that accompanied the population displacement and growth of cities. At the present time many industrial centers have become "boom towns" on a large or small scale through the expansion of war industries, and again raise fundamental social problems concerning the community's obligations to industry and industry's obligations to the community. Such questions are time-honored ground

for the investigations of social scientists and are certainly relevant for the understanding of industry's place in society.

4. Political and Legal Controls of Industrial Activity. The most controversial aspect of industry's relation to society is that concerning the appropriate amount and type of social control which should be exercised through the operation of government and the law. It is the rare individualist who will insist that the political organization of the society should not wield even the minimal control necessary to maintain the public peace and limit the more nefarious activities of the unscrupulous. But there is no real agreement as to what constitutes minimal control, and certainly no agreement as to how much further the regulation of industry ought to go. In the entire controversy there has certainly been more heat than light. One of the tasks of the scientific observer of industry therefore is to examine the interdependence of the economic and political activities of the community, and particularly the whole range of questions concerning the controls that are necessary to maintain social stability and ensure the rough compatibility of economic and other interests in the community. It is particularly important to examine the connection between increasing complexity of economic life and the increased legal control of economic organization, as well as the basis for the opposition to political control of industrial production. Some of the most fundamental problems of modern society lie in this much-debated field.

The organization of the book reflects the two major aspects of the social characteristics of industry, namely, the industrial plant as a complex social organization, and the relationship of industry to society. Parts Three, Four and Five deal with the various internal aspects of industrial organization and industrial relations, in the narrow sense. Parts Two and Six are concerned with industry and society, the former tracing the social historical and cultural setting, the latter the dynamic, or functional, relationships between industrial production and other aspects of societal organization.

It must be apparent that all of these questions constitute different aspects of a complex and interrelated industrial society and that any division is likely to be in some sense arbitrary. However, until it becomes possible to say everything important at the same time, it is necessary to start and stop somewhere.

REFERENCES

GARDNER, BURLEIGH B., and WILLIAM FOOTE WHYTE, "Methods for the Study of Human Relations in Industry," *American Sociological Review*, 11: 506–512, October 1946.

MILLER, DELBERT C., "The Social Factors of the Work Situation," *American Sociological Review*, 11: 300–314, June 1946.

MOORE, WILBERT E., "Industrial Sociology: Status and Prospects," *American Sociological Review*, 13: 382–391, August 1948.

WHYTE, WILLIAM FOOTE, ed., *Industry and Society* (New York: McGraw-Hill Book Company, Inc., 1946).

PART TWO

DEVELOPMENT OF MODERN INDUSTRY

CHAPTER II

THE FACTORY SYSTEM AND ITS FORERUNNERS

IN HISTORY all starting points and ends of epochs are arbitrary. The temporal sequence of events neither starts with the opening sentence nor stops at the end of the volume. With regard to the origins of modern industry, the standard solution to this problem has been to date all developments from the so-called *industrial revolution* around the end of the eighteenth century. Aside from the increasingly evident difficulty of determining when the industrial revolution started, when it ended, and in what it consisted, it is important for an understanding of modern large-scale production and distribution to look briefly at the principal technological, economic, and social transformations that preceded the "factory system" and converged to make it possible.

GUILD AND HANDICRAFT SYSTEMS

Modern industry has very few roots in feudalism, although some direct historical sequences can be traced. For present purposes it is not necessary to go further back than the guild and handicraft systems in order to show the social causes and social results of changing industrial relationships.

Towns and the Guilds. Over a long period of time, beginning at least as early as the eleventh century, and at different tempos and with some different results in various areas of western Europe, the immobile, self-sufficient agrarian economy of the feudal system underwent gradual relaxation and transformation. There is no need to follow all the intricacies of that development here; it is

17

sufficient to note that a variety of factors, including a gradually increasing trade and commerce and the extension of the direct power of the kings over the incipient trading centers, operated to cause establishment of a series of towns which formed an avenue of escape for the peasants and serfs previously bound to the soil. An expanding economic demand by the feudal lords, which could not be satisfied solely by enlargement of the manorial production systems, contributed to the ultimate downfall of the strictly autonomous economic life fostered by the feudal system. The towns created a market, and stimulated a market interest on the part of the lords and peasants.

The release of the laborer from traditional feudal dues and duties was thus the first significant change on the way to ultimate industrialism. The townsmen were a group of persons who had no definite status in the hierarchy of the feudal system. Veblen speaks of them as "masterless men" or men who were "ungraded." [1] From the traditional viewpoint the townsmen were very nearly socially dead, since they did not fit the system. The townsmen, however, showed embarrassing signs of life in their own world.

The establishment of the towns was a change of far-reaching importance. Independent artisans, producing for the market, banded together as approximate equals in organizations known as *guilds*. The craft guild, with which we are primarily concerned, was an organization of workers who specialized in a given craft and enjoyed the exclusive right to the practice of their trade in a local area—a right protected by public authority. Merchant guilds, generally of slightly later origin, monopolized trade in many areas on the same basis as the craft guilds monopolized production.

Occupational specialization in the earlier guilds was rarely carried beyond the finished product. That is, different stages in the productive process were not separated; the guild attempted to carry production from raw materials to market within a single organization. The guilds were a combination of trade union, manufacturers' association, mutual benefit society, and, to some extent, professional or-

[1] See Thorstein Veblen, *Absentee Ownership and Business Enterprise* (New York: B. W. Huebsch, 1923), pp. 40–49.

ganization. In the most general terms, they functioned by internal regulation of the work of the craft and external monopoly of services and production against outsiders. Control of the quality of the work depended on regulation from within the association rather than on the operation of external pressure through market competition. These regulations were strongly traditionalistic in tone and were often carried to what would now appear ridiculous extremes. Specifically, meticulous attention was given to the form and source of raw materials, the processes of production, the form of tools employed, and the quality necessary before goods could be placed on the market. These regulations may have resulted in economic benefits for the consumers, at least through standardization of quality, but were clearly designed to protect the interests of the members of the guilds by preserving their equality. A new technical process which would allow one man to produce a better product or the same product in less time was considered to be improper, and its introduction was deemed a mark of disloyalty to the group.

By controlling the supply of raw materials, the amount and type of production, and the price and the method of distribution, the guild system provided a *controlled* economic life. Internally, there was a measure of equality of opportunity within rather rigid and traditionalistic limits. The three ranks of apprentices, journeymen, and masters were in theory simply different stages in a worker's career. There was, however, some tendency for these status differences to become more rigid, and passing from a lower rank to a higher one required more time, if it could be accomplished at all.

Externally, the system was well designed to monopolize production. This monopoly was by no means automatic. The chief competitors of the guilds were monastic orders, rural craftsmen, and independent artisans. Against the first the guilds were never completely successful, although their marketing facilities were apparently superior to those of the monasteries. Against the rural craftsmen the guilds were more successful, although town merchants occasionally used this source of goods to hold down the monopolistic prices of the town producers. Within the towns the advantages to political authorities of complete organization of craft workers—

for purposes of regulation and taxation—were sufficiently numerous to give added weight to the guild demands for compulsory membership. The centrifugal tendencies did not completely disappear, however, for the guilds also attempted to limit membership and make advancement more difficult. Despite these competitive difficulties the guilds in general won the day, at least in establishing an effective if not a complete monopoly of production.

The relationship of the guild system to modern capitalistic production is certainly not direct. Our economic organization is based at least in theory upon the idea that one should have the opportunity to excel, and should have the rewards of excellence, as long as the competition is fair. The fundamental principle of the guild system was equality, with little room for differentiation. Despite these apparent and important differences, however, the guild system was important (1) for establishing a system of free labor and production for the market and (2) for its part in the sequence of economic changes which *gradually* produced capitalistic enterprise.

The Decline of the Guilds. Around the latter part of the thirteenth century some economic consequences of the guild system appeared. One of these, which may be noted as the first reason for the decline of the guilds, was inherent in the craft type of organization—*it was not at all obvious where the proper sphere of one left off and that of another began.* Gold beaters and silversmiths, for example, might each come into conflict with the guild of jewelers. It was thus possible for one guild to rise at the expense of and to the detriment of others.

With the multiplication of products and processes, specialization in terms of finished goods became confused. As production of goods requiring more distinct stages developed, separate guilds were established for different operations. Thus in textiles, four or five guilds might process the raw materials, from spinning and weaving to tailoring. These guilds often came into conflict, and such conflicts were won at times by the organization whose work required the largest capital, so that other guilds were forced into their service. Most often, however, the guild controlling the final stage of production prospered at the expense of the others, because of the importance to production of knowledge of the condition of the market. This constituted, in short, an *internal* breakdown of the guild system of production, by a type of rational development of division of labor. However, certain external circumstances—particularly a market favorable to multiplication of products and increasing refinement of processes—fostered the internal conflict.

This tendency for conflict to develop among the guilds was accompanied by a second cause of breakdown of far-reaching importance, namely, the gradual expansion of the market beyond local limits. The local craft groups became dependent upon importers for costly raw materials, and some guilds depended upon exporters as well. This meant, in fact, that the craftsman was producing for a merchant rather than a consumer. This was a minute adjustment, but important. Workers maintained "handicraft" production, but the merchant began to determine the types of goods produced. The loss of direct contact with the consumer demanded some "middleman" to bring together the labor and ability of the producer and the demands of the consumer. A further modification of productive relationships occurred when the merchant began to furnish raw materials for the craftsman, and deducted their cost from the price of the finished product.

These changes were very gradual and, taken individually, seemingly inconsequential. Taken together, and examined closely, they add up to a fundamentally different productive system. Far from controlling all stages of the productive process from raw materials to consumer, the guild depended upon a system of exchange at each end of the process. Increased complexity and specialization made every guild dependent upon the next preceding one in the productive chain for its materials, and the next succeeding one for handling its products. This involved not only the adjustment to an increased quantity and variety of impersonal circumstances beyond the control of the guildsmen—that is, the state of the market as represented by a system of exchange—but also the increased necessity of authoritarian controls to put into effect the required transformations in traditional policy. The death of the guilds was slow and relatively painless. Presently, however, they were definitely dead.

THE PUTTING–OUT SYSTEM

A further change, apparently very small but of sufficient import to prompt economic historians to give its results a distinct name, came about when the merchant began to supply the materials and agreed to take the finished product. Although in theory the worker was free to make and fulfill these obligations with various merchants in turn, his freedom over his own productive labor was further reduced by a more or less permanent debt relationship to the merchants. Other methods of control by the merchant included contracts with the entire guild for a year. The merchant did not always come from outside the guild organization, for very often he was a master who had broken traditional restraints on technical development and assumed a position of dominance through competition with his fellow craftsmen.

The demands of an expanding market placed heavier strains on the closed and meticulously regulated economy of the guild system than it was prepared to bear. By slow, and at any given time largely unnoticed, degrees a more complicated system of production and distribution, involving greater division of labor, was supplanting the simple life.

The Semblance of Craftsmanship. From the point of view of the worker the relationship remained nominally the same. The putting-out system maintained at first a semblance of individual craftsmanship. The worker could theoretically work at his own speed and as his own boss. Usually he worked in his own home or shop. In fact, this home production was such an outstanding characteristic of the whole arrangement that it is often called the *domestic* system. By and large the individual home and family remained the productive unit in the society. There was no apparent cause for alarm.

As the pressure for more and cheaper production became more acute, very nearly the whole family might engage in getting out the quota demanded by the merchant or necessary to support the family. Thus by slow degrees the older craftsmanship had to give way to standardized and fairly routine work, often facilitated by hand-powered "machines." For example, in the development of the textile industry and trade in England, hand looms were essential. These looms were rather more costly "tools" than most workers could well afford to buy, and were customarily rented or leased by the merchant to the family. In all this gradual transformation the entrepreneur was exercising greater control over the worker. The merchant, because of his contacts with market conditions and consumer demands, had to determine quality, quantity, and time of delivery of the finished goods. The craftsman had become essentially an employee.

Preface to Revolution. It must be noted that these transformations, although following a definite pattern toward increased specialization and division of labor and involving greater and greater dependence of the workman upon others, took place slowly. Moreover, the various changes which have been briefly sketched here should not be taken as definite historical stages. The tempo of change varied from one locality to another and from one "industry" to another. Various levels in the process coexisted.[2] This was all the more reason for attaching very little significance to the seemingly minute variations which might be observed in the same locality. Nevertheless, the social structure, the statuses and roles, the reciprocal rights and duties among persons in the productive process had shifted from independent artisanship to an economy largely *beyond the control of the individual workman.*

How fundamental were the structural changes may be seen from a brief summary of the situation that existed as a result of the eco-

[2] The review of developments herein presented is almost a "history without dates" and necessarily so. A sufficient number of these transformations had taken place in England by the end of the eighteenth century to give a certain uniformity to the economic life of the time. But the change from handicraft production to factory production is still going on as new products are transferred to the "machine" side of the ledger. For a fairly recent case, which very nearly duplicates the development which presumably ended in the industrial revolution, see S. McKee Rosen and Laura Rosen, *Technology and Society* (New York: The Macmillan Company, 1941), Chap. XI. This is a study of a cigar company, formerly organized on the putting-out system and only fully mechanized within the last decade. The contemporary problem of "industrial homework" indicates the persistent advantages of the domestic or putting-out system in production not requiring fixed capital. The regulation of industrial homework is discussed in Chap. XXIV.

nomic developments after the decline of the guilds and *before* the so-called industrial revolution.

1. The worker did not buy the raw materials; he worked on materials supplied by the merchant.

2. The worker did not always own the "tools" with which he worked. He rented, leased, or was loaned machines supplied by the entrepreneur.

3. The worker did not determine the type, quality, or amount of goods to be produced. He simply filled orders placed by those more aware of the condition of the market.

4. The worker did not sell the finished product to the consumer. In fact, in the full development of the putting-out system he did not own the materials but was paid on a piece-rate basis.

Of the older handicraft production there remained only production (1) under the worker's own roof (which he might also rent from the landlord-merchant) and (2) at a time and rate subject to the worker's discretion, but subject also to the reality of hunger if he were slow or dilatory. Over the course of a few centuries a "revolution" had already taken place!

FACTORY PRODUCTION

In the latter part of the eighteenth century "modern" industry got its start in the factory system. Since contemporary industrial organization and production stems directly from the first crude attempts at mass production under a single roof, it is pertinent to review some of the economic circumstances that fostered the development, as well as some of the basic features that prompted contemporaries to think that the change was revolutionary.

The factory system did not suddenly unfold out of the invention of power-driven labor-saving machines. These were important, even essential, to industrial expansion. But the factory system and industrial reorganization were revolutionary only by subsequent judgment of their far-reaching effects. The elementary social relationships of employer and employee, of capitalist and laborer, had already been developed by the rise of the merchants and the use of the putting-out system. The relation of the worker to the machine and to raw materials and the market which we associate with modern industrialism was thus not a sudden innovation. Often even the machines of the early factories were precisely those already used in the putting-out system. The change in the place of work was about the only new element in the first establishment of factories. Looked at in retrospect, this change was scarcely any more important than any one of the series of minute changes that had preceded it. It was, however, an obvious change and one which entailed wide social transformations that no contemporary witness could overlook. Some of these nonindustrial consequences of factory production are discussed later. For the moment we may limit our view simply to the causes and conditions of the transfer of production from the home to the workshop.

Although economic historians tell us that forms of shop production (as opposed to home industry) are very old and very common in human society, and often have involved rather large numbers of workers, the essentials of the factory in the modern sense are: (1) shop industry, requiring (2) fixed capital, and (3) free labor.[3]

Shop Production. Shop production means unified and coordinated production within a single establishment for that purpose. Although usually thought of as denoting a small establishment, shop in this sense might apply to manufacturing units ranging from the very small to the extremely complex. It is not even necessary that all the operations take place "under the same roof" as long as the units are located in close proximity, are interdependent, and are subject to a unified control.

There are certain inherent advantages arising from the centralization and close supervision provided by shop production, particularly for large-scale production or for manufacturing that entails a series of closely related processes. Among the advantages which early (and modern) factories enjoyed over domestic production were: minimizing the transportation of goods, especially those at different

[3] The present analysis of the principal features of the factory system and factors in its establishment follows closely the discussion of Max Weber, *General Economic History*, tr. by Frank H. Knight (New York: Greenberg, Publisher, Inc., 1927), pp. 162–164, 174–177.

stages of completion; saving of time and effort of agents and "factors"; reducing irregularities of quality and quantity resulting from inadequate supervision. It does not follow that these advantages were in every case crucial; often they were outweighed by the failure of other necessary conditions for factory production. They are, however, sufficiently important to merit the attention of those who think that the use of natural power alone "caused" the industrial revolution.

The first factories were not large, but did combine several processes in manufacturing or else brought a number of similar machines together for centralized supervision. Often the interests of the entrepreneurs were technical as well as commercial; the "capitalist" was frequently his own technical designer both for machines and for shop arrangement. Others relied chiefly on managerial ability. In any event, the impetus to further specialization and elaboration was provided by making the shop, not the craftsman, the productive unit in society.

Fixed Capital. The term *fixed capital* refers to investments in productive goods that are not easily transportable from one locality to another, or broken up into small units. A water wheel, heavy machinery, or a series of smaller machines that can be effectively operated only as interdependent units are examples of fixed capital. It was the introduction of fixed capital that often prompted transfer of production from scattered homes to a unified productive establishment. Occasionally, it is true, other advantages of the factory system (or rather of shop production) made even the use of fixed capital unnecessary. However, once established—for whatever reason or combination of reasons—the buildings and equipment became fixed capital themselves.

The early development of textile manufacturing in England, which may be taken not as typical of industrial transformation, but rather as its vanguard, illustrates the early advantages gained through centralization of production. The introduction of the power loom, together with the utilization of nonhuman energy in the form of water power, made the decentralized putting-out system definitely outmoded. There is no need here to follow through the various important inventions and innovations that gave England its supremacy in industrial production. It is simply to be noted that the establishment of the "factory system" was actually the introduction of unified production with fixed capital in one manufacturing industry in one country—cotton production in England. Why this was so will become evident from the subsequent analysis of other characteristics of factory production and the essential conditions for its successful operation.

Free Labor. The characteristic use of free labor saved capital investments in slaves, removed the risk of such investments, and made possible an insistence on technical efficiency in the labor force. This is one of the chief distinctions between the modern factory system and the "factories" of the ancient world. Actually, of course, enterprising capitalists in England and western Europe did not have to face this issue; they simply benefited, especially in England, from the presence of a large supply of cheap labor.

In the gradual disestablishment of feudalism in western Europe the lot of the peasant fell out in quite different ways. In general, the French serf became in time a free tenant or even proprietor on the ancestral plot of land. Not so the English *villein*. His complete freedom from feudal obligations was achieved for the most part much earlier than on the continent. (The principle of *mortmain* whereby the property of a peasant dying without legitimate heirs reverted to the lord or patron was maintained in France until the time of the French Revolution.) As sometimes happens, the English freeman paid for his liberty by lack of economic security. "Enclosures" which removed communal areas from the use of tenants started as early as the thirteenth century, and the process went on at an accelerating rate until, with the complete collapse of feudalism, tenants were evicted from their ancestral holdings. The extent of poverty and unemployment in England is attested by the famous Elizabethan Poor Laws of the sixteenth and early seventeenth centuries. By 1750 the tenant evictions and general agricultural poverty had created such a large unemployed population that labor supply was no problem, at least in regard to quantity. These same considerations also guaranteed that it would be cheap.

Bitter things have been written about the exploitation of labor in the early factories.[4] Some of the early social results of industrialism will be discussed in a subsequent part of this chapter. For the moment it is sufficient to repeat that an essential characteristic of modern factory production is the use of wage labor, and an adequate supply of such labor was at hand for the first factories established.

Necessary Economic Conditions. As previously noted, the establishment of factories did not simply grow out of the invention of power-driven machines. In the beginning, there was economic demand—a mass demand, fostered by the long-developing trade and commerce and greatly enhanced by colonial expansion and the opening of markets in the New World.

It was only in a situation of *large* and *steady demand* that it was possible, or at any rate profitable, to tie up investments in land, buildings, and machinery. Although laborers could be dismissed during a slack season, the material investment could not. It would often cost almost as much to maintain the plant's physical equipment during a shutdown as during full operation. It is true, as we are often told today, that the economies achieved through organized and mechanized production tended to reduce prices and thus bring many manufactured products within the purchasing power of those formerly unable to buy. But the reverse relationship—the effect of actual (or reasonably certain) demand on industrial expansion—was certainly an important consideration in the early days of the factory system and cannot be lightly dismissed even today. Moreover, it is clear that whenever specialized production is established it presumes *a monetary basis of exchange;* the manufacturer must produce for the market, not for his own use. This is further evidence of the high importance to the factory system of a pre-existing commercial development. The routes of distribution had already been established, and the idea of purchasing at least part of the necessities and comforts of life, rather than producing these within the household, was no novelty.

[4] "Exploitation" when used in reference to labor resources apparently always carries emotional overtones of condemnation which the same term does not have when used in reference to "natural" resources.

Again it was primarily in England that these necessary conditions were most fully met. Not only were there large numbers of people who were no longer "tied to the soil" and economically self-sufficient, but the expansion of British trade and commerce, particularly in the New World, had been going on for about a century and a half. The "colonial economy," whereby outlying possessions furnished raw materials for English factories and provided part of the market for finished products, was already well established by the time of the American Revolution, and continued with respect to Southern cotton long after American independence. Small wonder, then, that England is regarded as the home of the industrial revolution.

Subsequent Technical Developments.[5] Again contrary to the prevalent notion of a rapid and wholesale transformation of economic life with the introduction of the factory system, this type of production actually gained headway rather slowly until the middle of the last century. Early factories were limited by inadequate technical and scientific knowledge, particularly in the transition from human to natural sources of power, and in developing transportation and other marketing facilities. Inventions do not appear out of thin air to revolutionize industrial life, and complex inventions depend upon a combination of simpler mechanisms that precede them. Water power, for example, is limited in its usefulness as a direct source of power, not only because of possibly inadequate supply, but also because the factory locations that are satisfactory for supply of water power are not necessarily near the sources of raw materials, the markets, or transportation routes. It was thus not the application of nonhuman sources of power that was of primary importance to further expansion of mechanized production. Domestic animals, wind, and water had been used for thousands of years. It was

[5] The developments noted are, of course, of a general nature, not a catalogue of specific inventions. In a very real sense the transformations discussed are inherent in the factory system. That is, the establishment of unified and mechanized production requires certain further innovations beyond the minimum essentials of factory production. This interpretation is of course one-sided, since it overlooks the necessity of conditions favorable to industrial expansion—in the most immediate terms, an expanding market. Assuming these conditions, however, since they have in fact prevailed in the Western world during the last two hundred years, it is important to observe some of the refinements of the factory system.

transportable natural power in the form of coal that was of outstanding significance for industrial expansion, for with the invention of the steam engine heat could be transformed into energy for power-driven machinery. The power thus available was generally greater, more certain, and less restricted in use or location. Other more recent technical developments in industrial power, such as the use of petroleum products (either as an additional source of heat for steam or in the internal combustion engine), electricity, and possibly atomic energy, share with coal the advantages just noted, and in a sense are simply refinements of the basic principle of transportable power.

The greater power made possible by harnessing steam and other sources of energy required more *durable machines* if rather large investments were to be protected without too much breakage and replacement. Although iron had previously been used fairly extensively for tools, weapons, and other consumption goods, it came into its own as a part of capital or productive goods. Iron, especially when alloyed to make steel of various types, became the primary material of mechanized production. The refinement and elaboration of steel are still going on, and now as in the last century are making possible higher speeds with less wear and greater standardization of products.

The introduction and development of durable machines have of course depended in large part upon another important outgrowth of factory production—the *utilization and combination of new resources*. In response both to the demand for more efficient production and to the pressure for *diversified* production, new materials have been developed, such as aluminum, the rarer metals, and the recent plastics, and old materials have been put in new combinations. Industrial research serves the interests of large manufacturing corporations, just as the early textile factories benefited from the availability of large quantities of short-staple cotton after the invention of the cotton gin, or from the perfection of new colors and dyes.

Finally, *technical specialization and coordination* started very early in the modern industrial era. Although early factories often represented but a single stage in the productive process and comprised a collection of nearly identical machines, the advantages of combining a number of processes under one roof and with unified supervision soon became apparent. The elaboration of the technical processes for various stages in the manufacture of such a complex mechanism as a modern bomber often still prevents a complete unification within one plant. What has happened is that specialization has proceeded by leaps and bounds, with coordination taking place within the plant or division of the plant and then further coordination being provided either by over-all direction or more impersonally through contracts, agreements, or simply buying and selling on the market. It is the assembly line that symbolizes modern mass production of complicated mechanisms involving many distinct operations. Some of the units are made within the plant, some are manufactured by subsidiary plants, and some are purchased from other manufacturers. The factory system not only allows but fosters the integration of specialized activities.

A minute division of labor, directed, officially at least, toward a common goal, could scarcely be accomplished by any other system of production. Much of the remainder of this book will be concerned with the social significance of this outstanding characteristic of factory production. For it has not been simply a question of building the necessary specialized machines and putting them in the appropriate locations, but a problem, at least equally important, of organizing the human resources for production. The factory system, in other words, has produced some concrete social situations that are fairly new in human society, and the process of adjustment to these innovations has been a good deal less than automatic.

EARLY RESULTS OF THE FACTORY SYSTEM

Hitherto we have examined the economic and technical changes that preceded the factory system and the transformations made possible by factory production. This is by no means the whole story. Aside from the cultural environment that made a diversified and monetary economic life possible, which will be outlined in Part Six, there were immediate social situations that helped and hindered the industrial changes. If specialization and mass production created new social relationships within the factory, they also created new problems within society as a whole.

In casting up the social balance sheet for the factory system one would, by general consent, put on the credit side such things as "store clothes" and tufted tooth brushes, to say nothing of radios, automobiles, telephones, and other items of modern urban living, and on the debit side industrial accidents and diseases, child labor, urban slums, and unemployment. But whether the net balance would be black or red cannot be scientifically determined. This is true for a number of reasons. One cannot find universal agreement as to the side of the ledger on which some items ought to be entered. For example, there are some who do not regard the almost universal use by women of finger-nail polish and nylon hose as an unmixed blessing, or "child labor" as an unmixed evil. Even if such agreement could be found within our society, it would rest on value judgments rather than statements of fact. Not only that, but each item cannot count as one, for some are certainly considered more important than others. How these are weighted depends in general not upon scientific but upon ethical judgment. Even to speak of the "social problems" resulting from early factory production implies that situations existed that contemporary observers and subsequent reviewers found to be contrary to their conceptions of ethics, morals, or social order and stability. One must be very cautious here, for an impartial view has knowledge and understanding as its goal, not reform or pointing the finger of shame. In reviewing the social "problems" or "dislocations" resulting from the early adjustments to factory production it is therefore important to note: (1) the facts in regard to the disruption of previous patterns of social life and activities, without regard to the beneficial or harmful effects of such disruptions, and (2) what people have said and how they have acted in reference to the first set of facts, for these reactions are also important facts for an understanding of the relation of industrial production to the community and society. Rather than attempting to set off against one another the advantages and disadvantages, it will be more fruitful to examine the factors hindering factory production, and the community changes resulting from centralized direction of machines and labor.

Factors Hindering Production. The factory system, established well before 1800 in English textile manufacturing, proceeded rather slowly elsewhere and in other industries. We have already noted the convergence of economic and social transformations that facilitated factory production. However, it was not all smooth going. Factories represented a new type of investment, and one not regarded with particularly high favor by the wealthier classes whose chief interest was in land. Merchants who had accumulated a little capital under the putting-out system were the most numerous class of factory entrepreneurs, but others who had technical and managerial ability as well as enterprise often found it difficult to get the necessary capital. Apparently this caution of potential investors was not entirely mistaken, for the risk and uncertainty were certainly large. This risk was bound to be larger in the early days when transportation, the condition of distant markets, and other conditions beyond the capitalist's control but upon which he was dependent, were likely to be uncertain. Moreover, a small enterprise was scarcely equipped to weather heavy storms, since the margin of safety was often very small. The disruptive influence of wars and even piracies, of a poorly established credit system, and of capricious machines still in experimental stages of development contributed to a fairly high mortality rate for new industrial enterprises. Nor did the difficulties end there.

The factory system, it has been noted, is characterized by free contract labor, preferably cheap. In England, especially, the quantitative supply was certainly adequate. In America the availability of lands on the frontier was offset early in the nineteenth century by the recession of the frontier and a rising tide of immigration.[6] But in neither area was there any guarantee that the quality of the labor would be adequate. Machines, especially the early machines, did not remove the necessity of skilled labor; rather they demanded workers with new skills for operating the machines. The factory

[6] See Wilbert E. Moore, "Migration and Social Opportunity," *Rural Sociology*, 7: 86–89, March 1942.

system has long been charged with replacing skilled workers with machines. This is only one side of the picture, for the history of modern industrial development shows just as clearly the continual creation of positions requiring new technical abilities. The problem, however, is not completely dissolved by this observation, for the skills required are not those existing in the laboring population.

The transfer of production from the home to the factory frequently meant the necessity of drawing upon a much wider area and population than the local village or town in which the factory was located. In the early days of factory production in England there was a notable reluctance of workers to leave their homes and work in factories at some distance. During slack periods the workers had a tendency to drift back to their homes or former homes. The factories, even by standards prevalent at the time, were not exactly attractive places for work. Then, as until fairly recently, laborers were thought of as a cost of production, or at most as cogs in the industrial machine, and not as private persons. Factory discipline was harsh, the work often tedious, and the surroundings dismal. Lighting and ventilation were often rather primitive, and other conditions of work suffered by comparison with former home or shop production. Although the hours were long, this was by no means peculiar to factory production and became a grievance only because other working conditions were regarded as unsatisfactory. The wages also were low,[7] but probably did not compare too unfavorably with incomes available to the same persons elsewhere. Then, as now, complaints about wages and hours were frequently made *in view of working conditions considered unsatisfactory.*

We have already observed that the basic social structure of the factory system, as far as the relations of capitalist and laborer, employer and employee are concerned, was established before work moved to the factories. The transformation up to that point had been gradual and unobtrusive. Many changes took place while things appeared to be about the same as ever. But the establishment

[7] Contemporary evidence indicates that in 1770 the average industrial wage in England for a day of ten to twelve hours was about seven pence, or about the price of a loaf of bread. See Edward Henry Hempel, *Industrial Political Economy* (New York: Pitman Publishing Corporation, 1939), pp. 229–230.

of factories, with direct and insistent supervision of the laborer, made the relatively disadvantageous position of the employee apparent. He worked on the premises of another, often at a great distance from his home. He started work at a specified hour and stopped work when the plant closed for the day. The quality of his work was subject to constant scrutiny, as were his speed and general efficiency. If he lagged in one or the other he was reprimanded by his employer or one of his employer's representatives. The controls to which he had formerly been subject were often almost as great in net result, but they had been introduced gradually, and were in general more formal and impersonal. As an individual craftsman he was controlled by the impersonal market and the reality of hunger, not by particular persons. As an employee of a merchant under the putting-out system he was subject to the same controls, plus those of his employer whom he saw infrequently and to whom it still seemed that he was selling goods and not services. But with the factory system this illusion of liberty could no longer be maintained. That factory workers were newly conscious of their subservience is attested by many riots, acts of sabotage, disorderly strikes, and other signs of bitterness at their lot. Despite stringent laws attempting to suppress organizations of workers—some of which traced direct descent from independent guilds—machines were destroyed, tools broken, and factories burned around 1800 in England. The repressive power of the law, together with some greater regulation of working conditions, gradually reduced the effect of the opposition to industrialism on the part of labor.[8]

Ecological and Structural Changes. One of the most spectacular results of the early development of manufacturing was the widespread redistribution of the population. Cities, even rather large cities, are by no means exclusively modern novelties, but the rapid growth of rather numerous large cities is certainly an outstanding accompaniment of industrialization. The movement of the population to the factory towns and cities has been significant in itself, and important in its wider results.

Early as well as recent factories were located chiefly in reference

[8] *Ibid.*, pp. 223–228.

to sources of power, raw materials, markets, and the transportation facilities necessary to coordinate these essential factors in production. It was true that a labor supply was also necessary, but this was in general a relatively minor problem, since the mobility of labor resources could be counted on to a large degree, and not at the capitalist's expense. This meant that laborers seeking work crowded into villages, towns, and cities which were unprepared to house them. Crowded living arrangements, with meager sanitary facilities and a generally low level of living, combined to provide the dismal picture of early industrialism with which most of us are familiar.

Manchester, England, provides an interesting case in point. A center of textile products from around 1300, it saw the rise and fall of guilds and the domestic system. With a population of less than 5000 in 1650, the introduction of early factories, with a number of hand looms under a common roof, gave Manchester a population of 17,000 by 1750. The use of power looms, first with water power and subsequently with coal and steam, gave added impetus to factory development. By 1800 the population had reached 70,000. Another half century brought the number of inhabitants to 400,000. At no time during this period did housing or sanitary facilities keep pace with the expanding population.[9]

Although the growth of American cities for the most part came later, it proceeded just as rapidly and with the same general consequences.[10] The cluster of dwellings in the area surrounding the factory in a small community, or the tenement slums in the metropolitan areas, entailed many readjustments in patterns of living and social relationships for a hitherto predominantly rural population. This page in industrial history is ordinarily called black. Be that as it may, it is certainly full, for the problem has persisted with continued industrial expansion.

[9] The data are from G. H. Tupling, "Old Manchester: A Sketch of Its Growth to the End of the Eighteenth Century," *Journal of Manchester Geographical Society*, 45: 5–23, 1935, cited by Stuart Alfred Queen and Lewis Francis Thomas, *The City* (New York and London: McGraw-Hill Book Company, Inc., 1939), pp. 29–30.

[10] See Queen and Thomas, *op. cit.*, Chap. III, "The Growth of Cities since 1800."

The social changes that accompanied these ecological shifts are too numerous to be reviewed here. Many of these will be further discussed in Part Six. One basic change in the social structure was of sufficient importance to require a few words here. The character of the family, always a highly important segment of society, underwent a number of modifications with the introduction of new methods of economic production. The family under older systems of production had always been a producing unit. It actually continued to be so under the changed conditions of factory production. Although formally the same, it was in fact one thing for the whole family to engage in economic production under the domestic system, and quite another thing for the whole family to work from early morning until late at night in a factory. Although subsequent changes "reduced" the family to the role of consuming unit, early factories moved the family out of the home into the workshop. This was the beginning of the "problem" of the labor of women and children.

It is against such a background of economic history that many modern industrial problems are to be understood. Other problems can only be understood in terms of another important social innovation—the industrial corporation, discussed in the following chapter. First, however, it is appropriate to gain a little further perspective on the industrial system by turning attention to some characteristics of industrial organization where the factory is a recent and external innovation rather than the product of social evolution in the areas of early industrialization.

THE SPREAD OF THE FACTORY SYSTEM

The industrial mode of production, from its beginnings in England and Northwestern Europe, has shown a remarkable expansive power over the face of the globe. Even in the United States, where industrialism has been given its most elaborate development in terms of productivity, industry was an importation and not the outgrowth of guilds and the putting-out system. However, the American population at least shared the same historical background and traditions and the same types of economic interests were applied to markedly different resources and social conditions. These similarities have not prevailed in other areas to which industry has spread —Eastern Europe, Japan, the Soviet Union, China, India, Latin America, and many smaller areas.

As the factory system has moved to new areas it has been in each case a "foreign" importation, regardless of the degree of local initiative in sponsoring industrialization. This circumstance has two closely related implications of importance here: (1) far from developing out of the pre-existing modes of economic organization, industry in these new industrial areas commonly stands in marked contrast with locally evolved ways of producing and distributing goods; (2) there has been no necessity for complete recapitulation of the development of industrial organization and techniques, although in a rather general way some processes, such as the movement from low capitalization per worker to more capital-intensive production, have been repeated.

The important point for present purposes is that the factory system developed out of the particular combination of historic circumstances, but is no longer limited to precisely the same circumstances. Industrialism has been partially severed from its historic roots in the culture of Western Europe and its overseas outposts, and planted as an exotic plant in other climates.

Whether industrialism fares as well under conditions of state sponsorship and even ownership, or under circumstances of foreign rather than domestic investment, it now exists in such circumstances in rather important areas of the world.

Although the industrial mode of production has a very considerable adaptability to variations in market demand, quality of labor, and types of social and legal regulation, it is more often subversive of nonindustrial economies than successfully grafted to them.[11]

This result arises from the fact that certain organizational features of industrialism are intrinsic; their adaptability to varying social conditions and diverse policies is rather narrow. It follows that industrialism has common features that are not peculiarly those of capitalism in its historic sense. These features will be explored at

[11] See Wilbert E. Moore, *Industrialization and Labor: Social Aspects of Economic Development* (Ithaca: Cornell University Press, 1951).

appropriate junctures in the balance of this book. At the moment it is only important to recognize that the industrial mode of production and way of life may be inventions of the West, but they are no longer its peculiar property or problem.

REFERENCES

BEARD, CHARLES A., and MARY R. BEARD, *The Rise of American Civilization* (New York: The Macmillan Company, 1930), Vol. I, Chap. XIV, "The Sweep of Economic Forces."

COLE, G. D. H., "Industrialism," in *Encyclopaedia of the Social Sciences*, 8: 18–26.

COMMONS, JOHN R., ed., *History of Labor in the United States* (New York: The Macmillan Company, 1921), Part I, "Colonial and Federal Beginnings," by David J. Saposs (Vol. I, pp. 25–165).

COOKE TAYLOR, R. WHATELY, *The Modern Factory System* (London: Kegan Paul, Trench, Trubner & Co., 1891).

GAY, EDWIN F., "Putting Out System," in *Encyclopaedia of the Social Sciences*, 13: 7–11.

GRAS, N. S. B., *An Introduction to Economic History* (New York: Harper & Brothers, 1922), Chap. IV, "Town Economy."

HAMMOND, JOHN LAWRENCE, "Factory System," in *Encyclopaedia of the Social Sciences*, 6: 51–54.

HEATON, HERBERT, "Industrial Revolution," in *Encyclopaedia of the Social Sciences*, 8: 2–12.

KNIGHT, MELVIN M., "Handicraft," in *Encyclopaedia of the Social Sciences*, 7: 255–260.

MARX, KARL, *Capital* (New York: The Modern Library [1936]), Chap. XV, "Machinery and Modern Industry."

MOORE, WILBERT E., *Industrialization and Labor: Social Aspects of Economic Development* (Ithaca: Cornell University Press, 1951).

PIRENNE, HENRI, "Guilds, European," in *Encyclopaedia of the Social Sciences*, 7: 208–214.

ROSEN, S. McKEE, and LAURA ROSEN, *Technology and Society* (New York: The Macmillan Company, 1941), Chap. II, "Manufacture," and Chap. XI, "Machines and the Worker: A Case Study of the Cigar Industry."

SCHLESINGER, A. M., *Political and Social History of the United States, 1829–1925* (New York: The Macmillan Company, 1926), Chap. I, "The Rise of the Common Man."

TODD, ARTHUR JAMES, *Industry and Society* (New York: Henry Holt and Company, Inc., 1933), Chap. V. "The Earlier Background of Modern

Industrialism"; Chap. VI, "Later Phases of the Industrial Revolution: The So-Called Age of Man."

VEBLEN, THORSTEIN, *Absentee Ownership and Business Enterprise* (New York: B. W. Huebsch, 1923), Chap. III, "Law and Custom in Recent Times: I. Handicraft and Natural Right."

————, *Imperial Germany and the Industrial Revolution* (New York: The Viking Press, 1939), Chap. VI, "The Industrial Revolution in Germany."

————, *The Instinct of Workmanship* (New York: The Macmillan Company, 1914), Chap. VI, "The Era of Handicraft," and Chap. VII, "The Machine Industry."

WEBER, MAX, *General Economic History*, tr. by Frank H. Knight (New York: Greenberg Publisher, Inc., 1927), Chap. IX, "The Craft Guilds"; Chap. X, "The Origin of the European Guilds"; Chap. XI, "Disintegration of the Guilds and the Development of the Domestic System"; Chap. XII, "Shop Production; The Factory and Its Fore-Runners."

CHAPTER III

THE CORPORATION AND
PROFESSIONAL MANAGEMENT

THE EARLY factories were chiefly the handiwork of single individuals with money to invest and sufficient technical or managerial ability to secure a return on the investment. As an organizer and manager, as well as investor, the individual industrialist has been known as an *entrepreneur*. In his relations with laborers he was known as an *employer*. The traditional culture of capitalism has usually made the "entrepreneur" the central figure in the industrial scene. If our economic system is "capitalistic," it is seemingly an obvious conclusion that the "capitalist" runs the show.

With this chapter, however, we turn to a consideration of the modern organization of industry. And the first aspect of that organization which strikes the eye is that, although the old-style entrepreneurs are not an extinct species, their numbers are decreasing and their importance sadly diminished. The picture of the capitalist managing his own plant, employing fifty to a hundred laborers, is not a false picture; on the other hand, it is not typical of contemporary industrial organization. What has happened in the organization of productive enterprise to eclipse the importance of the captain of industry is indicated in a general way by the title of this chapter: the corporation and professional management. Just how this came about and what it means for the social relations in industry the present chapter and the five chapters of Part Three will attempt to show.

Although individual enterprise as understood in the classical theory of industrial capitalism has not exactly passed from the scene, the bulk of American manufacturing is done in plants that are not owned and managed by single individuals.[1] Moreover, it is the large, rather than the small, industrial enterprise which dominates and sets the pace in contemporary production. This transformation from small to "big" business has largely been made possible by a rather recent *social* invention: the corporation.

NATURE OF THE CORPORATION

The corporation as an officially constituted group of persons acting as a unity is very old. Any society with a legal structure sufficiently formal to recognize the elementary social principle that a number of persons may combine for their mutual advantage probably has some provision for treating such combinations as distinct entities. Yet the modern corporation is truly modern in its peculiar status in society, and in the unique combination of principles which guarantee its economic importance. In Roman law two types of combinations were recognized, neither one of which was a close approximation to the modern corporation. The *societas* was a purely voluntary association. Although for some purposes it was accounted a group, its rights and obligations actually rested with the members, individually and separately. The *universitas* was something more like the modern corporation, since it was treated as an entity, but it had no legal existence apart from the state. It was simply regarded as an official agency (something like a modern governmental bureau) to which the individual member owed various duties, but which was not regarded as in any sense a private organization.

Origin of the Modern Corporation. The independent corporation, between the two Roman types, seems to have been a Germanic invention. In its early forms it antedated industrial capitalism, since it was a response to the problem posed by large-scale overland and overseas trade and commerce. That problem was in reality a dual one: the cost of capital equipment (ships, warehouses, wharves,

[1] An estimate of the situation in 1929 indicated that about ninety-four per cent of all manufactured products were made by corporations. See Adolf A. Berle, Jr., and Gardiner C. Means, *The Modern Corporation and Private Property* (New York: The Macmillan Company, 1933), p. 39.

etc.) and the risk of loss in transit. Although some earlier Italian combinations had been formed, chiefly on the basis of extended partnerships, the merchants of the Hanseatic League found it to their advantage to establish their commercial ventures on a more permanent footing and to spread profits or losses over a longer time. The two commercial corporations (or joint stock companies) which marked the acme of this type of organization were the Dutch East India Company and the British East India Company. The latter company in particular became so extended in its enterprises that it had its own army and navy and for a number of years constituted the political government of India. In the light of this early corporation history, some of the modern civic and political activities of large corporations may not appear so strange.

Not only was the social invention of the corporation a response to commercial and similar economic interests, but its acceptance paved the way for an industrial development of a quite different character than would have been possible without such combinations.

Limited Liability and Corporate Unity. Whatever the economic pressures and advantages embodied in the formation of the corporation, this manner of mutual association owes much to the law and to lawyers. For it is in the elaboration of the legal theory of corporate enterprise that the privileges and limitations of collective economic action are to be found. The lawyers started (and the presumption remains in the Anglo-American legal system) with the premise that the state can grant a *franchise* or freedom to a group of persons to carry on certain activities, subject to the limitations set forth in the original terms of the agreement. But, as pointed out in a famous work on the modern corporation,

The real privilege which the state grants is that of corporate entity—the right to maintain business in its own name, to sue and be sued on its own behalf irrespective of the individuals; to have perpetual succession—i.e., to continue this entity although the individuals in it changed. From all this necessarily flowed a limited liability of the associates. Since only the entity was liable for debts, which did not attach to the various individuals, it followed that a stockholder was not normally liable for any of the debts of the enterprise; and he could thus embark a particular amount of capital in the corporate affairs without becoming responsible beyond this amount, for the corporate debts.[2]

An outstanding innovation of the corporation, therefore, was the limitation of liability for the debts of the enterprise. A partnership is in the eyes of the law simply an agreement to do business jointly, but each partner is individually held responsible for the whole. Whereas the partnership is simply a voluntary arrangement among distinct persons, the corporation is recognized as a legal entity, apart from its membership. Thus these organizations are said to have *corporate personality,* which means that for most purposes of administrative and civil law (although usually not for criminal law) the corporation is treated *as if* it were in fact a private person.

The unitary character of the corporation, moreover, plus the advantage of limited liability, made possible or at least facilitated the tapping of a much larger amount of capital than could a manageable group of investors in partnership. Except, apparently, for the perennially amusing cases of law and brokerage firms (such as Smith, Smith, Smith, Smith, and Jones) extensive partnerships are unwieldy, and it is difficult for them to arrive at a quick decision. The invention of the share of stock as a unit of participation in industrial enterprise opened up the individually small but cumulatively large sources of capital of the small investor. Trust funds, small savings accounts, and all manner of small amounts of money were no longer limited to direct loan on mortgages or to the money-lending activities of banking establishments. Outside of metropolitan areas with regular stock exchanges and brokerage houses, the banks and similar financial concerns became salesmen for stock issues, more or less sound. By purchasing shares ranging from "wild-cat stocks" to "gilt-edged securities" (the predictions were often erroneous in both cases), many ordinary citizens became participants in Big Business.

The Nature of Corporate Ownership.[3] The law of corporations is one of the most complex features of our legal system, and its principles

---

[2] Berle and Means, *op. cit.,* pp. 128–129. (Quoted by permission of The Macmillan Company, Publishers.) See also the article "Corporation" by the same authors in *Encyclopaedia of the Social Sciences,* 4: 414–423.

[3] Several of the following paragraphs appeared in a slightly different form in Wilbert E. Moore, "The Emergence of New Property Conceptions in America,"

are by no means certain or consistent. One major reason for the complexity and uncertainty is that it is actually difficult in theory, and more difficult in practice, to maintain a clear-cut distinction between the organization as a legal person, and the character and activities of the "actual" persons who constitute its membership.

This is an outstanding problem in the assignment of personal responsibility for the actions of the impersonal "corporate personality." A manufacturing corporation is actually made up of a great many persons who have many different rights and duties in regard to the organization as a whole. Our first concern, however, is not with those persons who may be regarded as employees of the corporation, but rather with those who "own" the business. That is, the problem arises as to who controls the policies of the enterprise and benefits from its operation. And this problem arises precisely because the personality of the corporation is for many purposes *only a legal fiction.*

This is not so difficult a position to maintain, or even so "fictional" as is sometimes claimed, if one is aware of the existence and importance of organized groups as social units. But the legal theory of the corporation cannot stop simply with the organized unit and assume that the internal distribution of privileges is communal, or at least of no legal concern. Actually the corporation is normally a device for unitary control and action in the interests of numerous persons with various claims upon the organization.

Viewed as a private organization comparable in purpose and general activity to the individual manufacturing or commercial enterprise or the partnership, the corporation is made up of stockholders. The theory of this organization of official ownership and control is a type of application of the democratic theory of government. That is, each unit in the total system is given as much weight as every other unit: each counts as one. The initial peculiarity of corporate democracy, however, is in the nature of the unit—the share of stock, not the stockholder. It is not sufficient to say, therefore, even in theory, that the managers of a corporation are

Journal of Legal and Political Sociology, 1 (3–4): 34–58, April 1943. Reprinted by permission of the editors.

the elected representatives of the stockholders; they are representatives of the shares of stock. Put in terms which are only slightly oversimplified, the corporation in legal theory is a fictional person whose behavior is determined by its elements, which are pieces of paper.

The corporation in contemporary economic life does not completely fulfill the expectations of the legal theory. This failure is of course partly due to the very unreality of the theory: it is not possible to separate the abstractions such as corporate personality, or the voting power of a share of stock, from the actions of particular persons in particular relations with other persons. But the corporation departs from theory in other respects also, and it is in these further problems involving such things as "ownership," "management," and "control" that we are primarily interested. In a general way the character of the problems may be seen from a few summary statements which will be elaborated in the pages that follow. Among the characteristics of the industrial corporation, which make its place in society of crucial significance for the classical theory of business enterprise, are the following: no one "owns" the corporation in the strict sense; the management of the corporation is often carried on by people who have no money invested in it; and the locus of control of the corporation rarely rests with the majority of the stockholders, and often is difficult to find at all. In short, the corporate system of capital is an innovation ranking with the factory system of production in its relative effect upon economic organization. Together (and the two have operated together) they determine the contemporary characteristics of Big Business.

CONCENTRATION AND DISTRIBUTION OF CORPORATE OWNERSHIP

As noted in the preceding section of this chapter, a major advantage of the corporation is the amount of capital, held in rather small amounts, which can be concentrated within a single business enterprise. This leads, in other words, to rather widespread distribution of the benefits (or some of the benefits) of ownership in major business enterprises. There are approximately 8,500,000 stockholders who own one or more shares in one or more of the 1710 corporations with securities listed on a national exchange.[4] This is a very rough estimate, since, it will be recalled, the corporate unit is the shareholding, not the shareholder. At any rate, this represents a widespread dispersal of ownership, at least in the sense of capital investment. Despite this dispersal of capital ownership, however, there is a notable "concentration of economic power" in the American economy. In the most general sense, this concentration arises from two facts: not all corporations are of equal size and importance, and not all shareholdings are of equal size, or confined to a single corporation.

Importance of Large Corporations. In a monograph prepared for the Temporary National Economic Committee, the Securities and Exchange Commission sponsored a study of characteristics of the two hundred largest nonfinancial corporations for the period 1937–39.[5] In number, these represented but two-tenths of one per cent (0.2%) of all domestic corporations, yet, as might be expected, their importance in the national economy was out of all proportion to their number.[6] The authors summarized the comparison with the other corporations as follows:

> Measured either by number of shareholdings, market value of securities, dividends paid, or total assets, the two hundred largest nonfinancial corporations studied in detail in this report . . . represent between two-fifths and one-half of all nonfinancial operations.[7]

These corporations, some of them interdependent, wield a major influence in manufacturing, utilities, railroads, and to a lesser degree in retail distribution and service.[8] In addition, many of the largest corporations maintain effective control over subsidiary corporations not included in the group.[9]

---

[4] See Raymond W. Goldsmith, Rexford C. Parmelee, and Others, "The Distribution of Ownership in the 200 Largest Nonfinancial Corporations," United States Congress, Temporary National Economic Committee, *Investigation of Concentration of Economic Power, Monograph No. 29* (Washington: U. S. Government Printing Office, 1940), pp. 10, 150–168.

[5] *Ibid.* Berle and Means, *op. cit.*, made a similar study a decade earlier than that represented in the TNEC monograph.

[6] Goldsmith, Parmelee, and Others, *op. cit.*, pp. 22–23.

[7] *Ibid.*, p. 23.   [8] *Ibid.*, p. 4.

[9] *Ibid.*, pp. 2–4. See also the numerous volumes of *Hearings* before the Temporary National Economic Committee, and the following in the series of

Concentration of Corporate Control. We have noted that in theory each share of stock carries an equal weight in determining the policies of the corporation as a whole. Thus, the man who owns one hundred shares of voting stock in a large corporation has one hundred times more voice in the management of the corporation than the man who owns but one share. In practice, however, the person owning a single share will have no significant voice in the affairs of the corporation, nor will the man owning one hundred shares if the corporation is a large one. Not even in theory must a person own all the shares of a corporation in order to control it; he need own only a bare majority. In practice, if the shareholdings are in general very widely dispersed, a substantial block of stock (which may be considerably less than a majority) will serve to dominate the organization. Thus persons who do not in any real sense "own" a corporation may in fact control its financial policies.

This is not to say that persons who own sufficient concentrations of shares to control the financial policies of a corporation have unlimited control over the entire resources of the corporation. They (or their representatives) cannot act in flagrant violation of the interests of other stockholders. Their position remains officially one of trusteeship. What is at stake is fundamentally a distribution of power.

The concentration of economic power is in fact chiefly made possible by dispersion of capital ownership. Very few corporations are in fact "owned" by a single family—only three of the two hundred largest corporations are so owned.[10] An additional four of the largest corporations show a single family owning the majority of the stock, and several are apparently so dominated by two or more related family groups.[11] The control of other large corporations, and to a lesser degree all corporations, rests in the first instance upon substantial or even small minority shareholdings, together with the "proxies" of other stockholders.

---

monographs: Roy C. Cook, "Control of the Petroleum Industry by the Major Oil Companies," *Monograph No. 39* (1941); "Review and Criticism on Behalf of Standard Oil Co. (New Jersey) and Sun Oil Co. of *Monograph No. 39* with Rejoinder by Monograph Author," *Monograph No. 39-A* (1941).

[10] Goldsmith, Parmelee, and Others, *op. cit.*, pp. 105–106.

It is possible to control an even larger financial empire through the pyramiding device of the *holding company*. Since the corporation as a legal personality can hold property rights, it is possible for one corporation to own stock in another corporation. If companies are pyramided a number of times, a bare majority stock control of the parent company and a similar bare·majority stock control by one company of each succeeding lower layer would allow "majority" control of the total financial empire by a very small proportion of the *total* capital. Since it is rarely necessary to own a majority of the shares of a widely held corporation, the capitalization necessary for financial control is much smaller than would be indicated by the requirement of majority stock ownership at each stage.

These control devices are, however, increasingly difficult in view of legal regulations and increasingly old-fashioned in terms of corporate organization. As large financial interests, such as insurance companies, pension trusts, and investment trusts, tend increasingly to be themselves representatives of many individuals, there is less attempt to mix the financial interests of security of and return on investments with the managerial interests in production and profit. Financial control of managerial policies is to an increasing extent likely to start with the large corporation and extend to its subsidiaries and affiliates and, less overtly, to its suppliers and customers, rather than starting with stockholders as such.

The advantages in a presumably competitive economy of centralized financial control are very great. The bases of concentration may be various, such as "horizontal" control of many enterprises of the same type (the most obvious type of "monopoly"); "vertical" control of raw materials, and various stages in production, including by-products; control of distribution of the products of the manufacturing corporations; or various other advantages arising from large-scale business operations.[12]

[11] *Ibid.*, pp. 106–107.

[12] See Willard L. Thorp, Walter F. Crowder, and Others, "The Structure of Industry," United States Congress, Temporary National Economic Committee, *Investigation of Concentration of Economic Power, Monograph No. 27* (Washington: U. S. Government Printing Office, 1941), especially Part II, "The Integration of Manufacturing Operations," by Walter F. Crowder and K. Celeste Stokes.

Effects of Economic Concentration. One fairly obvious result of the widespread capitalization of industrial corporations, plus their co-ordination through centralized financial control, is that of sheer magnitude of industrial operations. Without the "public" (that is, widely owned) corporation, large-scale manufacture without governmental subsidy would be nearly impossible. There are very few individuals or families in the United States at the present time who would have sufficient capital without outside assistance to enter one of the major industrial fields and compete successfully with present companies. Even in the establishment of new industries, the advantages of size are such as to discourage purely "individual" enterprise.

For our purposes, this characteristic large-scale organization has immediate implications for selection of materials and points of emphasis. Many of the social relationships in industry that are to be discussed are only to be found in the large industrial plant. The characteristics of industrial organization with which this book is concerned are fully developed only in the larger units. This emphasis is justified both by the tremendous weight which big business carries in the total economic life of our society and by the apparently increasing importance of large and complex organizations in manufacturing and distribution.[13]

Another aspect of the corporate structure of industry—an aspect closely related to that of size of industrial units—is that of the implications of this type of financial or capital organization for the character of the actual management of the industrial unit. Even in the classical theory of individual enterprise, the returns from capital investments have been thought to be separable from the returns for managerial ability. For the most part, however, this division amounted to very little outside of the textbooks of theoretical economists. The captain of industry did not often inquire too closely into the theoretical nature of his income; necessarily, his primary interest was in its size. But the modern corporation has to a large degree

[13] See United States Congress, Temporary National Economic Committee, *Investigation of Concentration of Economic Power, Hearings . . .* (Washington: U. S. Government Printing Office, 1939–1941), 36 vols.; and series of monographs, especially those previously cited.

translated abstract theory into hard fact. This has been accomplished by a fairly clear-cut distinction between the function and even the personnel of financial investment, on the one hand, and the actual operation of large organizations, on the other. With perhaps a little more brevity than is completely appropriate, this transformation in our economy has gained some recognition in the expression "the separation of ownership and management."

SEPARATION OF OWNERSHIP AND MANAGEMENT

It is often said that one of the institutional bases of our economic system is that of private property. What this means in concrete terms is that particular individuals are allowed to maintain most of the rights or advantages arising from the control of valuable things— whether those valuable things be tangible real estate or intangible patents. The word *most* is important, for the nature of property in human society is such that complete and unlimited control of valuable things is likely to be contrary to the interest of social order. These rights include such things as simple possession; use in a number of ways; appropriation of natural increase, if any; gift, exchange, sale, and inheritance; renting or leasing to another in return for money or other consideration. As we shall see in Part Six, the control of the economic life of society through the regulation provided by property institutions is a fundamental aspect of the relation of industry to society. What is of immediate significance for the organization of the modern corporation is the fundamental principle that *"property" consists in a number of rights, many of which may be held by a single person, but need not be.* In no case does society allow unlimited exercise of power over valuable things.

The usual limitation in a system of private property is expressed in the phrase "subject only to the police power of the state." We may note one or two examples. If one owns a rifle or other dangerous weapon, that ownership by no means carries with it the right of unrestricted use. It may be licensed, taxed, confiscated for military use, or its serial number registered with public officials. Above all, it must not be used to kill other persons, or even to destroy animals except as stipulated in statutes and regulations. If someone owns a city lot, he cannot so use it, or so fail to use it, that it becomes a public nuisance; he must pay any assessments for city-sponsored improvements, keep the weeds mowed, and possibly sell it at a price determined by a jury if the governmental unit exercises its right of "eminent domain" because it is needed as a street right-of-way or as the location of a municipal building. All of these limitations upon private property as ordinarily understood indicate that property involves many rights, and that some of these rights are always reserved to the community.[14]

Since property rights are in principle and in practice divisible, it follows that different persons or groups of persons *may hold different rights in the same valuable thing.* This is a proposition which is absolutely fundamental for understanding both the nature of corporate property and the division of function that the modern corporation exhibits.

Who Owns the Corporation? In the traditional view of private property, the owners of the corporation are the stockholders. But this view is subject to such limitations as to make it almost meaningless. For one thing, it will be recalled that the corporation itself is regarded as a legal person. This means that the corporation may itself hold property rights, including shares of stock in corporations. (This invites the logical conclusion that it would be possible for a corporation to own all its own stock, and thus become independent of "actual" persons.) Through the device of the holding company, for example, it is possible for individuals to control the policies of corporations which they do not in any traditional sense "own." Actually, in any corporation the stock of which is not completely owned by a single individual, or at most a single family (and these are understandably rare since the usual advantages of incorporation are in such cases nonexistent), there is a significant separation between the rights of ownership (as expressed in return

---

[14] The nature of property institutions and the control through the rules of property of both economic production and distribution are more fully treated in Chap. XXIV. The question is raised here only as a means of indicating the peculiar character of corporate organization.

on an investment) and the rights of control that are commonly associated with ownership.[15]

As far as the physical wealth, patent rights, undivided surplus, and other valuable assets are concerned, there is no question about their legal ownership; they belong to the corporation. The stockholder owns a right to a possible return on an investment, plus a *theoretical* right to share in the control of the total organization. The extent of the modification in the traditional view of property may be seen concretely in the fact that an owner of a share of stock can claim no particular share in the physical wealth of the corporation. He can claim no piece of equipment or manufactured product as rightfully his because he owns part of the company. He owns only an investment, which probably carries no real rights of control over the investment.

It is the theoretical right to share in control and in the success or failure of the business that chiefly distinguishes the stockholder from the bondholder or other creditor of the corporation. With widespread dispersion of capital ownership, this additional property right is likely to disappear for all but a few of the investors (who thus exercise control *beyond* that represented by their share in "ownership").

The first degree of separation of ownership and management is thus practically coextensive with the corporate type of organization, and arises from the nature of the corporation itself. This first step is the separation of capital ownership from the control over its productive or other uses.[16]

---

[15] This is always true for "minority stockholders" who are not actually represented in positions of control, and may be true of majority stockholders if their actual interests are limited to financial ones.

[16] Failure to understand the fundamental character of property relations has apparently caused a good deal of confusion on this point. Even the writers of the TNEC study of the ownership of the two hundred largest nonfinancial corporations (Goldsmith, Parmelee, and Others, *op. cit.*) obviously confuse ownership with substantial control. Thus they write,

"In about 140 of the 200 corporations the blocks of stock in the hands of one interest group were large enough to justify, together with other indications such as representation in the management, the classification of these companies as more or less definitely under ownership control." (*Ibid.*, p. 104.)

Even under the legal theory of the corporation, one cannot have "ownership

The separation is likely, however, to be even more complete, especially in very large corporations. That is, when the dispersion of ownership is sufficiently broad that no combination or "interest" group can carry any considerable weight in control, management becomes largely self-perpetuating and free from any but a limited legal control.[17] Thus management is independent of the control of stockholders, or of any group of them who might seek to combine to exercise financial control. The classic case of this separation between an investing public and the management of the corporation is that of the largest American corporation, the American Telephone and Telegraph Company. Only two of the twenty largest stockholders are individuals, and those two together own less than one-third of one per cent of the total stock. The other leading shareholders are insurance companies, investment trusts, banks, and brokers. The leading twenty shareholdings account for less than four per cent of the outstanding stock.[18] Although this case is admittedly ex-

control" without owning a majority of the stock of the company, and the legal theory of the corporation involves so much of the principles of trusteeship in regard to minority stockholders that it bears little relation to the ideas of "private property." The materials presented in the study cited thus in no way bear out the writers' conclusion concerning the convergence of "ownership" and control. Actually, in a very small proportion of the stock issues of two hundred corporations do the highest *twenty* shareholdings represent a majority of the stock, and in nearly all cases the highest twenty shareholdings are held in part by other corporations, trusts, foundations, and financial concerns representing a number of stockholders. (See *ibid.*, pp. 624–1439, where the twenty highest shareholders of the various stock issues of the two hundred largest corporations are listed, together with the percentage of shares outstanding represented by each holding and by the entire group of twenty.)

[17] This was pointed out in a work that is by now a classic, that of Berle and Means, *op. cit.*, especially pp. 47–125. The advantages of a control that is to a marked degree independent of a number of distinct shareholders are so clear that even in corporations in which members of a single family dominate the shareholdings, resort to a family holding company to give unified control is frequent. See Goldsmith, Parmelee, and Others, *op. cit.*, pp. 115–131.

Peter F. Drucker argues that the absence of control by stockholders, which is the actual situation in large corporations, be officially recognized through nonvoting stock and other devices in order to clarify legal, managerial, and lay thinking on the responsibilities of management as distinct from investment. See his *The New Society: The Anatomy of the Industrial Order* (New York: Harper & Brothers, 1950), pp. 339–343.

[18] See Goldsmith, Parmelee, and Others, *op. cit.*, pp. 684–685.

treme, the general situation of apparent absence of a dominant control group is not rare among large corporations.[19]

In regard to the actual control over policies and activities of the corporation and its assets, therefore, we must distinguish three different situations: complete ownership, financial control, and managerial control.

Complete Ownership. It is not only theoretically possible for one person or immediate family to own all the securities of a corporation, but this actually occurs in two or three very large corporations. Thus all rights to use, transfer, buy, sell, appropriate increase or profits, control, and so on nominally rest in the corporation as a legal person, but actually rest in the individual or family. As previously intimated, such corporations lack the ordinary advantages of incorporation, such as larger capitalization and limited liability. Some of them are apparently "historical accidents" in the sense that a single individual or family, formerly dependent upon "outside" capitalization, is able to buy all outstanding shares. This was true, for example, of the Ford Motor Company. Others have apparently been established for purposes of tax reduction, anonymity of control, and the like. At any rate, such corporations are extremely rare among actual operating concerns, and these must for our purposes be regarded as only nominally or technically incorporated. They amount simply to a peculiar form of individual enterprise.

Financial Control. The control situation in a majority of the large corporations rests apparently upon control of substantial blocks of stock. This is, of course, even truer of small corporations, since these have a smaller capitalization and hence allow an individual or an interest group to attain more easily a dominant position among the security holders. In such circumstances there is a complex ownership-control situation, involving ownership of investments, corporate ownership of various assets, with actual control vested in "control centers" of stockholders holding major or minor portions of stock.

[19] About sixty of the two hundred large corporations studied by the Securities and Exchange Commission experts were reported as being without an apparent center of control by ownership (of stock). (*See ibid.*, pp. 103–104.)

The financial control of a corporation usually rests upon owner-ship of certificates of stock, whether a majority, substantial minority, or small minority. As previously indicated, the proportion of stock necessary to control the corporation is smaller the more widely dispersed the general ownership and therefore, to a certain degree, the larger the capitalization. It is not unknown, however, for bond-holders without vote to control the policies of a corporation by their position as powerful creditors.

The most obvious and most frequent method of domination of a corporation by financial "control centers" is that of self-election, or election of closely controlled representatives to executive and directorial positions. The Securities and Exchange Commission experts found, for example, that in large corporations the holders of controlling bodies of stock were commonly represented in management to an extent quite exceeding their proportional share of the total capitalization.[20] Even this evidence, however, is not, as we shall see, conclusive demonstration of actual participation in the affairs of management. Corporation directors are not notorious for their complete interest in or familiarity with the operation of the corporations they "direct."

Managerial Control. It is possible, as we have noted, to carry the separation of ownership and management (or rather the division of various property rights) to such an extreme through very wide dispersion of security ownership that no actual financial control centers do or can exist. Stock ownership in such a situation carries with it no control rights for any investors, making their position similar to that of dispersed majority or minority shareholders in corporations under financial control. Thus control is in fact vested in a self-perpetuating management, acting in the dual capacity of salaried employees of the corporation and "trustees" of the investor's funds. The situation of even top executives, therefore, is not greatly different from

[20] *Ibid.*, p. 113. In a few of the two hundred largest corporations individuals or groups which appeared to be in a "control" position were underrepresented in management. (*Ibid.*, p. 112.) The writers recognize, moreover, that executives and managers may well have achieved their positions on other grounds than ownership of stock and subsequently acquired small blocks of stock in the corporation. (*Ibid.*, p. 113.)

their position under "financial control," except that under managerial control the "intrusion" of financial interests and demands into managerial policies is likely to be less immediate or nonexistent.

The question as to whether in particular corporations financial control or managerial control prevails may at times be determined

FIGURE 1. *Degrees of Separation of Ownership and Management*

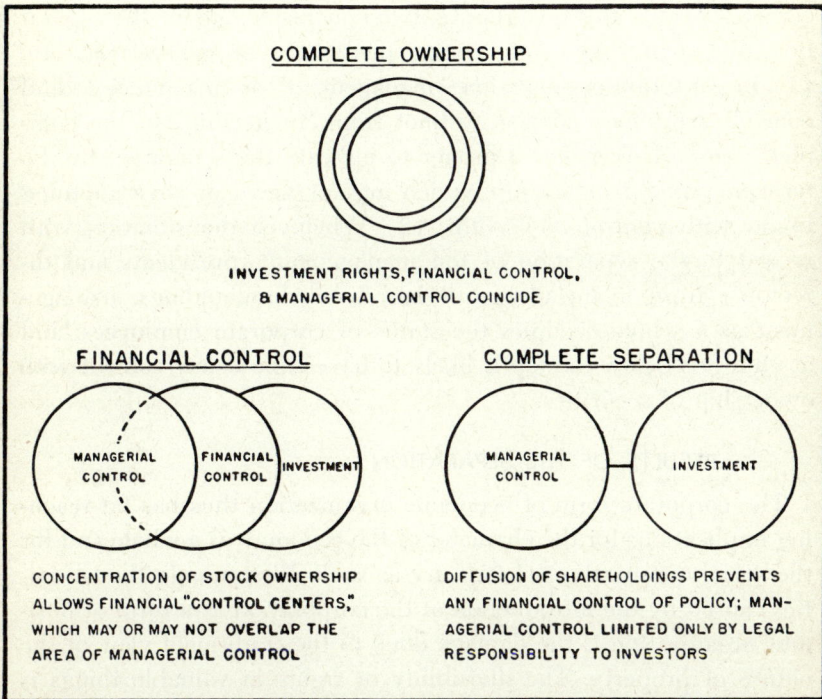

COMPLETE OWNERSHIP

INVESTMENT RIGHTS, FINANCIAL CONTROL,
& MANAGERIAL CONTROL COINCIDE

FINANCIAL CONTROL

MANAGERIAL CONTROL   FINANCIAL CONTROL   INVESTMENT

COMPLETE SEPARATION

MANAGERIAL CONTROL   INVESTMENT

CONCENTRATION OF STOCK OWNERSHIP
ALLOWS FINANCIAL "CONTROL CENTERS,"
WHICH MAY OR MAY NOT OVERLAP THE
AREA OF MANAGERIAL CONTROL

DIFFUSION OF SHAREHOLDINGS PREVENTS
ANY FINANCIAL CONTROL OF POLICY; MAN-
AGERIAL CONTROL LIMITED ONLY BY LEGAL
RESPONSIBILITY TO INVESTORS

simply on the basis of known concentration or dispersion of stock ownership. Other cases may be decided on the basis of the correlation, if any, between stock ownership and top managerial positions. The conclusion of financial domination does not, as we have seen, necessarily follow either from concentration of stock ownership or from stockholders in managerial positions, although the presumption would lie in that direction. The center of control is often very difficult to discover, and may in fact lie with one group as far as financial policies are concerned and with a quite different group as far as actual operation of the enterprise is concerned.[21] The three types of "ownership situations" are represented diagrammatically in Figure 1.

The final degree of separation, that between financial control and active management, is in a sense the debatable no-man's-land in corporate organization, at least as far as general principles are concerned. Despite this uncertainty, two conclusions about the separation of "ownership" and "management" are of general validity. (1) In corporate organization, "management" or "management and control" are almost always distinct from "ownership" in the complete sense. This makes it proper to indicate the separation by the term *investment ownership,* which may or may not have anything to do with *control ownership.* (2) Whatever the situation with regard to the separation of top management (presidents and directors) from financial control based on shareholdings, management as a whole occupies the status of corporate employees, and at all levels below the top is likely to have little if any contact with ownership of securities.

RESULTS OF THE SEPARATION

The corporate form of economic organization thus has far-reaching implications for the character of the economy as a whole and for the social organization of industry as such. First among the casualties caused by the introduction of the corporation as a form of business organization is the damage done to the traditional view of the nature of property. The divisibility of rights in valuable things is pointedly illustrated in the general problem of the ownership of corporate wealth.[22]

The Profit Motive. A second modification that is prompted by the separation of management from ownership is that required in the

---

[21] See Robert Aaron Gordon, *Business Leadership in the Large Corporation* (Washington: The Brookings Institution, 1945).

[22] The implications of the corporation for the "traditional logic of property" have been pointed out by Berle and Means, *op. cit.,* pp. 333–339. The discussion of the modifications necessary in the customary view of the "profit motive" is also very close to that of the same authors, *op. cit.,* pp. 340–344.

classic view of the efficacy of the profit motive. Profits have been justified as a reward for enterprise and an incentive to shrewd business practice. Under this view, profits should then go to the locus of control, not to the stockholder. This is of course exactly contrary to the "private property" view which vests beneficial ownership in the stockholders. In any event, salaried managers without direct financial risk in the enterprise can scarcely be claimed to be driven by the profit motive. It is true that various corporations have attempted, either through urging stock purchases by management or by bonus systems, to motivate industrial managers to increase corporate profits. These methods, however, must be judged in the same light as various "profit-sharing" and wage-incentive plans for any industrial employees, and not as approximating the profit making of the individual entrepreneur.

The opposite of profit is loss; the one is justified in our culture in terms of the possibility of the other. The innovation of "limited liability" plus the growth of salaried management makes this view of profit pointless. Moreover, the importance of large corporations in our whole economic and social life is such as to make it contrary to public interest to allow them to fail. Investors without control cannot, according to traditional ethics, be expected to take the consequences of business policies which they did not determine or help determine. If profit is the reward of enterprise and business acumen and loss the penalty for failure in these respects, both should devolve upon the control group, and not upon the passive investor. Such a policy, however, would not only run contrary to the traditional view of private property which the lawyers and courts strive vainly to maintain in face of corporate organization, but would undermine a basic principle of the corporation—that of limited liability.

The fact is that profit calculation as a yardstick of operations and the role of profits in avoiding current loss and guarding against future hazards is an important part of corporate policy. As Drucker has pointed out,[23] this requirement of profit calculation has no intrinsic relationship to the "profit motive" nor to the way in which profits are used or distributed. The requirement is as basic in na-

[23] *Op. cit.*, pp. 52–63, 68–73.

tionalized industry as in the "free enterprise" system. The principal difference in the latter system, aside from the possibility of direct financial pressure on managers in some corporations, is the role of distributed profits (stock dividends) in the competition for new capital. Even this competition in the capital market may be avoided by the large corporation that accumulates new capital out of its own current earnings and thus accentuates its independence from outside financial control.

The present point is simply that the separation of ownership and management means the loss of the individual entrepreneur or captain of industry, and with him goes part of the accepted explanatory principles concerning profit-motivated private initiative as the dominant influence in determining the actions of individual managers. To the extent that business leaders continue to justify their actions on the basis of the outworn rhetorical models and fail to emphasize the functions of management and profit calculation in the large corporation, to that extent they probably deserve the public distrust of which they currently complain.[24]

The Passing of "Capital-Labor." The foregoing considerations have even further and for present purposes more important ramifications. If one must distinguish investment ownership, financial control, and management, it follows that the twofold distinction between capital and labor becomes very nearly meaningless in large corporate industrial enterprises. It becomes meaningless because *it is next to impossible to identify one party to the conflict: capital.* Although as we have already observed it is sometimes difficult to determine just how dominant a position financial control of a corporation may hold in regard to general and specific policies, it generally devolves upon management to "deal" with labor. This is one reason why contemporary officials, newspapers, and various leaders of labor and business speak of the relations between *management* and labor, rather than capital and labor.

---

[24] In an official statement of principles, for example, the National Association of Manufacturers insists on the term "individual enterprise system." See National Association of Manufacturers, Economic Principles Commission, *The American Individual Enterprise System: Its Nature, Evolution, and Future* (New York: McGraw-Hill Book Company, Inc., 1946, 2 vols.)

Management in fact lies intermediate between the demands of capital (chiefly as represented by the center of financial control) and the demands of labor groups. It has ends and functions distinct from both. This is, of course, in terms of formal structure. It is not equally true that the actual alignment of forces finds managers uniformly or even frequently hostile to the claims of financiers. The formal structure would accordingly allow a greater diversion of interests than in fact appears. The actual separation of functions makes it legitimate to speak of the bulk of managerial activity in terms of the operation of a going concern. The discussion in the following paragraphs is mainly cast in that mold, but the importance of the sympathies of the top ranks of managers should be borne in mind.

Professional Management. Since management is in general distinct from capital ownership in corporate enterprise, it follows that the position of management is one directly related to the corporation as a unit. The official or legal view, it will be recalled, is that the corporation as a legal personality can employ its executives and administrators as well as its minor employees. The position and rights of management are in fact sufficiently distinct from the shareholders that the official view comes close to representing the actual situation. This is especially true as regards the direct relation of the management to the corporation as a whole. The principal shortcoming of the official view is that the management is likely to occupy a position of power over many or most affairs of the corporation, rather than the other way around.

The ends of capital, as represented by all or part of the holders of securities, and the ends of labor, as represented by unions of individual employees, are therefore interests to some degree independent of those of management. Since management occupies a position in many ways intermediate between these two types of interests, the latter may be regarded as *conditions of managerial action.* In other words, the interests of stockholders and trade unions are not unimportant for the managerial group as a whole, but they must in general be regarded by executives and administrators as *part of the situation,* not as the goals of management itself.

The nature of the managerial position may perhaps be clarified by comparing the "prerogatives" of management with managerial "functions." Many demands by labor unions have been rejected or resisted with the claim that they invaded managerial "prerogatives." Now these prerogatives have customarily been justified as resting upon the prior claims of the company's proprietors, whom management represents. This argument, as we have seen, is likely to be in various degrees fallacious as a statement of management's position and authority. There are indeed managerial functions. These are not unique to the "free enterprise" system, nor are they essentially changed by the changing *environment* of operation presented by collective bargaining or even by nationalization of industry. This changing environment modifies the structure of ultimate responsibility and even many details of operation, but does not change the responsibility for operating a going concern.

Yet salaried managers whose abilities are those of the policy-forming executive, the expert in personal and social relations, or the administrator of a research laboratory cannot persistently overlook the conditions imposed by other interests in the total corporation. Investors expect at least some reasonable return on capital, and the annual balance sheet cannot be viewed as another scrap of paper. In pursuing the general goal of "efficient" operation, the executive is expected also to act in a way consistent with profitable operation.

Because of the possibly close connection between centers of financial control and top executives, the management is not in general likely to forget its duties to the investors. Even if those who manage the firm have no money invested in it, market competition applies to the business unit, and profits for the corporation are regarded as an important mark of a successful professional manager.

The orientation to the interests of capital is often facilitated by another circumstance as well: the executive is likely to view himself as an old-style entrepreneur despite his position as a professional manager. Thus one is treated to the rather amusing spectacle of a salaried executive, with little or no actual ownership of the stock of his company, engaging in a controversy with governmental agencies or labor representatives and maintaining his individualistic rights of running his own company in his own way. This is, of course, not to be particularly wondered at in view of the persistence of cultural conceptions which do not precisely fit the contemporary characteristics of corporate organization.

However, the executive must also take into account the general position and interests of those employees who constitute the bulk of the personnel and are likely, correctly or not, to be lumped together under the general heading of "labor." It is always part of the managerial function to maintain "industrial morale" even if the interests and aspirations of machine and bench workers are given no formal expression. In view of recent increases in labor organization fostered by the legislation protecting the right of collective bargaining, the demands of labor are often as vocal and insistent as those of investors. The limitations placed upon the freedom of action of the industrial manager in operating a complex organization are consequently often acute.

To the extent that the interests of management are primarily technical and productive rather than financial, an actual conflict of interests may appear. Thus, technological developments which would adversely affect the immediate market situation of the corporation may be fostered by a technically oriented managerial group, only to be withheld in view of the overriding importance of financial interests. Patents, for example, may be secured and frozen to prevent a disruption of product organization. Designs that would prolong wear and decrease consumption may be sacrificed for designs that maintain existing levels of production. Processes that would increase unit costs of production but decrease the waste of raw materials may be withheld in view of the possible reduction in profits or impaired ability to compete for the market.[25] It is note-

[25] See United States Congress, Temporary National Economic Committee, *Investigation of Concentration of Economic Power, Hearings* . . . (Washington: U. S. Government Printing Office, 1939–1941), Part 3, *Patents—Proposals for Changes in Law and Procedures* (1939); Part 30, *Technology and Concentration of Economic Power* (1940). See also Walton Hamilton, "Patents and Free Enterprise," United States Congress, Temporary National Economic Committee, *Investigation of Concentration of Economic Power, Monograph No. 31* (Washington: U. S. Government Printing Office, 1941). See also Thorstein Veblen, *The Engineers and the Price System* (New York: The Viking Press,

worthy that, although these practices may illustrate potential conflict between business interests and *some* managerial interests, the business interests will ordinarily prevail.

It is the distinction between the role of the businessman and the role of the qualified manager which provides the first justification for speaking of the role of the latter as a professional one. In other words, the corporation executive (not the "silent director" whose name graces the corporation letterheads) or the administrator is a professional first of all because his occupation consists in management. The expression has even further justification in that the "professional manager" is a person presumably technically qualified in various aspects of administration. His position is, moreover, one of considerable responsibility and high status, and is officially oriented toward goals of service requiring specialized abilities, not toward the acquisition of profits.[26] Although not an "independent" professional (any more than the clergyman or college professor), his position in society and in industry tends to qualify him for the appellation.

It is, of course, erroneous even to imply that management constitutes an undifferentiated group or a society of equals. The following four chapters indicate the degree of specialization among those falling within the general category of management, as well as the various relations existing among these specialists. However, the discussion of the nature of the corporation and the very general divisions of function in large economic organizations has served to indicate not only the complexity of those organizations, but also the importance of the recent and often unrecognized arrival on the economic scene—the professional manager.

1933), Chap. II, "The Industrial System and the Captains of Industry," and Chap. III, "The Captains of Finance and the Engineers"; *The Place of Science in Modern Civilisation* (New York: The Viking Press, 1932), "Industrial and Pecuniary Employments," pp. 279–323. Veblen deals with numerous aspects of the divergence of financial and industrial or technical interests in many different essays. A fairly complete list of these essays is included in the general references for this chapter.

[26] For a general statement of the role and status of the professional in our society, see Talcott Parsons, "The Professions and Social Structure," *Social Forces*, 17: 457–467, May 1939.

REFERENCES

ARNOLD, THURMAN, *The Folklore of Capitalism* (New Haven: Yale University Press, 1937), Chap. V, "The Use of the Language of Private Property to Describe an Industrial Army"; Chap. VII, "The Personification of Corporation."

BAKER, JOHN CALHOUN, *Directors and Their Functions: A Preliminary Study* (Boston: Harvard University Graduate School of Business Administration, 1945).

BERLE, A. A., JR., and GARDINER C. MEANS, "Corporation," in *Encyclopaedia of the Social Sciences*, 4: 414–423.

BERLE, A. A., JR., and GARDINER C. MEANS, *The Modern Corporation and Private Property* (New York: The Macmillan Company, 1933).

BROOKINGS, ROBERT S., *Industrial Ownership* (New York: The Macmillan Company, 1925), especially Chap. I, "The Separation of Ownership from Management," and Chap. II, "Management Now a Trustee."

BURNHAM, JAMES, *The Managerial Revolution* (New York: The John Day Company, 1941), especially Chap. VII, "Who Are the Managers?"

DIMOCK, MARSHALL E., and HOWARD K. HYDE, "Bureaucracy and Trusteeship in Large Corporations," United States Congress, Temporary National Economic Committee, *Investigation of Concentration of Economic Power, Monograph No. 11* (Washington: U. S. Government Printing Office, 1940), Part I, "The Nature and Scope of Big Business."

DONHAM, WALLACE B., "The Professional Side of Business Training," in Henry C. Metcalf, ed., *Business Management as a Profession* (Chicago: A. W. Shaw Company, 1927), pp. 215–230.

DRUCKER, PETER F., *Concept of the Corporation* (New York: The John Day Company, 1946).

———, *The New Society: The Anatomy of the Industrial Order* (New York: Harper & Brothers, 1950).

FOLLETT, M. P., "How Must Business Management Develop in Order to Become a Profession?" in Henry C. Metcalf, ed., *Business Management as a Profession* (Chicago: A. W. Shaw Company, 1927), pp. 88–102.

GOLDSMITH, RAYMOND W., REXFORD C. PARMELEE, and OTHERS, "The Distribution of Ownership in the 200 Largest Nonfinancial Corporations," United States Congress, Temporary National Economic Committee, *Investigation of Concentration of Economic Power, Monograph No. 29* (Washington: U. S. Government Printing Office, 1940).

GORDON, ROBERT AARON, *Business Leadership in the Large Corporation* (Washington: The Brookings Institution, 1945).

GRANBY, HELENE, "Survey of Shareholdings in 1,710 Corporations with Securities Listed on a National Securities Exchange," United States Congress, Temporary National Economic Committee, *Investigation of Concentration of Economic Power, Monograph No. 30* (Washington: U. S. Government Printing Office, 1941).

HAMILTON, WALTON, "Patents and Free Enterprise," United States Congress, Temporary National Economic Committee, *Investigation of Concentration of Economic Power, Monograph No. 31* (Washington: U. S. Government Printing Office, 1941).

LYNCH, DAVID, *The Concentration of Economic Power* (New York: Columbia University Press, 1946).

MEANS, GARDINER C., "The Distribution of Control and Responsibility in a Modern Economy," in Benjamin E. Lippincott, ed., *Government Control of the Economic Order* (Minneapolis: University of Minnesota Press, 1935), pp. 1–17.

MOORE, WILBERT E., "The Emergence of New Property Conceptions in America," *Journal of Legal and Political Sociology*, 1 (3–4): 34–58, April 1943.

NATIONAL ASSOCIATION OF MANUFACTURERS, Economic Principles Commission, *The American Individual Enterprise System: Its Nature, Evolution, and Future* (New York: McGraw-Hill Book Company, Inc., 1946, 2 vols.), Vol. I, Chap. IV, "Types of Business Organization"; Chap. IX, "Profit and Loss in the Enterprise System"; Vol. II, Chap. XII, "Competition and Monopoly."

SCOVILLE, JOHN, and NOEL SARGENT, compilers, *Fact and Fancy in the T.N.E.C. Monographs* (New York: National Association of Manufacturers, 1942).

SHARP, MALCOLM, and CHARLES O. GREGORY, *Social Change and Labor Law* (Chicago: University of Chicago Press, 1939), Part I, Chap. III, "Industrial Management in the Law."

SHELDON, OLIVER, "Management," in *Encyclopaedia of the Social Sciences*, 10: 76–80.

———, *The Philosophy of Management* (London: Sir Isaac Pitman & Sons, Ltd., 1924), Chap. II, "The Fundamentals of Management," and Chap. VII, "Training for Industrial Management."

SOMBART, WERNER, "Capitalism," in *Encyclopaedia of the Social Sciences*, 3: 195–208.

STAUSS, JAMES H., "The Entrepreneur: The Firm," *Journal of Political Economy*, 52: 112–127, June 1944.

THORP, WILLARD L., WALTER F. CROWDER, and OTHERS, "The Structure of Industry," United States Congress, Temporary National Economic Committee, *Investigation of Concentration of Economic Power, Monograph No. 27* (Washington: U. S. Government Printing Office, 1941).

UNITED STATES CONGRESS, Temporary National Economic Committee, *Investigation of Concentration of Economic Power, Hearings* . . . (Washington: U. S. Government Printing Office, 1941, 30 vols.).

VEBLEN, THORSTEIN, *The Engineers and the Price System* (New York: The Viking Press, 1933), Chap. II, "The Industrial System and the Captains of Industry," and Chap. III, "The Captains of Finance and the Engineers."

———, *The Place of Science in Modern Civilisation* (New York: The Viking Press, 1932). See "Industrial and Pecuniary Employments," pp. 279–323.

———, *The Theory of Business Enterprise* (New York: Charles Scribner's Sons, 1936), Chap. VI, "Modern Business Capital."

———, *The Vested Interests and the State of the Industrial Arts* (New York: B. W. Huebsch, 1919), Sec. 5, "The Vested Interests."

———, *Absentee Ownership and Business Enterprise in Recent Times* (New York: B. W. Huebsch, 1923), Chap. VI, "The Captain of Industry"; Chap. VIII, "The New Order of Business"; Chap. IX, "The Industrial System of the New Order"; Chap. X, "The Technology of Physics and Chemistry"; Chap. XI, "Manufacturers and Salesmen."

WORTLEY, B. A., "Legal Aspects of Property," in T. H. Marshall, ed., *Class Conflict and Social Stratification* (London: LePlay House Press, 1938), pp. 17–35.

&ৎ PART THREE

INDUSTRIAL ORGANIZATION: MANAGEMENT

INDUSTRIAL BUREAUCRACY

IN MOST nonindustrial societies of the present and past, the major sphere of deliberate organization and planning, of delegation of authority, of selecting individuals with at least some regard for their competence for particular assignments, has been the political. Especially in the equipment of an army, the governing of an extensive territory, and the collection of taxes and tributes, more or less elaborate formal organizations have emerged in the great historic civilizations.

"Management" in this sense is not new. The modern significance of management consists primarily in the extension of elaborate organization into the sphere of daily productive activity—an area of human activity often rather simply arranged in older civilizations, even where the activities required a very considerable mass of workers.

The organization of even a fair-sized industrial plant in these modern times is extremely complicated. Much of this complexity arises inevitably from mere size, although size is not the only important factor in the division of industrial labor. Whether the character of the products, the agencies of distribution, the financial arrangements, or the quality of personnel be in question, one must be impressed by the necessity of bringing about coordination between specialized activities. Under a simpler economy all stages of operations from raw materials to sale and delivery of the finished product might very well be under the direct supervision and control of a single person, but it frequently taxes the abilities of modern administrators to bring order into a single minute phase of the process.

In the present chapter are outlined the *structural* features of industrial organization, and the importance of such problems as size, specialization, and division of authority is noted. The first concern is with general types of organizations, then with the implications of formal organization for the activities and relationships of persons.

ORGANIZATION IN GENERAL

The growth of professional management, particularly as a corollary of the dispersion of capital ownership in the modern corporation, has already been noted. Quite aside from the peculiar characteristics of corporate economy, all business enterprises beyond the very smallest and simplest today demand the services of managers: those whose chief function is direction, coordination, or technical advice. That this should be so arises from an elementary fact that may be unnoticed because of its very obviousness: the production and distribution of economic goods is a *human* as well as a *mechanical* activity. The secret of relating many machines and many persons in particular ways toward the achievement of certain goals is to be found in all the implications of the single term *organization*.

Organization in the social sense refers either to *the pattern or structure of relationships among a number of persons oriented to a set of goals or objectives, or to the group as a whole viewed as a unity.* Actually, any seeming ambiguity or looseness in the term is likely to be more apparent than real. Either use in fact implies the other. This is true because the structure is pointless save as a basis for concerted and unified action, and a collection of individuals without established patterns of relationship cannot long [1] maintain any semblance of unity or collective action.

Persons in a social system or, more explicitly, in an organization may be related to one another in many ways. The relationships among them may be few or many (a club compared with a family); on terms of authority and subordination or on terms of equality (as

---

[1] The qualification "long" is necessary because of the possibility of relatively "unorganized" or at least essentially unstructured aggregates of persons achieving a temporary unity of purpose with cooperative activity to achieve that purpose. This occasionally occurs in mob and crowd behavior, for example.

the army in contrast to a fraternity). The diversification of individual activities may be small or great (a collectors' society compared with a modern factory). These are but a few of the ways in which organizations may vary. But the variability of organizational arrangement is not simply an "academic" question. The nature of the patterned relationships among individuals—that is, the organization —in an industrial unit is an essential aspect of the effective operation of that unit. It follows that organization is a problem of "management" in the broadest sense. And since management itself is customarily made up of a number of distinct persons doing specialized jobs, not the least of the managerial worries is the organization of management.

In view of even the foregoing simplified summary of the nature and significance of organization, there is little cause for wonder at the vast amount of interest in and attention to industrial organization by executives, administrators, and experts in "scientific management."

The concept of organization includes the basic fact that individuals comprising a social system do not all occupy the same position in relation to other individuals (*status*) or carry on the same activities (*roles*). Whether one looks at a manufacturing plant from the point of view of the existing social structure that binds the personnel together into a cooperative system of more or less effectiveness, or from the point of view of the executive who seeks to maintain or improve the existing structure, two fundamental bases of distinction between persons are to be noted: relative authority and specialized function.[2] The two are not absolutely independent of one another, but are sufficiently so to make possible variations in emphasis upon one or the other, and consequent variations in the internal character of the organization as a whole. Among students

---

[2] There are, of course, other conceivable bases of distinction among organizational personnel besides rank and function. Such distinctions as sex, "race," and other determinants of social status prevalent in the general community are, however, only incidentally relevant to the industrial organization. The present reference is to those modes of distinction that are intrinsic to complex organization, not to those that may, more or less arbitrarily, be selected as significant in particular situations.

of industrial management (including, notably, industrial managers), organization that places primary emphasis on differences in rank and authority has come to be known as *line* organization, while attention to specialization and diversification has been called *staff* or *functional* organization. An examination of the primary characteristics of each may properly serve as an introduction to the *formal* (or official) character of industrial organization.

"LINE" ORGANIZATION

The simplest form of social structure in industry is not that of a society of equals. Rather it is the direct relationship of leader and follower, or of executive and operator. It is to be seen in the relative positions and activities of the boss and his workmen. For relatively small operations, where the goals to be achieved by organization are fairly immediate and not unduly complex, this type of organization has the advantage of simplicity and unitary control.

Vertical Extension of the Line. Line organization is not limited to situations involving few employees and only one or two ranks of managers, although it is likely to exist in anything like pure form only under those circumstances. Since differences in rank and authority are in principle extensible almost limitlessly, it is quite possible in fact to have a line organization with eight or ten positions on the direct line from the chief executive to the bench or shop worker. Aside from the obvious increase in organizational complexity, such an extension of line organization differs from its simplest form in the use of the principle of delegation and subdelegation of authority. Thus each person at any rank intermediate between the very top and the very bottom stands in a position of authority in relation to those "below" him, but in a position of responsibility or accountability to those "above" him. It is this characteristic of a system of ranks carrying various degrees of control of power according to the relative position on the scale that prompts the frequent comparison of this type of organization to the military hierarchy.

There is, of course, little need for the extension of the line of authority through many ranks in a small organization. Indeed, such an extension would be wasteful of time and would increase the likelihood of ineffectual transmission of orders and directions, or the downright subversion of authority. This is the sort of situation that gives basis to the charge that too many "figureheads" stand between the policy-forming executive and the workman. However, a large industrial unit organized on the line principle will in fact require many intermediaries, since the number of persons under a single person's *direct* authority must always be fairly small.[3] This is true even where no question of specialization, requiring different types of direction, is at issue. Again, this may be seen from the organization of the largest army unit, the infantry.

Organizational Characteristics. The principle of delegation and subdelegation of authority as a basis for line organization has two significant implications for the character of the relationships between different ranks.

1. The directions and policies determined by the executive or executive group are not ordinarily transmitted intact through a number of persons until they reach the operator at the machine. Rather, the orders normally start out in the most general terms and are made increasingly specific as they proceed down the line. As we shall note in the following chapter, line officers do not simply *pass along* orders: they *apply* them. This means concretely that willy nilly there is some specialization or functional distinction between the activities of managers at different stages in the organization.

2. The extension of delegated authority through a number of ranks, at each of which it is further subdelegated, gives a general pyramidal character to the organization as a whole. Apart from any functional specialization, therefore, persons widely separated at or near the bottom of the pyramid are only subject to a common authority by proceeding well toward the top of the pyramid. (See Figures 2 and 3 for illustration of the possible simplicity or complexity of line organization.)

[3] Because of the large number of independent variables (such as spatial arrangement, extent of routine, frequency of contact with subordinates, degree of specialization among subordinates, etc.), it is difficult to state a precise numerical rule for the maximum of direct subordinates. In practice it rarely exceeds twenty or thirty even at routine tasks, and is considerably less than that at higher managerial ranks where the variables just noted ordinarily work against extension beyond four or five.

Line organization has the advantage of simplified central-office control, as well as the related advantages of ease in fixing responsibility and unquestionable location of authority from any position.

FIGURE 2. *Possible Simple Types of Line Organization*

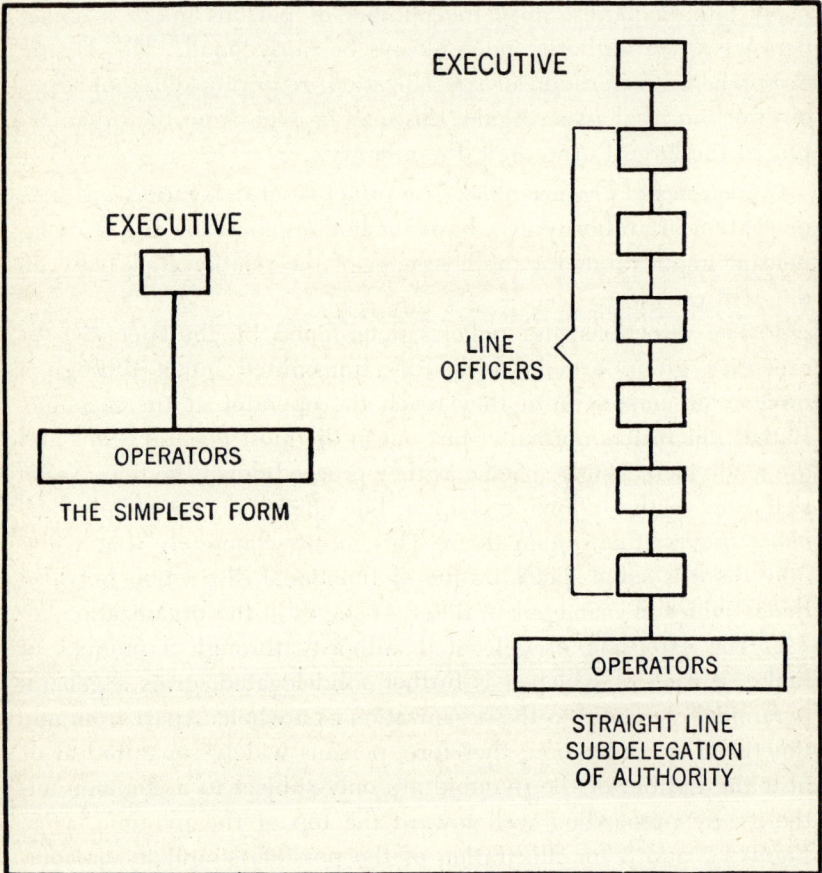

The chief disadvantages are those associated with the outstanding characteristic of line organization: the lack of specialization. Thus authority and decisions tend to reach a "bottleneck" at the top, with executives forced to pass judgment on essentially minor points of policy or practice. More critical than this, however, is the fact that a modern industrial plant does not comprise an undifferentiated mass of employees, directed by managers distinguished only by differences in rank. Division of labor, which is so characteristic of industrial production, has implications for managerial organization

FIGURE 3. *Pyramidal Subdelegation of Authority on Line Principles*
(Much Simplified)

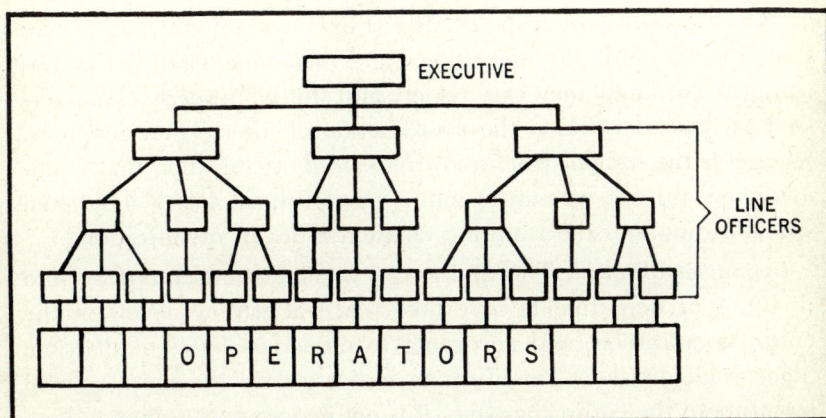

as well, for no executive can reasonably be expected to be expert in all phases of industrial operation. In short, functional specialization is demanded in modern industrial organization.

"FUNCTIONAL" ORGANIZATION

The term *functional* is often used rather loosely to refer to several varieties of relationship between parts or units of an organization. This is in fact not to be wondered at, since the term in its most general sense may refer to any type of specialization accompanied by coordination. That is, any organization that requires different but interdependent activities, performed by diversified but coordinated personnel, may be conveniently viewed as a "functional unity." The "function" of any activity, or any unit of the entire organization, is thus determined by what it contributes to the operation of the whole.

Formally considered, the function of any aspect of an entire organization is directly related to the basis of specialization in that organization. Thus a departmentalization on the basis of supplies and stores, maintenance, research, processing, distribution, and finance—the possible divisions can be multiplied almost endlessly—determines at once the general structural and functional relationships of the units. It reveals little or nothing, however, of the internal organization of any of these units, the character of the authority, or the distribution of responsibility. Functional specialization may thus refer to quite different things, and the character of the organization accordingly may vary widely and still be properly characterized as dependent upon the coordination of interrelated activities. Since it is the formal structure of *industrial* organization that is immediately at issue, we may examine some of the modes of functional specialization and the resulting characteristics of organization.

Departmentalization. The division of an industrial enterprise into divisions or departments may take place at various levels in the entire organization, and according to numerous bases of division. Since such divisions are likely to indicate only the most general structure of the entire company, it is not necessary to examine these in any great detail. It may simply be noted that the whole organization may be broken down horizontally (that is, into separate branches carrying on roughly the same activities), vertically (with separate branches representing different stages in the productive process), or on the basis of complementary activities or products.[4] Within a given establishment, the operations may be broken down according to the unit-product (as in a multiproduct company, or one producing a final product comprising many diversified units), according to the raw material handled, similarity of mechanical processes, the general nature of the service rendered, or quality of personnel required.

Regardless of other bases of distinction, a division between shop

[4] See, for example, Walter F. Crowder and K. Celeste Stokes, "The Integration of Manufacturing Operations," in Willard L. Thorp, Walter F. Crowder, and Others, "The Structure of Industry," United States Congress, Temporary National Economic Committee, *Investigation of Concentration of Economic Power, Monograph No. 27* (Washington: U. S. Government Printing Office, 1941), Part II.

personnel and office personnel is very nearly universal. Although not always rational or logical, this distinction is significant precisely because it is thought to be so in the organization itself. We shall return to this point in the following chapter.

Specialization in the form of departmentalization has little relation to the general character of executive control and the distribution of authority and responsibility. After the initial division is made, with the appropriate superintendents or general managers responsible to the "head office," the organization may proceed on straight-line principles or on some further basis of specialization.

Division of Competent Authority. A fundamental principle of social organization in general that is highly relevant to industrial organization in particular is that authority may not only be delegated, it may also be divided into spheres of competence. Even in a seemingly pure line organization, for example, it is the function of intermediate managers not simply to transmit orders, but to make orders increasingly explicit. When this is combined with the recognition of the necessity of technical knowledge in particular fields of activity —a knowledge not shared by the policy-forming executive—the delegation of authority takes on added significance. Since it is highly improbable in any but the simplest shop units that any person in the organization will be equally able to perform any job, the division of labor is likely to be based largely on special competence. This raises fundamental problems for the integration of activities and especially for the nature and responsibilities of managerial roles. Several solutions to these problems have been suggested, which singly or in various combinations provide the key to the formal structure of contemporary industrial management.

1. Line-Staff. The incorporation of specialists into an industrial organization may be accomplished with little modification of the line principle if the specialists are limited to an advisory capacity at the several appropriate ranks where their services are demanded. Their affiliation with the line managers may be directly "horizontal," that is, they may be called upon directly by the line officer needing their services, or the staff officers may be directly responsible only to a high line official, and only indirectly in contact with others down

the line. (A general diagram of line-staff organization is represented in Figure 4.)

2. "Functional." The type of managerial organization that has been popularly known as "functional," following the early exposi-

FIGURE 4. *Line and Staff Organization*

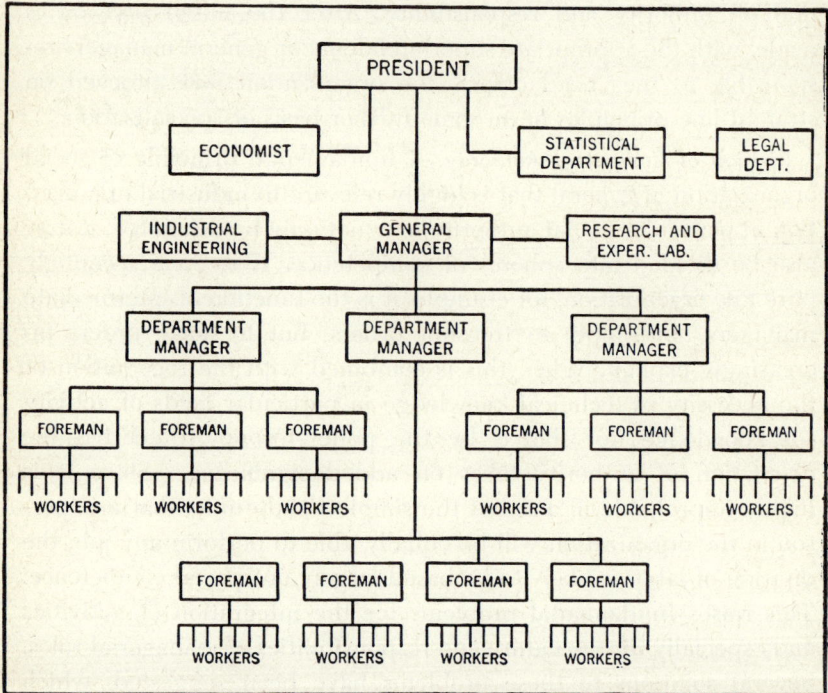

Reproduced by permission from Arthur G. Anderson, *Industrial Engineering and Management* (New York: The Ronald Press Company, 1928), p. 43.

tion of F. W. Taylor,[5] rests upon an almost complete division of authority among specialists. In Taylor's view the functional specialization of managerial officials ought to extend downward to the foremen or others directly in charge of bench workers and machine

[5] See F. W. Taylor, *Shop Management* (New York: Harper & Brothers, 1911), *passim.* See also E. H. Anderson and G. T. Schwenning, *The Science of Production Organization* (New York: John Wiley & Sons, Inc., 1938), pp. 108–117, 193–202.

tenders. Thus each person in the managerial organization would be a specialist, carrying authority only in his special field. A single worker might be directly subject to the direction of six or eight managers, including planners, directors, instructors, inspectors, and those responsible for discipline. As many authorities have pointed out,[6] such a division of authority would require an almost impossibly neat division of spheres of competence and coordination of activities. Without this complete mapping out of "zones of influence," the problems of overlapping authority, evasion of responsibility, or contradictory orders would easily disrupt all semblance of co-ordinated effort toward the common goals of the organization. In multitude of counsel there may be wisdom, but scarcely any guarantee of purposeful action without a "priority rating" in case of division of opinion.

3. Line-Staff-Functional. The advantages of specialization and division of authority into spheres of competence are so numerous in the modern industrial plant that a pure line organization is rare or nonexistent. At the very least the plant is broken up into departmental units, each with a responsible head. On the other hand, the disadvantages of overmanagement, and particularly the confused organization resulting from a functional arrangement in the sense used above, call attention to the unity of direction and direct responsibility allowed by line organization. It is thus quite understandable that, although the proportions and points of emphasis may and do vary, most modern establishments combine two or three methods of organization.

Some specialists are usually conveniently attached directly to the president, general manager, or other policy-forming executive. If these operate as individual advisers, without subordinates other than clerical assistants, their position is primarily that of staff specialists. But other specialists also occupy the position of line managers in the sense of directing the work of assistants and heading a functional division of some proportions. Thus their roles may be advisory as

[6] See Anderson and Schwenning, *op. cit.*, pp. 133–137, 172–181; Arthur G. Anderson, *Industrial Engineering and Factory Management* (New York: The Ronald Press Company, 1928), pp. 51–53; William N. Mitchell, *Production Management* (Chicago: University of Chicago Press, 1931), pp. 217–222.

far as their relation to the central structure of the organization is concerned and supervisory in regard to their corps of assistants or subordinates. Others in the managerial personnel are chiefly responsible for the relaying and applying of general directions originating with the policy-forming executive. In the previous diagram (Figure 4), if one were to add subordinate staffs, occasionally extending through numerous ranks, to the staff specialists represented by the horizontal extension of the chart, something approaching the formal organization of this combination-type would be represented. Such an organization recognizes, for example, the special sphere of authority of the director of the research staff in regard to the activities of his unit, without subjecting machine tenders to the direct supervision of an industrial engineer or a research chemist. The specialist both directs and advises.

One is led to suspect here that general principles of social organization are applicable to industrial plants as well as to other varieties of social systems. Under modern conditions of the necessity of utilizing many different types of materials and mechanical processes, and the accompanying necessity of coordinating the activities of many persons toward the achievement of goals many times removed from the immediate actions of most of those persons, both delegation and division of authority seem inevitable. This generalization is given further support by comparison with the nature of modern military organization. Although army discipline is the most generally recognized aspect of military management, functional specialization is by no means lacking. Not only is there a "departmentalization" of the armed forces, with unified direction only at or very near the top of the control group, but there is the distinction between line and staff officers. The latter do not in general command troops or carry on direct operations on the field. Although staff officers may have high rank, they do not under ordinary circumstances have any *direct* authority over men in any of the major service divisions. They do, however, have specialized spheres of competence in which their authority is direct. *The simplicity or elaborateness of the division of duty and the delegation of authority will in general depend upon the size of the unit and relative importance of the*

*particular unit to the achievement of the general goals of the or-
ganization.*

In the very largest industrial corporations, and particularly those
with a diversified line of products, there has been in recent years
an increasing emphasis on *decentralization* of decision-making and
responsibility. This policy of decentralization, or "federalism," [7]
has several implications for managerial functions that will be discussed in subsequent chapters. As an organizational principle it has
one especially important consequence in the present context. Where
decentralization is along lines of product divisions, for example,
many of the same staff functions will be appropriately carried out
in each division, modified only by the peculiarities of the particular
operation or product (or, in practice, by the peculiarities of the divisional managers). At the same time, these same staff functions may
be necessary at a more general level for the company as a whole.
Thus, advertising and public relations, engineering development,
accounting, personnel and industrial relations, and many other departments may appear in each product division and at the "general
staff" level. Now decentralization implies the authority and responsibility of the divisional manager for successful operation of the
division, including its specialized staff, while a functional division
along lines of spheres of competence implies responsibility of the
highest staff officials for operation of staff specialists. In practice,
divisional staff members are commonly made *administratively* responsible to the manager and *functionally* responsible to the general
staff. As the latter may outrank the divisional managers and in any
event are likely to be party to most high-level decisions for the company as a whole, this mode of organization places both the decentralized line and staff officials in a potentially difficult position.
In this feature of complex organizations, also, the industrial corporation is not unique; the problem has long faced large military
organizations. As a practical matter of operating policy, at least
superficial solution to the problem is easiest where a single criterion

[7] In this connection see Peter F. Drucker, *Concept of the Corporation* (New
York: The John Day Company, 1946), especially Chaps. 2–5; also his *The
New Society: The Anatomy of the Industrial Order* (New York: Harper &
Brothers, 1950), especially Chaps. 29–31.

of success of the divisional chief has clear priority over other considerations—for example, military success or business profit. In many circumstances, however, no such easy solution exists and a variety of devices are used to achieve the advantages of both specialization and unified authority.

Although not generally recognized, the principles applying to complex formal organizations are in fact of sufficient generality to allow the social observer to consider industrial organization as a particular example of a more general type. And despite the unsavory reputation of the term in some quarters, there is little possibility of evading the designation of the general type as *bureaucracy*. Holding in mind the foregoing discussion of the various modes of industrial organization as elaborated by industrial managers and industrial engineers, we may proceed to a discussion of some of the general characteristics of the formal social structure of large industrial plants.

ON THE NATURE OF INDUSTRIAL BUREAUCRACY

As noted in the previous chapter, the old-time boss is a member of a diminishing species. Because of both the separation of ownership and management and the tremendous increase in the size of managerial personnel (both closely related to the introduction of corporate enterprise and the various advantages of bigness), the paternalistic or exploitative employer has been largely replaced by the professional officeholder. In a period characterized by the multiplication of governmental bureaus and their functionaries—often viewed bitterly by industrial representatives—industry has also moved in a similar direction, namely, full-blown bureaucracy. Lest this should be understood as simply a name-calling characterization, it may be well to examine the features of bureaucratic organization and see if the term is indeed aptly applied to contemporary big business.

Specialization. An outstanding feature of the type of organization that may be properly called *bureaucratic* is specialization. More than any other variety of organization, bureaucracy rests upon a selection and distribution of personnel according to specialized abilities and particular duties.[8] It is thus in marked contrast to social units like the family or community that recruit their members chiefly by natural reproduction, and must therefore limit the division of labor in accordance with the quality of the human resources available.

Bureaucratic specialization depends not only upon an adequate recruitment process, but upon an effective classification and coordination process as well. Specifically, the high degree of division of labor characteristic of modern industrial organization rests upon three types of differences in the personnel available for productive labor. (1) It assumes and utilizes differences in native ability. One important distinction between bureaucratic principles of organization and those operating in other types of cooperative social systems is that the former frankly take into account both qualitative and quantitative differences in ability. These differences are not only taken into account negatively, as a limitation to possible occupational diversification, but positively as available human resources for particular positions. (2) The differences in native ability, however, are in general meaningless or useless without specific training along the lines of existent or possible future occupational demands. In fact, bureaucratic specialization goes so far beyond any "natural" (untrained) differences in ability that it calls for high degrees of skill often requiring long preliminary training or apprenticeship. (3) Since, as will be noted, position in a bureaucratic organization demands a good deal of loyalty to the system as a whole (sometimes called *esprit de corps*) and to the duties required by the individual's particular place in that system, it may be said to depend upon differences in occupational interests. This expectation sometimes poses some neat problems, for the individual in our society is in general supposed to be dissatisfied with his particular place in society, yet

[8] The classic analysis of bureaucratic organization is that of Max Weber. See *From Max Weber: Essays in Sociology*, trans. and ed. by H. H. Gerth and C. Wright Mills (New York: Oxford University Press, 1946), pp. 196–244. See also the following: Marshall E. Dimock and Howard K. Hyde, "Bureaucracy and Trusteeship in Large Corporations," United States Congress, Temporary National Economic Committee, *Investigation of Concentration of Economic Power, Monograph No. 11* (Washington: U. S. Government Printing Office, 1940), Part II, "Causes and Manifestations of Bureaucracy."

proud of his importance to his occupation, business organization, industrial plant, or independent profession. It is precisely in the bureaucratic organization that this pull-hauling upon the individual's occupational sentiments is reduced to a minimum by various devices which will be discussed in subsequent paragraphs.

Ideally, the three types of differences in the available personnel are expected to operate together. That is, the methods of selection and training are expected to provide a general sifting process on the basis of ability (as defined by the particular standards of selection considered important), and to induce the appropriate sentiments in regard to the specialized task and the system as a whole. In American society, where *choice* of occupational interests exists to an unusually high degree, the recruitment of the necessary qualified personnel for specialized industrial positions depends to a marked extent upon the advantages that such positions seem to offer to the individual. It is thus not simply necessary that the quantity and quality of the laboring population should have the necessary native ability, but that ability must be translated into usable skills through training, mediated by interest. (These points are further discussed in Chapter XIX.)

A shortcoming in any one of the three prerequisites to bureaucratic specialization may reduce the possible diversification of activities. Given a reasonably satisfactory solution to the general problem of personnel supply, however, the organizational problems resulting from specialization are not all taken care of.

Coordination. Whether in society as a whole, or in a smaller social system like a branch plant of a large steel corporation, *the higher the degree of specialization, the greater the necessity of coordination.* The integration of almost countless activities toward the achievement of the goals of the organization as a whole is one of the most persistent sources of difficulty in industrial management.[9] This would be true even if labor were simply *divided.* It is all the

---

[9] The recognition of the importance of coordination of diversified activities is implicit in most of the treatises on industrial management, but is perhaps most clearly stated in that field by Anderson and Schwenning, *op. cit*, pp. 203–210.

more true since the division takes place in the form of functional specialization.

The industrial executive, technical specialist, junior manager, line supervisor, and to some degree the productive laborer have special *spheres of competence* based upon particular abilities of functional importance to the organization as a whole. Within these broad or narrow spheres of competence the individual specialist reigns supreme. Thus a given riveter or welder may know considerably more about his job than does the foreman who supervises his work. The equivalent situation is most certainly true in the relation of the research chemist to the president or general manager. This is the reason, as intimated earlier in this chapter, that a "pure line" organization will not ordinarily work in a contemporary manufacturing plant. Authority, we noted, is divided as well as delegated. Of this we shall have more to say presently, but it should be observed at once that this does not settle the issue of coordination: it simply documents its importance.

A good deal of the coordination of diversified activities is ensured by the character of the formal organization itself. Thus every person's (or at least every "manager's") status in the organization is, formally considered, a well-defined position or office. This means that the rights and duties of the person occupying the office are largely determined by the relation of the *position* to others (and only incidentally, or even accidentally, by the relation between concrete persons). Under the triple assumption that the system is already established, that it is perfectly integrated, and that the occupants of the various positions will in fact fulfill precisely those official expectations demanded by the positions (no more, no less), the coordination might properly be viewed as automatic. That this result is rarely if ever achieved implies that ordinarily one or more of these assumptions are not in fact borne out. Nevertheless, the organizational advantages of the typical bureaucratic formalization merit some further consideration.

Routine and Formalization. One of the most consistent criticisms of bureaucratic organization, and one that usually makes of the term *bureaucracy* an epithet, is its emphasis upon routine and form.

From certain points of view (that is, with certain ends in mind) the criticism is undoubtedly justified. But from the point of view of maintaining a smoothly operating social system with a complex structure and diversified personnel, the criticism loses some of its merit. The elaborate ritual associated with interpersonal relations in a bureaucratic structure is well designed to maintain the division of spheres of competence, and to a certain degree the coordination of these. To the layman, or the person seeking help or information, the characteristic "passing the buck" is a sign of inefficiency. To the bureaucratic officeholder in government or industry, this is simply a process of referring a problem to the person or department within whose sphere its solution lies. Failure to follow this pattern would destroy the efficacy of the organizational specialization and cause general confusion of well-defined roles in the total system.

A major function of "rules and regulations" in any social organization is that of ensuring predictability of behavior within the organization. Thus the formal pattern of relations fixes responsibility for various decisions and standard activities. In this way it prevents overlapping authority, gaps in responsibility for important duties, and the arbitrary exercise of authority. To the extent that the rules are formal and the expected activities attach to the office and not to the particular occupant, the organization can maintain a high degree of stability with a changing personnel. (This principle is most strikingly illustrated, of course, in the organization of the army, where the most general rule is that a subordinate reacts to the uniform, and not to its wearer.)

A further corollary of the function of rules in ensuring predictability is their function in reducing or eliminating friction. The importance of this function is directly related to the highly diversified personnel making up the organization. The abilities, training, and interests represented are ordinarily such as to make impossible a friendly informal cooperation throughout the organization. Formal rules make it possible even for potential enemies, and especially for those who would under informal conditions remain indifferent toward one another, to maintain cooperative relations. To the extent that the person's significance for the system is determined by his position, and his relations with others follow predetermined routines, the significance of the total personality is minimized. What is of primary importance in a highly formal structure is rather the "organizational personality." Again this principle is of much more general application than its usefulness in a governmental bureau or a business main office. The elaboration of rules of etiquette in "polite society," for example, allows strangers who are familiar with the rule book to act properly toward one another, and minimizes the necessity of making personal adjustments. Its relevance to operation of an extended bureaucratic organization is enhanced, however, by the diversity of the personnel, the specialization of activity, and the necessary coordination if the goals of the entire organization are to be achieved. It is in bureaucracy that a social system most closely approximates the coordinated complexity of the modern machine.

Hierarchical Organization. The distinctions among personnel in any social organization are not all representable on a "horizontal" plane, for authority is never distributed evenly throughout a social system. Even if the source of the authority is a "popular mandate" expressed through some democratic procedure, the importance of responsibility and unified direction are such as to require a demarcation of persons on a "vertical" plane. The wide extension of functional specialization does not remove the necessity for centralized administration and control, but rather increases it. Thus bureaucratic organization, wherever its field of operation, is typically characterized by definite gradations in relative rank.

The discussion of "line" and "functional" organization earlier in this chapter pointed to the significance both of delegation and of division of authority. Part of the necessity of a rather elaborate hierarchy, it was noted, is to be found simply in the size of the industrial organizations, since convenience and effective organization require that the number of persons directly supervised by a single administrator not be large. This means that general policies of goals are passed down from one rank to the next, becoming more definite at each step, until they become explicit directions for the performance of those activities that will produce the general results desired.

The importance of "functional authority," that is, authority within special spheres of competence, has led some observers to minimize the importance of "final authority." [10] They argue, quite reasonably, that this specialization reduces the *area* of explicit authority of the executive. But they also argue that there is no final authority, but only the functional coordination of specialists. This is a sufficiently important issue in determining the general character of industrial organization, as well as the specific roles of members of the managerial personnel, to merit close examination.

One striking result of functional division of authority is that the executive ceases thereby to be the most skilled workman, or even the most competent "authority" in the organization. But this does not mean that the necessity for hierarchical organization is removed. On the contrary, the reduction of the area of the explicit authority of the executive increases the importance of the coordinating function of the "line" official. Besides coordination, which might conceivably be maintained by the formal structure of the organization, a "final authority" is further necessary for two reasons: (1) the overall policies of the organization must proceed from the responsible center of control of that organization, and (2) this is more particularly true since the organization must be prepared to adapt itself to changed conditions.

The function of coordinating specialized activities is, in practice, not adequately guaranteed by the formal relationships between specialists. There are a number of reasons for this, which are discussed more fully in the following chapter, but one of the outstanding ones is precisely the problem of organizational elasticity to allow for major or minor changes in the goals of the organization. In an elaborate social system, part of the units may be viewed as "structural," that is, as integrating the actions of various distinct units.

The addition of the problem of coordination to the general necessity of subdelegation of authority in a large organization increases, rather than decreases, the necessity of hierarchical arrangement of ranks and corresponding authority and responsibility. In fact, *the*

[10] See especially M. P. Follett, "The Meaning of Responsibility in Business Management," in Henry C. Metcalf, ed., *Business Management as a Profession* (Chicago: A. W. Shaw Company, 1927), pp. 319–338.

wider the horizontal extension of functional specialization, the greater the necessity for vertical subdelegation of authority. This, in the absence of a better term, may be called the *pyramidal principle of bureaucratic organization.*

Professionalization. The growth of professional management, noted in the previous chapter, is further evidence of the bureaucratic character of industrial organization. The amount of technical training required for specialized offices in a modern business or manufacturing establishment goes a long way toward ensuring that the individual officeholder will think of a career in terms of the organization. This does not necessarily mean that he expects to end his working life in the position he held when he first became a part of the system. On the contrary, he will ordinarily expect considerable advancement through various ranks during the course of his active career. How well these expectations are satisfied, or their failure justified and accepted, may well determine the extent of effective *esprit de corps* throughout the organization, and the presence or absence of an attachment to the organization as a whole.

Perhaps governmental bureaucracy, particularly as exemplified in the British and American "permanent civil service," has achieved this professionalization and regularized advancement through clearcut ranks more completely than has industrial bureaucracy. This is probably due partly to the longer period of development of complex governmental administration and partly to the more rapid changes in industrial organization demanded by the constant orientation to an expanding technology.

In political administration and, to a lesser extent, in industrial administration, the attachment of the individual to the organization as a whole has been ensured by a number of interrelated devices. (1) No matter what major department or section of an organization the individual enters, the steps to the top of the organization are sufficiently well defined to leave little doubt as to the usual line or direction of promotion. (2) The absolute and relative importance of any particular position is recognized not only by salaries proportional to rank, but by honorific titles ("coordinator," "director," "specialist," "executive secretary," and so on almost indefinitely), glass doors, large desks, letterheads, and the like. (3) The intrusion of a too highly competitive spirit in a cooperative organization is largely made unnecessary by the elaborate formal definition of rights and duties attaching to the particular office, and the likelihood of its appearance is often further reduced by basing advancement upon the relatively nonrational seniority principle rather than on technical qualification as determined on other grounds. It has been only within the comparatively recent past that industrial managers have given much consideration to the character of the promotional system, both as a part of the general problem of adequate selection of personnel and as a method of maintaining "morale" within the organization. Since this constitutes one of the major functions of management, fuller treatment of the various specific problems raised will be deferred to Chapter VI. It is important here simply to note its relevance to the integration of complex organizations.

If the career bureaucrat understands his position in the organization and complies with the organizational expectations in fulfilling his various duties, he must of course accept the rules and routines which presumably lead to the ultimate goals of the organization. This raises a series of problems, however, in a complex and partially elastic organization. Devotion to duty, that is, strict compliance with all the technical regulations, may persist in the face of their obvious inefficacy in attaining the officially prescribed end. A widespread characteristic of bureaucratic organizations of all kinds is this tendency of the officeholder to treat the rules as ends in themselves. Since in an extremely complex system the relation of any particular activity to the general goals of the organization may be difficult or impossible for the functionary to see, and since he is likely to feel that his only security in the organization is in a religious devotion to duty (narrowly defined), it is understandable that he should attach high significance to strict conformity with the rule book. To an outsider, who is much more likely to have his attention fixed upon the general goals and to fail to appreciate the problems of technical specialization, this lays the functionary or the entire organization open to charges of becoming enmeshed in "red tape."

In a very real sense, the "career man" who occupies a particular position in an elaborate organization has a "vested interest" in the preservation not only of the entire organization, but of the various formal activities and relationships that characterize his role in it. Subjectively considered, preservation of the formal relations is necessary for his security.

The characteristic routine and professionalization of bureaucracy make it a system that operates more effectively in a stable social order than in a changing one. External changes as reflected in modifications or transformations in general policies may also require changes in the social machinery. Within the organization, however, there is a profound resistance to change. Since manufacturing companies must be oriented to changes in the market, in technology, in labor relations, and in legislation, this conservatism becomes a critical problem in industrial management.

Indirect Lines of Communication. The essence of social interaction, and a primary condition for the existence of any social group, is to be found in communication. It is impossible to talk about a social relationship, or social organization, without implying the existence of communication among the several units (persons) said to be related or organized. But unlike animal societies, the human capacity for abstract and symbolic communication through various forms of language makes it possible for those not actually in one another's presence to maintain a social system. All large organizations are likely to maintain at least some indirect communication among the membership through the sheer necessities created by size. A large organization that is also formally organized and functionally specialized will rely on indirect communication to an even higher degree. Thus we arrive at an outstanding, although little recognized, attribute of industrial bureaucracy.[11]

Individuals who initiate action of the highest importance for a given workman, or foreman, may exist for that person simply by name and reputation. Even within the direct line organization, the executive may be separated by several or many stages from those

[11] See Chester I. Barnard, *The Functions of the Executive* (Cambridge: Harvard University Press, 1938), especially pp. 82–91, 106–111, 217–226.

expected to carry out the activities necessary to implement an executive order. With functional specialization the lines of communication become even more indirect, for specialists are chiefly bound together in formal organization through the line officer or executive charged with coordinating their activities and, if necessary, putting their recommendations into effect.

Well-established bureaucracies have definite arrangements for various types of communications. Ordinarily these will emphasize vertical channels rather than contact among equals in rank. This is, as previously implied, due to the coordinating functions of the executive, and to the necessity for orders to go "down" through the staff through regular patterns of superiors and subordinates. A consequence of the indirect lines of communication that is always a potential threat to effective operation is the tendency for the intermediate functionary or the executive to be overloaded with masses of routine business and thus act as a bottleneck to the free passage of directions and information. A deluge of interoffice communications, which may or may not have to proceed by way of a common superior officer, will tend to hold up essential information or provide work for endless secretaries and filing clerks without necessarily contributing to the effective operation of the entire system.

On the other hand, the executive who wants to cut out the "red tape" by reducing the volume of routine correspondence is faced with possible human forgetfulness, errors in interpretation, conscious or unconscious errors in passing along verbal directions. These are problems of managerial activities that will receive further elaboration in the following chapters.

Indirect lines of communication cannot avoid increasing the formality of an organization already formally established. By reducing personal contact to a minimum and eliminating it almost entirely among persons widely separated in rank and function, the operation of the whole system by reference to the rule book is made easier. That is, the difficulty of distinguishing the concrete person from his specialized position and roles is not great if one's relation to that person is not only formally prescribed, but indirect. Thus in so far as the existing structure and the formal rules adequately provide for the activities and social relationships necessary for effective operation of the organization, indirect lines of communication may actually enhance the strength of that organization. To the extent that personal contact and informal relationships are essential, or are thought to be, the very formality of the established structure may be a barrier to cooperative action. The latter possibility has been inadequately recognized by industrial managers, who understandably are inclined to view the formal organization as a mechanical contrivance ensuring "efficiency" (whatever that may be).

The shortcomings of established systems of communication are often recognized implicitly by the formation of new devices to aid coordination and decision-making. Both standing and special committees may be formed for cutting across official lines of specialization or for establishing new services. Moreover, many companies in recent years have experimented extensively with conference methods for achieving new channels for the flow of information and opinion. These devices are appropriate not only to the solution of new problems for which the existing formal structure is unprepared, but also for an attack upon some persistent problems of most complex structures. Notable among the latter problems are those of competition for spheres of competence among functional divisions and the unnecessary duplication of activities. The interdepartmental committee may serve to adjudicate such difficulties, which are likely to be most acute precisely in a situation of deliberate decentralization of authority and responsibility.

Peculiarities of Organizational Charts. Earlier in this chapter we noted the relative ease with which the formal outlines of an industrial organization can be plotted in the form of a chart. The use of charts is in fact widespread among industrial managers as a method of graphic summary of the delegation and division of authority, functional division of responsibility, and lines of communication.[12] This general practice is further evidence of the bureaucratic

[12] For discussion and illustration of the use of organizational charts, see Arthur G. Anderson, *Industrial Engineering and Factory Management* (New York: The Ronald Press Company, 1928), Chap. IV, "Organization for Management," and Chap. V, "Modern Industrial Organizations"; Anderson and Schwenning, *op. cit.*, pp. 117–123; Mitchell, *op. cit.*, p. 238.

structure of modern industrial organization, and gives basis for the reference to "blueprint organization."

The pyramidal principle of bureaucratic organization is well illustrated by most organization charts, and this has further significance in the actual attitudes and policies of industrial management. Although pyramidal in form, an organization chart is rarely consulted by a person whose position is at the bottom of the pyramid. In other words, the arrangement of the chart assumes that one is looking at the organization from the top down. This is symbolic of the tendency for precision of lines of communication, specialization of roles, and so on to "blur out" as one approaches the bottom of the pyramid. It is symbolic precisely because the organizational chart is consulted and relied upon by those at or near the top, and the tendency for these persons to be in touch with those at the bottom by extremely indirect lines of communication poses a general problem of complex formal organization—the relation of the worker at the bottom with the policy-forming executives at the top. This peculiarity of the organizational chart has been aptly summarized by Roethlisberger:

We . . . find the observer in the office of the general manager of a large industrial enterprise. The latter is poring over something which is to be a never-ending source of astonishment and mystery to the observer —an organization chart. The general manager's desk, which the observer had noticed when he entered the room was free of all objects except a telephone and a calendar pad, is now littered with blue charts which show the formal relations each person in the company is supposed to have to those people who work for him as well as to those people for whom he works. He is being initiated by the general manager into such mysteries as "staff and line," "centralization and decentralization of authority," "straight-line production," "functional as opposed to product-shop organization."

Although our observer's mind is in a whirl over all these new terms, he is still capable of making two simple observations: (1) The people at the top of the organization, including the person to whom he is talking, appear to be separated by many steps from the people at the bottom of the organization. (2) Although every place on the organization chart has a label attached to it, the labels at the top and middle of the chart refer to single persons, whereas the labels at the bottom, such as "workers," "clerks," etc., refer to groups of persons. These observations raise three questions in the observer's mind, so he asks the general manager: (1) Do the people at the bottom of the organization have any difficulty in understanding the economic and logical objectives of the people at the top? (2) Do the people at the top have difficulty in understanding the way the people at the bottom feel? (3) Although this chart shows how management is organized, how are all the people labeled "workers" (who, he understands, constitute two-thirds of the population) organized? [13]

Professor Roethlisberger's observer received no satisfactory answer to these questions from the general manager, and indeed, the basis for a satisfactory answer is often lacking in managerial circles in contemporary industry. Yet the questions raised have an important bearing on the activities and functions of management (and thereby on the general adequacy of the organization as a whole).

The integration of the industrial bureaucracy, even at managerial and executive levels, is a model and not a statement of complete fact. At several places in the preceding pages actual or potential trouble spots in the operation of industrial organization were indicated. Some of these arise from the very formality of the organizational structure, and the inclination of any member to view the whole system from his particular vantage point. But group (collective) action is also a likelihood in such organizations, and at managerial levels. The potentialities for "collective bargaining" between formally constituted units and between informally organized factions and cliques have been persistently obscured by the preoccupation of managers and scholars alike with management–labor relations. The industrial bureaucracy is not simply divisible at one level in the hierarchy; it is fissionable. How these considerations affect various types of industrial managers the two following chapters explore.

[13] From F. J. Roethlisberger, *Management and Morale* (Cambridge: Harvard University Press, 1941), Chap. V, "A Disinterested Observer Looks at Industry," pp. 73–74. Reprinted by permission of Harvard University Press.

REFERENCES

ALFORD, L. P., *Principles of Industrial Management* (New York: The Ronald Press Company, 1940), Chaps. 7 and 8, "Organization for Control."

ANDERSON, ARTHUR G., *Industrial Engineering and Factory Management* (New York: The Ronald Press Company, 1928), Chap. IV, "Organization for Management," and Chap. V, "Modern Industrial Organizations."

ANDERSON, E. H., and G. T. SCHWENNING, *The Science of Production Organization* (New York: John Wiley & Sons, Inc., 1938), Chap. IV, "Organization Structure"; Chap. V, "Types of Organization"; Chap. VI, "Comparison of Organization Types"; Chap. VII, "Organization Principles and Laws."

BARNARD, CHESTER I., *The Functions of the Executive* (Cambridge: Harvard University Press, 1938), Chaps. V–VIII, X, XI, XII, XIV.

——, *Organization and Management* (Cambridge: Harvard University Press, 1948).

DIMOCK, MARSHALL E., and HOWARD K. HYDE, "Bureaucracy and Trusteeship in Large Corporations," United States Congress, Temporary National Economic Committee, *Investigation of Concentration of Economic Power*, Monograph No. 11 (Washington: U. S. Government Printing Office, 1940), Part II, "Causes and Manifestations of Bureaucracy."

DRUCKER, PETER F., *Concept of the Corporation* (New York: The John Day Company, 1946).

——, *The New Society: The Anatomy of the Industrial Order* (New York: Harper & Brothers, 1950).

FARQUAR, HENRY H., "The Anomaly of Functional Authority at the Top," *Advanced Management*, 7: 51–54, 83, April–June 1942.

FAYOL, HENRI, *Industrial and General Administration* (London: Sir Isaac Pitman & Sons, Ltd., for International Management Institute, n.d.).

FIREY, WALTER, "Informal Organization and the Theory of Schism," *American Sociological Review*, 13: 15–24, February 1948.

FOLLETT, M. P., "The Meaning of Responsibility in Business Management," in Henry C. Metcalf, ed., *Business Management as a Profession* (Chicago: A. W. Shaw Company, 1927), pp. 318–338.

GARDNER, BURLEIGH B., *Human Relations in Industry* (Chicago: Richard D. Irwin, 1945), Chap. I, "The Factory as a Social System," and Chap. IV, "Segmentation of the Structure."

GRAICUNAS, V. A., "Relationship in Organization," in Luther Gulick and L. Urwick, eds., *Papers on the Science of Administration* (New York:

Institute of Public Administration, Columbia University, 1937), pp. 181–187.

GULICK, LUTHER, "Notes on the Theory of Organization," in Luther Gulick and L. Urwick, eds., *Papers on the Science of Administration* (New York: Institute of Public Administration, Columbia University, 1937), pp. 1–45.

LANSBURGH, RICHARD H., and WILLIAM R. SPRIEGEL, *Industrial Management* (New York: John Wiley & Sons, Inc., 1940), Chap. VI, "Organization Development," and Chap. VII, "Organization Types."

LASKI, HAROLD J., "Bureaucracy," in *Encyclopaedia of the Social Sciences,* 3: 70–73.

MERTON, ROBERT K., "Bureaucratic Structure and Personality," *Social Forces,* 18: 560–568, May 1940.

MOONEY, JAMES D., *The Principles of Organization* (New York: Harper & Brothers, 1939), Chap. II, "The Coordinative Principle"; Chap. III, "The Scalar Principle"; Chap. IV, "The Functional Principle"; Chap. V, "The Staff Phase of Functionalism"; Chap. XXI, "Internal Problems of Modern Industrial Organization."

PETERSEN, ELMORE, and E. GROSVENOR PLOWMAN, *Business Organization and Management,* rev. ed. (Chicago: Richard D. Irwin, 1948), especially Chap. IV, "The Levels Theory of Organization"; Chap. VII, "Line, Staff, and Functional Organization"; Chap. VIII, "Authority, Responsibility, Accountability."

PORTER, ROBERT W., *Design for Industrial Coordination* (New York: McGraw-Hill Book Company, Inc., 1941), Chap. IV, "Jurisdictional Processes of Industrial Coordination," and Chap. V, "Functional Characteristics of Industrial Organization."

ROBINSON, A., "Problem of Management and the Size of Firms," *Economic Journal,* 44: 242–257, June 1934.

SELZNICK, PHILIP, "Foundations of the Theory of Organization," *American Sociological Review,* 13: 25–35, February 1948.

SHELDON, OLIVER, *The Philosophy of Management* (London: Sir Isaac Pitman & Sons, Inc., 1924), Chap. IV, "The Organization of the Factory."

URWICK, L., "Executive Decentralization with Functional Coordination," *Management Review,* 24: 355–368, December 1935.

——, "Organization as a Technical Problem," in Luther Gulick and L. Urwick, eds., *Papers on the Science of Administration* (New York: Institute of Public Administration, Columbia University, 1937), pp. 47–88.

CHAPTER V

EXECUTIVE FUNCTIONS

As ONE walks through the corridors of the central office building of a large manufacturing plant, one must be impressed by the large number of people whose labor seems to be largely concerned with papers, typewriters, and telephones. Some of these persons are secluded behind paneled doors and protected by businesslike secretaries in "outer offices." Their presence, or affiliation with the organization, is known to the stray visitor and even to many persons employed by the company only by the evidence of a neatly lettered name and a door marked "Private." These persons, both those exposed to casual observation and those shielded from the gaze of the unworthy, are the company's managers.

The managers do not produce the company's products, but it is safe to say that the products could not be produced without their services. Ordinarily they do not, individually or collectively, "own" the company, but the dividends to investors and the price of the securities on the market would stand at zero were their services to collapse. As a unit of an industrial organization, *the general function of management is to be found in the establishment of organizations and in the operation of going concerns.* This is called a single function because organizing and operating are, at least in practice, simply two aspects of the same thing. An organization is pointless (except as an artistic creation) unless it operates, and unified operation is impossible without organization. It is the purpose of the present chapter to indicate the general division of managerial labor, and to consider in some detail the specific functions of executives. Other managerial groups will be discussed in Chapter VI.

MANAGERIAL FUNCTIONS IN GENERAL

What was previously referred to as the "growth of professional management" is not simply a substitution of management-labor for the older capital-labor dichotomy. Such a conclusion would be justified if the change were simply a division of the duties or functions of the older entrepreneur into those of capital investment and finance on the one hand and management on the other. Although the *general function* of management is not appreciably different from that of the "captain of industry" except in the sense of being narrower, this general function is in fact carried on by a great variety of specific managerial functions performed by a diversified personnel. The intricacies of organization outlined in the preceding chapter make it clear that management itself constitutes a cooperative system involving a great deal of division and delegation of specific rights and duties. Thus, viewed distributively and formally, the functions of management are achieved through the performance of duties according to the individual's place in the organization.

Division of Managerial Labor. For the sake of convenience in discussion of the specific functions of management, we may distinguish six groups in a large industrial organization whose relations to the operation of the whole are sufficiently similar within each group and sufficiently distinct between groups to warrant classification. The six categories are (1) executives, sometimes called "top management"; (2) technical specialists, known by a variety of specific designations; (3) junior line supervisors, often called "middle management"; (4) secretarial and clerical workers of various kinds and ranks; (5) first-line supervisors, known as foremen, section chiefs, bosses, and so on, whose outstanding common characteristic is that they relay orders and directions to those who do not in turn pass them on, that is, "workers"; (6) shop and bench workers who may be known as the rank and file, operatives, operators, or simply as employees.[1] It is significant of the correspondence between complex

---

[1] This classification is adapted from that given by F. J. Roethlisberger, *Management and Morale* (Cambridge: Harvard University Press, 1941), pp. 35–36. The chief difference in the list here presented is in the distinction be-

organization and the importance of management that five of these six groups are managerial, although the sixth may well constitute a sizable majority of the entire personnel. Actually, this represents a managerial bias symbolized by the expectation that the organizational chart will be viewed from the top down. Indeed it is noteworthy that many employees commonly considered in this last category are not in a direct sense production workers, even by the loose test of handling the product—for example, watchmen and guards, janitors and elevator operators, and chauffeurs of company cars. However, the present concern is with the distinctions as commonly made, and not with the many occupations that may at the moment best be characterized negatively as nonmanagerial.

It is not meant to imply that the formal organization of large industrial concerns is adequately described in terms of five or six categories of personnel. On the contrary, as subsequent sections of the present and following chapter will indicate, many distinctions of high importance for the specialization of work must be made within each of these categories. They are treated as units only because, and in so far as, their membership occupies roughly the same position or represents roughly the same interests in the organization as a whole.

"Unofficial" Aspects of Management. Neither is it meant to imply that the actual operation of an organization—that is, viewed distributively, the activities of the personnel—is adequately described by a statement of the formal, structural ("blueprint") relations. Over and beyond the officially expected rights and duties, lines of authority, and rigidly defined relationships, any managerial system is characterized by a great variety of informal, unofficial activities, attitudes, sentiments, and symbols. These "unexpected" social manifestations take many different specific forms that are only partly dependent on the character of the individuals' formal positions. Thus some individuals, for one reason or another, may do work of less quantity or lower quality than is officially demanded of one in that position, and other individuals, for one reason or another, do more. Questions of policy may in fact be referred to the unofficial

tween "middle management" and "first-line" supervisors, which seems to be dictated by the peculiar responsibilities of the latter group. (See Chap. VI.)

keeper of traditions who is a minor official with long service, rather than to the person in "authority." Such informal symbols of status as double pedestal desks, private offices, private secretaries, the posting of names on an office directory, the wearing of ties and white shirts, or ready access to water coolers furnished with paper cups may, to the initiated, symbolize more than endless charts, diagrams, or official pronouncements of managerial organization.

In reference to each of the several managerial categories we shall note the additional weight or intrusive influence of relationships, sentiments, and symbols that are informal and unofficial in character. Informal, however, does not mean unorganized. It means rather those relationships that tend to include more elements of the personality than do the official, segmental ones, and more sentiments and traditions. Although it is possible for informal organizations to be deliberately created, they always appear to their membership to be spontaneous. It is this characteristic spontaneity that is rarely guaranteed by formal organization and yet is of importance for maintaining what is often called the *morale* of the organization. This implies a consideration that will be documented in some detail in the discussion of specific managerial functions: the utilization of informal organization to supplement official expectations may be one of the primary techniques of successful management.

It follows from the foregoing that managerial functions and activities *will always include elements not planned in the organizational scheme.* For example, the "personalities" of executives and the peculiar office customs of the organization will not appear in the report to stockholders, but will comprise part of the total scheme of organization. This is a generalization that has been formulated only very recently,[2] but has been intuitively recognized by successful ex-

[2] Attention has been focused on the social character of managerial organization by a number of recent books, particularly the works of a group that roughly centers around the industrial research activities at the Harvard Graduate School of Business Administration. The present discussion has borrowed heavily from a number of these, notably Roethlisberger, *op. cit.;* Roethlisberger and William J. Dickson, *Management and the Worker* (Cambridge: Harvard University Press, 1939); Elton Mayo, *Human Problems of an Industrial Civilization* (New York: The Macmillan Company, 1933); T. N. Whitehead, *Leadership in a Free Society* (Cambridge: Harvard University Press, 1937) and *The*

ecutives or coordinators since time immemorial. In fact, it has probably been better recognized and acted upon in the past than in a great many modern industrial organizations. This seems to have been true for a number of reasons to be discussed in Chapter VII, but which for the present may be summarized as the peculiarly modern tendency to think of the persons comprising the membership of complex organizations as exclusively logical and economically rational beings. The informal aspects of organizational attitudes and activities arise, on the contrary, from three related considerations: (1) the heterogeneity of the personnel, and the fact that each is a concrete person, with interests, qualities, habits, and opinions beyond those technically required for his job; (2) the fact that in complex organizations individuals tend to define the operation of the whole from the only vantage point they have, namely, their own; and, consequently, (3) that sentiments of rights and duties, customs, traditions, symbols of status, small signs of favor or disfavor, figure largely in any individual's orientation to his immediate situation, and thus to the organization as a whole.

The importance of the first, which might be called the "personality" factor, is indicated by the difference the replacement of a grouchy official by a pleasant one will make in the actual work of the organization, although no change in official duties has taken place. The importance of the second, which might be called the factor of "organizational nearsightedness," is illustrated by every jealous administrator, foreman, or worker who is sure that his work is the most essential in the entire organization, and takes steps to keep it so and prevent encroachment by others. The importance of the third, which we may term the factor of "custom and ritual," arises at least partly from organizational nearsightedness, and is illustrated by the attention given to location of desks, a cheerful "good morning" from the boss, or keeping well stocked with the quality of humorous story demanded of one's station.

The industrial executive or shop supervisor neglects these social

---

Industrial Worker (Cambridge: Harvard University Press, 1938, 2 vols.); and Chester I. Barnard, *The Functions of the Executive* (Cambridge: Harvard University Press, 1938).

considerations at his own peril, or at least the peril of the effectiveness of management as a whole.

EXECUTIVE FUNCTIONS

Who Are the Executives? A first problem in discussing the functions of industrial executives is to discover them. This is not always easy, even by reference to organization charts, for the separation of managerial control, financial control, and investment ownership often confuses the picture as to the location of ultimate and active responsibility for the establishment as a going concern. Thus organization charts often represent the hierarchy of control at the top of the organization as:

Stockholders
Directors
President or General Manager

This is about as sensible as representing the executive department of the Federal government as being controlled at the top by:

Electorate
Electoral College
President

and only slightly more reasonable than viewing the "top management" of the distribution department of a manufacturing establishment as:

Consumers
Consumer Analysts
Sales Manager

Those persons or groups whose opinions are heard and possibly followed occasionally, or whose interests must be taken into account in the operation of an organization, do not stand in the position of executives. In fact, the executives must be defined in terms of their general functions: *the person or persons in responsible and continuous control of the organization as an operating unit and in a position to formulate general objectives of the organization.* Whether the executive is an individual or a committee, the method of his or their selection, the titles given, and so on, are not concretely irrelevant, but they are incidental to the general position of the coordinator and responsible authority in an operating organization.

The most general of the managerial functions are *specifically* the functions of the executives. Barnard [3] views the entire managerial organization as in an executive position. This is to a significant degree true, but, as Barnard also recognizes, within that organization there are at least two bases of division of function: amount of authority, and type or area of authority. The two are not completely independent, or yet the same thing. Executive functions in the managerial organization are performed by persons who have a *large amount* of authority, which is of a *general or coordinating type*.

The executive is not necessarily the most skilled person in the organization; skills in widely disparate fields are not easily comparable. Thus it is largely meaningless to inquire concerning the relative skills of an industrial executive and a research chemist, and it is a question not often raised in practice. The executive is, on the other hand, presumably the most skilled coordinator. That is, it is officially assumed that he has some grounds for wielding the amount and type of influence that his position gives him.

The higher the position a person occupies in a line of authority, the more general must his abilities be. This is about the same as saying that the abilities of higher executives are more readily transferable from one phase of organization to another, and is a corollary of the principle that the more general the objective, the higher must the responsibility rest for its attainment. Thus it follows that, in a large and highly specialized organization, there will be numerous "coordinators," that is, persons in major or minor executive positions all up and down the line. Since strictly executive functions are more closely represented at the top, however, and since it is only at the top that the activities apply to the entire organization, it is convenient to limit the term *executives* to the chief administrators.

Specific Executive Functions. The functions of the executive are clearly those activities which he carries on, officially or unofficially, which contribute to the character and operation of the organization

[3] *Op. cit.*, pp. 215–216.

as a whole, and, more particularly, those demanded of his peculiar position in the organization. In a formal organization, "functions" are intimately related to position, so that activities not ordinarily a part of the task of the executive may be useful without being executive functions. Thus if the executive is also a cost accountant, a salesman, or a first aid expert for the organization, these no doubt useful services are not a part of his executive functions. On the other hand, if the general objectives that he formulates are actually based upon the predictions of his favorite astrologer (or his emotional antipathy to labor organization), he may not be a good—that is, effective—executive, but he is performing services appropriate to his position.

The idea of "function," moreover, is always to be understood in reference to some end or result. In other words, one must ask, "function for what?" Thus the functions of the executive may be very limited if expressed in general terms, but since the general ends or results require a chain of more and more explicit activities for their achievement, the place at which the line is drawn in detailing the work of the executive is a matter of convenience determined by the goals of understanding and general knowledge. Since it is the combination of minute activities in particular ways that constitutes the achievement of more general results, it is not convenient to carry the analysis to the point of endless lists of particular operations performed by the executive office. For example, it is essentially meaningless to say that it is an executive function to write (or dictate) letters, since this is a particular means that may be, and is, used by persons who are not performing executive functions.

It is necessary in discussing functions to speak of their relation to ends *or* results because of the likelihood in any social organization that the two may be different. This is not true simply because of the possibility of failure in achieving ends, but because of the additional possibility that the *results* of some activities or aspects of the organization will contribute more to the functioning of the whole than the avowed reason for the activity or organizational paraphernalia. Again, this arises from the informal aspect of structure. For example, the large desks of high executives are customarily justified in terms of their specific usefulness to the executive. Since the desks, however, are ordinarily clean and only a small part of the area is in frequent use, this may well be dismissed as a specious explanation. As Roethlisberger has commented, "there seems to be in fact, an almost inverse correlation between the size of a person's desk and the technical need for the size." [4] It is also significant, however, as Roethlisberger observes, that the size of the desk is directly correlated with the social status of the person using it. We may, therefore, from the functional point of view maintain that such symbols of status contribute to the general aura of authority surrounding the executive, which in turn is important for carrying on his general functions. Indeed, we might say that it is a specific function of the executive to sit behind a large, unlittered desk. This statement does less violence to the principle of the inconvenience of overspecification of detailed activities as "functions" than does the illustration of letter writing, but may yet be regarded as simply a part of broader, and therefore more significant, functions.

Following Barnard,[5] we may distinguish four chief functions of the executive, which may in turn be subdivided as far as convenient —at least to the extent of indicating the chief principles and problems that affect their adequate performance. These specific functions are: (1) establishment and maintenance of lines of communication, (2) selection and retention of personnel, (3) securing essential services from individuals, and (4) the formulation of general purposes or objectives.[6]

Lines of Communication. Since the industrial establishment is, among other things, a particular type of *social* system, it follows that the

[4] *Management and Morale,* p. 77.

[5] *Op. cit.,* pp. 161–184, 215–234. Our treatment borrows heavily from Barnard, whose book should be consulted for more complete coverage of the points under discussion.

[6] This list differs in detail from that of Barnard (*ibid.,* pp. 217 ff.), chiefly in our consideration of selection and retention of personnel as distinct from the function of establishing and maintaining lines of communication. See also Luther Gulick, "Notes on the Theory of Organization," in Luther Gulick and L. Urwick, eds., *Papers on the Science of Administration* (New York: Institute of Public Administration, Columbia University, 1937), pp. 1–45, especially pp. 12–15.

maintenance of that system depends upon *communication* among its various members. The obviousness of the general principle should not obscure the problems posed in the actual establishment and maintenance of that communication. In a small, intimate group the problem of communication does not often arise, or at least not in the same way and with the same stringency in which it appears in large and complex organizations. This is true because a great deal of the "contact" and reciprocal influence of persons in large social systems is indirect, mediated either through mechanical contrivances, intermediate persons, or both. Thus the general scheme of organization, the delegation and division of authority, determines through what formal channels communications pass. In its simplest form this scheme of communication may be viewed as a passage "up and down" of information, the passage down of orders or directions, and possibly the passage up of suggestions. But the "horizontal" extension of technical specialization raises the additional question of "crosswise" contacts. In formal organization generally, such contacts are established through the lowest common line officer, that is, coordinator. In other words, such communications generally go "up and down" in the process of going "across" the organization. The actual operation of the communication system will be partly affected by the extent to which executives insist on ritualistic observance of the formal principles of hierarchical organization. This again may be affected by the necessity of the executive's knowing "what is going on" and possibly rendering decisions. Thus the foreman of an operating unit may not be required to address the foreman of the stock warehouse through their common superior if the matter is "routine," but may be required to submit some requests "for decision." This difficulty in the communication system arises from the tendency for bureaucratic structures to be "overorganized" in terms of the generally accepted objectives. The executive may be faced with the difficult decision between maintaining the strictly formal lines of communication in view of the advantages of predictability, order, and so on, or cutting across these lines in particular cases in order to avoid "red tape."

For the scheme of organization to provide an effective system of communication, even from a strictly formal point of view, a number of requirements must be met.

1. *The scheme of organization, and its attendant provisions for regularized communication, must be known.* The arrangement of positions, of superiors and subordinates, of colleagues and helpers, must be a part of the factual orientation of any member of the organization to the system as a whole. Actually, the extent of necessary information about the entire system varies directly with the position and responsibility of the individual in using and maintaining the system of communication. For many individuals this may be limited to a relatively small aspect of the organization. Yet, even within these limits, the importance of definite knowledge of the status and roles—and consequently of the character of the communicative relationships—of other meaningful persons in the system is such that appointments are publicly announced, the minor officials are instructed in the fine art of reading organization charts, and care is taken to avoid wholesale turnovers of official personnel or changes in positions and titles. This is further implemented by various informal badges of status or authority, such as business suits (even if unpressed) worn by supervisors, and possibly white coats or uniforms affected by members of the health service. Since the individual must know *to whom* as well as *for what* he is responsible, and from whom he may expect essential services, order and predictability can only be adequately achieved through knowledge of organizational relationships. A communication system, such as the resort to labor spies, that depends upon secrecy for its effectiveness is a clear confession that management has failed in one of its primary functions in the organization.

2. *The system of communication must reach everyone who is part of the organization.* Again, the principle is axiomatic, or "true by definition," but its effectual operation is nevertheless problematical in large and diversified organizations. American popular humor is replete with stories of some individual working in a plant for weeks at odd activities until finally asked by a supervisor what he is doing there. The principle of complete coverage of the personnel by formal lines of communication fixes every individual's relation to

the whole by establishing his relationship to the well-defined parts, and it is only in rapidly expanding bureaucracies, or organizations undergoing considerable transformation in positions or personnel, that the problem is likely to be acute.

3. *The line of communication should, for the sake of economy and increased certainty, be as short as possible.* This is a principle that must be taken into account in connection with the complementary principle noted in the previous chapter that the number of persons under the effective direct authority of a single person is limited. This latter principle tends to extend the lines of communication in a large organization. A balance between the two is frequently maintained by the decentralization of decision-making. Long lines of communication (that is, with a great many intermediaries between the initiator of the request, for example, and the performer of the operation) are dependent upon the adequacy of transmission and application of the directions at each stage in the line. This is one reason for the volume of interoffice correspondence in large managerial organizations. Much of what appears to be "red tape" may in fact be a necessary guard against the frailties of verbal understanding and the shortness of human memory. In practice, even very large and "highly organized" systems rarely have more than ten distinct stages in formal lines of communication.

4. As we have just implied, *a necessary aspect of establishing and maintaining lines of communication is the assured competence of those members of the personnel who serve as communication centers.* This accounts in part for the bureaucratic emphasis upon routine, systematic "clearing the desk," and the virtues made of punctuality, methodicalness, dependability, and so on. Although these policies often have the appearance and frequently the reality of ritual, they should be understood in terms of the problems of keeping a highly complicated social machine hanging together.

5. Except under extraordinary circumstances *all of the line of communication*—that is, all of the line between the initiator of the information or request and the ultimate recipient—*should be used.* This principle is not only important in maintaining the "orderliness and predictability" of formal relationships, but is intimately related

to the maintenance of authority. An officer who acts in regard to an indirect subordinate without going through the ordinary channels has gone a long way toward the subversion of the intermediate officer's authority. It is frequently practicable to have regular procedures of "appeal," but this is not the same as "going over the head" of the immediate superior. Nothing is quite so devastating to the morale (that is, the loyalty to the organization) of a junior supervisor as to have his authority lightly cast aside by his superiors. Subordinates themselves will ordinarily not welcome the interference of the "higher-ups" or "big shots" whose directions they are not accustomed to follow.

6. *The line of communication should not be interrupted when the organization is operating.* This is a principle that is complied with in formal organizations by a number of relatively standardized procedures. These include emphasis upon the office rather than the person to protect against disruption through changing personnel; maintenance of as much personnel stability as possible in view of the informal aspects of communication systems; available substitutes who take over duties during absence of the regular officeholder; and well-understood shortening of lines when the organization is operating at unusual times or with limited personnel. The last-named policy is most common in manufacturing plants that operate during the night in some departments. Higher executives and the "office force" are usually not on hand, and the plant supervisor on duty is for the time top executive. If the shift is one using only part of the usual daytime employees, other intermediate officials may be eliminated. It is interesting to note that shortened lines of communication usually mean decreased formality, and that some workers prefer the night shifts for that reason.

These principles are those applying to the system of communication, the establishment and maintenance of which is an important executive function. System alone, however, is not enough, for the most painstaking compliance with the principles indicated would not achieve the general objectives of the organization if *what is communicated* is trivial, nonsensical, or incapable of fulfillment. From the executive point of view, this is the problem of making requests or giving directions that have a reasonable chance of being carried out. Thus a few principles which apply to the nature of the executive order may be indicated.

1. *Communications must carry authority,* that is, come from the proper source and be well authenticated. This may be taken care of by official stationery, personal signatures, verbal confirmation, and similar devices. The importance of these may be seen from the general unwillingness of subordinates to obey orders relayed from a superior through unofficial channels. The subordinate reasonably maintains that he "won't believe it until the boss tells him personally."

2. *Orders and directions must be limited to those which can be and will be obeyed.* Although the official policy may be maintained that executive authority is unlimited, a wise executive will not run the risk of loss of prestige by issuing orders that cannot be carried out. Moreover, what is less generally recognized, every authoritarian situation in formal organizations is strictly limited by the general character of organization and the well-understood rules and established patterns of conduct that form the basis of conduct and moral allegiance to the system by its members. In other words, the authority of the executive must be in conformity with the individual's understanding of the general objectives of the organization. It is even important for the executive order to be in conformity with specific interests and objectives, unless it is adequately explained as more general, or unless the individual is induced to comply on other grounds. The amount of outright disobedience, and especially of minor or major evasions of official expectations, may be enormous even in "tight-knit" industrial organizations. Some of these evasions are widely accepted, and in fact become unofficial but effective rules of conduct. For example, a company executive may establish the official working day for all employees as 8:00 A.M. to 5:00 P.M., with one hour off for lunch. By long-established custom, however, higher administrators may not arrive at their offices before 9:00 A.M. and may take two hours for lunch, making up the difference if necessary by working several nights during the week.

Such a situation, of course, allows executives to issue orders expected of their positions with reasonable certainty that the orders will not be obeyed. Frequently, unexpected obedience is as embarrassing as unexpected disobedience. Thus, to follow our previous example, the administrator who followed the letter of the law about his working hours might seriously disrupt the whole organization. The effective executive will recognize both the official and the unofficial rules of conduct, and will compute the chances of success or failure of a given policy in terms of both. This does not mean an abdication of formal authority, nor does it mean a denial of the importance of the formal rules. It simply means a recognition of the sociological facts of institutional conformity, and the "institutionalized evasions of institutional rules." [7]

3. *The order or request must be understood by the person who is expected to perform the activity.* Barnard comments, "A communication that cannot be understood *can* have no authority." [8] This principle raises a number of concrete problems of at least three different types. (a) A consideration of the first order may be called the *denotative* problem: what, in an intellectual or cognitive sense, does the communication mean? Thus, use of ambiguous, overtechnical, or obscure language may defeat the purpose of the communication (although, in the last case, it may be impressive on other grounds). (b) A second type of problem in understanding may, for want of a better term, be called the *predictive*. This difficulty is closely related to the first, but is most crucially seen in the necessity of increasing definiteness and specificity as the communication goes down the line. At various stages in this process, but especially in the later stages, the actual fulfillment of the order may require a number of decisions involving more or less fundamental policies, unusual financial expenditure, or other critical circumstances which the executive may not have foreseen or at least concerning which he

---

[7] This term is borrowed from Professor Robert K. Merton, whose analysis of organizational principles is unusually shrewd. See his "Bureaucratic Structure and Personality," *Social Forces*, 18: 560–568, May 1940. Barnard (*op. cit.*, pp. 162–168) emphasizes the same principle and notes that it is convenient (that is, wise policy in view of general objectives) for executives to recognize the limitations on their authority, but not to publicize them.

[8] *Op. cit.*, p. 165.

has not forewarned. Unless the order is "understood" in the complete and meaningful sense of the word, the persons to whom the order is directed are either forced to go ahead and hope for the best, or else seek a clarification "in view of such and such circumstances." Part of this difficulty is inherent in the complexity of activity in large social systems, and part is no doubt avoidable by more explicit directions or a statement of some possible circumstances under which the recipient of the communication is relieved of responsibility for performing the action requested. (c) An aspect of communication in general that is little recognized, and one which is of peculiar importance in a system with a socially heterogeneous membership, is its *connotative* aspect. A great deal of language functions to convey attitudes and to imply subjective states of mind, rather than to convey cognitive ideas. But the peculiar quality of language in this respect is that *the same words often symbolize quite different attitudes and emotional states when used by different persons.* To take a simple illustration, it is not at all improbable for an executive to start word down the line that one of the goals of the organization for the ensuing period should be greater efficiency of production. Now "efficiency" is a word used in a great many different senses, and in this case is likely to be interpreted differently by the various persons who are expected to react to this executive request. Among those at the "bottom" of the organization, that is, those who only receive directions and do not give them, this is quite likely to be interpreted as just one more instance of "slave driving" or "exploitation" (which are also words connoting sentiments). In other words, the communication is likely to be *misunderstood* because the executive has not taken account of the connotative qualities of language.[9]

The executive who has established an adequate system of communication and exercises care in regard to the nature of the communications transmitted has gone a long way toward assuring the continued operation of a complex industrial system.

[9] The importance of the various qualities of language in industrial organization has been most clearly pointed out by Roethlisberger in *Management and Morale*, Chap. VI, "Of Words and Men," and pp. 27–33.

Maintenance of Personnel. Exclusive emphasis upon schemes of organization and lines of communication would, however, be an obvious error in view of the rather elementary consideration that social systems are also groups of persons. This is, of course, not the same as saying that an industrial organization is "simply" an aggregate of a certain number of persons and a certain amount of material equipment. The terms *organization* and *system* imply that the persons stand in definite relationships to other persons in the industrial unit. That is, each person has a position in the organization and therefore carries on certain activities which include his contacts and communicative interactions with other persons. Viewing an industrial establishment as a complex *formal* organization places primary emphasis upon the system of *interrelated positions.* Viewed in this way, the qualifications of the personnel are established or determined by the character of the organization, or, more explicitly, by the character of the position to be "occupied" or "filled." This is the point of view assumed when the problem of selecting personnel is said to be one of *fitting the man to the job.*

It is necessary, however, to note certain further characteristics of industrial recruiting and placement of persons in appropriate positions.

1. No formal scheme of positions exhausts the personal relationships that characterize the social system in actual operation. In addition to the formal criteria of competence for performing certain strictly defined duties, it is also necessary to take into account the personal and general community sentiments which may affect social relationships. Unofficial, and often rather nebulous, criteria of selection are used in practice. These include "race," religion, nationality, appearance, general conduct, and the residual catch-all "personality." At best (from the point of view of organizational effectiveness), the formal criteria of competence constitute a necessary minimum that must be supplemented by other qualifications. At the worst (from the same point of view), the unofficial criteria are made so paramount as to supersede the formal ones, and through nepotism, favoritism, or "pull," incompetent persons are selected for various positions. The important point is that the relevance of personal

qualities that are valued positively or negatively in other social situations are not, and cannot be, completely ignored in the selection of personnel for positions in a formal organization.

A limited and, in a sense, "pure" theory of formal organization defines interpersonal relations only in terms of the segmental relations between positions, each with its technical specification of activities and sphere of competence. However, the technical character of many positions, and especially of executive positions, involves responsibilities to and for persons much more immediately than mechanical processes and materials. Only very limited attempts have been made to study the intrinsic, technical basis of these social relations as distinct from "intrusive" elements of friendship and social acceptability that may have little to do with job requirements.[10] This problem is accentuated by a further important characteristic of bureaucratic organization. Such a social system presumably represents a type case of the "secondary group" as contrasted with the intimate, continuous, face-to-face relationships characteristic of the family, rural neighborhood, or juvenile gang as "primary groups." But note that the work organization (as compared for example with the service club or urban church) also involves continuous face-to-face relations among small numbers of persons. If the inclusion in these relations of personality characteristics not technically demanded of the positions is "unexpected" from the model of the secondary association, it cannot be unexpected on other sociological grounds.

The relevance of interpersonal relations of day-to-day operations and more acutely in the making of decisions leads to an additional specification of managerial talent. The manager needs "organizational sense," a major component of which is sensitivity to the

[10] In this connection, see Delbert C. Miller, "The Social Factors of the Work Situation," *American Sociological Review*, 11: 302–314, June 1946. Miller approaches the problem of determining social demands of the job mainly in terms of what informed respondents consider these demands to be and how they are weighted for any particular job. This gives an empirical, operational specification of demands and expectations, predictability depending on adequacy of the sample. It does not answer the question as to which demands are intrinsic in the more fundamental sense that their removal would not damage, or indeed might improve, the effectiveness of work organizations.

nuances of interpersonal relations. This talent, which has been little studied, involves detecting strain, knowing the kind of impression the person himself is making, hearing what has not been said behind what is said. Such abilities are by no means uniquely valuable to executives, for the demand for them is pervasive in modern society. It does appear, however, that their absence gives a dim prognosis of executive success.

2. Because it is virtually impossible to "blueprint" the exact duties, activities, and particularly the "tone" of social relationships associated with particular positions, *it is extremely unlikely that any two individuals who successively occupy the same position will in fact perform their official and unofficial activities in the same way.* Again, from the executive point of view, this fact introduces the necessity of care in the selection of personnel and in provision for stability and predictability in the organization. In concrete terms it means that any change in personnel will introduce slight modification in the character of the organization and may sometimes go so far as to change official expectations in the formal scheme of organization. Therefore, in any organization, consciously or unconsciously, there is also a constant process of *fitting the job to the man.* This process is most notable in positions where the duties are general (not rigidly specified in the formal scheme of organization), and it arises as a crucial problem in the process of "finding a place" for a man considered valuable to the organization because of his particular combination of abilities.

The problem of changing organization through changing personnel is somewhat reduced by a policy of internal promotion to higher positions. Many of the largest industrial organizations follow such a policy consistently, and some attempt to discover executive talent very early in the individual's career and thereafter plan the individual's moves within the organization so as to maximize his relevant experience. The overt basis for internal recruitment is the maintenance of morale through fulfilling expectations of a graded career. Whether recognized or not, the practice also has the great virtue, from an organizational standpoint, not only of assuring continuity in policy but also of satisfying the demand for social competence as previously discussed. In technical terms the process may be called "selective socialization," as there is an inevitable weeding out of persons who do not "fit" with the technical and attitudinal demands of the organization, and a shaping of attitudes by those who survive and have an ever greater commitment to the organization and its established policies. The great disadvantage to the organization of internal recruitment and its attendant "inbreeding" is that it eliminates the valuable contributions of the dissenter, the questioner of assumptions. Occasional "new blood" at top levels may therefore be essential to overcome the insulation from fresh points of view inherent in the bureaucratic selective process.

3. The executive, or executive department, must be assured of competent personnel in satisfactory working relationships, but cannot be expected to carry out the details of selection and placement. In other words, the executive is forced to place reliance upon the judgment of others. This may involve an "internal" delegation of responsibility to subordinates such as line supervisors and foremen, or the establishment of a personnel department to attempt "scientific" personnel administration through job analyses, employment records, aptitude tests, and the like. The delegation of "personnel work" to specialists does not evade the responsibility of the executive for assuring himself (and others) of the adequacy of personnel policies in terms of the objectives of the organization as a whole.

The selection of high-ranking technical specialists may mean reliance upon the judgment of "outsiders," that is, other specialists in the field in which a vacancy is to be filled or a man promoted. This has a number of further implications for the executive's position and duties. As noted in the discussion of industrial bureaucracy, the functional division of labor places predominant emphasis upon special spheres of competence. Moreover, the incorporation into the system of a number of persons with high technical abilities in very specialized fields places a special burden on the coordinator. Beyond the judgment of specialists technically qualified in the same field as the specialists in question, the executive's judgment of competence can only be in terms of the fulfillment of objectives over a fairly long time span. *The coordinator (executive) judges results, not methods.*

The function of the executive in assuring competent personnel, and competent performance of personnel, is thus attended by several possible difficulties in the case of technical specialists. (a) An incompetent person with a special "sphere of competence" is considerably insulated from direct surveillance, and his shortcomings may thus escape detection longer than those of an incompetent supervisor or an incompetent workman. (b) Conversely, a competent person may be judged incompetent on irrelevant grounds if the executive expects too much, too soon, or fails to recognize the adverse conditions over which the specialist has no effective control. Many an executive has hoped to solve all his problems by hiring some sort of "efficiency expert" armed with note pads and a slide rule, and then has been disappointed or outraged when this modern equivalent of primitive magic has not achieved prodigious and spectacular results. (c) Although specialists are insulated from the whole organization in varying degrees, rarely is it to the extent of limiting their roles *solely* to the segmental one of specialist. This means that individuals selected on technical grounds alone will not necessarily make satisfactory members of an operating organization. This is the more particularly important since part of their contacts, direct or indirect, are with those not technically trained, or at least not similarly trained. In fact, the specialist is likely to initiate action on limited (that is, logical or technical) grounds without any adequate knowledge of the social situation. The antipathy to the expert is not confined to popular humor, and the burden of the coordinator is increased by this fact. The limitations that social organizations, industrial or otherwise, place upon the endless elaboration of "efficiency" are discussed in the following chapters.

Securing Essential Services. Much of what was noted in the preceding paragraphs concerning the problem of maintenance of personnel has implied the necessary corollary of that function: the securing of essential services from the personnel. If an industrial organization were completely static, or simply a classificatory system whereby individuals were assigned to particular categories, only a series of more or less arbitrary judgments should be necessary to "staff" the organization. However, with few exceptions (some corporation vice-presidents, for example), persons are selected to do something for the operation of the organization in achieving its general objectives. And the standards of selection presumably have something to do with standards of performance expected of the particular position to be filled. But competence and actual performance are not the same thing. The former is a necessary minimum for the latter, but does not guarantee that it will be forthcoming. Between the two there must be inserted the necessary incentive to secure the services expected. It is therefore a function of the executive to provide, or see to it that some regularized system provides, the impetus to adequate performance. How executives do this, and what relevant facts must be considered in providing for the necessary incentives, are discussed in the following chapter. For the moment it is simply important to note that a social machine, perhaps even less than a material machine, does not run itself. To pursue the analogy, the source of the power need not be the operator of the machine, but the operator must at least be able to assume that the motivation will not fail.

Formulation of Purposes and Objectives. Despite the importance of habit, unthinking adherence to established custom, and behavioristic responses to "stimuli," a great deal of highly important human action is purposive in character. That is, it is direct toward the achievement of general or concrete ends or goals. It is, perhaps, a sad commentary upon the extent of "growing pains" in the social sciences that this purposive character of human activity—long recognized by "practical" and not altogether unintelligent persons—has only recently gained renewed recognition in scientific theory. Probably the clearest, and certainly the most extensive, evidence of purposive activity in the modern world is to be found in the vast cooperative organizations deliberately created for the achievement of certain objectives.

The most general purpose of such organizations may be to make profits, or to provide a feeling of useful activity for the founders. More specifically, a business or industrial organization will be "for" the carrying on of a particular variety of production or distribution. Obviously, from the point of view of economic activity, how general or how specific is the aim of the organization is directly related to the size of the organization and the specialized or coordinated character of its product. In these terms, the general objective of an industrial organization may vary, for example, from making stove bolts to making stoves.

Once this most general objective is determined, not only are many technical aspects of the organization determined, or at least limited in variability, but the policies of the executive are also limited. Short of a redefinition of ultimate objectives, as in conversion to armament production, the task of the executive might appear "routine." This seeming simplicity of activity is disproved not only by the problems arising from the functions already discussed, but by other considerations as well. Although one of the general policies of the executive is certainly to keep the organization going, the organization operates in an environment that is actually or potentially *unstable*, both internally and externally, and toward goals that are customarily elastic and quantitatively indeterminate. By way of illustration of the latter point, it should be noted that, even if the general objective be that of profit, this may range all the way from avoiding or decreasing loss to a theoretically limitless goal of more profits. If the next more specific goal be "efficiency of operation" in the sense of reducing waste, again this may be approached more or less closely, but from the engineers' viewpoint is never reached completely.

Ideals may perhaps be formulated without regard to their potential realization. Executives, as participants in our general, or some special part of it, may quite readily express "would't-it-be-nice-if" sentiments. But the task of the executive in an industrial organization is not confined to—perhaps does not even include—the expression of socially pious or socially reprehensible ideals. The purposes and objectives he formulates must be those capable of achievement or approximation in view of relevant existing conditions. The executive must take into account both the amount of real authority he has within the organization (the likelihood that a given order can and will be obeyed) and the external situation toward which the organization must make an active or passive adjustment.

To repeat an earlier point, the executive is not the most skilled workman in any meaningful sense, and certainly not in the sense of "leading" by performing the necessary activities of the organization better than those whom he directs. Rather the executive must have the *general* qualifications of the administrator and coordinator. As an administrator he must possess a high degree of responsibility for the fulfillment of the codes of the organization as a whole, as well as the various personal moral codes that have a bearing on his activities.[11] Moreover, in the process of reaching decisions and putting them into effect, the executive *creates* moral codes for others, especially codes that have a direct bearing on the operation of the organization.[12] Part of this may appear to be automatic, that is, the authority of position in a formal organization carries with it the right and duty of initiating action and securing cooperation. But the complexity of the situation means that the qualities of the person occupying the position are also important, for the executive's tasks are not all routine and predetermined. What Barnard[13] calls the "environment of decision" includes the sentiments of members of the organization as well as the "technical" problems of securing cooperation. Any change in general or concrete policies can be successful only to the extent that the executive can count on or create the necessary sentiments of loyalty to the organization and to the existing distribution of authority.

The practical character of the foregoing observations is further reinforced by two sets of circumstances: (a) the highly rigid tendencies of bureaucratic organization, already noted, and (b) the highly mobile character of the significant "external" social environment of the industrial organization. Some of the aspects of the organizational environment that are only partially, if at all, subject to direct control by the organization, and yet to which some ad-

[11] This point is succinctly stated by Barnard, *op. cit.*, pp. 272–278.
[12] See *ibid.*, pp. 279–281.
[13] See *ibid.*, pp. 185–199, where the complexity of the social environment of the executive is noted. This is a useful antidote to the possible overemphasis on the machine-like operation of formal organizations.

justment must be made, are: market conditions, legal controls, technical processes, raw material supplies, labor supply, and labor demands. Part of the orientation to change, whether through attempted control or simply through up-to-the-minute knowledge, is the special function of the technical specialists who stand in an advisory capacity to the executive. But the responsibility for decision as to changes in general objectives and, if necessary, in the scheme of organization rests with the executive.

The executive has been referred to here in the singular, but this is an oversimplification of the complex process of decision-making. The actual process is always somewhat hidden behind the formal structure, although organizations differ in the degree to which explicit attention is given to decentralization, the interdepartmental committee, and other decision-locating devices. Although the executive-of-record may have a deciding vote in a formal or informal sense, the presentation of both facts and recommendations, and their possible countering by other facts and recommendations, precludes the idea that all initiative springs from the single official. The managerial group must always have areas of potential conflict that are both intrinsic and recurrent in a changing environment. Sphere of authority (especially with regard to new functions) and competition for the budget are inherent sources of tension and must be resolved by what amounts to group action.[14]

Since the emphasis of any social organization, viewed as a series of relationships according to morally endowed codes, is contrary to change, and yet the emphasis of contemporary economic life and technology is primarily on change, the executive group must be able to maintain a tenuous balance between bureaucratic rigidity on the one hand and scientific and societal change on the other.

We have devoted what may appear to be an undue amount of attention to the activities and responsibilities of persons whose numerical weight in a large industrial corporation is extremely small. However, in matters of social organization the doctrine that "each

[14] Whenever a large industrial corporation goes outside its own staff to secure advice on policy, that action alone most probably indicates a conflict within management.

should count as one" is rarely fulfilled, and it cannot be fulfilled in an organization where social differentiation and division of labor are present. This is not to say that an executive is "worth" as much as thirty, or a hundred, or twenty thousand employees. Such a statement could only be an expression of sentiment, not a statement of fact: the requisite elements of judgment are not at hand. It is not even to be maintained that differences in income between corporation executives and unskilled employees reflect in any *precise* way societal judgments of their proportional worth to the organization. The income differentials are likely to reflect roughly the social valuation of various services, as well as available supply. In the case of the salaried executive there is some evidence that high salary reflects in addition the general confusion of his position with that of the older entrepreneur as a risker of capital as well as a manager. More importantly, these incomes are a function of the attempt to represent hierarchical differences by salary with the result that an organization with many "layers" may have a very high salary scale at the top.[15] On the other hand, the modern corporation executive is in a highly strategic position, since he is the man upon whom the detached "owners" are almost entirely dependent. In any event, attention has been focused on the executive because his position so succinctly crystallizes the general problems of managerial organization and the modern characteristics of industrial leadership in a changing social order. The executive obviously does not constitute an industrial organization, or even its management. He does not even "control" it in any complete sense. But his position as chief coordinator is an important one in the operation of industry.

[15] See Peter F. Drucker, *The New Society: The Anatomy of the Industrial Order* (New York: Harper & Brothers, 1950), pp. 92–95. Drucker points out that top executive salaries, although not representing a large proportion of the company's "wage bill," are a constant source of annoyance and therefore of propaganda for wage adjustments. It is doubtful that this is as insoluble a problem as he indicates, however, for even if the requirement of salary differentials be admitted, there is no necessity of keeping them at the same ratio among the highest ranks.

REFERENCES

BALDERSTON, C. CANBY, *Executive Guidance of Industrial Relations* (Philadelphia: University of Pennsylvania Press, 1935).

BARNARD, CHESTER I., "Functions and Pathology of Status Systems in Formal Organizations," in William Foote Whyte, ed., *Industry and Society* (New York: McGraw-Hill Book Company, Inc., 1946), pp. 46–83.

——, *The Functions of the Executive* (Cambridge: Harvard University Press, 1938), Chap. XII, "The Theory of Authority," Chap. XV, "The Executive Functions," Chap. XVI, "The Executive Process," and Chap. XVII, "The Nature of Executive Responsibility."

DIMOCK, MARSHALL E., *The Executive in Action* (New York: Harper & Brothers, 1945).

FAYOL, HENRI, *Industrial and General Administration* (London: Sir Isaac Pitman & Sons, Ltd., for International Management Institute, n.d.), pp. 42, 70–73.

FRANKLIN, B. A., *The Industrial Executive* (New York: The Ronald Press Company, 1926), Chap. III, "Organization for Operation."

GARDNER, BURLEIGH B., *Human Relations in Industry* (Chicago: Richard D. Irwin, 1945), Chap. II, "The Line of Authority and Communication," and Chap. III, "The Functions and Problems at Each Level."

GORDON, ROBERT AARON, *Business Leadership in the Large Corporation* (Washington: The Brookings Institution, 1945), especially Chap. III, "Business Leadership in Practice," Chap. IV, "The Chief Executive and the Diffusion of Decision-Making," and Chap. V, "The Executive Group and the Problem of Coordination."

HOLDEN, PAUL E., LAUNSBURY S. FISH, and HUBERT L. SMITH, *Top-Management Organization and Control* (Stanford University, Calif.: Stanford University Press, 1941), especially Part A, "Summary and Conclusions."

LEWISOHN, SAM A., *Human Leadership in Industry: The Challenge of Tomorrow* (New York: Harper & Brothers, 1945), Chap. III, "The Mind of the Employer," and Chap. IV, "Managers of Tomorrow."

MITCHELL, WILLIAM N., *Production Management* (Chicago: University of Chicago Press, 1931), Chap. XIII, "Control of Production Activities."

PETERSEN, ELMORE, and E. GROSVENOR PLOWMAN, *Business Organization and Management,* rev. ed. (Chicago: Richard D. Irwin, 1948), Chap. III, "The Executive and His Activities."

ROETHLISBERGER, F. J., *Management and Morale* (Cambridge: Harvard

University Press, 1941), Chap. III, "Understanding: a Prerequisite of Leadership," and Chap. VI, "Of Words and Men."

TANNENBAUM, ROBERT, "The Manager Concept: A Rational Synthesis," *Journal of Business of the University of Chicago*, 22: 225–241, October 1949.

——, "Managerial Decision-Making," *Journal of Business of the University of Chicago*, 23: 22–39, January 1950.

URWICK, L., "The Function of Administration, with Special Reference to the Work of Henri Fayol," in Luther Gulick and L. Urwick, eds., *Papers on the Science of Administration* (New York: Institute of Public Administration, Columbia University, 1937), pp. 115–130.

WHITEHEAD, T. N., *Leadership in a Free Society* (Cambridge: Harvard University Press, 1937), Chap. V, "The Evolution of Modern Leadership," Chap. VI, "The Social Function of the Administrator," and pp. 101–107.

CHAPTER VI

SPECIALISTS AND SUPERVISORS

MANAGEMENT, in its total organization, comprises so many people of such diverse talents that one might wonder that it is "organized" at all. This diversity of personnel and function in the modern economic enterprise has long been hidden by two types of oversimplification: the conception of the single, decision-making entrepreneur with perhaps a small staff of assistants, and the constant emphasis on the management-labor division without adequate attention to other functional distinctions.

The only reasonable hope for order and understanding of the total managerial organization is to be found in arranging individuals in social space and defining their duties and activities with respect to the cooperative system as a whole. To do this completely would of course involve a long series of "job analyses"—summaries of the requisite skills and actual duties of each distinct position in the organization, with a slightly or greatly different set for each organization. Yet for many practical purposes, including the purpose of understanding the general principles of managerial operation, it is sufficient to determine the general functions of a few distinct classes of managerial workers, while recognizing that the division of labor in fact proceeds much further.

Although it is only from the "broad view" that such groups as technical specialists, middle management, office and clerical workers, and first-line supervisors constitute homogeneous units, this view in itself has some merit for understanding the operation of the whole without becoming involved in a maze of minute specializations. On the other hand, it is also necessary to indicate something of the range of variation within each group, not only as further documentation of the constant tug of war between specialization and coordination, but as a basis for more adequate appreciation of the general functions of the group as a whole.

Since it is both impossible and unnecessary to describe an actual or hypothetical managerial organization in all its manifold details, "as it concretely exists," we may focus our attention upon a group of related questions or problems as they apply to each group. The chief points of interest in an analysis of managerial functions as they are carried out in a complex social system are:

1. What is the general position of each managerial group in relation to the organization as a whole? (This will determine the general and official function of each.)

2. What are the general characteristics of the personnel, officially and unofficially? How are they typically recruited, and what concrete "interests" does each group demonstrate that may be significant for social relations within and outside the group?

3. What formal and informal techniques and activities are instrumental in facilitating or hindering the accomplishment of their functions?

The answers to these questions will leave unsaid many things about industrial management, but will serve to summarize the considerations relevant for managerial functions in industrial organization.

TECHNICAL SPECIALISTS

In the central offices and the manufacturing plants of any large industrial corporation the careful observer can see, either in the flesh or by unmistakable signs, a rather large number of persons with peculiar titles of office and mysterious duties to perform. These are the technical specialists. They sit at desks behind glass doors, or on stools before test tubes, or walk about the shops bearing blueprints and leather-encased slide rules. Their positions are designated as "motion economy engineer," "research assistant," or "product designer." If, to the layman, their titles mean little more than do some of the more fanciful offices in lodges and fraternal organizations, their language is likely to be even more esoteric than that of the ritual of the Exalted Knights of Such and Such. Yet to the properly initiated their titles carry a fairly complete indication of their duties, and their language is that of persons trained to think precisely and express their thoughts in technical terms presumably without ambiguity. Aside from the separation of investment ownership from industrial management, perhaps no recent change in industrial organization is so noteworthy as the increased importance, numerically and functionally, of those who extend and apply "technology" to the operation of industry.

In the most general terms, the specialists' function is advisory. On the basis of knowledge and skill not readily available to executives and supervisors, the technical specialist advises on the feasibility of projected changes, or suggests changes on his own account. Since no hard and fast line can be drawn between the division of authority and the delegation of authority, the specialist may also occupy an administrative position. This is especially true of those who are in charge of entire departments which serve a specialized function within the organization, and of those with assistants. In customary organizational terminology, as noted in Chapter IV, some specialists will therefore hold purely "staff"—that is, advisory—positions, whereas others will represent a line-functional organization. In either case, their formal position is represented by the horizontal, not the vertical, extension of managerial organization.

Varieties of Specialists. The similarity of function of all technical specialists must perforce be found on a very general level: the application of technical knowledge to the achievement of specific or general organizational objectives. Beyond this, the specific functions obviously are as various as the organizational ends that specialists serve. However, we may note a few of the larger categories of specialized services that demand a highly trained personnel.

1. By far the largest group of technical specialists in a large manufacturing corporation is the one primarily concerned with the effective *internal* operation of the organization. These may again be divided into several classes which are more or less distinct:

(a) Those who are primarily concerned with the arrangement

and maintenance of production, narrowly considered. These, in common speech, are the "engineers" whose special fields include such things as plant, maintenance, safety, motion economy, architectural design, machine design, and so on. Since the term *engineering* has come to refer precisely to the application of scientific knowledge to the achievement of concrete ends, it is obvious that the number of possible varieties of engineers is as large and the range as various as the specialized fields of science and the concrete ends to be achieved. This is the reason why of all the so-called learned professions that of engineering is the least homogeneous and the most subject to expansion and subdivision. As is noted below, however, the industrial engineers have much in common despite the variety of their titles and the special objectives that they seek to achieve.

(b) Those who are primarily concerned with the statistical and financial aspects of the organization. These will include cost accountants, treasurers, and similar specialists.

(c) Those whose special abilities are required for the various problems associated with the maintenance of personnel, their health, satisfaction, and various personal interests. Thus the large modern industry will have some sort of personnel department or personnel expert, and may have a number of such specialists. Likewise in this group are staff physicians, nurses, social workers, or others rendering personal services which the company thinks wise on some grounds or other.

2. An additional group of qualified persons is ordinarily required for what may be viewed as the *external* or "foreign" relations of the organization. Such persons, for example, are the lawyers who advise on the relation of the corporation to the political authorities and the law. Others, such as product designers, market analysts, and advertising executives, seek both knowledge of and control over the demands of the consumer. In recent years still another "foreign ministry" has appeared, that of the "public relations counselor." In older, and undoubtedly less respectable, times, these functionaries were known in the entertainment business as press agents and publicity men. Their incorporation into modern industrial organiza-

tion is sign of an awareness of a significant public besides the government and the consumer. The staff handling union contract negotiation and general management-labor policy may or may not be integrated with personnel departments. Because of the increased importance of collective bargaining and grievance machinery, there is a growing tendency for the larger enterprises to establish special departments. Whether the industrial relations executive is to be regarded as an internal manager or foreign ambassador is a thorny and sensitive issue, and must await discussion of management-union relations in Part Five.

3. A third group which is to be found in some of the larger industrial units is scarely concerned directly with the general operation of the organization. This is the group that largely accounts for present-day technological inventions, both in processes and in products: organized industrial research. Much of the research program sponsored and supported in large-scale enterprises is of the "fundamental" sort; that is, the research scientists are limited only by the general field and are not asked monthly to "show cause" for their continued support in immediately marketable inventions. This results in some product modifications, some product additions, and some results of no immediate practical importance. Although the independent inventor is not completely a thing of the past, he is by no means typical of modern research or its practical applications.[1]

Some Peculiarities of Specialists. Strictly speaking, the high degree of division of labor typical of large industrial organizations makes almost every member of the organization a specialist. But the term as here used does not refer to those whose specialties are readily learned and easily transferable from one worker to another. Yet an obvious problem arises when the distinction to be made involves not "unskilled" workmen but highly skilled machinists,

[1] In 1938, 1769 companies reported the operation of research laboratories. See George Perazich and Philip M. Field, *Industrial Research and Changing Technology*, Works Projects Administration National Research Project (Washington: U. S. Government Printing Office, 1940). There is little doubt that the advantages of sponsored research lie most heavily with the larger companies which can better afford the overhead and are in a better position to use any practical results.

electricians, paint-gun operators, operators of movable cranes, and the like. The problem is that of drawing a line somewhere, and that line is difficult to draw in view of the rather continuous character of variation in requisite skills for the achievement of organizational objectives. Between the skilled workman and the technical specialist, however, there is a more or less definite line which is the result of the operation of three interrelated differentiating factors: (1) the position of the technical specialist and his authority are advisory and supervisory in nature, as opposed to a position of more or less passive performance of assigned tasks in the case of the skilled workman; (2) the amount of technical training of the specialist is likely to be greater in amount, and different (perhaps more difficult) in quality; (3) the staff specialist ordinarily gets very little of his formal training within the organization, or another of a similar type, but rather is trained very largely outside the industrial field in which he works, and is thus not typically recruited from the ranks of the industrially employed.

The characteristics of what may be called the professional personnel of a large and "rationalized" [2] industry are aptly summarized by Roethlisberger in a series of points noted by a "disinterested observer":

(1) Each specialist has a set of logically interrelated activities or functions to fulfill.

(2) Each specialist tends to see the total organization from the point of view of his own specialty.

(3) The function of coordinating the functions of these different specialists is not explicitly the function of any of these specialists but of a line executive.

(4) Most of the specialists are experimentally minded and technically trained and talk a great deal about "efficiency."

(5) The word "efficiency" is used in at least five different ways, two of which are rather vague and not clearly differentiated: (a) Sometimes,

[2] The "rationalization" of industry refers to the application of the principles of managerial organization to the coordination of specialized activities. It includes the related ideas of job specification and of recruiting of personnel in accordance with the general and specific objectives of the organization. In its more extreme form, "rationalization" involves what is currently called "scientific management" and as such will be discussed in the following chapter.

when talking about a machine, it is used in its technical sense, as the relation between input and output; (b) sometimes, when talking about a manufacturing process or operation, it is used to refer to relative unit cost; (c) sometimes, when talking about a worker, it is used to refer to a worker's production or output in relation to a certain standard of performance; (d) sometimes, its referent becomes more vague, and it is used as practically synonymous with "logical coordination of functions"; (e) sometimes, it is used in the sense of "morale" or "social integration."

(6) Some of the activities of these specialists tend to make for originality and change in the organization, particularly at the bottom.

(7) Many of the plans and systems which these specialists devise are intended to help the workers; for example, the wage incentive system is designed to assist the worker in earning a wage proportional to his effort.

(8) Some of these plans are based on the assumption that the worker is primarily motivated by economic interest.

(9) Most of the specialists come from a stratum of the community different from that of the workers and lower ranking supervisors. On the whole, they have more education and training than the workers and lower ranking supervisors. Many of them have a better logical training than they have training or experience in dealing with people; the opposite is more likely to be true of the lower ranking supervisors.

(10) Some of the specialists tend to move into the management or executive group as they become older and more experienced.

(11) Some of the specialists have more prestige and authority to initiate action than others.

(12) Some of the staff specialists have administrative as well as advisory functions. At times, they originate action directly on the line, not only in devising new systems but by seeing that they are carried through.

(13) Each staff specialist has relations not only with his immediate superiors and subordinates, as shown on the blueprint chart, but also with other staff specialists, supervisors, and workers.

(14) Among these specialists there exist certain codes of behavior which define their relations to one another and to other groups in the organization. Although their behavior toward the problems they are solving is logico-experimental, their relations to one another are, for the most part, socially determined.[3]

One of the outstanding characteristics of the work of specialists, as noted by Roethlisberger, is the attempted application of "science"

[3] From F. J. Roethlisberger, *Management and Morale* (Cambridge: Harvard University Press, 1941), pp. 76–77. Reprinted by permission of Harvard University Press.

to social as well as physical data and relationships. The limitations to the effectiveness of this policy will be discussed fully in the following chapter. We must note here that the importance of specialists in the operation of the entire organization is not adequately summarized by a statement of formal position, or even by the notation that they are scientific "problem solvers." The problems to be solved include many aspects of industrial organization that are not susceptible of solution by resort to slide rules. The outside recruitment, the tendency of specialists to generalize from particular specialities, and the very uncertainty concerning the position and duties of these fairly recent additions to industrial bureaucracy, all tend to lend support to the suspicion or outright hostility with which the "efficiency expert" is viewed. Wherever the responsibility rests, the specialist is frequently poorly integrated into the industrial organization as a going concern.[4]

MIDDLE MANAGEMENT

In any large formal organization the executive officer or officers will be separated from those who are expected to carry out the orders and directions in their most explicit form by a number of stages or steps of graded authority. This is no less true in a governmental bureau or industrial concern than it is in the army. Excluding, for reasons to be noted in a subsequent section, those who represent the last stage of managerial authority (the first-line supervisors), the intermediate group may be called "middle management."[5] In the language of organizational experts the persons comprising this managerial group are customarily called *line officers,* managers in *direct line of authority,* or simply *junior executives.* Although there is a notable recent tendency for this group to be submerged or displaced by increasing functional specialization of personnel, the functions of the middle managerial group remain sufficiently distinct from those of the technical specialists to merit separate consideration. In fact, there is considerable evidence that the functions are

[4] See Melville Dalton, "Conflicts between Staff and Line Managerial Officers," *American Sociological Review,* 15: 342–351, June 1950.
[5] See Mary Cushing Niles, *Middle Management* (New York: Harper & Brothers, 1941).

sufficiently distinct to demand a separate personnel if organizational effectiveness is to be achieved.[6] In any event, modern industries do have such a distinct personnel despite the inroads made by the specialists.

The Role of the Junior Administrator. The very position of the "middle managers" indicates that in the most general terms their function is that of serving as channels of communication. This is not to say that they simply pass along, without change, directions handed down from above. As such, their positions would scarcely be worth the expense of paying to have them filled; on the contrary, the ineffectiveness of direct verbal communication as opposed to a circular letter or a bulletin board announcement might prove a detriment to the operation of the organization. It is rather the characteristic duty of intermediate managers to make the statements of objectives and the form of orders more and more explicit and specific as they pass down the line.

Since objectives are in principle almost endlessly subdivisible, on this basis alone the number of ranks of junior supervisors might be very large. It has already been noted, however, that the necessity of keeping lines of communication reasonably short operates against extensive subdivision. Nevertheless, the intermediate managers represent several different ranks and differences in authority, and in a large organization may include five or six or more. Their common characteristics include the basic similarity that each receives "orders" and that each applies these orders and sees that they are carried out by those "down the line." Since for the fulfillment of objectives it is

[6] The limits to the effective combination of technological and administrative duties have been inadequately recognized by executives and enthusiasts for "scientific" management. It is not an uncommon observation, even in the field of school and university organization, that the appointment of a specialist (teacher or researcher) to an administrative post results in the loss of a good specialist and the acquisition of a poor administrator. A number of reasons for this lack of transferability may be noted: (1) the specialist is highly trained in his particular field, and may be very poorly equipped for administrative work; (2) administration is only partly dependent upon a detailed knowledge of technical processes and operations, and considerably more dependent upon peculiarly administrative abilities; (3) if nothing more, there is a time factor involved, as in the case of the specialist who is also an administrator and complains that his time and attention must be focused on a welter of administrative "red tape."

essential at each stage that the appropriate services of persons be rendered, each junior administrator must assure himself of the active participation of his subordinates, as well as his own responsibility to superiors.

The functional division of labor and departmentalization of modern industry, together with multistage subordination, produce a situation wherein every line administrator or manager has some special competence or area of responsibility. Thus the *amount* of authority is not the only relevant difference among intermediate managers. Nevertheless, the common problems of administration and coordination, together with the structural position of these persons in the "center" of the organization, result in more homogeneity of duty and attitude than might appear at first glance.

In the strictest formal organizational terms—as frequently represented in organizational charts—all of the junior administrator's social relationships are either "up" or "down" in the line of authority. If this were in practice followed strictly, as some higher executives primarily concerned with formal authority insist that it should be, administrators of the same rank but in widely separated departments could only maintain indirect communication through the lowest common coordinator. Few organizations so operate, although most industrial executives and administrators will expect to be informed of interdepartmental agreements or discussions engaged in by their subordinates. The "line" principle will in any case ordinarily operate to the extent that "horizontal" communication will be effected between exact or approximate equals in rank, so that questions of policy, procedure, and so on, may traverse considerable distance up or down before they go crosswise of the organization.

Qualifications and Characteristics of Personnel. It follows from the position and general functions of the junior administrator that a primary qualification of office consists in the ability to interpret and apply organizational objectives as they concern him and his subordinates. This means not simply a reasonable knowledge of the general apportionment of duties within the entire organization, but the ability to make orders and directions understood by those to whom they apply. In this sense every member of middle management occupies an executive position and must have a modicum of executive ability. This is more particularly true in that every administrator is a coordinator of diversified activities. The level of generality of the coordinating abilities required will vary directly with the administrator's amount of authority (or position in the hierarchy). Thus, like the executive, the intermediate manager is expected to show loyalty to the organization (and incidentally to his superiors, unless the latter are subverting the objectives of the organization) and responsibility.

Because gradations of authority are most apparent, and relative rank most easily ascertainable, in the direct line of authority, many of the characteristics of the personnel and activities of middle management closely follow the popular conceptions of "bureaucracy." The narrow definition of spheres of competence, "passing the buck," acute consciousness of symbols of status and the prerogatives of office: all these bureaucratic tendencies, frequently annoying to the layman, make sense within the confines of an elaborate managerial hierarchy. It is within middle management that mobility, with significant changes in title, position, and possibly income, is expected as part of a normal career. Since the difference between one position and another is not likely to be great, and the personal authority (aside from the office) is minimal or nonexistent, it is understandable that managers in this category feel they cannot afford any reduction in the informal symbols of authority or any challenge to the privileges and immunities traditionally attaching to the office.

The fact that the symbols of status or the various traditional rights and duties may have little logical relationship to the demands of the organization as a whole—this is especially likely after the passage of some time during which the general environmental situation of the organization has undergone significant change—does not destroy their significance. On the contrary, it enhances their importance as part of the relevant social circumstances which must either be utilized or in some manner circumvented. Let us suppose, for example, the fairly common situation of a department which has expanded in personnel and functions to the point of requiring subdivision. Although strict principles of organization might seem to demand a new department head with a status equivalent to the older one, such a change may seldom be undertaken abruptly. The older functionary is likely to interpret the reorganization as reducing his sphere of authority. His traditional rights and duties, and the loyalty of his subordinates, may perhaps be preserved and utilized by putting him in charge of both departments and appointing two assistants to supervise the separate divisions. Or the executive may remain only in nominal authority over the new department, with almost complete freedom of decision given to the new official. The forms may be preserved simply in titles and organization charts, or by a perfunctory consultation with the official superior, submitting orders for rubber-stamp approval, and similar face-saving devices. The overrational outsider may sniff at such "childishness"; the experienced administrator will not.

The junior executive must learn not only the technical requirements of his office, and the technical requirements of his rights and duties in regard to other officers, but he must learn the appropriate social behavior which follows from his formal position. Failure to take account of the unofficial demands of fellow managers may defeat the utility to the organization of the individual who seems to be most gifted in the *technical* competence appropriate to the formal position. This principle is constantly illustrated in the failure of presumably competent persons to "get along" in an organization, and is in practice recognized by executives who insist on interviewing prospective subordinates and on giving promotions on other than strictly technical grounds.

Managerial Cliques. It is within middle management that the intrusion of informal organizations which run at cross purposes to the formal managerial organizations are most in evidence. We have repeatedly noted the importance in industrial management of relationships that are not adequately summarized or predicted on the basis of organizational charts. These informal relationships, customs, symbols, and so on may serve to implement and "round out" the integration of activities toward the achievement of general objectives or the fulfilling of essential functions. *But formal and informal bases of organization are capable of independent variation.* An informal grouping of persons representing common interests which are at variance with their official capacities and relations, and which cut across formal patterns of contact and authority, is commonly known as a *clique*. The possibility, indeed the probability, of the appearance of cliques is from the managerial point of view the besetting sin of governmental or industrial bureaucracy. Why cliques should, in managerial circles, appear chiefly among junior supervisors and their immediate associates merits some attention.

The relationships existing in a complex formal organization are officially those characterized by the "logical coordination of functions" or the integration of offices or positions. Only incidentally are these relationships between persons, and then only to the extent defined by the official relationships. In other words, the bureaucratic relationship is minimal, essentially impersonal, and thus highly segmental. It is segmental in the sense that the persons interacting are not assumed to be total personalities, but only segmental persons united by a functional division of labor. Actions taken, opinions expressed, motives assumed, and so on are thus not those of the concrete person, but those of the officeholder as officeholder.

Many organizations approach this "ideal" state of affairs in a few or many sectors of the organization; none achieve it completely. To the extent that departures from the formal and impersonal norm parallel the formal organization, they may actually be advantageous in the operation of the official system. To the extent that departures from the norm represent the introduction of "machine politics," or devices for the protection of incompetents on extraneous grounds, a clique situation has developed. This form of deviation may appear in any section of the organization, but in the general managerial group is most likely to appear among those who are most directly in a mobile and competitive situation, in frequent contact, and judged to a large extent on poorly defined criteria. That is precisely the situation in the group which we have distinguished as middle management.

Technical specialists, top executives, and even clerical workers can be judged for retention, dismissal, or promotion on well-understood standards of performance. Of course, they are rarely judged *exclusively* on those grounds. But the very general and diffuse character of the qualifications of the junior administrator, plus the highly formal character of his official relationships, constitute the conditions under which informal cliques thrive. Irrelevant considerations, such as nationality, fraternal affiliation, family connections, and a host of others, may thus play into the relationship between functionaries. Intensified solidarities and intensified antagonisms come to mark the social interaction of persons who are presumably expected to carry on certain activities in an impersonal fashion. Leadership within the group *may* correspond with formal rank in the organization, but more often does not. It is not unknown for those of higher rank to be rather unwilling parties to the intrigues and the formation of hostile groups arising from a semipublic difference of opinion between officials or an unpopular promotion. Indeed, an official may be considerably embarrassed by the strong sentiments and perhaps by the political maneuvers of his own supporters. Active support may end the possibility of compromise.

It must be emphasized that clique formation arises partly from the very character of formal organization because of the many possible bases of cooperation or hostility that are neglected by a "social machine." It is most easily combatted, not by insistence upon the rigid limitations of formal organization, but by informal lines of association that parallel and supplement the formal ones. It is most difficult to combat where the competitive elements are strongest and the rules of the competition (that is, the criteria of judgment) are weakest. The clique functions to reduce purely individual competition through the substitution of group action and to establish standards of conduct that are well understood, even though at complete variance with the primary objectives of the organization as a whole. The primary bases of inclusion or exclusion in the matter of clique membership may be as various as the socially meaningful similarities and differences among human beings. Thus in a particular central office the college men may form a cohesive group, and the noncollege men perforce another; or the male managers may unite to exclude women from higher managerial positions; or members of the "right set" may consistently favor one another and overlook errors while consistently undermining the position of capable but socially unfortunate "climbers."

It is not meant to imply that every managerial organization is completely permeated by a confusion of petty feuds and jealousies; some are. But it is important to note the likelihood of such unofficial modes of association, particularly in the "line" organization.

Promotion and "Trained Incapacity." As noted in an earlier chapter, the ideal of an individualistic social order is that of impersonal competition within well-defined rules and automatic rewards according to merit. The bases of judgment and relative valuation have never been limitless, and have in fact been largely those of "productive efficiency"; ideally, the automatic rewards (or penalties) have been those meted out in the market. This set of ideals and assumptions, which corresponds closely to what is popularly known as the "American success pattern," is hailed and upheld by such adages and old wives' tales as "You can't keep a good man down," and "There's always room at the top." Yet the appearance of the large industrial corporation and complex industrial organization has served to reduce whatever importance individual competition in the market place may have had for the population as a whole. Even though most of our great corporations were built up by outstanding individuals (the "captains of industry"), once these companies are established, that sort of achievement is virtually impossible. So far is this true that the ideal has actually shifted from that of progress from small to large business operations—the older type—to that of office boy to corporation president. The way to the top, in other words, is through promotion in the bureaucratic structure.

A factual appraisal of industrial placement and occupational mobility removes a considerable portion of the truth from even the modified ideal.[7] Many high-ranking individuals, including nearly all of that group that we have called the "technical specialists," enter the organization somewhere near the "top" on the basis of formal training in technical schools or universities. The entire managerial group above the rank of first-line supervisors is cus-

---

[7] The whole question of the relation of occupational mobility to general social status and social classes is discussed in Chap. XXIII.

tomarily recruited outside the organization (despite official pronouncements to the contrary). Our present concern, however, is with a modification of the ideal of a somewhat different order. And that modification, particularly within the group of line administrators, is the decreased possibility of purely impersonal competition. Put bluntly, promotion in the bureaucratic structure depends to a marked degree upon the *personal* judgment of superiors.

If the requisite qualifications for various positions, that is, the standards of judgment, are highly standardized, the "personal" judgment may itself be more or less automatic. At least the judgment may be "objective" in the sense that any person who knows the demands of the position and the characteristics of the available personnel will arrive at the same conclusion in regard to the relative merits of the prospective appointees. But in the case of junior administrators, and of line executives generally, the criteria are unstandardized and the requisite abilities are general. It is precisely in this situation that cliques appear, and it is in this situation that advancement may depend upon favoritism, nepotism, or other officially irrelevant grounds. This is also the reason that adherence to the customs and traditions of the informal organization, or pandering to the egotism of a superior, may be a better preparation for "reward" than is meritorious service to the company.

The plain and simple truth of the matter is that, in the present state of knowledge, administrative competence and incompetence is difficult to judge in any precise fashion. Utter failure will ordinarily be detected—unless compensated for by others—in the failure of the organizational unit to fulfill formal expectations. Beyond this minimum the variation is great, and the guiding lines few. Thus higher administrators often are forced to rely upon various homely virtues as bases of judgment, upon the shaky assumption that these are in fact important for the performance of the job and are alone adequate as evidences of capacity. Thus strict obedience to orders, punctuality, a show of enthusiasm for the work at hand, and similar qualities may be fastened on as adequate evidence of competence and availability for promotion.

Where favoritism, nepotism, and "political" action by cliques threaten reasonable stability, as they may well do in managerial circles, industrial or political bureaucracies customarily fall back on the *seniority principle* of promotion. So well established is this practice that its organizational advantages and disadvantages may be briefly summarized.

Promotion on the basis of length of service has the advantage of certainty in operation, and therefore the reduction of the chances of disorganizing competition. If the rules of occupational competition are difficult or impossible to formulate—that is, the criteria of judgment are not agreed upon—promotions may be effected upon some noncompetitive standard. Among the various imaginable systems of selection, seniority bears the closest *apparent* relationship to merit in the organization. To the extent that a higher position requires experience of the sort that a person in an inferior position will have gained, or if the abilities required are not only general but involve some knowledge of the particular organization, the seniority principle may be a reasonably adequate basis for moving men up in the organization. To the extent that previous experience (or at least the actual experience of potential appointees) is not essential for the position to be filled, the seniority principle has no more logical claim to consideration than promotion on the basis of any other arbitrarily selected differentiating factor. That is, unless the experience of those long in the organization actually fits them for occupying higher positions, promotion on the basis of size, golf score, or position in an alphabetical list would be as sensible as advancement on the basis of organizational age.

There is even an outright organizational disadvantage involved in the seniority principle of promotion in any system that includes considerable differentiation in the duties and requisite abilities of various managerial offices. This disadvantage arises from the same source as the general and characteristic difficulty of bureaucracies in adapting themselves to changed conditions, previously noted in Chapter IV. To perform an occupational role effectively, it is necessary not only to perfect the appropriate skills, but also to learn and uphold the attendant attitudes. This provides a profound resistance to change. Thus, the individual who has effectively mastered the demands of his position, and through long habituation has thoroughly accepted and promoted the special attitudes appropriate to that position, has a *trained incapacity* for other offices.[8] The longer the individual has been in a particular position, or in a particular branch of the organization, the harder is the transition to another position or organizational unit. *The more highly developed is bureaucratic specialization, the more prevalent is trained incapacity, and the less reasonable is a system of promotion by seniority.*

The seniority principle is likely to be regarded with considerable favor by the individual office holder in a junior supervisory position. Despite the slowness of reward, its certainty and possibility of achievement, without a constant expenditure of effort in competition for somewhat whimsical favors, are conducive to careful, punctual, almost ritualistic devotion to duty. From the point of view of effective achievement of general objectives by securing essential services from the personnel of all ranks and varieties, some reasonably standardized and acceptable "merit system" may be preferable.

Competition is often thought to be a highly constructive force in calling forth the particular abilities and services of individuals necessary for the achievement of general objectives. Yet *unregulated* competition is completely destructive of morale and subversive of the very basis of cooperative action. The organizational position of the junior administrator presents in a crucial way the difficulties arising from a system of rewards that must rely either on poorly formulated rules of competition or on some arbitrary noncompetitive factor.

OFFICE AND CLERICAL WORKERS

Every "front office" of an industrial plant, and any business concern of a size beyond that of the small retail store, has a smaller or larger group of workers who may in general be called *clerical*. This group of persons has received very little attention in all the masses

---

[8] The term *trained incapacity* is borrowed from Thorstein Veblen, and its present application follows closely the discussion of Robert K. Merton, "Bureaucratic Structure and Personality," *Social Forces*, 18: 560–568, May 1940, reprinted in his *Social Theory and Social Structure* (Glencoe, Ill.: The Free Press, 1949), pp. 151–160.

of literature on industrial management and industrial relations, yet obviously carry on activities of considerable importance in maintaining the organization as a going concern. Several reasons for this lack of attention may be suggested, since they are likely to reveal something of the peculiar position of the group in the administrative hierarchy. (1) The customary twofold classification of capital and labor or management and labor obviously leaves no place for those whose duties are neither administrative nor directly productive. (2) The services rendered are likely to be easily included as part of the duties of executive or administrative officers. The assistance given, if thought of at all in the formal scheme of organization, is therefore likely to be considered as "mechanical." (3) Because of the general dispersion of clerical workers, even in the spatial sense, problems of employer-employee relationships do not ordinarily arise with the same frequency or force as they do with respect to supervisors and workers in the shop. The dispersion of the clerical workers as a group also has another aspect, in that they customarily stand in a much closer personal relation with their bosses and supervisors than do other employees. This tends to cut down antagonisms and misunderstandings arising from social distance.[9]

In terms of formal organization of management and the official hierarchy of authority, the clerical staff is in an anomalous position. Secretarial and clerical workers are not, in general, highly paid, and their official position is roughly that of "workers." Yet these workers are arranged in units or clusters at *every* stage in managerial organization. An executive or a supervisor does not delegate work solely down the line; the duties of his position may require the services of a number of immediate assistants whose work is clerical.

---

[9] The usual social spatial dispersion of clerical workers has a notable exception in such offices as those of insurance companies or very large merchandising concerns where the bulk of the employees may be clerical. The introduction of typing and stenographic "pools" including a number of workers whose services are on call for many administrators, and who are under the immediate supervision of a special official, illustrates the organizational differences most forcibly. Some attention has been given to this situation by organizational experts. See, for example, George S. May, "Stepping Up Production in the Office," *George S. May Business Foundation Report* No. 104, September 1, 1940, reprinted from *Commerce*, August and September, 1940; Niles, *op. cit.*, especially Chap. VIII, "Dealing with the Rank and File."

It is instructive to note that clerical workers have shown themselves less amenable to unionization than have production workers.
They maintain, moreover, a clear line of distinction between their
status (which is symbolized in methods of remuneration, dress,
circle of acquaintances, and so on) and that of the "working class."
In management-labor disputes, clerical workers are usually to be
found aligned with managers and not with those whose income they
rarely exceed and frequently fail to match.

FIGURE 5. *Official and Unofficial Lines of Authority and Managerial
Relationships*

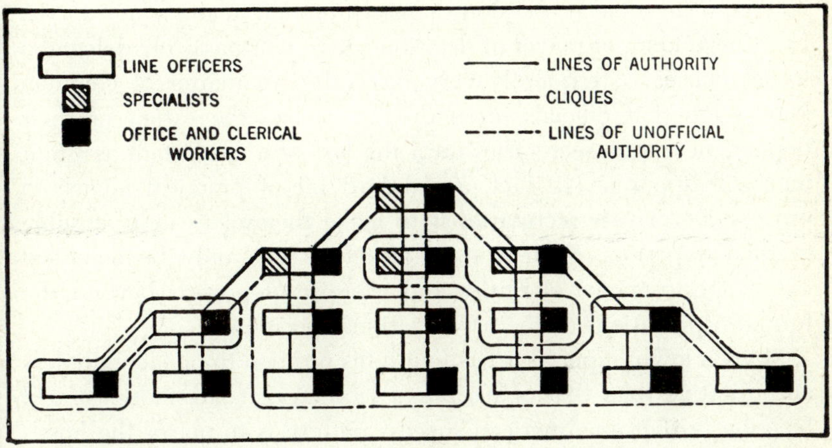

Partly because of spatial and organizational dispersion, the work
and interests of office and clerical workers are more likely to reflect
the differences in position and function of their immediate supervisors than their own low official position. This dispersion of clerks,
stenographers, and secretaries throughout the managerial hierarchy
gives to these persons a *reflected status,* based upon the relative rank
and authority of the administrators for whom they work. In fact, the
whole official hierarchy may be in large measure duplicated by the
unofficial distribution of privilege and rank in the clerical staff.
This and other complicating features of managerial organization are
represented in Figure 5.

Not all of the differences in effective rank and prestige among the clerical workers are based solely on a reflection of the official hierarchy, however. The positions of secretaries to important officials carry considerable actual (although still not formal) power. This arises from the delegation of executive activities and responsibilities to the secretarial staff, and the likelihood of private secretaries being entrusted with a great deal of confidential information. It is frequently possible for the effective lines of communication to by-pass the formal hierarchy by resort to the corresponding informal hierarchy of secretaries. Although in principle this semi-official system of communication would handle only routine matters not requiring official decision or interpretation at any stage in the line, the amount of power of decision actively or passively delegated to secretaries is frequently very large. It is a matter of common knowledge that officials often do not realize the extent of their dependence upon secretaries until the loss of a competent assistant makes it apparent. In fact, a standard bit of practical advice to prospective private secretaries is to make themselves indispensable to their superiors. Such a state of affairs can only be achieved by the performance of duties and exercise of powers beyond the formal expectations of the organizational position.[10]

Many a lowly supervisor has found his position to be factually less authoritative than that of his boss's secretary. It is sometimes said facetiously that an American success pattern is to marry the boss's daughter. However that may be, it is sound advice to the industrial manager to get and remain on good terms with his superior's secretary. In this regard, one simple but practical rule is: "Give to secretaries the deference which is not their official due, but which they expect." (An official in any large organization is rarely offended by deference beyond that called for by his position.)

The organizational functions of office and clerical workers are chiefly those of facilitating the collection and retention of necessary

---

[10] It is interesting that, in making the difficult decision as to who is an "employee" and who a "manager," the National Labor Relations Board includes most clerical workers in the former group, but excludes "confidential secretaries." The latter are considered to be in a managerial position, "regardless of method of compensation."

information, and maintenance of lines of communication. If they also serve functions usually thought to be the exclusive responsibilities of executives and administrators, as they frequently do, it is in the interest of understanding of managerial operation to take into account these significant departures from the "blueprint" organization.

FIRST—LINE SUPERVISORS

In a large manufacturing plant the largest single managerial group is one that spends relatively little time in the "front office," and for that reason alone is often scarcely considered a part of managerial organization. That group comprises the foremen, bosses, supervisors, inspectors, and so on, whose work is directly concerned with the supervision of workers or "operators." The uncertainty concerning the position of the first-line supervisor in management is symbolized by the distinction between the offices and the shops, but has much wider ramifications for the operation of industrial concerns. The foreman represents the last stage in the managerial hierarchy and thus stands in a crucial position with regard to the continued flow of production, the interpretation of executive orders, and the relations between management and the worker.[11]

Problems of Communication. We have earlier noted the high importance in a complex cooperative system of establishing and maintaining lines of communication. The responsibility for this duty was noted as one of the functions of the executive, but at the same time it was pointed out that the entire group of administrators and line officers have delegated responsibilities in this regard. The reason for this, it will be recalled, is that requests, directions, and policies must be interpreted and made more and more specific as they reach those whose specialized but coordinated efforts will (at least in theory) actually produce the desired results. It is the first-line supervisors who have the responsibility for interpreting and applying general

[11] The number of practical reference books outlining the duties and qualifications of first-line supervisors is very large. See, for example, Ralph Currier Davis, *Shop Management for the Shop Supervisor* (New York: Harper & Brothers, 1941); George D. Halsey, *Supervising People* (New York: Harper & Brothers, 1946).

objectives to those who maintain and operate the machines in the shops.

Although it is perhaps improper to select one link in a chain and claim it is *the* critical one, the position of the foreman is frequently to be so considered. It is at this point that general objectives must be translated into the most specific terms, and procedures adopted for conforming with them. Moreover, this is not by any means an automatic process, for the foreman must also possess discretion and the ability to determine the likelihood that orders can and will be obeyed.

It is frequently said that the foreman, to be successful, must have the respect of his men. In terms of formal organization, this is the same as saying that, like the executive, the foreman must have *authority*. That authority cannot be maintained if the foreman, as a link in line of communication, gives impossible or conflicting orders, or shows his incompetence by constant referral of all decisions to his superiors.

Since the potential difference of interest between the worker and management is most acutely symbolized in the direct relations of managerial representatives and operators, the first-line supervisor's problems of maintaining authority are especially critical. To a marked degree the success of the foreman may depend upon the extent to which he makes his directions genuinely understood in terms of the worker's position in the entire organization.

Ambivalence of Interests and Position. The position of the foreman is such as to make his loyalties subject to contradictory claims. As the connecting link between management and labor, the first-line supervisor is always potentially, and frequently in fact, in the rather uncomfortable middle ground between the devil and the deep blue sea. On the one hand, he is a representative of management and has the responsibility of interpreting managerial orders and seeing that they are carried out. On the other hand, the foreman is most frequently promoted from the ranks of laborers, and because of training in the attitudes of the workers plus an understanding of the concrete difficulties besetting the translation of requests into action, he is likely to represent the workers as well.

Even if the foreman's loyalties are unquestionably bound to the managerial hierarchy, his superior knowledge of shop conditions and workers' sentiments may force him to modify or subvert managerial expectations. With reference to orders that cannot be obeyed because of technical difficulties which higher administrators have failed to take into account, the foreman's inability to carry out the orders may expose him to little risk. With reference to orders that cannot be obeyed because they transgress the existing sentiments of the workers to whom they apply, the foreman may be on less certain ground. His position is more subject to attack from above because the assumptions of higher managers and technical specialists about "efficiency" are frequently based upon an erroneous conception of the data at hand—namely, the interests and social characteristics of workers. Thus, many industrial plants, including some of the largest and most "rationalized," have fixed managerial rules against conversation among employees. So far as any available evidence shows, these rules are *customarily* broken, and usually with the active or passive connivance of supervisors who know that attempted enforcement would lead to greater organizational disadvantages than possible losses in maximum "efficiency" through casual conversation.

In so far as the line of communication is allowed to work as a two-way system, the foreman may stand in the position of representing management to the worker, and the worker to management. In any event, the foreman stands apart from the workers by virtue of formal title and informal symbols of status, yet may hold his position by virtue of his ability to work effectively in direct contact with persons whose interests are not necessarily those assumed by management. The task of the first-line supervisor is to satisfy the demands of top management within the existing or any concretely attainable social and technical conditions.

During World War II and in the years thereafter the peculiar position of the foreman in industry was increasingly recognized by higher management and commented on by scholars.[12] The immedi-

[12] See, for example, Donald E. Wray, "Marginal Men of Industry: The Foremen," *American Journal of Sociology*, 54: 298–301, January 1949.

ate and precipitating causes of this concern were (a) the complaints of foremen, who were customarily on salary, that workers with overtime pay were earning a considerably larger wage than were their supervisors, and (b), for this and other reasons a movement to organize foremen into independent unions made some headway. However, other and more fundamental changes came to be recognized as attention shifted to the status of foremen. For a long time there had been a steady attrition of the supervisors' sphere of authority by the addition of staff functions—for example, personnel selection and up-grading, instruction and counseling of the worker, and discipline. This diminution of authority by the development of industrial bureaucracy came to be recognized largely as a result of a more sudden and overt change—the role of the union representative in the shop organization. The foreman was often in the position of having to share his authority with the union business agent or shop steward, and indeed might find his authority undermined by his own superiors when the shop steward by-passed the foreman with a worker's grievance or a disputed disciplinary action. Many, but not all, of these difficulties have been reduced by regularizing management-union grievance machinery at the same time that higher management has taken many measures to integrate the foreman more definitely in the operating and communications system.

There is, however, an even more fundamental problem in the morale of the first-line supervisor. Now that he has been newly discovered by policy-forming executives, he is being told that he is on the bottom rung of the managerial ladder, "one of the team." What he is not told, but can usually appraise for himself, is that there may be no further rungs on his ladder. The way to the top is increasingly by way of another ladder that starts with the training programs for college graduates selected for their potential managerial ability. The foreman has recently received much attention as the "man in the middle," practically none as the "man in a dead end." It is doubtful that his sense of frustration is eased much by constant emphasis on the lowly beginnings of current top executives if there is no evidence of continued operation of the full length of the line of ascent.

REFERENCES

ALFORD, L. P., *Principles of Industrial Management* (New York: The Ronald Press Company, 1940), Chap. 11, "Administrative and Managerial Control."

BICHOWSKY, F. RUSSELL, *Industrial Research* (New York: Chemical Publishing Co. of New York, Inc., 1942).

CARTER, WINTHROP L., "Industrial Management and Accounting," *Journal of Accounting*, 60: 345–356, November 1935.

CHEVENARD, PIERRE, "On the Function of Science in Works," *The Engineer*, 162: 279–281, September 18, 1936.

COOPER, ALFRED M., *How to Supervise People* (New York and London: McGraw-Hill Book Company, Inc., 1941).

DAVIS, RALPH CURRIER, *Industrial Organization and Management* (New York: Harper & Brothers, 1940), Chap. 8, "Office Management."

———, *Shop Management for the Shop Supervisor* (New York: Harper & Brothers, 1941), Chap. 5, "The Foreman's Responsibility for Production Control," and Chap. 12, "Labor Management and the Shop Supervisor."

DENT, A. G. H., "The Era of Management," *Fortnightly*, 150: 312–321, September 1938.

DIMOCK, MARSHALL E., and HOWARD K. HYDE, "Bureaucracy and Trusteeship in Large Corporations," United States Congress, Temporary National Economic Committee, *Investigation of Concentration of Economic Power, Monograph No. 11* (Washington: U. S. Government Printing Office, 1940), Part III, "Managerial Correctives of Bureaucracy."

GLICK, PHILIP M., "The Role of the Lawyer in Management," *Advanced Management*, 5: 68–71, 85, April–June 1940.

HALSEY, GEORGE D., *Supervising People* (New York: Harper & Brothers, 1946).

LANSBURGH, RICHARD H., and WILLIAM R. SPRIEGEL, *Industrial Management* (New York: John Wiley & Sons, Inc., 1940), Chap. XXIII, "The Foreman—A Representative of Both Men and Management."

LEITER, ROBERT DAVID, *The Foreman in Industrial Relations* (New York: Columbia University Press, 1948).

MAYNARD, HAROLD B., ed., *Effective Foremanship* (New York: McGraw-Hill Book Co., Inc., 1941).

NILES, MARY CUSHING, *Middle Management, The Job of the Junior Executive* (New York: Harper & Brothers, 1941).

PETERSEN, ELMORE, and E. GROSVENOR PLOWMAN, *Business Organization and Management*, rev. ed. (Chicago: Richard D. Irwin, 1948), Chap. XIII, "Supervision," and Chap. XVIII, "The Young Executive."

ROETHLISBERGER, F. J., *Management and Morale* (Cambridge: Harvard University Press, 1941), Chap. III, "Understanding: a Prerequisite of Leadership," and Chap. V, "A Disinterested Observer Looks at Industry."

ROSS, THURSTON H., "The Engineer's Responsibility in Management," *Mechanical Engineering*, 63: 524–526, July 1941.

SHELDON, OLIVER, *The Philosophy of Management* (London: Sir Isaac Pitman & Sons, Ltd., 1924), Chap. VI, "Production Management."

SMITH, CHARLES COPELAND, *The Foreman's Place in Management* (New York: Harper & Brothers, 1946).

CHAPTER VII

SOCIAL AND TECHNICAL EFFICIENCY

ALTHOUGH many problems of industrial organization are primarily or exclusively the concern of "management," it is always a little abstract to speak of management and labor separately. Each one tends to imply the existence of the other in actual industrial organization. In other words, an obvious fact deliberately overlooked, or at least somewhat neglected, to this point is that managers *manage*. Now it is true that partly they manage persons who in turn manage other persons. This has been discussed. But management is also concerned with the operation of the whole organization, and especially with the supervision of those who in turn manage no one.

It was pointed out in Chapter I that industrial relations are customarily thought of as including the position, power, and attitudes of management as one party and employees as the second party. In accordance with this usage, management-union relations and collective bargaining will be taken up in Part 5. Yet it is clear that no discussion of industrial organization can fail to be at the same time a discussion of industrial relations. An organization without relationships among its parts or elements is a self-evident contradiction. The character of the managerial organization, and of the policies in regard to supervision, maintenance of personnel, wages, and "working conditions," must be regarded as highly significant for the broader problems of industrial relations.

This chapter and the following one are concerned with the beliefs, policies, and practices of management in the supervision of employees. The general assumptions made by managerial groups about their powers, rights, and duties with regard to employees, and about the nature of the workers whom they direct are first noted. This might be called the "philosophy of management," except that to dignify the mixture of fact and fiction, belief and sentiment, by such a high-sounding title might give the impression of considerably more orderly thinking than in fact prevails. From an examination of the managerial "climate of opinion" the discussion then proceeds to a consideration of the more detailed and much more explicitly formulated ideas of so-called *scientific* management. What managers think about labor, what they do about it, and what effect the beliefs and activities have in the social organization of industry are the questions at issue.

ORGANIZATIONAL ASSUMPTIONS OF MANAGEMENT

A person in any concrete situation will carry on his daily activities under a number of assumptions as to the nature of those activities, their relationship to personal goals and social values, and so on. He walks to work in the morning under the assumption that the route he followed yesterday will not lead him in the opposite direction today; that it is his privilege or obligation to be going to work and not going fishing; that walking to work is good for his health and beneficial to his limited budget. These assumptions may not be explicit; indeed, they are seldom so. Yet careful observation of the individual at his round of activities, plus a few well-directed questions starting "Why . . . ?" will reveal that he is acting in accordance with certain principles and attaching some significance to what he does. Industrial executives and administrators are no exception to this basic principle of human behavior.

Personal Beliefs and Convictions. Although frequently confused in practice—that is, in the thoughts and actions of individuals—the assumptions that any person has concerning his social position and the nature of his activities may be conveniently divided into two types. The first comprises views, opinions, and presuppositions of a *factual* order. Whether completely, partially, or not at all correct, these assumptions are capable of formulation as statements which may be subjected to verification in the scientific sense. Such, for example, are managerial views concerning the motivation of workers, the efficacy of various types of supervision, or the unit cost of a manufactured article. The second type of assumption includes personal *ethical and moral codes,* which may correspond neatly or very roughly to the official ethical code of the society or the particular organization. In this category, for example, are judgments concerning the relative worth of individuals whose work is not readily comparable, or views about what employees *should* be interested in.

This second type of assumption is present in almost all social behavior, and is frequently confused with the first type. This is understandable, since the sort of unverifiable "value judgment" that the individual starts with is more than likely to color his view of the factual situation. To revert to our previous illustration, the man who walks to work may confuse his belief that "walking is a virtue—a sign of good character" with the assumption that walking is good for him in the physiological sense. As a matter of fact, walking may be very bad for his health. In other words, it is common for persons to engage in a considerable amount of wishful thinking, whereby they make judgments of "fact" that conform to their assumption of what the facts ought to be under the given circumstance. This makes it possible for otherwise intelligent individuals with considerable practical experience to make perfectly erroneous statements about the nature of industrial organization and relationships.

Even in the face of a large body of evidence to the contrary, many experienced managers will maintain that workers heed only the jingle of the pay envelope. The explanation of this perversity seems to lie in a widespread "factual" assumption with regard to the motivation of human behavior, reinforced by an evaluative assumption that it is only fitting and proper for workers to be so motivated. If the interest of industrial officials (or any other group of persons) were or could be confined to scientific appraisal of established facts, it is safe to say that many persistent errors in the interpretation of industrial relationships would lose their force. The truth of the matter is that the "irrationality" of employees who object, let us say, to a new wage-payment system or the "irrationality" of the manager who objects to a change in his title do not ordinarily indicate simply a failure in the "factual" assumptions of management concerning the concrete situation. The unexpected re-action of the workers also will violate managerial attitudes of right and wrong in the ethical sense.

What is sometimes called the "logic of the sentiments" [1] is not the same as the characteristic mode of thought which marks the work of the careful scientist. This is not to say that ordinary human be-ings, including industrial managers, indulge in a manner of think-ing that is not as "good" as that of scientific researchers. But it is different, and necessarily so, because the active participant in social affairs is operating in an environment of ethics and sentiments as well as of facts. The point of present interest is that the "factual" assumptions or conclusions of management more often follow from subjective values than from unbiased observation. This, in itself, is one of the more important facts relative to the problems of indus-trial organization and management.

To the extent that managers desire an effective ordering of com-plex human phenomena toward the achievement of the goals of the organization, they will take account of, and if necessary discount, their own ethical assumptions. Thus the superintendent who believes that responsibility should be rewarded more highly than skill will be well advised to recognize that this is a sentiment, and that this sentiment may not correspond to the beliefs of those whom he directs. A boiler repairman from the maintenance shops may be convinced that dirt and discomfort should be offset by greater re-ward than the pay for mere responsibility. There can be no scientific solution to such a difference of opinion, although there may be a "practical" solution based either on the greater power of the super-

---

[1] This is a term frequently used by Vilfredo Pareto in his well-known treatise on general sociology. It refers to a variety of departures from formal logic in situations where values or sentiments are involved. Notable among these char-acteristic modes of thinking are the holding of mutually contradictory views by explaining away the contradiction, and the very common tendency to observe or recognize only those facts that bolster a particular ethical or evaluative judg-ment. See *The Mind and Society* (New York: Harcourt, Brace and Company, 1935), 4 vols., §§ 480–484, 514–515 (Vol. I, pp. 291–292, 307–311), and § 1416 (Vol. III, pp. 896–898). See also F. J. Roethlisberger and William J. Dickson, *Management and the Worker* (Cambridge: Harvard University Press, 1939), Chap. XXIV, "An Industrial Organization as a Social System," especially pp. 562–568.

intendent or on some mutual agreement as to relative payment. The point is that the person in a position of policy determination is tempted to think of the difference as that between scientific right and wrong, rather than in terms of differences of sentiment and attitude.

The following paragraphs note some of the more important assumptions of management about the nature of industrial organization and personnel. It must be constantly borne in mind that in concrete situations fact, fancy, and value judgment are likely to be mixed in various proportions, and that a demonstration of factual error may not remove the foundation of the policy which is presumably based upon that error. Thus, even if the impartial observer can demonstrate that the "ordering and forbidding" technique of supervision has major shortcomings as a method of social control, he may find a tremendous resistance to abandonment of the policy deriving from sentiments about the "right" of employers to "run their own businesses."

We must also guard against the common fallacy of "proof by assertion," whereby the unwary are trapped. If an observer questions the validity of a managerial assumption, he may be met with the reply, "Why, sir, all competent authorities (or right-thinking men) agree that it is so." This assertion may be true by definition, since the person who disagrees is "clearly" incompetent, or a wrong-thinking man. Yet the assumption may be utterly false from the scientific point of view, whatever the sentiments of "right-thinking" men.

Labor as a Cost of Production. We have earlier noted (Chapter V) that, although the main concern of management is with organization, or the operation of a going concern, this must be consistent with the economic demands of capital. In other words, the element of *cost* must enter into computations and decisions in regard to policy. Just as in the case of a technologically more efficient process that cannot be introduced because of prohibitive cost, the cost of labor may prohibit the utilization of policies of organization that would lead to greater effectiveness in administration. The introduction of a new and extremely expensive machine for production of better quality in a shorter time may involve a cost of purchase and installation more than enough to offset any savings in operation. Similarly, a hiring and wage policy that would ensure the highest level of loyalty to the organization and effectiveness of organization may have to be passed by because of the competitive demands of the market or the more vocal demands of stockholders.

From a *strictly economic* point of view, the interests of capital in any concrete situation are likely to be in the lowest possible labor cost consistent with continued production.[2] From the same point of view, the interests of labor are likely to be in the highest wage consistent with continued operation of the industry (that is, with the continuance of employment). But even a "strictly economic" point of view must assume the existing devices for the apportionment of returns in a competitive economy, with a free market and free labor, or else some alternative system of fixing income. Thus we recognize the legitimacy of the claims of monetary income of investors, managers, and wage earners, but we leave the determination of relative amounts or proportions to competitive devices and differences in bargaining power. It is therefore understandable that the wage scale of laborers constitutes a troublesome and often acute problem for industrial management, just as the interest of management in maximizing profits may at times constitute a similarly acute problem for labor.

There can be no scientific argument about ultimate ethical questions concerning the appropriate distribution of wealth, although scientific knowledge about conditions and consequences may enter into nonscientific decisions. While recognizing that opinions differ as to the "fair share" of any party to the productive effort, we cannot make an objective judgment of the merit of the conflicting claims. Assuming the general system of rewards as given, a few of the *economic* considerations that industrial managers must take into ac-

---

[2] Discussions of wage policies, like most other policies, are likely to involve a conglomerate mixture of statements of fact and expressions of sentiment. No policy can be judged scientifically, except in the case of the efficacious means for the achievement of *given* ends or in the case of judging the probable results of a particular course of action.

count in determining wage policies may be noted. These are quite aside from questions about the adequacy of balance-sheet accounting as the sole factor in labor policy. The economic considerations follow:

1. An increased mechanization will ordinarily increase the productivity of the labor unit (usually, for sake of convenience, expressed as the *man hour*). Simply from the point of view of cost accounting—that is, without regard to social dislocations or ethical obligations—this raises the question for the management of any industry as to the point at which it is cheaper to invest in machinery in preference to continuing the existing cost of labor.

2. A corollary of the previous proposition is that a great increase in mechanization and decrease in man hours per unit of production means a corresponding decrease in *direct* labor costs. (Obviously the buildings, machinery, and other equipment, together with the raw or semifinished materials which the manufacturing plant processes, all represent considerable amounts of *indirect* labor expense, since labor costs are included in the market prices of these goods.) In modern large industrial units direct labor costs may constitute as little as ten per cent of the total production cost per unit, and thus only major variations in wage scales are likely to have much effect upon the competitive position of the manufactured product on the open market.

3. The productivity of the labor unit may be increased without introduction of machinery. This has been accomplished with more or less success by time-and-motion studies, by reorganization of productive tasks to reduce them to routine and rhythm, by the stretch-out, and by the introduction of compensation on a piece-rate basis. The wider social problems arising from such innovations will be noted in our discussion of scientific management. But simply from the economic point of view, and assuming a relatively high potential mobility of labor—that is, a condition of free labor—the wage payments of employees cannot fall below those necessary to command the work of persons possessing the requisite skills and abilities. This *tends* to place a floor under wages without formal and deliberate

restrictions.[3] On the other hand, even if sole or primary reliance is placed on wages as an incentive to increased productivity, wage increases for such purposes can only be effective to the point at which labor ceases to be the important variable. Thus, a wage policy designed to keep machines operating at their maximum efficiency will cease to be an effective stimulus to further productivity at the point where the maximum speed of the machines has been exploited. Beyond the point of maximum utilization of technical resources and the maximum utilization of the time, energies, and skills of the laborer, further increases of wages are likely to be costly. The increased cost may, of course, be passed on to the consumer, absorbed in decreased managerial salaries, or absorbed by decreased profits or dividends to the investors of capital. But assuming all these to be constant, and viewing labor simply as a cost of production, this set of considerations tends to put a ceiling above wages.

To the extent that labor is viewed simply as a cost of production one may suppose an attitude favorable to rationally efficient methods of labor exploitation. This attitude, all things considered, is not so surprising as the assumption that such a "penny wise" policy will work in long-term practice.

In questioning the wisdom of the "balance-sheet" policy, no attack is implied upon the ethics of managers who think in such terms. But even for the highly practical ends and conditions which constitute the relevant environment of managerial decision, it is demonstrably true that not all reductions in labor cost are wise. The *net results* may be decreased efficiency, increased waste, increased labor turnover, absenteeism, or deliberate restriction of output. That the unfavorable net results may be due to nonrational reactions upon the part of employees is not only possible but likely. *This does not*

---

[3] This is a modification of the so-called "iron law of wages" which holds that wages can never rise above the subsistence level for any extended period of time. The modification is necessary on at least two counts of present interest: one must take into account the possible quantitative variation in the available labor supply, and, more important, one must recognize the differential supply of various skills and abilities and the probable necessity of having to pay for the special skills demanded.

increase the "rationality" of the managerial policy which fails to take such "irrational" reactions into account.

Just as the slave represents a peculiar kind of wealth, so the free laborer is a peculiar kind of industrial expense. For the labor force in modern industry provides more resistance to efficiency of exploitation than do natural resources, capital funds, and productive machinery.

Laborers as Logical and Economically Rational Units. Closely associated with the managerial assumption that labor is adequately viewed as a cost of production is the presumption that laborers may be viewed as self-interested and logical units. In its crudest form—and this is by no means statistically "exceptional"—this assumption is stated as a realistic and hard-headed "fact" that laborers' sole significant interest in industrial employment is in higher pay for less work. It is interesting to note that this is the exact and logical counterpart of the managerial emphasis upon more productivity for less pay. But it is also interesting to note that, in situations where the assumption is manifestly *not* true, managers tend to *complain* that the workers are acting "irrationally."

Thus workers who make no protest about hours and wages, but wish to be consulted on changes in productive processes, or have a voice in management, may raise the ire of the superintendent or executive. The reason for the anger is not hard to find; the workers are acting contrary to expectation. But let us see how expectations have been disappointed. In the first place, workers who want a voice in management, or time off to fish or "loaf" (even at the loss of time and one-half for overtime) have belied the "factual" assumption that their only interest is in maximizing wages. To allow the change might well involve considerable hardships for management. One must suspect that this managerial error in factual prediction would arouse considerably less emotional disturbance, however, if it were the only source of difficulty. Available evidence seems to indicate that the failure to act "rationally" (in terms of the balance sheet) is also felt to be a dereliction of *duty*. In other words, this situation is a further example of the mixture of sentiment and fact, or assumed fact. And if the assumed fact is shown not to be true, this does not, from the managerial point of view, remove the onus of having violated a widely accepted sentiment: that one should be reasonable.

The crux of the difficulty is likely therefore to hinge upon an interpretation of what mode of behavior is "reasonable." It is understandable that, from the point of view of formal organizational relationships, the laborer's affiliation with the organization should be regarded as a segmental one. That is, the complete and unique personality of the individual, with all his habits, values, and interests, cannot be taken into account in fixing his duties in the organization. The worker must be thought of as playing a certain role in the productive activities of the entire organization—that of the drill-press operator, for example. From the organizational viewpoint, this role defines the operator's duties, and his interests are taken to be "reasonable" within the meaning officially prevailing in an industrial concern. Thus it is assumed that, in order to achieve his private goal of a certain wage or income, he will agree to follow the officially specified means to that end: productive labor of a certain quantity and quality. Since the goal of monetary return is assumed to be an elastic and relatively insatiable one, it follows that the method of eliciting greater productivity is to pay him more money.

But such a view begs many questions. For one thing, it fails adequately to take into account the complex problem of motivation, which will be discussed in Chapter XI. Moreover, and intimately related to the motivational problem, it overlooks the great importance of the subjectively meaningful conditions in which the laborer works. What this means in practice, for example, is that if the laborer feels that he should have "some say about working conditions," this goal makes behavior "reasonable," *even if contrary to managerial expectation.*

It is undoubtedly true, as we shall see in subsequent fuller treatment, that, other things being equal, the laborer will act as an economically rational, self-interested person. It would be surprising in our culture to find a workman who had no interest in money or in his own economic welfare. The difficulty of the managerial view here under discussion, however, is that it tends to neglect the very important qualification "other things being equal." In concrete situations, other relevant conditions are rarely equal in the worker's interpretation of his situation. The managerial assumption concerning the economic rationality of employees neglects other important considerations, both rational and nonrational: method (not amount) of wage payments, *relative* income for various types of labor, pride in workmanship, desires for security and for some measure of predictability and control in the employment situation, and various customs, rituals, and informal relationships to which the employee attaches significance.

The assumption that economic rationality and logic adequately characterize the orientation of the employee to his job reveals a type of thinking that may be called the "mechanistic fallacy." This fallacy consists in thinking of human reactions solely in terms of stimuli and responses. It is illustrated in such logical but erroneous propositions as: if ten units of payment motivate ten units of production, twenty units of payment should double the production. The first error implicit in this way of looking at phenomena is one common to all scientific predictive situations: the neglect of the *principle of limits*.[4] Simply stated, it is the principle that a causal or functional relationship will operate in a certain way only within certain limits, and beyond those limits may actually be reversed. Thus in the field of mechanics, increases in power may increase the speed of a machine only to the limit set by the characteristics of the machine. An increase of power beyond that limit may break or destroy the machine. Likewise, the harder a gong is struck with a hammer, the louder the noise up to the point at which the gong itself will be broken. Similarly, wage increases can motivate the worker no further than his physiological and mental capacity to produce. Actually, the limit may be further restricted by the

[4] The "principle of limits" has been formulated in reference to social and cultural variation by Pitirim A. Sorokin. See "The Principle of Limits Applied to the Problems of Causal or Functional Relationship between Societal Variables and of the Direction of Social Processes," *Publications of the American Sociological Society*, 26: 19–27, August 1932. The principle has received explicit theoretical formulation in the field of economic phenomena in the conceptions of "marginal utility" and of "diminishing returns."

worker's *level of aspiration,* which will be determined by habit, class and community expectations, and so on.

Managers are less likely to neglect the principle of limits which applies to all phenomena over which they have some degree of control, than they are to neglect a further consideration which applies solely to the human agents in production. It may be summarized as the neglect of the worker's *definition of the situation.*[5] The worker, in other words, will react to any new situation in terms of its meaning for him, and that meaning may or may not correspond with the significance attached to the change by the managerial personnel. It almost certainly will not correspond if the change has been based upon the assumption that the worker's only meaningful orientation to his job is an economically rational one.

A fairly common employment situation may serve as an example of the relevance of the worker's definition of the situation. The person who, by misinterpretation of various "signs" (such as a frown from the boss or a transfer to another machine), fears that he will be dismissed may so allow this fear to disturb his effectiveness at his job as to produce the very change he fears. It is sterile to argue that the worker is irrational or stupid. The fact of his dismissal only serves to convince him of the correctness of his "hunch." A narrow definition of what is reasonable behavior would leave no interpretation open but that of the operation of some vague attribute of "human nature." A mechanistic view of stimulus (incentive) and response (expected reaction) will not account for real or imagined stimuli that produce important, if unpredicted, responses. A managerial policy based primarily or exclusively upon such partial views of the pattern of human action overlooks highly relevant and

---

[5] The importance of the subjective mode of orientation (definition of the situation) is great both for the theoretical sciences of human action and for the practical understanding of concrete behavior. It was long ruled out by orthodox behaviorists among American psychologists, who found themselves in the uncomfortable position of being able to draw few if any distinctions among the billions of environmental "stimuli." It has been recently rediscovered in the form of "field theory" and the relevance of the "frame of reference." For the phrase *definition of the situation* and early exposition of its importance, the social sciences are indebted to W. I. Thomas. See W. I. Thomas and Florian Znaniecki, *The Polish Peasant in Europe and America* (Boston, Richard G. Badger, 1918), 5 vols., "Methodological Note," Vol. I, pp. 68–70.

practical facts. We shall note in the following section of this chapter that this set of considerations has profound significance for the success or failure of so-called *scientific management*.

The Command Theory of Authority. The final major assumption of management in regard to industrial organization which merits attention because of its bearing on policy may be called the *command* theory of authority. Again, in practice, this assumption is closely related to, and frequently indistinguishable from, those previously noted. This is quite understandable, since the attempt to maintain a cooperative enterprise by reliance upon the techniques of "ordering and forbidding" derives its logic from the presumed validity of the other assumptions.

Stated in terms of "practical" policy, *the command theory of authority holds that decision and direction are exclusively managerial functions, so that in the most general terms the worker's duty is to obey orders.* The worker is presumably induced to obey commands by receiving a wage for his services. This view, like the other mentioned, is usually closely associated with certain sentiments. The sentiments are ordinarily expressed in terms of the "right" of the employer to give orders. It is again not necessary or profitable to inquire into the ethical standing of such sentiments, but it is important to observe that the employer (manager) may well be more interested in preserving his right "to run his business as he sees fit" than he is in the command theory of authority as a truly effective policy.

As will be noted more fully in discussion of management-union bargaining (Part Five), there is a strong temptation for managers to refuse labor representatives any voice in the affairs of the organization, even when improvement of organizational effectiveness would result. The explanation must lie in the prevalent sentiments about authority and discipline, and not in the factual judgment that such a policy is adequate for practical purposes.

As a practical policy, the ordering and forbidding technique has certain disadvantages. It is likely to be based on one of the oversimplified views of employee reaction already noted, and thus to produce only grudging compliance or possibly outright disobedience. Thus, if the manager relies simply upon a wage inducement to purchase obedience, he is inviting attempts of employees to have their cake and eat it too; in other words, to collect their pay and evade responsibility. If the worker thinks the order given him is silly, unreasonable, or impossible of fulfillment, any opportunities that arise for evading the order may be grasped with delight. With reference to the authority of the executive (and this is equally true for management in general) it was noted in Chapter V that an order which is not understood can carry no authority. It is not of course either uniformly possible or necessary for the employee to understand all of the wider ramifications of the productive process with which he is asked to cooperate. It is, however, at least necessary for him to be able to translate the directions given into the particular operations required of him. Furthermore, the likelihood that the order will be obeyed in a manner completely satisfactory for achieving the goals of the organization—both in the short run and in the long run—is materially increased if the directions are so given that they become part of the *meaningful* situation of the employee.

Let us take as an example of the point under discussion a worker in a modern steel mill turning out armor plate. If the worker is operating a cutting machine and is told to cut the continuous strip of steel into three-foot lengths, it may be wise policy to inform him also of the possible margin of error. Will an inch or two one way or the other make much difference? The amount of care and precision, as opposed to the amount of speed demanded, may depend upon the purpose of this operation and how it fits into previous and subsequent processes. Is this a preliminary operation or a final one? How frequently should a check be made on the operation of the machine, or are there special inspectors somewhere "along the line"? These and similar questions may never be answered by the foreman who barks, "I said three feet!" but the effective cooperation of the employee may well depend upon some understanding of the order.

But there is a further difficulty with unadorned commands, which has already been partly implied: it is the high possibility, because of the division of authority that accompanies a division of labor, that any given job will entail *elements of decision*. Even in highly mechanized and routinized plants, with a preponderance of "semi-skilled" workers, the potentially variable factors bearing upon any operation are numerous. The worker who has been given detailed but fixed directions may know what he is to do under ordinary circumstances. He is at a loss in any unusual circumstance unless he knows something of the general character of the work he is doing. Returning to our previous illustration, let us suppose that the worker notices a change of approximately one-eighth inch in the thickness of the steel plate feeding into his cutting machine. His orders do not give him any basis for deciding whether this is significant unless he has also been told something of the nature of the work and the subsequent operations. If he allows the change to pass by him, he runs the risk of a dressing down for his "stupidity." Yet if he stops operations to make inquiry, he may also run the risk of the double charge of stupidity and "soldiering" on the job.

It may be that the command theory of authority operates effectively, "in view of the circumstances," if the laborers are as "stupid" as the theory implies. It may also be that the workers are not in fact so stupid and that the policy fails to make use of the workers' abilities. It is certainly true that *the manager who places no trust in his workers has no grounds for complaint if the workers show no initiative in adapting themselves to slightly variable conditions.*

It would be clearly erroneous to maintain, or even imply, that the managerial views discussed are uniformly characteristic of industrial policy. Rather the assumptions noted are to be regarded as extreme statements of views and presuppositions that are usually *not* formulated as propositions or articles of faith. The evidence of their presence and importance derives only partly from linguistic expression of the "philosophy" underlying policy. However, the policies current in industrial management reveal or imply various degrees of approximation to these assumptions, without which the policies do not "make sense." Perhaps this is nowhere more clearly illustrated than in the industrial adoption of "scientific management."

"SCIENTIFIC MANAGEMENT"

The possible application of science to the practical aims of industrial organization and administration has received a great deal of attention during the present century. This attention has indeed been exhibited in two quite distinct "movements" in the practice of management. The first in time has gone by the name of "scientific management," and represents the application of mechanical engineering to the increased efficiency of the worker as a machine. The second is much more recent and currently very much in the forefront of managerial policy; it represents an attempt to apply the human sciences to the increased cooperativeness of the worker as a social being. Both of these movements present common problems in applied science, but each in rather different ways. Because the mechanical engineering approach is older, and also because it illustrates some of the fundamental problems of the use of science for nonscientific purposes, it is appropriate to explore first its difficulties. In the following chapter some of the peculiar problems of the "human relations" approach are discussed.

Stemming in America from the work of Frederick W. Taylor (1856–1915), the movement to apply technology to human organization as well as to physical materials has built up an extensive following among both theoretical experts and active administrators. It is accordingly a matter of some importance to examine the policies that pass for scientific management and to note some of the theoretical and practical difficulties attendant upon the development of a technology of human relationships in industry.

The aim of Taylor, and that of his followers and interpreters, appears at first glance to be that of building up an inductive science of management on the basis of concrete observation and experimentation. Taylor's own experimental work extended for as long as fifteen years on a single project.[6] The observations ranged from char-

[6] For a general exposition of the nature of scientific management, see Frederick Winslow Taylor, *The Principles of Scientific Management* (New York, Harper & Brothers, 1911); *Shop Management* (New York: Harper & Brothers, 1911). See also the more recent collection of essays, H. S. Person, ed. for the Taylor Society, *Scientific Management in American Industry* (New York: Harper & Brothers, 1929).

acter of materials and machine design and speeds to the better known time and motion studies designed to eliminate wasteful and fatiguing effort and to increase man-hour productivity. Some of the specific types of studies will be noted in subsequent paragraphs. It is pertinent at this point, however, to note that the "scientific" observations have been carried on under two types of limitations: the ordinary limitation of any scientific research to those selected aspects of total reality that are relevant to a particular conceptual scheme or frame of reference, plus a limitation confining the studies to those that seem—under certain assumptions—to be most fruitful for increased "efficiency" and reduction of unit cost.

All precise or scientific knowledge is "abstract." In the present connection this implies that a criticism of the scientific management movement on the grounds that it has not studied *everything* about industry is not a legitimate one. To be relevant the criticism must assert that facts are overlooked that are significant for the scientific or practical objectives at hand. It is suggested therefore that it is the second limitation—the concern for efficiency—that needs scrutiny. Our concern in this scrutiny, it should be observed, is with the scientific adequacy of the approach to the problems of management, and not with the ethics of scientific management except as ethical controversy is revealed as relevant to understanding.

Problems of a "Science" of Management. To talk about scientific management at all implies that there are relevant scientific principles dealing with the problems of management, and that those principles are readily applicable to concrete administrative situations. Just how well the policies and procedures of administration that carry the label of "science" merit that designation may be examined in terms of a number of specific problems.

1. *The Problem of Empiricism.* The movement known as scientific management had, at least in its initial stages, a type of handicap that we may call the reliance upon "empiricism." Although the term *empirical* has recently come into use as practically synonymous with *factual*, or *observable*, an older and still valid usage refers to knowledge that is based solely on personal experience. Particularly in the field of medicine, the term *empirical* refers to the trial-and-

error practice of medicine without adequate or exact knowledge of principles. The field of scientific management, from the time of Taylor to the present day, has been characterized by empiricism in that sense.

Exact scientific research covering the various critical aspects of industrial organization and production has developed rather slowly, and one result of this has been the necessity of developing and applying science at the same time. For example, in speaking of the long period of experimentation in metal cutting at the Midvale Steel Company, Taylor notes that

the motive power which kept these experiments going through many years, and which supplied the money and the opportunity for their accomplishment, was not an abstract search after scientific knowledge, but was the very practical fact that we lacked the exact information which was needed every day, in order to help our machinists to do their work in the best way and in the quickest time.[7]

Now there are certain persons who maintain that this is as it should be, since the only true, and especially the only useful, knowledge is learned in the "school of hard knocks." Without attempting to discredit the importance of practical experience, which is especially valuable where principles are uncertain or unstandardized, we must note that science and experience are not the same thing. Thus many facts of theoretical (that is, scientific) importance are practically useless at any given time, and many facts of the greatest practical import will have few if any reverberations in the body of scientific theory. But it should be noted that scientific investigation which is not forced to show practical applications at every juncture may have considerable subsequent use. Taylor was able, in the Midvale Steel studies, to show enough practical results to keep the experiments going, but much of the information collected was of no use until combined and converted into formulas, and a slide rule designed to make it usable.[8]

The reliance upon trial-and-error procedures, with occasional and

[7] *The Principles of Scientific Management*, p. 106. Quoted by permission of Harper & Brothers, publishers.
[8] *Ibid.*, pp. 104–116.

apparently accidental success, results not only in inadequate theoretical formulation, but in considerable limitations on sound practice. Why this difficulty has been particularly acute in the case of
scientific management will become evident from its association with
the other problems to be discussed.

2. *The Problem of Scientific Selection.* No science describes reality
completely: selection and abstraction are therefore fundamental
characteristics of scientific procedure. Thus every generalization
about a series of phenomena will overlook perfectly well-known
characteristics of those phenomena because those characteristics
are irrelevant for the question at issue. Thus, to use an illustration
from Taylor's work on the "art of cutting metals," the relation between cutting speed and nature of the metal cannot overlook chemical composition, hardness, qualities of the machine tool, thickness
of the metal to be cut, and so on. The generalization may safely
neglect the origin of the metal, its geological age, how it was mined,
its reaction to hydrochloric acid, and so on. However, scientific
adequacy and certainly practical usefulness demand that the characteristics of the phenomena that are overlooked be truly irrelevant.
The assumptions made concerning the nature of the data may
dictate a false or too-limited posing of the problem, and the results
reached may have little practical bearing on the concrete circumstances which are supposedly studied. Thus, scientific managers ordinarily start with the assumption that the workers' interests are
adequately described as economic, that is, high pay.[9] Thus the generalization that workers can be induced to increase their man-hour
productivity (by following the directions of the foreman who is
attempting to eliminate waste motion) simply by increasing his
pay, may be true under the assumption noted and utterly false in
practice.

The studies carried on by the adherents of scientific management
have for the most part taken as given the ordinary managerial views
in regard to labor costs, the rational (almost mechanical) orientation of the worker, and the command theory of authority. This

[9] Taylor, for example, repeatedly asserted that the worker's motives were
simply those of high wages. See his *Principles of Scientific Management, passim.*

has vitiated much of the research, both from theoretical and practical points of view, not because the facts noted have been categorically wrong, but because *too much has been taken for granted.* As is noted below, the "scientific" determination of wage policies, piece rates, and standards of performance (on the basis of ideal computations of maximum production in the shortest time and the least waste motion) has rested to a certain extent upon observation and generalization in true scientific fashion. The problem arises from the fact that the results may be true under certain conditions, but these conditions may never prevail.

Those aspects of labor productivity and industrial relations have been selected for study that correspond to the usual managerial assumptions concerning the relevant considerations in industrial administration. If workers indeed were only rational or mechanical units, or if those characteristics constituted the only relevant qualities for understanding their relation to industrial production, the abstractions made by scientific managers would be perfectly proper. To the extent that the abstractions fail to account for significant aspects of the total situation, their utility and accuracy are correspondingly decreased. For example, if the worker is asked to do four times the usual amount of work for one and one-third his usual pay (Taylor recommends this), his undoubted interest in higher pay may be more than offset by his equally real sentiment that he should get a "fair" return for his labor. This difficulty is related to the following problem, namely, the application of science to concrete situations.

3. The Problem of Scientific Application. Contrary to popular impression, the immediate application of scientific principles to the solution of a concrete situation is rare. Aside from the question of ends to be served in applying science—a problem we shall presently discuss—there is the difficulty which follows from the abstractness of science. Put simply, every practical situation—and especially one involving social elements—contains phenomena and relationships normally treated in a number of scientific fields. In other words, this is a practical problem closely related to the preceding theoretical one. The application of one type of scientific discipline under the pretense that the other elements in the situation do not exist or do not matter is the most flagrant violation of scientific cogency (and of practical utility).

Perhaps this difficulty of applied science may be illustrated by a type of "problem situation" in the field of industrial production. Suppose that in a highly mechanized manufacturing plant production is falling off, waste is increasing, and a large labor turnover indicates dissatisfaction among the employees. A whole series of scientific experts might be called in to solve this problem. A chemist might find that the materials used were incorrectly proportioned, causing undue breakage in processing. An illuminating engineer might call attention to improper lighting; a mechanical engineer to excessive speed of machines; a time-and-motion study expert might find the workers spending too much time and energy per unit of production; a physiologist might find signs of fatigue in the presence of lactic acid in the workers' blood. Understandably enough, each of these experts would very likely insist that *the* problem was capable of solution by reference only to one body of scientific principles—his own. Yet the actual difficulty might well be a combination of all of these, *or none of them.* There are still aspects of the situation that none of the experts mentioned would be likely to take into account, or at best would only account for somewhat mystically as the "human factor." Wages and wage policies, methods of payment, feelings of insecurity, of being held in low esteem, and of never being consulted on any changes undertaken in the interests of "efficiency"— all these may be concretely relevant but beyond the range of vision of scientific experts whose views are limited to particular segments of human knowledge. The activities of scientific managers sometimes leave an impression analogous to the fable of the blind men and the elephant: each may be segmentally right and totally wrong.

The problem under discussion has, it is true, received widespread recognition. It is frequently expressed as the difference between science and art. Thus it is claimed that the practice of medicine rests not only on the developments in the laboratory, but also upon the "art" of the physician in complex human situations. What this really means is that the physician must call upon knowledge other than medicine, and if such knowledge is not available, or not known to him, he must resort to "empiricism" in the sense noted above. It is because the scientific knowledge taught the physician is inadequate for the practice of medicine that an experienced practitioner may have more success than a younger man who has more knowledge of experimental developments. It is for this reason also that an experienced manager of the "old school" may have better success (as measured by achievement of the ends of the organization) than the scientific specialist whose knowledge is limited to his specialty.

Critics of scientific management—including many of the more recent experts in industrial administration—have frequently objected that the policies of Taylor and his successors are "too scientific." This charge seems to indicate a very common confusion of "science" with quantitative and laboratory techniques as developed chiefly in the natural and biological sciences. If this were indeed the only meaning properly given to the term *science,* the charge might be well founded. For it is certainly true that the indiscriminate application of the "technology of physics and chemistry" to human situations is very likely to turn out in anything but a practical fashion.

Illustrations which seem to indicate the difficulties involved in being "overscientific" are readily available in modern industry. Time-and-motion study, for example, is designed to reduce operations to their simplest components and to find the number of time units required for each motion. Taylor explains the procedure as follows:

First. Find, say, 10 or 15 men (preferably in as many separate establishments and different parts of the country) who are especially skillful in doing the particular work to be analyzed.

Second. Study the exact series of elementary operations or motions which each of these men uses in doing the work which is being investigated, as well as the implements each man uses.

Third. Study with a stop-watch the time required to make each of these elementary movements and then select the quickest way of doing each element of the work.

Fourth. Eliminate all false movements, slow movements, and useless movements.

Fifth. After doing away with all unnecessary movements, collect into one series the quickest and best movements as well as the best implements.[10]

But applied alone, without reference to accidents, shortages of materials, differences in manual dexterity, the complicated physiological-psychological problem of fatigue, and so on, such studies can provide only approximate standards of performance. Of the use to be made of the standard Taylor says,

> This one new method, involving that series of motions which can be made quickest and best, is then substituted in place of the ten or fifteen inferior series which were formerly in use. This best method becomes standard, and remains standard, to be taught first to the teachers (or functional foremen) and by them to every workman in the establishment. . . .[11]

Such a procedure results of course in an ideal of some sort, but one must question whether it can regularly become a "standard" performance. It may rather result in a highly unrealistic composite which no workman could hope to master. One is reminded in this connection of the difficulty of finding the "average man," who has been married one and one-half times, has 2.6 children, and lives in an uninhabited field in central Iowa. A standard which is abstracted from characteristics of different units in different places can scarcely be expected to correspond exactly to any one of those units or any others.

The variable elements, noted above, which have been neglected in establishing the standard provide a source of some difficulty to rate setters. Some of these factors (such as fatigue) have been studied in their relation to productive efficiency, but large elements of "judgment" still enter into the actual application of such findings to concrete situations. Concerning this difficulty Taylor writes:

> The elements of the art which at first appear most difficult to investigate are the percentages which should be allowed, under conditions, for rest and for accidental or unavoidable delays. These elements can, however, be studied with about the same accuracy as the others.

[10] Taylor, *The Principles of Scientific Management*, pp. 117–118. Quoted by permission of Harper & Brothers, publishers.
[11] *Ibid.*, p. 118. Quoted by permission of Harper & Brothers, publishers.

Perhaps the greatest difficulty rests upon the fact that no two men work at exactly the same speed. The writer has found it best to take his time observations on first-class men only, when they can be found; and these men should be timed when working at their best. Having obtained the best time of a first-class man, it is a simple matter to determine the percentage which an average man will fall short of this maximum.[12]

This show of confidence seems considerably overoptimistic, since the procedure, as noted above, consists in observing the best unit times of several best workmen working at their best speed, and then combining these unit observations into an artificially constructed sequence for the standard. *The fact that a "principle" or standard is based on observation does not alone make it "scientific," much less practical.* One might, for example, observe that cows have several stomachs, dogs chase cats, rabbits have short tails, and mules cannot reproduce themselves, but one would hesitate to make a composite standard of these and similar selected elements and ask all animals to conform. One might even hesitate to determine the percentage of nonconformity. It might reasonably be asserted that the example is far-fetched; it is. But the point at issue is whether the abstract standards arrived at by generalization from artificially selected units constitute an "overscientific" approach to the problems of management.

Perhaps even more striking are the difficulties attendant upon a "scientific" wage policy. Not only is the wage expert likely to oversimplify the worker's interest in wage incentives, but he is likely to overestimate the worker's interest in and ability to understand complicated wage formulas. The question of incentives will receive fuller treatment in Chapter XI, but some of the peculiar assumptions of wage setters should be noted here. Especially noteworthy is the practice of attempting to determine the elements in wage differences, (such as skill, responsibility, occupational hazards, physical effort, dirtiness of work, etc.) and then weighting these elements by some numerical scheme and deriving the "proper" wage by resort to mathematical formula. There are at least two classes of

---

[12] *Shop Management*, pp. 167–168. Quoted by permission of Harper & Brothers, publishers.

variables in such a system: the variation of each unit (as one type of work may involve twice as much skill or one and one-third times as much responsibility as another) and the weight to be attached to each unit (as responsibility may be weighted twice as much as hazards). Quite aside from the question of whether any such complicated wage policy can have any but a negative effect as an incentive, there is still the question whether this procedure is truly scientific. The scientific manager is likely to maintain that wage scales and wage differences so determined are objective and scientific, as contrasted with the selfish or sentimental views of workers whose judgments differ from those of the manager.

But the judgment of the relative weight to be attached to various factors in determining wage scales is clearly arbitrary from any strictly scientific viewpoint. The interpretation of the judgments is likely to be that they are "right" in so far as they conform to the sentiments of the person making the judgment and "wrong" in so far as they fail to do so. There is no conceivable procedure for determining the share of any individual or group of individuals in the total value of the product or services produced by the company, without sooner or later resorting to nonscientific judgments of differential worth or merit. *The fact that an arbitrary judgment is given numerical expression and manipulated with a slide rule does not make that judgment scientific.*

The original question that prompted the illustrations of time-and-motion study and wage policy was whether the difficulty of scientific management consist in its being overscientific. The illustrations just examined indicate that such a claim would be a fundamental error in interpretation. Rather, *scientific management frequently errs in applying too little science.* The charges that scientific management neglects, among other things, the highly relevant sentiments of the workers seems well founded.[13] But to stop at that observation leaves

[13] The concrete importance of the "sentiments" in industrial relations has been documented very fully by the extended period of observation and experimentation carried on at the Hawthorne Works of the Western Electric Company. See especially Elton Mayo, *The Human Problems of an Industrial Civilization* (New York: The Macmillan Company, 1933); Roethlisberger and Dickson, *op. cit.*; T. N. Whitehead, *Leadership in a Free Society* (Cambridge:

the way open to all sorts of mystical, "intuitive," and haphazard interpretations based on the "intrusion of the human factor." It is only from a highly abstract and unrealistic point of view that the "human factor" (sentiments about a fair day's work, for example) can be regarded as intrusive or unexpected in any social situation. It is intrusive only if one forgets that it is with human beings and their social values that we are dealing. Either because the scientific knowledge of human relationships is not available (which in the past has been to a certain degree the case), or because of failure to apply scientific knowledge that has been developed (which is more nearly the contemporary situation), scientific management fails on at least one count to be adequately scientific.

What knowledge is to be applied for the practical solution of concrete situations? This question can only be answered by the general statement that one must apply *all* of the relevant knowledge about the units and relationships in question. In other words, successful management requires the utilization of the "technology of human relations" in addition to the ordinary use of the technology of the natural sciences. The truly scientific manager would no more confuse a series of rapid motions with a workman than he would a mathematical formula with a machine. But we have still left untouched one of the most critical problems in reference to the application of science to practical situations: toward what ends is the technology to be applied? The answer is scarcely as simple or as automatic as the general neglect of the issue would seem to indicate.

4. The Problem of Ends. The application of scientific principles to the solution of concrete problems is not wholly a scientific or technological procedure. It can be so described only if the goals to be achieved are taken as given—not problematical. The determination of those goals is not in itself a purely scientific procedure. Thus, an expert in industrial reorganization may assume that it is fitting and

---

Harvard University Press, 1937). A more positive formulation of the type of information frequently overlooked by the technically trained manager is given by Roethlisberger in his *Management and Morale* (Cambridge: Harvard University Press, 1941), especially Chap. VII, "What is Adequate Personnel Management?"

proper to attempt to reduce labor costs. But the conclusion that "labor costs should be reduced" could be reached by the scientific procedures of observation and generalization only under the circumstance of the assumption of a more general goal, such as reduction of market price of the manufactured article, reduction of loss to the company, increase in dividends to stockholders, increase in the friendship of competitors who pay lower wages, and so on. In that case, the formulation of the principle would be, "If you want to lower your price, and still hold all other factors constant, you should lower your labor costs." Such "If . . . , then . . ." principles can be pushed back to the next preceding factor that is subject to modification, and so on. Thus, the next formulation may be, "If you want to reduce labor cost, and still retain your present volume of production, you should reduce wages, increase the task of each worker, or substitute machines for work now requiring human labor." But sooner or later the scientist or technologist comes up against goals that are no longer a question of applied science; their source is ethical and not matter of fact. The ethical judgments may be as far removed from the concrete situation as the general assumption that the corporation ought to be run at a profit, not at a loss to be made up by contributions of wealthy stockholders. Or the ethical judgment may be inserted on a fairly concrete level, with little idea of its relation to more general goals, as in the sentiment that "Workers are being paid to work and not to talk, and therefore we must find ways of preventing their talking."

It is perhaps not widely recognized that scientific principles are applicable in many different directions, and whether or not they are applied at all is presumably a matter of supreme indifference to the scientist. To repeat, the *ends* that scientific managers serve are not in themselves scientific. Nor are those ends as relatively unchallenged as, for example, those of medical practice. (It is interesting to note that even in medicine any departure from the goal of saving life at all costs, as in euthenasia, arouses considerable controversy.) From this point of view, if from no other, the term *scientific management* is clearly a misnomer, for the problems are those of technology, not of science.

The ends that experts in management serve are those of the organization as a whole, or, more narrowly, those of management itself. The assumption that such ends adequately represent the sentiments of the entire personnel in a modern industrial plant is a notoriously impractical and invalid one. The hiatus between the interests of management and of labor is in fact usually assumed by management itself. Correctly or incorrectly, the work of managerial experts is usually viewed by those most directly affected by their policies—the laborers—as a further method of advancing the interests of management *as opposed to the interests of labor.* For this view there is some foundation. Taylor himself first became interested in analyzing the content of a day's work when he, as a supervisor, became involved in a wage controversy with his men.

Taylor, of course, claimed that the introduction of his version of scientific management satisfied the demands both of management and labor. This was to be accomplished by increasing the productivity of each laborer by two hundred to four hundred per cent, and thus reducing labor costs; at the same time wages were to be increased by thirty to one hundred per cent, and thus satisfy the primary interest of employees.[14] But even where it can be demonstrated that the introduction of new working methods redounds to the immediate economic advantage of employees, the question of goals which are common to manager and worker is not so easily settled. Even though the worker is given higher wages, there is no evidence that this advantage will consistently offset the rather obvious fact that he is being paid a smaller proportion of the benefits distributed by the company. The worker may also fear for his

[14] See Taylor, *Shop Management,* especially pp. 17–30; and *The Principles of Scientific Management,* pp. 9–16. Taylor is much given to "proof by assertion," as in his simple statement that what the workman most wants is high wages. Such a statement can only be true under certain conditions, and those conditions will include satisfactory working conditions as defined by the employee. Similarly, the following assertion assumes considerably more than it says: "No one can be found who will deny that in the case of any single individual the greatest prosperity can exist only when that individual has reached his highest state of efficiency; that is, when he is turning out his largest daily output." Among the important conditions assumed by this statement is one that is by no means commonly agreed upon, namely, that the individual is going to receive an appropriate reward for his efficiency.

long-time security, or regret the loss of former customs, routines, and informal social relationships. The opposition to differential piece-rate systems of wage payments, time and motion study, and other "scientific" introductions is understandable, and even "logical," under the assumptions of the laborers affected by these innovations. Just as in the field of medicine there is no scientific ground for maintaining that the sentiment favorable to saving life is more valid than the sentiment of the patient that he should die, so in the field of managerial technology, the differences of management and labor over the question of "rationalization" of productive methods are likely to turn upon matters of sentiment and not questions of fact. Indeed, the pattern of such controversies indicates that facts are selected and arrayed in support of or in contradiction to sentiments. *This is perhaps the reason why managerial technologists have been far more successful in demonstrating efficient procedures for maximum productivity than they have been in getting such procedures accepted by the workers.*

It is not meant to imply that the sentiments of workers are always, and necessarily, contrary to the ends of the organization as a whole. There is certainly no *a priori* reason for thinking that the loyalty of those who are classed as "operators" or "laborers" is intrinsically more difficult to capture than that of any other (especially managerial) employees of the corporation. But there is evidence to show that modern industrial laborers will maintain that their individual sentiments are as worthy of account as those of the organizational personnel classified as "management." Even assuming for the moment that the ends of management and those of labor are different, the latter are certainly sufficiently a part of the relevant situation to command the attention of the administrator who is formulating policy and instituting changed procedures.

The difficulty in many controversies seems to be less a question of basically antithetical sentiments—although these are not to be dismissed, as we shall see in subsequent chapters—than a failure by managers to recognize in the social situation of the *operator* those elements which he recognizes habitually in relationships with his *fellow managers*. Thus we observed (Chapters V and VI) that executives and administrators follow many customs and routines that are not in the rule book; modify their relationships with other managers in accordance with personality traits and characteristics that have no relation to the official demands of formal position; and set great store by a change in title and rank that may have no other significance, or may give greater freedom of action without increase in pay. Yet considerations of the same order in the relationships among employees, and of employees to their superiors, are customarily disregarded in the attempt to increase "efficiency." To use an illustration from an earlier chapter, until such a time as an "efficiency expert" reduces the size of the executive's desk to the area actually used for the executive's work, the objections of laborers to time and motion study that would eliminate conversation cannot be considered unreasonable.

(References for Chapters VII and VIII are given at the end of Chapter VIII.)

SOCIAL AND TECHNICAL
EFFICIENCY (Cont'd)

W<small>E</small> A<small>RE</small> now in a position to summarize the problem of fitting together the technical efficiency exemplified in modern industry and those human relationships that are no less real in industry than in any other social system. We have just been noting that managerial experts following procedures frequently called *scientific management* tend to deny (in action if not in words) that any such problem exists, whereas the present stage of enlightenment among their critics is largely confined to imprecise and somewhat mysterious references to the "human factor." There seems to be some need, therefore, to clarify the limits to the elaboration of technical efficiency, as well as to assemble some orderly knowledge of the human relationships that lie beyond those limits.

EFFICIENCY AND EFFECTIVENESS

The Meaning of Efficiency. As the contemporary observer of industrial relations, quoted at the end of Chapter VI, has noted, there is little consistency in the use of the term "efficiency," even (or especially) among those who are most concerned about its achievement in business and industrial concerns. However, apart from its meaning in mechanics as the relation between input and output, a common and acceptable use of the term in reference to human action may be stated. From this point of view, *efficiency involves the adoption of the means most suited to securing a particular end, without reference to sacrifice of other ends (cost) and without any restriction on the selection of means except that of intrinsic relationship to the end.* Thus if the end be doubled production of a particular commodity, the most suitable means may turn out to be the substitution of expensive machinery for skilled labor. The fact that the expense may reduce dividends, force the company out of business, or require that all managers accept a major cut in salary has no bearing on the immediate question of efficiency. Likewise, the fact that a group of laborers are thrown out of employment, that a collective bargaining agreement with employees forbids such an action, or that the economic life of the community is seriously upset does not affect the efficiency of the action taken. The only relevant question, from this limited point of view, is, Will this change produce the immediately desired result in the shortest possible time and with the least expenditure of effort?

It may be safely asserted that in concrete human action this can be at most a goal for approximation and not a characteristic of actual behavior. We have already implied the basic reasons why this is so: the element of cost, and the element of values or rules. Since any person has more than one goal, and does not have unlimited means for achieving all of them, expenditure of time and money for one purpose must necessarily involve some sacrifice in other ends. Similarly, a manufacturing company cannot long pursue a policy of greater and greater efficiency, and "hang the cost." (The only exception would appear to be the special circumstance where speed, for example in war production, is more important than cost, and the latter can be shifted to taxpayers.) Likewise, the possibility in a social situation of using others as means to one's own ends introduces the necessity of social control in the interests of social order. Thus, one method of reducing the unit cost of production might be to use forced labor, or pay the laborers in counterfeit money, or pay them their wages and subsequently have company representatives take the money from them by force. But these actions, however efficient, are not taken because of the necessary rules that limit such complete freedom in the choice of means.[1]

Subject to these limitations, which are not to be regarded lightly,

[1] See Talcott Parsons, *The Structure of Social Action* (New York: McGraw-Hill Book Company, Inc., 1937), especially pp. 89–94.

it is possible to picture an ideal network of rational (that is, efficient) actions, with each end becoming itself a means to a more general end until the goals of the system as a whole are reached. Thus, to increase the production of synthetic rubber, additional raw materials must be brought to the plant, the speed of operations must be stepped up or additional machinery installed, and the accomplishment of each stage in processing becomes the means for the achievement of the next immediate objective, until finally the increased amount of synthetic rubber becomes available for whatever use the market or national interest indicates. Each specific efficient action (greatly oversimplified in our example) would be ultimately designed to secure efficient achievement of the general purposes of the organization. All this is an abstract and theoretical way of stating the view of managerial experts who seek to approximate this state of affairs by increased efficiency "all up and down the line," avoiding "bottlenecks" that hold up the forging of subsequent links in the chain.

Limitations to the Elaboration of Efficiency. If it is possible to *think* of such a network of chains of means-end relationships, extending from the most particular to the most general, it is not possible to *observe* such a system in fact. Not only do the limitations already noted apply, but others as well. For any particular segment of the activity carried on within the organization the considerations of cost and social norms might be taken into account and simply regarded as conditions over which the actor has no control. Thus, the order of the day may be, "Without violating any laws or well-established rules, and without material increase in unit cost, increase the output of machine No. 24." But the complexity of any social situation, and the impossibility of carrying on efficient activity in a "social vacuum," introduce the strong probability that activities that seem to be efficient will have unforeseen consequences. Thus, the method used to increase the output of machine No. 24 may achieve that end, but at the expense of replacing the operator of machine No. 25, who quits his job because the company now asks him to process the increased materials turned out by the preceding machine at no increase in pay. These unforeseen consequences may or may not aid in achieving the general goals of the individual, or the organizational ends toward which his efforts are presumably directed. There is little assurance that they will always do so.

A careful analyst of the shortcomings of planned social behavior has referred to this set of considerations as the "unanticipated consequences of purposive social action." [2] We may follow his analysis in summarizing the sources of breakdown in efficiency as applied to human action.

1. The first and simplest source of unpredicted results following a deliberate line of action is to be found in *ignorance*. Any sort of rational or planned action or scheme of organization assumes adequate knowledge of the significant elements in the situation, whether or not those elements are subject to control. Insufficient knowledge may well lead to unforeseen results. The ignorance may be that of the person instituting the action (for example, the poorly trained manager who expects the impossible) or simply a reflection of the general state of usable knowledge bearing on the question at issue. Thus unexpected signs of fatigue and voluntary absenteeism may result from a policy of longer working hours, and the ignorance may not be chargeable to anyone in management, since in the present state of knowledge the precise conditions that determine the maximum work week can only be guessed at.

When results of particular policies can only be predicted within narrower or broader limits because of the complexity of the variables involved, the decision as to whether or not to pursue the policy must rest upon a calculation of probabilities. Thus the manager may be able to say, on the basis of previous experience or knowledge of scientific observations in the field, that a particular policy has a better than even chance of success. This is, of course, a makeshift or partial solution to the problem of ignorance. It is one that must be frequently employed by the manager who would have any measure of assurance concerning the consequences of various activities.

[2] See Robert K. Merton, "The Unanticipated Consequences of Purposive Social Action," *American Sociological Review*, 1: 894–904, December 1936. Our discussion consists essentially of an application of Professor Merton's analysis to the particular problems of industrial efficiency, although some elaboration has been undertaken in view of the special issues involved.

Just as in selling products on the open market the businessman must *expect* occasional, and in each particular instance unexpected, losses, so the industrial supervisor must "make allowances" for his ignorance of what to expect.

Where the operation of forces is so complex that no application of general principles will serve to indicate the results of those forces, the results are said to be due to *chance or accident.* This is not to say that the exact operation of those forces is not conceivably knowable, but only that it is in fact unknown. Even in the application of precise natural scientific principles to mechanical situations, as has been noted, the concrete circumstances may be sufficiently unique to require modification in view of accidents (unforeseen results). This is even more necessary in situations involving social relationships, both because of the unquestionably greater complexity of the variables that are significantly involved in any situation and because the state of knowledge concerning the operation of those variables is considerably less advanced than in the case of the natural sciences. If in tossing a single coin the resulting "heads" or "tails" is unpredictable by the laws of physics, so the reaction of a particular workman to a managerial policy may have to be set down as due to chance.

2. A second source of failure of actions to produce the desired results is *error.* In a certain sense it might be claimed that error is in reality simply the result of ignorance, so that no separate attention would need to be given to it. However, error may in fact arise where the person attempting to achieve some particular end (such as increased production) is in possession of the essential facts, but errs in his weighting of the factors or in his inferences drawn from them. Thus the wage setter may be perfectly aware of the workers' opinions about relative worth, but err in thinking those opinions unimportant. From a strictly rational point of view, error is a failure, not of information, but of logic. (To maintain that error and ignorance are the same thing would be to argue the false position that "facts speak for themselves" and necessarily indicate the course to be followed without exercise of reason.)

One of the most persistent sources of error in practical everyday activities in the factory and machine shop is to be found in the "common-sense fallacy." This fallacy consists in thinking that a person with a great deal of practical experience will be able to judge a particular situation by reference to previous experience. More particularly, it is the common assumption that actions that have produced the desired results in the past will continue to do so in the future. *This policy will work only if the immediately relevant conditions remain constant.* Hasty generalization, or "jumping at conclusions," is of course not confined to industrial managers; it is, on the contrary, an extremely common error in thought and action. The visitor who has asked one or two policemen for directions and comes to the conclusion that all policemen are dumb; the consumer who has been cheated in a purchase and concludes that businessmen are dishonest; or the army sergeant who operates on the assumption that the way to secure the confidence of his men is to curse them— these are commonplace illustrations of the common-sense fallacy.

Fortunately for the experienced manager there is sufficient constancy of type situations to allow considerable predictability. We have already noted, in fact, that the knowledge of the practical administrator may lead him to fewer errors than that of the narrowly trained specialist. Nevertheless, habitual employment of certain procedures may fail to produce the expected results if some change in organization, in characteristics of employees, or other relevant condition has taken place. Thus, the manager who has developed habitual policies for dealing with unskilled immigrant laborers may make the error of applying these same policies to skilled craftsmen who are strongly organized in trade unions. The possibility of errors of this sort constitutes one of the primary reasons that large concerns find it expedient constantly to train and retrain their supervisors. Their previous experience may not be worthless in general, but may become "dated" under rapidly changing conditions.[3]

---

[3] The classification of elements in a concrete situation as means (those factors subject to control) and conditions (those not immediately subject to control) is not necessarily constant. Some elements that are subject to modification, utilization, or control for certain purposes may not constitute means for the given end sought. For example, if the end be that of increased production, a number of factors become relevant: the number of workers, and their speed and efficiency;

The error of a policy that is assumed to be efficient may arise therefore from simple neglect of pertinent aspects of the situation, although, to repeat, those circumstances may be perfectly well known to the person attempting to achieve the end. At the other extreme is the case where error arises from what Merton calls a "pathological obsession" indicated by the "refusal or inability to consider elements of the problem." [4] This is illustrated by the insistence of many managers on some specific "factor" which may or may not be important in the particular case. For example, it is not unknown for managers to attribute every dispute between management and labor as attributable to "Communists and agitators." Other managers may get "bugs" on temperature or illumination; still others may want to supervise everyone's diet to ensure proper vitamin intake. Probably these examples of "riding a hobby" are more commonly recognized as such than the more frequent obsession with "economic motives," and the surprise, not to say ethical outrage, when the actions do not produce the desired results. The emotional reaction arises, of course, from the previously noted fact that judgments of a factual order and those of a normative or emotional order are frequently confused in social behavior. Thus interest in economic gains is held to be not only a realistic description of human motivation, but a positive duty. Needless to say, this complicates the problem of error.

The preoccupation of the administrator with the formal duties of

---

the adequacy or inadequacy of handling of materials; the state of repair of the machines, etc. If any one of these factors is selected as the means for increasing production, the others become conditions for the immediate purpose at hand. In other words, their presence is not irrelevant, but rather the end is actually subject to continual minute or major restatement in terms of the relevant elements of the situations to be brought under control. Thus, if it is decided first to attack the problem of repairing machines, the goal may be stated as "to increase production by increasing the efficiency of the machines." Each of the other factors, with greater or lesser difficulty, may subsequently be brought under control. The element that is crucial at any given juncture in the total plan of action is called by Barnard the "strategic factor." See Chester I. Barnard, *The Functions of the Executive* (Cambridge: Harvard University Press, 1938.) Chap. XIV, "The Theory of Opportunism." Neglect of this dynamic aspect of purposeful activity is a special case of the error of assuming constancy of conditions.

[4] See Merton, *op. cit.*, p. 901.

those whose actions must be directed may explain the frequent neglect of certain conditions of the situation: the motives, interests, and so on of the persons who are being directed toward the achievement of organizational goals. Putting persons into formal relationships also induces informal patterns of action and reaction. It was noted in earlier chapters that the formal organization never completely summarizes the actual relationships existing among the personnel. These informal patterns thus constitute unanticipated consequences of the formal ones, and become in turn part of the relevant conditions for future action. For example, attempts to change the informal standards of a "fair day's work," even if financial inducement is given, may fail because of the neglect of such relevant conditions as the sentiments concerning working relationships, feelings of distrust, fear of exploitation, and so on. That some of these sentiments may be "objectively" unfounded does not destroy their relevance. *It simply enhances the possibility that the manager will neglect them.*

The relevant social conditions overlooked by the technical specialist may be neglected because the assumptions concerning the nature of the data are drawn from the physical sciences, not the social sciences. This is *not* to say that social data must be treated differently because they are completely unpredictable. It is to say that the predictive principles must take account of the elements and the conditions of their relations. The physicist or mechanical engineer can no more neglect important properties of his data if he wishes to predict and control their behavior than the social scientist or "social technologist" can neglect the properties of his data. It is as meaningless to think of a social ssytem without ethical rules and sentiments as it is to think of a physical system without temperature. In either case it is more or less feasible to reduce the effect of certain properties by holding them constant or reducing their relevance. A formal social system will attempt to rule out the factor of norms and sentiments by rigid definition of rights and duties, and limitation of the individual's role to his official one. Since the units of such a system are, however, organic personalities, this limitation is never completely effective.

3. A third way in which an extended system of "efficient" actions may fail is through what Merton refers to as an "imperious immediacy of interest." [5] This involves such a concentration on immediate goals that further consequences may be neglected. Thus the immediate end may be achieved, but at the expense of the more general goals of the organization. A very common form of this source of noncorrespondence between immediate activity and general goals is to be found in the "ritualism" of organizational employees.[6] Ritualism in this sense implies an almost religious devotion to duty, even if that duty is no longer effective in producing results. If we were to find a clerical worker who insisted on writing official correspondence in longhand with a quill pen, or an accountant who spent hours over a column of figures rather than trusting any "new-fangled" machine like an electric calculator, we would suspect the existence of ritualism. What were formerly means have now become ends in themselves.

Administrators may be concerned with the achievement of a particular goal at all costs, and those costs may in fact be the sacrifice of more general goals. Some trained experts in management show such a concern for "efficiency" that their special formulas for increasing efficiency come to have first place in their thinking and acting. Occasionally this interest takes the form of complicated mathematical formulations (for wage determination, for example) which apparently have an aesthetic appeal but which clearly fail to facilitate the organizational goal of production of goods and services.

The exclusive concern with one segment of an extended chain of actions may, paradoxically enough, neglect "economic" elements.

[5] *Op. cit.*, pp. 901–902.

[6] The effective negation of general goals through ritualistic observance of rules regardless of their effectiveness was noted in Chap. IV. Merton is one of the very few social scientists who has recognized this as a form of social deviation; most deviant behavior of course consists in failure to obey rules. The layman who is interested in the goals may note that the "red tape" blocks rather than facilitates their achievement, and even within the organization the executive must be concerned with results as well as methods. See Robert K. Merton, *Social Theory and Social Structure* (Glencoe, Ill.: The Free Press, 1949), Chap. IV, "Social Structure and Anomie."

That is, the pursuit of one particular type of activity may be carried on at the expense (that is, sacrifice) of alternative uses of scarce resources. Notable among the scarce resources in practically any situation involving choice are time and money. The latter is more likely to be recognized and checked, since a business or industrial concern is accustomed to some form of cost accounting. Nevertheless, cases can be found where such an elaborate system of efficient production has been introduced that the savings effected are more than offset by the system itself. Thus the constant attention of a mechanical engineer may increase the average speed of machines in a shop unit by ten per cent, but the cost of the inspection may be greater than the savings from increased production. From the strictly economic point of view one might think it axiomatic that an efficiency expert who is hired to reduce costs must save more than his salary or the goal may be achieved in only an illusory way. In practice, the ritual attachment to "efficiency" is so great that the axiom is frequently forgotten.

No less significant is the possibility of such a diversion of time and energy to a small segment of the total scheme of organization that other necessary activities suffer. A special case of this "noneconomic" concern with immediate objectives is to be found in the situation where an overcautious administrator desires to reduce the effects of probability or chance to zero, and thus wins the battle but loses the war. All of these illustrate the paradoxical irrationality of being too rational.

The preoccupation with "doing each small job very, very well" neglects the complexity of social action systems. Each small job is simply part of much larger ones, and the primary concern of the organization must be to get the big jobs done. The problem arises from the fact that in an integrated social system the activities that are designed to produce the desired results have other effects as well. Thus every action has further reactions of greater or lesser degree throughout the interrelated parts of a complex organization. For example, a battery of aptitude tests may demonstrate that two men are both ill-fitted for their particular assignments, but should work more effectively if they trade. The shift in jobs may be made and the improvement in production result as expected (at least temporarily), but further unexpected repercussions follow in its wake. Either or both may feel that the transfer is a demotion; the informal patterns of social relationship previously established among the men are broken, and each is treated as an outsider in his new group; other workers may unconsciously reduce their productivity because of neurotic fears that they may soon be transferred. These results may sound like speculative nonsense, but a wise and seasoned administrator will not overlook their possibility.

The unexpected, and possibly negative, results of any change will of course be most noticeable in case of a change in habitual pattern of working relationships. Some of these reactions will contribute directly or indirectly to the general objectives of the organization. Others may operate in the opposite direction. *It is axiomatic not only that the likelihood of important repercussions will increase with the magnitude of the change, but that the chances for the consequences to operate entirely in favorable or unfavorable direction are correspondingly decreased.*

Oversimplifying for a moment, it is possible that a given change C will achieve its immediate purpose or end E and a series of further favorable results R^+. It may, however, also produce other results R^- which are unfavorable to the general goals of the organization. Thus the total situation might be expressed as

$$C \longrightarrow E + (R_1^+, R_2^+, R_3^+, R_4^+) + (R_1^-, R_2^-, R_3^-)$$

giving a net favorable balance. This is oversimplified in two ways: it assumes that equal weight is to be attached to each consequence, a situation that almost never exists, and it assumes complete predictability of significant consequences, which is more a standard for approximation than a likely description of fact.

Nevertheless, it is important to note that, in a complex cooperative system, it is necessary to think of consequences other than immediate efficiency; specifically, it is necessary to compute the *net balance of results*. If the net balance is favorable to the ends of the organization, the results may be said to be effective,[7] whatever the immediate efficiency rating of the action taken. This is simply stating some of the formal principles that support the actual experience of executives, who have the advantage of concern with general purposes and objectives. And that experience is to the effect that measures that look good in the immediate situation may seem quite the contrary "from the long view" or "everything considered."

4. A final way in which an efficient policy may be ineffective is peculiarly disturbing to precise predictability in human behavior. It is the way in which the intention to introduce change, or even the prediction of change, may become a part of the relevant conditions and modify or defeat the intention or prediction. Anyone who has had his future predicted by a fortune-teller will recognize the possibility of deliberately (and, in this case, probably unnecessarily) disproving the seer's forebodings by avoiding that course of action. Unlike the situation with regard to changes in the mechanical facilities in the factory, or prediction of the possible date that a machine will be no longer useful (the calculation of obsolescence), changes or predictions concerning policy, working conditions, and the like will very probably affect the actions of the units whose behavior is supposed to be controlled. Thus the manager who announces his intention to increasing efficiency may by that act alone make his task more difficult or impossible in a situation where the workers, however erroneously, confuse efficiency and "exploitation."

The operation of this principle is widely recognized in concrete circumstances, but rarely applied or taken into account in all the situations where it applies. For example, safety directors in manufacturing plants may make use of the principle in their "propaganda" campaigns to reduce accidents. This frequently takes the form of posters announcing that during a certain period a certain number of accidents will occur because of carelessness. The intention, ob-

---

[7] This use of the term *effective* follows that of Barnard, who notes that "'effectiveness' of cooperation is the accomplishment of the recognized objectives of cooperative action." (*Op. cit.*, p. 55.) We have not followed Barnard's special use of the term *efficiency*, which he makes apply to the ability of the organization to offer sufficient inducements to secure cooperation. (*Ibid.*, p. 93.)

viously, is precisely to make the prediction false through emphasis on greater care. Yet the same official may forget himself and predict a great decrease in lost-time accidents through the introduction of new and foolproof machinery, only to find that habitual care is relaxed to the point of increasing the accident rate.

The mechanical engineer can study the operation of a machine and calculate ways and means of increasing its efficiency without noticeable effect on the machine, other than that deliberately undertaken as the result of the investigation. On the other hand, a rate setter for piece work may study the actions of workers in order to recommend changes in behavior with a view to increasing their productivity. *The fact that the rate setter is making his study will in itself change the situation in respect to the behavior of the workers, and the purpose of the study may thus be defeated in advance.* The latter unanticipated consequence arises from the fact that the change or predicted change in standard rate, or in the performance of particular operations, will frequently be offset by a deliberate slow-down (even by piece workers) while the expert is making his observations.

Effectiveness of industrial management, as distinct from efficiency, rests therefore in part upon gradual elimination of the disturbing factors of ignorance and error, but more especially upon the recognition of the relevant social circumstances (including even the plans of management), the operation of which may either facilitate or hinder programs deemed sound on mechanical grounds.

"MANAGERIAL SOCIOLOGY"

The most extensive attempt to apply social scientific principles to managerial problems, and the second of the two major movements to give management a more scientific foundation, may be called "managerial sociology."[8] Although sometimes made synonymous with industrial sociology, the narrower term has special aptness as it applies to one major group of investigations and publica-

---

[8] This is the term used by Harold L. Sheppard, "The Treatment of Unionism in 'Managerial Sociology,'" *American Sociological Review*, 14: 310–313, April 1949.

tions in the field—that deriving from the work of Elton Mayo and his associates.[9]

At first glance, the recommendations to management made by this group and applied in many other studies would seem to meet most of the criticisms of "scientific management." The proponents of managerial sociology place central emphasis precisely upon the social character of the productive system and the human qualities of the individual components. Even a bare and abbreviated list of points recommended to managerial groups is impressive in its contrast to the mechanistic preoccupation of the followers of Taylor: (1) insistence on the importance of the informal work group, and the individual's membership and status in it, for employee morale and productivity; (2) emphasis on the relevance of "sentiments" and the individual's definition of the situation for predicting response to managerial action; (3) emphasis on the meaning as well as mechanical efficiency of communication within the organization; (4) a correlative prescription of consultation, of hearing advice and criticism by those supervised; (5) recommendations concerning machine design and placement and on avoiding unduly elaborate specialization of component tasks and functionalization of departments, in order to preserve some sense of personal participation for the worker; (6) to the same end, recommendations concerning decentralization of decision-making.[10]

These recommendations are based on a combination of important empirical research and an appreciation of sociological principles unknown to the older proponents of scientific management.

[9] See Elton Mayo, *The Human Problems of an Industrial Civilization,* 2nd ed. (Boston: Division of Research, Harvard Graduate School of Business Administration, 1946); Mayo, *The Social Problems of an Industrial Civilization* (Boston: Division of Research, Harvard Graduate School of Business Administration, 1945); F. J. Roethlisberger, *Management and Morale* (Cambridge: Harvard University Press, 1941); F. J. Roethlisberger and William J. Dickson, *Management and the Worker* (Cambridge: Harvard University Press, 1939); Thomas N. Whitehead, *The Industrial Worker* (Cambridge: Harvard University Press, 1938, 2 vols.).

[10] See, in addition to works cited in previous footnote, Peter F. Drucker, *The New Society: The Anatomy of the Industrial Order* (New York: Harper & Brothers, 1950), especially pp. 157–182; James C. Worthy, "Organizational Structure and Employe Morale," *American Sociological Review,* 15: 169–179, April 1950.

Despite the notable improvement of the second attempt to apply science to managerial problems over the first, managerial sociology still shares most of the fundamental difficulties discussed in the previous chapter with respect to scientific management. Of those difficulties, certainly the most crucial is that of the *ends* to which applied research is to be directed, and it is precisely this difficulty that justifies the designation, "managerial sociology." Mayo and his associates seem to be peculiarly insensitive to the problems of ends and values, despite the emphasis on "sentiments." The prescription given to the solution of industrial disorders and indeed all problems of modern civilization is the development of the "skills of cooperation." [11] Nowhere are answers provided to the vexing problems of current management: cooperation for what, in whose interests, and with what rewards and powers assigned to the co-operators? [12]

The fact is that much of the research into the social factors in industrial relations has been explicitly designed to avoid industrial disputes, to improve morale, and to enhance productivity, but without attention either to the differing interests and definitions of problems internal to the productive enterprise or to the fact that the factory as a social system or production as a goal are neither isolated nor paramount in society as a whole. [13] In this connection, it is not accidental that the "human relations" program of research

[11] Mayo, *The Social Problems* . . . , especially pp. 15–33. Indeed, Mayo judges the immaturity of social science by its lack of this skill, thus indicating (as in his persistent comparison with medicine as a science rather than a part of technology) his failure to comprehend scientific method. His position is one of radical empiricism.

[12] See Wilbert E. Moore, "Current Issues in Industrial Sociology," *American Sociological Review*, 12: 651–657, December 1947. See also the following later criticisms of the Mayo group: Reinhard Bendix and Lloyd H. Fisher, "The Perspectives of Elton Mayo," *Review of Economics and Statistics* 31: 312–319, November 1949; C. Wright Mills, "The Contributions of Sociology to Studies of Industrial Relations," *Proceedings of the First Annual Meeting, Industrial Relations Research Association.* Cleveland, Ohio, December 29–30, 1948 (Champaign Ill.: 1949), pp. 199–222; Sheppard, *op. cit.* The paper by Mills is the most fully documented of these.

[13] See, in addition to the author's "Current Problems . . ." cited above, Georges Friedmann, "Philosophy Underlying the Hawthorne Investigation," trans. by William J. Goode and Harold L. Sheppard, *Social Forces*, 28: 204–209, December 1949.

and action in large enterprises is being used as a tool in the attempt of management to compete with unions for the workers' loyalties.

Social research in the factory has been commended to management on grounds that attention to human relations will improve morale and productivity, which is indeed possible within limits if joint management-union sponsorship is secured. But not all of the social problems of an industrial civilization can be solved within the factory gates. There may be changes in the organization of work, and therefore in managerial policy, that are dictated not on grounds of increased productivity and lower absenteeism and turnover, but rather on grounds that production cannot be the sole goal of society or of an individual. Although the industrial enterprise is organized for production, it must accomplish that function within limits set by other social functions that are also essential. How this applies to the relaton of the worker to the machine will be explored in the following two chapters.

REFERENCES

BARNARD, CHESTER I., *The Functions of the Executive* (Cambridge: Harvard University Press, 1938), Chap. V, "Principles of Cooperative Action," and Chap. XI, "The Economy of Incentives."

CAREY, H. H., "Consultative Supervision and Management," *Personnel*, 18: 286–295, March 1942.

DAVIS, RALPH CURRIER, *Industrial Organization and Management* (New York: Harper & Brothers, 1940), Chap. 17, "Time and Motion Study"; Chap. 23, "The Personnel Organization"; Chap. 26, "Labor Relations and Employee Morale"; Chap. 28, "Personnel Research, Standards, and Control."

——, *Shop Management for the Shop Supervisor* (New York: Harper & Brothers, 1941), Chap. 8, "Motion and Time Study," and Chap. 12, "Labor Management and the Shop Supervisor."

FRANKLIN, B. A., *The Industrial Executive* (New York: The Ronald Press Company, 1926), Chap. II, "Operating Policies."

GOMBERG, WILLIAM, *A Trade Union Analysis of Time Study* (Chicago: Science Research Associates, 1948).

KNOWLES, ASA S., and ROBERT D. THOMPSON, *Industrial Management* (New York: The Macmillan Company, 1944), Chap. XVIII, "Motion Study and the Worker"; Chap. XIX, "Time Study"; Chap. XX,

"Job Evaluation"; Chap. XXI, "Merit Rating—Measuring Manpower Performance."

LANSBURGH, RICHARD H., and WILLIAM R. SPRIEGEL, *Industrial Management* (New York: John Wiley & Sons, Inc., 1940), Chap. VIII, "Morale Building as a Factor in Organization."

MAYO, ELTON, *The Human Problems of an Industrial Civilization*, 2nd ed. (Boston: Division of Research, Harvard Graduate School of Business Administration, 1946).

———, *The Social Problems of an Industrial Civilization* (Boston: Division of Research, Harvard Graduate School of Business Administration, 1945).

MERTON, ROBERT K., *Social Theory and Social Structure* (Glencoe, Ill.: The Free Press, 1949), Chap. IV, "Social Structure and Anomie," and Chap. XIII, "The Machine, the Worker, and the Engineer."

———, "The Unanticipated Consequences of Purposive Social Action," *American Sociological Review*, 1: 894–904, December 1936.

MILLER, SPENCER, JR., "Labor's Attitude toward Time and Motion Study," *Mechanical Engineering*, 60: 289–294, 338, April 1938.

MILLS, C. WRIGHT, "The Contributions of Sociology to Studies of Industrial Relations," in Milton Derber, ed., *Proceedings of the First Annual Meeting, Industrial Relations Research Association*, Cleveland, Ohio, December 29–30, 1948 (Champaign, Ill.: 1949), pp. 199–222.

MOORE, WILBERT E., "Current Issues in Industrial Sociology," *American Sociological Review*, 12: 651–657, December 1947.

PERSON, H. S., ed. for The Taylor Society, *Scientific Management in American Industry* (New York: Harper & Brothers, 1929).

PETERSEN, ELMORE, and E. GROSVENOR PLOWMAN, *Business Organization and Management*, rev. ed. (Chicago: Richard D. Irwin, 1948), Chap. XII, "Efficiency."

ROETHLISBERGER, F. J., *Management and Morale* (Cambridge: Harvard University Press, 1941), Chap. VII, "What Is Adequate Personnel Management?" and Chap. VIII, "Concerning People Who Deal with Cooperative Phenomena."

ROETHLISBERGER, F. J., and WILLIAM J. DICKSON, *Management and the Worker* (Cambridge: Harvard University Press, 1939), Part II (Chaps. IX–XI), "A Plan for the Improvement of Employee Relations," Part II (Chaps. XII–XVI), "A Conceptual Scheme for the Understanding of Employee Dissatisfaction," and Part V (Chaps. XXIV–XXVI), "Applications to Practice of Research Results."

SHELDON, OLIVER, *The Philosophy of Management* (London: Sir Isaac Pitman & Sons, Ltd., 1924), Chap. V, "Labour Management."

Schneider, Eugene V., "Limitations on Observation in Industrial Sociology," *Social Forces*, 28: 279–284, March 1950.

Sheppard, Harold L., "The Treatment of Unionism in 'Managerial Sociology,'" *American Sociological Review*, 14: 310–313, April 1949.

Taylor, Frederick Winslow, *The Principles of Scientific Management* (New York: Harper & Brothers, 1911).

———, *Shop Management* (New York: Harper & Brothers, 1911).

Thompson, Clarence Bertrand, ed., *Scientific Management* (Cambridge: Harvard University Press, 1914).

Todd, Arthur James, *Industry and Society* (New York: Henry Holt and Company, Inc., 1933), Chaps. XXVII and XXVIII, "The Humanizing of Industry."

Whitehead, T. N., *Leadership in a Free Society* (Cambridge: Harvard University Press, 1937), Chap. VIII, "Progressive Management," Chap. IX, "The Financial Reward," and Chap. X, "The Care of Personnel in Industry."

Worthy, James C., "Organizational Structure and Employee Morale," *American Sociological Review*, 15: 169–179, April 1950.

PART FOUR

INDUSTRIAL ORGANIZATION: LABOR

CHAPTER IX

THE WORKER AND THE MACHINE

IN THE shops and mills, in the mines and factories, there are two classes of "objects" that bear the main brunt of directly productive work: the workers and the machines. And although there is a general tendency for the machines to become more "human" and, it is frequently claimed, for the workers to become more machinelike, the two are not to be confused. It is in the relations between these two classes of producers that many claim to find the substance of modern industrial relations. Indeed, the machine is frequently endowed with belligerent emotions by persons with more imagination than good sense, and the worker is pictured as a hapless Frankenstein, destroyed by a monster of his own or someone else's devising.

Behind the poetry and metaphor that encumber the literature in this field there are certain fundamental facts that seem to give point to the literary flights of fancy. Although we have already indicated some of the general principles of the "relationships of production" in the factory system (Chapter II), a recapitulation at this point may be helpful. (1) The modern worker no longer typically owns his own tools. This is mainly because factory production has made possible the use of tools that are far too large, complicated, and expensive to be owned by the single workman. Although the distinction is only a rough one, the "tool" has been replaced by the "machine." (2) The worker is employed by the person or corporation that owns the machines. The customary formality and impersonality of the source of ownership and the immediacy of the machine thus make it appear that he serves the machine. Actually, the machine is simply symbolic of a rather more basic fact: the worker no longer controls the conditions of work. (3) The rate and quality of work, the length of the working day, the location of employment—all tend to be increasingly standardized. And the standardization again takes place most often through the medium of the machine, and according to the demands of a machine technology. (4) It is possible by mechanization to reduce the number of workmen as well as the skills required of them. Thus the machine may truly appear as the direct and often successful competitor of the workman, as well as his master in determining the conditions of his employment.

In view of these rather well-known circumstances it is really not surprising to find the machine personified as a willful force for good or evil, and the position of the laborer something like that of the sinful soul in the hands of an angry god. It may be repeated that this is perhaps permissible literary license, but it is not an accurate description of the worker's position in modern industry. The machines are invented, installed, and regulated to fulfill conscious human goals. They are means for the achievement of efficient production. To a certain extent, so are the workers. Of the two, the human agents of production are the more adaptable to changing circumstances, and this has given rise to the policy of determining changes on mechanical grounds and then fitting the working behavior of the laborer to the machine technology.

This does not remove the problem of the relation of the worker to the machine. It simply phrases the situation in slightly less grandiloquent terms than is customary, and with a little more accuracy. The fundamental issue seems to be: What significance has industrial mechanization for the worker? This in turn may be put more concretely. (1) What are the relations between mechanical efficiency and physiological efficiency? This is usually expressed as the problem of industrial fatigue, and raises the issue of the physiological limits to exploitation. (2) What is the significance of the fact that the human agents of production are not simply organic units of exploitation, but social persons who react in terms of complicated learning, emotional states, and social interests? (3) What effect has mechanization and rationalization upon the worker's satisfaction with his job, and on his economic and social position in the community? It is our purpose to consider the first two questions in this chapter, and the last in Chapter X.

ROUTINE AND THE PROBLEM OF FATIGUE

Only since the second decade of this century have various scientists been concerned with what they consider to be a major problem of contemporary industrial employment—*fatigue*. The relative recency of concern with the problem calls for some comment. Did not the medieval peasant returning from the fields show signs of weariness? Were farmers who worked from sun to sun, and women whose work, by an old adage, was never done exempt from "that tired feeling"? It would be naive to think so. Except for the natives of some rather idyllic tropical isles (which, incidentally, are often more mythical than real), man has been accustomed to earn his bread by "the sweat of his face." Why all the to-do? Two logical alternatives suggest themselves: either the weariness resulting from labor is more acute under modern conditions of production, or the same old human frailty has some new significance in the modern world. It is of course possible that both situations exist.

An Old Condition Becomes a New Problem. We may postpone for the moment the question of whether modern industry actually creates more fatigue, and note some of the reasons why the undoubted wearisomeness of labor is increasingly recognized and considered significant.

1. There can be little doubt that, even if modern conditions of employment created no more fatigue than other modes of production, or even less, the fatigue would be increasingly recognized. This is partly because increased "rationalization" of industrial organization allows a rather close check upon variations in individual performance at routine tasks. Individual production records, piece-rate and bonus systems of payment, careful inspection of quality as well as quantity of work, and so on, not only symbolize the oft-noted subservience of the worker to the machine, but allow *measurement* of his productivity. The control over the conditions of employment afforded by the factory system even allow quasi-experimental varia-

tion of conditions to determine the significant factors in observed variations in efficiency of production. Standardization may reveal, even if it does not cause, the worker's inability to maintain a constant level of performance over an extended period of time. There is even the likelihood that standardization makes a "normal" amount of fatigue more *significant*, since machines do not slow down or relax standards of quality to match the worker's weariness.

2. There are many new techniques for the measurement and study of variations in individual performance. Those techniques that derive from the organization of production itself have been paralleled by partially independent developments in medical, physiological, and psychological research. This again presents the possibility that, even if there is no more fatigue, it may be increasingly recognized and subjected to analysis.

3. The recognition of a problem not only implies the possibility of solution, but also the normative judgment that it *should* be solved. In other words, a problem is always formulated in terms of some ideal, and a change in ideals therefore creates new problems without necessarily creating any new conditions. There is substantial evidence that ideals of the comfort, "happiness," and similar aspirations of workers have been revised upward, at least in the democratic societies. This also tends to give fatigue a new significance without necessarily changing its amount. The heightened interest in fatigue during wartime labor shortages and pressure for accelerated production further illustrates this point.[1]

Possible Increases in Fatigue. The foregoing considerations do not rule out the possibility that modern industry makes fatigue more prevalent or more acute. It must certainly be assumed that the type or conditions of work have something to do with the response of the human body to that work. To the extent that present-day jobs make different physiological demands upon the worker there exists the possibility that those demands are more onerous than those that formerly prevailed. Thus, a farmer may produce far more

---

[1] We shall refer below to the English studies made during the first World War and to the more nearly contemporary researches. The present interest is simply to indicate the relation between ideals of maximum productivity and recognition of fatigue as a "problem."

"horsepower" or foot-pounds of work during his long working day than does a drill-press operator making holes in steel plate. Yet the latter may show far more actual physical deterioration during the course of his shorter day, because he is using the *same* muscles time after time and thus not allowing the tissues sufficient time to recuperate. This is part of the reason that fatigue as a peculiarly modern problem is usually thought to be associated with the routinization of industrial work assignments. It should be noted, of course, that intensified and commercialized agriculture provides numerous illustrations of job assignments just as routinized as factory employment. Chopping cotton, transplanting rice, and hand cultivation of vegetables are cases in point.

But fatigue is by no means a simple phenomenon, or even a single one. As a practical matter "mental exhaustion" is at least as important as the physical variety, even if less subject to objective analysis and measurement. Thus it is well known in terms of personal experience that an interesting task is less tiring than a boring (we even say "tiresome") one. And this reaction appears to be almost independent of differences in required muscular exertion. This is the other part of the reason that fatigue is usually thought to be associated with routine, because the latter is frequently confused with the evaluative and subjective term *monotony*. To the extent that contemporary employment is more likely to bore the worker, or bore him more quickly, "fatigue" of some sort has increased. It is evident, therefore, that we can no longer put off some consideration of the nature of this phenomenon which is supposed to be a product of the worker's bond service to the machine.

Determining the Nature of Fatigue. The general inability of the human individual to work hard and continuously without rest is well known. But it is also apparent that individuals vary in their physical stamina, and even that the same individual reacts differently under changing circumstances. The "symptoms" of fatigue may range all the way from chemical changes in the blood as revealed by laboratory test to absenteeism and excessive labor turnover as revealed by comparison of employment records and statistics. The tired worker may reduce the quantity or quality of his output, become surly and ill-tempered, or deliberately jam his machine. Yet many of these same results may be due to other causes, and it is obvious that no single and simple cause could produce such otherwise unrelated results. This can only mean that we are dealing here with a complex series of relationships, which must be analyzed in detail if we are to find any useful principles.

This difficulty in determining the nature of fatigue arises from the fact that the human animal has the rather vexing habit of reacting to stimuli in a nonmechanistic fashion. If fatigue were simply a physiological reaction of the organism, the attempt to analyze and possibly control the phenomenon would be considerably easier than it is in fact. Complaints of weariness, monotony, boredom, exhaustion, and so on are made under circumstances where no physiological fatigue does or could exist. It is partly for this reason that many students of fatigue in industry adopt a pragmatic view of the nature of fatigue: whatever it is in industrial work that results in a decrease in the worker's production.[2] But this would seem to get us no farther on our way than calling this mysterious force X, a *gremlin*, or some other modern counterpart of an old-style demon or evil spirit. If fatigue is a "problem" in the dual sense of something to be understood and something to be reduced, it is axiomatic that its sources—be they as objective as temperature or as subjective as unreasoned fear of a machine—need to be examined and isolated.[3]

Determining the Causes of Fatigue. The variables involved in an investigation of the reaction of the industrial worker to his employment may be conveniently classified as: *the worker, the job, and "working conditions."* Each of these is in turn a complex union of

[2] See, for example, Joseph Tiffin, *Industrial Psychology* (New York: Prentice-Hall, Inc., 1942), pp. 219–220.

[3] It is not meant to imply that industrial psychologists and others who define fatigue pragmatically in terms of reduced output dismiss thereby the importance of causal factors, but only that the concentration on a single symptom is likely to obscure those factors. This is true because the same situation, such as reduction of output, may signify physiological deterioration, deliberate "spinning out" of work to make it last longer, avoidance of reduction in piece rates, and so on. Moreover, the motives behind the last two may result in types of behavior other than reduction of output (such as a collective bargaining contract guaranteeing tenure and rate of pay), and even physiological weariness may show itself only in curtailment of activities after working hours.

variables. The job or task, for example, is subject to major or minor modification such as changes in machine speeds, variability of materials, degree of watchfulness or judgment required of the worker, and so on. Workers differ not only in physical stamina, inherent mental ability, and trained skill, but in their emotional and other psychological reactions to their "environment." This is the reason for the repeated assertion that the reaction of the worker to his job and working conditions is not a mechanistic one. The worker reacts to his environment in terms of its meaning for him. This we have already referred to as the worker's "definition of the situation." Whether or not this definition, or the worker's reaction, corresponds to the expectations of the observer or experimenter depends on the skill and knowledge of the latter. More particularly, it depends upon the awareness on the part of the observer of the character of the human variables with which he is dealing. This set of considerations must be borne in mind as we examine the research evidence concerning the reaction of the worker to the conditions of factory production.

RESEARCH EVIDENCE ON FACTORS IN FATIGUE AND PRODUCTIVITY

Two commonplace observations may be regarded as fundamental points of interest in studies of industrial fatigue: workers at the same type of job and the same overt working conditions do not have the same production records, and the same worker over the period of a day or week may show marked differences in speed and accuracy of work. These observations have prompted a great many studies, under more or less controlled conditions, to determine the explanation of these differences. In the following pages we shall summarize the major findings of these studies without any attempt at a complete report. We shall, however, attempt to judge the range of accuracy of the conclusions suggested.

The Organism and the Environment. The simplest relationship of the worker to his job is the elementary one of the organism and the external environment, and it is on this level that we may first examine fatigue.

1. *Simple Muscular Fatigue.* If the same muscle or set of muscles is used continuously over a period of time, the muscle gradually loses its effectiveness until sufficient time elapses for the body to restore equilibrium. This reaction may be summarized as to the temporary exhaustion of energy-producing materials, and the corresponding accumulation of waste materials in the muscles and blood.[4] Combined with the partially offsetting effect of practice,[5] this is

FIGURE 6. *"Normal" Production and Fatigue Curve*

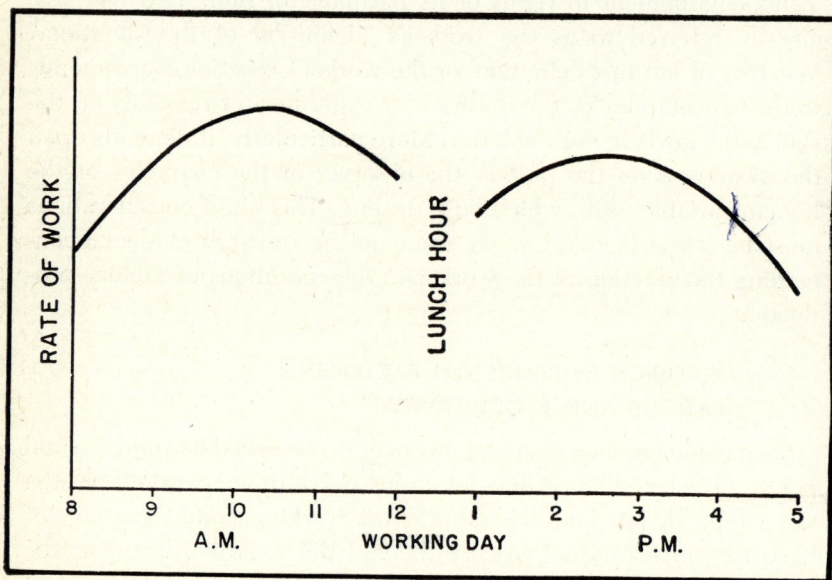

1. *Simple Muscular Fatigue.*

supposed to yield the "normal" production curve illustrated in Figure 6. It should, however, be especially noted that the translation of muscular fatigue into production curves can only be significant at a type of work genuinely involving repetitive or extreme muscular exertion with insufficient rest to maintain the equilibrium between productive material and waste. Other types of work show

[4] See, for example, Morris S. Viteles, *The Science of Work* (New York: W. W. Norton & Company, Inc., 1934), especially pp. 286–287.
[5] The relation of practice and fatigue is discussed by H. M. Vernon, *Industrial Fatigue and Efficiency* (London: George Routledge & Sons, Ltd., 1921), p. 13 and *passim*.

slower loss of productivity, and in some light rhythmical work the overt effect of any possible fatigue is not apparent.[6]

Although the machine has largely made work "easier" as measured by the total amount of energy or force expended by the laborer, the specialization and routinization customary in "unskilled" and "semiskilled" factory labor has not necessarily made work less onerous for those ranking lowest in the productive hierarchy. Motion economy studies following the "scientific management" movement may remove part of the effort normally expended in doing a work assignment, but whatever gains are made in production may reflect more a saving of time than of the worker's vigor. In any event, the relation between muscular exertion and presence of lactic acid in the blood as tested by laboratory techniques is considerably more direct and subject to experimental control than the effect of muscular fatigue in actual factory work.

2. *Physiological Reactions to Working Conditions.* The response of the organism to its environment is somewhat more directly (or at least more demonstrably) significant in industrial employment in the case of *atmospheric conditions*. Although a good deal of nonsense has been written about the "artificiality" of the modern industrial environment (what typically human environment is not?), it is undeniably true that some extreme variations in temperature, humidity, and oxygen supply seriously curtail the effectiveness of the human organism as a productive force. For example, workers in steel mills, especially those working near the furnaces and molds, were seriously bothered with "heat exhaustion" until observation and tests revealed that the excessive sweating reducd the salt content of the body below the minimum necessary for normal functioning. Simply replenishing the water supply through fresh drinking water had no effect, but salt tablets or a slightly saline drinking water have greatly reduced this type of "fatigue." Other studies have indicated the debilitating effect of humid heat (as in lumber dry kilns and similar drying rooms), where the problem is not one of excessive sweat but of insufficient evaporation of sweat, thus allow-

[6] See Charles S. Myers, *Industrial Psychology* (New York: The Peoples Institute Publishing Co., 1925), p. 70.

ing body heat to rise beyond the limit of vigor and possibly even of safety.[7] Excessive pressure (as in diving and underwater tunneling) results in dissolving nitrogen in the blood and producing "bends" if work is long sustained and return to normal pressure too rapid. Recently the great increase in the effective "ceiling" of the airplane as a machine has made possible (and in war, militarily expedient) the carrying of human beings into regions of low atmospheric pressure and reduced oxygen supply. The pilot or passengers may lose consciousness or even die from the effect of environmental conditions more extreme than those to which the human body can adjust unaided.

These physiological reactions to conditions of employment do not always represent the *direct* effect of mechanization as ordinarily understood, but do indicate some of the ways in which a machine technology may place greater demands on the human organism than the ordinary range of human adaptability permits. An "artificial" environment in these cases has to be created to offset the effects of "abnormal" environments.

A much more complex aspect of the physiological effects of working conditions is presented in the problem of the *alternation of work and rest*. The complexity is chiefly due to the number of variables and the practical difficulty of experimental study of their relations. It is safe to say that the capacity of the body to work reaches a vanishing point under continued activity without change or rest and sleep. But for the most part the research evidence concerning the maximum length of the work interval, the work day, or work week is based simply on production records. Reasoning back from variations in production to the physiological capacity to produce is fraught with the gravest dangers. Interest and boredom at work, sentiments of a "fair day's work," and the counterbalancing of financial incentives on the one hand and desires to maintain out-of-hours social activities on the other are all possibly involved. We may review some of the results of studies in the field, while noting the difficulties in interpretation of their results.

[7] See National Research Council, Committee on Work in Industry (Report of the Committee by George C. Homans), *Fatigue of Workers* (New York: Reinhold Publishing Corporation, 1941), pp. 23–28.

With regard to the length of the uninterrupted work period, the obvious variables of the physical capacity of workers and the nature of the job make extensive generalization difficult. Most investigators have found, however, that the introduction of rest pauses increases total production despite the slight shortening of the work day.[8] Yet Elton Mayo found in an early study[9] that certainty of rest pauses was more important than making them dependent on a certain amount of work done (which would seem to invalidate any simple fatigue hypothesis), and accounted for their effectiveness as being due more to interruption of "pessimistic revery" than to relief of muscular or postural fatigue. The investigators in the extensive research program carried on at the Hawthorne works of the Western Electric Company, which we shall review later in the chapter, found that the introduction of rest pauses raised the level of production, but that subsequent elimination of the rest periods had the same effect. Such results make even the "pragmatic" test of relationship between rest pauses and production open to some question, and certainly incapable of uncritical extension without taking into account other possible variables.

Just as the introduction of rest pauses has in general resulted in a greater amount of production, so some shortening of the work day seems to increase not only the relative productivity per time unit, but the absolute amount as well. But here the limits of this relationship must be investigated, as well as its explanation. It is one thing to shorten the work day from fourteen hours to ten and find total production increasing, and quite another thing to expect the same results from a reduction from eight hours to six. There is simply no reliable evidence indicating the maximum length of the work day in terms of the worker's physiological capacity to produce. Long-term comparisons between man-hour productivity under the old twelve-

---

[8] See the summaries of studies in Viteles, *op. cit.*, pp. 296–299, and in the same author's *Industrial Psychology* (New York: W. W. Norton & Company, Inc., 1929), pp. 470–482. Several investigators have found that authorized rest periods do not actually decrease work time, since workers take voluntary rests anyway. See Rex B. Hersey, "Rests—Authorized and Unauthorized," *Journal of Personnel Research*, 2: 37–45, June 1925.

[9] Elton Mayo, "Revery and Industrial Fatigue," *Journal of Personnel Research*, 3: 273–281, December 1924.

hour day and the modern eight-hour day are obviously vitiated by the important factor of increased mechanization. On the other hand, short-term comparisons which *seem* to indicate the physiological advantages of shorter hours may actually indicate the effectiveness of the goal of increased leisure, the erroneous belief that work is thereby spread out, and so on.

These same strictures apply with equal or even greater rigor in the case of the work week. The British studies made since the days of the first World War indicate an optimum work week of around fifty-four hours.[10] An absolute increase was usually recorded in the reduction of longer work weeks to approximately the optimum figure. Yet it is difficult to judge what characteristics of working conditions, normal pace, customary standards, and the like may be reflected. In the absence of any comparable American studies, it is interesting that a canvass of industrial executives, employment administrators, and other managers elicited an almost unanimous agreement that the "optimum" work week is forty-eight hours.[11] Since various types of plants with different classes of workers were represented, it is safe to say that this was at least as much a statement of sentiment as a generalization from experience.[12]

The general principle that summarizes the evidence with respect to the physiological reaction of the worker to conditions of work is easier to state than the precise applicability of the principle in concrete cases. The general principle is that the range of adaptability of the human organism to conditions of production sets

[10] See Great Britain, Medical Research Council, Industrial Health Research Board, *Hours of Work, Lost Time, and Labour Wastage*, Emergency Report No. 2 (London: H. M. Stationery Office, 1942), Max D. Kossoris, "Hours and Efficiency in British Industry," *Monthly Labor Review*, 52: 1337–1346, June 1941; United States Department of Labor, Bureau of Labor Statistics, "Industrial Efficiency and Fatigue in British Munition Factories," *Bulletin No. 221* (Washington: U. S. Government Printing Office, 1917); H. M. Vernon, *The Health and Efficiency of Munition Workers* (London: Oxford University Press, 1940).

[11] J. Douglas Brown and Helen Baker, *Optimum Hours of Work in War Production* (Princeton, N. J.: Industrial Relations Section, Princeton University, 1942).

[12] Even when the generalization from experience was genuine, as when companies reported that longer work weeks increased absenteeism and thus reduced the effective work week to about the optimum, it is likely that something besides the wearing down of the organism is involved. See *ibid.*, pp. 9–10.

upper and lower limits to variations in atmospheric conditions, periods of rest, and length of employment, if production is to be maintained at the highest level. The determination of those limits is "only a practical matter," but nevertheless attended by greater difficulties the more variables are included.

3. *Mental Ability and Boredom.* A relationship of a slightly different order, but one still capable of phrasing in the rather simple terms of the relation of the organism and the environment, is that between mental ability and boredom. Comparing boredom, as determined both by testimony of workers and by correspondence of their production curves to the characteristic "monotony curve" showing mid-period depression, and intelligence by various standardized tests, research seems uniformly to indicate that intelligent workers employed at repetitive work or other tasks below their ability become bored and dissatisfied. The "boon of stupidity" [13] has been rather generally hailed as one solution to the human problems of mechanization. Aside from questions of accuracy of judgment of mental ability and boredom, or even of possible "hidden" variables in any such relationships (such as differences in levels of aspiration), it is clear that insufficient intelligence might equally result in boredom with work assignments beyond the worker's abilities. This would seem to be another instance of the characteristics of the organism setting limits to effective variation in types of work or conditions of employment.

THE PERSON AND THE SIGNIFICANT ENVIRONMENT

If the number and complexity of the variables at the rather simple level of organism and environment makes precise statement of applicable principles difficult, how much greater is the difficulty once the complete person is brought into account. For here we must begin to differentiate the environment into the significant and the insignificant, and recognize that it is the individual worker's classification that is chiefly important, not the observer's. We may start with rather simple examples which pretty closely approximate the

[13] The phrase is that of Viteles, who also summarizes the studies in *The Science of Work*, pp. 329–333.

mechanistic relationship of stimuli and responses, and proceed to some of the less obvious types or signs of work weariness.

1. *Illumination and Noise.* Although there is some slight evidence of a more direct effect of insufficient or excessive illumination and of noise on "nervous strain," the significance of these factors seems to depend more on individual differences in perception and sensitivity. In the case of illumination there seems to be some definite strain and fatigue of muscles through necessity of repeated change in focus, glare, and so on,[14] yet complaints about lighting may be more symptomatic of other causes of dissatisfaction than genuinely productive of weariness. In the Western Electric studies, for example, both increases and decreases (down to the approximate illumination of moonlight) resulted in constant or increased production, and at one time a complaint about the lighting was adequately met by a substitution of a new set of bulbs of the same size as the old ones.[15] Reports on the effect of noise on productivity are also variable, some indicating no decrease in production with increased noise (though perhaps with increased signs of muscular effort), and others indicating a definite decline.[16] None of the studies seem to have taken into account differences in auditory sensitivity or habituation or in type of work being performed, nor to have established the upper (and, conceivably, the lower) limits of noise variation as conditions of work. We must therefore report the evidence on illumination and noise as inconclusive, although possibly indicative at least of an aggravating role when coupled with other circumstances.

2. *Incentives, Financial and Otherwise.* The importance of goals in the orientation of the worker to his job has been accepted in general by all researchers concerning fatigue and productivity, and of course by administrators. But the interrelation of physiological fatigue, monotony and boredom, and the effectiveness of various incentives in counterbalancing or eliminating complaints of weariness has not received adequate attention. Work is rarely an end in itself, although

---

[14] See Viteles, *The Science of Work,* pp. 299–301, where various studies are summarized.

[15] F. J. Roethlisberger and W. J. Dickson, *Management and the Worker* (Cambridge: Harvard University Press, 1939), pp. 14–17.

[16] See Viteles, *The Science of Work,* pp. 293–295; Tiffin, *op. cit.,* p. 223.

the circumstances in which work is performed may be regarded by the workman as so satisfactory that little further incentive is required. On the other hand the work or its attendant conditions may be so unsatisfactory from the workman's standpoint that only exceptional incentives will secure his continued cooperation. It is customarily maintained that for the great bulk of laborers in contemporary industry the latter is more nearly an accurate characterization of the situation than the former. And it is certainly true that in nonindustrial societies a very common barrier to voluntary labor recruitment for new industrial enterprises is the time-discipline and routine of manufacturing jobs.[17]

We shall return in the following chapter to the question of "workmanship" and its substitutes in mechanized and routinized production, and in Chapter XI we shall review the goals of laborers as participants in industrial production. Our concern at this point is to note the possibilities with respect to offsetting the effects of fatigue and monotony by wages or other incentives.

As a general principle, it would seem possible partially to offset fatigue and maintain production if incentives are sufficiently strong. This seems to be the basis for bonus systems on piece rate, where the rate is increased after the production of some standard number of units. An extra rate of pay for overtime work is also sometimes justified on this basis. But it is apparent that, if the "physiological fatigue" is genuinely a deterioration of the capacity of the organism to act, no amount of incentive can possibly motivate sustained productivity. On the other hand, it is probable that even short of genuine exhaustion (which is actually rare) the individual can overcome his own weariness "by taking thought thereto." [18]

---

[17] See Wilbert E. Moore, *Industrialization and Labor: Social Aspects of Economic Development* (Ithaca: Cornell University Press, 1951), Chap. II, "Barriers and Antipathies."

[18] It is possible that in the case of fatigue, as in many other cases, the dualism of the mind and body is an inaccurate assumption. It is well established that subjects who show physiological symptoms of fatigue, such as the presence of lactic acid in the blood, also complain of general weariness. It is not beyond the realm of possibility that this relationship may work in reverse: that is, that what is called "mental fatigue" may produce physiological results. Such a relationship is already known in the case of emotional states and the endocrine

Boredom and monotony are by definition indicative of insufficient incentive. It follows that the greater the negative reaction of the worker to the nature or conditions of his working assignment, the greater must be the counterbalancing incentive. The worker's official duty in the formal structure of industrial organization is to cooperate in production. But short of the unlikely event of production being a goal in itself (an event almost equally unlikely in all ranks of the hierarchy), his interest must be purchased by other means, and the work assignment becomes a means for the satisfaction of his private ends. There is no evidence that reliance on any single incentive—even including the theoretically limitless goal of income—will consistently and uniformly offset the various disadvantages the worker finds in his employment.

As the worker is asked to increase his pace, or confine his activities to a few repetitive ones for which he is "best qualified," greater and greater strain is placed on his enthusiasm for those few activities. This seems to be the basic consideration in the attitudinal relation of the worker to his job. Not only is there less likelihood that the activities will be intrinsically interesting, but the chance of his finding incidental compensations in satisfactory social relationships is decreased. If the worker is expected to have a "singleness of purpose," that purpose must be strong indeed.

The effectiveness of income in overcoming boredom is dependent not simply on the relative importance of money in the worker's scale of values, but upon the whole context of wage payments in the worker's definition of the situation. Thus various studies indicate that piecework wage systems will induce greater production at routinized work than will straight hourly wages.[19] Yet investigations of a number of repetitive work situations indicate that the significance of wages to the worker may be in terms of competitive status within the organization;[20] it may be the sole symbol of value in the

---

glands of internal secretion, and indeed in the whole area of psychosomatic medicine.

[19] See Arthur G. Anderson, Merten Joseph Mandeville, and John Mueller Anderson, *Industrial Management* (New York: The Ronald Press Company, 1942), Chap. 26, "Wages—Comparison of Wage Plans."

[20] See Roethlisberger and Dickson, *op. cit.*, pp. 133–134, 576–577.

community for work of such a new and specialized character that it can have no other significance; [21] and it is quite possible that both wage complaints and signs of boredom are attitudinal indicators of the general orientation of the worker to his job rather than isolated and specific sources of difficulty.[22] The mistake of finding some cure-all like wages for some symptom of dissatisfaction like boredom is simply another example of mechanistic interpretation of stimuli and responses.

The substitution or addition of other incentives to cooperation does little to change the conclusion with regard to the effectiveness of income goals, except in so far as they increase the satisfactoriness of the entire work situation as viewed by the worker. Extra "spurts" of production, or reduction of complaints about servitude to mecha-nized processes, can be temporarily gained by contests, patriotic appeals, and so on. But these wear off and call for new and greater efforts to induce the next temporary burst of activity unless they become a part of the daily life of the man at the machine. The longest and most comprehensive single industrial research project— the Western Electric studies—attempting to discover the factors in rate of production, employee morale, and related problems docu-ments the primary importance of the "human relationships" of production: the relation of the worker to his superiors and to his fellows. Compared to the importance of this factor (which is really a great complex of factors), questions of repetitive work, fatigue,. and boredom lose their supposed significance. The routine or repeti-tive character of work simply accentuates the importance of the subjectively significant working conditions.[23]

[21] *Ibid.*, p. 574.

[22] See Elton Mayo, *The Human Problems of an Industrial Civilization* (New York: The Macmillan Company, 1933), Chap. II, "What Is Monotony?"

[23] For reports on various phases and aspects of the Western Electric studies, see Mayo, *Human Problems of an Industrial Civilization;* Roethlisberger and Dickson, *op. cit.,* T. N. Whitehead, *The Industrial Worker* (Cambridge: Har-vard University Press, 1938) 2 vols.; T. N. Whitehead, *Leadership in a Free Society* (Cambridge: Harvard University Press, 1937). For briefer summaries see National Research Council, Committee on Work in Industry, *op. cit.,* Sec. IV, "The Western Electric Researches"; F. J. Roethlisberger, *Management and Morale* (Cambridge: Harvard University Press, 1941), especially Chap. II, "The Road Back to Sanity."

3. *Routine and Security.* An aspect of mechanization and routinization of work that frequently escapes attention is the security provided by a regularized and predictable environment. This is not to say that *any* kind of working conditions are subjectively satisfactory as long as they are known. That is a question that can only be answered by reference to the worker's expectations as determined by his previous "conditioning." But it is to say that the "deadliness" of routine has often been overemphasized and incorrectly stated. Human existence as a whole depends upon the daily, and even hourly, observance of major and minor (even petty) rituals. Many of these can be as demanding of conformity as the most implacable machine or hard-hearted foreman. Certainly any industrial job, ranging from the lofty heights of the executive to the lowly estate of the pieceworker, is replete with routine and repetitive work. But there are certain differences in the relation of the pieceworker to his work that distinguish his situation. (a) The cycle of repetition is likely to cover a shorter time span. This is apparently what has been most apparent to industrial observers, but is likely to have less significance than some other differences, or at least to gain significance only in combination with the others. (b) The length of the repetitive cycle is largely beyond his control and is most often determined without attention to his wishes. This is more a question of degree, and chiefly significant in relation to still another difference. (c) The general social context in which routine work is set is likely to be neglected in the case of the workman, and changes in that context not only are less subject to his choice, but are more likely to destroy routines in which he had formerly found satisfaction.

As we observed in discussing management, placing persons in formal relationships also induces informal patterns of interaction. Many of these are of a *routine* character, but they are *crescive, not imposed.* This fits into our preceding observation about the "human relationships" offsetting the effects of repetitive work and suggests that complaints about the latter are indicative of interferences with the former.

4. *Unanticipated Participation in Experiments.* If the studies referred to in the last few pages point to any conclusion, they point anew to the difficulty of applying experimental procedures to human activities and relationships. This is not to say that experimentation with respect to the conditions of industrial employment is simply impossible, but only that it must be approached with extreme caution. In controlling the "environment" and varying one condition at a time, many other conditions may unwittingly undergo change. Chief among these is the knowledge of the test group that they are undergoing observation. Whether the results are "short" of expectations, as in the case of slowing down for the observation of the rate setter, or beyond expectations, as in the case of workers obligingly increasing production to make the experiment a "success," the organism is not reacting to its environment, but human personalities are reacting to the environment as it exists in their "definition of the situation." This is nowhere more clearly brought out than in the Western Electric studies. The effects of rest pauses, wages, illumination, the work week, and so on were tested in relation to production. Production increased. But the "crucial experiment"—that of a return to previous conditions—failed to yield the expected results: production still went up. The investigators were forced to recognize that in setting up controlled conditions for experimental variation of conditions of work they had changed practically every significant circumstance of the social environment: size of group, informal relationships, supervisory situation, and so on.[24] This indicates that the range of data subjected to analysis must be considerably broader than ordinarily assumed by industrial experi-

[24] For a convenient summary of this aspect of the results of the studies, see Roethlisberger, *Management and Morale,* Chap. II, "The Road Back to Sanity." The investigators seem to place main emphasis on the change in supervisory control and the amount of "consultation" with workers about the experiments. The evidence reported supports the significance of this factor, but not necessarily the relative weight attached to it as compared with other changes equally evident. The difficulty here seems to be that the *positive* analysis was concerned with various aspects of working conditions as ordinarily understood. Failure of these studies to account for the observed behavior of workers turned the attention of the investigators to the social situation or human relationships as a residual category. This simply indicates the area for investigation, but not the

menters. Roethlisberger, one of the researchers and reporters of the Western Electric study, has indicated this situation by a diagram, reproduced as Figure 7. The first part of the diagram indicates the level of ordinary "experiment," the second the level of attitude recognition, the third the level of social analysis. This unquestionably makes the study of the reaction of the worker to working con-

FIGURE 7. *Levels of Analysis of Workers' Reactions*

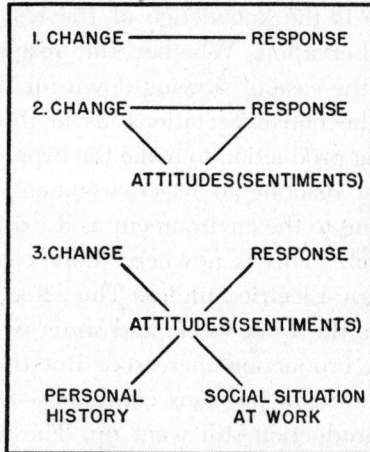

Adapted by permission of Harvard University Press from F. J. Roethlisberger, *Management and Morale* (Cambridge: Harvard University Press, 1941), p. 21.

ditions more difficult, but promises to yield results of much greater reliability (and therefore utility) than the type of experiment that Professor Mayo refers to as "essentially trivial tricks." [25]

Conclusion. The first part of our review of the relations of the worker to the machine (or to "conditions of work") indicates that, although the effects of speed, muscular effort, temperature, humidity, and similar conditions are not negligible, their direct signifi-

significance of various factors in that area. The positive research into the social factors took the form of the "undirected interview" and is subject to some doubt as an accurate scientific technique if unaccompanied by other methods of controlled observation. See Roethlisberger and Dickson, *op. cit.*

[25] Elton Mayo, "Changing Methods in Industry," *The Personnel Journal,* 8: 326–332, February 1930.

cance is likely to appear only at the extremes of variation. Short of these extremes, the effects of mechanization, routine, speed, and so on depend upon the interrelations of workers' previous conditioning (emotional and otherwise) and the "social situation." To the extent that the former can be taken as fairly common, the individual worker's reactions to the social situation can be predicted, and even partially controlled by manipulation of the latter. However, the limits to control are determined by the worker's orientation to his environment, and not by a mechanistic process of stimuli and responses.

Thus, increasing the speed of a machine may increase the man-hour productivity of workers to the limit of the organism's ability to keep up the pace, *providing the worker is somehow induced to make the effort.* No amount of incentive can produce a continuous effort beyond his abilities. But whether the "incentive" is genuinely such or not will, short of that limit, depend on the "state of the worker's mind" and not on the "state of the organism."

REFERENCES

ANDERSON, ARTHUR G., MERTEN JOSEPH MANDEVILLE, and JOHN MUELLER ANDERSON, *Industrial Management* (New York: The Ronald Press Company, 1942), Chap. 21, "Fatigue among Workers."

BROWN, J. DOUGLAS, and HELEN BAKER, *Optimum Hours of Work in War Production* (Princeton, N. J.: Industrial Relations Section, Princeton University, 1942).

BROWNE, HAROLD F., "Length of Work Week and Total Output," *Conference Board Management Record*, 2: 109–111, 113, September 1940.

CATHCART, E. P., D. E. R. HUGHES, and J. G. CHALMERS, *The Physique of Man in Industry*, Great Britain, Medical Research Council, Industrial Health Research Board, Report No. 71 (London: H. M. Stationery Office, 1939).

CHASE, STUART, *Men and Machines* (New York: The Macmillan Company, 1937), especially Chap. VIII, "Robots."

DANA, RICHARD T., *The Human Machine in Industry* (New York: Codex Book Co., 1927).

FLINN, FREDERICK BONNER, "Industrial Aspects of Human Fatigue," *Journal of Personnel Research*, 2: 285–293, November 1923.

FLORENCE, P. SARGANT, *Economics of Fatigue and Unrest and the Effi-*

ciency of Labour in English and American Industry (New York: Henry Holt and Company, Inc., 1924), Chap. IV, "The Theory of Fatigue and Unrest," and Chap. XII, "The Significance of Fatigue and Unrest."

FLORENCE, P. SARGANT, "A Scientific Labour Policy for Industrial Plants," *International Labour Review*, 43: 260–298, March 1941.

GREAT BRITAIN, Medical Research Council, Industrial Health Research Board, *Hours of Work, Lost Time, and Labour Wastage*, Emergency Report No. 2 (London: H. M. Stationery Office, 1942).

GREAT BRITAIN, Medical Research Council, Industrial Health Research Board, *Industrial Health in War*, Emergency Report No. 1 (London: H. M. Stationery Office, 1940).

KOSSORIS, MAX D., "Hours and Efficiency in British Industry," *Monthly Labor Review*, 52: 1337–1346, June 1941.

MARX, WALTER JOHN, *Mechanization and Culture* (St. Louis: B. Herder Book Co., 1941), Chap. IV, "Machines and Human Work."

MAYO, ELTON, *Human Problems of an Industrial Civilization* (New York: The Macmillan Company, 1933), Chap. I, "Fatigue," Chap. II, "What Is Monotony?," Chap. III, "The Hawthorne Experiment," Chap. IV, "The Development of the Western Electric Inquiry," and Chap. V, "The Meaning of Morale."

——, "Psychopathologic Aspects of Industry," *Transactions of the American Neurological Association*, 1931.

——, "Revery and Industrial Fatigue," *Journal of Personnel Research*, 3: 273–281, December 1924.

MURRAY, H. M. L., "Bases of Worker Efficiency," *Personnel Journal*, 21: 131–145, October 1942.

MYERS, CHARLES S., "The Study of Fatigue," *Journal of Personnel Research*, 3: 321–334, January 1925.

NATIONAL RESEARCH COUNCIL, Committee on Work in Industry, *Fatigue of Workers* (New York: Reinhold Publishing Corporation, 1941).

PATTERSON, S. HOWARD, *Social Aspects of Industry*, 3d ed. (New York: McGraw-Hill Book Company, Inc., 1943), Chap. IX, "Industrial Strain and Fatigue: Increased Leisure and Improved Working Conditions."

ROETHLISBERGER, F. J., *Management and Morale* (Cambridge: Harvard University Press, 1941), Chap. II, "The Road Back to Sanity."

ROETHLISBERGER, F. J., and William J. Dickson, *Management and the Worker* (Cambridge: Harvard University Press, 1939), Chap. III, "Experiment with Rest Pauses," Chap. IV, "Experiment with Shorter Working Days and Weeks," Chap. V, "Testing the Fatigue and Monotony Hypotheses," and pp. 570–574.

STERN, BERNHARD J., *Medicine in Industry* (New York: The Commonwealth Fund, 1946), Chap. V, "Preventive Services."

TIFFIN, JOSEPH, *Industrial Psychology* (New York: Prentice-Hall, Inc., 1942), Chap. 8, "Work, Fatigue, and Efficiency."

UNITED STATES DEPARTMENT OF LABOR, Bureau of Labor Statistics, "Hours, Fatigue, and Health in British Munition Factories," *Bulletin No. 221* (Washington: U. S. Government Printing Office, 1917).

UNITED STATES DEPARTMENT OF LABOR, Bureau of Labor Statistics, Industrial Efficiency and Fatigue in British Munition Factories," *Bulletin No. 230* (Washington: U. S. Government Printing Office, 1917).

UNITED STATES DEPARTMENT OF LABOR, Bureau of Labor Statistics, "Industrial Health and Efficiency," *Bulletin No. 249* (Washington: U. S. Government Printing Office, 1919).

VERNON, H. M., *The Health and Efficiency of Munition Workers* (London: Humphrey Milford, Oxford University Press, 1940).

VITELES, MORRIS S., *The Science of Work* (New York: W. W. Norton & Company, Inc., 1934), Chap. 9, "Making Work Easy," and Chap. 10, "Machines and Monotony."

WHITEHEAD, THOMAS N., *The Industrial Worker* (Cambridge, Harvard University Press, 1938), Vol. I, Part II.

WYATT, S., and J. N. LANGDON, *Fatigue and Boredom in Repetitive Work*, Great Britain, Medical Research Council, Industrial Health Research Board, Report No. 77 (London: H. M. Stationery Office, 1937).

CHAPTER X

THE WORKER AND THE MACHINE (Cont'd)

THE PRICE of industrial mechanization—sometimes called *progress*—is undeniably high. It may well be questioned, however, whether the cost is to be attributed to mechanization as such. In the cases of fatigue and monotony, discussed in the previous chapter, the difficulty appeared rather to be the failure to integrate the social with the technological organization. This difficulty becomes more apparent when attention is shifted to some of the other costs customarily charged to changes in industrial techniques. These additional costs may be grouped under two principal indictments, which we shall examine in this chapter: (1) mechanization is claimed to have destroyed "workmanship" in the sense of pride in individual creation traditionally associated with independent creative effort, and (2) technological change is charged with causing outright loss of livelihood to some workmen, reduction in skills to others, and increasing insecurity to all. It may be expected that the place of the workman in contemporary industrial organization is to be judged in large measure by the relative truth or falsity of these claims.

"WORKMANSHIP" AND ITS SUBSTITUTES

The pride of the workman in the product of his industry, the esteem which attaches to a "good job well done," the loving care with which a craftsman treats his tools—these are supposed to be traditional examples of the "workmanship" sacrificed to the machine process. So fundamental is the value attached to useful work in Western culture, especially as associated with individualistic philosophies, that the burdensome character of labor perhaps has been less emphasized in the past than the intrinsic joy of creative effort. Indeed, Veblen suggested early in the century that the goal of workmanship was instinctive in the human species.[1] Modern evidence indicates considerable lack of uniformity in the value attached to labor in various societies, or at least in the definition of usefulness. Moreover, any explanation of complex, socially mediated activity in terms of "instinct" is suspect. Yet there is little doubt that pride in work has stood as a positive goal in the development of modern production.

The "Loss" of Workmanship. It requires little more than passing familiarity with the organization of industrial production to note the dissimilarity between the role of the machine operator or tender and that of the craftsman producing finished articles for the trade. Two differences seem especially to catch the eye of the casual observer: mechanization and standardization give the worker little but a negative control over work methods or quality of product, and the minute subdivision of labor blurs out the part of any single workman in the total process. The latter circumstance removes any semblance of "property" relationship between the producer and the product of his toil. Thus in the mechanization of shoe manufacture many of the niceties of distinction in quality and style are lost, as are the individualized "custom-built" variations in filling the order of a particular consumer. But the mechanization also is accompanied by a division of labor, so that even with reference to the standard styles the workman cannot say that he is making shoes; he is only making parts of shoes. Or with the assembly-line method of productive organization, the worker (or some spokesman viewing with alarm) may well ask: "What merit is there in the endless putting of nuts on bolts, or mounting the left front wheel on a moving chassis?" Examples like these seem to lend support to the usual dreary picture of robots or automatons serving machines which seem to be gifted with superhuman cunning.

But we may pause here and inquire what it is we are comparing. Is the comparison between the modern machine tender and the

---

[1] See Thorstein Veblen, *The Instinct of Workmanship* (New York: The Macmillan Company, 1914), pp. 1–37.

cloth weaver during the later stages of the "putting-out system"? The loom of the latter may have made less clatter, and even may have been supplied with power by the workman's feet, but the product was specified in quantity and quality by the merchant. And the weaver neither sheared the sheep nor made garments for "gentlemen." Or is the contrast to be drawn between the modern workman and his guildsman ancestor in a late medieval town? The latter, it is true, may have carried the productive process from raw material to ultimate consumer—that is, before he became dependent upon merchants at both ends of the process—but his freedom of choice concerning quality of materials, methods of work, and method of disposal were not appreciably greater than those of the "machine slave." From the modern view, he was a "slave of tradition."

In short, if we compare the modern administrator or machine designer with the independent craftsman of other years, or the modern routinized workman with the guild journeyman or "common laborer," the supposed modern loss of workmanship seems overdrawn. It seems that the comparison is made with a modern ideal rather than a genuine past state of affairs.

This does not dismiss the problem of the supposed effect of industry in blighting creative individuality. Several further possibilities suggest themselves. For example, it might be claimed that the question is one of number or degree. Thus the loss of workmanship as commonly understood would still be a partially correct assertion if an increasing proportion of the productive population were doomed to standardization and routine. This posing of the problem begs some questions, notably, at what point routine and standardized service violates pride in work. However, it is noteworthy that the division of labor involves not only the simplification and routinization of some tasks, but also a diversification of talents and an increased demand for designers, inventors, administrators, and so on. In fact, we shall note in Chapter XXIII that the general trend of occupational distribution is toward a *smaller* proportion of interchangeable automatons, and a larger proportion of persons whose work may be called professional and administrative. Although it might with some justice be claimed that the complexity and interdependence of modern life tend to an increasing standardization of all productive activity, this is certainly less apparent than the past subservience to ritual. Even now standardization is more noticeable with reference to minimum requirements and skills for any given occupation than for the range of variation within and between occupations.

On the other hand, it might be claimed that, if the possibility of pride in creative effort is not less in modern industry, its lack is more keenly felt because the ideal is shared by a larger proportion of the productive work force. The general rise of educational level and the democratic educational emphasis on individualism and occupational mobility bear out the validity of this hypothesis. Far from being an instinct formerly satisfied and now frustrated, pride in work may rather be a fairly recent ideal for many workers who in former times would have been more "contented with their lot." As noted in the previous chapter, a "problem" arises from the lack of correspondence between ideal and actuality. And the conclusion inevitably follows that a change in ideal creates a problem as surely as a change in the factual situation.

Lack of Social Recognition. It appears that the proportion of workers who have some control over the type and quality of their productive output (that is, have some chance for decision or innovation) is not much smaller in modern economic organization than in former years, but that more of the unprivileged in this respect seem to share the ideal of independent accomplishment. However, the attitude of the worker toward his job is not simply a function of its intrinsic demands upon his skill, imagination, resourcefulness, and similar virtues. Suppose a workman has suggested an improved method of ensuring uniformity in thickness of steel armor plate, or distinguishes himself in finding the "bugs" in an airplane instrument panel, or develops a knack for handling a new and tricky machine. Who cares? His supervisors likely, and possibly a few of his fellow workmen. And these are not unimportant. But it is extremely unlikely that the workman's superior ability will have any meaning outside the factory, or even outside his unit in the factory. It is doubtful if the inventor of a superior mousetrap these days (there are a number of superior ones on the market) would get even a small proportion of the world beating a path to his door, but at least most of the population would know its purpose by hearsay if not by experience. The same cannot be said for the skill of the modern workman under highly specialized conditions of production. What Veblen mistook for the "instinct" of workmanship seems rather to be a common desire for social recognition commensurate with one's demonstrated ability in productive activity. Diversification of labor does not remove the value of skill in the organization of production; it frequently does remove the job from the comprehension of the community. A semiautomatic machine accomplishes a number of distinct but continuous processing operations to the open-mouthed awe of the visiting dignitary. It may depend for its continued operation on a workman who checks dials and gauges, makes decisions, and bears the responsibility. But the machine is more spectacular than the workman and gets the bulk of the credit (only partly shared with the inventor). A workman's pride is very nearly pointless unless it is upheld by the esteem of the community.

It would be a mistake to assume that the workman's useful activity must be recognized by the entire community in order for him to take pride in his work. Except for the rather monetary interest of authors and entertainers in satisfying the "public," or the politician's desire to satisfy the voters, few persons are genuinely interested in public opinion in general. They are interested in the opinion of that portion of the public that is close enough to the individual's pattern of activities to make opinions count. The family, a greater or smaller circle of acquaintances and friends, companions and colleagues at the daily activity, supervisors and subordinates constitute the significant public of the individual workman. But if those persons have no conception of his job, and it is completely unrelated to the rest of his social activity, little satisfaction can derive from his accomplishments, however exemplary. Thus, *specialized work that is insulated from recognition by the worker's significant community violates the sentiment of "workmanship."*

Mechanization and Social Isolation. There is one final characteristic of the dependence of the worker on the machine that has significance for the loss of workmanship: the tendency to make the worker's orientation to the machine take precedence over his position in a group of workmen. This tendency toward social isolation in the shops may be the product of the "stretch-out," which we shall discuss below, meticulous supervision in an attempt to keep the worker's devotion to duty whole-souled, or simply by the spatial arrangement of job assignments which deliberately or unconsciously prevent the formation of informal relationships among workmen. Subservience to the machine is never so apparent (whether "real" to the observer or not) as when the machine or the conveyor belt forms the sole aspect of the environment taken into account by those responsible for the assignment of tasks.

Machine design, the sequence of operations, and the spatial relationships of work have been regarded as purely engineering matters. Only reluctant attention has been given to the anatomy and physiology of the worker, virtually none to his social characteristics. To suggest that machines should be located with reference to both power sources and sequence of mechanical operations on the one hand and the "sociography" of work groups on the other is to invite condemnation for madness. Yet this kind of consideration may be as important for effective operation as mechanical engineering.

Some contemporary industrial researchers are inclined to attach more significance to "satisfactory social living" within the work situation than to "workmanship" in its traditional form.[2] The two may in fact go together if the factory group also esteems good work. To the extent that the contemporary organization of production interferes with "satisfactory social living" it will also probably violate sentiments of workmanship.

Substitutes for Workmanship. In the absence of an intrinsic interest in work, or of pleasant working relationships and community esteem, the workman's labor must be directed toward some other end. If the worker's only interest is in payment for a certain number of hours or a certain amount of effort expended, his membership in the coopera-

---

[2] See, for example, T. N. Whitehead, *Leadership in a Free Society* (Cambridge: Harvard University Press, 1937), especially Chap. VIII, "Progressive Management."

tive unit is not only limited, but his effective cooperation is uncertain. Yet there is some evidence, to be reviewed in the following chapter, that modern industrial organization has increased the concern of workmen over wages and hours. Put another way, industrial wages are less a recognition of merit than a bribery to overcome unpleasantness. This is not, as we shall see, the whole story, but there is little doubt that preoccupation with income bears some relation to negative attitudes toward the way in which the income must be earned.

Likewise, the shortening of work hours and of the work week seems to bear a close relation to dissatisfaction with modern conditions of employment. Again, the loss of workmanship or its equivalent is not the only significant variable. The increased productivity of labor through the introduction of labor-saving machinery, which we shall note later in the present chapter, has made possible shorter hours for equivalent or increased production. Likewise, the desire to "spread the work" in view of a presumed limited demand for labor has been important. But these do not explain the fact that the demand for reduction in hours of work has been made by, or on behalf of, commercial and industrial employees, and not other sections of the working population. Certainly physiological fatigue is not a primary factor in reducing a forty-eight-hour week to a forty- or thirty-hour week. The fact that physicians, lawyers, some clergymen and teachers, occasional administrators and many researchers work long days and a long week seems to cause little concern to them or to the general public. The weight of evidence suggests, if it does not demonstrate, that fewer hours in the factory are sought because the work is less satisfactory to the workman than other types of activity.

This evidence also suggests, therefore, that the great recent concern about "training for leisure" is largely an attempt to make out-of-work activities supply the creative activity that industrial work fails to provide. Again, the problem may be, and usually is, viewed from the other side: the shortening of working hours made possible by increasing mechanization poses the question of the use to be made of this time. But the arguments put forth about relief from monotony, development of hobbies, and the necessity for relaxation point to the attempted use of leisure as a respite from dreary and largely unrewarding toil. The Lynds found this to be a common reaction in their survey of industrial Muncie, Indiana ("Middletown"),[3] and again indirect evidence comes from the lack of concern for the out-of-hours activities of the business and professional man.[4]

Other substitutes for pride in work that have been used by so-called "progressive" managements include vacations with pay (leisure again), contests, planned recreation, and factory social affairs. All of these rely on a reward after the work is accomplished as a goal for the completion of the task. And for that reason all of them may be viewed as only partially effective in creating interest in work. In some cases these rewards may be positively detrimental to the continuance of satisfactory effort, for the goal may be so important that the required means (work) loses significance save as a hurdle to be cleared.

There is a further possible substitute for workmanship in the immediate sense, and that is to be found in pride in cooperative effort, whether of the plant as a whole, a large unit, or a small group. There is no doubt that simply working for some large and well-known firms carries prestige, whatever the particular nature of the job. But this is most likely to be true only if nearly all jobs are at least on the "craft" level, and is certainly not true of mass-production industries in general. Interest in cooperative effort is of course enhanced if the worker knows how his job fits into the total scheme. Yet it is amazing how many industrial managers neglect such simple initiation ceremonies as a tour through the plant for a new workman. Under wartime conditions of production those workmen employed in making articles most directly and obviously designed for combat,

[3] Robert S. Lynd and Helen Merrell Lynd, *Middletown* (New York: Harcourt, Brace and Company, 1929), Part IV (Chaps. XVII–XIX), "Using Leisure," especially p. 311.

[4] It might, of course, be objected that the problem of the "wise use of leisure" is an educational one, and that business and professional groups need no guidance with respect to alternative uses of their time. This is true in a certain sense, namely, that their leisure activities may be expected to follow middle and upper class ideas of what constitutes fun. Not only their educational background, but their level of income allows this. This not only indicates a class-biased judgment, however, but also does not account for the indubitably smaller concern for the *amount* of leisure for these groups.

such as guns, tanks, and planes, may take some pride (supported by community esteem) in their role as "war workers." Yet the same factor may serve to draw an incorrect but significant invidious distinction operating against productive activity less obviously related to the battle. Even in peacetime, fads in popular interest and the development of new products or services may give to the workman a temporarily honorable place in the community. There seems to be no reason why something akin to workmanship should not be derived from cooperative activity, provided that it is truly cooperative and the individual worker understands his place in the total scheme of things. Under conditions of extreme specialization, this is difficult, but apparently not impossible. It may perhaps bear repeating that the relation of the worker to the machine tends to be less problematical if the relationship is part of a satisfactory context of social relations. Failing the latter, less effective substitutes will be sought, either by labor or by management.

MECHANIZATION AND PRODUCTIVITY

Viewed statistically, the modern laborer has more, not less, to show for his work than the handiworkers of the past. That is, the total volume of products, whether agricultural or industrial, has increased more than the number of man hours required to produce them. Thus, in terms of volume alone the contemporary cooperator in production is more *productive*.

Change in Productivity. Anything like adequate statistics of employment, volume of production, hours actually employed, and so on, are of fairly recent origin. It would be interesting to know how much less labor is required to produce a given product now than, say, a century ago. Slichter gives as a rough estimate that for the American economy as a whole the output per man-hour in 1940 was six times the output in 1840.[5] Of course, even if we had adequate knowledge of the situation a hundred years ago, our comparison would have to be limited to types of products then manufactured or produced, and still produced. In view of the rather recent addition to our

[5] Sumner H. Slichter, *The Challenge of Industrial Relations* (Ithaca: Cornell University Press, 1947), p. 88.

economic life of such industries as wire and wireless communication, automobiles and aircraft, electrical goods and supplies, and so on almost endlessly, such a comparison would lose much of its point. But during the last quarter of a century records have been kept and statistical indexes made, to indicate something of the trend in labor productivity.

The most comprehensive study of productivity in manufacturing in the United States is that made under Works Progress Administration auspices as part of the National Research Project, published in 1939.[6] Comprising a large number of detailed studies for various industries and specific problems, the series of volumes provide a careful analysis of mechanization and its effects on employment and productivity.[7]

The summary of increasing labor productivity in fifty-nine manufacturing industries indicates a steady growth of volume output per man hour (or, put another way, a steady decrease in the amount of labor required for a single unit of output), and over the eighteen-year period covered by the study the change might be called "tremendous." It is apparent that the changing character of industrial production adds effectiveness to the unit of labor as far as volume of production is concerned, whatever the situation with regard to quality.

Although such indexes are but rough indicators of the complex transformations which industrial enterprises undergo, and do not indicate what factors are responsible for the increasing productivity of labor, what changes in quality may have taken place, what skills

[6] The most general picture of increasing productivity is that given in Harry Magdoff, Irvin H. Siegel, and Milton B. Davis, *Production, Employment, and Productivity in 59 Manufacturing Industries, 1919–1936*, Works Project Administration, National Research Project on Reemployment Opportunities and Recent Changes in Industrial Techniques, *Studies of the Labor Supply, Productivity, and Production*, Report No. S–1 (Philadelphia: 1939), especially Part One, "Purpose, Methods, and Summary of Findings." For a brief summary of the study, see United States Department of Labor, Bureau of Labor Statistics, "Employment and Production in Manufacturing Industries, 1919–1936," *Monthly Labor Review*, 49: 1397–1404, December 1939.

[7] Besides the studies in the series previously referred to (Labor Supply, Productivity, and Production), the reports include a General series, Studies in Types and Rates of Technological Change, and Studies of Effects of Industrial Change on Labor Markets.

have been necessary to put in a "man hour" of labor, and so on, they do indicate the direction and something of the magnitude of the trend toward labor-saving. Because of the importance of these questions, however, we may examine some further aspects of technological change and the productivity of labor.

Factors in Increased Productivity. The common-sense interpretation of increased productivity of labor (thus making less employment necessary to maintain or even increase production) is that this is the result of mechanization. The displacement of workers by labor-saving inventions, resulting in "technological unemployment" as discussed below, has been so much in the public eye that other factors in the upward trend of man-hour productivity have been neglected. We may summarize briefly some of the more important factors in lowered labor requirements per unit of output.[8]

I. Direct Technological Changes
    A. Replacement of manual processes by machine processes
    B. Improvement of capital equipment to carry a heavier burden
    C. Substitution of continuous belt-line operations for discontinuous ones
    D. Product simplification
    E. Improvement of quality of raw materials
II. Economic and Social Factors
    A. Use of capital equipment
        1. Degree of utilization of plant capacity
        2. Ratio of maintenance and repairs

[8] The outline of factors in labor productivity has been compiled, with some modifications, from the following sources: Testimony of Theodore J. Kreps, in United States Congress, Temporary National Economic Committee, *Investigation of Concentration of Economic Power, Hearings . . .* , Part 30, "Technology and Concentration of Economic Power" (Washington: U. S. Government Printing Office, 1940), pp. 16214–16231; Testimony of Isador Lubin, in *ibid.*, pp. 17244–17252; John W. Riegel, *Management, Labor, and Technological Change* (Ann Arbor: The University of Michigan Press, 1942), Chap. II, "Types of Technological Change"; David Weintraub, "Unemployment and Increasing Productivity," in National Resources Committee, *Technological Trends and National Policy* (Washington: U. S. Government Printing Office, 1937), Part I, Sec. V; Arthur Wubnig, "The Measurement of the Technological Factor in Labor Productivity," *Journal of the American Statistical Association*, 34: 319–325, June 1939.

B. Organization
1. Effective job placement
2. Reduction of top-heavy management or similar organizational inefficiencies
C. Managerial Innovation
1. Increase in job assignments ("stretch-out")
2. Increase of work pace through machine speeds ("speed-up")
D. "Morale"
1. Reduction of fatigue
2. More effective incentives
3. Improvement of management-labor relations

Few of these changes call for much further comment; some have already been discussed, and some will be discussed more fully in the final section of this chapter. The sheer number of possible factors involved in explaining increased productivity makes it apparent that the machine, or even the technologist, is not the only force tending to reduce employment. Indeed, many of these changes take place within a given plant at the same time, and certainly all of them are involved in varying, indeterminable degrees in any over-all statistics of man-hour productivity. All of them may be said to be indicative of increasing "rationalization" of industry in its broadest sense, and as such are aspects of the problem of worker and "machine" in the same broad sense. Since efficiency improvement and cost reduction may center on the nontechnological as well as the immediately mechanical factors, we may neglect the distinctions for a moment and turn to consideration of the determinants in technological change.

Determinants in Technological Change. The obvious basis for the technological changes that increase man-hour productivity is the simple one of reducing unit labor cost or increasing production of products for sale on the market. But the management of an industrial concern is oriented toward the market in other respects besides quality and the margin between cost and price. Technological changes are therefore sometimes undertaken with labor productivity as a secondary consideration. Thus, the company's product may be improved in quality as a device for getting a larger share of market demand. Or an entirely new product may be put on the market. It is this creation of a new market that is commonly claimed as one of the "automatic" solutions to the displacement of workers through rationalization of production. On the other hand, even the economies of labor-saving machinery need not exclusively benefit investors. They may be passed back to laborers in the form of higher wages, shorter hours, or improved working conditions; they may also be passed on for the benefit of consumers. The latter may possibly increase an elastic demand for the product and thus increase the labor requirements for production, or else allow the consumer to divert a larger share of his expenditures elsewhere with the same effect. This is supposed to be the other principal "automatic" solution to the problem of technological unemployment.

It is clear that the important economic variables in the decision to introduce new products or processes are numerous and their precise operation uncertain. Even if it were possible to isolate a single technological change apart from other modifications in industrial production, it would still be next to impossible to trace all of its repercussions. It is extremely doubtful that any manager will be able to do so, nor does he need to beyond the point where the effects, direct and indirect, cease to have some clear bearing on the situation of the industry he represents. In fact, the initiative for any given change may be more in the nature of a protective reaction than a freely chosen policy. This is the case where the competitive situation demands that the manager meet price or quality, the investors demand greater returns, or laborers demand higher wages or other benefits. There is even some possibility that technologists and executives like to keep up with the Industrial Joneses with respect to methods and equipment without any clear appraisal of the economic situation. Certainly the repercussions on the employment situation in other plants or industries cannot be a matter of immediate concern,[9] although his own organizational problems may well be.

[9] Weintraub (*loc. cit.*, p. 79) suggests four indirect ways in which technological change may reduce labor requirements: (1) diversion of production from a competing plant, (2) making a substitute product and thus forcing another industry to reduce employment, (3) reducing the labor necessary to make raw

These considerations are introduced, not in order to confuse the situation unnecessarily, but simply to indicate that it is dangerous to oversimplify the question of the productive ratio between machines and men. Above all, it must be noted that, contrary to certain popular views, technical change is not the simple equivalent of "progress." Defining the latter as a change in an approved direction (whatever the direction, and whoever does the approving), it is apparent that the decision to introduce changes in methods or products is always conditional upon a complex balancing of conditions and interests. Some of those interests are capable of phrasing in terms of the economic ends of the industrial organization; others have to do with internal affairs, not the least of which is the concern of the workers for their jobs.

TECHNOLOGICAL CHANGE AND THE WORKER

The contemporary industrial laborer lives and works in an environment predominantly characterized by change. Although the human being has considerable adaptability to environmental variations, and the recent character of Western culture has placed peculiar emphasis on change and "progress" as positive goals, the nature of the changes affecting the worker prohibits their ready acceptance. This is the other side of the situation already observed with respect to repetitive work and routine: the changes are for the most part neither subject to the worker's control nor necessarily oriented toward the worker's interests and sentiments. Since our present concern is with the position of the laborer in industrial organization, we may note the chief "problem areas" in the effects of technological change on the situation of the industrial employee. For sake of convenience, these may be grouped under three heads, although all are very closely related. Stated negatively, the workman faces the loss of *liberty, status,* and *security.*

Servitude to the Machine. From the beginning of the factory system, the necessity for coordination and control of specialized activities has progressively reduced the worker's range of choice with respect

---

materials or capital goods through reduction of waste, and (4) quality improvement of output, thus requiring less labor for upkeep by industries using the product.

to the character or conditions of his employment. The free and untrammeled economic individual, we have noted, is not represented by the wage earner. Nor has the disharmony between traditional ideal and contemporary fact always escaped the notice of those brought under factory discipline. One reason why the change to factory production has been frequently confused with a "revolution" is the very real, if sporadic, violence which the transition occasioned. Then, as now, the visible agents of "enslavement" were likely to be machines rather than men, and it was upon machines that violence was visited.[10] Although there are indications that questions of status and even of security were involved, it was the loss of traditional (if rather ephemeral) liberties which apparently occasioned the greatest dissatisfaction. The enjoyment of a status subjectively considered as fitting is in fact likely to be defended as a "liberty," and even absence of fear and uncertainty is currently labeled a "freedom." But the essential point at issue is the range of conditions subject to the worker's control.

As the factory system spreads to new areas, where workers are lacking in "industrial discipline" just as workers were in the early factories of the West, reluctance to work and even hostility to the impersonal service to the machine are repeatedly encountered. The particular context varies, as does the complaint—loss of socially recognized skills, the arbitrary regimen of time rather than task, the loss of social relationships upon which the worker depended for security. Despite the great differences among nonindustrial societies, the introduction of the machine process creates situations common enough to be recognized (and thus predicted) from one place to the next.[11]

The question of decreasing liberty is, of course, partly a function of change. Thus a restraint such as custom or traditional ritual is not

[10] See Karl Marx, *Capital* (Chicago: C. H. Kerr and Co., 1906–1909, 3 vols.), Vol. I, Chap. XV, Sec. 5; Elliott Dunlap Smith and Richmond Carter Nyman, *Technology and Labor* (New Haven: Yale University Press for the Institute of Human Relations, 1939), Appendix A, "The Industrial Revolution and the Application of Engineering Methods of Labor Management."
[11] See Wilbert E. Moore, *Industrialization and Labor: Social Aspects of Economic Development* (Ithaca: Cornell University Press, 1951), Chap. II, "Barriers and Antipathies."

regarded as an incursion upon the liberty of the person who is properly socialized in the group practicing such routine patterns of action. But any *new* restraint, especially one that is at the same time apparent, leads to "frustration" and possibly even to aggression against the real or supposed source of the control. On the other hand, the increasing restraint is not simply "all in the mind." An objective view yields a result that supports at least in part the subjective impression of increasing dependence. The very perfection of the mechanical processes may seem to remove them from the ordinary field of human fallibility. The impersonal character of bureaucratic management only serves to reinforce the very real and widespread dissatisfaction with job assignments which are almost entirely geared to the demands of a machine technology. The testimony of assembly-line workers points to the existence of considerable animus against the all-controlling moving belt, and even some tendency to personify the machine as a worker of good or evil. Although groups of employees these days rarely destroy machinery simply as a means of escaping the control of mechanized processes, it is not unknown for a single workman to "jimmy" his machine, even at some loss of piece-rate pay, to show at least a negative mastery over his employment situation.

There is a further change in work organization attributable to advanced stages of mechanization, and that is the virtual necessity of treating workers as groups—as collectivities. Routinization of work and subdivision of tasks make the department rather than the individual the effective unit for many purposes. Labor unions did not always create collective relations of workers with management; they became a way of reacting to an already established fact.

We do not mean to attach undue or simply poetical importance to the worker's loss of freedom in modern factory production. Again, it is more likely to be the *change* which upsets previous habits, routines, and working relationships that is viewed as a violation of independence, rather than the precise *amount* of control. It should even be noted that with increasing mechanization of repetitive tasks, the worker is restored to some measure of mastery over tools. This movement has not proceeded to the same extent in all factories, and it is questionable whether all industries lend themselves to such complete mechanization, even over a long span of time. In any event, it is clear that, although the worker's liberty of action has suffered a great affront, the extent of subservience depends partly upon the future course of technical innovations.[12]

Machines and the Loss of Status. Closely related to the reduction in the worker's liberty through rationalization of industry is the effect of mechanization in speeding the obsolescence of skills. Although technological change may ultimately extend to virtual elimination of unskilled, repetitive work, such is not its ordinary or first effect. The replacement of handicraft production of textiles by the early factories and the recent mechanization of cigar manufacture illustrate a common tendency: the initial blow of the new processes is likely to fall most heavily on skilled workmen. Even if the result of such displacement is not complete loss of employment, the workman who has spent a good portion of his working life perfecting skills and gaining a good position in his plant and community cannot be expected to view the machine that replaces him as a blessing of "progress."

It is not an adequate answer to this problem to point out that technological change also creates demand for new skills, even within any given industrial plant. The new skills are very unlikely to be sufficiently similar to those of the displaced craftsmen to provide genuine employment opportunities. In fact, we have already noted that the increasingly technical character of managerial direction prompts recruitment of labor for those positions *outside* the plant, not from among technologically displaced employees. Various studies indicate that skilled workmen who are replaced by some technological or similar modification remain unemployed longer than the less skilled. This suggests that, understandably enough, the crafts-

---

[12] The probable course of further innovation in increasing the directing role of the industrial laborer has received little recognition. It has, however, been pointed out by Lewis Mumford, *Technics and Civilization* (New York: Harcourt, Brace and Company, 1934), especially pp. 410–417, and by Herbert von Beckerath, *Modern Industrial Organization* (New York and London: McGraw-Hill Book Company, Inc., 1933), p. 99. An especially able analysis is that of Georges Friedmann, "Automatisme et Travail Industriel," *Cahiers Internationaux de Sociologie,* 1: 139–160, 1946.

man will attempt to seek reemployment in his own kind of work, or at least at his customary level, and only reluctantly seek retraining or employment at a lower level.[13] It is also not surprising that the man with a useless skill will insist that the product of his mechanical competitor is not as good as his craftsmanlike output. Although quality may at times be sacrificed for cost-saving through speed and standardization, it may also be increased. In any case, the worker's judgment is ordinarily one of sentiment, not of fact. This does not reduce its importance, but simply changes its significance.

Although the change in the worker's status as a result of technological changes is frequently dismissed as an incidental result of a competitive economy, it is apparent that for any given workman the competition is unequal or nonexistent. He is not for the most part competing with other workmen for a position based upon skill, but with a deliberate process of change that makes his previous training and expectations irrelevant. It is as though a winning football team finds its victory nonexistent because its coach has forfeited the match as a stake in a poker game. The disgruntled wage earner may be pompously informed that he "can't fight progress," but he may enter a private and somewhat bitter minority opinion about the nature of progress.

Technological Change and Insecurity. Certainly the most important question that the industrial wage earner faces with respect to increasing mechanization is how it is going to affect his means of livelihood. In this general sense, the problems of decreasing liberty and threatened loss of status are simply aspects of the broader problem of insecurity. We have already emphasized that the fact of change alone accounts for a good deal of the subjective loss of liberty. Now this should be modified as "significant but unpredicted and uncontrolled changes in the worker's position in the organization." Mechanical and other labor-saving reorganizations are customarily undertaken by management without either consultation or official

---

[13] Various studies of reemployment of technological displaced skilled workmen are summarized by Weintraub, *loc. cit.*, pp. 84–85. See also Smith and Nyman, *op. cit.*, pp. 14–17; Testimony of Corrington Gill in *Hearings* of the Temporary National Economic Committee, Part 30, pp. 17232–17234; Testimony of Philip Murray in *ibid.*, pp. 16461–16469.

forewarning. In the absence of the latter, "signs" and rumors may make the expectation worse than the fact. Fears already present are easily fed by a multitude of circumstances, all of which may in fact be misinterpreted. One is tempted to conclude, in fact, that the problem of insecurity lies close to the heart of the problem of the relation of the worker to the machine.

The most obvious and troublesome fear of the workman is that of outright loss of employment. Economic experts continue to study and debate the nature of technological unemployment. In view of the complexity of factors involved in increased labor productivity (in the immediate case, labor displacement), as well as the equally complex situation with regard to the development of new avenues of employment, it is understandable that the over-all relationship between technological change and labor demand is by no means clear.[14] But nation-wide statistics on labor productivity and employment in all industries are likely to be close to meaningless to a particular workman, or even to all the workmen in a particular plant. The laborer is most aware of those changes in the equipment or organization of his own plant which lead to a reduction of the labor force. Periodic shutdowns, or even loss of jobs by some of the workers, may be the indirect results of technological improvements elsewhere that reduce the plant's markets, change the quality of its raw materials, and so on. These changes may be more readily accepted by workmen because they can be blamed on the impersonal market rather than on their own supervisors. Similarly, the "stretch-out" which increases the definite work assignment of some employees and displaces others is more apparent than the "speed-up" where increased work loads are imposed indirectly and technological displacement is not immediately evident. Likewise, an occasional displaced workman may be lost in the normal labor turnover, but the closing down of an entire department or even a whole mill or industrial area is not easily dismissed.

Particularly over recent years in the United States, with high

[14] For a summary of the general problem of technological unemployment, see Weintraub, *loc. cit.*, and the entire volume of the Temporary National Economic Committee *Hearings*, Part 30, especially the testimony of Corrington Gill (pp. 17220–17242), and of Isador Lubin (pp. 17242–17263).

wages in manufacturing resulting both from union pressure and from the generally high demand for labor, the power to make labor-saving innovations has been used as a scarcely veiled threat by management to keep workers tractable.[15]

Thus the immediate and apparent displacement of workers through technological change is certainly the most obvious factor in the worker's fear and insecurity. But there are other relevant conditions that may either increase the uncertainty or tend to offset it. Following Riegel and Smith,[16] these may be briefly reviewed. (1) The past record of the company's employment policies, such as the reputation for hasty and faddish changes, whimsical discharges, and so on. (2) The competitive position and earnings of the company. If the company is making profits, employees will ordinarily see no point in change; on the other hand, if the company is in a poor economic condition, change may be viewed as inevitable, although not necessarily welcome. (3) The steadiness of past employment—a person periodically or spasmodically laid off already fears the worst. (4) The trend in the number of persons employed. If the number has been increasing, displaced workers may be absorbed without much difficulty; if employment has been falling off, the addition of technological displacement means further difficulties. (5) The recency and customariness of change. A long-established routine and organization are given up with greater reluctance than short-time adjustments to frequent changes. (6) The number of persons affected. We have already noted that sheer numbers of persons displaced or demoted appears to bring the change closer to other employees. (7) The speed of change. Investigators agree that a precipitous change is more devastating to morale than a gradual and cautious transition, and a gradual change is much more likely to be worked into existing customs and routines. (8) The degree to which past habits, informal relationships, and so on are respected.

---

[15] See Robert K. Merton, *Social Theory and Social Structure* (Glencoe, Ill.: The Free Press, 1949), Chap. XIII, "The Machine, the Worker, and the Engineer."

[16] The list here presented is adapted from discussions of factors in employee attitudes toward technological changes in Riegel, *op. cit.*, Chap. V, "Variables Affecting Technological Changes," and Smith and Nyman, *op. cit.*, pp. 59–62.

We have repeatedly insisted that the technically minded administrator neglects this range of conditions at his peril, to say nothing of the insecurity feelings of workmen who have not been consulted. (9) The degree to which commonly accepted differentials such as seniority, skill, and need are respected. In the case of actual severance of employment, the workman will at least expect to know where he stands, and will resent and fear haphazard dismissal. (10) The past history of the new method in other plants. Thus, the "stretch-out" and "scientific management" have both gained rather unsavory reputations in the course of recent industrial history, and the names alone may incite all kinds of pessimistic neuroses among the workers in a plant where some such method is due to be installed. (11) The state of industrial unrest, either in the particular plant or in the economy as a whole. Thus during a period of depression and falling labor demand, fears of any technological changes are disproportionately increased. Likewise, any move by management during periods of labor disputes is likely to be considered as simply one more example of "slave driving," whereas any objection to managerial policies may be blamed on "reds and agitators" and called a slow-down, sabotage, or resistance to progress. Suspicion breeds suspicion, and in tense times suspicions may be subjectively translated into certainties, whatever the external facts.

It is likely that the foregoing is far from a complete catalogue of fear-producing factors in the relation of the worker to "efficiency" of industrial operation. Certainly the exact weight to be attached to any of them will vary in particular cases. Yet they indicate something of the range of problems faced by the opposing forces of management and labor, and certainly destroy the validity of any assumption that principles of mechanical engineering alone are sufficient to "manage" labor.

In fact, the most evident characteristic of the modern worker (or his representatives) in his reaction to technological change is his rather insistent demand to be heard. And if he is heard, the question he poses is seen to be pretty fundamental in the whole issue. That question is, Who should bear the cost and who should derive the benefit from increased technological efficiency? Spokesmen for labor, as well as some managers and independent experts, are now insisting that simply to improve methods of labor utilization in the interests of market competition or increased dividends is not an unmixed and automatic blessing. The idea that technological change is self-generating, self-directing, and inevitable is increasingly recognized as naive (and, of course, from the standpoint of interest groups adversely affected, vicious). Labor representatives are asking that the cost of technological displacements be borne by those who benefit: either investors or consumers. Managers are beginning to make such adjustments as guaranteed employment for those taken from their previous jobs because of a labor-saving change, and retraining programs for those whose skills are displaced. Others would add the payment of a substantial dismissal wage to those who cannot be reabsorbed into the plant where their jobs have been lost to the machine.[17] The principle, as Dr. Isador Lubin has pointed out, is already recognized in compulsory workmen's compensation laws, compulsory unemployment insurance provisions, and the like.[18] Organized labor has frequently included similar provisions in collective bargaining contracts.[19] Although prediction of future policy in any matter as complex as this is extremely hazardous, it seems probable that the future direction of change will be toward greater recognition of the employee's stake in industrial organization, and particularly toward greater security in his relationships with machine technology.

[17] See, for example, Riegel, *op. cit.*, Chap. VII, "Obtaining Employee Cooperation in Methods Improvement," and Chap. VIII, "Safeguarding Employee Interests When New Techniques Are Introduced"; Testimony of Isador Lubin in the Temporary National Economic Committee *Hearings*, Part 30, pp. 17252–17264; Testimony of Philip Murray in *ibid.*, pp. 16508–16509.

[18] See Testimony of Isador Lubin, *loc. cit.*

[19] See Richmond C. Nyman and Elliott Dunlap Smith, *Union-Management Cooperation in the "Stretch Out"* (New Haven: Yale University Press for the Institute of Human Relations, 1934); Riegel, *op. cit.*, Chap. IX, "Collective Agreements on Technological Change."

REFERENCES

AHEARN, DANIEL J., JR., *The Wages of Farm and Factory Laborers, 1914–1944* (New York: Columbia University Press, 1945), Chap. VIII, "Wages, Production, and Productivity."

BARGER, HAROLD, and SAM H. SCHURR, *The Mining Industries, 1899–1939: A Study of Output, Employment and Productivity* (New York: National Bureau of Economic Research, 1944).

BECKERATH, HERBERT VON, *Modern Industrial Organization* (New York: McGraw-Hill Book Company, Inc., 1939), pp. 98–105.

BROWN, DOUGLASS V., JOHN T. DUNLOP, and OTHERS, "Industrial Wage Rates, Labor Costs, and Price Policies," United States Congress, Temporary National Economic Committee, *Investigation of Concentration of Economic Power, Monograph No. 5* (Washington: U. S. Government Printing Office, 1940).

COOKE, MORRIS LLEWELLYN, and PHILIP MURRAY, *Organized Labor and Production* (New York: Harper & Brothers, 1940), Chap. 13, "The Impact of Technology on Employment."

DRUCKER, PETER F., *The New Society: The Anatomy of the Industrial Order* (New York: Harper & Brothers, 1950), Chap. 17, "Men at Work."

DUGGINS, G. H., and F. R. EASTWOOD, *Planning Industrial Recreation* (Lafayette, Ind.: Purdue University, 1941).

FABRICANT, SOLOMON, *Labor Savings in American Industry, 1899–1939,* National Bureau of Economic Research, Occasional Paper 23 (New York: 1945).

FRIEDMANN, GEORGES, "Automatisme et Travail Industriel," *Cahiers Internationaux de Sociologie,* 1: 139–160, 1946.

HOPPOCK, ROBERT, *Job Satisfaction* (New York: Harper & Brothers, for the National Occupational Conference, 1935). See especially Part I (Chaps. I–II), "Summary and Interpretation of Results," and Chap. VI, "Relationships between Job Satisfaction and Other Factors: A Review of Other Investigations."

INTERNATIONAL LABOUR OFFICE, *The Social Aspects of Rationalisation,* in Studies and Reports, Series B, No. 18 (Geneva: 1931).

JEROME, HARRY, *Mechanization in Industry* (New York: National Bureau of Economic Research, 1934).

LONIGAN, E., "Effect of Modern Technological Conditions upon the Employment of Labor," *American Economic Review,* 29: 246–259, June 1939.

LORWIN, LEWIS L., and JOHN M. BLAIR, "Technology in Our Economy," United States Congress, Temporary National Economic Committee,

Investigation of Concentration of Economic Power, Monograph No. 22 (Washington: U. S. Government Printing Office, 1941).

LYND, ROBERT S., and HELEN MERRELL LYND, *Middletown* (New York: Harcourt, Brace and Company, 1929), Chap. VIII, "Why Do They Work So Hard?"

MAGDOFF, HARRY, IRVIN H. SIEGEL, and MILTON B. DAVIS, *Production, Employment, and Productivity in 59 Manufacturing Industries, 1919–1936,* Works Project Administration, National Research Project on Reemployment Opportunities and Recent Changes in Industrial Techniques, *Studies of the Labor Supply, Productivity, and Production, Report No. S–1* (Philadelphia: 1939), especially Part One, "Purpose, Methods, and Summary of Findings."

MAGDOFF, HARRY, "The Purpose and Method of Measuring Productivity," *Journal of the American Statistical Association,* 34: 309–318, June 1939.

MARX, WALTER JOHN, *Mechanization and Culture* (St. Louis: B. Herder Book Co., 1941), Chap. I, "Machines and Unemployment."

MERTON, ROBERT K., *Social Theory and Social Structure* (Glencoe, Ill.: The Free Press, 1949), Chap. XIII, "The Machine, the Worker, and the Engineer."

MUMFORD, LEWIS, *Technics and Civilization* (New York: Harcourt, Brace and Company, 1934), Chap. VIII, "Orientation."

NYMAN, RICHARD C., and ELLIOTT DUNLAP SMITH, *Union-Management Cooperation in the "Stretch Out"* (New Haven: Yale University Press for the Institute of Human Relations, 1934).

PETRILL, JACK, *After the Whistle Blows* (New York: The William-Frederick Press for the Industrial Recreation Bureau, 1949).

RIEGEL, JOHN W., *Management, Labor and Technological Change* (Ann Arbor: University of Michigan Press, 1942).

ROSEN, S. McKEE, and LAURA ROSEN, *Technology and Society* (New York: The Macmillan Company, 1941), Chap. XI, "Machines and the Worker: A Case Study of the Cigar Industry."

SIMONS, A. M., *Personnel Relations in Industry* (New York: The Ronald Press Company, 1921), Chap. VIII, "Interesting Labor in Industry."

SMITH, ELLIOTT DUNLAP, and RICHMOND CARTER NYMAN, *Technology and Labor* (New Haven: Yale University Press for the Institute of Human Relations, 1939).

SMITTER, WESSEL, *F. O. B. Detroit* (New York: Harper & Brothers, 1938). A fictionalized account of the reaction of the worker to automatic machines and assembly-line routine.

STAGNER, ROSS, J. N. RICH, and R. H. BRITTEN, JR., "Job Attitudes I. Defense Workers," *Personnel Journal,* 20: 90–97, September 1941.

TODD, ARTHUR JAMES, *Industry and Society* (New York: Henry Holt and Company, Inc., 1933), Chap. XIV, "Hours and Leisure."

UNITED STATES CONGRESS, Temporary National Economic Committee, *Investigation of Concentration of Economic Power, Hearings . . . ,* Part 30, *Technology and Concentration of Economic Power* (Washington: U. S. Government Printing Office, 1940).

UNITED STATES DEPARTMENT OF LABOR, Bureau of Labor Statistics, "Employment and Production in Manufacturing Industries, 1919–1936," *Monthly Labor Review,* 49: 1397–1404, December 1939.

UNITED STATES DEPARTMENT OF LABOR, Bureau of Labor Statistics, "Productivity of Labor and Industry, Technological Changes and Labor Displacements," *Bulletin,* 616: 709–734, 1936.

VEBLEN, THORSTEIN, *The Instinct of Workmanship* (New York: The Macmillan Company, 1914), Chap. VII, "The Machine Industry."

WEINTRAUB, DAVID, "Increased Productivity and Unemployment," *Personnel Journal,* 16: 171–178, November 1937.

———, "Unemployment and Increasing Productivity," in National Resources Committee, *Technological Trends and National Policy* (Washington: U. S. Government Printing Office, 1937), Part I, Sec. V.

WUBNIG, ARTHUR, "The Measurement of the Technological Factor in Labor Productivity," *Journal of the American Statistical Association,* 34: 319–325, June 1939.

YODER, DALE, *Personnel and Labor Relations* (New York: Prentice-Hall, Inc., 1938), Chap. XVII, "Employee Morale, Interest, and Discipline."

◆§ CHAPTER XI

THE QUESTION OF MOTIVES

SOME YEARS ago the Lynds entitled one chapter of their report on a small industrial city, "Why Do They Work So Hard?" The question might be phrased even more generally: "Why does the laborer work at all?" The question is not entirely pointless, although at first glance it may appear so. The laborer works, it is true, to avoid starvation for himself and his dependents. Yet he ordinarily does not stop there, and some further explanation for his continued effort must be found.

It can scarcely be startling to anyone who at one time or another has worked for a living that any work is at least occasionally dull, tiresome, demanding, and uncomfortable. It is noteworthy that in many religious systems heaven is pictured as a place replete with creature comforts, ample wealth, and luxurious leisure. Yet to those who have stood at factory gates, tramped the streets, scanned "Help Wanted" advertisements, or worked on public relief projects, those who were working in the factories and shops were highly fortunate persons.

Traditional doctrine concerning the motivation to labor has been a mixture of two interpretations, with emphasis falling sometimes on one, sometimes on the other. The one emphasizes the positive goal of self-interest, for which work is a necessary and even intrinsically desirable means; the other emphasizes the negative goal of avoiding misery and starvation, for which work is a necessary evil. Both emphasize a money wage or its strict equivalent as the mediator of the workers' interests, and thereby create some difficulties in understanding the observable behavior of industrial workers.

In preceding chapters we have noted in numerous specific instances how inadequate is the traditional view of economic motivation. As a preface to more positive statement of the motives operating throughout all ranks of the industrially employed we may summarize briefly the shortcomings of *homo oeconomicus* as a stereotype of the observable behavior of workers.

1. The positive formula of "wealth-getting" as the sole significant desire of the human individual neglects the impressive range of goals and aspirations evident in actual behavior, while the negative formula of "struggle for existence" not only neglects nonbiological aspirations but provides no explanation for acquisitive behavior after the bare subsistence is assured.

2. The tendency to "biologize" the explanation of human motives, either with reference to ends pursued (such as the familiar economic trilogy of food, clothing, and shelter) or with reference to the source of motives (such as the "acquisitive instinct") finds no confirmation in individual behavior or in the actual process of acquiring motives through socialization of the young.

3. The emphasis on "economic rationality" has obscured both the rational behavior directed toward nonmonetary goals and the important elements of nonrational and irrational (including magical and ritual) behavior of managers and workmen alike.

The whole question of labor motivation has become such a source of contention in the social sciences that it often appears that economists have become partisans of the wage incentive and sociologists of the nonwage incentive. Each discipline has entered its respective candidate in the contest and the two groups have then constituted themselves into rival cheering sections. Each rooting section has a sort of vested interest in the outcome, it is true. The behavior that does not conform to the "maximum principle" translated as monetary maximization must be treated by the economist either as irrelevant or as a disturbing variable that upsets the outcome of rigorous analysis. And the sociologist, often envious of the theoretical rigor of the economist, has not bothered to conceal his delight wherever "economic man" turned out to be a fraud. It should be added that the contest has often been spurious, as the gladiators were contesting in different arenas. Economists have been concerned in both empirical and theoretical work with the operation of market and especially industrial economies. There they have had the great boon of a mensuration device—money. Their gladiators have been *prize* fighters. Sociologists have tended to use head-hunters, priests, and aesthetes from the far places of the world to defeat the worldly "economic man." Needless to add, in such circumstances there is scarcely a contest to decide the issue.

Men will work for as many reasons as they have interests that can be served, either inherently in the work situation or in its rewards, monetary and otherwise. It is axiomatic that society cannot have as its sole function material production, or even the production of "services" on a purely rational, market-oriented basis. Similarly, the individual cannot have production or its monetary rewards as his sole purpose in life. (The rare individual who may come close to such a life-organization is and must be definitely pathological in the strict sense, according to the canons of any operating society.)

The typical social situation, including productive organization, is one of multiple motivation. The work group is in most economies typically composed of persons who stand in many relationships to one another in addition to their cooperative productive relationships. The elements of social recognition and affectional response, of play, and even of aesthetic and religious attitudes are commonly present as an intrinsic part of work organization.

Our knowledge of human motivation indicates the large role of the early socialization process, and the *moral* character of social action and social conformity. This is as true of occupational activity as it is, say, of familial or religious activity. Economic motivation cannot be regarded as the primal urge to acquisitiveness which is *limited* or *liberated* by differing institutional systems but exists independently of them. There is no factual basis for such an attribution of acquisitiveness to "human nature," or rather "animal nature," outside the normal operation of social learning, and there is no necessity of making such a claim in order to establish the validity of ordinary economic analysis as applied to areas of rational utilitarian production and distribution.

Yet it is characteristic of the industrial system to have "impoverished" motives by reducing both rewards and penalties toward the absolute minimum of wages and hunger. As this may be regarded as a serious charge, and indeed has been regarded as an incriminating one by critics and reformers for a century and a half, it is appropriate to find its explanation. Three closely related aspects of industrialism, both in its historical development and in its contemporary expansion to new areas, deserve attention in this connection.

1. Industrialism is a way of organizing for production, perhaps more fundamentally than it is a system harnessing natural power, intensifying capital relative to labor, or similar characteristics. The rational efficiency in industrial production rests upon a maximum emphasis on technical competence at work, unmixed with play, ritual, or social intercourse. In technical terms, the entire occupational structure emphasizes, *as moral principles, universalism* (selection and treatment of persons without regard to previous social ties or obligations) and *functional specificity* (relations determined solely on technical grounds related to the occupation as such).[1] These principles are exemplified in casual trading relations, where any buyer may seek the best bargain with a seller and the momentary or more formal future-delivery sales contract comprises the whole sum of the social transaction. But they are also exemplified in the strict form of bureaucratic organization, as we have seen, and presumably characterize the relations among workers and between superiors and subordinates.

2. At the same time that the industrial system minimizes ranges of social ties not relevant to productive organization, it has been a "great mixer of peoples."[2] Both because the industrial system draws workers from different regions and even different language and ethnic groups and because the occupation is separated in both space and time from other social activities, the worker is torn from nearly all the traditionally sanctioned forms of social organization

---

[1] See Talcott Parsons, *Essays in Sociological Theory, Pure and Applied* (Glencoe, Ill.: The Free Press, 1949), Chap. VIII, "The Professions and Social Structure," and Chap. IX, "The Motivation of Economic Activities."

[2] See Everett C. Hughes, "Queries Concerning Industry and Society Growing out of Study of Ethnic Relations in Industry," *American Sociological Review*, 14: 211–220, April 1949.

that gave life meaning and security. To accomplish this transformation, pressure and bribery have been the effective incentives, particularly prior to the institutionalization of the industrial system of placement and rewards.[3]

3. The specialization of labor, which is both a major key to the productivity of industrial societies and a major source of social tension, requires a monetary system of exchange. Since the worker and family or village do not produce for themselves, they must have means of laying claim to the general product. Two further points accentuate this basic principle. (a) Increased specialization and the shattering of traditional reciprocities based on kinship or neighborhood result in an increasing movement of "services" into the market, thus heightening the pecuniary incentive. (b) The mass market, upon which advanced forms of production depend, is itself possible only by virtue of rising material consumption of producers and their families. It is indeed this upward trend in "wants" that is generally lacking in nonindustrial societies and is typical precisely of the most completely "integrated" workers in industrial societies. Whether from lack of industrial tradition [4] or from repeated frustration,[5] it is the lowest ranks of unskilled industrial labor that also show the least anxiety to "move ahead" or greatly expand their consumption by the avenue of job mobility.[6]

[3] See Wilbert E. Moore, *Industrialization and Labor: Social Aspects of Economic Development* (Ithaca: Cornell University Press, 1951), especially Chaps. I–III. Even bribery has direct and immediate shortcomings in an economy with a poorly developed market and a low customary standard of consumption and "wants."

The idea of individual mobility by merit, for example, is rare as an aspiration expected of all active participants in production. It requires a special kind of social system and set of normative injunctions. It is also, incidentally, an unstable system unless hedged about with safeguards and new forms of social cohesion.

[4] See Melville Dalton, "Worker Response and Social Background," *Journal of Political Economy*, 55: 323–332, August 1947.

[5] See Allison Davis, "The Motivation of the Underprivileged Worker," in William Foote Whyte, ed., *Industry and Society* (New York: McGraw-Hill Book Company, Inc., 1946), Chap. V.

[6] See also William H. Form, "Toward an Occupational Social Psychology," *Journal of Social Psychology*, 24: 85–99, 1946; Lloyd G. Reynolds and Joseph Shister, *Job Horizons: A Study of Job Satisfaction and Labor Mobility* (New York: Harper & Brothers, 1949).

In a somewhat oversimplified way, one can say therefore that money is so important as a work incentive in industrial societies because there are so few other types of interests directly consistent with the industrial mode of division of labor, and because money is such a useful thing to secure the fruits of production and at least some other interests as well.

WEALTH AND POWER AS "UNIVERSAL MEANS"

Much of the seeming evidence in support of traditional doctrine of economic motivation stems from the important and apparently increasing role of money as a means to a great variety of other goals. Indeed, the increasing commercialization of values makes otherwise incommensurable things reducible to a common denominator: how much does it cost? Money, as the textbooks in economics put it, is a means of exchange. Put somewhat differently, within our social system money is a type of "universal means," owing much of its value precisely to this quality of adaptability. Yet the significance of wages or income is both narrower and broader than we have implied. It is narrower in that some values or goals are not readily capable of commercialization, and therefore are independent of, and possibly even contrary to, economic aspirations. It is broader in that the significance of money in our society is not limited to its direct purchasing power, since it serves as a symbol as well as an intrinsic means to purchasable ends.

Symbolic Character of Income. The increasing commercialization of values has had not only the direct effect of making more goals of the individual purchasable, but the indirect effect of making wages or income symbolic of social position.

In a small and relatively immobile community differential valuation (status fixing) of individuals is a product of a great many standards of judgment: family, occupation, education, political and religious affiliation, informal circle of acquaintances, and so on. In a large and mobile community many of these standards lose their significance, and income assumes a much greater relative importance. Income then becomes symbolic of other standards of valuation.

It is only by recognition of this aspect of the economic demands of laborers that some forms of behavior can be understood. For example, a very small increase in pay may have a significance far beyond the direct monetary advantage if this is understood as constituting an acceptable form of social recognition.

Whitehead has observed that methods of income payment, including frequency of payment, have symbolic significance without direct reference to amount.[7] The difference between a "salary" and a "wage" persists without reference to relative amounts. In fact, it is ordinarily true that the lower ranks of salaried workers earn considerably less than the higher ranks of skilled wage earners. Among wage earners those paid on time rates within the shop frequently have higher status and lower incomes than those paid on piece rates. It is of course true that the presumably greater security of income of the former accounts for part of the preference, but it is also certainly true that income and methods of payment symbolize standards of valuation other than mere productivity.

Wage experts with slide rules to the contrary notwithstanding, it is impossible to assess relative worth or productivity throughout an industrial organization by any single standard or convenient group of them. Although rationalization of industrial organization places great stress on rewards for immediate productive activity, other considerations cannot be eliminated. The individual has statuses and roles outside the plant that call for differential reward, partly in economic terms. Thus age, sex, seniority, family responsibilities, educational background, nationality, and a host of other distinctions affect wage scales. They are likely to be more, rather than less, important in the future. Income may have little relevance to intrinsic worth (if that can be defined) or to buying power, and yet not lose its significance as a symbol of relative valuation.

Relativity of Hours and Wages. The foregoing considerations make it evident that hours and wages, disputes over which figure largely in industrial controversies, are highly relative matters. Even in economic terms, wages are obviously relative to cost of living, and from

---

[7] T. N. Whitehead, *Leadership in a Free Society* (Cambridge: Harvard University Press, 1937), pp. 131–134.

this arises the necessity of distinguishing *money wages* and *real wages*. But considerations of income levels are also relative to standards of wage payments typical of the industry or type of work. This, in turn, will correspond fairly closely to the standard of living (level of "reasonable" aspiration) thought proper for the occupation or stratum in question. Wages and hours are also relative to sentiments concerning a "fair day's work" and "appropriate" return for contributions to the productive effort. The workman who complains that his wages are too low may mean that the money does not buy enough, that he is paid less than some prevailing or otherwise fair standard, that he is not sufficiently repaid for the unpleasant character of his work, or that his work is worth more in comparison with the work of another. He may mean all of these things in combination. The actual complexity of human motivation in particular cases points up the extreme oversimplification of views such as those of Taylor that higher wages represent the sum and substance of the interests of laborers.[8]

Acquisitiveness in a Pecuniary Society. What we have been saying about the intermediate rather than ultimate character of income as a goal, its frequently symbolic rather than intrinsic significance, and its relativity to other considerations should not be thought to imply that the "wages question" is of minor importance. On the contrary, economic demands of the laborer assume large proportions partly because income has such varied meaning and utility.

The preoccupation with monetary aspirations should not be thought of exclusively in terms of physiological comfort, or even material possessions. Veblen pointed to the high importance in our society of what he called "pecuniary emulation." He noted the appearance of standards deriving from the ideals and practices of the leisure class: conspicuous consumption, leisure, and waste. Paradoxically, a great deal of money is necessary to show one's apparent unconcern for money.[9] Veblen was observing late in the nineteenth

---

[8] It was noted in Chap. VII that Frederick W. Taylor, founder of "scientific management," maintained that workmen could be induced to double or triple their productivity through the payment of slightly higher wages and adoption of "scientific" standards of performance.

[9] See especially Veblen's *The Theory of the Leisure Class* (New York:

century what several more recent scholars have stated more explicitly: the preoccupation with acquisitiveness as a desperatio̶ measure for the achievement of goals not otherwise obtainable a relatively poor substitute for other values. Mayo and others have observed the way in which the headlong pursuit of wealth grows out of the "poverty of social existence," and Mayo characterizes this situation as "the acquisitiveness of a sick society." [10] This is simply a more general formulation of a principle frequently illustrated in everyday industrial relations. Compensation is very often sought for sacrifices of interests, for discomfort and unpleasant working conditions, for jobs having low prestige value, and so on. It is commonly true, for example, that dirty unskilled jobs must be paid for at a higher rate than clean ones. As previously observed, the managerial tendency to overestimate the importance of financial incentives indirectly validates the assumption through the neglect of other incentives.

The fact that money is a generally accepted, if intermediate, aspiration has a further significance. To the extent that the goal is strongly emphasized (and this is especially easy with a quantifiably expanding goal) and the means for achieving the end are not uniformly available, strong pressure is created for departing from customary and ethically approved methods for getting ahead in the world. These "antisocial" methods are likely to include force and fraud, and account not only for a great deal of professional criminality, but for part of the coercive tactics in industrial disputes as well.[11]

All of this concern over income should not suggest that income is more than rarely an ultimate end (that is, an end in itself), or even that income is the sole or primary intrinsic means for the accom-

B. W. Huebsch, 1918), Chap. II, "Pecuniary Emulation"; Chap. III, "Conspicuous Leisure"; and Chap. VIII, "Industrial Exemption and Conservatism."

[10] See Elton Mayo, *Human Problems of an Industrial Civilization* (New York: The Macmillan Company, 1933), p. 153. See also F. J. Roethlisberger and William J. Dickson, *Management and the Worker* (Cambridge: Harvard University Press, 1939), p. 574; Whitehead, *op. cit.*, Chap. IX, "The Financial Reward," especially pp. 125–126.

[11] See Robert K. Merton, "Social Structure and Anomie," *American Sociological Review*, 3: 672–682, October 1938.

plishment of all goals. Aside from those ends that are ordinarily not ~~~hasable, which we shall note below, we have so far neglected ~~ ~termediate aspiration, that of power.

~ss of Power. So generally useful is power that like income it may be termed a "universal means." Power and wealth may, in fact, be converted into one another, so that there is an understandable tendency for the two to appear together.

The significance of power is fairly simple, yet frequently overlooked. In all social situations, other persons are potential means to any given person's ends. That is, if he can exert control over the actions of others, he can use their talents or labor for his own purposes. The exercise of power (or "authority," if its legitimacy is socially recognized) was traditionally assumed to be the exclusive prerogative of the industrial entrepreneur, and was thought to be connected in some manner with private property rights. When an industrial owner, or a modern industrial manager, insists on "running his business as he best sees fit" he is asserting not only a right over material assets but power over the actions of persons comprising the organization. But the advantages of power are not limited to those actually in positions of authority in industrial organization. Although in the past the individual workman had little opportunity to acquire power over industrial labor, this does not mean that it held no interest for him.

We shall note in subsequent chapters that one of the most immediate goals of combinations of workers into unions is the changing of the balance of power in industrial organization. Many of the so-called direct economic activities of unions, such as the strike, are in reality types of acquisition and use of power. Although the usefulness of power is sometimes obscured by the heavy emphasis on wealth, the modern industrial situation indicates that it is an increasingly important goal.

Power is sometimes viewed as an end in itself, and in some rare cases—comparable to the solitary miser—it may be. The claim that laborers, or anyone else, are simply interested in power for its own sake is usually a misinterpretation of the *symbolic* means-end relationship. Just as income may give social distinction without reference to its use for other ends, so power (especially if legitimized as authority) may constitute a significant element in relative ev~~~~ ~~tion, even if that power is not exercised toward other en~~~~ ~~or as individual. Until very recently the factory laborer, if he~~~~ ~~appreciable power at all, gained no immediate advantage except in use of that power to implement his demands for wages, shorter hours, better working conditions, and so on. To the extent that some measure of control is socially recognized as permissible for laborers, power may be expected to take on the character of a symbol of social esteem without being used as a weapon.

Income and power may each be used to gain the other, and both are likely to be directed immediately or ultimately to other ends. They do not constitute the only methods of satisfying the worker's aspirations, for despite the readily transferable and adaptable nature of both they are not truly universal means. In any event, we must note what appear to be the more ultimate ends of labor, whether those are dependent on wealth and power or not.

THE WORKERS' ASPIRATIONS

Although any reduction of the complexity of human motivation to convenient types is in some measure arbitrary—some might even say foolhardy—part of the difficulty is offset by confining the treatment to a single society and by bearing in mind that any basis of classification can only be judged in terms of its utility for specific purposes. It should be noted that on the very concrete level the range of aspirations or ends is extremely wide. It is only necessary to recall the previous discussion of the importance of "sentiments" and of irrational, symbolic, and obsessive thinking to understand that the ideals and values that motivate laborers (or any other group) are not likely to comprise a logical system of means-end relationships. Thus, the fact that one worker tries to gain security by restricting output and another aims to secure the same end by working extra hard to catch the eye of the foreman does not destroy the importance of security as an aspiration. Whether or not the observer judges the manifestations of the motive as efficient makes no difference in the relative importance of the motive; it simply makes the task of the observer in discovering the goals of activity more difficult, since he cannot derive them solely by observing results or from the assumptions of logic.

Despite these difficulties, the weight of available evidence seems to justify a roughly threefold classification of ends, not necessarily separable in particular cases. The goals that appear to be dominant in the worker's orientation to his job are *security, pleasant working relations, and status in a competitive society.*

Security. One hears a great deal these days about "security." The fairly recent beginning of discussion and controversy about its importance should not be taken to mean that security is a new fad, or a newly invented goal. Rather, there is a sound basis for maintaining that it is a new problem in the sense that modern conditions of labor satisfy the desire for security less well than older conditions. In any case, it is undeniably true that security is a matter of considerable concern to the industrial employee.

Some of the interest in income is obviously in terms of the necessary purchasing power for survival, or, more frequently, for survival at a particular level of living which may be considerably above that necessary for mere preservation of life. Because of the nature of the goal, much of the action oriented toward security is protective or defensive in character. The desire for security is thus frequently expressed as a conservative tendency: the preservation of the status quo, such as continuity of employment or keeping well-loved habits and routines. Security may mean, in fact, simply a guarantee that other ends will be satisfied.

Relative emphasis on security may, of course, be offset by a more active orientation toward mobility and advancement. But the two are not always antithetical, since advancement and increases in income are frequently sought simply as further safeguards or evidences of security. So strong, indeed, is the desire for security that even competition and mobility must take place within well-defined rules. A widespread uncertainty about the rules, or an impression of utter disorder, is likely to prompt withdrawal and defense rather than more active competition. The rapidity of social (including technological) change in modern industry makes this a highly important consideration in understanding the behavior of workers.

Since the goal of security involves not only the necessity of predictability but also that of control (to prevent an otherwise predictable and undesirable change), it is clear that power is frequently more useful to this end than money. We shall see in the following chapter how some of the control devices are developed in the informal organization. Restriction of output, for example, is almost always oriented toward security, although it may have considerably less relevance for income and employment security than for control of the conditions of work and resistance to what is viewed as "exploitation." [12]

It is clear that security is a very general goal, and may mean different things to different people. Wealth and power, because of their general usefulness, are therefore convenient security-devices. But both of these together may not be able to obtain for the worker that emotional security and sense of personal integrity which are also valued components of the general class "security." [13] The informal organization, aside from its possible operation as a power mechanism, seems to have the potentiality of fulfilling that function. It is perhaps significant that this is rarely recognized as an "incentive" to cooperate, and that if this goal of the workman is satisfied in industrial organization it will ordinarily be in spite of management, not because of it.

Pleasant Working Relations. It is also primarily in the informal organization, if at all, that the worker's goal of satisfactory working relations is achieved. If officially recognized at all, this aspect of the worker's orientation to his job is usually viewed in terms of "working conditions." The phrase itself immediately signifies that the

[12] The significance of output restriction for social (not simply economic) security has been observed in the Western Electric research. See Roethlisberger and Dickson, *op. cit.*, Chap. XVIII, "The Output Situation in the Bank Wiring Observation Room," and pp. 531–534. J. A. Hobson noted some years ago the importance to the worker of control of "near" conditions of labor in small groups. See his *Incentives in the New Industrial Order* (New York: Thomas Seltzer, 1923), especially pp. 116–119.

[13] See Chester I. Barnard, *The Functions of the Executive* (Cambridge: Harvard University Press, 1938), Chap. XI, "The Economy of Incentives," especially p. 148.

laborer is not expected to be *primarily* interested in his surroundings, but only that "improvement" of his surroundings may make his attention to his official duties more single-minded. The surroundings ordinarily viewed as constituting the "working conditions" lend support to this view, for attention is ordinarily focused on the physical environment and the physiological reaction of the organism to that environment.

We have already observed in Chapters IX and X that "working conditions" as ordinarily understood are precisely conditions, and that their direct and immediate significance is apparent only at the extremes of variation in those conditions. But we also noted in that same connection that temperature, humidity, dirt, noise, illumination, and so on do not constitute the total of the worker's significant environment. Rarely do those conditions, or changes in those conditions, constitute positive incentives to cooperation. On the other hand, the social environment, the customs and relationships established in informal groups, are not necessarily so limited and essentially negative in the worker's scheme of things. In fact, achievement of pleasant working relations may well constitute a positive goal, and one not ordinarily purchasable or capable of attainment through power.

So little attention has been paid to this goal that the means for its achievement are not generally known, either to workmen or to outside experts. The establishment of pleasant working relations depends upon the interplay of complex and often highly divergent personalities, and therefore within the present state of knowledge is subject to considerable chance and unpredictable error. It is in general easier to recognize symptoms of failure to achieve this goal than it is to formulate any but some negative rules for success.[14] Significantly, the rules of avoidance—the "Thou Shalt Not's"—that

[14] The symptoms of failure to achieve satisfactory social relations obviously include many of those commonly recognized by psychiatrists as neurotic and psychotic reactions. Guilt feelings, paranoid fears of social disapproval and persecution, delusions of grandeur, and a host of other symptoms of the disorganized or maladjusted personality are evidential of social "frustration" in the broadest sense. See V. V. Anderson, *Psychiatry in Industry* (New York and London: Harper & Brothers, 1929), Chap. II, "Work Failures—Their Study and Treatment," and Chap. VI, "Psychiatry in Industrial Health Work"; Roethlis-

are capable of ready formulation have to do with protection of informal group standards against disruption and against the interference of outsiders, chiefly management. But, like the rules of
etiquette for polite social discourse, these set minimum requirements
for "getting along" socially, but do not necessarily guarantee the
positive achievement of personally satisfactory relations.

It is, of course, a function (not necessarily a conscious purpose)
of informal organization to provide the appropriate means for satisfactory social relations. The universal appearance of such informal
standards and the tremendous attention given to their preservation
and elaboration in spite of managerial efforts in prevention are
ample testimony to the strength of this motive. But since for any
particular person those informal practices and expectations are very
little less arbitrary than official expectations, the existence of well-
developed informal organization is still no guarantee of achievement of the goal. Industrial personnel records are replete with examples of men who could perform their official duties very satis-
factorily but who seemed not to "get on" well, or not to have "found
themselves" yet. The cult of happiness in our society does little to
dispel such maladjustments; on the contrary, it accentuates the
contrast between the ideal and the actual for those persons who are
poorly integrated into occupational life.

Status in a Competitive Society. A final, and much more generally
recognized, group of ends are those involving respect, esteem, and
other modes of differential valuation. Now "status," as these ends
are usually summarized, is not a simple goal, nor are the means for
its achievement constant. Taking a position in the social structure
(or in some segment of it) as given, the goal may be to fulfill the
expectations attaching to that position and to command the respect
appropriate to one's position. This assumes a highly developed institutional structure if there is to be any close correspondence between
subjective expectation and objective fact. Otherwise, the person is
likely to be overanxious in seeking deference and respect where

---

berger and Dickson, *op. cit.*, Chap. XIV, "Complaints and Personal Equilibrium," and Chap. XVI, "Complaints and Social Equilibrium."

it is not due. The present point, however, is simply that status does not need to be mobile, such as "improving one's status," to be a focus of attention and an incentive to action. Thus, those who speak of status as a "noneconomic incentive" appear very frequently to be referring to *social recognition or prestige attaching to a position*, taken as given, and not to promotion or other methods of enhancing the person's relative rank. This might preferably be expressed as the desire for prestige accruing to the position, and of esteem for fulfilling the obligations of the position in an approved fashion.[15]

Closely related to the foregoing aspect of "status" as an end is the very commonly recognized importance of a sense of accomplishment or pride in workmanship. Although this is frequently expressed as a purely individual matter, it is clear that accomplishment and workmanship cannot be far removed from the prevalent standards of prestige and esteem and still remain significant goals. Short of positing an instinct of workmanship or some variant of it, there is no reason for assuming that individuals find any particular joy in accomplishments (even if very difficult) that are commonly regarded as useless.

It may, of course, be noted that the same abilities and achievements will not be rated equally in all segments of society, or even among all members of a complex cooperative system. Like the small boy's virtuosity in spitting between his front teeth, the accomplishment may in some quarters be viewed with positive disfavor, while it may in other quarters be simply ignored. It is a truism that the worker is most interested in the good opinion of those who are in a position to appreciate his work, and whose opinions are also important to him in other respects. Thus praise from a supervisor or an increase in wages will not under ordinary circumstances be insignifi-

---

[15] These and other aspects of differential position and evaluation have been carefully worked out by Kingsley Davis, "A Conceptual Analysis of Stratification," *American Sociological Review*, 7: 309–321, June 1942. The importance of social recognition as a goal of industrial workers has been noted very extensively in the literature; see, for example, Charles A. Drake, "When Wage Incentives Fail," *Advanced Management*, 7: 42–44, January–March 1942; K. O. Schulte, "Grading of Labor Occupations," *Seventh International Management Congress*, Washington 1938, Production Papers, pp. 152–157; Whiting Williams, *Mainsprings of Men* (New York: Charles Scribner's Sons, 1925).

cant satisfactions, but may be considerably less important ways of achieving the general end of recognition than the approval of his informal group of fellow employees. Since accomplishment in this sense is known to be very poorly measured or rewarded by income, it is properly regarded as a "noneconomic" incentive.[16]

Still another variant of the end of social recognition for a position or for the fulfillment of its duties is to be found in what Barnard refers to as the incentive of an approved altruism.[17] This may simply take the form of fulfilling the minimal expectations of the community for the breadwinner by being a "good provider," or may involve loyalty to some larger and less immediately personal organization. The significance of such aspirations has been widely recognized by armament manufactures during wartime, and indeed the patriotic value of almost all kinds of work has been asserted, with varying degrees of success. The importance of production for military victory is of course most readily apparent in the case of plants manufacturing arms and munitions, and the evidence seems fairly clear that the extra incentive has been real and productive.[18]

The examples of the goal of "status" discussed have all been concerned with the value attached to a given position or its appropriate duties. But in a competitive social order it is normally expected that the individual will seek to change his status, chiefly by "climbing" along well-defined paths of advancement. In industrial terms, this will ordinarily be expressed as the desire for promotion. Although, as was noted in discussing managerial organization, the way to the top is by no means limited to starting at the bottom, it remains true that the goal of higher position is a very common one among industrial employees. Many laborers, it is true, have been frustrated in

---

[16] See Barnard, *op. cit.*, pp. 146–148; Walter Brown, "Our Way of Putting Creative Interest into Humdrum Jobs," *Factory*, 33: 39, 137, July 1924; Harry Tipper, *Human Factors in Industry* (New York: The Ronald Press Company, 1922), Chap. XV, "Incentive"; same, "Personal Aspirations More Important to Worker than Economic Laws," *Automotive Industries*, 47: 682–683, October 5, 1922; Robert B. Wolf, "Non-Financial Incentives," *Advanced Management*, 5: 168–170, 176, October–December 1940.

[17] *Op. cit.*, p. 146.

[18] See *Factory Management and Maintenance*, "Case Studies in Building the Will to Win," 100 (6): 64–71, 188, 190, 192, 194, 199–200, June 1942; and 100 (7): 68–73, July 1942.

their ambitions, either through inadequate ability or through inadequate opportunity. The former frustration is no more acceptable than the latter if the selective processes are *thought* to be unfair. It is also important that seeming acceptance of nonpromotion usually takes the form of an embittered and cynical reaction, which by no means diminishes the general importance of the goal. It simply means that the worker will direct his attention to other ends as compensation for his lack of success in gaining this socially approved goal; from the managerial point of view, this means that a heavier burden is thereby placed on other incentives to cooperation. We shall return in Chapter XXIII to a consideration of the ideal of occupational mobility in an ascending scale, and its significance for the open-class system. Our present concern is to note the existence of the ideal, and the possibility that frustration in competition for status may lead to behavior less satisfactory from the managerial viewpoint. However, the possibly disruptive effects of competition should also not be forgotten, and this is an especially important consideration if the gap between the end and the available means is large. There is some recent evidence of greater managerial interest in promoting those already within the organization ("up-grading") and in making the normal path for improving status more clear-cut.

It is not meant to imply, as we have previously noted, that our list of the worker's aspirations is exhaustive, especially on the concrete level. It is likely, however, that other examples will be found to fall fairly readily into the three groups indicated. As we turn our attention to the informal and formal (union) organization of workers, it is suggested that the ends of labor as evidenced in the work-day behavior of industrial employees will also aid in an understanding of some of the less obvious activities of these forms of association.

REFERENCES

BARNARD, CHESTER I., *The Functions of the Executive* (Cambridge, Harvard University Press, 1938), Chap. XI, "The Economy of Incentives."

DALTON, MELVILLE, "Worker Response and Social Background," *Journal of Political Economy*, 55: 323–332, August 1947.

DAVIS, ALLISON, "The Motivation of the Underprivileged Worker," in

William Foote Whyte, ed., *Industry and Society* (New York: McGraw-Hill Book Company, Inc., 1946), Chap. V.

FORM, WILLIAM H., "Toward an Occupational Social Psychology," *Journal of Social Psychology*, 24: 85–99, 1946.

GLOVER, JOHN G., and COLEMAN L. MAZE, *Managerial Control* (New York: The Ronald Press Company, 1937), Chap. XI, "The Relation of Wage Systems and Incentives to Cost."

GOLDEN, CLINTON S., "What Labor Wants from Management," *Advanced Management*, 6: 7–12, January–March 1941.

HOBSON, J. A., *Incentives in the New Industrial Order* (New York: Thomas Seltzer, 1923), especially Chap. V, "Incentives to the Efficiency of Labour."

KORNHAUSER, ARTHUR, "The Contribution of Psychology to Industrial Relations Research," in Milton Derber, ed., *Proceedings of the First Annual Meeting, Industrial Relations Research Association*, Cleveland, Ohio, December 29–30, 1948 (Champaign, Ill.: 1949), pp. 172–188.

LYND, ROBERT S., and HELEN MERRELL LYND, *Middletown* (New York: Harcourt, Brace and Company, 1929), Chap. VIII, "Why Do They Work So Hard?"

MEADOWS, PAUL, "The Motivation of Industrial Man," *American Journal of Economics and Sociology*, 6: 363–370, April 1947.

MILES, G. H., *The Problem of Incentives in Industry* (London: Sir Isaac Pitman & Sons, Ltd., 1932).

NATIONAL INDUSTRIAL CONFERENCE BOARD, *Some Problems in Wage Incentive Administration*, Studies in Personnel Policy No. 19 (New York, 1940).

PARSONS, TALCOTT, *Essays in Sociological Theory, Pure and Applied* (Glencoe, Ill.: The Free Press, 1949), Chap. IX, "The Motivation of Economic Activities."

POLANYI, KARL, "Our Obsolete Market Mentality," *Commentary*, 3: 109–117, February 1947.

REYNOLDS, LLOYD G., and JOSEPH SHISTER, *Job Horizons: A Study of Job Satisfaction and Labor Mobility* (New York: Harper & Brothers, 1949).

ROETHLISBERGER, F. J., and WILLIAM J. DICKSON, *Management and the Worker* (Cambridge: Harvard University Press, 1939), Chap. VI, "Testing the Effects of Wage Incentive," Chap. XVIII, "The Output Situation in the Bank Wiring Observation Room," and pp. 531–534.

STEIN, EMANUEL, "Financial Incentives and Profit Sharing," In Emanuel Stein and Jerome Davis, eds., *Labor Problems in America* (New York: Farrar & Rinehart, Inc., 1940), Chap. 23.

VEBLEN, THORSTEIN, *The Theory of the Leisure Class* (New York: B. W. Huebsch, 1918), Chap. II, "Pecuniary Emulation," Chap. III, "Conspicuous Leisure," and Chap. VIII, "Industrial Exemption and Conservatism."

WHITEHEAD, T. N., *Leadership in a Free Society* (Cambridge: Harvard University Press, 1937), Chap. 18, "The Financial Rewards," and pp. 248–253.

WILLIAMS, WHITING, *Mainsprings of Men* (New York: Charles Scribner's Sons, 1925).

——, *What's on the Worker's Mind* (New York: Charles Scribner's Sons, 1920).

CHAPTER XII

INFORMAL ORGANIZATION
OF WORKERS

THE TARDY discovery by scholars and executives of "human relations" in industry has led in recent years to a consideration of the
worker as an individual and as a member of groups at the work-
place and of more formidable groups, called unions. The failure in
the past to consider the crescive, spontaneous group of workers
derived in part from a preoccupation with the official structure of
the cooperative system. Any social relationships not accounted for
by that system were accordingly regarded as irrelevant, or possibly
as subversive, of managerial authority. And the theorists of organization apparently forgot or did not know that the formal organization
that constitutes a daily place of work for persons in continuous contact provides also the conditions for deletions and elaborations of
the "expected" relations.

The present chapter examines the patterns of action among employees, particularly with respect to (1) the bases for the formation
of cohesions and hostilities, (2) the attributes of membership in
spontaneous groups, and (3) the positive or negative relationship
between the formal demands of the organization (or "management") and the informal expectations of fellow employees.

ORGANIZATION CHARTS AND ORGANIZATION FACTS

The dangling squares or "berries" of an organization chart refer
to formal positions in a cooperative system, and only incidentally to
persons who happen to be filling those positions. Nowhere in industrial organization is this official impersonality (not to say un-

reality) more evident than in the case of those who take but do not give orders. Rarely do the berries suspended at the very bottom refer to single persons; rather, they indicate the position of workers or "operators," allocated according to the technical division of labor in production.

Even on technical grounds, however, organization charts fall far short of representing the actual division of labor. Like small-scale maps of large areas, only the major boundaries and place names are indicated. Many places of importance from some points of view simply "aren't on the map." But, to follow this metaphor for a moment, the map is specialized: it shows some features in more detail than others. Most especially, it indicates lines of formal authority much more clearly than lines of "horizontal" organization and division of labor. Yet our previous discussion of managerial organization would lead us to expect that among workers also there is more than meets the map-reader's eye.

Inevitability of Informal Patterns. Whenever persons are placed in continued formal contact, in whatever circumstances, their relationships become characterized by actions and reactions over and above the formal expectations. This elementary principle of social behavior has already been noted with reference to industrial managers, and indeed is intuitively recognized *by* industrial managers. But elementary principles are frequently the ones most taken for granted, and therefore overlooked in the observation of unfamiliar situations. To assume that the relations of a machinist and his helper are adequately characterized by their official duties, that the "personalities" of both are irrelevant, and that the relationship is exactly comparable wherever the formal division of labor is defined in the same way is to make a common but fundamental error in interpretation.

Nor is it simply sufficient to know of the existence of friendships and hostilities, of grumbling and joking, and similar manifestations of the interaction between persons. If the knowledge of these matters is not only commonplace but irrelevant for the understanding of industrial organization and relations, there is no point in singling out the obvious for special comment. However, even if the informal relations among employees were of no especial significance for management (an idea that even managers reject when they forbid conversation, for example), there is no particularly good reason for maintaining that this is the sole important viewpoint in the organization. When an employee is assigned to do a certain job, he is also, perhaps unwittingly, assigned to the task of getting along with certain people. And however unimportant or matter-of-fact this incidental assignment may be to the employment manager, it is likely to figure fairly large in the thinking of the man involved.

Reverting to the previous metaphor, the blank areas on the general map of the cooperative system do not mean that nothing is there, or even that nothing of any importance has been left out. Our problem is to augment the usefulness of the chart by a series of descriptions of local areas.

GROUP MEMBERSHIP AND STATUS

Workers entering the factory gates are scarcely a homogeneous mass of interchangeable parts. The characteristic specialization and division of labor of modern economic organization deny that possibility. But our remarks in the last few paragraphs lead to the expectation that the technical allocation of manpower is not the only set of similarities and distinctions that these employees will exhibit, and that as they go about their business other relationships will be apparent. Perhaps the easiest way to understand these other relationships is in terms of *cliques* and how these are formed.

Cliques—Technical Distinctions. From what has been said about the inadequacy of a technical division of labor for understanding the groupings of laborers it must not be assumed that technical distinctions are simply irrelevant. On the contrary, occupational role is one of the major bases of inclusion and exclusion of group members. This does not mean, however, even where occupation is the important demarcation line, that the occupational role precisely *determines* the character of the relations among those of similar skill and duty. An illustration or two may serve to indicate the distinction. Among railroaders, as reported by Cottrell,[1] occupational distinc-

---

[1] W. Fred Cottrell, *The Railroader* (Stanford University, Calif.: Stanford University Press, 1940), especially Chap. III, "Technological and Social Grouping."

tions figure largest in the informal customs and working relationships. From the "aristocracy" of railroading (firemen, engineers,
brakemen, and conductors) down to the lower ranks of mechanical
repairmen and maintenance-of-way section hands, the job is the
primary criterion of social group membership. The emphasis on
craft, moreover, ensures against a grouping based on rank alone,
since clerks, station agents, administrators, and traffic department
representatives are not even accepted as true railroaders. But even
craft similarities are not sufficient to incorporate Pullman conductors
into the groups of "regular" trainmen. And the ritual devotion to
time requirements, technical slang, non-Puritanical modes of recreation, and so on, are relevant to occupational role, but by no means
determined by that role. Even the craft distinctions are based more
on "monopolizability" of training and selection than on genuine
competitive achievement. The railroader's technical job is simply
the point of reference for customs typical of the industry.

In their detailed study of a small productive unit at the Western
Electric Hawthorne plant, Roethlisberger and Dickson [2] found a
rather inconsequential technical difference of work assignment—
that between "connector" and "selector" wiremen—having an effect
on social distinctions and clique formation through the idea that
connector wiremen were superior, or that the work was easier. But
the cliques observed also cut across lines of specialization, partly on
functional lines of the smallest productive unit (three wiremen, one
solderman serving the three, and one inspector) and partly on
"extraneous" grounds which we shall note subsequently.

Occupational distinctions as a basis for informal organization may
be based on genuine differences in skill and technical interest or
on minor differences which are, from the technical standpoint,
arbitrarily selected as significant. Some differences, perhaps greater,
are overlooked. Other occupational distinctions include income differences or methods of payment, ease or difficulty of job (aside from
skill), and possible lines of advancement either in formal position

---

[2] F. J. Roethlisberger and William J. Dickson, *Management and the Worker*
(Cambridge: Harvard University Press, 1939), Chap. XXI, "The Internal Organization of the Group in the Bank Wiring Observation Room," and pp.
513–516.

or in informal prestige. Even where craft distinctions are considerable, informal patterns of conduct will follow those distinctions only to the extent that the technical role is genuinely a focus of interest, or is made to seem so by other bases of common interest that are more or less related to the technical positions, possibly through historical accident. Thus, certain jobs sometimes become associated with age, nationality, or similar lines of demarcation. The occupation thereby becomes the focus of a group of sentiments in addition to simple interchangeability of job assignments, pride in craft, and so on.

Cliques—Spatial Arrangements. One of the factors in the correspondence between semiofficial (technical) distinctions and informal groupings is the simple one of location of work. Those performing the same jobs, especially in a large manufacturing plant, will ordinarily also work in the same area. In some cases the specialization of labor will correspond almost exactly with architectural and mechanical arrangements, so that job titles and place names are interchangeable. For the most part, however, plant divisions like "hot strip mill," "maintenance shops," "planing mill," or "wheel assembly" demarcate a number of functionally interdependent workers, rather than similar job assignments. Since any social organization depends upon communication, spatial arrangements are always relevant to organizational patterns.

Although informal contacts, and even rudimentary "organization" supported by customs and sentiments, can be maintained by off-the-job meetings, rest period and washroom get-togethers, messengers, and the like, cliques will ordinarily be limited to the range of face-to-face relationship. This range will depend upon the mobility allowed the worker, and the effect of noise or a watchful overseer on conversation or other means of communication. Although placing persons in close functional relationships and frequent face-to-face contacts does not guarantee that they will love one another, it does assure the appearance of some mode of interaction over and above the strict demands of duty.

The location of job assignments will frequently result in group loyalties and recognizable group characteristics that may have very little to do with the intrinsic demands of the job. Thus boiler-room gangs, loading-platform outfits, and second-floor groups may speak of themselves and be recognized by others as unofficial groups. Workers may even seek transfers to jobs located in a favored unit, not because of the correspondence of technical skills and the demands of the job, but because "all my friends work there," or "they're a good bunch of fellows to work with."

Rate of pay, presence or absence of dirt, heat, noise, or similar "working conditions" undoubtedly affect the informal activities of workers. However, their status in the plant, the supervisory situation, and other social relationships are certainly not overlooked by the workman. Roethlisberger and Dickson found that the distinction between selector and connector wiremen had been given a spatial basis in the large department from which their observation group was drawn. Connector wiremen worked at the front of the department, with new men being started at the back of the room on selector equipments and gradually moving forward until shifted to the connectors.[3]

It is apparent that the precise significance of spatial adjacency for the relationships among employees cannot be predicted simply from knowledge of the physical layout; on the other hand, once social significance becomes attached to the location of workers, that becomes a fact of considerable importance in the attitudes of workers about their jobs.

Cliques—Formal and Informal Status. The ideas of the company about the relative worth of various official duties are ordinarily reflected in wage differentials, closeness or looseness of supervision, titles, and similar devices. Although these distinctions among employees are not irrelevant, they never account for all of the significant differences in social position recognized by employees, and may be offset or even reversed by other scales of valuation adopted by fellow workers. Informal symbols of status such as size of desks, privacy and size of offices, and individual listing of directories, prevalent in managerial circles, have their counterparts among shop

[3] *Op. cit.,* pp. 495–496.

and bench workers. In neither case do the informal symbols need to correspond to official positions.

We may distinguish two chief varieties of informal status in the development of leadership and deference among workers: that attaching to the position, but not officially recognized, and that attaching to the person, based upon particular qualities and achievements not germane to official demands. Examples of the former type can be found in almost any establishment, since the rating adopted by management will rarely correspond to the workers' sentiments about the relative skill demanded, the usefulness of the task, the compensations due for unpleasant working conditions, or the relative weight to be attached to any of these factors. We have already noted an example of this in the deference due to connector wiremen in the Western Electric study.

As in the case of private secretaries and some other clerical workers, an individual may enjoy a sort of "reflected status" because of close association with persons having an official or unofficial position of prestige. Roethlisberger and Dickson report that in the Bank Wiring Observation Room the solderman serving the high-prestige clique could assert his superiority over the solderman serving the inferior group.[4] Bosses' helpers and other carriers of communications, possibly including real or fictitious "inside information," may enjoy a deference far beyond that expected from their immediate skills or monetary reward.

In the examples just noted the prestige seems to attach to the position, although it is safe to say that personal characteristics of the person in that position may either enhance or reduce that prestige. Many individuals, however, will be accorded respect and deference by their fellows without much reference to their particular jobs. The qualities and achievements so recognized may be as diverse as the ways in which workmen differ, and will always depend on a constellation of on-the-job and off-the-job sentiments. The time is not far past when sheer physical dominance played a part in the relations among rough construction workers and in the "heavy industries." Even supervisory positions sometimes depended

[4] *Op. cit.*, pp. 496–498.

on the ability to trounce any man in the outfit rather than on superior training or greater technical skill. In the contemporary industrial plant the storyteller, the man who, by repute, has a way with the women or serves useful functions in the employees' relations with management is more likely to speak with authority or receive offers of assistance from his fellows. Even in very small groups "functional leadership" may be developed to the point of having one person who speaks for the group when dealing with supervisors, another who maintains the internal organization and routines, and possibly a third who thinks up practical jokes for the group to play on some rival clique. The person who thinks these distinctions are trivial should look more closely at the nature of social living.

Cliques—Internal and Community Distinctions. By no means all of the alignments and distinctions found in an industrial establishment are based simply on the work situation or behavior during the working day. Off-the-job attitudes and modes of association may be, and frequently are, carried over into the shops. The most obvious examples of this are to be found in the preservation of religious and ethnic demarcations in shop relationships. Not only is the American Negro thus practically restricted to special (and not very desirable) positions, and frequently barred from informal contact with white workers, but other groups may be given virtually the same treatment. Catholics are under a disadvantage in a Protestant community, and Protestants find their position unfavorable in a Catholic community. Immigrant groups of all sorts may be relegated to inferior informal status, and frequently barred from formal advancement as well. If management disregards the sentiments of workers and places an "inferior" person in a position presumably reserved for the elect, the presumptive social climber's position may be made uncomfortable or downright intolerable by various control devices available to his fellows—silence and shunning, verbal invective, practical "joking" which is scarcely good-humored, "framing" the individual to secure his dismissal, and other means too numerous to mention.

Incidentally, this type of distinction among workers places the sociological consultant in an extremely awkward position. As an expert in social structure, and particularly in those features of informal organization most likely to be overlooked, he may have to recommend taking ethnic or other distinctions into account in recruitment and supervision. It should be noted, however, that the fact of existing prejudice among workers may be taken into account without confirming or supporting it, through careful planning and joint action with labor leaders.[5]

Such distinctions as those holding between union and nonunion employees, or the continued exclusion of former strikers, or strikebreakers, from high-ranking informal groups long after the event are further indications of the breadth (and frequently the depth) of workers' sentiments and their overt manifestations. Groups of high school or college students working during the summer may form cliques of self-conscious exclusiveness, whereas the single student may be well advised to obscure his background.

To repeat, the criteria of membership and status in the informal organizations of workers are multitudinous, and although they fall into recurrent types, their specific form in any establishment is likely to be unique in some respects. Whether the newcomer is a supervisor or a sweep-up boy, he will not "know the ropes" until he has learned, and at least partially respects, the local rules about "who's who and what's what."

MANIFESTATIONS OF GROUP ACTIVITY

These cliques are somewhat more than merely honorary societies; nor are the distinctions merely casual and superficial. The whole point of the present discussion is that the informal organization makes a difference, and that the groupings genuinely result in *joint activity*. We may now turn to some of the ways in which the informal organization of workers shapes and determines the pattern of daily activities, and some of the more important functions which those activities serve.

[5] See Everett Cherrington Hughes, "The Knitting of Racial Groups in Industry," *American Sociological Review*, 11: 512–519, October 1946. See also Orvis Collins, "Ethnic Behavior in Industry: Sponsorship and Rejection in a New England Factory," *American Journal of Sociology*, 51: 293–298, January 1946.

"Initiation" Ceremonies. The stranger or newcomer is always the object of some suspicion and distrust, and is made to feel "out of things" until fully accepted or definitely rejected by those with whom he is thrown in contact. The informal industrial group is no exception to this general rule. A new worker may gain admittance to previously established relationships very gradually and without fanfare, or he may actually be "tested" by a more or less deliberate policy of initiation.

The newcomer may be given the poorest job assignment for his rank and classification (perhaps as an official policy) but find that he is also expected to render other services which the other workers claim are part of his assignment. The new recruit may find himself running errands, helping out other workers, or handling the poorest material until he gets "wised up" or can pass on the duties to a more recent recruit. Practical jokes of all kinds, especially the standard and favorite ones of the group, are tried on the "greenhorn." How he reacts to these impositions may well determine his future acceptability in the group.

A very frequent type of initiation ceremony functions to emphasize the greater knowledge and experience of the old hands. A new man in a lumber planing mill is sent after a board-stretcher, the new apprentice in a glass factory is told to secure a mold-stretcher from the stock room, and from time immemorial mechanics' helpers have been told to go and fetch a left-handed monkey wrench. In other cases some simple mechanism on a machine is "jimmied," and the new man is forced to call upon the services of the maintenance and repair crew. By all these ways and many others the outsider goes through tests for being a good fellow or "right guy," as well as for gradual acceptance as an occupational equal. The tests need have little or nothing to do with occupational skill, as in cases of insistence upon initiation into the the fine art of chewing tobacco or snuff, or the ability to use obscene language without visible discomfort. Although rarely stated in so many words, it is apparent that members of the informal group feel that their acceptance or rejection of a prospective member makes a difference—that acceptance confers advantages worth trying for.

Level and Pattern of Communication. The newcomer in the machine shop, factory, or section gang, or an inconspicuous observer of the behavior of workingmen, is likely to be impressed by two characteristics of the ordinary conversation: he is likely to find much of it incomprehensible, even though individual words sound like English, and he is likely to find profanity and obscenity coloring every sentence, even the most commonplace "small talk." Although technical terms and occupational argot (a specialized slang) have been commented on rather frequently by observers, the scarcely respectable tone of everyday factory or roundhouse speech has received scant attention. Both may be regarded as manifestations of informal organization.

Every occupation reserves to itself the right to invent or accumulate a technical vocabulary for common objects, processes, or situations in that occupation. Obviously the learned professions and the older crafts have a more richly developed vocabulary of this sort than newer types of specialization. Part of this technical language refers to objects and processes for which there are no other names —a truly technical vocabulary. Other words and phrases are in the nature of substitutions for ordinary methods of expression, and constitute an occupational argot. To a certain extent the argot also serves "technical" ends, since its meaning is likely to be more precise, and often the mode of expression is briefer, than the ordinary language of the layman in reference to the same objects or actions. But the additional function of specialized vocabularies in serving as identification of group members and exclusion of the uninitiated should not be overlooked. This seems to be characteristic of any group where occupational role is sufficiently important to occasion "talking shop." An industrial group that has no such idiom tends to develop one, perhaps of purely local significance. Old and highly mobile crafts like those of the railroader have developed occupational argot to a high degree.[6]

---

[6] See Cottrell, *op. cit.*, especially Chap. VII, "Railroad Language," and "Glossary." No disrespect for railroaders is implied by the observation that professional criminals also satisfy the criteria of carrying on "crafts" of long standing and involving considerable mobility, and have a highly developed

The qualification of almost every noun by blasphemous or obscene words in many shop and factory situations is undoubtedly to be accounted for in part simply as a special variety of occupational language. Yet its appearance is not confined to a narrow range of occupations, but rather seems to be typical in varying degrees of the entire class of industrial laborers. Perhaps because squeamish investigators have thought the subject unworthy of their attention, the circumstances in which the use of four-letter Anglo-Saxon words is common and the reasons for their virtual nonappearance among other groups are not fully understood. Certain observations may, however, be hazarded. (1) Such levels of discourse are most evident in unisexual groups, and most especially among men, although blasphemy and some verbal nastiness is not unusual among factory women. A heterosexual situation seems to induce more nearly "normal" speech, with perhaps greater emphasis on the risqué joke. (2) Strong language is also closely associated with lower income groups, highly mobile occupations, and other departures from "middle class" expectations. To a certain extent, therefore, it may simply reflect differences in class standards of (verbal) morality. (3) Verbal invective and filth also seem, at least in some cases, to be defiant forms of expression of individuality (note the virtuoso who claims to have the best cursing vocabulary for miles around) and may therefore be associated with lack of interest in and esteem for occupation. This is very nearly the same as suggesting that aggression against the prescribed moral vocabulary of the community may be the product of frustration of more socially approved methods of gaining attention.[7] In what combination of these or other

argot. See Edwin H. Sutherland, ed., *The Professional Thief, by a Professional Thief* (Chicago: University of Chicago Press, 1937), especially "Glossary."

[7] This is the suggestion of Whiting Williams, one of the few first-hand observers of industrial labor who has made any effort to account for, or even to notice, the linguistic sins of the "proletariat." See his *What's on the Worker's Mind* (New York: Charles Scribner's Sons, 1920), especially pp. 193, 274–275. Williams also notes the tendency for "improper" language to be considered as a symbol of membership in informal groups. (See also *ibid.*, p. 247.) It is perhaps instructive to note that various branches of the armed forces, particularly noncommissioned ranks of the army and apparently most ranks of the navy and marine corps, indulge in language ranging from the "salty" to the completely obscene. Although the factors suggested in explanation of the language

circumstances the explanation of the origin of the linguistic pungency of industrial workers is to be found, it is difficult or impossible to say. For any given workman, the problem may be less complex: he conforms to group-imposed standards in this as in other modes of social behavior.

Not only does the conversational pattern of workers differ from the ordinary standards of the community in *form,* but it is also significantly different in *content.* Aside from necessary communication demanded of technical relationships and some tendency to "talk shop" (more noticeable with the skilled than with the unskilled except for "gripes" and complaints), the two most common topics of conversation are sports and sex. This should perhaps be qualified as applying chiefly to male workers, since employed women seem more concerned with clothes and "gossip." The latter, however, is likely to include, perhaps prominently, sexual irregularities.

Now to a certain extent these conversational topics simply reflect sexual distinctions in adult roles and interests, and for either sex may represent the "least common denominator" of subjects interesting to persons of different backgrounds. It is noteworthy that these topics of conversation pervade all ranks in the industrial organization. This would still not account either for the vocabulary used or for the range of stories and jokes told among the men. By numerous reports, the preoccupation with sex is not confined to the fairly standard lot of "smoking car" stories, but extends to discussion of personal sexual interests and relationships, even including marital relationships—a subject completely taboo even in so-called "enlightened" sections of the rest of the community. Although the explanation for this characteristic of informal group activity is by no means clear, there is some reason for believing that it may be related to lack of other bases for personal distinction or "the poverty of social existence." [8] It is certainly true that, with persons occupying higher positions, the pattern of communication shows more

---

of factory workers undoubtedly operate here also, probably in differing relative significance, the factor of release of tensions in dangerous circumstances is also to be suggested.

[8] This is the suggestion of Williams, *op. cit.,* pp. 303–305, who also attaches some importance to fatigue and general dissatisfaction with working conditions.

sophistication, and ordinarily a broadening of content. This does not mean, of course, that the relationship between job assignment and level of informal communication is a direct one, since it may depend upon prevalent standards of acceptability over which particular individuals may have little control.

Recreational Activities. Many activities of informal groups take the form of change of pace, or adding fun to the work situation. Indeed, much of the conversation and storytelling is of a recreational character, having nothing to do with the formal demands of the job. It seems evident from our previous discussion of the problem of monotony and fatigue (Chapter IX) that workers cannot and will not be single minded in their devotion to technical duty unless that duty carries with it sufficient breadth of activity to ensure satisfactory social relationships. It is an old wheeze, but probably a valid one, that work is most satisfactory from the worker's viewpoint if it includes elements of play. It is not surprising, therefore, to find that the informal organization of workers provides outlets of playful tendencies, even if those activities are directly contrary to the demands of the formal organization.

But the recreational activities of informal associations do not simply provide a release from boredom and dissatisfaction. The activities are not simply random and haphazard, or purely individual inventions. They are preeminently *group* activities, and serve group ends as well as the release of individual tensions. Nowhere is this more evident than in the common occurrence of "horseplay."

A brief and casual observation of workers at play in mills and shops, during both work periods and rest periods, might give the impression that "rough stuff," tricks, and general "horsing around" appear quite spontaneously and unpredictably. Yet more careful study will ordinarily reveal patterns even in these activities. For example, we have already noted that the newcomer in the group is made the butt of practical jokes. At least part of those same tricks were used on other initiates before him, and will be used on others who come after him. As in a lodge initiation, some of the stunts are traditional with the group. This does not mean that individual inventiveness is stifled, but variations or additions must ordinarily receive the approval of the group before they are tried. To a large extent, therefore, the members of the informal group are *controlled* quite as much as the person against whom the jokes are directed. The participant, however, has the impression of spontaneity.

In some instances the "horseplay" takes the form of a standard custom, with every member of the group being equally subject to playful attack by the others. In others, however, particular persons are considered the appropriate recipients of the playful attentions of the group, either because of their subservient position (which is also the case with the temporary inferiority of the newcomer) or because of personal characteristics. Roethlisberger and Dickson report that the trucker serving the observation group of wiremen and soldermen was harassed continually by the latter, and this had nothing to do with particular personalities. A second trucker who replaced the first was treated in the same way.[9] In a glass factory an observer noted that the "spare boy" (a young apprentice and handyman) and "sweep-up boys" (who were called "boys" regardless of age) were subjected to "ribbing" and tricks of various sorts. If the spare boy on the night shift was caught sleeping he was doused with water.[10]

Some employees are made the butt of jokes and tricks without particular regard to their position, or at least the "treatment" is modified to fit the particular case. In the glass factory just mentioned one sweep-up boy in particular was judged by the observer as "moronic," and fell for the same tricks and practical jokes repeatedly. Other cases may range from near-cruelty directed against an unacceptable person, to what looks like a peculiar variety of deference toward the inveterate "good sport."

A variant of the customary horseplay is more directly a control device: inflicting a standard form of punishment for offenses against the customs of the group, or as a penalty for personal affront. Among the Western Electric workers the observers noted the use of "binging" (a hard blow on the muscle of the upper arm) as such a con-

[9] *Op. cit.*, p. 498.
[10] The writer's informant is James Lewis, a former student at The Pennsylvania State College, 1941.

trol mechanism.[11] Similar practices are probably more general than available evidence indicates.

Whether the object of horseplay is seemingly only that of spontaneous recreation, or is more directly used as a status-enforcing and control device, it is apparently an expression of joint activity—an attribute of membership in the informal groupings of industrial employees.

Another very common form of informal recreational activity among workers is *gambling*. The range of gambling activities to be found may include card playing, placing bets on horse races, forming betting pools on the outcome of sports events or the serial numbers on pay checks, lagging coins, and so on. Contrary to the reputation of the army on payday, the amounts of money involved are ordinarily not large. The main criteria seem to be that an element of chance be involved and that those included in such games be from the same cliques.[12] It is quite possible that the interest in gambling has a significance beyond that of simply joint activity; for example, it may represent a release from humdrum activities and daily routine of the official job assignment, where decision and chance are largely the prerogatives of management. In any event, it is clear that this is another evidence of the "spontaneous" activities of informal associations, and that these activities modify and direct the behavior of the individual workman.

In work situations where a "no-smoking" rule prevails in the interests of safety, cleanliness, or simply managerial whim, a common form of "unofficial" behavior is *wash-room smoking*. It is rare for the official rule to be modified by an official exception of the wash room or other places "out of bounds," yet the testimony of observers is uniform that such exceptions exist. This, of course, is almost inevitably with the unofficial sanction of supervisors.

Informal organization, as our examples show, is not simply a device for preserving and enforcing standards of conduct over and above (or even contrary to) the official demands of job assignments,

---

[11] Roethlisberger and Dickson, *op. cit.*, pp. 421–423, 500–502.

[12] *Ibid.*, pp. 500–502. The writer's own experiences and the information given by former students bear out these observations.

but also gives at least the subjective impression of liberty and spontaneity of individual behavior. With this background we may now turn to a more direct consideration of the junction of formal and informal organizational demands upon the workman, and the significance of these for the position of the laborer in industrial establishments.

INFORMAL *versus* FORMAL EXPECTATIONS

Little further need be said of the official expectations concerning the orientation of the workman to his job. We have already dealt with the "organizational assumptions of management" in some detail in Chapter VII, and need only translate those assumptions into terms of the expected role of the workingman in cooperative industrial enterprise.[13] Briefly, the laborer's role is expected to be *a strict devotion to technical duty* (for example, sweep-up boy), *mediated by a competitive orientation toward reward and advancement*. Together, these assumptions presumably define the worker's position in the organization and the direction of his interests. It follows that the formation of cliques, the determination of position on nontechnical grounds, the addition or substitution of duties applying to the position or to the person, and the modification or subversion of competitive orientation constitute the "unexpected" results of informal organization.

The discussion of informal organization to this point has been largely concerned with practices that violate the first assumption just noted; that is, they indicate that the activities and relationships of the workman are not limited to those demanded of his formal

---

[13] The phrase "cooperative industrial enterprise" may seem at first glance to refer only to a peculiar and rare type of industrial establishment: one "owned," managed, and possibly completely staffed by a group of co-acting equals. It is unfortunate for the understanding of industrial organization that competitive and conflicting interests have been so much emphasized that the cooperative character of the whole has been neglected. Viewed as a whole, any industrial establishment is comprised of a number of persons performing differentiated tasks toward the achievement of the ends of the organization. The individual ends and motives that induce people to cooperate are not unimportant in general, and certainly influence the effectiveness of the organization, but differences and antipathies in individual ends do not change the cooperative character of the whole.

position. Put somewhat differently, they represent the intrusion of other personal and social considerations into an officially limited and segmental cooperative arrangement. But the two assumptions are not discrete variables; rather, they are two aspects of the same thing. Thus, any departure from a strict and exclusive devotion to technical duty must of necessity imply that the direction of the worker's interests is more extensive than an interest in organizational reward and advancement, and may not even include the official orientation. Indeed, the whole of informal organization seems to imply a substitution of group ends for competitive individual ends. *This does not necessarily mean that the general ends of the formal organization are not being served; it does imply that the means to those ends are not those formally assumed, but are on the contrary those consistent with the activities and security of the informal group.* Whether or not the substitution adversely affects the achievement of the cooperative goals of the entire organization will depend on the particular circumstances. We have already discussed the primary considerations with reference to the problems of management. They may be summarized as the extent to which managers recognize the abstractness and consequent inadequacy of the formal system as a cooperative arrangement.

With these considerations in mind, we may review some of the expectations of the informal organization and note their consistency or inconsistency with the over-all ends of the industrial establishment.

Expectations of Informal Groups. To the extent that informal groups exist at all, they modify the behavior of their members along the lines of common interest and joint activity. This is by definition: otherwise, no group exists. In industrial organization, at least part of the rules of behavior determined by informal associations are directed toward group and personal security. On the basis of the Western Electric study Roethlisberger and Dickson concluded that there were four general rules operating:

(1) You should not turn out too much work. If you do, you are a "rate buster."

(2) You should not turn out too little work. If you do, you are a "chiseler."

(3) You should not tell a supervisor anything that will react to the detriment of an associate. If you do, you are a "squealer."

(4) You should not attempt to maintain social distance or act officious. If you are an inspector, for example, you should not act like one.[14]

Although these rules are phrased in terms of a situation involving a group piece-work payment system, and omit consideration of rules relative to recreational activities, conversational patterns, and initiation practices, they are undoubtedly of general validity with respect to the informal limitations on competition and authority.

Limitation of Output. The limitation on output, to which the Western Electric researchers paid a great deal of attention, is of course very common in industrial plants. On straight time payment plans, the limitation may be "justified" as a device for spreading the job out over a longer time or larger number of workmen, or simply as a way of maintaining a comfortable and congenial pace. Under a piece-rate system, its explanation is more difficult to find, except as a way of avoiding reduction of the rate of pay. This was the most common explanation given by the workmen in the Hawthorne plant and explains the epithet *rate buster.* Yet the investigators found a confusing welter of opinions and explanations, no factual evidence that rates had been cut in the past, and no evidence of a logical appraisal of the work situation. In fact, Roethlisberger and Dickson think it preferable not to call the action a "restriction," since its function and apparent aim was not a deliberate violation of official expectations of competition, but rather a manifestation of group concern for social (not simply economic) security.[15] Complete and constant attention to the job as narrowly defined, even if proportionally rewarded in wages, would prevent many activities and relationships that are important parts of the job as viewed by the workman. An additional factor of significance is the way in which primary or exclusive concern for competitive performance is not only destructive of informal group morale, but *may actually subvert the general ends of the cooperative system by destroying the basis of*

---

[14] *Op. cit.,* p. 522. Reprinted by permission of Harvard University Press.

[15] *Ibid.,* Chap. XVIII, "The Output Situation in the Bank Wiring Observation Room," and pp. 531–537.

joint activity. The line between trying to outdo the other fellow in "legitimate" competition and trying to outdo him in any event is really very thin. The latter attitude tends to be produced by an extreme emphasis on official expectations and is destructive of the bases for general cooperation toward the goals of the organized system.[16] To interpret the limitations imposed by informal organization as uniformly unnecessary and "illegitimate" is to overlook the "limits to the elaboration of efficiency," discussed in Chapters VII and VIII.

Prevention of "Sabotage." Sabotage, in Veblen's sense of "conscientious withdrawal of efficiency," will be prevented by the informal group whenever the failure of some workman to do his duty overburdens his fellows or injures their position in some other way. This does not mean that an occasional lapse will not be forgiven, and certainly not that an unintentional failure will be condemned. But the "chiseler" is inimical to the standards of fairness in the group. To the extent that official duties are incompletely specified, the informal prevention of "chiseling" may be the only safeguard the organization has against minimal, letter-of-the-law performance.

Condemnation of "Squealing and Officiousness." A rule clearly designed as a security measure is the very general practice of condemning the "tattler," "stool pigeon," or "squealer" as he is variously called. But the "no-squealing" rule is not simply a device for protecting individuals from supervisory discipline; it is a mark of loyalty to the informal group. Since all of the activities and relationships of the informal organization of workmen are "unexpected" in terms of the formal organization, and many of them are likely to be clearly contrary to official rules, the "squealer" endangers the whole fabric of customary practices. Carrying tales also implies or accentuates

---

[16] An exceptionally clear-cut case of an overcompetitive situation has been reported by William A. MacIntyre, Jr., "Technical versus Informal Organization in a Soda Fountain Group" (unpublished Honors Thesis in Sociology, Harvard University, 1940). This study compares the general effectiveness (not "efficiency") of a small business organization under a situation of contravention of formal expectations and under a situation of strict adherence to formal duties. The former was far superior.

the hostility of immediate supervisors to the informal organization. Although the official (and in some cases the actual) policy of the management may be to search out and eliminate every violation of company rules, the first-line supervisor, we have noted, can scarcely adopt such a policy and maintain his effectiveness. When the supervisor avoids officiousness and thereby becomes part of the informal group, the "squealer" may be at least as obnoxious to him as to fellow workmen.[17]

Both the condemnation of "squealing" and the disapproval of officiousness violate the ordinary managerial assumptions about obedience to rules and the exercise of supervisory authority. Yet again it may well be doubted that these informal expectations are genuinely antithetical to the stability or effectiveness of a complex cooperative system. In fact, the informal structure of working relationships *may* contribute as much or more to the achievement of organizational objectives as attempted strict compliance with the formal demands. In view of the certainty of some form of informal organization among industrial laborers, the alternative is false anyway. The worker certainly has as great an interest in the preservation of his personally satisfactory activities as does the junior administrator. And both are equally likely to become rebellious or neurotic if these are changed in the interests of Efficiency or some other impersonal and pagan god.

The informal organization ensures the individual workmen against the loss of his personality in an impersonal system; it also ensures the group of workmen against attack from within or without. Seemingly spontaneous, it has however form and substance. It is, in fact, within the unofficial structure that one may find the major elements of the workers' social environment on the job.

---

[17] A complaint to a supervisor (or any person in authority) about a violation of rule places that person in the frequently uncomfortable position of having to take action or openly admitting and condoning the violation. Only the most naive person can believe that widespread and consistent violations of rules are not known to the persons responsible for their enforcement. However, the violations may not "officially" come to their attention and thus require no action. If complete conformity is impossible to secure, or can only be secured at too great a cost (not necessarily economic), an "institutionalized evasion" passively permitted by the authorities is in order.

REFERENCES

BARNARD, CHESTER I., *The Functions of the Executive* (Cambridge: Harvard University Press, 1938), Chap. IX, "Informal Organizations and Their Relation to Formal Organizations."

COLLINS, ORVIS, "Ethnic Behavior in Industry: Sponsorship and Rejection in a New England Factory," *American Journal of Sociology,* 51: 293–298, January 1946.

COTTRELL, W. FRED, *The Railroader* (Stanford Univ., Calif.: Stanford University Press, 1940). Entire book is pertinent.

DONOVAN, FRANCES R., *The Saleslady* (Chicago: University of Chicago Press, 1929).

DURKHEIM, EMILE, *On the Division of Labor in Society,* tr. by George Simpson (New York: The Macmillan Company, 1933), Preface to the Second Edition, "Some Notes on Occupational Groups."

FIREY, WALTER, "Informal Organization and the Theory of Schism," *American Sociological Review,* 13: 15–24, February 1948.

HUGHES, EVERETT CHERRINGTON, "The Knitting of Racial Groups in Industry," *American Sociological Review,* 11: 512–519, October 1946.

KOENIG, SAMUEL, "Ethnic Groups in Connecticut Industry," *Social Forces,* 20: 96–105, October 1941.

MILLER, DELBERT C., "The Social Factors of the Work Situation," *American Sociological Review,* 11: 300–314, June 1946.

MYERS, RICHARD R., "Myth and Status Systems in Industry," *Social Forces,* 26: 331–337, March 1948.

RODNICK, DAVID, "Status Values Among Railroadmen," *Social Forces,* 20: 89–96, October 1941.

ROETHLISBERGER, F. J., *Management and Morale* (Cambridge: Harvard University Press, 1941), Chap. II, "The Road Back to Sanity," and Chap. IV, "The Social Structure of Industry."

ROETHLISBERGER, F. J., and WILLIAM J. DICKSON, *Management and the Worker* (Cambridge: Harvard University Press, 1939), Chap. VII, "The Test Room Operators; Their Individual Differences and Interpersonal Relations"; Part IV (Chaps. XVII–XXIII), "Social Organization of Employees."

WHITEHEAD, THOMAS N., *The Industrial Worker* (Cambridge: Harvard University Press, 1938, 2 vols.), Vol. I, Chap. 18, "Organization of Social Activity for Its Own Sake," and Chap. 27, "The Organization of the Relay Test Group."

———, *Leadership in a Free Society* (Cambridge: Harvard University Press, 1937), Chap. III, "The Relay Test Group"; Chap. IV, "The Meaning of Social Integration"; and pp. 95–98.

WHYTE, WILLIAM FOOTE, *Human Relations in the Restaurant Industry* (New York: McGraw-Hill Book Company, Inc., 1948).

WILLIAMS, WHITING, *Mainsprings of Men* (New York: Charles Scribner's Sons, 1925) Chap. III, "His Working Conditions," and Chap. VII, "The Mainspring: the Wish for Worth."

———, *What's on the Worker's Mind* (New York: Charles Scribner's Sons, 1920).

CHAPTER XIII

UNION ORGANIZATION

In the American economy, labor unions have been an intrinsic part of industrial organization for so short a time that the phenomenon still has some capacity for shock. Despite a fairly long history of trade unionism in various skilled crafts—including some craftsmen in manufacturing plants—the union as a typical aspect of the conduct of industrial operations was barely established prior to World War II. The growth of union membership *and influence in daily operations* has been so recent and rapid, and marked by so much heated controversy with management, that even yet the role of the union as part of the internal organization of industrial units is not widely recognized.

The American experience with unionism is in some respects unique. Although workers' organizations have widely differing powers and concrete functions in other industrial countries, the United States is the only major industrial country in which such organizations were successfully excluded from major parts of the industrial system until recent years. For this historical development there are a number of related explanations, which will be discussed in later chapters. They may be summed up here as the ideology of individualism, which despite the inherently organized, and even mass-organized, character of industrial production was represented not only in the law but to a remarkable degree also in popular sentiment.

Because of the peculiar and peculiarly recent development of American collective bargaining and management-union relations, unions may be viewed in two seemingly contradictory ways. By selecting cases and aspects of cases, unions may be viewed both as intrusive, outside, hostile organizations and as intrinsic parts of modern industrial organization. The latter view is perforce recent and not yet widely accepted.

This chapter deals with union structure, purposes, and functions, except as these relate directly to the conduct of management-labor relations. This may seem an artificial distinction, as it is, but the separation is useful. For with the increasing size, power, and security of American labor unions, the strike or the negotiating session falls far short of encompassing all of the important organizational features of the unions. The union, in a far more fundamental sense than management, exists *for* bargaining, in the present American institutional setting. But it also serves other ends, and uses other means for their attainment. Much of the union structure is the direct result of management-labor relations, much more the indirect result of this primary historic and contemporary rationale for the union's existence. Collective bargaining and the legislation and rulings of governmental administrative agencies that relate to collective bargaining have a major influence on the size, jurisdiction, and even internal powers of unions. It will, however, be useful to examine the formal structure of unions and their confederations, the translation of this structure in operating procedures at the shop level, and the aims and functions of unions as service agencies for their members.

THE STRUCTURE OF UNIONS

Both because of the actual diversity of union aims and functions, and because of the variable impact of industrial conditions and society at large, union organization is far from standardized. Contemporary unions may still reflect the peculiar historic circumstances of their founding, the whims of a leader long departed, and also the very present internal factions or threat provided by a rival union.

Moreover, union organization has received far less study either by the unions themselves or by students of organization than has management, and virtually no "expertizing" by organizational specialists such as those who operate as managerial consultants, write books both technical and uplifting ("How To Be a Better Manager"), and teach countless courses in the colleges and universities. Aside from the recency and rapidity with which unions have become large and important structures in the industrial system, there are several other considerations that account for the neglect of union organization as a topic of study. With regard to the "experts" in organization, whether professional consultants or members of university faculties, there have been both financial and ideological links to the business and industrial managers, virtually none to the labor leaders. Managers have had both the funds and the disposition to seek and use technical advice, and to an increasing degree industrial managers are themselves college trained. Unions have lacked not only the funds for use of consultants or hiring staff specialists, but perhaps more importantly have had few contacts with the academic and professional communities and slight disposition to trust anyone not definitely a part of the "labor movement." For this distrust there has been a very considerable justification in view of the traditional American hostility to unionism, but the effect has been two-edged—the unions have not developed standardized principles of organization appropriate to their aims and problems, and the actual internal practices and policies of unions are very inadequately known by students of industrial relations.[1] Recent establishment of workers' education programs and of industrial relations research and instructional centers in a number of universities may be expected to improve the state of knowledge about unions, whatever the effect on the unions themselves.

Almost by definition the "official" structure of unions is more easily accessible than is the translation and modification of that structure under conditions of actual operation. It is to the official order that we may first direct our attention, and subsequently to what we know or may reasonably guess about operations.

[1] Secrecy and resistance to objective study are by no means peculiar traits of unions, as many social scientists seeking to study corporate records and policies can testify. Any organization will resist observation, and particularly publication of results, if it fears damage to internal morale or possible aid to rivals.

The Union as a Representative Government. The form of American union organization is typically that of a voluntary association, with sufficient common interests of members to justify their membership and with democratic modes of selecting leaders and representatives for carrying on the association's activities. The terms of office of leaders, their powers and responsibilities, as well as the powers reserved to the membership meeting, are determined by constitutions and by-laws, as well as by custom and precedent. The "actual" democracy of unions is a matter of much discussion, both within the unions and in circles in various degrees friendly or hostile to unionism, but of formal democracy there is a great deal in American trade unions.

Although there are a variety of exceptions, the typical union member belongs to an organization which regularly operates at three levels: (1) the union "local," in which the member presumably acts as a participant in a direct democracy through the membership meeting as well as a participant in the non-governmental aspects of union activity, (2) the national or "international" (the latter usually, although not necessarily, implying Canadian or possibly Latin American affiliates), and (3) the confederation of national unions (the American Federation of Labor or the Congress of Industrial Organizations).

Some notable exceptions to this typical structure require brief comment. There are, in addition to unions affiliated with the AFL or CIO a number of "independent unions." Now an "independent union" may be a purely local affair, limited to a particular shop or locality. Most independent unions, however, have the local and national levels of organization, lacking only affiliation with one of the two confederations. The railroad brotherhoods are the most widely known independent unions, but there are also other powerful unions not members of the AFL or CIO. The International Association of Machinists, for example, occupies a strategic position in several capital goods industries and in a number of other industries as well. Some unions have been organized as independents and have subsequently affiliated with a confederation—e.g., the Communications Workers of America, CIO. Other unions have been expelled from the confederations on policy issues, such as the United Electrical Workers and many smaller unions expelled from the CIO on charges of following the Communist line. One important national union, the United Mine Workers, was an important constituent of the AFL prior to the formation in 1935 of the Committee for Industrial Organization (which became in 1938 the Congress of Industrial Organizations). The president of the UMW, John L. Lewis, was a leading agent in the formation of the CIO, but the UMW again became independent in 1940 over the issue of support of the Roosevelt National administration, which Lewis did not favor. In 1946 the UMW again affiliated with the AFL, only to "disaffiliate" again in 1947.

Within the confederations there are some exceptions to the typical three-level organization and some modifications for particular purposes. In both AFL and CIO there are some directly chartered locals in occupations or industries where for one reason or another national membership is small. Particularly in the CIO there are, from time to time, also units affiliated with the parent body only through "organizing committees." Several of the most powerful CIO affiliates, including the steel and textile unions, started as "organizing committees," having been constituted as chartered national unions with locals only after the success of the organizing drive. Both the AFL and CIO have a partial territorial subdivision as well as functional constituents, through state and city Federations (AFL) or Councils (CIO). For the most part these geographical subdivisions do not figure in collective bargaining or most other union activities except local political action and policy. National unions often have regional directors representing a coordinating stage between the local and national levels.

Typically, therefore, a worker is a member of the AFL or CIO and of a national union by virtue of his membership in a particular local, although he may secure his transfer from one local to another in the same union. So fundamental is this principle of local membership that most line and staff officers of national unions and the big confederations are members of a particular constituent local. Since the local is the basic membership unit, it is at this level that policies

with regard to membership and jurisdiction, settlement of grievances, and most union "services" are translated into operating procedures.

One of the most difficult problems of union organization is the
basic one of membership criteria. The problem appears in many
guises—the question of jurisdiction as between rival unions, the
question of the "closed" shop or union security provisions with the
corresponding requirement of membership, and the question of
exclusion of certain groups such as Negroes on grounds irrelevant to
the professed jurisdictional claims of the union.

The classic jurisdictional debate is that between rival principles
of union membership, commonly called "craft" and "industrial"
types of organization. Until the second half of the 1930's the predominant form of union organization was the "craft" unit comprising
persons of similar skills. In an environment essentially hostile to
independent unionism, the occupation of a strategic position in the
productive process was an important and often essential aspect of
union strength.

The strength of the local or national craft union lies chiefly in its
monopoly of some skill, and the ability through joint action to bargain collectively with employers requiring skilled laborers of the
type represented by the union. On this basis some of the craft unions
affiliated with the AFL, as well as the independent Railroad Brotherhoods, have had some measure of success. On the other hand, this
type of organization holds little promise for the "unskilled" or mass-
production worker, nor is it well adapted to the fairly rapidly changing organization and technology of industry. Of the former difficulty we shall have more to say presently, but the latter difficulty
spells internal trouble for federations of craft unions. It is understandable that a given union will want to represent as many workers
as possible, not only for dues payable but also for support in collective bargaining. But the character of expansion and modification
of labor skills raises questions concerning the jurisdiction of the
traditional crafts. Perhaps the classic example of this is the controversy over the affiliation of tin roofers, who are claimed by carpen-
ters and metalworkers. Such jurisdictional problems seem to mul-

tiply endlessly in modern industry, partly because of the rather unspecific character of the charters granted to potentially rival unions.

The "industrial" principle of organization rests not on particular occupations but on major industrial specialties, that is, principally products. Its outstanding advantage stems from its inclusive criteria of membership, which brought unions to large numbers of employees in manufacturing, and the correlative principle of matching the jurisdiction of the employer.

Neither the craft nor industrial basis of union organization is as clear as some arguments about their characteristics imply. Most craft unions do, in fact, include persons of somewhat different occupation, and many industrial unions experience difficulty in defining the boundaries of an industry in view of multi-product companies, industries whose products are components in other industries, and many other problems. Although the AFL is commonly regarded as espousing craft unionism and the CIO as uniting industrial unions, both organizations actually use both principles in various mixtures and combinations.

On the craft *vs.* industrial principle of union jurisdiction, the actual union membership and structure is more likely to be affected by bargaining advantage than by preference for abstract principles.

Rival unionism does not end with the way craft and industrial principles cut across one another or by the overlapping jurisdictions of craft unions. Other instances of disputed jurisdiction or competition for membership are likely to arise from "dual" unionism, that is, two or more organizations with similar jurisdictional claims but with dissimilar ideologies or affiliations. Thus an AFL and a CIO affiliate may compete for members on exactly the same membership criteria, whether craft or industrial. District 50 of the United Mine Workers has recruited members without regard to either craft or industry. Some of the unions expelled from the CIO for Communist domination were immediately faced with new unions set up within the confederation in order to win back the non-Communist rank and file membership. Indeed, many organizational characteristics and policies of American unions are now to be understood in terms of rival unionism rather than management-union rivalry.

Another much debated aspect of union membership is the somewhat "involuntary" union membership implied in the "closed shop" or other union-security devices. As an organizational principle union security has both positive and negative potentialities. On the one hand, union security not only provides the union with assured financial support from those benefiting from union activities but also with an assured membership against managerial policies designed to weaken the union, rival unions, or the simple but important attrition of interest that any voluntary association must face. On the other hand, the closed or union shop is likely to bring in reluctant members who regard union dues as a tax and union membership as something to be taken as lightly as possible. This attitude is not helpful to the union as a conflict group or to unionism as a "social movement."

At the opposite pole from involuntary inclusion of members, although sometimes paradoxically in conjunction with it, is the policy of exclusion of persons from membership. The paradoxical combination occurs when the closed shop is supplemented by the closed union, so that persons otherwise eligible for employment are barred by the restrictive policy of the union. This organizational principle is commonly designed to supplement monopoly of skill with limitation of supply in order to protect or enhance the earnings of those already in the union. However, if a union that excludes Negroes from membership on grounds of racial discrimination also achieves a closed shop, the effect is to deny employment as well as membership to the excluded group. Many unions continue to exclude Negro workers, either by rule or by custom, but many of the newer industrial unions have consistently emphasized non-discrimination, often without support or enthusiasm at the local level.

The union local is a self-governing body, both within the terms prescribed in its charter and in the constitution and rules of the national union. Local union officers are elected by membership vote and accountable to the electorate, but also to the parent body for carrying on union activities in a way consistent with national union rules and policies. This dual accountability is subject to the difficulties inherent in any federal political system. Local pressure may bring union officials into conflict with national union policy. Although often discussed in terms of the degree of union democracy, that is not in fact the essential issue. National policy may be determined by the perfectly democratic procedure of majority rule within a constitutional framework, and yet not meet the approval of a local unit. Thus the essential issue is the degree of *local* self-government as opposed to self-government by a more inclusive electorate. Clearly any solution to this problem of the powers and responsibilities of the local unit and its leadership depends upon specification of the *level* in the representative government where various decisions are made and activities carried out. There is no common pattern among American unions concerning the degree or sphere of local autonomy, but there is a notable tendency in this, as in other aspects of modern life, to increase the powers of the central agency. This tendency is especially the result of the developing character of management-union relations, discussed in Part Five.

The national or international union is in form a government responsible to a representative legislature (the convention), in which locals are represented according to dues-paying membership. There are many variations around this pattern, however, including devices for giving minimal representation to certain affiliates in order to preserve the powerful position of others. Manipulation of the franchise is thus one of the "legal" means for achieving undemocratic representation and control. The financial support of the national union derives from a share of initiation fees and from a continuous "head tax" on the membership in the form of a share of union dues.

Except for unions with some very large and prosperous locals, it is at the national level that most union staff functions become an important part of the structure. Unions differ widely in their development of specialized staff functions and officers. Some of the principal issues in this connection will be discussed below with reference to problems of union bureaucracy. At this point two observations are in order. (1) The extent and type of staff specialization will primarily depend upon (a) the union's understanding of its principal aims and functions, its "services" to the local unit or the membership at large, and (b) its relations with other organized or unorganized "interests," including management, organs of government, and the general public. (2) Depending to a large degree upon the character of management-union relations, national officers may be entirely "staff" in that they advise but do not direct local officials, or include genuine "line" officers whose decisions are binding at the local level; the latter is by far more common, as is consistent with the federal principles of organization already discussed.

The confederation (AFL or CIO) may be viewed as standing to the national union as the latter does to the local. However, the confederation has fewer officers elected at this level by the representative convention as a governing body. With the exception of the president and secretary-treasurer, executive committees are composed of the officials of all (CIO) or part (AFL) of the constituent national unions. In fact, union federalism as a governmental structure stops at the national level, the confederation having no direct authority except that of controlling affiliation. The officers of the confederation are therefore solely in an advisory position except with regard to their own national unions. However, additional staff functions of relevance to the confederation as a whole or to its membership without regard to particular union affiliation are organized at the confederation level.

The Union at the Shop Level. Much of the preceding discussion of union government could, with a change of names and terms, be taken as describing many other large associations—for example, a religious denomination or a fraternal organization. The difference lies for the most part not in the general form of organization but in the particular ends that organization is designed to serve, in the particular ways activities are carried out, and, most importantly, in the criteria of membership.

The simplest key to an understanding of the union as both a distinct association and as a *part* of industrial organization is the nature of union membership. A union member is such by virtue of his participation in productive organization. As union membership remains in the United States to a considerable extent voluntary, not all persons even at the rank-and-file level in productive organizations belong to unions. But, with the exception of full-time officers and those for one reason or another not employed at their usual occupations, union members are producers of goods and service in the economic system. There may be a certain degree of probability that a member of a religious denomination will have a particular political affiliation, belong to certain types of clubs, and that he or the bread-winner of the family will have a certain level of income or broad type of employment. The relationship, however, is not in the same sense intrinsic as that between the union and the industrial organization.

At the shop level, the union is intrinsic to industrial organization by virtue of its membership and by virtue of its operation as a part of the system of industrial government. This point will be discussed in subsequent chapters as an aspect of management-union relations. In the present context it is important to note that whatever the level at which collective bargaining takes place the daily life of the worker is affected by the way agreements are translated into daily relations with supervisors and with union officials.

Two union officials not yet discussed are the "business agent" and the "shop steward." These officials carry on much the same function and within any particular union structure the offices tend to be mutually exclusive. The titles are in fact somewhat interchangeable, but a structural distinction can still be drawn regardless of titles.

The "business agent" is ordinarily a full-time official of the union who moves from one work unit to another to check on compliance with collective agreements and take up workers' grievances through the established machinery or on a more informal basis. In a very real sense he is the representative of the union *to the worker* as well as to management.

The "shop steward" is ordinarily a regular employee in the work unit, elected by his fellow union members to represent them in disputes with supervisors. A common practice is for the union to recompense the shop steward on a "lost time" basis. (A similar practice is often followed with respect to other local officers.) The structural distinction mentioned is that the shop steward as a regular fellow employee is likely to be more directly responsive to rank and file pressure and at the same time a direct symbol of the union members' partial control over the concrete operation of the productive organization as it affects them.

Leadership and Democracy. With the growing size and power of unions in the United States, there has also been an increasing concern for the internal structure of union with regard to leadership and democracy. Naturally, much of this discussion has been extremely partisan, and at least some of it has been "disinterested" but hopelessly muddled. Thus democracy has been confused with open opportunities for membership, although exclusion does violence to democracy only if the union professes to represent those excluded, however reprehensible exclusion may be on other grounds. Similarly, long tenure of union officials is only undemocratic if opposition candidates are prevented from running for office or are defeated by "illegal" means. The absence of an organized opposition in the form of the political party does not prove the absence of a democracy in a voluntary organization with somewhat greater chance of consensus on matters relevant to organizational purposes than has the modern state.

If union organization is approached in terms of its leadership, it is clear that an essential requirement of the union officer is that he be a politician.[2] This implies not only a sensitivity to rank-and-file pressures, but also the probability of a "political machine" and of patronage with respect to appointive officials. These in turn are not undemocratic if opposiiton is not crushed by ejection, denial of free speech, or other incursions on "civil liberties" within the organization.

Inherent in any such organization, however, and particularly one without an independent judiciary, is the possibility of illegal domination by a leader, or more properly, by a tight power group. This makes possible a "dictatorial" leadership that may indeed gain

---

[2] See Benjamin M. Selekman, *Labor Relations and Human Relations.* (New York: McGraw-Hill Book Company, Inc., 1947), Chap. VIII, "Wanted: Mature Labor Leaders."

power only to dispense with democratic procedures in order to retain power.[3]

In order for a small minority of the union membership to gain and retain dominance it is not, however, absolutely essential to use undemocratic means. Indeed, a favorite weapon of a Communist minority is to use the very paraphernalia of democracy, and especially parliamentary procedure, to defeat opposition and provide a leadership that would not be supported by the membership at large if it took the trouble to replace it. In order to understand this phenomenon it is necessary to grasp the characteristics of a special-interest association. Many, and often most, members of such a group belong for very limited reasons, even if membership is entirely voluntary. As long as the organization fulfills those special interests—say periodic pay increases—there is likely to be little inclination to attend meetings, serve on committees, or form an opposition caucus to unseat the leadership. In most specialized associations most members are not good "organization people," in the sense of wide and consistent participation in organizational activities. This means that a small group of determined individuals can capture elective offices because of their obvious willingness to serve even at some seeming sacrifice. Coupled with the tactic of wearing out the opposition—"come early and vote late"—the concerted and persistent action of the minority leadership can retain power without majority support but with the passive acquiescence of the majority.

The power of union leaders is more widely recognized than is the fact that these "new men of power" do not have prestige in the community at large commensurate with either their power or their income.[4] Only rarely does union leadership extend to community leadership, except as the community is affected indirectly by the internal organization and decisions of unions. Given the ad-

[3] See Wellington Roe, *Juggernaut: American Labor in Action* (Philadelphia: J. B. Lippincott Company, 1948).

[4] See C. Wright Mills, *The New Men of Power: America's Labor Leaders* (New York: Harcourt, Brace and Company, 1948), especially "Introduction," and Chaps. 3–5; Eli Ginzberg, *The Labor Leader* (New York: The Macmillan Company, 1948).

ditional fact that union leadership constitutes a fairly important new channel of mobility for those not moved up into managerial ranks in the industrial system, an insight is provided concerning the anxiety of union officials to protect their internal power in the unions. Within the organization prestige accompanies power. The "maturity" of labor leadership so often sought probably depends in some measure upon professionalization of the position and its recognition within the prestige system of the society. Such a solution would in turn, however, have rather serious implications for the rather rough-and-tumble democracy prevalent in many unions.

The problem of union leadership and democracy arises in still another context in contemporary public discussion. That discussion revolves around the "responsibility" of union leaders, usually in the sense of reliability and trustworthiness in dealings with management. The plea for increased responsibility of union leaders is often made by those who at the same time criticize the lack of grass-roots democracy in the union. But clearly union "irresponsibility" in keeping a collective agreement may arise from the very real *responsibility* (that is, accountability) of union leaders to members. Because of the very democratic or quasi-democratic structure of the unions, agreements entered into by union representatives may be rejected by the membership, violated subsequent to approval, and leaders deposed if they attempt to be "responsible." The external responsibility of the union leader depends in considerable measure on his internal political security, but paradoxically that security may best be fostered by a conflict orientation toward management or other interest groups. Just as in other aspects of the industrial system, failure of the individual to think in terms of the operation of the organization as a whole leads to pressures that may damage the continuous effectiveness of the union as a going concern. From this point of view the union leader may need to do more than "represent" the members distributively, especially by way of "education" in aims and policies of the union as such. In this the union official is like the executive of any large organization, whether elected or appointed—he must view the organization as a whole. Representative democracy places a special burden on this responsibility, a cost to be justified on other grounds.

Problems of Bureaucracy. Since the rapid growth and even the establishment of many labor unions is fairly recent, it is not surprising that organizational procedures have not kept pace. Even more acutely than in industrial management, a constant tone of crisis pervades decision-making. The prevalence of short-run plans, of decisions made *ad hoc* in each situation, has two outstanding organizational results—failure to utilize the efficiencies of routinization and decentralization of authority, and failure to develop staff functions that would supply on a continuing basis the information needed for policy.

It is true that some idealists of the "labor movement" dislike the trend toward rationalized organization because of its actual or probable effect upon the enthusiastic and even sacrificial efforts of the crisis leader and the correlative sense of participation by the rank and file. Development of organizational routines, however, is an intrinsic penalty of success, and one that cannot be avoided even by finding ever new and larger enemies to conquer, for even large-scale conflict requires an extensive "bureaucracy."

Some of the concern of sympathetic observers over "union bureaucracy" undoubtedly stems from the tendency for appointive and even elective officials to treat their positions as sinecures if they are politically secure.[5] This, however, is not a problem of "bureaucracy" as such but of ineffective means for enforcing the accountability of office holders. Of bureaucracy in the strict sense of technical specialization and its associated features previously discussed, the typical labor union probably has too little for optimum operation rather than too much.

Staff specialization in particular tends to be very meager even at the national union level. This is partly a function of recent establishment or rapid growth, already mentioned. The more fundamental reason for failure to develop staff functions, however, de-

---

[5] See Irving Howe and B. J. Widick, *The UAW and Walter Reuther* (New York: Random House, 1949), Chap. 11, "The Life of a Union: Democracy and Bureaucracy."

rives from the fact that most unions still are in considerable measure *conflict organizations*. Several implications follow from that conflict orientation: (1) The union tends to have funds inadequate to provide a "war chest" for industrial disputes and still employ expensive technical talent on a continuing basis. (2) Securing a competent staff is made additionally difficult in that the employer (the union) has little prestige comparable to that offered by positions with established and "respectable" organizations. (3) As the nature of industrial conflict is not territorial but in some degree "ideological," organizational loyalty is likely to be a very important basis for staff appointments, with a definite tendency for such positions to be awarded to faithful incompetents. (4) The staff officers actually employed are likely to be assigned tasks dealing with the union's external relations and only very indirectly with the formulation of internal policy. This in turn is due not only to the concern of the union over its relations with management, the government, or the general public, but because there is likely to be very little disposition to trust the recommendations of the "intellectuals" against the intuitive judgment of the experienced leader scarred by successful conflict.

Bureaucracy in union organization is likely to increase in the measure that unions achieve security in membership and stability in industrial relations. It is also likely to increase proportionally to the extension of union aims and functions discussed in the following section of the chapter.

AIMS AND FUNCTIONS OF UNIONS

Unions may be regarded as collective means for the achievement of individual goals, but also as collectivities with aims and functions that are not merely the sum of individuals' goals. The union will have different values for various members, and the only (not necessarily the least) common denominator of those values may simply be the survival of the organization.

Many of the aims of unions are expressed through the medium of collective bargaining, for the avowed purpose of union organization as such is ordinarily the representation of workers in industrial organization. By a somewhat artificial separation, the aims and procedures of unions in their relations with management are postponed to the several chapters of Part Five. Here attention may be given those aims and activities of unions that do not in a *direct* way depend upon the union's relations with management.

Status in Shop and Community. It is an essential characteristic of industrial organization that it unites in cooperative effort not a group of "whole" persons but rather a group of fragmental persons who participate in production through the demands of an occupation. It has already been observed that among factory operatives, as among their managers, there is a considerable and indeed overwhelming pressure to add to the technical status in the organization a variety of social relations.

In the nature of the productive process with its great emphasis on the efficiencies of routine and specialization, it has been more difficult for production workers than for other groups to indulge this common desire for social meaning and satisfaction in daily activity.

The unions are often accused of stereotyping the individual, of substituting group ends for individual ones, of thwarting individual initiative. The important fact in this connection is that the unions for the most part have not created standardization and impersonality; they are a product of modern industrial organization and a reaction to some of its characteristics.

Whether recognized as an important aim of unions or not, one of the functions performed by the union is to give its members some standing in the shop and community. In the shop the worker, through his union membership, has some assurance of a hearing for his complaints, protection against whimsical superiors, and even a measure of control over his daily working conditions. In short, the worker may become a *participant* in modern productive organization in a more meaningful sense than when he was treated (or thought he was treated) only as a recipient of directions and an adjunct to the machine.[6]

[6] See Joseph Shister, "Trade Union Policies and Non-Market Values," in Milton Derber, ed., *Proceedings of the Second Annual Meeting, Industrial Relations Research Association*, New York City, December 29–30, 1949 (Champaign, Ill.: 1950), pp. 85–99.

The union gives the worker not only a new standing in the industrial organization but also in the community at large. Warner and Low, in their report on an old New England industrial community, place considerable emphasis on union membership and activity as an outgrowth of the steadily declining community status of the factory workers.[7] Hart, on the other hand, found in a relatively new Canadian industrial community that there were no traditions of graded skills of artisans to lose, but only the standardized mass production of the automobile industry. Here, too, the "working masses" became, through their unions and its activities in the community as well as the shop, persons with a definite place in community life.[8]

Participation and Services. Although presumably organized primarily as a conflict or bargaining agency, unions may and to an increasing extent do provide types of participation and services not provided for workers by other agencies or provided only in a grudging and patronizing way.

As an association primarily related to the economic sector of social life, it is not surprising that many union services involve the pooling of funds for the achievement of various economic aims. Thus some unions have experimented with the reduction of distribution costs through cooperative buying and the organization of consumers' cooperatives. A few unions have entered the field of banking and credit, and the Amalgamated Clothing Workers Union even undertook to sponsor cooperative housing.

Despite the wide discussion of union pension demands in collective bargaining after World War II, social welfare and insurance benefits have long figured in union activities, often through benefit plans financed solely by contributions of union members. In the future the unions' aspirations for various kinds of insurance are likely to swing between demands upon management and pressures on national and state governments, depending upon the current

[7] See W. Lloyd Warner and J. O. Low, *The Social System of the Modern Factory; The Strike: A Social Analysis* (New Haven: Yale University Press, 1947), Chap. IX, "The Workers Lose Status in the Community."

[8] See C. W. M. Hart, "Industrial Relations Research and Social Theory," *Canadian Journal of Economics and Political Science*, 15–53–73, February, 1949.

strength of the union and the temper of corporations and legislatures.

It would be a mistake, however, to view the union's functions as entirely confined to the market, whether the labor market or the commodity market. As already noted, the union tends to give the worker a new standing in the shop and community. And for some workers the very existence of the union provides a sense of "belonging" and of social participation. This "service" of the union is likely to be particularly important to the isolated urban worker and the member of a disadvantaged group. Both may find themselves cut off from more "normal" or at least more traditional forms of social activity. By no means all urban workers are "isolated," and it appears probable that careful study would reveal an inverse relationship between the intensity of union activity and the extent of participation in the more traditional forms of familial and neighborhood life and types of voluntary associations. It is certainly true that at least some "minority" groups have become especially staunch union members.

Some unions such as the International Ladies Garment Workers Union have developed extensive forms of intellectual and recreational activities for members. Many of these activities seem designed to bring various middle-income services to factory workers, but they are likely also to be defended in terms of their value to the "labor movement." There is some doubt whether the unions with the most extensive programs have ever carefully appraised the priorities to be assigned to the several activities should the union treasury be reduced. There is even more doubt that either unions or students of labor have carefully appraised the significance of union attempts to act as a sort of encompassing community for its members. The importance of the occupational position is so great in modern life that there may be increasing pressure to make it, and its formal expression in the industrial organization or the union, the central focus of all social activity. Although this tendency would appeal alike to believers in the broader aspirations of the "labor movement" and to social scientists with an implicit ideology that the good society is the perfectly integrated one, it is doubtful whether any largely voluntary, special-interest association is structurally suited to serve the functions of a complete community.

Political Action. For the greater part of American history, organized labor did not fare well at the hands of legislators, judges, and law enforcement officials, the difficulties being partly doctrinal and partly political in the narrow sense of effective power. For these and other reasons labor organizations have found themselves opposing the forces of "law and order" more frequently than they have been allied with the government and its agencies. And although the suffrage has been progressively widened, especially by the reduction or elimination of property qualifications, organized labor in the past exerted very little influence toward fundamental modification of doctrine or the activities of local officials. This was partly due, of course, to the absence of a consistent doctrine or program. Moreover, many workers have been and are unorganized—often the minority represented by unions has been very small—and at least on a national scale other interests and cleavages have assumed greater importance than class or occupational distinctions.

Organized workers and their sympathizers have not, however, totally neglected considerations of political power. Direct political action through the support of prolabor candidates or even putting labor party tickets in the field has had some local success. Indeed, local political action has considerable advantage as an indirect labor weapon, since the control of law enforcement officials is primarily local. Thus the election of union men as mayors or members of town or city councils may yield immediate benefits in the way the laws are interpreted and applied, with little or no change in formal statutes. Pragmatically considered, of course, the law is what the courts will apply and the police will enforce, and these are preeminently local affairs.

Nationally the program of organized labor has consisted less of party action than of pressure-group action. The support or nonsupport of a sizeable and organized constituency of whatever sort is not without significance for elective officials. Although labor officials have not been uniformly successful in "delivering the vote," their prestige in this respect has increased in recent years. There is still considerable, and often acrimonious, debate as to the value of the support given to the national administration since 1932, and as to whether the debt was underpaid or overpaid. Yet it is certainly true that the position of organized labor on questions of public policy is not only increasingly expressed, but also increasingly heard and at least partially followed.

Since the passage and support by the courts of such acts as the National Labor Relations Act, the Fair Labor Standards Act, the Norris-La Guardia Act, and various other national and state laws, organized labor has found and used the weapon of the courts, formerly reserved almost exclusively for management. Changes in the law not only strengthen such weapons as the strike and picketing already in use, but modify the balance of power in such a way that the labor organization may use the less expensive (and incidentally less violent) indirect weapons provided by government. Labor organizations thus have access not only to such weapons as injunctions—or "cease and desist" orders issued by administrative agencies and upheld by the courts, which amounts to the same thing—but can add weight to their propaganda by being leagued with the government. Thus, after the passage of the National Labor Relations Act, union organizers could claim with considerable accuracy that the national government itself desired the organization of workers. Labor unions lost national political status as a result of the passage of the Taft-Hartley Act, perhaps less because of its direct provisions, designed to correct various labor "abuses," than because of the unions' strong but unsuccessful opposition to the legislation.

In the present context it is important to note that with the increasing size and power of labor unions in the industrial system they have also shown increasing interest and partial effectiveness in political participation. Although the difficulty of "politicizing" the American labor movement has been the despair of various minority political groups inside and outside the unions, a kind of pragmatic but often very active political effort is increasingly common. In many local areas persons scarcely noticed by the standard party machines have shown both enthusiasm and talent in electioneering.

Aside from the obvious benefit to any interest-group in having friendly elected officials, the fact of political action itself may serve to enhance the importance of the union to its membership and provide avenues of activity for those politically oriented members who might otherwise become dissidents within the union.

The union, we have implied, is scarcely fitted to be all things to all people or even to all members, but it may occupy a fairly wide place in the life of the union member both within the industrial organization itself and in the community at large. The way the union modifies the structure of industrial management itself and creates new patterns of group relations in modern society will be explored in subsequent chapters.

REFERENCES

AARON, BENJAMIN, "Protecting Civil Liberties of Members within Trade Unions," in Milton Derber, ed., *Proceedings of the Second Annual Meeting, Industrial Relations Research Association,* New York City, December 29–30, 1949 (Champaign, Ill.: 1930), pp. 28–41.

BARBASH, JACK, *Labor Unions in Action: A Study of the Mainsprings of Unionism* (New York: Harper & Brothers, 1947), 83–90.

BERMAN, EDWARD, "The American Labor Movement," in Emanuel Stein and Jerome Davis, eds., *Labor Problems in America* (New York: Farrar and Rinehart, 1940), Book II (Chaps. 10–13).

BLOOM, GORDEN F., and HERBERT R. NORTHRUP, *Economics of Labor and Industrial Relations* (Philadelphia: The Blakiston Company, 1950), Chap. 4, "Union Structure and Government," and Chap. 9, "Union Structure and Government," and Chap. 9, "Union Institutionalism and the Scope of Union Activity."

BRAUNTHAL, ALFRED, "American Labor in Politics," *Social Research*, 12: 1–21, February 1945.

BROOKS, ROBERT R. R., *When Labor Organizes* (New Haven: Yale University Press, 1937).

COMMONS, JOHN R., DAVID J. SAPOSS, and OTHERS, *History of Labour in the United States* (New York: The Macmillan Company, 1921–1935, 4 vols).

CUMMINS, E. E., *The Labor Problem in the United States* (New York: D. Van Nostrand Co., 1932), Part III (Chaps. V–XII), "The Wage Earner."

DANKERT, CLYDE E., *Contemporary Unionism in the United States* (New York: Prentice-Hall, 1948).

DAVID, HENRY, "Labor in Politics," in Emanuel Stein and Jerome Davis,

Labor Problems in America (New York: Farrar and Rinehart, 1940), Chap. 20.

FELLER, ALEXANDER, and JACOB E. HURWITZ, *How to Deal with Organized Labor* (New York: The Alexander Publishing Co., 1937), Part One, Chap. I, "Organized Labor—Immediate Objectives"; Chap. IV, "The American Labor Movement"; Chap. V, "Organization, Structure and Government of Unions."

GINZBERG, ELI, *The Labor Leader* (New York: The Macmillan Company, 1948).

GOULDNER, ALVIN W., "Attitudes of 'Progressive' Trade-Union Leaders," *American Journal of Sociology*, 52: 389–392, March 1947.

HART, C. W. M., "Industrial Relations Research and Social Theory," *Canadian Journal of Economics and Political Science*, 15: 53–73, February 1949.

HOWE, IRVING, and B. J. WIDICK, *The UAW and Walter Reuther* (New York: Random House, 1949).

MACDONALD, LOIS, *Labor Problems and the American Scene* (New York and London: Harper & Brothers, 1938), Part Six (Chaps. XX–XXIX), "The Labor Movement."

MILLS, C. WRIGHT, *The New Men of Power: America's Labor Leaders* (New York: Harcourt, Brace and Company, 1948), especially "Introduction," and Chaps. 3–5.

PETERSON, FLORENCE, *American Labor Unions: What They Are and How They Work* (New York: Harper & Brothers, 1945).

PIERSON, FRANK C., "The Government of Trade Unions," *Industrial and Labor Relations Review*, 1: 593–608, July 1948.

ROE, WELLINGTON, *Juggernaut: American Labor in Action* (Philadelphia: J. B. Lippincott Company, 1948).

ROSE, CAROLINE BAER, "Morale in a Trade-Union," *American Journal of Sociology*, 56: 167–174, September 1950.

SELEKMAN, BENJAMIN M., *Labor Relations and Human Relations* (New York: McGraw-Hill Book Company, Inc., 1947.)

SHARP, MALCOLM, and CHARLES O. GREGORY, *Social Change and Labor Law* (Chicago: University of Chicago Press, 1939), Part II, Chap. I, "The Common Law in State and Federal Courts."

SHEPARD, HERBERT A., "Democratic Control in a Labor Union," *American Journal of Sociology*, 54: 311–316, January 1949.

SHISTER, JOSEPH, "The Locus of Union Control in Collective Bargaining," *Quarterly Journal of Economics*, 60: 513–545, August 1946.

——, "Trade Union Government: A Formal Analysis," *Quarterly Journal of Economics*, 60: 78–112, November 1945.

——, "Trade Union Policies and Non-Market Values," in Milton Derber, ed., *Proceedings of the Second Annual Meeting, Industrial Relations Research Association,* New York City, December 29–30, 1949 (Champaign, Ill.: 1950), pp. 85–99.

SLICHTER, SUMNER H., *The Challenge of Industrial Relations: Trade Unions, Management, and the Public Interest* (Ithaca: Cornell University Press, 1947), Chap. IV, "The Government of Trade Unions."

——, *Union Policies and Industrial Management* (Washington: The Brookings Institution, 1941), especially Chaps. I–XIII.

WALSH, J. RAYMOND, *C. I. O. Industrial Unionism in Action* (New York: W. W. Norton and Co., 1937).

WARNE, COLSTON, "The Workers' Approach to the Labor Problem," in Emanuel Stein and Jerome Davis, eds., *Labor Problems in America* (New York: Farrar and Rinehart, 1940), Book III. See Chaps. 14–17 and 19.

WARNER, W. LLOYD, and J. O. Low, *The Social System of the Modern Factory; The Strike: A Social Analysis* (New Haven: Yale University Press, 1947), Chap. IX, "The Workers Lose Status in the Community."

WHITEHEAD, T. N. *Leadership in a Free Society* (Cambridge: Harvard University Press, 1937), Chap. XI, "The Function of Trade Unions."

PART FIVE

MANAGEMENT—UNION RELATIONS

CHAPTER XIV

MANAGEMENT AND UNION ORGANI-
ZATION AS RELATED TO BARGAINING

To MOST persons not directly involved in the factory system of production, and to many persons who are, the outstanding feature of modern industrial life is the state of relations between management and the unions. Among the myriads of relations inherent in the industrial mode of production, those between corporations and labor organizations are commonly known as "industrial relations." The claim of the unions to a place in the industrial system was long opposed with some success, and the continued uncertainty about the exact nature of that place gives rise to continued disputes. It is scarcely surprising, therefore, that these two substructures of modern industrial organization are often pictured as opposing armies, their leaders adopting the customary posture of gladiators.

As indicated in previous chapters, management necessarily and the union probably exist for purposes besides that of achieving their aims by bargaining with each other. Yet the importance of the union in modern industrial organization is such that many policies and decisions, and even the continued operation of the productive system, are contingent upon the participation of the union as a sector of the total organization. Under systems of public ownership or the corporate state the union and some of its functions are likely to persist, although the character of management-union relations is likely to be very different. With the union operating with more or less autonomy in the industrial system, the character of management-union relations may greatly influence the nature of the productive system.

Although management and unions are each likely to have ends

and activities not directly tied to the nature of their joint relations, each structure is molded in part by its relations with the other and indeed by the very existence of the other. Two simple illustrations may be in order. First, examine the case of a corporate management with a plant not yet organized by an independent union. Only the most naïve would suppose that management is therefore "free" of union influence. Actually, nearly all policies with respect to wages and conditions of employment will be adopted in the light of trends in collective bargaining. The preventive measures taken by management to avoid union organization may be somewhat less military than the older weapons of the mercenary army and well-paid spies, but they are likely to be important in the actual operation of the managerial organization. Second, consider the case of the union with a great deal of autonomy of local units at the shop level, which finds that essential decisions affecting labor policy are made by top executives for all plants of the company, or even by a trade association for the industry as a whole. The very existence of this managerial structure, and particularly the attempts of the union to penetrate it, will almost certainly produce a parallel concentration of union power for determining bargaining policy.

There are many other aspects of reciprocal influence between management and the union, ranging from the obvious to the fairly subtle. The purpose of this chapter is to examine what might be called the essential structure of management and union as it bears on the relations between them, but also on the way the operating organizations are modified by the character of their interrelations.

MANAGERIAL STRUCTURE AND THE BARGAINING FUNCTION

The structure of management, which was examined in some detail in Part Three, may here be reappraised in terms of the bargaining function. This reappraisal will focus on three questions: the location of labor relations policy, the expansion of joint determination, and the expansion of staff and services.

Location of Labor Relations Policy. Our previous discussion of managerial decision-making indicated that the formal structure of management is authoritarian but that the top executive alone cannot possibly make all decisions. This means concretely that managerial policies always represent some sort of balance of diverse facts and opinions, and often of opposing views. The closest approximation to the formally authoritarian power of the executive is that of "consultation," with divergent views perhaps freely expressed prior to decision, but ending with a binding decision by a single executive or small group. If disgruntled groups, or those who claim that new developments demand reopening the discussion, are given no hearing, managerial flexibility depends entirely on the top executive group.

The relevance of this aspect of managerial structure at once becomes evident if one considers the problem of determining managerial policy on collective bargaining in a large multi-plant and multi-product company. The increasing policy of decentralization to accomplish flexibility and broaden the base of managerial responsibility encounters the difficulty that problems of labor policies are of a more *general* character than most other matters requiring decision. At the same time, the growth of national industrial unions with centralized policy-determination may create the necessity of additional managerial centralization. Dubin has pointed out that bigness alone tends to require standardization of managerial policy with respect to labor,[1] and Baker finds that there has been a trend toward increased concern of top management in determining labor policies.[2] Indeed, even if contracts are negotiated locally the essential policies may be determined for the company as a whole by the highest executive group.

Despite the increased attention of top executives to management-union relations or perhaps because of it, Baker finds that by comparison with 1937 the principal industrial relations officer now generally appears at a higher position in the managerial structure.[3]

---

[1] See Robert Dubin, "Decision-Making by Management in Industrial Relations," *American Journal of Sociology*, 54: 292–301, January 1949.

[2] See Helen Baker, *Management Procedures in the Determination of Industrial Relations Policies* (Princeton: Industrial Relations Section, Princeton University, 1948).

[3] *Ibid.*

In many of the largest corporations the principal industrial relations officer now figures as a ranking vice-president, administratively attached to the central executive staff. In some companies relations with unions have been regarded as sufficiently important to add an entirely new department to the organization, in addition to an existing personnel department.

The process of moving decisions on management-union relations "higher" in the managerial structure and nearer its "center" in terms of line executive interest is naturally in large measure the effect of the impact of centralized union policy. Where the industrial union is itself decentralized for bargaining, these managerial changes may be less evident. Similarly, the fractioning of unions along product or craft lines may indicate a policy of managerial decentralization of the bargaining function.

It should be noted that management is under no such normative pressure for democratic determination of policy as is the union. Indeed, elaborate decentralization runs the risk of condemnation as "abdicating of executive responsibility." Yet to an increasing extent the very complexity of industrial organization and the growing concern for morale and utilization of talents "down the line" may prompt attempts to generate discussion and determine policies at lower levels. Although it is probably not true that such policies if adopted earlier and without union pressure would have prevented the appearance or great influence of unions, it is certainly true that the representation of the lowest ranks of industrial organization by an organization with power to force concessions and agreements from the top levels provides management with serious problems of organization.

Expansion of Joint Determination. The union, we have observed, is not simply an external element in industrial organization; to an increasing extent, it *permeates* it. The implications of the broadening scope of collective bargaining are discussed in Chapter XVII. In the present context it is appropriate to examine some intrinsic features of managerial structure that slow down the process of sharing authority.

In the nature of the case the union is in the position of challenger to managerial authority. This means that management is likely to resist changes sought by the union on principle, somewhat independently of momentary market advantages in quick settlement. The union demands are likely to narrow, and in any event will certainly change, the area of autonomous authority of many managers, from president to foreman. And since those powers have been supported by ideological claims to legitimacy, questions of sentiment as well as rational calculation are likely to be raised.

Resistance *on principle* does not necessarily imply that all types and grades of managers will uniformly oppose union demands. Nor should it be assumed that line managers are more intransigent opponents of the union than staff men. Those not faced with regular relations with union members or officers, such as lawyers and treasurers, are likely to be more concerned with abstract rights and principles than those on the firing line. Some managers may favor concessions for reasons of practical operation in the immediate situation, others because they regard the process as inevitable in the long run and seek as orderly a development as possible. Some few may see advantages in morale and "communications" in the entrance of the union into various areas of decision-making.

The norm of authoritarianism in management has an additional significance in this context. In this, as in other matters, cleavages in the managerial structure are by no means unlikely. They are, however, commonly "private" disputes, for the power to influence the decisions of top executives is not a "right," and the norm dictates hiding disputes both before and after decisions are made.

Quite apart from questions of sentiment or principle, managerial structure is resistant to change by the very nature of bureaucratic organization. As pointed out in Chapter IV, an elaborate formal organization with its intricate specialization of functions and routinization of activities is best fitted to operate in a stable environment. Achievement of flexibility is one of the most pressing problems of any such organization under conditions of external change.[4] In the

---

[4] Dubin, *op. cit.*, greatly overstates the extent to which managerial structure is keyed to change. One of the major functions of scale in industrial operations is to control or cushion market, technological, and other relevant changes.

management of industrial organizations market and technological changes are regarded as more or less inevitable and even "right," although large organizations will attempt to control these changes. But governmental regulation, whether legislative or administrative, and union demands do not come within the theory of impersonal inevitability, and the disposition of management may be to contain or defeat the change rather than adapt to it.

Despite these resistances the areas of joint determination by management and union have increased and are likely in the near future to continue to do so. As the union "permeates" the industrial organization it will inevitably affect the operation of staff activities previously not directly concerned with union relations. This leads to the likelihood of wider staff participation in decisions regarding management-union relations or else a greater "interference" in staff operations by line officers negotiating union agreements. The latter alternative would then constitute a new form of "business" consideration bearing on technical operations. Just as the company's market position may dictate the direction of engineering development, so its relations with the union may alter the training of apprentices or the character of its pension system.

Expansion of Staff and Services. It follows from the preceding discussion that with the inclusion of the union in the industrial system the structure of management is changed both in order to bargain and as a consequence of union demands and agreements. This same duality appears in the expansion of staff and services. The increased importance of contract negotiation and of administration of agreements through grievance procedures has led to the direct expansion of personnel or industrial relations staffs. The capacity for negotiations and even administration to consume managerial (and union) time is very considerable. From this standpoint decentralization of bargaining or even the fractioning of unions fostered by the Taft-Hartley Act may have distinct disadvantages to management.

Some of the consequences of labor agreements for staff expansion have already been implied in the discussion of the expansion of joint determination. Such expansion may not only affect the operations of existing staff units but result in the creation of entirely new units ranging from market analysis to pension plans.

There are even more indirect and occasionally subtle changes to be noted, however. To a marked degree management has defined its relations with the union as one of competition for the loyalties of workers. Thus the very popular development of "human relations" programs, of conferences and therapeutic counseling, and of more or less elaborate employee benefit plans, have been in no small measure due to the growth of unionism. Similarly the plight of the foreman as the "man in the middle" has been given greatly expanded attention by management because of a combination of related developments: (1) union wage scales, particularly coupled with penalty rates for overtime work during periods of high production, often resulted in larger pay for workers than for their supervisors; (2) foremen often found their authority greatly diminished as a result of union success, not only because of the power of the shop steward but also because of the tendency for the foreman's superiors to settle issues "over his head" on an emergency basis; and (3) independent unionism for foremen made considerable headway for a time just prior to and after World War II. The result of these developments has been greatly increased managerial attention to selection and training of supervisors, coupled with attempts to enhance their authority and prestige.

Where management has admitted the possibility of different spheres of workers' loyalties to the union and the company, other types of changes in staff organization are likely to result. Thus even outside the direct areas of current negotiation, management may find it wise as a preventive measure or even positively advantageous to consult the union concerning contemplated changes in policies or procedures. By the same token, the union may serve as a more effective medium of communication than the direct line organization or the posted bulletin.[5]

[5] See Helen Baker, *Company-Wide Understanding of Industrial Relations Policies: A Study in Communications* (Princeton: Industrial Relations Section, Princeton University, 1948), especially Chap. V, "The Influence of Unions on Communications"; Sumner H. Slichter, *The Challenge of Industrial Relations: Trade Unions, Management, and the Public Interest* (Ithaca: Cornell Univer-

UNION STRUCTURE AND THE BARGAINING FUNCTION

The formal structure of unions is, as already observed, considerably less elaborate than that of modern industrial management. The organization also tends to be less explicit and rationalized, more the product of particular personalities and events. The fluidity of the union organization is partly a result of recent and rapid growth, partly the result of the more specific orientation of the union toward the shifting character of collective bargaining.

Primacy of the Bargaining Function. Unions perform a variety of services for their members and serve a number of functions that may not be explicitly recognized. It remains true, however, that securing concessions from employers and the representation of the worker in the daily conduct of management-labor relations are central to most unions' activities. In a more fundamental sense than with respect to management it may be said that the bargaining situation is the major determinant of union structure.

Historically, unions were successful only as their members occupied strategic positions in the technical or marketing structure of industry.[6] This was true not only because such workers were difficult or impossible to replace, but because the legally-sanctioned power of employers to combat unions was less effective against those strategically placed. The unions representing large numbers of employees in mass-production industries required concerted action by large numbers of individually replaceable workers, abetted by changed legislation that allowed and even encouraged such organization.

Thus just the question of size of the union unit engaged in bargaining depends in considerable measure upon the degree to which numbers are a necessary component of bargaining power. Until modified after World War II by the Taft-Hartley Act, the National Labor Relations Board under the Wagner Act rather consistently

---

sity Press, 1947), Chap. II, "The Effect of Trade Unions on the Management of Business Enterprises."

[6] See John T. Dunlop, "The Development of Labor Organization: A Theoretical Framework," in Richard A. Lester and Joseph Shister, eds., *Insights into Labor Issues* (New York: The Macmillan Company, 1948), pp. 163–193.

settled questions of the "appropriate bargaining unit" in terms of matching the power of the employer. With many exceptions where craft organizations had long-established bargaining relations with the employer, the tendency of the NLRB was to judge an "appropriate bargaining unit" the one that covered approximately the same sphere as the employer's labor relations policy. If this policy was determined on a company-wide or, through a trade association, an industry-wide basis, the approved bargaining unit tended to have the same jurisdiction.

So closely geared is the union to the nature of its relations with management that there is a tendency to develop matching jurisdictions even in the absence of administrative decision. However changes in structure themselves constitute potential weapons in the conduct of bargaining. Thus unions may attempt to "pick off" one employer at a time but subsequently seek to "take labor out of competition" by industry-wide bargaining. In view of its greater flexibility the union may be able to move decision-making from a local to a national level and back again more quickly than can management.

The general tendency in union organization, however, is to secure as broad a basis of common standards as possible, and thus to centralize decisions and the conduct of bargaining at the level of the national organization. When coupled with a multi-stage grievance procedure, this is likely to produce a union hierarchy with something like the number of stages in managerial organization. The result is that of parallel, interrelated, but competing organizations with a common membership at the rank-and-file level.

There is a by-product of the centralization of the bargaining function in the union that also merits attention. That by-product is the change in local union structure when the officers are no longer centrally concerned with the major issues in the union's relations with management. Since those issues are settled at higher levels, the local union and its officers can pay greater attention to other aims and functions of unions in the plant and community.

Union Politics and Collective Bargaining. Union policies in relations with management are a complex balance of pressures to an even more marked extent than are managerial policies. This arises primarily from the interplay of two characteristics of union organization: (1) most union membership is voluntary and not a condition of continuing employment, although "union security" agreements tend to reduce this source of strain on union organization. The voluntary character of membership means that relations with management must be sufficiently acceptable to keep members in the union. Dissent from managerial decision by a member of management is likely to mean dismissal from employment. In the union without a maintenance-of-membership agreement, dissent means loss of a supporter. (2) In any case, the norm of democratic organization makes union decision-makers in some degree responsible to the organization, so that policies are likely to reflect membership opinion either expressed by actual vote on issues or expressed by selection of officers.

To these characteristics of voluntary and democratic organization as factors in the often tenuous balance of union policy should be added a feature of union organization that still is of major importance in structure and policy. That feature is the role of conflict. The importance of conflict in the development of management-union relations lies deep in the "organizational memory" of unions. The inherent position of the union as the challenger to the established arrangements of industrial organization, plus the very real and "principled" opposition of management, have combined to emphasize conflict leadership as a criterion of union officialdom.

According to the general state of management-union relations the appropriate union leader may be the warrior, the shrewd bargainer, or the internal administrator. According to the scope of those relations all may be needed at the same time or at short intervals, in addition to a variety of staff officials for the development of decisions and the conduct of joint determination with management.

Primary emphasis on the conflict role has led to a kind of "leadership principle" in unions, whereby the warrior's intuitive judgment is trusted above the administrator's. This tendency is given further support by the problems of democracy and potential dissidence in the internal affairs of the union. The responsibility of the leader to the membership enhances the role of the warrior as a builder of morale and therefore as a defeater of rival factions and leaders.

The importance of industrial conflict in the cohesiveness of unions and in the character of union leadership is such that many unions are faced with peculiar problems arising from their seeming security and prosperity. In the absence of conflict, membership interest tends to dwindle and the motives of the member to reduce to the least common denominator of wage benefits balanced against dues. Moreover, political factions are likely to arise based primarily on the claim of rivals that they can "deliver" more for the members than the current officials have done.

As long as bargaining retains a primary place in union functions, organizational strength is likely to depend in some measure on occasional conflict and even reverses as a factor in maintaining loyalty. The development of the non-bargaining functions of unions may provide some substitute for the dangers of peace and security.

In this connection it may be noted that union factionalism and attrition of loyalty are likely to be more pervasive and better known to management than are the latter's own internal difficulties. This again stems from the open discussion inherent in democratic forms. Knowledge of internal dissension in the union often strengthens the bargaining power of management, and it is not uncommon for management's bargainers to profess their belief and even sympathetic understanding that particular union demands stem from the leader's political difficulties within his organization. That management's position may stem from similar circumstances is not at all unlikely, but the relevant facts are not likely to be known to the union.

Staff Problems with Joint Determination. The expansion of the scope of collective bargaining, which will be discussed in some detail in Chapter XVII, raises difficult organizational problems for unions. As earlier noted, existing union staffs are not only customarily small but also of modest influence in the formation of policy. The technical functions, if any, thought essential by union policy-makers have been those concerned with "foreign relations" and particularly relations with legislatures, courts, and the general public. When coupled with the trust in intuitive leaders and a fairly pervasive anti-intellectualism quite unlike unions in other industrial countries, the meager staff development of unions necessarily limits effectiveness in unfamiliar technical areas.

The concern of unions over the rate of technological change, the increase of non-labor efficiencies, or the establishment of pension plans requires expert services. Whatever the merits of particular union requests for joint determination, organizational difficulties alone are likely to provide serious hurdles to union effectiveness in new areas. Although we shall see that it is rather difficult to state in general principles the "appropriate" area of union concern in managerial policy, it seems quite clear that the union will probably not be able to duplicate all managerial talents. If the union assumes joint responsibility for all managerial functions, it will act like management in many essential ways, and thereby lose its function as an opposition. Even an approximation to this situation will substantially change the position of the union in the industrial organization.

Apart from the central problem of union functions under conditions of joint determination, two further difficulties in union structure require attention in this context. The first is the question of the source of funds for staff expansion. The union is not a productive organization. Its funds depend upon members' dues or such funds as the employer may agree to deposit to the account of employees for various insurance and welfare benefits. The union would have to have an additional share in the allocation of industrial funds in order to compete for professional talent on any considerable scale. Second, the prestige of the union as an organization is commonly not such as to make the competition for staff talent particularly easy, as the professional employed by the union is not likely to receive the full measure of prestige commonly accorded comparable positions in other organizations. At the same time, the character of the union as a membership group, with a high emphasis on loyalty in view of actual or potential conflict, is likely to impede the free selection of staff officials on grounds of technical competence. The loyalty to the employer, which is by no means unimportant to management, is likely to have a special urgency in union organiza- tions in view of continuing fear of spies and "turncoats." The very fact that leaving the employ of the union for a better position with management is still regarded as something akin to treason indicates how serious is the difficulty in establishing union organization on a primarily rational basis. And in view of the functions of the union in supplying some of the types of participation and services not avail- able within the formal structure of productive organization, it is not self-evident that the union need aspire to match the staff or- ganization of management. An extension of its technical functions may be at the expense of the role of the union as a form of direct participation by workers in the industrial system.

REFERENCES

BAKER, HELEN, *Company-Wide Understanding of Industrial Relations Policies: A Study of Communications* (Princeton: Industrial Rela- tions Section, Princeton University, 1948), especially Chap. V, "The Influence of Unions on Company Communications."

————, *Management Procedures in the Determination of Industrial Rela- tions Policies* (Princeton: Industrial Relations Section, Princeton University, 1948).

BAKKE, E. WIGHT, *Mutual Survival: The Goal of Unions and Management* (New York: Harper and Brothers, 1947).

BLOOM, GORDON F., and HERBERT R. NORTHRUP, *Economics of Labor and Industrial Relations* (Philadelphia: the Blakiston Company, 1950), Chap. 5, "Management of Industrial Relations."

DUBIN, ROBERT, "Decision-Making by Management in Industrial Rela- tions," *American Journal of Sociology*, 54: 292–301, January 1949.

DUNLOP, JOHN T., "The Development of Labor Organization: A Theo- retical Framework," in Richard A. Lester and Joseph Shister, eds., *Insights into Labor Issues* (New York: The Macmillan Company, 1948), pp. 163–193.

HOWE, IRVING, and B. J. WIDICK, *The UAW and Walter Reuther* (New York: Random House, 1949).

LINDBLOM, CHARLES E., *Unions and Capitalism* (New Haven: Yale Uni- versity Press, 1949), especially Chap. IV, "The Politics of Unionism."

SLICHTER, SUMNER H., *The Challenge of Industrial Relations: Trade Unions, Management, and the Public Interest* (Ithaca: Cornell Uni- versity Press, 1947), Chap. II, "The Effect of Trade Unions on the Management of Business Enterprises."

CHAPTER XV

TYPES OF COLLECTIVE BARGAINING RELATIONS

SOCIAL LIFE in modern industrial societies is increasingly marked by collective relations, that is, by relations among individuals of such character that they can only be understood in terms of the groups or collectivities represented by such individuals. This is not the same as interaction of individuals in terms of positions and established patterns, which is characteristic of social relationships within social structures. Nor is the crucial issue the segmental character of collective relations. The whole personality of the individual is not, and indeed could not be, involved in any patterned social behavior in any society. The virtually unique feature of urban-industrial societies is that associations are deliberately organized around a narrow range of common interests and then these collectivities must find a mode of relationship when their several collective interests or the individual interests of their common membership overlap and conflict.

Social theory has made little progress in the analysis of collective relations. The theory of social organization is almost exclusively concerned with the internal structure of groups and associations. The theory of society has only recently emerged from a preoccupation with the evolution of Western society to turn attention to the common and essential features of all organized social life. Neither is irrelevant for an analysis of collective relations, yet at the present state of development neither provides clear principles and inferences for such analysis.[1]

[1] See Herbert Blumer, "Sociological Theory in Industrial Relations," *American Sociological Review*, 12: 271–278, June 1947.

Perhaps the essential difficulty in analysis of collective relations is that they are not only complex (which is a feature of most social phenomena) but also dynamic. Put crudely, collective relations will not hold still to be studied. The demand of labor union A upon the management of corporation X not only affects the latter, but the labor union itself is modified in the process. Moreover, the nature of the settlement of this issue will modify the continuing collective relations and become relevant for an understanding or prediction of subsequent issues. Thus to an acute degree collective relations are characterized by "interplay" and by "feedback." No simple model of influence and reaction will encompass these continuously changing relations.

The first step in bringing order into such a confusing situation is ordinarily to attempt a classification. A classification is a mode of ordering phenomena for further analysis; it does not itself constitute adequate analysis, particularly of dynamic relations. The popularity of classification in social science literature is itself an indication of the elementary stage of analysis. In the study of collective relations even classification is difficult because the variables are numerous and therefore reduction to "elements" and "essences" is difficult and hazardous.

The primitive state of analysis in this field is illustrated by one heroic attempt at a simple dichotomy of types of relations[2]—the most primitive of all classifications. That attempt, which is discussed later in this chapter, is interesting for its explicit hypotheses but more interesting for its failures by way of ordering management-union relations.

Even a classification involving a number of points along a scale, such as the one presented in the following section of this chapter, is fraught with serious hazards. Whatever the scale adopted, it will determine which characteristics of concrete cases are relevant to the classification. Unfortunately, there is no assurance that other important variables will move in the same direction or by comparable stages along the scale.

[2] See Frederick H. Harbison and Robert Dubin, *Patterns of Union-Management Relations* (Chicago: Science Research Associates, 1947).

The range of practice in contemporary American management-union relations is great and the character of bargaining rapidly changing (partly because of "interplay" and "feedback" and partly because of the changes in the relevant "external" environment—level of production, the state of labor market, legislation and judicial and administrative decision). This variety and rapid change has accounted for the fact that the relevant literature overflows with descriptive studies but seriously lacks sufficient repetition of features to permit even rough testing of hypothesis. In a sense, we know so little of predictive value about management-labor relations because we know so much about concrete cases.

THE RANGE FROM CONFLICT TO COOPERATION

The classification of types of management-union relations adopted here is one that will leave a number of otherwise important features out of account, but has the simple virtue of getting at the nub of the relationship—bargaining. The classification takes as its major focus the degree of mutual acceptance and understanding between management and the union. "Understanding" in this context refers to the development of accepted principles that are not bargained about.

It is appropriate to bear in mind that it is easiest to discuss and contrast polar types, that is, those lying at the two extremes of the scale, for the simple reason that they alone are likely to be "pure." By the same token, instances of these extremes are the most difficult to find in actual situations. This point has a special relevance in the present context, but that relevance can best be understood by reference to a more general principle of inter-group relations. The outcome of extreme conflict may be annihilation of one organization, and the outcome of extreme cooperation is likely to be fusion and absorption. To the extent that each organization performs differing functions that are essential or useful to the other, either annihilation or fusion is likely to be troublesome and costly for the remaining organization. Management and the union are caught in an involuntary relationship involving overlapping membership and jurisdiction and separate but interdependent functions.[3] Complete defeat or complete fusion may leave necessary functions unperformed or force their performance on the remaining organization.

Extreme Conflict. Extreme conflict is an essentially unstable form of collective relations. The reason for this instability is not hard to find; in the measure that conflict is successful, one party either ceases to exist or the relationship takes on some other form. If neither side emerges clearly victorious, continuation of the relationship depends upon some measure of accommodation, a sort of *modus vivendi.* The pattern of relations established as a result of inconclusive conflict does not bar a resumption of hostilities over new issues or when one party feels better able to defeat the other. The essential point is that extreme conflict as a type of management-union relations is an inherently temporary one.

A conflict-orientation in industrial relations in the sense of seeking to destroy the other organization is more probable on the part of management, despite the fact that in the nature of the case the union is usually the challenger. This arises from the fact that most unions recognize their dependence upon the continued survival of the business, whereas few managers have recognized or conceded the legitimacy of union functions. Only those radical unions which seek to disrupt the whole productive system would attempt the utter defeat of management. This could be the policy of unions under Communist domination in the event of war with a Communist state, or as a substitute for international war should the leaders feel strong enough to secure internal revolution. However, in the United States after World War II those unions under Communist leadership most often adopted a "bread and butter" approach to union demands in order to consolidate their membership support while some rival non-Communist unions were often more troublesome to management by seeking to extend the scope of bargaining.

---

[3] With respect to management-union relations this has been pointed out by Robert Dubin in his "Discussion" of Wilbert E. Moore, "Industrial Sociology: Status and Prospects," *American Sociological Review* 13: 382–391; August 1948, Dubin's discussion on pp. 391–393. Dubin regards this "necessary" characteristic of management-union relations as unique to them. It is actually true of all collective relations—for example, church and state, family and school, etc.— where there are separate but interdependent functions.

In the past, management carried on more vigorous and more varied warfare against unions. But the intention of this warfare was clearly to *prevent* bargaining, not to engage in it. This history is not forgotten, however, and fear for survival still characterizes unions. Thus the legacy of past relations conditions the present and gives rise to suspicions that particular proposals or resistances are designed to destroy rather than modify existing relationships. A fear for survival is also increasingly characteristic of management as unions attempt to expand the amount and area of their power.[4]

The strike and the picket line and other labor weapons as well as the devices used by management are not necessarily to be regarded as aspects of conflict in any more fundamental sense than a test of strength and strategy as a part of settling issues. Frequent strikes, for example, may stem from a variety of circumstances having little or nothing to do with extreme conflict as a mode of management-union relations. The test of basic conflict is not the occurrence of disputes, alone, but whether or not an early settlement that preserves the organizational continuity of the rival organizations is sought.

Issue Bargaining. Much of contemporary management-union relations must be interpreted as the constant redefinition of specific powers and functions, and of benefits accorded to workers by collective agreement. The type of bargaining that involves major attempts to specify the basic terms for continuing relationships between management and union may be called "issue bargaining." From the managerial standpoint this type of relationship is likely to involve an attempt at *containment* of the union.[5] From the union standpoint, this type involves the expanding assertion of the workers' interests in industrial policy.

Issue bargaining has also been called "pattern setting" and the "generating type" of management-union relations.[6] Harbison and

---

[4] See E. Wight Bakke, *Mutual Survival: The Goal of Unions and Management* (New York: Harper & Brothers, 1946).

[5] See Benjamin F. Selekman, "Some Implications and Problems of Collective Bargaining," in Louis M. Hacker and Others, *The New Industrial Relations* (Ithaca: Cornell University Press, 1948), pp. 33–65.

[6] See Harbison and Dubin, *op. cit.*

Dubin think that issue bargaining is associated with industrial "power centers," such as General Motors in automobiles and United States Steel in steel. The argument then proceeds to maintain the importance of the settlements made in these centers for the pattern of industrial relations as a whole. There is nothing essentially wrong with this argument except that it imposes a consistency of pattern on industrial relations, which does not in fact exist. This problem will be raised again later in this chapter in connection with the locus of agreement. At this juncture it is sufficient to note that issue bargaining is definitely not limited to a few large corporations, each of which holds a position of leadership in a particular industry. Indeed, attempts to predict the locus of issue bargaining have not been notably successful, except that the trend is definitely to larger or higher-status representatives. Thus national union leaders and top corporation executives are likely to be concerned over fundamental issues in their relations, local union leaders and plant managers over settlement of particular problems within the general framework.

It is issue bargaining that clearly generates most of the pressure to have the government settle the problem by specification of fundamental principles of managerial and union rights. Such a governmental policy would of course take many of the issues out of bargaining, but attempts to find an acceptable basis for settling management-union relations once and for all have been notably unsuccessful.

Problem Bargaining. Most specific cases of management-union relations most of the time fall within a fairly broad type that may be called problem bargaining. In these relations the parties do not directly address themselves to the question of the survival of either —that is assumed. Nor do they directly attempt to settle the scope of subjects bargained about or the fundamental question of the position of the union in the industrial system. Such issues are part of the framework within which bargaining and continued operations take place.

Some problem bargaining is possible because the issues are settled elsewhere. Such circumstances arise not only where pattern-setting in one important sector of the industry allows other companies and unions to act as "satellites," [7] but also where a more encompassing settlement sets the limits for local determination. But problem bargaining is also possible, and indeed more usual, where basic principles have been established by past agreements. This form of relationship is greatly accentuated by permanent arbitration machinery, as arbitration awards tend to become a set of common law precedents.

The basic weakness of a static classification of dynamic relations is especially revealed in this context. A continuance of issue bargaining may well lead to such settlements and accommodations that the type of relationship shifts to problem-solving. Perhaps only a basic change in some external factor such as legislation or the level of employment will tempt either party to seek a reopening of basic issues. On the other hand, a continuance of problem bargaining, even of the extreme degree often characterized as "business unionism" on the labor side, may result in a gradual restructuring of powers. The difference between bargaining on issues and on problems may be only those of rapidity and recognition of long-run implications rather than those of basic philosophy and current tenor of relationships. It follows that in two otherwise comparable situations a specific union contract demand or grievance in administration may in one instance be defined as a simple problem-solving case and in the other as a fundamental issue—not because the second company is a "power center," but only because its management is extremely sensitive to what it views as "the creeping paralysis of union encroachment." This possibility points up once more the hazard of limiting analysis to a typology of collective relations without appraisal of the internal structures of union and management.

Removal of issue settlement from the local level may have a tendency to stereotype management-union relations, as Warner and Low conclude.[8] In most instances, however, freedom of concern over basic rights and powers and even the wage bargain leaves a

---

[7] *Ibid.*

[8] See W. Lloyd Warner and J. O. Low, *The Social System of the Modern Factory: The Strike: A Social Analysis* (New Haven: Yale University Press, 1947), Chaps. VII–IX.

wide area for administration and local development of management·
union relations,[9] and of the non-bargaining functions and services
of the union.[10]

Management-Union Cooperation. As used in the literature of industrial relations, "management-union cooperation" has a number
of rather distinct meanings. Occasionally it is apparently meant to
apply to the attitudes and motives of officials of the two organizations—are they hostile or "cooperative"? In the literature of labor
economics for some curious reason, management-union cooperation
tends to mean only cooperation toward reduction of direct labor
costs relative to output.[11] The more acceptable use of the term refers
to a mode of relationships between management and union that
brings both organizations into the planning and administration of
various policies through regularized procedures.[12]

This last use of the term "cooperation" with reference to management-union relations still leaves open the question of degree and
the question of forms and procedures. Of these, the problem of degree is clearly the more troublesome in the typology used here, as
any collective bargaining involves some degree of cooperation, that
is, joint determination. As a type of management-union relations it
is perhaps most convenient to view cooperation as the situation in
which the basic issues of union survival and participation in a number of decisions are settled, along with many specific problems. In
these areas the term "bargaining" may then be inappropriate, and
actual negotiation is likely to be on matters that would extend the
scope of the agreement.

The aim or impact of cooperation may include labor recruitment,
discipline, efficiency including elimination of material waste, sales

---

[9] Harbison and Dubin, *op. cit.*

[10] See C. W. M. Hart, "Industrial Relations Research and Social Theory,"
Canadian Journal of Economics and Political Science, 15: 53–73, February 1949.

[11] See, for example, Joseph Shister, "Union-Management Cooperation: An
Analysis," in Richard A. Lester and Joseph Shister, eds., *Insights into Labor
Issues* (New York: The Macmillan Company, 1948), pp. 87–115.

[12] See Kurt Braun, *Union-Management Co-operation: Experience in the
Clothing Industry* (Washington: The Brookings Institution, 1947); Dorothea
de Schweinitz, *Labor and Management in a Common Enterprise* (Cambridge:
Harvard University Press, 1949), especially Chap. XI "The Outlook for Union-
Management Cooperation through Joint Committees."

promotion, trade practices, welfare plans, as well as wages and conditions of employment. In some instances the procedure may involve what Selekman[13] calls "deal bargaining," that is, settled relations that emphasize the common interests of top management and union executives at the possible expense of lower managerial ranks (especially supervisors) and the union rank and file. And the area and nature of management-union agreement may be such as to constitute collusion for the exploitation of the consumer.

The attempt to establish cooperation of the degree discussed here commonly encounters managerial opposition, both because management fears that it will result in increased costs of operation and more importantly because management fears invasions of established "rights." But it should not be assumed that unions view extensive cooperation as an unmixed blessing. A broadened base of union participation in policy and procedure implies a greater union responsibility for the results. Whether founded or not, there is a very considerable suspicion among the ordinary members of most unions that cooperation means "selling out" to management. And, it will be noted in Chapter XVII with regard to the scope of bargaining, the partial loss of the power of opposition lends just enough essential validity to this view to make the virtues of cooperation somewhat less than they may at first appear. Moreover, it has already been noted that the union structure is not ideally suited to supply or support an extensive range of staff functions implied by joint determination of a wide variety of fairly technical policies.

The appeal of cooperation as an ideal has blinded many enthusiasts to the functions of dispute and opposition in maintaining the individual's leverage on the industrial system. To these problems we return in Chapter XVII.

BARGAINING UNITS AND LOCUS OF AGREEMENT

We have noted in the previous section of this chapter that the type of management-union relations is dependent in considerable measure on the locus of agreement. Organizations away from the "firing line" for the settlement of the basic position of the union in

[13] Selekman, *op. cit.*

the industrial system are likely to have more stable, orderly relations. Local plant managers and union leaders may maintain a fairly even course of settling specific problems in an industry marked by more or less violent labor disputes at the national level. It is appropriate therefore to examine the nature of bargaining units as a feature of management-union relations, and to explore the question as to where negotiation of basic issues takes place.

Types of Bargaining Units. Although less hazardous than the classification of dynamic relations between management and union, a typology of bargaining units encounters considerable complexity. Thus, the loose term "industry-wide bargaining" may refer to negotiations between a single employer and single union (for example, the telephone industry), a number of employers with or without a formal association and a single union (for example, the coal industry), or a group of employers with a group of unions (this is rare). As the term is used, it may also inaccurately refer to negotiations between a national union and an employer with several plants and products (steel and automobiles, for example), or to negotiations between employers and unions in different industries in a labor market area (San Francisco, for example). In any of these instances the term may refer to local, regional, or national negotiations.

In view of this complexity it will be useful to build up somewhat systematically a "catalogue" of possible bargaining units. In order to cover the full range, it will be assumed that firms manufacture several products and have several local plants and that there is more than one firm in any industry. Fewer possibilities exist if either of these assumptions does not hold.

> LOCAL PLANT LEVEL
>   Occupation or craft
>   Product division
>   Plant as a unit
>
>   Local craft or industrial union
>   Unions of same employer [14]

[14] Multiple-union bargaining is rare, but in a sense does exist in sympathetic strikes and refusal to cross picket lines.

FIRM LEVEL
  Occupational or functional division
  Product line
  Firm as a unit

  National union
  Unions of same employer

INDUSTRY LEVEL
  Local
  Regional
  National
  (All ordinarily through trade association)

  National union
  Group of unions in industry

INTER-INDUSTRY LEVEL [15]
  Employers' association
  Labor union councils

The bargaining unit therefore is made up of one or more of the following components: occupation, product division, plant, firm, industry, trade association, local craft or industrial union, national union, inter-union council. As these components are somewhat independent, it follows that a progression from units to complexes is not necessarily as orderly as the list above implies. There is, however, a natural tendency, commented on in the preceding chapter, for the unit chosen by one party to be matched by the other, with the additional possibility that a shift in level by management or union may give a temporary advantage until matched by the other.

Before commenting on some problems of multi-unit bargaining, a few observations about the role of trade associations is in order. Many trade associations antedate strong unions and were indeed designed to prevent union organization or genuine collective bargaining. In a sense, therefore, they represented a collective refusal to bargain; often they also represented a collective refusal to hire

---

[15] In the United States this has developed only at the local labor market level. (See, for example, Clark Kerr and Lloyd H. Fisher, "Multiple-Employer Bargaining: The San Francisco Experience," in Lester and Shister, eds., *op. cit.*, pp. 25–61.) The national master agreement is a theoretical possibility, but probably only in a totalitarian state where government would essentially determine the terms.

known union members or sympathizers. All this, of course, was in the fine tradition of "individualism" as an argument against unions, but not against the collusion of employers.

Other employers' associations are defensive organizations, designed to avoid the "whipsaw" procedure of unions in pushing up wage rates by striking one plant at a time while the recalcitrant employer lost his market position to competitors with or without union agreements. In order to combat industry-wide bargaining the Taft-Hartley Act forbids unions to require employer membership in an association as a condition of bargaining, but indirect pressures such as the "whipsaw" principle are still available to the union.

Employers' or trade associations differ in their degree of centralization of labor policy. Just as the union local may lose its autonomy to the national organization in policy determination, the individual employer may find that the pressure of other employers and of the association itself forces policy into the collective sphere. The association staff is likely to abet this process to justify its own existence as well as to "keep peace" by avoiding labor competition among employers. Although avoidance of wage competition may have adequate legal sanction (even this is somewhat doubtful), the broadening scope of collective bargaining into non-wage issues may involve the association members in violations of antitrust acts through standardization of a broad area of business policies by formal agreement.

Problems of Multiple-Unit Bargaining. The growth of multiple-unit bargaining, whether strictly "industry-wide" or one of the other types indicated above, has led to various problems and implications not encountered at the strictly local level.

The first of these problems is that of increased *formalization* of relations. This is a departure only in degree from any collective relations, but the heightened degree is still of some importance. Multiple-unit bargaining necessarily centers on common problems, perhaps even a "least common denominator" of problems, at the possible cost of established local relations on a more informal level. This form of bargaining involves not only the standardization of rules and practices as they are distributively applied within the area of the agreement, but also new rules and forms for determining representation of bargaining agents, and degrees of sovereignty and autonomy reserved to the component units. To work effectively, multiple-unit bargaining requires solidarity of management and union representatives, respectively, and uniformity in application of decisions. Thus grievance machinery set up as the continuing judicial organ of the agreement cannot differ widely in its interpretations and decisions from plant to plant without endangering the whole structure of management-union relations. This raises problems of authority and accountability on both sides, as any given local manager or union leader may be forced to justify a policy in terms of problems faced by an entirely different plant or company or union local. If such instances are frequent the system is subject to a very considerable strain from sentiments for secession. Unity carries penalties that may not be perceived until standard treatment violates notions of local sovereignty.

A second problem of multiple-unit bargaining is that of *concentration of power*. Whatever the formal provisions for representation on negotiating committees, it is virtually certain that the several units affected will not have an equal weight in reaching decisions. On the union side representation or effective weight may be approximately proportional to membership. On the employer side, it is more likely to be on volume of sales or share of the market. Those units best able to secure a favorable bargain and, by the same token, best able to survive an unfavorable one, are almost certain to have a major voice in policies and decisions. On either side the result may be collapse or loss of sovereignty of weak units.

Although this problem applies to unions as well as plants or companies, the problems of the latter have been more commonly recognized because of their economic implications. If a number of firms are involved in bargaining, decisions relative to wage scales may raise problems concerning the survival of small and less efficient firms. (This problem is not unique to multiple-company bargaining, however. The unilateral drive by a national union for uniformity in wage scales may have the same effect.) Even if the bargaining is only company-wide, the impact of the agreement may be markedly more severe on some plants or product lines than on others.

If a principal function of multiple-unit bargaining is "to take labor out of competition" by standardizing wage rates, the problem of *securing inter-unit manpower transfers* is presented. Wage differentials in classic labor market theory are *the* effective means for securing allocation of labor supply to match labor demand. Detailed labor market studies have amply demonstrated the failures of the labor market to act according to form. However, wage differentials have played *some* role in securing manpower transfers, and wage standardization requires turning attention to other devices. The closest approximation to a difference in basic wage rates is a difference in actual take-home pay through varying availability of overtime pay. There are also many types of non-wage competition for labor, including "working conditions" in the broadest sense. Some of these also may be standardized in multiple-unit bargaining, but it is improbable that all local initiative would or could be removed. Finally, the union itself may take on responsibility for labor supply, which means use of union authority over the membership to secure transfers as needed.

Still another result of multiple-unit bargaining is the *increased security of the union,* which also presents problems for the rival union. A rival union may be able to secure a footing in an industry only by organizing one plant at a time. If employers present a united front owing to their current union commitments, inter-union competition may be impeded or prevented. This has obvious implications for the responsibility to its own membership of a union so powerfully protected.

Finally, multiple-unit bargaining allows widening and intensifying the area of cooperation. It does not guarantee it, for it also allows more severe conflict. A dispute may tie up not a single division or plant but an entire company or industry, with consequent disadvantages to the public at large.

Unless positively prohibited by law—a prohibition that might have results as mixed as have followed enforcement of the antitrust acts—it appears that despite disadvantages the "breadth" of bargaining is likely to increase. Localism and competition also have disadvantages to participants. The treatment of the weak by the strong, the degree and area of local autonomy, the compensations for rigidity and standardization—these are the leading issues that will have to be settled in some way as the scale of management-union agreements grows.

The Locus of Agreement. We are now in a position to appraise the developing practices with regard to where basic issues of management-labor relations are settled. Leaving aside for the moment the role of "external" factors—especially the government and the volume of employment, which may in given instances be decisive—where are "patterns" set?

The most ambitious attempt at an answer to that question is that put forward by Harbison and Dubin.[16] These authors propose a dichotomous classification of management-union relations as "pattern setting" or "generating" types and "pattern-following" or "satellite" types. The authors partially recognize the weakness of the classification by addition of a third category, "semi-isolated types," which upon inspection of the authors' classificatory criteria turn out to include most of the management-union relations in American industry. We have encountered this classification earlier in this chapter with reference to types of management-union relations. It is especially relevant here because of its bearing on the locus of agreement.

According to Harbison and Dubin, patterns of management-union relations are set in major industrial power centers (their principal case is General Motors). What constitutes a power center, independently of the circular test of pattern-setting, is not quite clear, as the authors refer to "mass-production industries," "basic industries," and "concentrations of economic power." Now these are not exactly the same thing. The telephone industry is certainly concentrated without being mass-production in the ordinary sense, and does not set patterns except, doubtfully, for itself. Coal is basic

---

[16] *Op. cit.* See also Frederick H. Harbison, Robert K. Burns, and Robert Dubin, "Toward a Theory of Labor-Management Relations," in Lester and Shister, eds., *op. cit.*, pp. 3–24.

without being mass-production, and its pattern-setting is quite different from what Harbison and Dubin have in mind.

In effect, the correspondence between mass-production industries and pattern-setting (or what we have called issue bargaining) is fortuitous and not intrinsic. The essential, structural basis for pattern-setting in the sense used by Harbison and Dubin is not at all the authors' specification but rather marked inequality in the size and power of productive units in the same industry and the absence of an employer united-front. The locus of agreement at the "power center" is simply inapplicable to a monopolistic industry (telephone) or a widely-scattered one (coal).[17]

What, then, can be said about the probable locus of agreement on basic issues? Several answers must be given, depending upon variable circumstances, and even so, subject to relatively low predictive value because of the complex interrelation of those variables. (1) In a multi-firm industry, without genuine industry-wide bargaining (even if enforced only by the union, as in coal), basic issues are likely to be settled by the union's agreement with one of the big firms; which firm will depend upon union strategy and upon changes in the light of collective relations with the union. (2) Where any form of multiple-employer bargaining takes place, even if the employers are less organized than the union, "pattern setting" and "pattern following" are determined internally to the organization of each party to the negotiation, with the formal agreement setting the pattern simultaneously for the industry; this does not necessarily reduce the importance of the "power centers," but does radically alter the mode of decision-making and the latitude of the less powerful unit in seeking modification of the pattern *before* it is established. (3) Where the union is tightly organized on a national level but the industry is not, the union is most likely to seek the best possible terms in its center of greatest numerical strength or other bargaining advantage, and then bring other employers into line if necessary

[17] The hazard of generalizing the particular study is especially exemplified in this instance. General Motors, identified by Harbison and Dubin as the likely place among the automobile "big three" for fairly continuous conflict because of bargaining over issues, early in 1950 signed a five-year contract with the UAW while Chrysler fought out a long strike.

by strikes that give a market advantage to employers with whom the agreement was initially concluded.

It should be emphasized that these principles will not include all cases; for example, inter-union competition may occasionally be more important than inter-company competition. Moreover, some "patterns" have a quite "unreasonable" effect, simply because they provide an available, external formula which will resolve an impasse while saving face on all sides. Thus in 1946 in the uncertain period of withdrawal of wage and price controls, a wage increase formula of 18½ cents an hour proposed for one industry (automobiles) on necessarily arbitrary grounds was accepted by major sectors of management and union negotiators in widely differing industries. This sort of "exception" provides a challenge still unanswered to reduce the area of uncertainty in the prediction of types and sequences in the relations of management and union.

REFERENCES

BAKKE, E. WIGHT, *Mutual Survival: The Goal of Unions and Management* (New York: Harper & Brothers, 1946).

BLOOM, GORDON F., and HERBERT R. NORTHROP, *Economics of Labor and Industrial Relations* (Philadelphia: The Blakiston Company, 1950), Chap. 6, "Industrial Jurisprudence," and Chap. 8, "Collective Bargaining—Scope and Breadth."

BLUMER, HERBERT, "Sociological Theory in Industrial Relations," *American Sociological Review*, 12: 271–278, June 1947.

BRAUN, KURT: *Union-Management Co-operation: Experience in the Clothing Industry* (Washington: The Brookings Institution, 1947).

CARPENTER, JESSE THOMAS, *Employers' Associations and Collective Bargaining in New York City* (Ithaca: Cornell University Press, 1950).

COMMONS, JOHN R., and ASSOCIATES, *Industrial Government* (New York: The Macmillan Company, 1921).

DE SCHWEINITZ, DOROTHEA, *Labor and Management in a Common Enterprise* (Cambridge: Harvard University Press, 1949).

DUBIN, ROBERT, "Union-Management Co-operation and Productivity," *Industrial and Labor Relations Review*, 2: 195–209, January 1949.

DUNLOP, JOHN T., *Collective Bargaining: Principles and Cases* (Chicago: Richard D. Irwin, 1949).

DYMOND, W. R., "Union-Management Co-operation at the Toronto Factory of Lever Brothers Limited," *Canadian Journal of Economics and Political Science*, 13: 26–67, February 1947.

HARBISON, FREDERICK H., "Some Reflections on a Theory of Labor-Management Relations," *Journal of Political Economy*, 54: 1–16, February 1946.

HARBISON, FREDERICK H., and ROBERT DUBIN, *Patterns of Union-Management Relations* (Chicago: Science Research Associates, 1947).

HARBISON, FREDERICK H., ROBERT K. BURNS, and ROBERT DUBIN, "Toward a Theory of Labor-Management Relations," in Richard A. Lester and Joseph Shister, eds., *Insights into Labor Issues* (New York: The Macmillan Company, 1948), pp. 3–24.

HART, C. W. M., "Industrial Relations Research and Social Theory," *Canadian Journal of Economics and Political Science*, 15: 53–73, February 1949.

KERR, CLARK, and LLOYD H. FISHER, "Multiple-Employer Bargaining: The San Francisco Experience," in Richard A. Lester and Joseph Shister, eds., *Insights into Labor Issues* (New York: The Macmillan Company, 1948), pp. 25–61.

LESTER, RICHARD A., and EDWARD A. ROBIE, *Constructive Labor Relations: Experience in Four Firms* (Princeton: Industrial Relations Section, Princeton University, 1948).

LESTER, RICHARD A., and EDWARD A. ROBIE, *Wages under National and Regional Collective Bargaining* (Princeton: Industrial Relations Section, Princeton University, 1946).

NYMAN, RICHMOND C., and ELLIOTT DUNLAP SMITH, *Union-Management Coöperation in the "Stretch Out"* (New Haven: Yale University Press for the Institute of Human Relations, 1934).

PIERSON, FRANK C., *Collective Bargaining Systems* (Washington: American Council on Public Affairs, 1942).

ROSS, ARTHUR M., *Trade Union Wage Policy* (Berkeley and Los Angeles: University of California Press, 1948), Chap. II, "The Trade Union as a Wage-Fixing Institution," and Chap. V, "Union-Management Relations and the Wage Bargain."

SELEKMAN, BENJAMIN M., *Labor Relations and Human Relations* (New York: McGraw-Hill Book Company, Inc., 1947).

———, "Some Implications and Problems of Collective Bargaining," in Louis M. Hacker and Others, *The New Industrial Relations* (Ithaca: Cornell University Press, 1948), pp. 33–65.

SHISTER, JOSEPH, "Union-Management Cooperation: An Analysis," in Richard A. Lester and Joseph Shister, eds., *Insights into Labor Issues* (New York: The Macmillan Company, 1948), pp. 87–115.

SLICHTER, SUMNER H., *Union Policies and Industrial Management* (Washington: The Brookings Institution, 1941), especially Chaps. XIV–XX.

TURNBULL, JOHN G., *Labor-Management Relations: A Research Planning Memorandum,* Social Science Research Council, Bulletin 61(New York: 1949), Chap. III, "Patterns of Interaction and Their Consequences."

TWENTIETH CENTURY FUND, Labor Committee, *Partners in Production: A Basis for Labor-Management Understanding* (New York: 1949).

UNIVERSITY OF PENNSYLVANIA, *Proceedings of the Conference on Industry-Wide Collective Bargaining* (Philadelphia: University of Pennsylvania Press, 1949).

WARNER, W. LLOYD, and J. O. Low, *The Social System of the Modern Factory: The Strike: A Social Analysis* (New Haven: Yale University Press, 1947), Chaps. VII–IX.

CHAPTER XVI

DISPUTES, CONFLICTS, SETTLEMENTS

MANAGEMENT-UNION cooperation, discussed in the last chapter, and conflict, discussed in this, are customarily regarded as virtue and sin, respectively. This view demands careful scrutiny, for complete peace and cooperation in the industrial sphere may be achieved at the expense of other values that are even more important in a liberal social order.

Despite the impressive area of possible joint determination by management and union, there is considerable doubt about the ability of unions to participate in all managerial functions and at the same time fulfill the function of an opposition in behalf of union membership. Management in a competitive economy, or indeed any other industrial economy, must represent consumer interests and investment interests. Under systems of nationalization of production, these interests are presumably the responsibility of government in its directives to management. This changes the mechanism of managerial responsibility, not the essential functions. Management is, however, poorly equipped to serve these functions and also represent "producer" interests in the terms and conditions of employment.[1] This is an important function of unions.

Disputes between management and union over these differing interests may be suppressed by complete emasculation of the unions, complete control by an administrative agency, or complete syndicalization of industry. None of these devices would resolve the differing interests, but only prevent overt disputes by shifting and con-

[1] See Peter F. Drucker, *The New Society: The Anatomy of the Industrial Order* (New York: Harper & Brothers, 1950), especially Chap. 10, "Can Management Be a Legitimate Government?"

straining the mechanism of protest, dissent, and leverage on the system. If interests are represented by independent, although inter-dependent, organizations, disputes are normal and to be expected. They are an indication of an area of voluntary action and expressed differences.

The notion that the proper goal of study of industrial relations is the achievement of industrial peace is likely to stem from some unexpressed ideologies pervasive in the social sciences—the econo-mists' self-regulating market, the political scientists' representative but completely orderly state, the sociologists' perfectly integrated society. In a complex society with many differing interests and be-liefs, the price of preservation of considerable latitude in voluntary individual action and group organization is an "area of tolerated conflict." Since such conflicts are likely to affect persons not directly involved in the disputes, and affect even disputants in ways not di-rectly related to the main points at issue, it is a matter of policy within what limits conflict may occur, and what measures for the settlement or repression of conflict are consistent with other ideals and norms. The importance of industrial disputes within these gen-eral principles is that with the increasing interdependence of the economy their impact on disputants and bystanders alike is likely to be more severe and far-reaching than is usually true of other organizational conflicts.

THE SOURCES AND POINTS OF CONFLICT

In the light of the preceding paragraphs, it is clear that industrial *disputes* are a normal aspect of collective relations between manage-ment and unions. What does this imply by way of industrial *con-flict?* Here some important difficulties of definition and meaning arise.

The language of public and even academic discussion of indus-trial relations is strongly flavored with terms that better fitted the past than the contemporary conduct of corporations and unions. For much of the history of American unionism an industrial dispute was likely to take the form of overt, violent conflict, with the union's own survival a major stake in the contest. This situation prevailed even into the late 1930's. Despite the National Labor Relations (Wagner) Act, it was not until a rapid rise in the level of employment, followed by the definite establishment of the position of the union through the procedures of the War Labor Board and other wartime governmental agencies, that the essential pattern of management-union relations was based on the definite existence and power of the union in the industrial system. As noted in the preceding chapter, this background of "extreme conflict" still conditions management-union relations. The present point is that it also conditions and obscures understanding of the genuine changes resulting from the fact that the union's existence and the practice of collective bargaining are no longer the essential points at issue in industrial disputes. Until that change took place, it made sense to discuss at least part of industrial relations in terms appropriate to warfare, for in fact violence was overt or incipient in many situations.

The basic nature of the change effected by the legalization of collective bargaining and the *recognition* of the union as a definite part of the industrial order may be illustrated by reference to the strike. The very term "strike" carries a flavor of violence, whereas the more cumbersome "concerted work stoppage" may also be the more accurate in its connotations. Even during the hectic interwar period, many strikes in areas of the economy long characterized by collective bargaining involved no more than a "failure to complete a transaction" over the contractual specification of the terms and conditions of employment. It was an instrument of bargaining, not an act of violence. But in industries long marked by weak unions, or none, the sudden flourishing of large unions often encountered a rejection by management of the union's right to exist and especially to represent workers in any dispute with management. The employer often attempted violence and intimidation, employment of non-union workers, and indeed an entire "arsenal" of weapons that will be briefly catalogued in the following section. Unions countered with mass picketing, including the use of "flying squads" of workers from other plants to intimidate non-union workers ("scabs") seeking to accept employment in the struck plant and to combat the professional strikebreakers hired by the company. These situations gave rise to industrial conflict in a far more fundamental sense than the simple jockeying for power, influence, and favorable terms of agreement inherent in management-union disputes. And violence was not the essential criterion of that fundamental conflict but rather its result. The basic question was the existence and survival of the union as a legitimate instrumentality of negotiation and protest. The settlement of that issue has not removed all "fundamental" disputes or made all "weapons" of management and union outmoded. But once that issue was settled in favor of the union's recognition as a part of the conduct of the industrial system, no other dispute could be so basic.

Industrial disputes and conflicts may be classified in several broad types: (1) disagreement over the basic terms of management-union relations—the "issues" as they were called in the preceding chapter; (2) disputes arising from the application and interpretation of basic terms or areas of agreement—these include both "problem bargaining" as previously discussed and some aspects of grievance machinery; and (3) disputes arising from complexities and tensions of personality and interpersonal relations.

Disputes of the first type represent the closest approximation to old-fashioned industrial conflict, for the recognition of the union has not settled its area of power and competence in the structure of industry. It is in this area, where principles are uncertain and subject to change with the shifting power of management and union and the variable environment of the industrial order, that "rights" are likely to be talked about with strong emotions and appeals to sentiment. It is this area, therefore, that is most important for analysis of the continuing evolution of the American industrial system. To use a somewhat appropriate metaphor, the issues are constitutional, not legislative, judicial, or administrative.

Disputes of the second type are the most pervasive in industrial relations. They range from the multitude of disputes and grievances in the shop to the settlement of the economic bargain over wages and hours. Because of the importance of wages as an issue in bargaining, and of wealth as a "universal means," it may cause surprise that the wage bargain is put in this category. The justification for this rests primarily on the fact that the wage issue is perhaps the most solidly established aspect of collective bargaining. This does not mean that no work stoppages will result from wage disputes or even that there is a fundamental agreement as to the "fair share" of labor in the industrial budget. What is generally agreed is that the unions have a "right" to ask for as high wages as they can get for their members, consistent with continued successful operation of the enterprise. The mooted issues are many—should workers accept substandard wages because of the competitive disadvantage of the firm, should workers alone benefit from improvements in productivity, what is the relation between wages, prices, and profits? These issues are of varying importance in particular management-union relations. In general, however, a dispute over wages is likely to be settled more easily than one involving new elements of union participation in joint determination or new "employee benefits" that have structural as well as financial implications for the firm.

The third type of dispute is the least homogeneous, but not necessarily the least important. Numerous students of industrial relations have emphasized that these may be the hardest to resolve precisely because they fall outside the conventional framework of collective bargaining. The only way to get the tensions and hostilities into the machinery of protest and adjustment may be a grievance or demand that is an acceptable rather than a real source of dispute.

Specific issues in industrial conflicts range as widely as individual aspirations and group interests. Moreover, industrial conflict is not always, or even usually, a rational affair. Its pattern is, on the contrary, typically one of strong sentiments and outraged sensibilities. Issues are frequently lost sight of in the interaction of discordant personalities. The generating spark may be a muttered oath or a thumbed nose. Its continuance may rest on the necessity of "keeping face," either as individuals or as organizations. Both sides are capable of a good deal of dissimulation, conscious or otherwise. Thus workers at a factory ranking low in the community's scheme of things may insist that they are underpaid. The argument by comparative statistics that the workers are not underpaid has little merit (or at least little effect). Similarly, an employer may genuinely believe that the quarter of a million dollars he pays annually to compete for workers' loyalties represents the fulfillment of his duty to protect his employees from the honeyed words of radicals and agitators. Conflict in any field of human activity ordinarily involves something more than a shrewd and calculating marshalling of forces; there is also the interplay of sentiments and emotions, giving the conflict its characteristic "unreasonableness." It follows that an examination of the specific issues in industrial disputes, the points of overt friction and conflict, may reveal little concerning the underlying sources of discontent and hostility.

THE "WEAPONS" OF MANAGEMENT

Despite the greatly reduced incidence of violence in industrial disputes due, it was noted, to the diminishing significance of union survival as the basic issue—it is still proper to refer in a metaphorical sense to the "weapons" of management and labor. The types of "weapons" have undergone major changes with the evolution of management-union relations, and those in current use may in turn be discarded as they prove inappropriate to the strategy or tactics of battle or the rules of warfare.

Before directing attention to some of the past and present devices used by management in dealing with unions, several general tendencies in the development of tactics may be noted. One such tendency is that of developing new weapons, or new tactical uses of weapons, in those areas of group relations poorly defined by law. Thus the invention of the company union, frequently with closed shop provisions, aided the managerial battle against independent unionism. Similarly, the employment of the "sit-down strike" by the growing industrial unions in the mid-1930's gained some temporary advantage for organized labor. That both of these weapons were subsequently judged to be contrary to public policy is simply illustrative of the logic of institutional growth in this field. That is, in a conflict situation within a social order, new tactical developments must either be fitted into previous rules, or else be upheld or rejected by new rules.

Another tendency that reveals the underlying problems of industrial conflict is to be found in the practice of regarding questions of legality as of distinctly secondary importance. In other words, victory over the enemy is viewed as more important than the or derly processes of peaceful adjudication.

Closely related to the foregoing tendencies is the practice of both parties to any conflict of *using* the rules or the rule-enforcing officials to their own advantage. This may range all the way from pressing an advantage inherent in the rules to outright subversion of the regulatory system through bribery, intimidation, and so on. The law itself, in other words, may be a powerful weapon in the hands of either party. In these cases—and indeed in all cases of extreme conflict—the divisive forces of special interests take precedence over the unifying factor of institutional regulation. However, the importance of the law remains at least as great as at other times for those who are not parties to the dispute. Even when the law is being used or circumvented by those in conflict, its force must always be taken into account. And it is manifestly true, almost by definition, that the force of the law will prevail in the long run.

The Scrap Heap of Weapons. In the history, including the fairly recent history, of American industrial disputes management had at its disposal a formidable array of instruments of combat, some of them weapons in the literal sense of the word. Because of their historic importance, and the comtemporary importance in turn of the background of extreme conflict, a brief catalogue of these largely discarded tactics is appropriate.

Coercion and show of force was of considerable importance in the attempts to prevent union organization and defeat strikes until just prior to World War II. Company guards were increased and armed, and by the device of "deputizing" these guards they became a sort of private police system in the entire community. Workers were beaten and occasionally killed. Several firms prospered in "industrial munitioning"—the supplying of rifles, machine guns, and tear gas to industrial concerns fearing "labor troubles."

Not all devices of management were so direct and potentially deadly. Various "preventive" measures were used. Notable among these was the *company union,* outlawed in major industrial plants by the Wagner Act (NLRA). The only reason for establishment of a company union, that is, one actually under the domination of management, is the threat of independent unionism. Widely used at one time or another between the two World Wars, it was a more or less effective device for convincing both employees and government agencies that there was no need for "outside organizers and agitators."

Another preventive measure, especially developed during the period of rapid union expansion in the 1930's, was *labor espionage and bribery.* Borrowing the revolutionists' tactic of "boring from within," private detective agencies were hired to ferret out the existence of a union, to identify members so that they could be fired and possibly "blacklisted" with other employers, to learn union plans, and even, occasionally, to capture union elections (the position of union treasurer being the ultimate triumph of espionage). Bribery of union officials was also undoubtedly attempted and may have occasionally succeeded, although the known cases chiefly involved a racket using a union front for "shaking down" employers "to prevent labor troubles."

Antiunion discrimination and individual contracts were long favorite devices of some leading corporations espousing the "open shop" (meaning a closed, antiunion shop). The extreme device was the individual ("yellow dog") contract making continued employment contingent upon the worker's being and remaining unaffiliated with any union (except possibly compulsory membership in a company union). Less obvious practices involved discrimination against union members in work assignments, promotions, discipline, and discharge. In the early years of the Wagner Act before World War II many cases before the National Labor Relations Board involved charges of this sort of "unfair labor practice." These tactics were also sometimes combined with a *blacklist,* which virtually prevented an employee discharged for union activity from securing employment at his regular occupation with another company.

The tactics associated with strikebreaking were often the most elaborate. *Professional strikebreakers,* who were almost always men with criminal records willing to continue their criminal careers under the august sponsorship of respectable corporations and local law enforcement officers, were often the shock troops of industrial warfare. Some agencies supplied a complete service: "strikeguards" or "nobles" used to supplement company and community police for any necessary violence; "finks" who pretended to be nonunion employees operating the plant (necessarily at pay above that demanded by the strikers and often with disastrous results to tools and materials); and "missionaries," who sought out "loyal" employees, stirred up discontent and discord among others.

Strikebreaking involved not only the use of hired gangsters, but the organization of *citizens' committees* and *back-to-work movements,* with management finding its sympathizers among some of the "thought leaders" in the community, some workers unemployed because of the strike but not sympathetic to the union, and the wives of some strikers. Threats to move or abandon the plant were coupled with promises of re-employment of all innocent employees at the previous terms.

Many of these tactics were locally and temporarily successful. Especially when they were successful they conditioned the union to violence and conflict and remain recorded in organization "memory." The tactics of management in combating unionism turned out to be the appropriate means for winning many battles and losing the war.

The Current Tactics of Management. The survival of the union and its incorporation in the industrial order was an outcome of industrial warfare greatly aided by legislative changes as well as by the increased enthusiasm for unions owing to the tactics of management. This outcome, despite the natural tendency for corporations to cry disaster, did not leave management unarmed.

Perhaps the most fundamental power of management, a power moderately limited by law and union power but not lost, is that of extending or withholding employment. Union power, with or without legal backing, may prevent discriminatory discharge and even prevent discharge of the incompetent union member, may require the employment of persons not needed, and may require that persons hired be union members.

Even the extreme union powers will not prevent the company from suspending operations for business reasons, and may not prevent a *lockout* as a tactic in labor disputes. The lockout is the employer's counterpart of the strike. In practice, however, it is very difficult to distinguish the strike and the lockout in a full-fledged industrial dispute, and it is not infrequently true that spokesmen for management will declare that the workers are on strike, whereas the union leaders will maintain that they are locked out. It is important to note that work stoppages hurt both the company and the workmen, and therefore constitute weapons in the hands of both. "Waiting ability" is likely to be an important aspect of relative bargaining advantage.

As long as the central issue in industrial disputes was the survival of the union, one of the major weapons of the employer was the use of law and law enforcement machinery to break the power of unions. After the defeat of the doctrine that any union constituted unlawful conspiracy, legislation and judicial interpretation was generally unclear on the positive rights of unions. However, most of the weapons used by unions in the course of disputes could be and commonly were enjoined by the courts. Continuance of strike activity in the face of a court injunction made the labor leaders liable to fine and imprisonment for contempt of court. In some cases, any violence in an industrial dispute, especially if the violence could be actually or conceivably attributed to the strikers, was also the basis for securing injunctions, and possibly criminal prosecutions. The courts usually applied existing legislation and judicial precedent fairly honestly; the law and precedents simply did not favor union activity. The same concern for legality often did not prevail among state and local law enforcement agencies, which were often used essentially as strikebreakers in conjunction with the employer's attempts to end the dispute, completely victorious over the union. Changes in the law coupled with increased political activity by unions on the local level have greatly altered the pattern of recourse to the courts and police in industrial disputes. Strikes still produce sporadic violence, but the occasions for violence are few if the company does not attempt to operate the plant with a large proportion of the regular employees on strike. The injunction was largely set aside as an instrumentality of the employer in the federal jurisdiction with the passage of the Norris-La Guardia Act, and restored only in very diminished degree with the Taft-Hartley Act. Governmental administrative and arbitration agencies still play an important part in the conduct of management-labor relations, and the possibilities of governmental "seizure" of companies in "essential" industries may be used by both sides as a factor in negotiation. In this and a number of other situations there is a tendency for the disputes to be settled by governmental arbitration. This circumstance makes difficult any generalized statement of the importance of direct governmental action for either management or labor.

Changes in the law and conduct of management-labor relations have changed but not decreased the importance of another management weapon—*antiunion propaganda*. An especially effective procedure for combating the power of independent unionism is to discredit the forces of organized labor as destructive of business prosperity, violators of individual initiative and freedom, and upholders of un-American doctrines and perpetrators of unpatriotic actions. Individual employers, and especially employers' associations, have thought this type of weapon sufficiently powerful to warrant the expenditure of untold millions for advertising, distribution of free texts for the schools, maintenance of "research" and editorial staffs, etc.

On a local scale, especially, management may theaten to abandon the plant or move it to some area less given to "labor troubles" as a means of bringing community pressure upon striking workers to admit defeat and keep their jobs. Because the public at large is likely to suffer some inconvenience during a labor dispute, and overt action is usually first precipitated by laborers (since they are challenging the previously existing conditions), management has the advantage of an incipient antilabor attitude as a basis for its propaganda.[2] If the strikers can be made to appear responsible not only for any inconvenience or sporadic violence, but for the loss of an industrial payroll and taxable property, continuance of a labor dispute may have to face the opposition of merchants, professionals, and "loyal" workers as well as the direct representatives of management.

The subtler advertising campaigns conducted by employers' associations are simply probusiness, or in favor of "unity." Thus, two favorite recent slogans have been "Prosperity Dwells where Harmony Reigns," and "What Helps Business Helps You." Like President Coolidge's pastor, the sponsors of such slogans are simply "against sin." More forceful campaigns, however, attempt to discredit labor leaders as swindlers, racketeers, or agents of a foreign government, and labor unions as gangs of cutthroats or misled dupes. As in any propaganda, effectiveness of the campaign is greatly aided by selection of instances that more or less bear out the contention.

Belief in the importance of public opinion in labor disputes has grown steadily, with the result that readers of metropolitan newspapers a thousand miles from the scene of action may be greeted in full-page advertisements by both management and union, each presenting the "reasonableness" of its position.

Arguments against unionism as such have largely subsided in the direct dealings of management with employees in plants where the union is firmly established. Under the Wagner Act such arguments constituted an "unfair labor practice" in companies subject to Federal labor jurisdiction through a loose interpretation of "interstate commerce." The Taft-Hartley Act modified this prohibition but the importance of arguments against any union representation is largely confined to companies experiencing new organizational drives.

[2] It is not meant to imply that attitudes favorable to the position of management on the part of the general public derive only from the inconvenience or personal loss occasioned by labor disputes. An individualistic ideal, together with the prestige and virtue attached to business success, tends to discredit in advance the efforts of labor organizations. This ideal is especially typical of tradespeople and independent professionals.

Internally to unionized companies an essential redefinition of managerial tactics has taken place. Having failed to defeat the union as an organized entity, many companies now define the situation as one of "competition for the loyalty of employees." This competition has led to extensive "human relations" programs and to the introduction of various "employee benefits." Many executives, with superior historical hindsight, now profess their belief that had these programs been introduced earlier, the unions would have had no chance in "capturing" worker loyalty. In view of the functional role of the union as an agency of bargaining and protest, managerial regrets are in most instances unjustified on these grounds.

The "competition for loyalties" is regarded as so important by contemporary managements that it deserves one or two additional comments. Every major association (and even minor voluntary groups) competes for the loyalties of its members, all of whom are perforce members of other groups. There is in the industrial sphere still a widespread failure to comprehend that loyalty is not an all-or-none matter, but differentiated according to the function of associations. Some of the more naïve social scientists have lent credence to the view that a kind of "totalitarianism of industry" can recapture the type of organizational integration more or less characteristic of primitive and peasant societies. This leads to the view, usually not succinctly stated, that the company or plant should take the place of the state, community, church, family, and all voluntary associations by "servicing" the employee in all respects. The industrial firm is an even less appropriate structure for fulfilling the functions of other associations than is the union. The nostalgia of managers is less surprising than that of the scholars. Neither is likely to find that industrial "integration" can be achieved by rivalrous courting of the worker.

The existence of factions within the union, however, may in some instances prove to be an advantage to the employer almost as effective as the real or alleged minority position of the union in the period of major union organizational drives. The employer may be able to find a "peace party" within the union and deftly encourage

either a change of union leaders or at least a change in union bargaining demands and tactics. Such a policy carries its own hazard
—the possibility that the membership backing of the leaders and of
the specific demands is sufficiently strong to defeat the internal
opposition and at the same time increase the morale and therefore
the bargaining power of the union.

The specific tactics of management in industrial disputes will
naturally depend in considerable measure upon market considerations and company prosperity. The relationship is not simple, however. The company with a large financial margin may be able to
afford a long strike but if the financial margin is due to continuing
high volume of sales the ease of passing any increased labor costs
along to the consumer may indicate quick settlement. Management's appraisal of short-run and long-run changes not only of the
market and the law in the loosest sense but also of the power of the
union, will be a major factor in its handling of any particular dispute.

The complaint is often heard that there are no longer any "normal times" which, if interpreted as rapid change and meager predictability of future change, is a fairly accurate statement. The
implication of this problem in the present context is that the level
of military operations, governmental controls in view of international conditions, and the level and type of industrial activity that
these involve must all affect managerial tactics in the conduct of
relations with unions. In these circumstances the past and present
are uncertain guides to the future.

THE UNION'S "WEAPONS"

Just as employers have taken precautionary measures to protect
that power already granted by law and custom, and definitely coercive measures to meet challenges to that power, so organized
groups of employees have developed over a considerable period of
time the fundamental strategy and varying tactics of battle. It is
understandable that some of the methods used by management and
labor are similar, and that each may learn "tricks" from the other.
Management may follow a "divide and conquer" policy by securing

individual contracts or by creating dissension between rival organizations; the striking labor union may find it expedient to settle with one employer in a competitive field while the remainder are forced to come to terms or lose part of their sales.

But there are also marked differences in the range of effective weapons available to management and labor arising from their different resources and normal power. Thus, the labor organization is usually in the position of the challenger (or "aggressor") in an industrial dispute, and must perfect the strategy of offense rather than defense. Furthermore, the management of a business enterprise is already a cooperative organization; this is not equally true of the employees. Thus, a good deal of the effort of the union leaders and members must be expended on maintaining unity of purpose, preventing "scabbing," and persuading workmen that concerted demands have more chance of success than individual petitions for redress of grievances or rewards for merit. These differences, and others that follow from them, account for the disparity in weapons and in the importance of those weapons available to both parties to industrial disputes. The significance of these observations may be pointed up by a survey of the battle resources of organized labor.

Some Discarded Tactics. Unions, like the corporations, have junkyards of weapons no longer necessary or appropriate to the current state of management-labor relations. Isolated instances of continued use may be found, for example in new organizational drives against a belligerent employer, but for the most part the weapons represent earlier historical epochs. Although normally not a part of the regular arsenal of American labor unions, *destruction* of plant and equipment, and possibly *violence* directed against nonstrikers and managers, have not been lacking in industrial disputes. The so-called revolutionary unions have occasionally used destruction as a regular instrument of labor policy, either to make immediate gains or for the more far-reaching purpose of contributing to the collapse of the economic and political system. "Sabotage," as the term is frequently used in common American speech, may consist primarily in wrecking equipment or product, whether designed as a weapon against an individual employer or as a blow at the productive system as such.

Like picketing, and, indeed, the bulk of labor's weapons, violence and destruction rarely appear as a distinct type of strategy, but rather as an accompaniment of a strike. Yet logically and actually, "terrorist" activities such as beatings and bombings may be used where a strike has for one reason or another not been called. However, the number of labor disputes actually won by violence and destruction seems to be very small, largely, of course, because law enforcement officers intervene. So effective is that intervention, in fact, that employers may find it possible to have their agents perpetrate violence that can be blamed upon workers as a means of getting official backing for breaking the strike. For these reasons violence and destruction clearly carried on by workers are much more likely to appear as a symptom of weakness and despair of victory in a dispute than as an ordinary policy.

A spectacular weapon of labor that was briefly used with great success by industrial unions in the mass-production industries in the middle 1930's was the *sit-down,* or, more properly, the *stay-in* strike. Aside from the element of surprise, the chief initial advantage gained by a strike which left the workers in control of the plant was the small likelihood of successful strikebreaking by any of the customary procedures. As long as the workers remained in the buildings there was no necessity for persuasive or coercive picketing to prevent "scabbing." It was even claimed by the workers, with considerable accuracy, that the plant and equipment were better protected by the presence of the regular workmen than they would have been if left to the tender mercies of professional strikebreakers.

The stay-in strikes as used principally in the rubber and automobile plants required a minimum of advance organization and could capitalize on spontaneous support partly due to the novelty of the situation. The avoidance of mass picketing provided less excuse for incidents leading to violence, and public authorities hesitated to attempt eviction by force with the strikers in the more advantageous position. However, the effectiveness of the weapon waned largely because of public disapproval. The disapproval might have been less insistent had the strikes been confined to major disputes and so authorized by regular union procedures. But the very novelty and spontaneity of the new weapon, together with its initial success, encouraged a sporadic outbreak of "wildcat" (unauthorized) strikes which served partially to discredit the organization of the unions. The new weapon in fact had been generally discarded as an important strategy at least a year before the United States Supreme Court effectively settled upon its illegality in 1939.[3] Although few if any full-fledged stay-in strikes may be expected in American industrial disputes of the future, brief sit-downs (temporary work stoppages) may continue to be an occasionally effective weapon for settlement of minor disputes where a show of strength seems necessary to break an impasse in bargaining.

The Indirect Tactics of Unions. Like the forces of management, labor unions have attempted with varying degrees of success to improve their position by indirect action, and to protect and consolidate by preventive measures gains achieved in industrial disputes. Such weapons tend to figure less prominently in union strategy than with management, because the union is more often the challenger than the defender. Moreover, in the past the customary relative strength of management and labor meant that defensive action by the former was designed to hold off some slight inroads on the amount of power wielded, whereas the latter often had to defend its very existence as an organized group.

Nevertheless, unions have not failed to explore the possibilities of supplementing direct action by various indirect pressures, and of holding on to gains without the expedient of battle.

[3] National Labor Relations Board *v.* Fansteel Metallurgical Corporation, 306 U.S. 240. The Court ruled that although the National Labor Relations Act recognized workers as "employees" for the duration of a labor dispute, violation of the property rights of the company would sacrifice that privileged status. There is sound ground for holding that the stay-in strike involves a *conflict* in property rights: that of the employees in their jobs (as granted in effect by NLRA and similar legal developments) and that of the company in possession and use of the physical assets of the plant. In this view, the Supreme Court simply held that in the case of the stay-in strike the older right of possession and use took precedence over the newer and still poorly defined property right of the worker in his job.

The public is always affected by labor disputes, and both sides attempt to win public favor, or work through public agencies to buttress their own forces. Actually, there are numerous publics, and of these one of the most important in the strategy of labor is that of the consuming public—especially those consumers upon whom the "enemy" depends for trade. The strike, as a primary boycott, attempts among other things to cut off the supply of products at the source. But either with or without the strike the union may attempt to bring the same economic pressures upon the company by reducing or stopping demand. To this end various devices for influencing the market have been adopted.

The *boycott* is a withdrawal of patronage or other business dealings in order to cause a loss to the individual or company boycotted. As a device used by unions the boycott has had a troubled history. Following *laissez-faire* doctrines the courts cannot interfere with a voluntary refusal to carry on business relationships, except to enforce contracts. Members of a union therefore cannot be prevented from boycotting an offending employer. On the other hand, the courts have also held that a business establishment has a property interest in uninterrupted trade, and that any attempt on the part of the unions to influence "third parties" to cease business dealings with a concern amounts to an illegal restraint of trade. But between these general principles the courts have taken various positions in specific cases. For example, picketing may be partially intended to induce a boycott as well as to dissuade possible strikebreakers. But a strict refusal to allow appeals to consumers during a labor dispute may interfere with another recognized legal principle, that of freedom of speech. In this regard, the courts have generally held that pickets may inform the public that a dispute is in progress, but may not attempt to restrain people from entering the place of business by intimidation or coercion.

In order to circumvent the judicial antipathy to the secondary boycott (that is, one used to prevent business dealings between an employer and "third parties"), unions have adopted other stratagems with some small success. Of these devices, the "unfair" or black lists of nonunion employers, or employers currently engaged in labor disputes, have received the harshest treatment by the courts, since they have been held to constitute a form of the forbidden secondary boycott. (As already noted, until the recent legislation protecting the right of workers to organize, the courts held that blacklists of union workers circulated among employers were perfectly proper.) Other techniques have avoided this pitfall. Thus the courts have been able to find no justifiable grounds for preventing the publishing or circulating of "white lists"—that is, lists of businesses which union members and their friends are urged to patronize. This is, of course, simply a blacklist in reverse, especially if the omissions are obvious. A similar subterfuge is that of the use of advertising space in union publications. Companies with a favorable record of negotiations with unions may find it to their advantage to declare their position as a basis for getting increased sales to union members, whereas nonunion companies might find it difficult to secure any advertising space, even if they so desired.

Perhaps the watered-down boycott that comes most to the attention of the consuming public is the union label. Like white lists or advertising clients, the union label constitutes a boycott only by omission and implication. As a part of union strategy the label is regarded both as a reward to cooperative employers and as a means of passive boycott on those employers to whom its use is denied. To make the distinction carry weight, unions may carry on advertising and propaganda campaigns in behalf of those firms entitled to use the label, and make purchase of union-made goods a mark of loyalty to or sympathy with the labor movement. Withdrawal of the union label may then become an effective weapon against an employer who gets out of line. On the other hand, the unions have not always been able to prevent pirating of the label by nonunion companies. Obviously, it would be extremely difficult to measure the effectiveness of these weapons, especially when they are used in conjunction with other tactics. Yet it is safe to say that they have had a major influence on the purchasing habits of organized workers and their families, and some effect on other consumers. The latter obviously depends greatly on the previously existing sympathies of those not directly involved in industrial controversy.

Thus a union label, for example, may be a highly effective element in the arsenal of unionism in a "union town," and an insignificant or possibly a negative factor in an open-shop community.

To match the propaganda campaigns of antiunion employers and employers' associations, labor organizations from time to time have endeavored to discredit the policies and tactics of big business. The qualification "big" must be made, since the majority of American labor organizations have not found it expedient—or for that matter, do not seem to have seriously desired—to question the older ideology of small and independent enterprise. Antitrust and antimonopoly legislation have been supported by unions fearing the power of sheer size in business organizations. Although much more haphazard and sporadic than the organized campaigns of corporate managerial interests, some union propaganda efforts have capitalized on a general fear of bigness in our economic system. The unions have gained some public support by calling attention to the spread in salaries and wages within an organization, to wastes and inefficiencies attributable to management, as well as to real or alleged violations of civil rights of employees by large corporations.

The propaganda campaign against big business has lacked organization and consistency because the unions have had no set of guiding principles clearly opposed to the doctrines supported by managerial and financial interests. In other words, the ideology of most of the American labor groups has not been anticapitalistic. Yet to the extent that a strictly individualistic doctrine was accepted by organized labor, unions themselves were subject to attack by real or self-styled rugged individualists. In a very real sense, therefore, the absence of an equally powerful counterpropaganda by labor unions has stemmed not only from ideological uncertainty but from a lack of comprehension of the significance of corporate enterprise for the older individualistic doctrines. For this reason, managerial circles have exhibited a great deal more "class consciousness" than have the forces of organized labor. It seems safe to predict that with the growth of large and powerful national unions there will emerge a more consistent set of doctrines which may be presented to the public either as propaganda or counterpropaganda.

Slow-Down, Overstaffing, and Restrictive Rules. Unions have resorted to a variety of expedients intended, in one way or another, to limit the worker's productivity, limit the competition of mechanization, spread the work, and so on. Of these techniques, the one supposedly given the most attention and elaboration is that of the slow-down. Variously called a "strike on the job," "soldiering," "ca'canny," and "sabotage," the slow-down may be used as a fairly direct weapon against management for an immediate goal and abandoned once the goal is achieved, or as a general defensive policy of resistance to "exploitation." Sabotage in its strict and original sense of conscientious withdrawal of efficiency may be developed to a fine art of wasting time, doing the wrong thing with presumed innocence, submitting every question to a superior for decision, fulfilling stupid commands with complete literalness, and so on. A definite, though passive, policy of noncooperation can be a powerful weapon in the hands of the seemingly unarmed. An administrator subjected to this kind of attack can be made to appear very silly without his having much ground for overt punitive action.

As it was observed in Chapter XII dealing with the problems of wastes of labor resources, restriction of output in one form or another is very widespread throughout the gainfully employed population (including managers and professionals as well as shop and bench workers). But it is apparently only in the labor organization that such restrictions are used as an offensive or defensive weapon. If a union is in a favorable bargaining position, the policy of work restriction or spreading the work may become not only a definite but also a formal and official policy. Thus unions may write into collective agreements provision for restriction on the introduction of labor-saving machinery, or investigatory and administrative machinery for decision as to what constitutes a "fair day's work." Some craft unions have become sufficiently powerful to insist on a minimum staff, even though the business of the employer does not require so large a group. In some cases, especially the unions of workers in the entertainment field, this may be extended to paying for services that are not used at all. For example, a radio broadcaster whose musical program consisted of records or transcriptions might be required to hire a "stand-by" orchestra. Such agreements are contractually legal unless forbidden by positive legislation, and represent a defense against the full burden of technological change being borne by displaced workers. In a sense these tactics, however they are viewed with respect to public policy, simply represent an extension of the craft union's aim of maintaining a monopoly on skills by preventing effective substitution for or obsolescence of that monopoly. In this regard it is noteworthy that labor unions share a practice with big business establishments: both are willing and anxious to interrupt any technological change which endangers private group interests.

The Strike. It is frequently asserted that for American organized labor the strike is the center and substance of organizational policy: that other tactics of conflict are either subsidiary to or designed to protect the weapon of collective refusal to work. Although objection might be made to this generalization in specific instances, it is certainly true in a statistical sense. That is, of the various weapons ued by various labor organizations, the strike is certainly the most frequent and the one customarily regarded by the unions as most effective.

Essentially the strike is an organized work stoppage, directed against the economic interests of the employer, but also against any sympathizers or supporters of the employer (including "loyal" employees).[4] It is true that strikes, like wars, may also be undertaken to

---

[4] The literature on such an important weapon of industrial conflict as the strike is, of course, enormous. For good general treatments, see the following: Robert R. R. Brooks, *When Labor Organizes* (New Haven: Yale University Press, 1937), Chap. IV, "The Strike"; Jerome Davis, "Industrial Disputes," in Emanuel Stein and Jerome Davis, eds., *Labor Problems in America* (New York: Farrar & Rinehart, Inc., 1940), Chap. 9; Lois MacDonald, *Labor Problems and the American Scene* (New York: Harper & Brothers, 1938), pp. 480–489; S. Howard Patterson, *Social Aspects of Industry*, 3d. ed. (New York: McGraw-Hill Book Company, Inc., 1943), pp. 284–392. For court cases indicating the legal status of the strike, see James M. Landis, *Cases on Labor Law* (Chicago: The Foundation Press, 1934), Chap. IV, "The Conduct of a Striker," and Chap. V, "The Ends for Which Men May Strike." The most comprehensive treatment of the strike as a complex type of organized social action is that of E. T. Hiller, *The Strike* (Chicago: University of Chicago Press, 1928). See also W. Lloyd

solidify the ranks of the combatants and thus gain a united front for future and more successful action. On the other hand, such unification is not likely to follow from resounding defeat by the selected "enemy," and a union will not willingly call a strike which is patently foredoomed to complete failure at the hands of the employer. Thus, even an "organizational" strike has as its immediate or ultimate goal a successful challenge to the power of management.

The strike is sometimes referred to as a "primary boycott," since its aim is to bring direct economic pressure on the employer by the members of the union and their immediate sympathizers. Although occasionally this pressure consists partly in withholding patronage for the products or services of the company, the strike is primarily designed to withhold the labor necessary for the employer to continue normal operation of the business. For this reason the strike is also commonly called an "economic weapon." However, such a designation should not be thought to mean too much. For example, it does not mean that strikes are called only to wrest economic concessions from employers, or even that during an actual strike the workers' sole hope of victory rests upon the cost of the strike to the company. The designation of a strike as an economic weapon certainly does not mean that it is also an "economical" one, since both parties to the dispute lose income while the plant is shut down. Whether or not the results of the strike are worth the expense even to the victors is a question to which there may be no answer capable of evaluation on a balance sheet. Both sides are likely to feel that there is more at stake in a strike than simply a question of monetary advantages and disadvantages.

A strike may be fairly spontaneous and unorganized, without benefit of elaborate campaign plans or of a previously existing formal union to provide leadership. Some such strikes may gain an immediate and fairly limited objective, partly because the very lack of preparation catches the employer with no effective defense. On the other hand, no very great gains are likely to be secured by such spontaneous stoppages, and even such minor advantages as may be

---

Warner and J. O. Low, *The Social System of the Modern Factory; The Strike: A Social Analysis* (New Haven: Yale University Press, 1947), Chaps. I–III.

secured are likely to be pretty temporary if there is no effective organization to protect the terms of settlement. In general, therefore, the weapon of the strike calls for a tightly knit organization, careful planning, and able leadership.

Viewed as a fairly standardized form of collective action, the strike involves preliminary planning and organization, the strategy and tactics of concerted stoppage of work, and a "settlement" that may range all the way from complete victory for the workers to various forms of defeat, the most disastrous of which may be not only the collapse of the organization but general loss of employment. Obviously, the exact outcome of such a complex and highly variable situation cannot be predicted exactly, although both managers and union leaders who have had long experience in industrial disputes are able to predict *and control* the outcome to a marked extent. On the other hand, strikes are not necessarily undertaken on purely rational grounds, and there is a notable and understandable tendency to overestimate the chances for victory. But even shrewd and cautious contestants may be forced to resort to trial by ordeal in order to determine relative power.

Whatever may be the grievances of the workers, or their more positive aims that can only be achieved through some form of exertion of power and control, a union leader must recognize that simple conviction in the justice of the cause is not sufficient to win battles. The order of decision is likely to be: whether, and if so, when? Naturally the decision to strike, and certainly the decision concerning the time of a strike, will depend upon a judgment of relative strength. Thus, the most propitious time for a strike is when the union is well organized and equipped with sufficient reserve funds, when the demand for labor is high and increasing, and when the employer is in the poorest bargaining position—especially, at a peak season in production, so that a shutdown will really constitute an effective weapon.

Although uncertainty concerning policy, and therefore concerning the amount and kind of support he may expect, may plague a local manager of an extensive corporation, these problems are much graver for a union leader. His efforts must be directed toward creating and maintaining disciplined cooperative activity among those who may be quite unaccustomed to united action in general, or to industrial conflict in particular. This means that the workers must be restrained from an ill-advised or ill-timed strike as surely as they must be expected to support a seemingly advisable and timely one. This difficulty is enhanced by the fact that union members and the general public are likely to insist not only upon democratically chosen leadership, but upon a large measure of *direct* democracy.

Once a strike is effectively called, the strikers must be prepared to "outwait" the employer. This requires not only some form of "strike relief" or other means of subsistence in the absence of regular wages, but also a sufficiently large and united stoppage of work to ensure serious curtailment or complete stoppage of production. A small but strategically important group of workmen may cause a complete stoppage of production, especially if they are also not readily replaceable. This, as we have previously noted, has been a source of strength for craft unions of skilled workmen. So-called production workers in the mass-production industries, on the other hand, must depend on concerted action by a much larger group to have any hope of winning a strike.

Provision of at least a minimum subsistence and maintenance of a united front are probably the two greatest factors in upholding the morale of the strikers. If the employer attempts to operate the plant, even minor defections from the ranks of the strikers may be played up by the employer as a means of inducing others to break ranks and scramble to secure jobs on the old or poorer terms. Since strikes are costly both for the employer and for the employees, and the employer is likely to have a greater reserve, a short strike is more likely to be successful than a long one. Although strikes have been won after a year and more of work stoppage, the problem of maintaining morale mounts with the passage of time.

Before noting the additional direct weapons of labor which may or may not be used in conjunction with a work stoppage, some of the well-known varieties of strikes may be briefly noted. The *sympathetic strike* takes several forms, all involving, as the name implies, work stoppages by laborers not directly involved in the original dispute. A sympathetic strike may be called by one craft union in support of the demands of another craft union in the same plant; it may be a refusal to work with nonunion materials (usually called *hot goods*); it may be a full-fledged sympathetic strike to force an employer to cease doing any business with struck plants, communication lines, and so on. The less direct the connection and interest of the sympathetic workers with the company originally involved in the dispute, the less acceptable is such action in the eyes of the courts. Since most forms of sympathetic strikes involve an attempted coercion of recalcitrant employers through "third parties," this weapon is likely to be judged as an illegal "secondary boycott." For this reason the sympathetic strike is most likely to be effective if directed against a common employer, or if some sort of demands independent of the original controversy can be made against the employers of the sympathetic strikers.

A *general strike* is in form simply an extension of the sympathetic strike to include all workers in an industry, in a local area, or even in the country as a whole. However, since a general strike affecting an area involves the almost complete cessation of all business activity, including the supply of essential consumer goods, it is generally regarded as a revolutionary weapon aimed primarily at the government rather than at commerce and industry as such. Although city-wide general strikes have been called a few times in the United States—most recently in San Francisco in 1934—their success has been debatable. The weapon has not been widely or successfully used in America primarily because the ranks of organized labor have been prepared neither in ideology nor in fact for a concerted, class-conscious revolutionary action.[5]

Picketing, Persuasive and Otherwise. Although there are strikes without picket lines and picket lines without strikes, the two weapons of labor are so frequently used together that they are frequently considered part of the same general phenomenon. Indeed, the nondisputing public is most frequently aware of strikes through the ap-

[5] For a comprehensive treatment of the general strike, see W. H. Crook, *The General Strike* (Chapel Hill: University of North Carolina Press, 1931), especially Chap. XV, "America."

pearance of picket lines around an industrial plant or place of business.

It is difficult to define picketing, precisely because its aim is by no means constant, either in theory or in fact. Apparently the original, and still the most legally acceptable, form of picketing is that illustrated by one or two persons walking back and forth in front of an entrance to a manufacturing or commercial establishment carrying placards proclaiming that a strike is in progress, or simply that the company is "unfair to organized workers." As such, the picket line is designed to be informative, with the potential worker or customer allowed to draw his own conclusions, or at most persuasive, urging support for the demands of the labor organization. To be successful, the use of such a completely "peaceful" weapon must depend upon a considerable body of sympathetic opinion, or at least a benevolent neutrality upon the part of the public, which may be changed into sympathetic support by persuasion. Very frequently organized labor has enjoyed no such sympathy or neutrality either from the buying public or from other workers. From this difficulty arise other types of picketing, the aims of which are much less persuasive than coercive.

If no attempt is made by management to reopen a struck plant while the dispute is in progress, picketing may be a mere formality or even dispensed with completely. On the other hand, a small group of striking employees may attempt to persuade the employees of other departments to "come out" in sympathy. Such picketing is based on the well-known reluctance of union members to "go through a picket line," even if that line has been established by an actually or potentially rival union.

Picketing becomes most obviously a directly coercive weapon in industrial conflict in *mass picketing*. The clear intent of mass picketing is informative or persuasive only in the sense of "it will be healthier for you if you don't go through." The encirclement of a building or grounds by pickets walking in double column and perhaps numbering several thousands is designed to dissuade "scabs" from seeking employment at the expense of the strikers. In union strategy this weapon is considered a necessary adjunct of a strike among unskilled or semiskilled workers whose jobs might be readily taken by nonunion workers. The presence of a large number of strikers or strike sympathizers is also regarded as an effective symbol of united strength, and useful in discouraging the intervention of unsympathetic law enforcement officers or professional strikebreakers.

It is apparent that in so far as picketing is designed to persuade or coerce nonunion workers not to take over the jobs of striking employees the weapon has point only in an industrial society where large numbers of workers remain unorganized. Thus, as between Great Britain and the United States, for example, the picket line has been a major weapon of American unions whereas the English unions for the most part find such strategy unnecessary. If one can assume that the clear tendency in the development of industrial relations is toward fairly complete organization by both employers and employees, most forms of picketing (as well as the whole strategy of strikebreaking by management) are seen to be indicative of immaturity. Those forms of picketing, in other words, are designed to produce at least a temporary "solidarity in the labor movement," which is not guaranteed by permanent organization.

The purpose of a picket line is, of course, not necessarily confined to prevention of strikebreaking. We have already noted that its purpose may be that of dissuading customers from buying goods from the company while a dispute is in progress. But picketing may also be extended to attempt complete economic isolation of the company through stopping of shipments in and out of the establishment. Thus trucks and trains may be halted, cars stopped and searched for contraband (possibly professional strikebreakers), and resistance will ordinarily produce violence. A picket line which operates in this fashion actually attempts to enforce a blockade in a war of attrition against the company; that the analogy is not far-fetched is indicated by the actual overturning of trucks and even freight cars, exchanges of gunfire between the blockaders and the convoyed truckers, and so on. Although there is no question that such tactics place the workers outside the law, we have had several occasions in our review of the weapons of management and labor to remark

that legality may be a merely academic matter in cases of conflict.

One final form of picketing differs somewhat from the others because of its complete independence of the strike. Most types of
picketing are designed simply to make a strike effective through
some form of pressure on other workers, or to add to the strike the
additional pressure of economic isolation of the company. However, picketing may be used as an independent weapon where no
strike is in progress in an attempt to force the employer to hire
union workers. Thus the employees in an "open" or nonunion shop
may refuse to join the union (possibly because to do so would im-
peril or definitely sacrifice their continued employment), while
representatives of the appropriate union proceed to picket the establishment carrying placards announcing the "unfairness" of the employer. State courts almost uniformly view such tactics with hostility, viewing the action as a secondary boycott and damaging the
property right of the employer in an uninterrupted business. Under
the Wagner Act the National Labor Relations Board was not uniformly unfavorable to picketing as an instrument of union organizing
efforts, but under the Taft-Hartley Act such action is illegal.

PREVENTION AND SETTLEMENT OF
INDUSTRIAL DISPUTES

It is apparent that the prospects for industrial peace, as well as
for the protection of public interests not directly involved in labor
disputes, depends in part upon stringent limitations upon the exercise of power. Without such limitations, there is strong pressure
for canons of efficiency to outweigh any nebulous ethical problems
of rights and duties. But legislative limitation upon violence and
coercion is not alone sufficient to preserve the peace. So long as
alterations in relative power are a paramount aim of groups with
divergent interests, the pressure for adopting short-cuts is ever-
present; and the use of such short-cuts is very nearly inevitable unless regular and reasonably acceptable procedures for adjudicating
claims and interests can be established. It is to accomplish this
adjudication that various types of machinery have been used, and

others suggested, for the peaceful avoidance or settlement of industrial conflicts.

We have suggested in the preceding paragraph that industrial conflicts can be minimized or prevented by resort to two types of procedures, both of which are necessary to accomplish the result. The first type might be called that of regulation and limitation of the power of the two interest groups, and especially the restriction of ways in which power may be exercised. The second type is that of providing more positive "interference" in industrial disputes in the form of adjudication and settlement. We may review some of the accomplishments and prospects in these two fields.

Balance and Limitation of Power. The course of recent labor legislation affecting collective bargaining has been in the direction of equalization and limitation of collective power. The power of the employer was subjected to a major curtailment by the passage of the National Labor Relations Act, which had the effect not only of denying certain weapons to the employer, but of adding positive powers available to employees. Further disarmament of the employer was provided by the restriction on the use of the injunction in industrial disputes (Norris-La Guardia Act) and the use of professional strikebreakers (Byrnes Act).

Over a much longer period of time the weapons legally available to labor have been reduced or their legitimate use curtailed—e.g., the regulation or prohibition of the secondary boycott, of coercion and intimidation through mass picketing, of occupation of plants, and so on. With the avowed purpose of restoring a balance of power between management and labor, the Taft-Hartley Act specifies a series of "unfair practices" by unions as well as employers, requires financial statements, and statements of non-Communist affiliation of union officers in order to secure the protection of the Act for unions.

Provision of Adjustment Machinery. The provision of collective bargaining with a roughly approximate equality in the power of the bargainers, together with a limitation on the weapons used to secure advantageous terms, cannot, however, guarantee a solution of industrial disputes. Even in such circumstances, it may be necessary finally to determine issues by resort to trial by ordeal, or by battle.

Any further governmental regulation of the course of industrial relations rests upon the thesis that in any conflict between special interests groups, the public willy-nilly becomes involved, and, indeed, that in the last analysis the public interest is preeminent. This amounts to saying that the government has the right (and some would say, the duty) to intervene and adjudicate disputes in the public interest.

The public interest is usually asserted as strongest with regard to labor disputes in "essential industries," but attempts to define such industries in advance of disputes have not been notably successful. There is some agreement that public utilities, medical, fire, and police protection, and basic food supplies constitute a minimum list of essential services. But the growing interdependence of the economy is such that seemingly minor disputes may become of serious importance, such as the tugboat strike in New York City in 1945 which for a time threatened both food and fuel supplies to the city. Moreover, a dispute may directly affect a very small proportion of the public in their daily lives and yet be of fundamental importance to national military security. With or without clear legal authority, responsible governmental officials are likely to intervene in such disputes.

The settlement of disputes may take a number of forms, differing chiefly in the nature and amount of compulsion involved in the initiation of the adjudication and in the acceptance of its results. *Conciliation,* strictly speaking, is simply the process of give and take involved in collective bargaining, without outside help or authority. It is, however, frequently used in the sense of *mediation,* which is sometimes called *industrial diplomacy.* Mediation involves essentially the selection of a person or group, private or official, to attempt to act as an adviser and go-between in negotiations that have reached an impasse. The selection of a mediator is possible only if there is a genuine interest of both parties to continue negotiations without resort to conflict, and if, moreover, a mutually acceptable mediator can be found. Mediation may, of course, be made to carry greater probability of acceptance if publicity is given to the terms proposed.

A representative of the government, even though he carries no direct authority to compel acceptance of his recommendations, may carry considerable weight in inducing settlement. This is the secret of the frequent success of the publicly appointed "fact-finding body." The device is usually a euphemism for public mediation, as the "facts" in the ordinary sense are not usually under dispute. The recommendations of such a public panel put the burden of proof on the party to the dispute who does not accept the suggested solution.

Mediation can at most offer the services of an outsider, with some nebulous pressure to accept his advice. If his diplomacy and prestige are insufficient to bring a rapprochement between the disputing parties, the disputants must resort to a contest of strength or to further and more authoritative settlement by an outsider. That further step is ordinarily called *arbitration*.

Arbitration differs primarily from mediation only with respect to the authority of the arbitrator to reach an independent decision and to make that decision binding. Arbitration may be classified as voluntary and compulsory, with respect both to its initiation and to acceptance of the arbitrator's verdict. This yields four logical types: [6]

Initiation	Acceptance of Decision
voluntary	voluntary
voluntary	compulsory
compulsory	voluntary
compulsory	compulsory

However, as Patterson has pointed out,[7] the first of these types is not arbitration at all, but mediation. The other three are customarily distinguished by the terms *voluntary arbitration, compulsory investigation,* and *compulsory arbitration,* respectively. They obviously represent an ascending scale of assertion and enforcement of public intervention. But public intervention is not necessarily the most important form of industrial arbitration, although it may be the most spectacular.

[6] See S. Howard Patterson, *Social Aspects of Industry,* 3rd ed. (New York: McGraw-Hill Book Company, Inc., 1943), p. 403.
[7] *Ibid.*

To an increasing degree, collective bargaining agreements provide for "compulsory" arbitration of disputes arising under the agreement itself. In some major industries and a number of minor ones where industry-wide bargaining is the rule, the companies and unions jointly hire a "permanent" arbitrator for the duration of the agreement. The primary function of such an arbitrator is with reference to the grievance machinery, where he is the court of final appeal, and not with contract negotiation as such. Particularly in the early stages of such an arrangement, there is a strong temptation for both management and labor to attempt rather essential changes in the terms of agreement through the device of arbitrator's decisions.

The general view is that "that arbitration is best that functions least," indicating a willingness of management and labor to bargain. However this is not simply a product of "maturity" of the bargainers but may reflect much more frequent arbitration at an earlier stage of management-union relations and the consequent development of a "common law" that is not repeatedly questioned.

It is clearly difficult for a collective agreement to provide for definite arbitration of issues upon the lapse of the contract and the negotiation of a new one, but arbitration is nevertheless used as a device to avoid a halt in production when bargaining has failed to remove a stalemate. It is at this point that the public interest is likely to be most evident. On the one hand, one of the parties to the dispute may suggest arbitration of remaining differences, either in the genuine hope of a favorable outcome or as a face-saving device. As such proposals are customarily public, the other party may face loss of public support if it refuses to submit to arbitration. On the other hand, it is clearly the threatened work stoppage that is most likely to bring appeals or pressures from public officials for settlement.

The reluctance of state and Federal legislators to insist on compulsory arbitration stems not only from uncertainty concerning the constitutionality of such "interference," but from the determined opposition of organized labor. Union representatives have argued that the best way to industrial peace is through collective negotiation, supported by proper safeguards and approximate equality. As we have noted, collective negotiation is no ultimate preventive of industrial conflict, although the unions can point to an increasing provision for arbitration in collective agreements. However, there is no immediate sign of universal adoption of collective agreements or their completely peaceful renegotiation to meet changing conditions. Where agreements are in effect, the unions have already accepted the principle of compulsory arbitration for the duration of the contract.

The more fundamental, and more tenable, objection of the unions is that compulsory arbitration takes from organized labor its most powerful weapon—the strike—and gives it no commensurate safeguards in return. Thus they point out that prohibiting the employer from resort to the lockout removes a very minor weapon from his arsenal, and still leaves him with the power to close the plant completely, change the conditions of work, and so on, without effective protest from the workers. This raises a fundamental problem of policy and of machinery for putting that policy into effect.

If it be maintained that the public interest in industrial peace is paramount, and that conflict is a "luxury" which must be sacrificed at least in "essential" industries and during periods of national emergency, some form of compulsory arbitration seems to be the only solution. But that solution depends upon adequate safeguards for the interests represented, according to some standard of justice. This means especially that the employer's bargaining power must be reduced to approximately that of the union through governmental interpretation of "fair" wages, "reasonable" hours, and so on.[8]

The fact-finding and administrative machinery for compulsory arbitration can be made to appear as a prohibitively gigantic undertaking, to say nothing of the incursions thus made on traditional liberties. But there is no reason to suppose that every industrial dispute would have to be decided by a national panel of arbitrators, or that every dispute would have to be treated as a *completely* unique case. Certain principles already exist in governmental policy, such

[8] The difficulties of compulsory arbitration are succinctly pointed out by Patterson, *op. cit.*, pp. 406–407.

as maximum hours and minimum wages. An arbitrator would no doubt have to take into account past policies and relationships in an industrial situation, regional and local standards and practices, etc. Such procedures are already practiced in collective bargaining, in mediation and voluntary arbitration, and in administrative decision of government agencies.

It is not meant to imply that the question of the machinery for compulsory arbitration is unimportant, for acceptance of the machinery and the general standards upon which it rests would be necessary for successful arbitration. Even "compulsory" arbitration cannot be used to force persons to work so long as we maintain any of the principles of a free labor system. But it is suggested that on this level it is not impossible to secure acceptance of compulsory arbitration with adequate guarantees under prevailing or some other standards of justice.

This still leaves untouched the question as to the fundamental policy of interference in industrial disputes. Although this is a question with which the social scientist cannot be directly concerned, the prediction may be hazarded that the tendency to exert emergency control, and the tendency to extend the definition of essential industry as the economic system becomes more highly concentrated, will lead to a gradual acceptance of compulsory adjudication of industrial disputes as a last resort.

REFERENCES

BAKKE, E. WIGHT, and CLARK KERR, *Unions, Management and the Public* (New York: Harcourt, Brace and Company, 1948).

BRADY, ROBERT A., *Business as a System of Power* (New York: Columbia University Press, 1943), Chap. VIII, "Social Policies: Status, Trusteeship, Harmony," especially pp. 274–287.

BROOKS, ROBERT R. R., *When Labor Organizes* (New Haven: Yale University Press, 1937), Chap. III, "Antiunionism," Chap. IV, "The Strike," and Chap. V, "Breaking Strikes."

CHALMERS, W. ELLISON, "The Conciliation Process," *Industrial and Labor Relations Review*, 1: 337–350, April 1948.

CHAMBERLAIN, NEIL W., "Grievance Proceedings and Collective Bargaining," in Richard A. Lester and Joseph Shister, eds., *Insights into*

Labor Issues (New York: The Macmillan Company, 1948), pp. 62–86.

COPELOF, MAXWELL, *Management-Union Arbitration: A Record of Cases, Methods and Decisions* (New York: Harper & Brothers, 1949).

DAVEY, HAROLD W., "Hazards in Labor Arbitration," *Industrial and Labor Relations Review*, 1: 386–405, April 1948.

DRUCKER, PETER F., *The New Society: The Anatomy of the Industrial Order* (New York: Harper & Brothers, 1950), Chaps. 7–14.

HARTMANN, GEORGE W., and THEODORE NEWCOMB, eds., *Industrial Conflict: A Psychological Interpretation,* First Yearbook of the Society for the Psychological Study of Social Issues, (New York: The Condon Co., 1939).

HILLER, E. T., *The Strike,* (Chicago: University of Chicago Press, 1928).

JONES, ALFRED WINSLOW, *Life, Liberty, and Property* (Philadelphia: J. B. Lippincott Company, 1941).

KELLOR, FRANCIS, *American Arbitration: Its History, Functions, and Achievements* (New York: Harper & Brothers, 1948).

KENNEDY, THOMAS, *Effective Labor Arbitration: The Impartial Chairmanship of the Full-Fashioned Hoisery Industry* (Philadelphia: University of Pennsylvania Press, 1948), especially Chaps. III–VI and X.

LESTER, RICHARD A., and EDWARD A. ROBIE, *Constructive Labor Relations: Experience in Four Firms* (Princeton: Industrial Relations Section, Princeton University, 1948).

PATTERSON, S. HOWARD, *Social Aspects of Industry,* 3rd ed., (New York: McGraw-Hill Book Company, Inc., 1943), Chap. XVI, "Labor Disputes and Weapons of Collective Bargaining: Problems of Industrial Conflict"; Chap. XVII, "Industrial Conciliation and Arbitration: Programs of Industrial Peace."

SEIDMAN, HAROLD, *Labor Czars: A History of Labor Racketeering,* (New York: Liveright Publishing Corporation, 1938).

SLICHTER, SUMNER H., *The Challenge of Industrial Relations: Trade Unions, Management, and the Public Interest* (Ithaca: Cornell University Press, 1947), Chap. V, "The Problem of Industrial Peace."

TELLER, LUDWIG, *A Labor Policy for America* (New York: Baker, Voorhis and Co., 1945).

UNITED STATES SENATE, Committee on Education and Labor, *Violations of Free Speech and Rights of Labor; Hearings before a Subcommittee . . .* (Washington: U. S. Government Printing Office, 1937–1941), 75 vols. (entitled "parts"). With some considerable overlapping, these volumes may be classified as follows: Labor Espionage and Strikebreaking: Parts 1–2, 5–8; Open-Shop and Anti-Union Activities: Parts 7–8, 52–53, 56–58; Industrial Munitioning: Part 7;

Organization and Activities of Various Employers' Associations and "Citizens' Committees": Parts 3–4, 16–22; 48–53, 55–58, 60–61; Particular Areas and Conflict Situations: Parts 9–14 (Harlan County, Ky.), Parts 23–34 (Steel, especially "Little Steel"), and 46–61 (California Agriculture and Industry); Supplementary Exhibits: Parts 15A–D, 35–45, 54, 62–75.

VINCENT, MELVIN JAMES, *The Accomodation Process in Industry,* University of Southern California Social Science Series, No. 2, (Los Angeles: University of Southern California Press, 1930).

YELLEN, SAMUEL, *American Labor Struggles* (New York: Harcourt, Brace and Company, 1936).

WARNER, W. LLOYD, and J. O. Low, *The Social System of the Modern Factory; The Strike: A Social Analysis* (New Haven: Yale University Press, 1947), Chaps. I–III.

CHAPTER XVII

SCOPE AND IMPLICATIONS OF COLLECTIVE BARGAINING

MANAGEMENT-UNION relations in the United States form a number of evolving patterns, which are to a marked degree inconsistent through time and space. The variables of organization, types of leadership, character of market conditions, and the impact of law and governmental action are too complex and their interplay too unpredictable for completely satisfactory scientific analysis with available knowledge and tools. Yet what is known about specific instances of management-union relations need not be left as completely isolated bits of knowledge. It is possible to appraise the broader and future significance of at least some aspects of the seemingly disorderly array of current practices.

In this chapter attention is directed to some underlying features of management-union relations, particularly as they concern the scope of joint decision-making in the industrial sphere and the implications of collective relations for the structure of the industrial order.

CHANGING CONCEPTIONS OF MANAGEMENT– LABOR RELATIONS

There is an archaic flavor in the legal language relating to the conduct of firms and employees, and even in the more flexible popular tongue. Some aspects of the employment relation may still fall within the law of "masters and servants," and popular speech concerning the policies of an "employer" toward an "employee" fail to reflect the fact that the employer is commonly not a real person and

392

the employee is commonly a representative of an organized collectivity. The idiom of industrial relations tends to connote a state of affairs that antedated not only the powerful union but also the corporation, and the arguments concerning "rights" of management are likely to reflect a notion of industrial organization quite different from the true situation.

Recognition of Collective Interests. The common law of England and America at the time of the introduction of factory production—that is, at the beginning of modern industrialism—had developed a pronounced emphasis on individual liberty of trade and freedom of contract. Thus when groups of workers quit work in protest over small wages, or the bidding down of wages by job-hungry workers, the law fell upon them with a heavy hand. By strict application of judicial doctrine, the worker had not only given up all claim to his job by his refusal to fulfill his "contract" with the employer, but the banding together of several workmen constituted a criminal conspiracy.[1] Although the doctrine of criminal conspiracy did not last much beyond the fourth decade of the nineteenth century, it was simply an extreme statement of the predominant view of the courts until fairly recent years. Stated in general terms, the employer-employee relationship was held to be an individual contract, entered into by official equals. "For value received," in the form of wages, the worker agreed to render a certain kind and amount of services under conditions and directions specified by the employer. If the worker did not like the wages or the conditions specified by the employer, he was free to "bargain" individually with the employer or refuse his services altogether. Among the conditions which the employer was free to set was the signing of an agreement not to join any independent labor organization—the "yellow dog" contract—which the prospective employee could accept, or refuse the employment entirely. By the same token, a labor organization could be treated as a conspiracy to secure the breach of such contracts. Even

---

[1] A good brief summary of judicial interpretation of early labor organization is given in Malcolm Sharp and Charles O. Gregory, *Social Change and Labor Law* (Chicago: University of Chicago Press, 1939), Part II, Chap. I, "The Common Law in State and Federal Courts."

under the Federal antitrust laws (Sherman Act of 1890, Clayton Act of 1914), conservative majorities in the United States Supreme Court held strikes, picketing, and boycotts by labor unions to be illegal if they were "in restraint of trade."

We are not immediately concerned at this point with the obvious fictitiousness of the assumptions implied or expressed in this body of legal thought, nor with the curious fact that apparently respectable and intelligent judges were only a few years ago still reaching decisions following this line of argument, and reading them with perfectly straight faces. Since the litigants at the bar were involved in serious business, it is probable that only the gods laughed. The important point of immediate concern is that the individualistic conceptions and the emphasis on market exchange and contractual equality were fully incorporated into the law, and were the basis for treating a labor organization either as legally nonexistent, or as a violation of criminal law or civil rights.

Independent labor organization, we have noted, existed before the 1930's only by a none-too-willing sufferance of the law. Although independent political activity, within the framework of constitutional democracy, could scarcely be denied to organized labor, direct economic pressure such as the strike and boycott was of doubtful legality. The reason for this view was clear (if a little unrealistic). A combination of workers seeking to persuade an employer to give them better terms, or to force him to do so by various degrees of pressure, was a violation of the legally supported ideal of individual freedom of contract and an interference with free competition in the labor market. They were, in the language of the antitrust acts, "in restraint of trade." If any organized or cooperative activity merits the same stigma, that principle has been less officially observed.

The difficulty with the doctrines of individualism as applied to labor organization is to be found in the fictional assumption of equality. A contractual system without equality for parties to the contract—equality, that is, for the purpose at hand—is a contradiction in terms. It is, strictly speaking, nonsense. Yet this is precisely the type of nonsense upheld by the courts until very recent years.

The tenuous legal status of the labor union has been very widely blamed upon the conservative character of the judiciary, and there is some evidence to support such a view in the form of dissenting opinions by the famous liberals of the Supreme Court during the first three decades of the present century. Yet the difficulty was more deeply rooted in legal tradition and legal fiction—and is still widely represented in a considerable body of lay opinion.

Perhaps the point at issue may be illustrated by a fairly recent industrial policy with regard to unions. During the early 1930's when the CIO's Steel Workers Organizing Committee was making inroads in large steel centers, at times capturing Employee Representation Plan units, various officials of the steel companies asserted their readiness to discuss any questions or grievances with individual employees but refused to talk to representatives of the union "as such." [2] Now this was a position in strict conformity with the "culture of capitalism." But suppose that this line of argument were pushed a little further. A union employee might just as reasonably refuse to talk to any representative of the mammoth United States Steel Corporation "as such," or even to any official in his official capacity. *An official position always implies representation of an organization.* The same "individualistic" reasoning would forbid talking to a clergyman, or a Red Cross campaign representative, or a majority stockholder, or a newspaper reporter "as such." All social, including industrial, relations would then become a series of heart-to-heart talks between private (if slightly self-interested) persons.

The foregoing illustration appears at the height of absurdity, and indeed we should regard it so if the disgruntled workman were to suggest that the difference of opinion be settled by a quiet little fist fight behind the boiler room. The point of present concern is not to poke fun at misguided industrial executives or representatives of the judiciary; it is rather an attempt to account for the peculiar quality of industrial relations as a separate category of social phenomena.

The key to the peculiarities of social thinking in this field is to be found in the character of the industrial corporation. Because of the

[2] See Robert R. R. Brooks, *As Steel Goes* . . . (New Haven: Yale University Press, 1940).

legal grant of corporate personality, which was discussed in Chapter III, *the modern employer is always regarded legally as an individual.* Mere questions of size of the corporation, or number of managers, or political and economic power wielded, are irrelevant in this view. Without legal recognition or existence, a labor organization was on doubtful grounds in using persuasion on an "individual" employer. It was only by direct grant of legislative recognition that a labor union could enter into negotiations with an employer in full view of the law.

"Union recognition," which often has been the goal of prolonged strikes in newly organized industries, thus carries the immediate implication of recognition of collective interests. That this implication was not missed by various managerial groups is indicated by the fact that in many instances no issues of wages or "working conditions" were directly involved in disputes that were bitterly contested by various corporations.

To a large extent, this is history. But it is important to note that the organized and standardized character of productive enterprise is intrinsic to the industrial system, although long obscured by the emphasis on the atomistic, impersonal relations of producers in the market. The union may accentuate common interests and minimize individual ones, and may even create new common interests—notably the survival of the union itself. The union, however, did not invent the collective treatment of workers. It represents one mode of reaction to the existence of collective interests, in a social system that encourages groups and organizations of many varieties.

Substitution of "Functions" for "Prerogatives." Within the older conceptions of the nature of industrial organization and the position of management, the very existence of the union was, as we have seen, a challenge to the "rights" of management. Management in the past has made unilateral decisions over a great variety of matters, ranging from those most obviously relating to workers such as wages and hours to those least directly affecting workers such as purchasing, market policies, and inventory. The claims to legitimacy, the normative justification, of the power exercised by management has rested on the notion of "prerogatives." When the justification has been pushed one further step, these "prerogatives" have been claimed to rest on property rights, which are prior to other claims—note the prefix "pre-." Now the property institutions of our society have been undergoing many changes, some of which were indicated in Chapter III. The nature of these changes has been such as to cast serious doubt on this claim to legitimacy. If the managers are the representatives of the owners, it is not quite clear of which owners, and of which type of ownership, the managers are representative, or to which they are by definite structure accountable.

The more general and at the same time more accurate equivalent of managerial "prerogatives" is "powers and responsibilities." Once this change in language is made, discourse is no longer prejudiced by the assumption of rights that are inviolable and unrelated to the representation of various interests.

Within the existing structure of powers and responsibilities, management performs various *functions* in the industrial system. The effectiveness with which these functions are performed is not itself a matter of right, but a matter of objective appraisal. The degree to which performance of managerial functions is limited or enhanced by variations in powers and responsibilities is also a matter of objective appraisal. The crucial point is that this changed conception of management no longer assumes the point to be proved —that the actions of management are proper and appropriate because they represent the interests of the owners as against all other interests.

In the most general terms, the function of industrial management may be stated as the organization of the factors of production, within the "degrees of freedom" allowed by the current balance of conditions and direct controls. The ways of holding management accountable, or the interests taken into account, are variable, as are the mechanisms for determining the nature and quantity of goods and services to be produced.

Whether management "can do its job effectively" in view of union pressures, demands, and other effects on the environment of decision, depends in the first instance on the closer specification of that job in terms of its relation to other interests that society permits or encourages. Management has always operated within some framework of values and interests other than those, say, of maximizing profits at all costs. A society simply could not survive if profits to "owners" (or even service to consumers) were always prior to other ends. There is no doubt that in concrete instances the entrance of the union into the industrial organization has complicated the life of managers, and has done so by changing the specific powers and responsibilities of managers. But it has also served to clarify a distinction that existed anyway, that between rights or interests on the one hand, and managerial operations on the other. Recognition of the union and the conduct of collective bargaining will change the rights and interests impinging on managerial operation, but the latter is not dependent upon any particular specification of the former. Were the business entirely "owned" by the employees there would still be a managerial function to perform.

Collective Bargaining as End and Means. As workers in all sorts of unions were attempting to establish their economic and legal power to act in concert, collective bargaining tended to be the goal of union policy. Only with the widespread establishment of collective bargaining has it come to be recognized that collective negotiation is a technique of presenting union aspirations to management without in any way settling the points at issue. There simply is no easy formula for determining those matters of organization, management, and general policy that directly affect employee interests and therefore equitably constitute a subject for bargaining. This circumstance gives rise to a steady increase in the scope of negotiations that the union will seek to undertake. It is given common expression in the desire of unions to have a share in policy formation and management.

Once collective bargaining is established and thus the position of the union in the industrial system assured, the character of management-union relations seems to rest on bargaining power. In this connection it is important to note once more that equalization of bargaining power does not assure agreement. In fact, equalized power only assures attritional warfare and stalemate unless there is a structure of interests and norms more fundamental than the issues bargained over, these interests and norms providing the basis of compromise.

For purposes of static analysis, the interests and rules within which collective bargaining takes place may be taken as given. Thus, given certain common interests in continuing production and certain values concerning the economic security of retired workers, certain disputes over pension plans may be negotiated. But the values and rules are not immune to purposive change at the hands of persons not directly involved in industrial relations, and, as we have seen, they are also not insulated from the effects of developments in collective relations themselves. The rules of collective relations, in other words, are constantly undergoing change as a result of the practice of collective relations. In such a dynamic aspect of contemporary society, experimentation (that is, trial-and-error) is widespread. This makes the statement of specific principles, such as the "proper" scope of collective bargaining, hazardous in the extreme.

THE SCOPE OF BARGAINING [3]

In the light of the preceding paragraphs, is it possible to detect any principles and tendencies with respect to the scope of collective bargaining? The answer is a qualified "yes." The principles derive in part from the structure of industry itself, in part from the interaction between industry and the normative order of society.

Groups Involved in Collective Bargaining. The first problem of "scope" of bargaining is a numerical and occupational one. To whom is collective bargaining available? The customary answer is in terms of "employees," but closer inspection reveals that once again the language connotes a type of industrial system that has ceased to exist in major sectors of the economy. The situation has something of the qualities of a child's riddle, except for the frustrating circumstance that there is no clever answer. The riddle

[3] With reference to the whole question of the scope of bargaining, see Neil W. Chamberlain, *The Union Challenge to Management Control* (New York: Harper & Brothers, 1948).

might go: If managers are employers then nonmanagers are employees, but if managers are also employees, who is the employer? The corporation, of course, but since managers form the policies of corporations and hire workers while they are themselves hired by other managers, that way lies madness.

Law and administrative decision may set definitions of employees for the purpose of determining eligibility for union membership and therefore collective bargaining as those are defined and regulated by law and administrative decision. This is a kind of "operational" definition, but it in no way answers the more basic issue. Its circularity can be avoided only by finding the principles and usages on which decisions rest.

As indicated in Chapter III, the "appropriate bargaining unit" has ordinarily comprised direct production workers as the reliably eligible union members, and has left uncertain the position of foremen, guards, and professional and staff groups not directly involved in corporate policy formation. The appearance of unions among foremen, clerical workers, and even professional groups has indicated that the issue is not purely academic, and shocked managers have taken a far from academic view of developments.

The reason unionism has not been more prevalent among supervisors in large companies, clerical workers, and professional groups stems from the same ideology of individual competition for advancement that long discouraged any independent unionism, and the greater accuracy of the ideology in many cases has further confirmed it. The common prestige differential favorable to white-collar workers of all sorts in comparison with production workers and the association of unionism with the latter has also discouraged formal unionization of the former. Among professional workers there has been the additional factor of the traditional association between professional activity and private practice—a tradition subject to increasing pressure in view of the predominantly organized, salaried character of most modern professional work.

Thus the current occupational scope of collective bargaining is potentially unstable aside from the fact that by no means all workers in occupations admittedly subject to unionization belong to unions. The occupational scope of bargaining is unstable because wherever conditions of employment and other relevant circumstances are standardized, there is the potentiality of collective bargaining.

At this point it is appropriate to emphasize once more that in the industrial sphere collective relations are not limited to management-union relations. In the corporation, the employer's bargaining is *always* collective, whatever the situation among those employed. Furthermore, there are many *group* interests within management, as noted before. These will almost inevitably be represented as such in various discussions and negotiations. The chronic shortage of skills for an expanding managerial staff has given collective bargaining power without the overt forms of independent unionism. In a sense, therefore, collective bargaining extended *from* other industrial groups *to* production workers with the rise of independent unions. It follows that part of managerial opposition to unions stemmed from the lowly position of the bargainers and not from the fact of group action itself. The forms of collective bargaining by other groups are likely to become overt wherever formal action seems required to secure aspirations and redress grievances, although the associations are likely to be called by another name and the sanctions to be less dramatic than the strike.

Decisions and Their Status in Collective Bargaining. In the paragraphs that follow a fairly large number of areas of industrial policy and decision are commented on briefly with regard to union interest in collective bargaining.

(1) The "economic bargain" between management and the workers as represented by the union centers primarily on the question of *wages*. If unions are accepted at all, wage bargaining is almost inevitably accepted as within the union's appropriate scope. But wages, whether direct or indirect through various "free" services, whether immediate or deferred through pension plans, are so central to the economic functioning of the enterprise and such a tangible aspect of union activity that acceptance of wage bargaining in general leaves many wage issues in disputed jurisdiction. If bargaining over piece rates, shift differentials, and overtime pay is

accepted, other wage issues may be regarded as solely a managerial matter. For example, can the union claim the right to bargain over the following: job evaluation for purpose of setting wage rates, wage differentials representing the company's comparative efficiency in the industry, a share in the increased productivity achieved by greater capitalization and improved technique? Can the union establish a relation between wages and profits without accepting a wage cut in the absence of profits? Various unions are concerned about all of these issues, but no clear line demarcates unilateral managerial decision from the area of negotiation.

(2) *Hours* of work are so closely related to wages because of the prevalence of hourly wage rates that the two areas of employee interests are commonly considered together. This connection is further confirmed by bargaining over penalty wage rates for overtime work, and even by vacation provisions which may either be regarded as pay for time not worked or extra pay for time worked. However, the historic interest of the unions in shorter hours although certainly in part a simple desire for more pay for less work and in part a desire to "spread the work," has also undoubtedly reflected also a desire for increased leisure as such. Few would deny the legitimacy of the union interest in hours, although legislative provisions have at least narrowed the range of potential bargaining over length of the work day and week.

(3) A third area of bargaining, even less homogeneous than the preceding two, is also commonly conceded to be within the appropriate scope of bargaining. That area is usually called *working conditions,* and since the coverage of the term is broad, agreement on the principle of bargaining about "working conditions" is somewhat greater than the agreement as to which working conditions are meant. Working conditions commonly subject to collective negotiation or grievance procedures include light and temperature, health and safety precautions, food and sanitary facilities, and shop rules. The standing of the union as a negotiator of shop rules or their modification is more likely to be hotly contested than in the case of other working conditions, for these rules represent the disciplinary powers of management and are therefore likely to be

viewed with possessive sentiment as part of managerial right—
or requirements "to do an effective job."

(4) Before the scope of bargaining can even be argued, the union must achieve one area of jurisdiction, that of its own *recognition
as bargaining agent*. Indeed, in some instances during the rapid
growth of industrial unions, management and unions had protracted
negotiations as to whether management would negotiate with the
unions. As questions of the numerical coverage of union representation were often at stake, this was not as completely ridiculous as it
sounds, but it had some elements of fantasy. Once the issue of union recognition is settled, at least temporarily, the related question
of *union security* is likely to rise. Here the scope of bargaining is
partially hedged about with legislation concerning the legitimacy or
illegitimacy of the closed shop, the check-off of union dues, and
other provisions for insuring the union against the employer's antiunionism, inroads of a rival union, or "free riders" among the workers in the union's jurisdiction. The issue of the closed shop is still
hotly contested, and the whole problem of union security is likely
to remain as long as the security itself is threatened. Even if the
union has no cause to fear company attempts at disestablishment,
rival unionism is likely to prompt a recognized union to seek the
employer's "cooperation" in preserving its position and thus in a
sense expand the scope of the company's decisions concerning union
affairs.

(5) The establishment of the union within the industrial system immediately affected *hiring* and especially *firing* policies, for
a major part of the antiunion campaign of many companies rested
on firing workers for union activity and failure to hire known union sympathizers. The virtual collapse of those tactics mainly through
governmental intervention on behalf of the unions resulted in neutrality at least with regard to the relevance of union membership
for employment. Introduction of the closed shop, preferential union shop, and occasionally even the "hiring hall" system whereby
the union provides the labor supply have made union membership a positive rather than a negative factor in securing and retaining employment. Other union efforts have also brought into ne-

gotiation and joint determination the enforcement of shop rules and resulting discipline including firing, and, of special importance, the seniority principle for layoffs and rehiring.

(6) Although unions are commonly considered to be interested in the general level of wages and in security of employment rather than advancement, they have actually shown an increasing interest in differential wage scales for various occupations within the plant and for the system of *promotion* and *demotion,* particularly below the rank of supervisor.

(7) Consistent with the motives of workers generally, and with the function of the union in giving its members a more definite standing in the industrial system, *individual security* is increasingly subject to joint determination by management and the union. In the past organized labor took a great interest in the provision of workmen's compensation for industrial accidents and diseases. Although this intrusion into the "prerogatives" of management (not to be concerned about the risks of employment) largely came about by governmental intervention, the principle has provided a precedent for many later union demands. Unemployment insurance (including severance pay from the employer), health and welfare plans, and retirement pensions have all been made subject to negotiation in some companies. Should unemployment become once more a serious problem, the proposal for guaranteed annual wages may be once more put forth. All of these attempts to insure against various risks faced by the worker not only extend the area of union penetration into decision-making but also tend to enhance the stake of the worker and the union in the continued prosperity of industry and of the economy generally.

(8) Although management-union cooperation for reduction of direct labor costs is understandably rare, occasionally unions have shown a positive interest in other aspects of *efficiency* of operations. The clearest incentive for union interest in operational efficiency arises from a situation in which management can reasonably claim that a wage increase would seriously damage its competitive position in the product market. In such instances the union may undertake to aid management in the discovery and elimina-

tion of various sources of waste and inefficiency. During the period of conversion to armament prior to American entry into World War II, several unions attempted to aid companies in organizing the change. Particularly because of the background of "one way" communications from managers to workers, the union often has access to the workers' knowledge of possible improvements in a way that even immediate supervisors do not.

(9) A major and troublesome area of union interest in the formation of industrial policy is that of *technological change*. Although some technical innovations may result in new employment opportunities while older job assignments remain relatively unchanged, and other changes may involve no loss of employment but only a reorganization of jobs, one of the main incentives for technical change has been reduction of direct labor costs. Most unions are not prepared to argue that the reduction of labor requirements relative to output is a bad thing in principle. (Musicians do argue that mechanization in the form of recordings, radio, and television could almost entirely eliminate the live musician, with consequent detriment to the culture.) The unions usually argue, however, that the costs of technical change are likely to be borne in large measure by workers through loss of skills and employment, whereas the benefits are likely to be shared by investors and consumers. Virtually every union with sufficient bargaining power will attempt to insure consideration of the workers' interests in decisions about technical innovation. Thus, should the change make possible centering production entirely in one plant rather than three, employees and others in the communities where plants are closed down are likely to suffer serious loss. Some attempts have been made to make the cost of moving workers a direct charge on the company. The unions sometimes argue with some logic that technical change involves many costs not ordinarily considered when the decision is made, because the costs are borne by workers or by various other persons and agencies. A similar argument may be used with respect to obsolescence of skills through mechanization. Collective agreements thus frequently include provisions for dismissal pay and for retraining and rehiring of displaced workers.

(10) *Purchasing policies* would at first appear beyond the range of union concern, but the combined attempt to secure widespread organization of workers and "to take labor out of competition" has occasionally prompted the unions to seek a ban on raw materials or other commodities produced under nonunion conditions ("hot goods"). As long as union organization is substantially less than complete and as long as union rivalry remains an important consideration, unions may attempt to further their cause by influencing the purchasing policies of companies.

(11) The participation of unions in industrial policy may even extend to price and sales policies. The instances that came to the widest public attention were largely in the period following World War II when accumulated savings and the continuing shortage of many consumer goods combined with other circumstances to produce inflationary pressures. At least one large national union attempted to influence managerial policy by claiming that manufacturers were building up inventories to secure higher prices in subsequent sale, and another large union attempted to insist that the wage increase demanded should result in no increase in prices set by the companies for their products. In both these situations the union directly challenged the traditional claim of managers that they represented consumers in the industrial system. The unions argued that labor organizations by their very size were more representative of consumers generally than was management. The arguments largely missed contact, for the unions were arguing the consumers' "best interests" and the companies were arguing the consumers' "real interests" by the pragmatic test of willingness to buy the products even at higher prices. The relation between wage levels and inflationary pressures is understood by some union leaders well enough to prompt a continued although not necessarily overriding concern for industrial price levels. Without the problem of inflation, or with the prospect of declining markets, the union may also show concern for volume of sales and the company's share of the market or, as in the case of fuels for example, the economic position of the entire industry. The outstanding cases of union participation in sales and marketing policy are still those of the garment

trades, but once the union can be sure of its own survival it may seek to enhance the prospects for industry.

These areas of possible management-union joint determination do not exhaust the particular points at which the union challenges managerial control.[4] They do comprise the policies most commonly settled by negotiation and provide some insight into the ways that decisions, seemingly farthest removed from union interest or competence, may enter into negotiation if not actual joint determination.

Any attempt at delimiting the area within which the union will seek to bargain or to protest decisions is likely to fail as long as the union maintains a measure of independence in the industrial system. Whether the union is able or willing to administer policies, or to generate policies in areas outside the ordinary interest and competence of union leaders and members, are different questions. The unions may broaden the scope of bargaining by protest and negotiation over particular issues in areas of managerial operation that remain primarily the unilateral responsibility of management. This is equally true of management's relations with courts and governmental agencies, with banks and other financial interests, and with itself in the form of departmental negotiations. The difference in the union pressure derives not only from its novelty and uncertain normative justification, but also from the fact that it brings to the level of general policy formation the interests of persons with a major stake and a slight voice in industrial affairs.

SOME IMPLICATIONS OF COLLECTIVE BARGAINING

Legally protected collective bargaining between large managerial and employee units cannot fail to affect not only the immediate conduct of industrial production but also the wider reaches of public policy. It goes without saying that all persons do not regard the change in the legal framework with pleasure; indeed, it would be hard to imagine *any* change in a complex social order that would redound to the advantage of everyone. This is a fundamental problem in any discussion of social planning, and can only be resolved by reference to some standard for determining whose interests shall be served.

[4] See Chamberlain, *op. cit.*

Our present concern is not so much with the merits of the change but with an understanding of its social significance.

The "Corporate" Principle Applied to Labor. We have noted at numerous points that the grant of corporate personality to the corporation allowed the development, by legal fiction, of the doctrine that the actions of the corporation were those of an individual, and that a contract of employment as offered by a large corporation was no different in principle from the action of a private householder in hiring a caretaker. Insistence upon the individual contract was upheld by the courts as proper in an individualistic economic order. The coercive power wielded by the employer (individual or corporation) in control of the means of production did not exist in the eyes of the law. Yet while these doctrines were being maintained the courts were shifting to the view of labor organizations as legally responsible entities. The responsibility of an unincorporated organization for the actions of its agents, and its possible prosecution for violations of antitrust legislation, were affirmed in the famous "Danbury Hatters Case."[5] Subsequent decisions followed this doctrine more or less closely. The failure to provide at the same time legal support for collective bargaining tended to give to labor organizations all the responsibilities of corporations, and none of the privileges. Although the courts have naturally been reluctant to say so, the legal support of collective bargaining is a recognition of *group* relationships and agreements, although still nominally within the framework of a "contractual" system. However, in connection with some other implications of collective bargaining that we shall note, extending a contractual system to group relationships puts some strains on traditional conceptions.

"Property" Interests in the Job. The modifications in the traditional views of private property made necessary by the inclusion of the corporation within our legal system have already been discussed (Chapter III). A close examination of the control of corporate assets, it was pointed out, involves the necessity of distinguishing different rights in the same valuable "things," since those rights

[5] Loewe *v.* Lawlor, 208 U.S. 274 (1908).

may be held by different persons. In fact, the unmistakable trend in the law of property is toward a wider recognition of rights in "intangibles" and a less naïve view of the divisibility of property rights.

It is quite in keeping with these tendencies to maintain that the NLRA and similar legislation reducing the authority of the employer to discharge at will grants to employees at least a partial "property interest" in the job. Although again such a conception is by no means without precedent,[6] the more positive provisions of recent legislation give new point to a slowly emerging idea.

This is not a conclusion formulated by the courts, but an inescapable conclusion in view of the facts. The legal recognition of collective bargaining as a "right" with workers maintaining their employee status during strikes or other labor disputes, with enforceable claims on employment if illegally discharged, and with back pay for the period of illegal withholding of employment—all this amounts to property, however unwilling the courts may be to offend traditional sentiment by use of the term.

There seems to be sound basis for predicting a further extension of this principle in view of the ever wider use of seniority and other tenure agreements, computing the cost to labor in considering technological change, the establishment of dismissal pay, and so on.

Syndicalization. The definite establishment of the union as part of the industrial system together with the expanding scope of collective bargaining results in a sort of "syndicalization" of industry. This is a result that is more by accident than by conscious design, for with few exceptions American union leaders have not been prone to develop any long range "philosophy" of the labor movement. But even the purest business unionism of the type made famous by

[6] See John R. Commons, *Legal Foundations of Capitalism* (New York: The Macmillan Company, 1924), Chap. VIII, "The Wage Bargain—Industrialism"; Elizabeth Paschal, "The Worker's Equity in His Job," *American Federationist,* 40: 1296–1303, December 1933; 41: 68–75, January 1934; 1212–1221, November 1934; 1332–1342, December 1934; 42: 44–52, January 1935; 149–154, February 1935; 275–277, March 1935; 748–753, July 1935; James P. Rowland, *The Legal Protection of the Worker's Job* (Philadelphia: author [?]; 1937); G. T. Schwenning, "The Worker's Legal Right to His Job," *American Federationist* 39: 26–32, January 1932.

Samuel Gompers' simple statement of "more and more" has, if successful, a fundamental effect upon the allocation of power and rewards. The process of syndicalization is enhanced by development of the areas of joint determination of policy, by the "peace and maturity" of industrial relations so commonly sought by the experts, and by the structural development of grievance machinery, impartial arbitration, and the accumulation of a body of common law of the industry.

There are, however, two closely related types of limitation upon the complete syndicalization of industry without the direct actions of the state. The first type of limitation is structural. Just as management by virtue of its responsibilities to investors and other interests is poorly equipped at the same time to represent workers, so the union as a dues-paying membership group with some form of representative democracy in selection of leaders is not ideally constituted for some kinds and degrees of managerial policy and administration. The second type of limitation is functional, and essentially follows from the first. If the union becomes an integral part of the management of enterprises it can no longer serve with assurance the functions of protest, of leverage on the system. Looked at from the point of view of the worker, a completely integrated system of control may simply mean that there is no longer any alternative avenue for pressure and attempts to redress grievances.

Here we are faced with the paradox that the worker may influence industrial management through elected representatives, but that to the extent that those representatives are successful in determining policies they must take responsibility for them. The more completely successful the union attempt to determine policy, the less the possibility of protesting the result or redressing grievances. For the union, as Drucker points out, is a political organization and not a productive enterprise, and a productive enterprise cannot be operated solely for the benefit of its members as long as they are not the sole or most important consumers.[7]

---

[7] See Peter F. Drucker, *The New Society: The Anatomy of the Industrial Order* (New York: Harper & Brothers, 1950), especially Chap. 10, "Can Management Be a Legitimate Government?" and Chap. 11, "Can Unionism Survive?"

The Unions and Industrial Efficiency. The special function of unions in representing what may be called "producer interests" as distinct from "consumer interests" is evident in the problem of the effects of unions on industrial efficiency. The problem is most acutely represented in "featherbedding," overstaffing, restrictions on technical innovations, and similar policies. But interference with the strict canons of economic efficiency is inherent in any limitation upon the treatment of labor as a pure commodity, subject only to competitive market principles for determining price (wages), and as a pure "factor" in production subject only to the criteria of rational efficiency of productive organization.[8] Collective action to prevent bargaining down of wages through competition of workers for jobs and to prevent the maximum output consistent with short-run or long-run physiological limitations is plainly contrary to maximum productive efficiency and therefore, assuming efficient distribution, to maximum consumer satisfaction.[9]

The fact is that maximum consumer satisfaction—"consumer sovereignty"—may be assumed as the sole important value affecting the productive system for certain purposes of economic analysis, but it cannot be assumed as the sole value for purposes of understanding the nature of industrial society. The "human factor" in production, which turns out to be a rather mystical way of expressing the bearing of social requirements upon a particular segment of society, inherently limits the treatment of workers solely as commodities or as instruments of production. The union is one formally constituted mechanism for bringing non-productive interests to bear on the productive system. Both the form and degree of this "interference" may

[8] Even without union or other interference in behalf of labor interests, there is an inherent anomaly in a market system between *labor* as a cost of production and *laborers* as consumers. A "cheap labor" policy, as long as it is consistent with the necessity of securing specialized skills, may be quite appropriate for any single producer, and yet inappropriate for the economy as a whole because only workers as consumers can possibly provide the mass demand necessary for efficiencies of scale and expansion of production.

[9] See Charles E. Lindblom, *Unions and Capitalism* (New Haven: Yale University Press, 1949); Joseph J. Spengler, "Power Blocs and the Formation and Content of Economic Decision," in Milton Derber, ed., *Proceedings of the Second Annual Meeting, Industrial Relations Research Association*, New York City, December 29–30, 1949 (Champaign, Ill.: 1950), pp. 174–191.

upset other interests and values and create pressures for organized control by other agencies. The reduction of efficiency may be greater than is required for the preservation of a viable social system. The essential point is that many other producers (such as independent farmers and professionals, and, notably, managers) are more amply protected from efficient exploitation of their productive services by self-regulation and appropriate style of life than are industrial workers in view of the necessary administrative organization of production and the necessary administrative concern for productive efficiency. To the extent that the union represents the range of interests of its membership it *must* promote the genuine stake of workers in security, pleasant working relations, a right to be heard, and other elements of the "human factor" including the money and time to participate in family, community, church, and recreational activities. In view of these considerations what occasions surprise is that scholars have come upon the union's interference with efficiency with an air of breathless discovery.

Class Orientations. Finally, it is sometimes claimed that the increased power and activities of the union in representing *worker* interests in the economic system implies an increasing emphasis on *class* relations.[10] The relation between the industrial order and social stratification will be more fully explored in Chapter XXIII. At this point a few observations are in order.

There can be no question about the implications of collective action in industrial relations for emphasizing the common interests internal to the collectivities and minimizing the common interests that cut across this division and the divisive interests internal to each. The laws establishing the rights of union membership and collective bargaining constitute a legal recognition of *status* differences in the industrial system. The actions of union representatives are necessarily such as to maintain internal morale by attention to con-

---

[10] See, for example, Frederick H. Harbison and Robert Dubin, *Patterns of Union-Management Relations* (Chicago: Science Research Associates, 1947), p. 194; W. Lloyd Warner and J. O. Low, *The Social System of the Modern Factory; The Strike: A Social Analysis* (New Haven: Yale University Press, 1947), pp. 159–196.

flicts in interests between workers and managers, although the importance of this consideration is rather variable.

There are, however, certain reservations that need to be entered here. Despite the importance of occupation and occupational position as a criterion of general social rank, "social class" ordinarily implies a division cutting through most aspects of significant social relations and affiliations. Whether an increased emphasis on differences of interest within the productive system means a definite division along the same lines in other aspects of social life is a question for inquiry and not to be automatically assumed. In this connection it is important to note that the concrete rank differences in the industrial organization yield many "strata," not just two. Moreover, the possibility of differences in attitude and interests within these strata, whether relevant to the productive system or not, remains. The union also has its hierarchy, and by many usual tests its leadership would have to be assigned a social position equivalent to managers. The complexity of social stratification in a society marked by many semi-autonomous associations is such that conclusions regarding "class" relations in industry are likely to represent acute oversimplification. And whatever else may be said about industrial societies, they are not simple.

REFERENCES

BLOOM, GORDON F., and HERBERT R. NORTHRUP, *Economics of Labor and Industrial Relations* (Philadelphia: The Blakiston Company, 1950), Chap. 6, "Industrial Jurisprudence," and Chap. 8, "Collective Bargaining—Scope and Breadth."

BROWN, DOUGLASS V., "Management Rights and the Collective Agreement," in Milton Derber, ed., *Proceedings of the First Annual Meeting, Industrial Relations Research Association,* Cleveland, Ohio, December 29–30, 1948 (Champaign, Ill.: 1949), pp. 145–155.

BROWN, LEO C., "The Shifting Distribution of the Rights to Manage," in Milton Derber, ed., *Proceedings of the First Annual Meeting, Industrial Relations Research Association,* Cleveland, Ohio, December 29–30, 1948 (Champaign, Ill.: 1949), pp. 132–144.

CHAMBERLAIN, NEIL W., *The Union Challenge to Management Control* (New York: Harper & Brothers, 1947).

DRUCKER, PETER F., *The New Society: The Anatomy of the Industrial*

Order (New York: Harper & Brothers, 1950), especially Chaps. 10–14.

KASSALOW, EVERETT M., "New Patterns of Collective Bargaining," in Richard A. Lester and Joseph Shister, eds., *Insights into Labor Issues* (New York: The Macmillan Company, 1948), pp. 116–133.

KENNEDY, THOMAS, *Effective Labor Arbitration: The Impartial Chairmanship of the Full-Fashioned Hosiery Industry* (Philadelphia: University of Pennsylvania Press, 1948), especially Chaps. VII–IX.

LINDBLOM, CHARLES E., *Unions and Capitalism* (New Haven: Yale University Press, 1949).

PASCHAL, ELIZABETH, "The Workers' Equity in His Job," *American Federationist*, 40: 1296–1303, December 1933; 41: 68–75, January 1934; 1212–1221, November 1934; 42: 44–52, January 1935; 149–154, February 1935; 275–277, March 1935; 748–753, July 1935.

PETERSON, FLORENCE, "Management Efficiency and Collective Bargaining," *Industrial and Labor Relations Review*, 1: 29–49, October 1947.

RIEGEL, JOHN W., *Management, Labor and Technological Change*, (Ann Arbor: The University of Michigan Press, 1942), Chap. IX, "Collective Agreements on Technological Change."

SLICHTER, SUMNER H., *The Challenge of Industrial Relations: Trade Unions, Management, and the Public Interest* (Ithaca: Cornell University Press, 1947), Chap. VI, "Trade Unions and the Public Interest."

SPENGLER, JOSEPH J., "Power Blocs and the Formation and Content of Economic Decision," in Milton Derber, ed., *Proceedings of the Second Annual Meeting, Industrial Relations Research Association*, New York City, December 29–30, 1949 (Champaign, Ill.: 1950), pp. 174–191.

TODD, ARTHUR JAMES, *Industry and Society*, (New York: Henry Holt and Co., 1933), Chap. XXVI, "Constitutional Government in Industry."

WALPOLE, G. S., *Management and Men; A Study of the Theory and Practice of Joint Consultation at All Levels* (London: Jonathan Cape, 1944).

PART SIX

INDUSTRY AND SOCIETY

CAPITALISM AND INDUSTRIALISM

IT IS generally supposed that the development of the factory system and modern industrial organization was "inevitable." This is true. It is true in the sense that any historical change is inevitable when viewed in retrospect. The proof is that it happened. But difficulties arise when, with scant scientific justification, peculiar and primary significance is attached to some of the antecedent factors in the situation and other factors are persistently overlooked or dismissed as "unimportant." Chapters II and III emphasized the technological and economic changes, that is, changes in methods and relationships of production, that marked the unfolding of modern industrialism. Standard interpretation stops here, but all this took place within a wider social and cultural framework of ideas and values, knowledge and sentiments. And these ideas made, and continue to make, a difference. It is with the cultural background of modern industry that this chapter is primarily concerned.

The developments outlined in Part Two were in a continual functional relationship with a system of ideas and values which prevailed, and were undergoing transformation, at the same time. These ideas are of continued import for modern industrial organization, for they form the general "climate of opinion" within which specific actions and attitudes are understandable. The cultural values and social institutions [1] that converge in their bearing on modern industrialism

[1] "Institution" is here used to mean a well-established rule of conduct having a normative sanction; that is, the infraction of an institutional rule evokes moral indignation or ethical disapproval on the part of the community. Thus "private property" is an institution, or rather a series of related institutions, with a definite bearing on the character of modern industrial production.

This use of the term "institution" is rather common but is not that of many

may be classified under the following heads: (1) general features of capitalism and industrialism, (2) science, (3) technology, (4) individualism, and (5) rational division of labor. Since these have been closely interrelated in fact, the lines of distinction between them are in particular cases likely to be a little artificial. This is more especially true since it is possible to expand the connotations of "capitalism" or "individualism" or "division of labor" to include all the others. Nevertheless, we may make some reasonable separation, and proceed from the characteristics of capitalism to those of its close relatives.

GENERAL FEATURES OF CAPITALISM AND INDUSTRIALISM

If the factory system in its modern expansion constitutes the characteristic type of productive organization in our society, its cultural counterpart is to be found in a system of ideas and values known as *capitalism*. Capitalism has been talked and written about a great deal; it has become a slogan for some and an epithet for others. The present discussion is concerned only with a series of interrelated characteristics, their cultural origins, and their relation to other social elements.

Early Capitalism. The accumulation of fluid capital in the form of money (or bills of exchange) and the development of cost accounting and exact computation of profits were known in Europe long before the modern industrial period. It is to the merchants of medieval Italy, who not only engaged in a lively commerce in the Mediterranean area but were not too proud to use the Arabic numerical system, that we owe the establishment of banking and credit with profits and losses entered in record books. Not only was *capital* in money thus put to use in buying and selling, but risks were shared by the pooling of capital and the *pro rata* apportionment of profits

---

introductory texts in sociology, where "institution" is hopelessly confused with "complex organization." For further explanation and illustration of the meaning adopted here, see R. M. MacIver, *Society, Its Structure and Changes* (New York: Ray Long and Richard R. Smith, 1933), pp. 15–17, 32. See also Talcott Parsons, *The Structure of Social Action* (New York: McGraw-Hill Book Company, Inc., 1937), pp. 399–408 and *passim.*

or losses. Thus economic historians speak of *commercial* capitalism in distinction from modern capitalistic *production*. For early capitalism had practically nothing to do with production. How the goods were produced or where they came from was of small importance. It was in trade and in the equipment for trade (as storehouses, ships, and wharves) that money was invested and profit taken. This type of economic activity took on fairly large proportions unaided by mass production in factories. The Italians and Germans bought and sold, and kept the difference. With the colonization of the Americas and the beginning of sea trade with the Orient this commercial capitalism became very nearly world-wide in character, and wondrously full of romance. The line between legitimate trade and piracy was occasionally thin, but the trade went on. Even in the North American colonies "Yankee ingenuity" first manifested itself, not in the machine shop or factory, but in the shipyards and ports serving the traders. This international trade, notable for its characteristics of great risks and great profits, as well as for its avid search for new products and new markets, has often been called *adventure capitalism*. It was remarked in Chapter II that these commercial interests, already well established, preceded the factory system, and that the effective demand so created was a necessary economic condition for the establishment of unified and coordinated production. Indeed, the term *capitalism* is often limited to these commercial interests, and their union with machine technology to form the modern economy is called a marriage of convenience. Be that as it may, the interests of the trader and the interests of the mechanic were actually combined with a number of other elements to produce the system that we know as *industrial capitalism*.

General Characteristics of Industrial Capitalism.[2] The system of ideas and principles that underlay factory production and complex industrial organization had—and continues to have—a number of distinct

---

[2] The present exposition is not by any means intended to be exhaustive, but is simply designed to give the broad outlines of the "culture of capitalism." The importance of this system of ideas and norms for conduct (institutions) as a basis for social control, and the various limitations made necessary in view of other social values, will be more fully discussed in Chap. XXIV.

but interrelated elements. In the most general terms these may be grouped under two principal characteristics: (1) free labor and (2) a free market. Because of the importance of these conceptions for an understanding of the social setting of industrial development, each will be considered in some detail in the following paragraphs. Some of the more important elements will then be considered in greater detail in the remainder of this chapter.

1. **Free Labor.** The expression *free labor* is here used in a very general sense to include not only free wage labor, but the independent economic activities of all classes of individuals in the production and distribution of economic goods. Perhaps a better term would be the customary catch phrase "individual initiative." For what is of fundamental significance in the culture of capitalism is its emphasis on the economic individual, that is, the rational, acquisitive, self-interested individual who goes about the pursuit of private ends (generally capable of expression in monetary terms in the forms of wages, rents, or profits) in the most efficient manner possible. His prototype is popularly supposed to be found in the ingenious Yankee, whether as an industrious laborer with reasonable hope of better things, the inventive manufacturer, or the shrewd trader.

This is so much a part of our philosophy that we have come to take it for granted as a part of "human nature." But acquisitiveness is a distinctly modern and Western phenomenon. It is associated, as we shall see more fully below, with the socially sanctioned dissatisfaction with what one has. It is based upon a moving goal, not a stationary one fixed by tradition. Thus under the feudal regime one simply did the appropriate duties required of one's station. Even under the arrangement of the guilds, production was controlled in the interests of the guild as a whole. But under modern capitalism the emphasis has shifted to the individual productive unit, with each individual making the greatest possible effort to achieve a place in the economic world.

This meant that the physical means of production not only were greatly increased—in contrast with primary emphasis upon land or simple tools—but the instruments of production were henceforth to be considered as the disposable property of separate industrial enterprises. The world has always known a good deal about "private property," particularly in consumption goods and in individual tools and weapons. But the emphasis on private property in capital goods, that is, productive goods, is fairly rare, and fairly recent even in Western society. We hear a good deal about the "sacredness of private property," but modern industrial property is not so sacred but that it can be bought, sold, and traded to the advantage of one or the other or (in theory) all concerned. For free labor, on individual initiative, demands that the individual shall have access to the productive property of the community and is not to be kept out of the running by reason of lowly birth or lack of traditional rights.

In summary, then, *the free labor characteristic of capitalism involves* (a) *emphasis upon the acquisitive individual,* (b) *individual technical efficiency, and* (c) *private ownership of productive goods.*

2. Free Market. Closely associated with the foregoing cultural values which we have grouped together under the general heading of free labor are other characteristics of capitalism that are implied by or follow from a "free market." Again in the most general terms a free market is one that is not positively regulated or manipulated by any social agency or organization, political or otherwise, but that is rather "determined" by the impartial operation of unregulated "supply and demand." Public regulation is presumably minimal and indirect, designed primarily to keep the market free. Without undue elaboration at this point, this simply means that individual consumers "come to the market" willing to buy at certain prices for certain qualities, whereas separate and discrete producers are willing to sell goods of a certain quality at a certain price. If the supply is small, demand remaining constant, the price goes up. If the demand is small, supply remaining constant, the price goes down. The important point in all this is that none of the three elements—demand, supply, price—is regulated from outside, but only by the operation of the other two. If one were to label the free market system with a catch phrase, it would be *laissez faire*.

It is not of present importance to worry about the ethics of *laissez faire*, or even to inquire into the failure of this set of ideas accurately to describe the actual operation of the market. It should simply be noted that this has constituted a basic "ideology" of industrial capitalism, and that to a significant degree a free market has in fact existed.

Not only does a free market imply freedom from regulation of any of the elements by governmental agency, by traditional restrictions upon demand, by traditional or other restrictions upon productive techniques, and so on, but it means that the market is not regulated or controlled through collaboration among consumers or among producers. Thus a consumers' boycott or a producers' "combination in restraint of trade" through monopoly or other price-fixing methods are violations of the tenets of the free market. Put more simply, and no less accurately, the free market involves *free competition* (within broad limits to ensure "fairness"). Thus the individual's efficiency is impartially and impersonally weighed (and presumably appropriately awarded) within the economic system itself.

Another aspect of the free market, or at least a conception closely related to it, is that of *freedom of contract*. This means that the individual is not only free to sell his goods or services to the one he wishes, or rather to the one with whom he can strike the best bargain, but is positively enjoined not to extend contractual obligations to more general and unspecified rights and duties. Thus in all economic relations, whether of employer and employee or buyer and seller, each interested person presumably acts as a free agent, bound only to those obligations to which he himself has willingly agreed. This is, for example, quite different from the feudal conception of customary duties associated with hereditary statuses, or from the traditional neighborly rights and obligations of peasant communities. The contractual relationship is voluntary, limited, explicit, and supposedly gives some advantage or "consideration" to all parties. All this in turn implies an *official equality of opportunity*. Without such equality of opportunity freedom of contract becomes a rather empty phrase, and bargaining in the market place a fairly one-sided affair. We have noted that this has been a very sore spot in the relationships of employer and employee.

As has already been observed, free labor in the widest sense under capitalism implies and involves individual ownership of the means of production and individual initiative in their operation. The interrelationship of all these characteristics may once more be noted in view of the close dependence of a free market upon the commercialization and transferability of property. By commercialization of property we mean simply the conversion of property rights and their appropriate values into monetary terms. This has an immediate advantage in the market, for it subjects capital goods to the same measuring sticks as all other economic values, and provides the basis for exchange. This was, in fact, a heritage from earlier commercial capitalism, which had already established a basis for rational capital accounting and the translation of property values into money, with paper symbols of ownership. Not only did this make it possible to compute "paper" profits and "paper" losses, but it gave capital its modern *fluid* character whereby vast industrial empires may be bought and sold in New York or London without disturbing production at the various plants, and cotton and wheat "futures" can be transferred in Chicago between individuals who do not so much as walk on the grass or water a window box. A market could conceivably be "free" without this commercialization and cost accounting, but certainly could not be very active. For a genuinely free market in all its ramifications it is essential that the means of production be available to those who can afford them. This would be next to impossible without the commercialization of all property values. Thus not only are consumption goods transferred on the market, but, through absentee ownership and paper symbols of property, the means of production also are subject to the counterbalancing pressures of supply and demand. To use a far-fetched illustration, it is possible for a person with sufficient capital (that is, money) to face a decision between buying a new yacht or a new factory.

Finally, a necessary condition for the operation of a free market is that not only must the trader or the employer be protected from positive outside control as long as he stays within the two boundaries set by force and fraud,[3] but the operation of the law must be certain and predictable. That is, *the legal framework must be regarded as a constant condition, so that knowledge of its operation is alone sufficient in the rational calculation of means to the end of self-interest.* Specifically, legal and judicial favoritism, or uncertainty in the law, or purchasable "justice" destroy equality in the market place, as they destroy the possibility of reasonable prediction of results. The idea of reasonable certainty in the law, and impartial justice, is so much a part of our culture that we may be tempted to forget that it is fairly recent in origin and not too extensive in the world today. The arbitrary actions of a monarch, or of administrative officials, the practice of only reaching decisions on legality *after* the act, are all inimical to the operation of a free market. Whether the law is in fact certain, and whether it may not often be used as a means rather than a constant condition, are matters for future consideration. We are again here simply outlining the interrelated elements which converge to make up the "culture of capitalism."

In summary, *the free market of industrial capitalism involves* (a) *free competition and impersonal judgment of efficiency;* (b) *freedom of contract and equality of opportunity;* (c) *commercialization and transferability of all property, including rational capital accounting, monetary exchange and paper symbols of ownership, and fluidity of capital; finally,* (d) *the whole presupposes certainty and predictability in the operation of the law.*

Many transformations have taken place in the machinery of production and in the social organization of industrial enterprise since the early days of capitalism. Some of these have forced modification in the underlying assumptions of capitalistic production, and others have led to demands for even further modification. These will be considered below. Nevertheless, modern economic

---

[3] It is noteworthy that the two most generally acceptable pleas for the avoidance of contracts are duress and fraud. In fact, the minimum conditions for the operation of a social order include the control of these otherwise highly efficient means for securing private ends. See Talcott Parsons, *op. cit.,* especially pp. 87–94; also, pp. 95–107, 121–122, 129–177.

life in the United States to a large degree operates under the assumptions just outlined, and against a cultural background that has united ethical and normative conceptions with the demands of the market place.

The Separation of Industrialism from Capitalism. It is sometimes argued that the particular combination of norms and patterns that characterized relatively "pure" private capitalism are so little intrinsic to industrial capitalism as a system of economic production that "capitalism" should be freed from its older historical context and the term applied to all systems involving capital accumulation, mechanization, specialized production on a large scale, and other features of modern industry. On the surface this is merely a question of terminology. What lies beneath the surface is a genuine change in the character of economic production in many areas of the world.

"Industrialism" turns out not to be dependent upon all of the peculiar features of Western capitalism as it developed historically. This is notably true in the basic pattern of private operation guided by the impersonal operation of a competitive market. Even in the United States and other industrial areas where basic industries have not been nationalized on a comprehensive scale, the combination of governmental regulation with the growth of "monopoly" and "oligopoly" has seriously modified the notions of a self-regulating economic system. In other areas, including most of the late-comers on the industrial scene, capital accumulation, enterprise, and even management have been strongly governmental in character.

Whether industrialism could have originated with the kind of direction and control now evident in most industrial and industrializing economies is a fairly academic question. Once the productive possibilities of industry became established in the centers of its original development, subsequent development in those and other areas was no longer independent of what had already been done. Industry does not develop now out of the indigenous social structure of some peasant society, but comes as an outside, intrusive, but powerful influence.

This leads to a kind of "acceleration" principle in the spread of the industrial system. For both political and economic reasons governmental leaders in undeveloped countries increasingly seek industrial development, and in doing so place that development under "forced draught" by governmental sponsorship and direction. This, in turn, is made possible under otherwise favorable conditions because it is not necessary for the late-comer to recapitulate all of the slow technical development characteristic of the original centers of capitalism.

The industrial system in its expansion, however, encounters quite different antecedent institutions from those that characterized the Western world at the time of the "Industrial Revolution." In general, those institutions and the social structures that they regulate include those characteristic of all nonindustrial (primitive or peasant) societies, and also those that are peculiar to each society.

Two outstanding and related features of nonindustrial societies are important in the present context. (1) Production and distribution are typically carried on by multifunctional organizations, such as the family and the village, with consequent motivational and security patterns that emphasize responsibility and mutual aid and do not emphasize minute skill differentials. (2) There is in such societies a lack of any *general* expectation of mobility of occupational or social position.[4]

The industrial expansion of Germany, Japan, and the Soviet Union, as well as the newer developments in many other areas of the world, give ample evidence to the fact that industrialism does not require, in the full sense outlined above, "free labor" and a "free market." It does require competition for occupational placement on the basis of skills and a consequent flexibility of labor supply. Where various systems of forced labor or stringent ethnic distinctions have been used in new industrial enterprises, as in some colonial areas, requisite skills have been supplied by the superordinate group and the impact of the industrial mode of production on the domestic economy has been radically minimized.

---

[4] The significance of these barriers to industrial development is explored in some detail in Wilbert E. Moore, *Industrialization and Labor* (Ithaca: Cornell University Press, 1951).

The mechanisms for achieving flexibility of labor supply are variable, and may include planned production of skills through early selection in the educational process. But it appears impossible to achieve an industrial mode of labor allocation without some mode of positive incentive and reward for scarce talents and skills, whether those rewards be contingent upon a "market" system of wage determination or an "administered price" for labor supplemented by other rewards.

Industrialism is possible under governmental rather than private initiative, planning, investment, and distribution. It does require, however, an area of political stability adequate to insure the supply of raw materials and a reasonable certainty of distribution. Although capital may not be treated as itself subject to market considerations, it must be fluid and transferable from one operating unit to another if technical development and changes in operating conditions and output goals are to be taken into account.

Moreover, governmental ownership or detailed regulation of productive enterprises does not obviate the necessity of rational capital accounting or of a monetary system of exchange in order to give specialized producers claims on the products of other producers as well as in order to effect capital transfers.

These requisites of an industrial system comprise the principal institutional features necessary for the operation of an industrial mode of production. They are in addition to the essential features of productive organization itself, which also is in a number of essential features not peculiar to capitalism. This is notably true of the managerial organization and hierarchy inherent in the combination of specialization with large size of concrete productive units. The arrangements for managerial responsibility and for the representation of other interests may vary in important ways, but the combination of coordination with specialization is intrinsic and not a peculiar sin of capitalism as an institutional order.

SCIENCE AND TECHNOLOGY

An outstanding characteristic of modern industry is its widespread use of exact knowledge. Science and industrial production are separate yet related aspects of our civilization. Thus in tracing the cultural background of industrial organization it is fitting to sketch the development of science before turning to its union with production through technology.

General Features of Science. Science rests as much upon metaphysical assumptions or "acts of faith" as does any other mode of orientation to the world about us. There is no need here, even were it possible, to examine the ultimate truth or falsity, or even the relative adequacy of those assumptions. It must be simply noted that among many types of "world views" science represents but one.[5] It assumes, for example, a certain orderliness in natural events: that what happens is not simply the result of chance, or luck, or the whimsy of a facetious or malicious divinity. It assumes, moreover, that this order is knowable, or discoverable, through sensory experience. Reality is what one sees or hears or smells or turns about in one's hands. Subject to the refinements made possible by mechanical aids, and to the checks provided by the experiences of others, science must assume that "seeing is believing," that this is not an illusory dream world, but a world of fact. These may be said to constitute the basic assumptions of science concerning the nature of the universe—of reality. But one must add to this a further basic assumption that is normative in character, that is, a view concerning the obligations that follow from such a conception of reality. The ultimate ethical judgment that supports scientific inquiry is that it is good to know. For science as a part of our culture consists not simply of abstract metaphysical preconceptions; it is also a set of beliefs relating to action. If knowledge is possible, it is also good; it is better to know more than to know less. These are the dicta that transform a philosophical conception into a program of action.

[5] See, for example, P. A. Sorokin, *Social and Cultural Dynamics* (New York: American Book Company, 1937, 1941, 4 vols.), especially Vol. I, Chap. II, "Ideational, Sensate, Idealistic, and Mixed Systems of Culture." The presuppositions of modern science and their comparatively recent development are outlined also by Lewis Mumford, *Technics and Civilization* (New York: Harcourt, Brace and Company, 1934), Chap. I, "Cultural Preparation"; and by Thorstein Veblen, *The Place of Science in Modern Civilization* (New York: The Viking Press, 1932), pp. 1–55.

It follows from the underlying "factual" and ethical assumptions of science that this sort of knowledge must place particular emphasis on doing things. The orderliness of nature is not adequately revealed by sudden inspiration, or by long and quiet contemplation. It must be actively sought. Thus the validity of the oft-repeated assertion that science is essentially a method. Knowledge of worldly affairs is the result of doing certain things, of going through regular procedures. Scientific knowledge is distinguished from common-sense knowledge not only in that the former is more often "right" (within the assumptions noted), but that it is more orderly, precise, and organized. It is not simply a question of looking at lots of things, but of ordering, classifying, noting similarities, observing sequences, and drawing conclusions. Thus the primary test of the validity of a statement of fact is not its correspondence with some system of absolute truth, but rather the repetition of the *procedures* whereby the phenomenon was observed. The importance of this aspect of science can scarcely be overemphasized, for it provides the key to an understanding of the *active* orientation to the knowable universe with which we are so familiar. More and more phenomena must be brought within the purview of the scientific observer, and the precision and exactness of the observations must be continually increased. Such are the conclusions to be reached from the basic assumptions of science.

Like many other important aspects of the culture that bear on the nature of modern industry, the preconceptions of science antedate capitalistic production. On the other hand, the modern rapid development of science and the expansion of industry have been not only parallel but also closely interdependent movements.

Science and Industry. Medieval churchmen would have understood expressions such as "natural order" or the "orderliness in nature," but they would not have understood them in the same way as the modern scientist. The scholar versed in the Scripture and the writings of the Church Fathers knew the world as an exemplification of the handiwork of God, about which it was unnecessary to ask further questions. The important reality was that of the Heavenly City, not the forces of nature. But the newer conceptions of time and space and movement made possible a new and mechanistic view of nature. Movements became connected through causation. The study of astronomy and discovery of order and regularity in the heavenly bodies that were amenable to quantitative expression provided the basis for "laws" based on observation, not on faith or philosophy.

But first and foremost there was a shift of interest from the perusal of sacred manuscripts and an other-worldly focus of attention to interest in natural events. Much of this development had taken place by slow accretions before the seventeenth century. The groundwork in basic conceptions had been laid through several hundred years. However, it is from the seventeenth century that we must date most of the rapid development of modern science.

Although it is true that much of the voluminous work of that century may be represented as simply combining principles previously established and multiplying their applications, the development was given a tremendous impetus by the same transformations which contributed to the ideology of capitalism. Notably, the Protestant Reformation transformed scientific interests from preoccupations contrary to or barely suffered by the teachings of the church, to positive goods.[6]

Much of the interest that has fostered scientific development has been primarily practical (technological), and only secondarily in knowledge for its own sake. Science may be either an intermediate or an ultimate value. For his protection, and with good grounds in

[6] The importance of Protestantism, especially Calvinism and related doctrines, for the development of capitalism was demonstrated in some detail by Max Weber. The essential part of his study is to be found in *The Protestant Ethic and the Spirit of Capitalism*, tr. by Talcott Parsons (London: George Allen and Unwin, Ltd., 1930). For a summary of Weber's treatment, together with a discussion of his methodology and the comparative study of other religious systems which he undertook elsewhere, see Talcott Parsons, *op. cit.*, pp. 500–578. See also Max Weber, *General Economic History*, tr. by Frank H. Knight (New York: Greenberg Publisher, Inc., 1927), pp. 352–369; Richard Henry Tawney, *The Acquisitive Society* (New York: Harcourt, Brace and Howe, 1920), and *Religion and the Rise of Capitalism* (New York: Penguin Books, 1926).

For a careful analysis of the role of religious influences in the development of science and technology, see Robert K. Merton, *Science, Technology, and Society in Seventeenth Century England*, in the series *Osiris*, Vol. IV, Part 2, pp. 360–632 (Bruges, Belgium: The Saint Catherine Press, 1938)

view of the notable gaps at least in time between theoretical and practical importance, the scientist often insists on the ultimate value of scientific knowledge. It is certainly true historically that reservation of judgment concerning the value of "pure science" has borne subsequent fruit in practical applications to mechanical production or new consumption goods. Nevertheless, science has been tied up with technology during most of its recent history.

Industrial Technology.[7] Technology, simply defined, is the application of scientific principles for the achievement of particular concrete ends, taken as given. These ends are "practical" within the given scale of values, although they may be regarded as illusory or wasteful according to different value schemes. For example, for approximately twenty years after 1918 the technology of armaments and destructive warfare was widely regarded in our society as wasteful, whereas during the second World War civilian production was often held to be wasteful of valuable resources, skills, and productive capacities needed in the war effort.

It is the utilization of science for technical organization and industrial production that has given modern industry its *economic* superiority over other systems of production. Whether this system is ultimately "better" than traditional handicrafts cannot be scientifically determined. What is of importance here is that a distinct body of culture, namely, technology, has been of profound importance in shaping the character of modern industry. Its particular manifestations include the large number of technical schools which not only carry on research of fairly immediate applicability to industrial processes and products, but the graduates of which find positions as technical specialists in manufacturing corporations. Although there are many actual, and more conceivable, varieties

---

[7] It would serve no useful purpose for the present analysis to attempt a historical sketch of technological inventions used in industrial production. From rather simple beginnings the combination and application of basic principles have resulted in an ever-increasing rate of inventions of all types. Thus some authorities speak of an "exponential rate" of culture growth. (See, for example, William F. Ogburn and Meyer F. Nimkoff, *Sociology* [Boston: Houghton Mifflin Company, 1940], pp. 791–793.) This, however, is a principle that must be limited to the field of technology in recent times, and must presuppose a cultural interest in the elaboration of techniques and products.

of "engineers," the large and growing profession of technologists finds its primary societal function in the service of productive enterprise. That science ought, sooner or later, to be useful is a widespread belief in our society. Contemporary industrial technology represents one fulfillment of that conviction.

The utilization of science in capitalistic production has taken three principal forms: increased complexity and coordination of semi-automatic (machine) production; increased and intensified production through greater and greater mastery of mechanical power; and multiplication and standardization of industrial products, giving a much wider range and larger quantity of articles of consumption.[8]

The ideas and values embodied in capitalism, science, and technology should provide warning against any crude economic or technological determinism in the analysis of modern industry. Together with the ideas of individualism and a technical division of labor, they form a general climate of opinion that had major importance in the formative stages of factory production and continues to influence the organization of modern industry.

INDIVIDUALISM

Individualism, when it is spoken of by leading industrial managers or their representatives, or by speakers at Rotarian luncheons, chiefly means individual acquisitiveness, unhampered by governmental restriction or organized labor. This is, of course, but one aspect of the emphasis upon the self-reliant individual, but it is the one which most often comes to attention in matters affecting economic policy. The first phase of individualism which we must distinguish, therefore, is economic individualism.

Economic Individualism. Briefly, economic individualism is tied up with the doctrine of *laissez faire,* namely, that each individual pursuing his own well-understood self-interest without undue restriction will contribute to the good of all. The emphasis of our economic system has been on individual opportunity and free enterprise. Other economic systems have emphasized family or kinship

[8] Adapted from Emil Lederer, "Technology," in *Encyclopaedia of the Social Sciences,* 14: 555.

solidarity, national interests, or the maintenance of traditional and hereditary relationships. Industry in our society is in times of peace preeminently a matter of "individual" concern. This is *not* to say that traditional common values and institutional controls have not operated in our economic order, but only to point out that these controls have been glossed over in the theory of economic activities, and minimized in fact. In time of war the necessity of hanging together becomes more clear-cut, and social (that is, national) interests may claim precedence over individual initiative and individual aspirations. But in "normal" periods of industrial production our culture has focused attention upon the interests of the individual. Concretely, this has involved a peculiar theory of individual motivation, a valuation of individual or distributive rather than common or collective ends, and a justification of the whole system of ideas both as scientific ("practical") theory and as a scheme of values.

Economic individualism assumes a pain-pleasure hedonism. The individual attempts to maximize his "utilities," or, negatively, to avoid losses. All this, of course, might be something like an accurate (if not very significant) explanation of individual behavior, were there some recognition of the source of the "pleasures" and "pains." Traditional economic individualism, as a theory of social behavior, has stumbled over this problem, but chiefly has placed the motivation within the individual. Thus well-understood self-interest is phrased in exclusively economic terms, and its source is found in some sort of acquisitive instinct or in the satisfaction of biological needs. This turns out therefore to be not only a focus of interest and value in the individual, but an emphasis upon material acquisition and consumption as the sole significant goal of individual behavior.

Economic individualism thus appears as both a theory and a doctrine. As a theory, it attempts to explain social behavior in terms of a rational, self-interested, acquisitive "economic man." As a doctrine it maintains that such an orientation of individual behavior in society is good and proper, for it leads to social and individual values.

As an explanation of the operation of the social order the theory will not stand close scrutiny,[9] but as an ideal and a doctrine, it remains of first-rate importance for the operation of the economic order. Linked with other aspects of individualism, it makes the individual, rather than the state or society, the responsible source for productive initiative, and the measure of the effectiveness of a given organization of production.

Individualism in Other Spheres. Economic individualism is given added support in the value system of our society by the prevalence of individualistic notions in other fields of activity. Although partly of independent origin, and certainly with varying applications, the ideals of individual responsibility in religion, government, and the family add weight to the expectation of economic self-help. A very few examples will suffice to call to mind how much importance we attach to the individual.

The religious tenets of Christianity provide the basis for both group-emphasis and individual-emphasis. In Protestantism the individual has the positive duty of making his own decisions. Political democracy and the protection of "natural rights" serve to confirm the individual's importance and self-reliance. In all of the major spheres of individualistic ideas distinctions have been made: the manufacturer or trader as opposed to the unskilled laborer; the religiously elect as opposed to the sinful; the politically worthy as opposed to the rule of the masses. All, however, have been found amenable to outward and downward extension. The concern over personality development, the emphasis on competitive courtship and individual choice of marital partners, and the development of psychiatry, social work, and medicine may be viewed with considerable accuracy as applications of individualistic doctrines.

Although traditions and groups are antecedent to particular individuals, at least in the chronological sense, in our society we have emphasized the individual's part in changing the world, and not its

[9] For a careful analysis of the inadequacy of economic individualism as a complete foundation for social order, and the fallacy of a "natural identity of interests," see Talcott Parsons, *op. cit.*, pp. 87–102. See also G. D. H. Cole, "Laissez Faire," in *Encyclopaedia of the Social Sciences,* 9: 13–20.

part in changing him. One may thus properly speak of a "cult of individualism," a major doctrine of which is the maximum achievement of the individual's capacities: the "unfolding" of the individual's personality.

Role of the Individual in an Industrial Society. Despite the ubiquity of individualistic conceptions in our culture, there are fairly obvious and rather stringent limitations to the extension of individualism in any society. No society can be so tolerant or so naïve as to develop *every* human capacity to its ultimate, or to place no barriers upon the fulfillment of unbridled appetites. The human organism is plastic, and its capacities and potentialities are extremely varied. Some special abilities, like the ability to kill, must clearly be limited and regulated; various outstanding skills such as superior cunning and effective trickery and deceit must be regarded as inimical to the stability of society. In short, *all special abilities must be in conformity with the requirements of social order in general, and of a given social order in particular.* This constitutes the ultimate difficulty of attempting to reason from the nature and worth of the individual to the social organization and culture of a society.

In other words, it is a scientific impossibility to attempt to construct a society with the sole aim of complete and universal individualism in all its forms. Yet in our society this has been more often a theoretical than a practical difficulty, for the conception of the *nature* of the individual has been pretty clearly linked with a particular kind of social organization which gave meaning to that conception. Thus we have not in fact looked with the same favor upon the development of individual aesthetic or mystical talents as we have upon shrewd economic rationality. It is only in the disordered and perilous households of certain believers in the wrongness of repressions and inhibitions that children develop their personalities in directions of property destruction and sudden death. It is thus *not* the complete and unrestrained individual who is the center and measure of modern industrial society, but rather the individual whose character most closely conforms to the ideals established in traditional doctrine.

This restraint upon individual talents and abilities and the focusing of those talents and abilities on activities and goals that are, in fact, of social origin explain the paradox that modern industry may exist in societies with a prevailing ideology of collectivism rather than individualism. In a sense, collectivism submerges the individual in the group and places an immediate and constant, rather than indirect and ultimate, test of group interest on individual activities. But in fact when collectivism is combined with industrialism, the social rationale of individual efforts is more insistently stated, and enforced in ways that modify the concrete structure of productive enterprise, but the emphasis on individual talents and competitive performance and placement is retained. Indeed, because the matter is no longer explained or justified in terms of individual self-interest, competitive performance and placement may be more strongly encouraged and enforced because of its importance to collective goals.

THE DIVISION OF LABOR

Social differentiation and division of labor are universal attributes of human society. Contrary to the view persisting into the recent past that primitive man lives in completely homogeneous and amorphous groups, modern knowledge of primitive and peasant communities reveals much complexity and specialization. Such knowledge also dispels the older view of the simple, "natural" man, unhampered by social conventions, completely dependent on his own efforts for his bodily needs. Modern specialization cannot therefore be contrasted with an assumed society or period having no division of labor. The difference is one of degree and not of kind.

What we know of the nature of the human organism and the simple necessity of the child to be cared for after birth indicates a minimum of organization below which not only society but also the human species ceases to exist. The character of that organization requires differentiation in the social positions and duties of individuals. Thus no society can completely ignore the great dichotomy of sex as a basis for social distinction. Neither is it possible to pass over the different capacities and acquired skills which accompany differences in age. It does not follow that the precise social significance attached to age and sex is the same, or more than roughly similar, in all societies, but no society can overlook these fundamental distinctions.

Bases for Division of Labor. Thus in all societies every individual has certain positions (statuses) that serve to ally him with some and distinguish him from other members of that society. Those statuses, such as the ones following from age and sex, over which the individual has no control, are said to be *ascribed.*[10] Ascribed statuses are important in the productive system in any society. This is true in regard to sex, whether the division of labor is that between men who hunt and make war and women who till the soil and rear the young, or that between men who work in factories and women who belong to clubs and do the family shopping. The principle holds in regard to age whether the adolescent boy goes through a public initiation and becomes a warrior or finishes his compulsory education and becomes a breadwinner. The aged may rule the tribe, be left to die because unable to keep up their share to work, or be pensioned at sixty-five by a state insurance system. Despite the impressive cultural variability, the underlying principle remains constant.

Assigning status by reference to broad categories without regard to individual competence is, in a highly specialized and integrated productive system, definitely limited in its applicability. This may be seen by brief examination of the various possible bases for a rigid and automatic division of labor. The distinction between the sexes allows only a dichotomous specialization. Even age provides relatively few convenient lines of demarcation. Moreover, if there are a great many specialized positions to be filled within a single career, the length of time available for each might well be inadequate for learning the particular techniques required. For example, we do not, and could not, expect every male to achieve competence

[10] See Ralph Linton, *The Study of Man* (New York: D. Appleton-Century Company, Inc., 1936), p. 115 and pp. 113–131, *passim.* See also his "Age and Sex Categories," *American Sociological Review,* 7: 589–603, October, 1942; Kingsley Davis, "The Child and the Social Structure," *Journal of Educational Sociology,* 14: 217–229, December 1940.

successively as a carpenter, barber, physician, lawyer, corporation executive, and research chemist. Indeed, we expect no such occupational career from *any* person, and if such a person were to gain such diversified skills, his ability in any one field would be seriously doubted for the very reason of his "dabbling" in others.

In view of the fairly independent variation of population distribution, there is no guarantee of an exactly appropriate age composition for a given degree of specialization on the basis of seniority. Thus a productive system might find itself with too many old administrators and too few young clerks, just as in a more limited field modern armies that operate on a seniority basis of distinction occasionally have too many generals and not enough privates. Even combining age and sex gives only a very few general divisions within the population.

A further basis for status ascription as a method of ensuring a social division of labor is the widely used one of inheritance of occupational position in family lines. The hereditary distinction between aristocrat and commoner, master and slave, or even the more elaborate hierarchy illustrated in European feudalism or the Indian caste arrangement, provide common examples of the utilization of kinship organizations as a mode of social differentiation. Again, however, as indicated in the foregoing illustrations, the possible number of divisions is fairly small. It is, of course, just conceivably possible to draw lines of occupational distinction between small, individual families, and so perpetuate any given fairly minute division of labor from one generation to the next. Such a system could only work if other significant elements in the situation were subject to complete control. Specifically, it would involve stabilizing the economic or industrial system at a particular level, so that no changes could occur that could change the demand for workers of a particular type. It would also involve such a control of population size and composition as to ensure that every family reproduced its quota of workers of the appropriate type, no more, no less. Imagine the difficulty in our rapidly changing industrial order where occupations go out of style over night, and in a population such as ours that overreproduces at some occupational levels and under-reproduces at others, of attempting to make each highly specialized occupation precisely hereditary.

There is, indeed, an even more general limitation upon the sole use of status ascription for widespread division of labor. Despite the previously noted plasticity of the human organism, the variability of the species is such that many individuals are born who lack even the minimum capacity for fulfilling their expected roles in society. If those roles are very specific, and peculiar to one or a few individuals, society stands to take too great a chance on individual ability. This problem is well illustrated by the difficulties encountered when a hereditary ruler turns out to be unmistakably feeble-minded. Again, imagine our present plight if a fair proportion of the hereditary stevedores should turn out to be physically incapable of lifting a ten-pound weight, and the members of any other hereditary calling could not be transferred to replace them.

The inevitable conclusion is that, as a basis for division of labor, status ascription is effective for marking off general categories but is inadequate for widespread specialization.[11] The obvious corollary of this principle is that any complex division of labor must depend upon at least some indeterminacy of occupational status to ensure a minimal relationship between the demands of the job and the abilities of the incumbent.

If one asks, perhaps reasonably at this juncture, what all this has to do with the structure of modern industry, the answer is fairly simple. Precise occupational position in modern industry is rarely ascribed, although general class status in the society may be in some

---

[11] We have not discussed all conceivable bases for status ascription, but only those more commonly used. Skin pigmentation as a mark of "race" is very frequently fixed upon as a method of categorizing the population into broad occupational groups. This is to a large degree evident in the treatment of the American Negro. Any other visible symbol of distinction might be used, such as color of hair or shape of nose. Since few, if any, of the available methods of status ascription have any necessary correspondence to native ability, societal choice is made on other grounds and then justified as representing true differences in capacity. It would be just as sensible, on grounds of biological ability, to confine left-handed persons to pitching professional baseball as to limit Negroes to carrying bags and shining shoes or to give special privileges to descendants of *early* immigrants.

degree.[12] The considerations advanced above give a partial, if negative, explanation of the nature of the social division of labor in contemporary society. Taking, for the moment, a manifold division of labor as given, it must be subject to explanation on other grounds than status ascription. But this is not to say that ascription of status is simply irrelevant for industrial specialization. Thus, employers may insist that tool and die workers shall be men, which of course immediately limits the field of competition to those having the appropriate ascribed status. The widespread belief, not only among women but also among male employers, that factory work is in general unsuitable for female laborers is a potent factor in determining the section of the population that is available for specialized industrial tasks. But after the broad categories have been determined on grounds that are in general irrelevant to particular abilities, it is still necessary to fill particular jobs by another method: status *achievement*.[13]

The general bases of status achievement are the qualities of the individual and how they relate to the values of the society. In industrial societies it is the person's productive usefulness that is primarily at issue, and it is upon that basis that an individual presumably arrives at a particular position in an industrial organization. In fact, the whole cultural background of industrial capitalism either supports directly, or conforms indirectly, to the expectation that each individual will do that useful work for which he is best fitted. Despite the very real inequalities of opportunity engendered by the necessity of qualifying for particular positions by first belonging to the appropriate age, sex, or similar category, we nevertheless place great value upon occupational diversification *grounded upon the achieved specialized capacities of particular individuals*.

Assuming the advantages or social value of occupational diversity, the first necessary step to allow widespread division of labor was to remove the traditional barriers provided by a rigid inheritance of

---

[12] The question of the relation of occupational position to general or class status in society will be discussed in Chap. XXIII.

[13] Linton, *op. cit.*, pp. 113–131.

occupation. Put more positively, and more correctly, the various types of individualism that have permeated the culture of capitalism have provided a positive incentive to specialization and to a correspondence between position and demonstrated ability. The situation, we have seen, is in this respect not radically different under industrial collectivism. Within the limits, therefore, of the necessary status ascription found in all societies, and its specific forms and types in any one society, modern industrial division of labor may be said to rest upon individual competition and achievement of position, supported by fundamental values in the culture. Specialization is not simply a major phenomenon in industrial organization; it is also an ideal.

Extent of Specialization. Occasionally the newspapers and popular magazines carry feature articles on newly discovered "strange and unusual occupations" whereby enterprising individuals in the population earn a living. In addition to such careers as winding clocks, tasting tea, or helping out-of-town shoppers get rid of their money, there are many others that make less sense to the uninformed layman. There is in the United States at least one water smeller, whose special skill is the detecting of unpleasant odors in city water. A number of "mattress walkers" stamp out lumps before the heavy pads are sold, to ensure the citizen's comfort while sleeping. The meat-packing industry employs workmen whose job titles, such as "tooth knocker out," sound truly satanic. One can even make a paying career out of spooning (cleaning out holes for dynamite in coal mines) and necking (putting on sweater necks in knitting mills). With such a diversity of legitimate occupations, to say nothing of skilled parasites like the pickpockets who specialize in particular pockets, the average American is fairly shockproof on the subject of the division of labor. From an occupational classification which could be fairly completely covered by fifty or a hundred callings about one hundred and fifty years ago, we have reached a degree of complexity that is truly astounding by any comparative standards.

The *Dictionary of Occupational Titles,* prepared by the United States Employment Service of the United States Department of

Labor,[14] has 1040 pages devoted solely to an alphabetical listing of titles with brief definitions. The dictionary defines 17,452 distinct jobs and classifies an additional 12,292 alternate titles. This is a total of 29,744 occupational titles defined. Yet this is not claimed to be a complete coverage of occupational specialization. The editors write,

It should be especially noted that the coverage of the Employment Service Dictionary, either occupational or industrial, is by no means complete. Reasons of economy, practicability, and efficiency, as well as administrative and budgetary considerations, imposed certain limitations, in some instances rather severe, but the book as it now stands is thought of as but a first edition.[15]

The positions and occupations defined range from "cheese sprayer" (confectionery industry) to "pharmaceutical botanist" (professional and kindred occupations). Arranged by industry the number of distinct jobs gives an even better indication of how far the division of labor has proceeded in modern manufacture. For example, there are approximately 375 different jobs in the petroleum refining industry, besides an additional 125 or so in petroleum and natural gas production. The textile industry, first on the field in the transition to the factory system and outstanding in the degree of mechanization and subdivision of processes, requires more than 1850 types of specialized abilities. This is exclusive of the cultivation and transportation of textile fibers, or of such specialized related industries as garments, hosiery, knit goods, and textile bags.[16] This is truly a far cry from individual economic self-sufficiency.

A random selection of definitions of occupations may illustrate not only the degree of specialization but also the degree of skill required in modern economic life. Some representative definitions of skilled and semiskilled occupations listed in the *Dictionary* follow.[17]

[14] United States Employment Service, United States Department of Labor, *Dictionary of Occupational Titles* (Washington: U. S. Government Printing Office, 1939), Part I, Definitions of Titles.

[15] *Ibid.*, p. xvi.

[16] The number of jobs by specific industries noted in this paragraph is computed from lists in *ibid.*, Appendix III, pp. 1117–1287.

[17] Quoted from *ibid.*, pages as indicated at the end of each definition. The

Heel-Seat Scourer; *seat scourer and tack remover* (boot and shoe) 6–61.811. Operates a heel-scouring machine and an insole tack cutter (m) to cut and remove nails from heel seats and insoles of shoes and to smooth the heel seats: holds heel seat tightly against revolving disk cutter of scouring machine, and turns shoe in a horizontal circular motion, thus cutting off any protruding nails and removing any unevenness in the heel seat; holds shoe with both hands so that disk cutter of insole tack-cutting machine is inside of shoe on the insole near the toe; makes a downward movement with the shoe while the insole is against the cutter, thus cutting any protruding tacks which may be in the insole, and removing any unevenness in the insole where the protruding tack was cut. [449]

Radio-Chassis Aliner; *intermediate frequency aliner; radio chassis test man; radio-frequency aliner; radio tester* (radio mfg.) 4–98.040. Adjusts completed radio chassis to obtain proper electrical frequencies: connects chassis to testing equipment; adjusts position of iron core in each intermediate frequency stage successively, using a neutralizer (type of socket wrench); adjusts with a screw driver or wrench, the trimmer condensers of radio frequency stages for maximum response in headset or on meter. [725]

Saccharate-Filtration Man (sugar) 6–10.632. Filters saccharate which is used in place of lime in treating raw sugar juice; manipulates wheel valves to control flow of fluid to and from filters (m); maintains proper level of liquid in the filtration reservoir; changes cotton twill cloths on filters periodically by releasing metal clamps; checks temperature of liquid coming to filter. [771]

Not all specialized occupations, of course, are so closely dependent on complicated machines and tools. Thus the following definitions indicate administrative and professional abilities:

Sales Engineer (whole. tr.) 0–19.04. Sells chemical, mechanical, and electrical equipment and supplies, and other products that require professional or technical knowledge based on familiarity with products sold: calls at factories and industrial plants, and on engineers, architects and other professional and technical workers, attempting to convince prospective customers of the desirability of purchasing from him; computes the cost of installing equipment and calculates saving in production costs anticipated by use of equipment; makes estimates from blueprints, plans,

---

numbers following the title are for use in coding occupations. The insertion (m) indicates a machine.

or other records submitted by potential customers; draws up and proposes changes in equipment or use of materials which would result in cost reduction or more efficient operation of enterprise. Usually specializes in selling one product or a group of closely related products, such as technical electrical equipment, industrial machinery, mechanical rubber equipment, chemical goods, or mineral products. *ref.* **Salesman, Wholesale; Salesperson** (any ind.). [773]

Secretary, Administrative; *secretary, executive* (any ind.) 0–97.03. Executes administrative policies determined by, or in conjunction with, other officials: prepares memoranda outlining and explaining administrative procedure and policy to subordinate supervisory workers; acts as intermediary between minor supervisors and policy-making officials. Makes confidential contacts, keeps special files and performs other responsible duties, varying according to policy of firm or organization. In small organizations, such as trade, civic, or welfare associations, often performs publicity work, *ref.* **Public-Relations Man.** [804]

Even those occupations coded as unskilled labor reveal a considerable degree of specialization and involve at least some special skills. Two sample definitions follow:

Gore Stapler (boot & shoe). A **Laborer, Process.** Cuts strips of rubber elastic tape (gore) and staples them to shoe ornaments: lays gore strip on finished side of ornament, centering the strip across the width of the part and over the metal strip on the underside of the ornament; sets ornament with gore strip in place under head of stapling machine, and drives staple through the ornament, and through the metal strip, clinching the end of the staple under the metal strip. [418]

Ham Grader; *ham selector* (slaught. & meat pack.). A **Laborer By-products Operations.** Turns uncured hams over and inspects them for blood cots around the bone, bruises, and broken bones; places bruised hams in truck for pork products, broken bone hams in truck for pickling, and perfect hams in truck for boiling or smoking. [431]

One might, of course, reasonably ask to what extent this tremendous specialization represents simply increased mechanization so that the laboring processes are diversified. In other words, is this an artificial specialization as far as the laborer is concerned so that workers might freely move from job to job without serious difficulty or retraining? To a certain extent, yes. That is, many of the diversified occupations listed and defined as found in modern industry are classified as "unskilled labor," implying that laborers occupying those positions could be interchanged with small relative loss. Recognizing the disadvantages of the minute classification of occupations for determining the degree of specialized and technical skills required by workers, a group of experts have undertaken the tremendous task of classifying many similar occupations found in various industries into "families" of occupational skills.[18]

To determine the degree of transferability of workers involves comparative job analysis and the computation of time required to learn the skills and routines that are to some degree different from others in the same family of occupations. The principal criteria used for comparative analysis were:

1. Working rapidly for long periods
2. Strength
3. Dexterity
4. Co-ordination
5. Estimation
6. Special senses
7. Memory
8. Social factors
9. Temperament
10. Miscellaneous worker factors
11. All C jobs in which all the worker characteristics were rated C, the amount possessed by the lowest 70 per cent of the general population
12. Training period on job, one week or less
13. Training period on job, one week to one month
14. Training period on job, one month to six months
15. Training period on job, over six months
16. Special knowledge required for entrance into occupation
17. Supervising
18. Public contacts
19. Use of measuring devices or graphic instructions
20. Use of tools
21. Use of machines

[18] See William H. Stead, Carroll L. Shartle, and Others, *Occupational Counseling Techniques, Their Development and Application* (New York: American Book Company, 1940).

22. Minimum formal education requirement
23. Seasonality
24. Working rapidly for long periods
25. Repetitive nature [19]

Even such a simplified list of important worker attributes and job requirements indicates that wholesale reshuffling of occupations would not be easy. A diagrammatic representation of degrees of transferability in various occupational groups has been presented by the same authorities, and is reproduced in Figure 8.[20] The author of the section of the report under consideration explains the figure as follows:

It is postulated that the higher one goes in this pyramid, the fewer will be the opportunities for transfers from one occupation to another in a horizontal direction. There will probably be families of occupations quite closely related in each level, permitting an interchange of workers within that particular group. The more complex the occupation the longer the training period required to become expert in the trade, the more difficult it will be to effect transfers.

. . . At the top of the pyramid is superimposed an inverted pyramid that represents the executive and administrative workers. Here once more is found a level wherein rather wide transferability from one industry to another is possible and occurs frequently, especially in large corporations. This is probably due to the fact that executive ability and adaptability are necessary to attain this position.[21]

Even this limitation of the degree of division of labor to the positions requiring approximately equal (and interchangeable) degrees of skills leaves but one clear-cut conclusion. The "laboring population" is by no means a homogeneous mass of workers who may be chosen at random for any industrial position. The fact that the degree of interchangeability of laborers decreases with an increase in technical skill required for the position, and thus somewhat with rank, has had far-reaching consequences for industrial organization,

[19] Quoted (main headings only) by permission of American Book Company from *ibid.*, Chap. X, "Occupational Relationships," by Raymond S. Ward, pp. 194–195. The first ten items are worker attributes, the last fifteen job characteristics.
[20] Reproduced from *ibid.*, Fig. 41, p. 205.
[21] *Ibid.*, pp. 203–205. Quoted by permission of American Book Company.

and for the relative strength of skilled and unskilled workers in labor organizations. Other implications following from a technical division of labor will be sketched briefly in the paragraphs that follow.

FIGURE 8. *Range of Horizontal Transferability of Workers in Various Groups of Occupations*

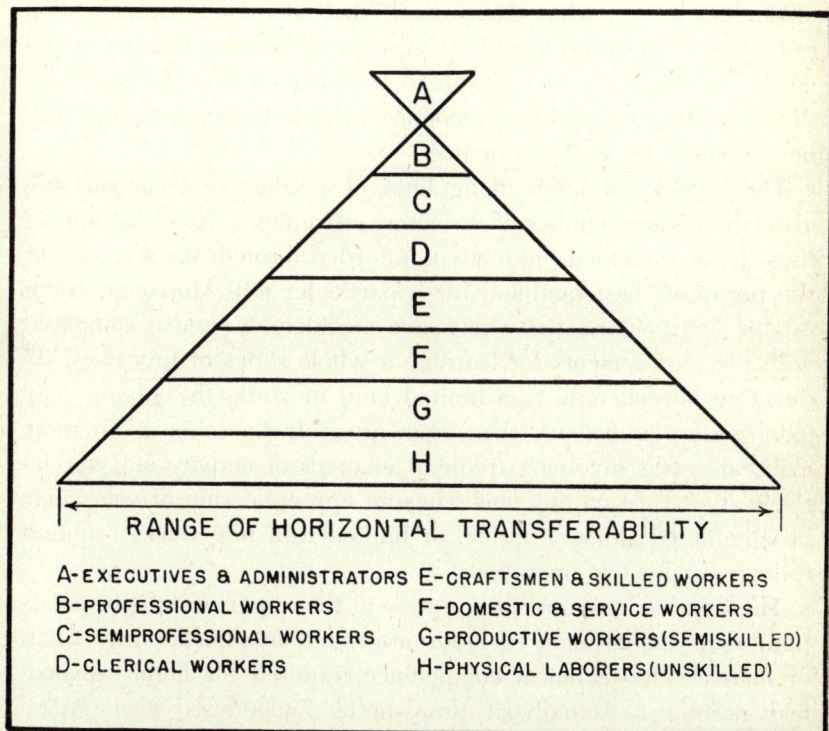

A-EXECUTIVES & ADMINISTRATORS E-CRAFTSMEN & SKILLED WORKERS
B-PROFESSIONAL WORKERS F-DOMESTIC & SERVICE WORKERS
C-SEMIPROFESSIONAL WORKERS G-PRODUCTIVE WORKERS (SEMISKILLED)
D-CLERICAL WORKERS H-PHYSICAL LABORERS (UNSKILLED)

Adapted by permission from Raymond S. Ward, "Occupational Relationships," in William H. Stead, Carroll L. Shartle, and Others, *Occupational Counseling Techniques, Their Development and Application* (New York: American Book Company, 1940), Fig. 41, p. 205.

Economic Significance of Specialization. The foremost fact of industrial significance that follows from an extended division of labor is that the greater the specialization the greater the problem and necessity of coordination and cooperation. As between independent producers, control is effected through buying and selling on the market.[22] This provides a largely automatic (that is, impersonal) coordination of productive efforts. Within a manufacturing establishment coordination is accomplished on a different basis: that of *authority*. Thus in contemporary industry a major task of management is that of maintaining coordination of effort and effectiveness of the entire unit in the face of large-scale diversification. It is axiomatic, if somewhat paradoxical, that increased diversification of individual positions in society requires at the same time increased cooperation because of widespread interdependence. Economic individualists have not always recognized this in theory, although they have done fairly well in practice.

The division of labor along lines of productive technical specialization has a number of economic advantages. Not least among these is the increased productivity afforded through the selection of the personnel best qualified for a particular job. Moreover, training for a particular activity may save considerable time as compared with the requirements for learning a whole series of processes. By devoting himself only to a limited kind of work, the laborer may gain greater proficiency than could possibly be achieved in more elaborate tasks involving frequent changes of activity and a relatively short time on any one. Thus an apprenticeship of years may be eliminated almost entirely, or limited to a few weeks required to learn one or two operations.

This raises a fundamental question in the economics of specialization: does the division of labor introduce simplification of tasks, or increase the technical competence required for highly diversified positions? Actually it does both. Economists since Adam Smith have emphasized simplification of tasks through division and subdivision of operations. This, it is argued quite rightly, saves time in changing from one operation to another, saves duplication of equipment for each worker, and is of special advantage in main-

[22] See Sumner H. Slichter, *Modern Economic Society* (New York: Henry Holt and Company, Inc., 1931), pp. 105–106. The treatment of "specialization" in this book, pp. 104–121, has been drawn upon at numerous places in the present section. Slichter also quite properly notes that division of labor takes place on business and territorial lines, as well as occupational. Naturally, our primary concern is with the last, although the three are not unrelated.

taining the labor force. The last named advantage can be seen in
the reduction of skilled labor costs to a minimum through breaking
down complex operations into easily learned component units, especially with the aid of machinery. It is likewise evident in the decreased dependence of the manufacturer upon a small number of
skilled workers not easily replaced, and in the control made possible
by the interdependence of the workers. Thus, as Slichter points out,[23]
a pace-setter at an early stage in continuous processing involving
many workers can regulate the speed of the others all down the line.

But what practically all treatises on economic specialization have
overlooked is that "division of labor" is a misleading term, since it
implies that a given amount of labor is to be divided or subdivided.
Modern specialization, however, involves more than that. The very
complexity of industrial organization, plus the special services made
possible by increased productivity through specialization, has increased rather than decreased the demand for *skilled* specialists.
True, the newer skilled labor may be in managerial and advisory
positions, rather than in "production" itself, but this is likely to be
an artificial distinction. The fact remains that in an American textile
factory one sees not simply division of labor illustrated by the
breakdown of processes to such a point that in some departments
each worker tends a number of identical or similar machines, but
also a *diversification* of labor involving technical specialists responsible for research, design, planning, and coordination. If the producer is less dependent on any given processor of the raw material,
he may be more dependent on highly trained specialists whose
knowledge of particular aspects of the organization is far greater
than his own.

It is, of course, not even true in economic terms that more specialization is always better than less. The degree of division of labor
as a basis for increased productivity must always be limited by the
optimum (most satisfactory) utilization of a worker's time and
energies. Thus the almost unbelievably extensive division of labor
fostered among large groups of slaves by Roman patrician slave-
holders was in the interests of conspicuous display and waste, not

[23] *Ibid.*, p. 108.

productive efficiency. Unless it is possible to find other work for an individual employee, or hire a part-time worker, it is probably not in the interests of efficiency so to subdivide operations that it takes four workers to do what one did formerly. This implies a further point, previously noted with regard to industrial organization: *the extent of useful division of labor is intimately related to the size of the establishment or complexity of the industry as a whole. Thus, as a general rule, the larger the concern, the greater the possible degree of specialization.*

Certain Social Implications. The division of labor, we have noted, is well grounded in the cultural background of modern industry. It is not enough simply to note the fact that specialization is rampant in our society. We must note also the fact that in general it is believed in as a positive good. But the assumptions upon which it rests—for example, the doctrines of individualism—and the conclusions to be drawn from the applications of the principle are not always in complete conformity. For example, minute subdivision of tasks has led some critics to maintain that specialization destroys individual self-reliance, pride in useful work, and so on, by reducing a worker to the status of a machine. It is certainly true, as noted in Chapters IX and X, that the relation of the worker to the machine as expressed in routine tasks has created serious problems in employee satisfaction and industrial morale. This implies the possibility, moreover, that individual specialization makes the worker more and more dependent upon society, yet more poorly integrated into the entire social system because he is too far removed from the common values toward which all this diversified activity is directed, and too little aware of his place in the entire structure. This was the classic problem posed by the French sociologist, Emile Durkheim. Put very simply, the question he raised was how to prevent extensive social division of labor, which should presumably lead to social interdependence, from producing instead a general social collapse through insufficient integration around common values.[24] This

[24] See Emile Durkheim, *On the Division of Labor in Society,* tr. by George Simpson (New York: The Macmillan Company, 1933), especially pp. 200–229, 353–373, and Preface to the Second Edition.

is a problem basic to the relationship of modern industry to society as a whole, and thus will merit fuller discussion in later chapters. It is sufficient here to note that, however strongly the belief in specialization may be rooted in the culture, its practical applications must meet the tests of social expediency and rough conformity with other values held in the society.

Related to the considerations just advanced is the problem of *controlled* specialization. It was noted that, although the division of labor requires coordination of labor, this is accomplished in an industrial plant by means of authority. Thus the general assumptions of economic individualism in regard to free and impersonal competition within a few well-recognized rules, resulting in an "automatic" judgment of appropriate position in the entire system, break down for all but a limited number of entrepreneurs and managers. If the capitalist is judged by the impersonal operation of the market, his laborers are judged by *him* or his representatives. The modern factory worker must not only satisfy the demands made upon his skill, but he must avoid being "sassy" to his foreman. He may, in concrete cases, be judged more quickly on the latter achievement (or its absence) than on the former. And therein lies the breakdown of some time-hallowed tenets of economic individualism that emphasize impersonal competition. Thus again it is clear that the cultural structure underlying industrial activity is not a consistent body of doctrine. Thus "individualism" may be deposed and "collectivism" put in its place, without changing the essential characteristic of competitive specialization and administrative coordination. The effects of the difference in doctrine are real and important, but they are exhibited in such questions as the toleration of independent unionism, the separation of political and economic sanctions upon the worker, and the less stringent insistence on detailed political orthodoxy, which are more or less characteristic of modified "individualism." The industrial system has shown a considerable adaptability to noncapitalistic doctrines and types of organization, while imposing its own requirements for specialization and coordination of specialized activities.

REFERENCES

AYRES, C. E., *The Theory of Economic Progress* (Chapel Hill: University of North Carolina Press, 1944), Chap. IX, "Technology and Institutions."

BEARD, CHARLES A., "Introduction I—The Development of Social Thought and Institutions. IX. Individualism and Capitalism," in *Encyclopaedia of the Social Sciences*, 1: 145–163.

BERNAL, J. D., *The Social Function of Science* (New York: The Macmillan Company, 1939).

BOGART, ERNEST L., and CHARLES E. LANDON, *Modern Industry* (New York: Longmans, Green and Company, 1927), Chap. III, "Specialization," and Chap. IV, "Division of Labor."

CLARK, HAROLD R., *Economic Theory and Correct Occupational Distribution* (New York: Bureau of Publications, Teachers College, Columbia University, 1931), Chap. VII, "Eighteenth Century Individualism and Occupational Distribution."

COMMONS, JOHN R., *Legal Foundations of Capitalism* (New York: The Macmillan Company, 1924).

DAVIS, JEROME, *Capitalism and Its Culture* (New York: Farrar & Rinehart, Inc., 1935), Chap. I, "The Rise of Capitalism," and Chap. III, "The Philosophy Examined."

DURKHEIM, EMILE, *On the Division of Labor in Society*, tr. by George Simpson (New York: The Macmillan Company, 1933), especially Book I, Chap. VII, "Organic Solidarity and Contractual Solidarity"; Book III, Chap. I, "The Anomic Division of Labor"; and Preface to the Second Edition.

HENDERSON, LEON, "Basic Assumptions of American Competitive Capitalistic System," in the United States Congress, Temporary National Economic Committee, *Investigation of Concentration of Economic Power, Hearings . . .* (Washington: U. S. Government Printing Office, 1940), Part I, pp. 167–168.

LEDERER, EMIL, "Technology," in *Encyclopaedia of the Social Sciences*, 14: 553–560.

LINDSAY, A. D., "Individualism," in *Encyclopaedia of the Social Sciences*, 7: 674–680.

LINTON, RALPH, "Age and Sex Categories," *American Sociological Review*, 7: 589–603, October 1942.

——, *The Study of Man* (New York: D. Appleton-Century Company, Inc., 1936), Chap. VIII, "Status and Role."

MARSHALL, LEON CARROLL, ed., *Readings in Industrial Society* (Chicago: University of Chicago Press, 1918), Chap. III, "The Coming in of

Capitalism," especially pp. 144–174; Chap. VII, "Machine Industry—An Expression of the New Technology," especially pp. 417–
436.

MARX, KARL, *Capital* (New York: The Modern Library [1936]), Vol. I,
Chap. XIV, "Division of Labour and Manufacture."

———, *The Poverty of Philosophy* (Chicago: Charles H. Kerr and Co.,
1920), Chap. II, "The Metaphysics of Political Economy," especially
Sec. II, "The Division of Labor and Machinery."

MERTON, ROBERT K., *Science, Technology and Society in Seventeenth
Century England,* in the series *Osiris,* Vol. IV, Part 2, pp. 360–362
(Bruges, Belgium: The Saint Catherine Press, 1938).

MUMFORD, LEWIS, *Technics and Civilization* (New York: Harcourt,
Brace and Company, 1934), Chap. I, "Cultural Preparation"; Chap.
II, "Agents of Mechanization"; and pp. 107–118, 316–320.

NATIONAL ASSOCIATION OF MANUFACTURERS, Economic Principles Commission, *The American Individual Enterprise System: Its Nature,
Evolution, and Future* (New York: McGraw-Hill Book Company,
Inc., 1946, 2 vols.), Vol. I, Chap. I, "Nature and Philosophy of the
Individual Enterprise System"; Chap. II, "Evolution of the Individual Enterprise System"; and Chap. III, "Fundamental Elements of the Individual Enterprise System."

PAGE, KIRBY, *Individualism and Socialism* (New York: Farrar & Rinehart, Inc., 1933), Chap. I, "The Theory of Individualism."

PARSONS, TALCOTT, *The Structure of Social Action* (New York: McGraw-
Hill Book Company, Inc., 1937), Chap. II, "The Theory of Action";
Chap. III, "Some Phases of the Historical Development of In-
dividualistic Positivism in the Theory of Action"; Chap. IV, "Alfred
Marshall: Wants and Activities and the Problem of the Scope of
Economics"; Chaps. XIV and XV, "Max Weber I (II): Religion
and Modern Capitalism"; and pp. 399–408.

POLANYI, KARL, *The Great Transformation* (New York: Farrar & Rinehart, Inc., 1944).

SALZ, ARTHUR, "Occupation," in *Encyclopaedia of the Social Sciences,*
11: 424–435.

———, "Specialization," in *Encyclopaedia of the Social Sciences,* 14: 279–
285.

SÉE, HENRI EUGÈNE, *Modern Capitalism, Its Origin and Evolution,* tr. by
Homer V. Vanderblue and Georges F. Doriot (London: N. Douglas,
1928).

SIEVERS, ALLEN MORRIS, *Has Market Capitalism Collapsed? A Critique of
Karl Polanyi's New Economics* (New York: Columbia University
Press, 1949).

SLICHTER, SUMNER H., *Modern Economic Society* (New York: Henry Holt and Company, Inc., 1931), Chap. VI, "Specialization."

SMITH, ADAM, *An Inquiry into the Nature and Causes of the Wealth of Nations,* Everyman's Library ed. (London and Toronto: J. M. Dent and Sons; New York: E. P. Dutton & Company, Inc., 1910), Book I, Chap. I, "Of the Division of Labor"; Chap. II, "Of the Principle which Gives Occasion to the Division of Labor"; Chap. III, "That the Division of Labor is Limited by the Extent of the Market."

SOMBART, WERNER, "Capitalism," in *Encyclopaedia of the Social Sciences,* 3: 195–208.

STEAD, WILLIAM H., CARROLL L. SHARTLE, and OTHERS, *Occupational Counseling Techniques, Their Development and Application* (New York: American Book Company, 1940). See especially Chap. X, "Occupational Relationships," by Raymond S. Ward.

TAWNEY, RICHARD HENRY, *The Acquisitive Society* (New York: Harcourt, Brace and Howe, 1920).

——, *Religion and the Rise of Capitalism* (New York: Penguin Books, 1926).

VEBLEN, THORSTEIN, *Absentee Ownership and Business Enterprise in Recent Times* (New York: B. W. Huebsch, 1923), Chap. X, "The Technology of Physics and Chemistry."

——, *The Instinct of Workmanship* (New York: The Macmillan Company, 1914), Chap. V, "Ownership and the Competitive System."

——, *The Place of Science in Modern Civilisation* (New York: The Viking Press, 1932). See especially the following essays: "The Place of Science in Modern Civilisation," pp. 1–31; "The Evolution of the Scientific Point of View," pp. 32–55; "The Preconceptions of Economic Science, I, II, III," pp. 82–179; "On the Nature of Capital, I and II, " pp. 324–386.

——, *The Vested Interests and the State of the Industrial Arts* (New York: B. W. Huebsch, 1918), Sec. I, "The Instability of Knowledge and Belief," and Sec. III, "The State of the Industrial Arts."

WEBER, MAX, *General Economic History,* tr. by Frank H. Knight (New York: Greenberg Publisher, Inc., 1927), Chap. XXII, "The Meaning and Presuppositions of Modern Capitalism"; Chap. XXVII, "The Development of Industrial Technique"; Chap. XXX, "The Evolution of the Capitalistic Spirit."

——, *The Protestant Ethic and the Spirit of Capitalism,* tr. by Talcott Parsons (London: George Allen and Unwin, Ltd., 1930).

——, *The Theory of Social and Economic Organization,* tr. by A. M. Henderson and Talcott Parsons (New York: Oxford University Press, 1947), pp. 216–254.

CHAPTER XIX

SOURCES OF LABOR SUPPLY

ONE OF the many ways industry is dependent upon society at large and in turn affects the total society is through the supply and utilization of industrial labor. Labor is one of the "resources" or factors of production, which, however, constitutes a substantial part of the very social system served by the productive organization. And, as a part of society, and being subject to human reproduction and socialization, laborers are a product of noneconomic segments of society before they enter the productive system. In this chapter attention will be given to four main problems: (1) the size of the "labor force" in the American population; (2) the *quantitative* problems of labor supply with reference to geographical mobility of labor; (3) the *qualitative* problems which hinge upon the social mobility of labor; and (4) the problem of specialized training in an industrial system characterized by extensive division of labor.

THE LABOR FORCE IN THE POPULATION

Even in a society that places strong emphasis on productive labor, not every one works for a living. Aside from individuals (a very small minority) who are "independently wealthy," and whose chief productive labor consists in clipping coupons from gilt-edged securities, there are large numbers of living Americans who by reason of age, sex, or physical infirmity must be supported by the nation's workers.

The Concept of Labor Force. The actual and immediately potential workers in the population comprise our "labor force." The labor force thus includes not only all the employed population, but those who are temporarily or involuntarily unemployed but are able and willing to work. It excludes the unemployables (even though willing to work) and those under age or not seeking work.

The concept of labor force is not and cannot be very precise in its reference. Part of the indefiniteness is due to questions of general definition. For example, are part-time laborers who work only a few hours a week and are not interested in additional employment part of the labor force? Are working children under fourteen, such as newsboys, delivery boys, and girls employed after school in domestic service, part of the work force? These and similar questions indicate difficulties in defining what we mean by workers in the population. However, the technical questions of definition can be met more easily, if somewhat arbitrarily, than can the problems that arise from the *inherently relative* character of the concept. To a highly significant extent, the size and character of the labor force depends upon the customs of society. Thus, if children were allowed to work as soon as any productive labor could be found for them, and without regard for considerations of future health or training for greater productivity, the labor force would be considerably larger. Similarly, if the American family structure were such that all adults were expected to contribute their share to total production instead of confining occupational selection primarily to males and single females, the number of actually or potentially gainfully employed persons would be much greater. In the following chapter these and similar restrictions will be noted as "institutionalized wastes" of labor resources. At this point it is sufficient to recognize that *the labor force at any particular time is relative to the actual situation in the institutional structure at that time.* Conversely, any large and rapid increase in the labor force must be made at the expense of existing institutional restrictions, as in the present widespread employment of women and pressure for the employment of children.

The labor force is not a constant factor, even aside from questions of definition, possible institutional modification, or the more basic consideration of population size and age-sex distribution. It is also relative to the existing or predicted future demand on the labor market. This is to say that the supply of labor and the demand for that labor are not completely independent variables. This is especially evident in the way the demand tends to affect the available supply. A few illustrations may serve to indicate some of the ways this relationship works.

In a period of rapid industrial expansion and increased demand for labor, persons who had not previously considered gainful employment enter the labor force either as workers or as persons seeking employment. Persons long unemployed and no longer actively seeking work, workmen beyond the normal retirement age, and youths who would normally continue their formal training or depend upon parental support until their maturity become part of the available supply of labor.

In a period of reduced industrial employment, as in the early 1930's, the labor force tends to shrink through the withdrawal of those who have the least necessity or chance of employment. This is not an exact relationship, however, because of the contrary tendency for the ranks of the unemployed to be swelled by members of the family of the unemployed breadwinner, seeking to compensate for the loss of normal sources of support.

Part of the relativity of the size of the labor force is due to the difference in quality of workers employable under different conditions. Thus persons who are classified as "unemployable" when the demand for labor is low may become fairly readily employable with increased demand, and without change in the qualifications of the worker. In other words, the margin or threshold of employability is raised or lowered in conformity with the condition of the labor market in general. If the pressure for manpower is acute, useful occupations can be found for the lame, the halt, and the blind.

The Size of the Labor Force. In view of this relativity of the concept of "labor force," it is understandable that any statement of the size of the employed and employable population in the United States must either be very approximate, or else assume the constancy of conditions which may not in fact remain constant. Nevertheless, it is possible to indicate, without too much error, the proportion of the American population that may be considered to constitute our work force.

According to the Sixteenth Population Census of the United States, 1940, the labor force then numbered 52,789,499 persons, of whom 5,093,810 were then unemployed and seeking work.[1] The labor force in 1940 thus comprised forty per cent of the total population of 131,669,275. By May, 1950, the labor force had increased to an estimated 62,788,000 persons, or about forty-two per cent of the estimated population at that time.[2]

Part of this increase was due to continued growth of the population; that is, more persons reached the age of employability (set at fourteen) than died or became too old for employment (set at sixty-five). A more important source of the increase, however, was the marked upturn in the employment of women not previously considered part of the work force. Some additional increment of workers resulted from lowering the threshold of employability accompanied by specialized training for the handicapped "unemployable." As long as the shortage of manpower for the armed forces and armament production continues, the increase in the size of the labor force from sources other than natural population growth may be expected to continue. Indeed, as is discussed in the following chapter, there is good reason for believing that the luxury of many riders and few pushers may be a thing of the past.

The present expansion of the labor force over and beyond the increase of the population thus documents its relativity in terms of industrial and general social conditions. The short-term variability in the proportion of the total population that may be considered part of the available labor supply is possible because of the normal existence of a large number of potential workers who neither work nor seek employment.

Peculiarities of Population Distribution. At the present time and for the near future the age composition of the American population

[1] Figures from United States Department of Commerce, Bureau of the Census, *Sixteenth Census, 1940, Population*, Vol. III, The Labor Force, Part 1, p. 3.

[2] Figures from United States Department of Commerce, Bureau of the Census, *Current Population Reports: Labor Force*, Series P–59, No. 17, August 2, 1950, and *Population Estimates*, Series P–25, No. 42, June 30, 1950.

shows a heavy concentration in the productive years—that is, among those actually or potentially part of the labor force. Whether this is to be regarded as fortunate or unfortunate depends upon other circumstances and upon point of view. In the pressure for man-

FIGURE 9. *Age-Sex Distribution of the Population: "Ideal" (If Everyone Died of Old Age), "Normal," and Actual (United States, 1949)*

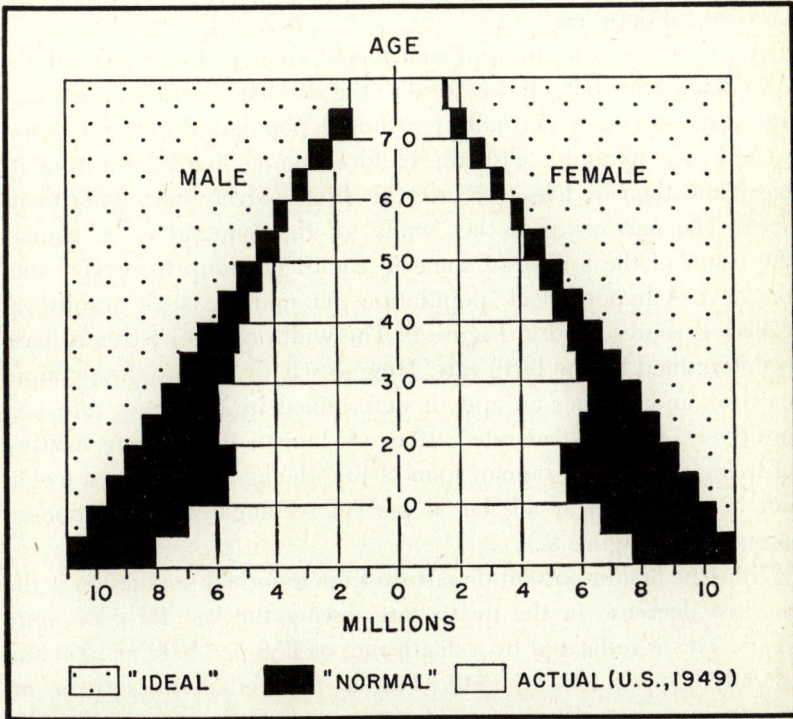

American population data for 1949 are official estimates of the Bureau of the Census in *Current Population Reports: Population Estimates*, Series P–25, No. 39, May 5, 1950, Table 2.

power in a war for national survival, the high proportion of producers must be regarded as fortunate. In the interwar years, when the pressure was not for manpower but for jobs, the number of actual or potential competitors was clearly disadvantageous to the individual laborer.

Aside from the disturbing factors of immigration and emigration, the size of a population is obviously determined by births and deaths. More specifically, the age-sex composition of the population is the result of past births and deaths which have determined the survival ratios in each age or sex group. It is axiomatic therefore that the source of the present "peculiar" distribution of the American population must be sought in the birth and death rates of the last several decades.

A convenient way to approach recent changes in the size of the American labor potential is to note the departures from a "normal" age distribution. A normally expanding population may be represented as a pyramid, with the children under five constituting its base, and then by five-year intervals progressively narrowing to its apex. The narrowing of the "walls" of the pyramid is, of course, the result of the failure of some in each age group to survive into the next. A hypothetical "population pyramid," as such graphs are called, is represented in Figure 9. The width of the horizontal base is determined by the birth rate. How slowly or rapidly the pyramid narrows and reaches an apex is determined by the death rate (or, positively, the survival rate). If every human infant were assured of living out the full human span of life, the age composition would not be pyramidal at all, but a perfect rectangle of superimposed strata. (See Figure 9.)

Now the first important departure from a normal population is the marked decrease in the death rate during the last forty or more years. This is indicated by a death rate of 17.6 per 1000 in 1900 and of only 9.7 per 1000 in 1949.[3] Part of this reduction is to be attributed to controlling of epidemics, improved sanitation, reduction of maternal mortality, and so on. Most spectacular, however, has been the reduction of infant mortality (that is, death within the first year of life). Thus one infant in ten (99.9 per 1000 live births) born in 1915 did not survive the first year, whereas less than one in thirty (31 per 1000) of those born in 1949 died during the

[3] Figures from U. S. Department of Commerce, Bureau of the Census, *Vital Statistics of the United States*, 1939, Part I (Washington: U. S. Government Printing Office, 1941), Table U, p. 11; and National Office of Vital Statistics, *Monthly Vital Statistics Bulletin*, 12: 1, March 31, 1950.

first year of life.[4] The infant mortality rates before 1915 (the first year of American registration) were certainly higher. What the reduction of death rates in general and infant mortality rates in particular signifies for the size of our labor force is that *many persons are alive and working today who would not have lived through infancy if previous conditions had continued.* Put in our previous graphic terms, the walls of the population pyramid have been straightened toward the perpendicular. This constitutes a significant approximation to the hypothetical situation of one hundred per cent survival to which we previously referred.

Yet we have only partially accounted for our present proportion of productive laborers. Although paradoxical at first glance, the relative size of the labor force has been increased by a reduction of the birth rate. The paradox is resolved by noting that the decline of the birth rate came later than the decline of death rate,[5] so that there are fewer nonproductive persons for the laboring population to support. Prior to 1950, the 1920 census was the last to show a larger percentage under five years of age than in the age group from five to nine. Even then the difference was only one-tenth of one per cent (0.1 per cent). Until about 1945, the population pyramid was contracting on its base. In conjunction with the earlier fall in the death rate already noted, this has produced a positive "bulge" in the age groups from which productive labor is chiefly drawn. This also is illustrated by Figure 9, which shows the age-sex composition of the American population by the 1949 estimates.

It may be noted that this situation is clearly a temporary one. As the "bulge" in the pyramid moves nearer and nearer the apex of the pyramid, representing the span of human life, more and more

---

[4] *Ibid.*

[5] In 1915 (the first year of anything like national registration), the birth rate was 25.1 per thousand, and in 1939 only 17.3. (*Ibid.* Table F, p. 6.) Estimates, based partly upon state statistics, indicate that in 1896–1900 the rate was 29.8, and in 1912, 26.4. (See Alfred J. Lotka, "Modern Trends in the Birth Rate," *Annals* of the American Academy of Political and Social Science, 188: 1–13, November 1936, Table I, pp. 2–3.) Although there is some evidence that the birth rate in the United States has been slowly declining since early in the last century, the marked decline is a relatively recent phenomenon. (See Warren S. Thompson, *Population Problems,* 2nd ed. [New York and London: McGraw-Hill Book Company, Inc., 1936], p. 126.)

persons will be too old for productive labor. Thus the dual problem of old-age security plus the manpower requirements of a competitive world power may be predicted in the future. The latter problem will be accentuated by the very circumstance which contributes to the national "good fortune" at the present time: *the declining birth rate means increased difficulty in the future in replacing the aged.* This is not the place to "view with alarm." The present concern is to focus attention upon the "sources of labor supply" and to indicate some temporary circumstances that will not hold in the future of the American labor force.

The remarkable recovery of the birth rate in the United States and other Western countries after World War II may reflect a trend toward higher average size of families, but seems to be more nearly the result of higher marriage rates at earlier ages, which in turn reflect a high level of employment. With a population generally practicing deliberate control of fertility, birth rates seem to parallel closely the level of employment and prosperity. They are thus subject to considerable short-run variations, with inevitable long-run effects on the age cohorts reaching working age. Since death rates remain rather stable short of major catastrophes, populations of working ages can still be predicted for a decade or two, but longer predictions require hazardous assumptions about future births. Thus the increasingly unfavorable ratio between accessions and retirements as far as those are a function of age may be reversed around 1960 when the postwar "baby crop" begins to enter the labor market.

QUANTITATIVE PROBLEMS AND GEOGRAPHICAL MOBILITY

In an earlier chapter it was noted that one of the characteristics of modern industrial capitalism is its reliance upon free labor. It was also observed that, throughout most of the modern history of industrial production, a fairly adequate supply of labor has been at the disposal of managers. Again there is evident a correspondence between historical fact and the assumptions of traditional economic theory, whereby the particular instance comes to be thought of as a universal rule. In this instance, labor and wage theory has been posited upon the presumption of a continued supply of cheap labor. In order adequately to understand the general position of labor in contemporary affairs we must place on record the customary assumption with regard to the numerical supply of laborers, and some of the factors that may and do modify those assumptions.

The Assumption of the Expanding Population. The ready supply of cheap labor to which we have referred has in the recent past existed over most of western Europe and America by reason of the technological improvements in agriculture and industry that allow each worker to produce more, and by reason of a rapidly expanding population. In so far as these conditions have prevailed, a problem of the amount of labor supply could not exist. That is, no problem could exist from the capitalistic or managerial point of view, whatever might be the difficulties with regard to low wages, underemployment, and insecurity from the laborer's point of view. The rapid expansion of the population that accompanied increased industrialization came to be thought of as another "natural law." The increase in numbers was held to provide a constantly expanding market for industrial products, and the arms and hands to tend the machines.

The validity of this line of reasoning becomes seriously impaired either under a situation of widespread withdrawal of potentially productive laborers for military or other duties (coupled in wartime with a demand for increased production), or in a situation of voluntary or involuntary reduction of the rate of population growth. Thus, for given levels of industrial production, labor *shortages* may actually occur. The effect of military action and war production is more immediate, since a reduction in the birth rate temporarily increases the *proportion* (but not the number) of workers. The latter trend may prove the more serious in the future. Recent and contemporary events illustrate the coincidence of these situations, in various degrees of urgency or immediacy. The various solutions of this problem through expansion of the labor force have already been discussed. Our present concern is to emphasize that, despite customary views to the contrary, a contemporary industrial system may be faced with quantitative problems of labor supply.

The Assumption of Spatial Mobility. Merely to have sufficient workers in the entire population is not, of course, enough. They must be at the right place at the appropriate time. Traditional economic theory has assumed the "fluidity" of the labor market, or in other words free geographical mobility in accordance with differences in "economic opportunity." Thus the movement of rural populations to urban industrial centers, the westward movement of land-hungry migrants, and the crowding of armament-producing cities are all explained by the "pull" of greater opportunity.

This fluidity of the labor market will hold true in any marked degree only under certain further conditions, and can never operate completely. The necessary conditions for its operation *at all* include the existence of a labor system allowing free occupational shifts, and the absence of barriers to territorial mobility. Economic opportunity as a factor in labor mobility would be meaningless if states or counties forbade the entrance or emigration of laborers. In any event, communication must be sufficiently well developed for workers in one area to hear of openings in other places. Then, too, it must be assumed that economic advancement is the sole significant motive for the residential choice of laborers, and that the potentially mobile worker can distinguish genuinely from fictionally greener pastures. A little reflection by anyone familiar with recent American migratory labor reveals how far the actual circumstances deviate from the assumed conditions.

Although there have been few official barriers to occupational shifts in the past, they have been present. The outstanding case has been the discrimination against Negro labor by employers, labor unions, and members of the community in general. Yet it is clear that the greater industrial (and social) opportunity for the Negro in northern cities has been chiefly responsible for the northward migration of rural southern Negroes. Thus the principle holds, but in a modified degree.

There have been attempts, almost entirely extralegal, to prevent free territorial mobility in order to protect the laborers or taxpayers of one area from the competition or public assistance burden of migrants from other areas. Within the United States such practices have been held by the Supreme Court to be unconstitutional.[6] Yet the restrictions on international migration clearly limit the fluidity of the labor market. Immigration laws, in fact, are designed to do for native laborers what tariff laws do for native industries. In both cases a free market has been set aside.

More important than these violations of the conditions of labor mobility, however, are those inherent in the institutional structure of the society. Property ownership, for example, especially the ownership of residences and real estate, is a potent source of immobility. The worker who has invested his savings in a home of his own has also given hostages to fortune (or at least to society). He has a stake in remaining at his place of residence and employment as long as possible, despite the pull of greater opportunity elsewhere. Likewise, residential and regional preferences, familistic and similar bonds, and the difficulty (real or imagined) of starting as a stranger in a strange land serve to reduce the casual wandering of a mobile laborer sensitive to slight differentials in opportunity.

Add to these limiting factors the expense of mobility, the frequently overcrowded residential conditions in expanding industrial communities, difficulties in the education of children, and so on, and the assumption of free geographical mobility loses its force.[7]

---

[6] See United States Congress, House of Representatives, Select Committee Investigating National Defense Migration, *Hearings,* Part 26, "Constitutional Rights of Destitute Citizens of the United States to Move from State to State —the Edwards Case" (Washington: U. S. Government Printing Office, 1942). This case involved the constitutionality of a California statute attempting to limit interstate migration. California, during 1935 and 1936, attempted by various devices to reduce the number of drought victims and other migrants entering the state. During 1936 the Los Angeles police illegally stopped migrants at the Arizona border and forced them to turn back. See *ibid.,* pp. 10148–10158.

[7] The writer has pointed out elsewhere that "economic opportunity" cannot be separated from the institutional framework of society, and that the "pull" of a serious labor shortage may be offset by the general social status that the available type of labor gives the worker. See Wilbert E. Moore, "Migration and Social Opportunity," *Rural Sociology,* 7: 86–89, March 1942.

A number of recent studies have been directed to the discovery of the actual extent of geographical and job mobility in the labor market. See, for example, Edward William Noland and E. Wight Bakke, *Workers Wanted* (New York: Harper & Brothers, 1949); Lloyd G. Reynolds and Joseph Shister, *Job Horizons: A Study of Job Satisfaction and Labor Mobility* (New York: Harper & Brothers, 1949).

The evidence from the large amount of labor mobility in the decade of the 1930's is that the "push" of highly unfavorable economic circumstances is more important under some social conditions than the assumed "pull" from the sources of labor demand. Without the push of unfavorable circumstances, the economic opportunity must be great enough (or rumored to be great enough) to offset the contrary factors which produce immobility.

In so far as the transactions of employer and employee resemble the conditions of a market governed by supply and demand, it is to the interest of employers to urge the in-migration of potential laborers, and of local workers to send the hopeful immigrant elsewhere. Both groups, therefore, may try to interfere with any total or partial operation of the "automatic" mobility of labor supply. This circumstance adds still another factor to the quantitative problem of available labor. Even in a period of pronounced increase in the demand for labor (that is, heightened economic opportunity), the combination of pushes and pulls, the erroneous operation of the "grapevine" system of communication, and the barriers to free mobility combine to produce "overages" of labor in some areas and shortages in others. In view of the differences in interest already noted, it is not surprising that *employers and laborers do not always agree about the existence of a surplus or deficiency of available labor.*

QUALITATIVE PROBLEMS AND SOCIAL MOBILITY

Even a sufficient number of laborers in the right places to satisfy the demands of industrial employment may still constitute an inadequate labor supply. *The workers must be of the appropriate quality.* We noted in the preceding chapter, with reference to the division of labor, that the ideal situation in the "culture of capitalism" is for every laborer to do that useful work for which he is best fitted. This, it was pointed out, involves a differentiation as well as a simple division of labor. The labor force of the nation is not a large mass of identical units (or interchangeable parts), but a group of specialized workers trained in the skills of industry. Under the assumptions of traditional theory, the higher the skill the smaller the supply of workers possessing that skill; consequently, there is a greater relative demand for those workers having greater ability, and the market price of labor (wages) reflects the situation and appropriately rewards the deserving.

Social Mobility of the Labor Force. Assuming for the moment that the basic potentialities exist in the human resources available for productive work, the over-all problem of getting the right persons for the jobs to be done might be called that of facilitating the social mobility of labor. Put in more concrete terms, if an industrial concern has too many sweep-up men and not enough toolmakers, its problem is to make skilled workers out of janitors. Actually, a single industrial concern is likely to fire the extra sweep-up men or transfer them to other unskilled jobs, and look elsewhere for toolmakers. If, however, a comparable situation develops for the entire industrial order, the problem cannot be so simply evaded: the fluidity of the labor market must compensate for shortages in skill as well as in numbers.

Overcrowding, the unemployment of the unskilled or those whose skills are no longer marketable, and acute shortages of some types of skilled workers may coexist in the same industrial order. Whether one assumes the traditional doctrine as a standard of judgment, or the contemporary necessity of maximum production, such a situation indicates that "something is wrong." From the viewpoint of the employer or manager, something is wrong with the quality of the labor he can secure. It might, of course, almost as reasonably be held that something is wrong with the organizational ability of the manager who has failed to take into account the quality of the workmen available.

In economic theory, a "correct occupational distribution" would presumably be one that showed neither shortages nor underemployment, with those of equal ability in various occupations receiving equal income.[8] Thus any barriers to occupational mobility, whether

[8] See Harold F. Clark, *Economic Theory and Correct Occupational Distribution* (New York: Bureau of Publications, Teachers College, Columbia University, 1931); Omar Pancoast, Jr., *Occupational Mobility* (New York: Columbia University Press, 1941).

due to conscious manipulation, ignorance, tradition, or whatever, would force a disruption in the equilibrium of labor and production.

Skills: Supply and Demand. It is essential for an understanding of the general position of labor in our society to examine briefly the sources of difficulty in the qualitative distribution of skills. The more important barriers to free occupational mobility that affect the quality of the labor supply are: (1) ignorance, (2) traditional restrictions on freedom of choice, (3) absence of equal opportunity, (4) the prevalence of "trained incapacity," and (5) the rapidity of change in industrial processes (and therefore in skills demanded).

1. We have often noted the fundamental assumption of classical economic theory to the effect that every individual will pursue his economic activities according to the canons of rational self-interest. Even were this a true characterization of human motivation, it would still face a formidable obstacle in lack of knowledge of facts essential for decision. In the absence of knowledge of opportunities the worker may either fail to develop his skills, or fail to use those he already possesses. No group has a monopoly on ignorance, however, and the industrial manager may fail to utilize potential skills by neglecting to discover them or by not recognizing the usefulness of those which he sees. The lack of vocational information on the one hand, and the tendency to be concerned only with machine technology on the other, may produce poor occupational adjustment.

2. But other difficulties arise from an error in the original premise. It is by no means certain that vocations will be chosen "wisely" (in terms of rational self-interest), even if knowledge is freely available. The marked tendencies for sons to follow their fathers' occupations frequently reflects a vocational choice (or simply a lack of choice by following the line of least resistance) that takes into account neither opportunities nor abilities. This is one example of what we have called traditional restrictions on freedom of choice. Another type of limitation is to be found in the customary distinction between "honorable" and "common" occupations. This distinction may correspond neither to the amount of ability required, nor even to

the income received. Thus the professions have long represented honorable vocational opportunities for children of the upper classes, regardless of the children's abilities and the degree of overcrowding in some of the professions. In industrial plants an invidious distinction is always drawn between office ("white collar") and shop workers, although the latter may be far more skilled and more highly paid. One of the difficulties that employment service representatives have had in recruiting women factory workers has been the consistent preference for lower paid clerical positions. It is frequently claimed that the schools, particularly the high schools and colleges, are responsible for much of the disdain for the work of the skilled artisan or mechanic. In any event, it is certainly true that the "brain worker," who may not use much of his brain, feels superior to the "manual laborer," who may use his hands (and his brain) rather well. It is also true that this represents a barrier to the development of an equilibrium between skills demanded and skills available.

3. The classical formulation of the equilibrium theory assumed a condition that does not completely hold in fact: an effective equality of opportunity. Partly through the family's contribution to rigidity in the class structure,[9] and partly through the deliberate controls exercised by interest groups, the individual worker may never have the opportunity to develop or use the ability or skill he possesses. Any close approximation to fluidity in occupational distribution— that is, a high degree of correspondence between supply and demand—must rest upon free access to the means of vocational training and advancement. Although the American nation has gone a long way toward the breaking down of hereditary privileges through tax-supported education, it is still not true that the opportunities are equal with regard to precisely those more skilled occupations where shortages are most likely to occur. Advanced technical education in colleges, universities, and technical schools is by no means free. The able son of an unskilled factory worker or tenant farmer has very little chance of becoming a professional engineer or machine

[9] See the discussion of institutional limitations on equality of opportunity in Chap. XXIII.

designer. Stories to the contrary are newsworthy because they are exceptional.

The inequality of opportunity is also fostered by those persons in critical occupations simply to protect their scarcity value. This is in conformity with well-understood self-interest, and could only be prevented by positive rule allowing equal access to specialized skills by all those capable of learning them. Certain professional groups, notably physicians and surgeons, have been outstanding in limiting the number of persons to be trained. Labor organizations of skilled craft workers have long attempted to maintain a monopoly over apprenticeship to prevent overcrowding and possibly unemployment or lower income. Such practices have great advantage for those in a position to monopolize a needed skill, but may operate to the disadvantages of less fortunate workers, employers, or even society as a whole if they serve to restrict production. The societal disadvantage from barriers to occupational mobility are of course most noticeable in a period of wartime production. As is discussed more fully in the concluding section of this chapter, the whole issue of the responsibility for technical training has been in a state of confusion, and under the impetus of national emergency major efforts have been made to remove some of the barriers to social mobility.

4. The very complexity of industrial division of labor has an adverse effect upon free movement from one occupation or rank to another. This point was discussed in the preceding chapter with regard to the "range of horizontal transferability," which was noted as decreasing with higher ranks and skills. We also noted in our analysis of industrial bureaucracy (especially Chapter VI) that an individual who develops a high ability in one sphere of competence develops also a corresponding "trained incapacity" to perform other (perhaps less skilled but different) tasks. This inelasticity of distribution of skills is most pregnant with difficulty when the character of the organization or the industrial order as a whole so changes as to demand either quite different skills, or at least a different proportion in the various types of technical abilities required.

5. As just indicated, the problem of the equality of labor supply

is largely significant precisely because the demand is not constant. The rapidity of change in industrial processes requires an ever-different distribution of requisite abilities, as well as the continual addition of new ones. This places a serious strain on the entire training system, for modern training is necessarily long and the problem of retraining is not easy of solution. The length of the training period implies that much of the education must take place with no adequate prediction of placement opportunities. The changes in industrial processes customarily have been made in view of mechanical and technical developments, and not in view of the quality of the labor supply. In other words, demand has affected supply more than existing supply has affected demand.

Labor Pirating. Even without major transformations in technical organization, a change in volume and product necessarily disrupts any previous equilibrium. Slight increases in production may, of course, take up existing slacks in employment, but rapid expansion as in wartime may create critical shortages of skilled workers (even though unskilled or uselessly skilled workers remain unemployed). This leads to the phenomenon known as "labor pirating." The so-called labor market in the past has operated almost entirely through an individual laborer seeking employment, or a single industrial unit advertising for workers. Some modifications have been introduced, such as union hiring halls, industrial labor pools through cooperation of several plants, and private employment agencies. During the industrial depression of the 1930's there was a growing tendency to consider the task of bringing employers and employees together a legitimate function of government. As the drive for increased defense and subsequently war production got under way, the older system of hiring showed increasing inadequacy. The obvious and, in the most immediate terms, easiest way to secure needed skilled workmen is to find those who are doing similar work elsewhere. On a national scale, however, this simply means robbing Peter to pay Paul unless the workers are shifted from nonessential fields of production.

A condition of widespread labor pirating dramatizes the rapidity of industrial change and the qualitative problems of labor supply.

An over-all shortage of workers of a particular degree of skill can only be met by additions to that segment of the labor force through training programs or by a change in industrial processes to allow the employment of less, or at least differently, skilled persons. The latter is usually called the *dilution* of job requirements. Such a program, however, seems to require over-all supervision, first taking the form of voluntary or compulsory elimination of pirating. It should be noted that an elimination of pirating reduces the worker's horizontal mobility (job shifting without significant change of occupation) in order to facilitate the upward movement of the less skilled.[10] This, of course, constitutes what might be called an intrusion upon the traditional liberties of workers (and employers), but might be justified on grounds of equalizing the freedom of mobility of the labor force in general.

In summary of the question of the quality of the labor force, we may say that, although the qualifications of laborers and the qualities demanded by industry are not completely independent variables, since training is normally undertaken in view of predicted occupational opportunity, neither are the two automatically consistent. It would certainly be improper to insist that the lack of consistency is the "fault" of the labor force, or even to maintain that regardless of responsibility the situation could only be rectified by a change in the quality of the supply. Industrial processes may be modified in view of human as well as mechanical requirements. Yet it may be maintained, in view of the size of the American labor force, its general potentialities, and the possibility of turning potentialities into useful skills, that the single most strategic approach to the problem of labor quality lies in the training system of the society. We are now in a position to examine that possibility in the concluding section of the chapter.

---

[10] The proponents of the uncontrolled labor market might hold that the competitive bidding for skilled labor would so increase wages that other workers would be "automatically" attracted to those occupations and thus eliminate the shortage as well as reduce the excessive wage payments. Aside from the limitations upon free mobility already noted, however, the time required for the new equilibrium to be established may be overlong, as under the necessity of immediate conversion to war production.

TECHNICAL EDUCATION FOR INDUSTRIAL PRODUCTION

Words like manpower, human resources, or labor force fail to convey the proper impression of the workers who operate American industry, whether in peace or in war. The expressions are too color-less; they connote only numbers and physical strength. An elaborate industrial system does not use manpower in the sense that it uses the horsepower of engines and machines. Rather it uses the hand-and-brain power of intelligent and highly trained persons.

It is true that a great many American workmen are classified in industry and by employment services as "unskilled." To many per-sons that term evokes a picture of a hulking brute of feeble intel-ligence ploddingly digging a ditch, or that of a frail and palsied workman casually tending an almost automatic machine. There are such individuals, and there are such jobs in American production. But there are not many of either. The term *unskilled* should always be preceded by the qualifier *relatively*. So qualified, the category of the unskilled would be understood to include those whose abilities and training are somewhere just beyond the minimum for industrial employability, *whatever that minimum may be*. We noted earlier in the present chapter that what we called the "threshold of employ-ability" is subject to short-time changes through increases or de-creases in the demand for laborers. We should also recognize that there is some tendency toward a long-term upward trend through wider education on the one hand and increasing industrial com-plexity on the other. In anything approximating the absolute sense of the word, *there obviously are no unskilled workmen in American industry*. We ask for and receive a quality of work from the con-temporary unskilled laborer that might well have been classified as at least "semiskilled" a generation or two ago. This means that the problem of training for industrial employment is always present in some degree, and with reference to all industrial laborers. That the difficulty is more acute with the more highly skilled should not be allowed to obscure its generality.

Who Should Do the Training? Except for the automatic increase in skill and possibly wider experience that come from continued industrial employment, industry typically has little if any training program as a means of creating its own skilled labor force. The industrial manager or foreman attempts to select needed workmen from among previous applicants for employment, applications in answer to an advertisement of an opening, or from men in the "bull pen" outside the factory gates. Depending partly upon the size of the plant and partly upon its degree of "rationalization," the applicant's ability may be judged on the basis of his appearance and manner, or his employment and job allocation may depend upon his showing in a more or less elaborate battery of interviews and aptitude tests.

In-service training is likely to be expensive for a small concern, and the supply of most types of skilled workers has been fairly adequate during periods of normal production. Some larger industrial units have had for some time their own training schools for certain classes of employees. These have ranged from a type of orientation class for all incoming employees to brief courses on special industrial processes for the technical staff. More recently some companies have given up the attempt to select foremen from outside the plant or to rely on haphazard promotion from the ranks, and have established foremanship and supervisory training programs. For the higher ranks of skilled workmen, and various types of technical specialists, industries have relied almost exclusively on the general labor market or on direct recruiting from colleges and technical schools. Some of the largest companies recruit persons directly from higher educational institutions not for a definite position but for a training course, which serves both a sorting and a specific training function. A single company may have as many as ten or fifteen such programs, but virtually all of them will be designed to supply various categories of *managerial* personnel, and all rely on previous advanced training.

It seems clear that an industrial plant could not rely on its own training resources completely for turning out persons with the skills needed in the operation of the organization. The instructional personnel would be a sizeable nonproductive group on the payroll. Moreover, the industry could not hope to give the necessary scientific and technical background for training specialists. It is widely conceded that at least for the higher groups of skills the individual or the community through its educational system has the responsibility for training. At what point the community's responsibility leaves off and that of industry's begins, however, is not easily determined, as we shall discuss presently.

Craft unions of skilled laborers have long attempted to maintain a monopoly on apprenticeship and training in order to keep an effective position for bargaining with employers. This means that the organized craftsmen are willing to accept responsibility for technical training, but claim the right to extend or limit the training in accordance with the state of the labor market. In this respect the craft unions maintain a position quite similar to that of the medieval guilds. Yet such a close monopoly may defeat itself if the training is so restricted that substitute methods or materials are introduced, or if the government breaks the "bottleneck" by instituting its own training program for industry.

To an increasing extent the tax-supported schools have taken over much of the task of fitting out workers with the skills demanded by business and industry. Not only are the schools offering specific vocational instruction at educational levels lower than the colleges and technical institutes, but there is an increasing emphasis upon information about vocational opportunities with a view to increasing intelligent occupational choice.[11] Smaller school systems, however, face a more acute problem than even the small industry, for the school is called upon not only to give a general background for further advanced training for those having the ability, but also to provide specific vocational training suitable to the level of ability of students. No school system, however large, could hope to offer competent instruction in each of the immense variety of industrial skills. The basis for limitation is naturally determined in part by local and regional occupational demands, but is likely also to reflect irrelevant considerations such as the preferences of teachers and school board officials, ideas of honorable employment, and so on.

[11] See Alfred Kahler and Ernest Hamburger, *Education for an Industrial Age* (Ithaca: Cornell University Press, 1948).

In some vocational fields the requirements vary so greatly from one establishment to another that specific training may range from the useless to the positively bad, since so much has to be "unlearned" before the student who takes industrial employment can learn the new rules demanded by his employers. This circumstance seems to be more prevalent in financial and general office work than in shop work, but may be true in the latter. The conclusion seems clear that in general the responsibility of the schools will be limited to giving general training and background knowledge, and that the specific job will continue to be learned "on the job."

Under a wartime economy the shortage of skills became more acute than normal methods of instruction could handle, and the Federal government, in cooperation with schools, colleges, and industrial organizations, established training programs of immense proportions.[12] The necessity of governmental training programs illustrates the contemporary difficulty in providing a skilled labor supply for industrial production.

Problems of Training in a Complex Society. The uncertainty concerning the responsibility for keeping up a labor supply of the quality needed for current industrial demands stems from a more basic uncertainty: the relation of general background and special training.

Modern industry demands specialists, not amateurs, dabblers, or dilettantes. The individual or those charged with formal education may therefore be tempted to start special training rather early in the educational career. "Practical" persons in the community constantly press for more useful education and fewer "frills." The temptation is enhanced by the fact that early specialization may allow either an earlier attainment of narrow skills or possible greater and greater specialization.

Even assuming that the individual child's adult occupational career can be precisely predicted early in the educational process, such an emphasis on "practical" teaching is likely to defeat its own purposes. That is, it runs great risk of being the most impractical

---

[12] See, for example, United States War Manpower Commission, Bureau of Training, Training Within Industry Service, *The Training Within Industry Report, 1940–1945* (Washington: U. S. Government Printing Office, 1945).

type of training in the long run. One of the major risks is that employment opportunities in a very narrow field, or even the occupation as a whole, may cease to exist before or soon after the completion of the training. A very narrowly trained person must then be entirely retrained because he has no general background to fall back on. It should take very little time to train a physician for the single skill of diagnosing smallpox and prescribing treatment. Such a physician would not only be completely incompetent if asked to treat scarlet fever, but might find that through universal vaccination he was among the "technologically unemployed." Similarly, a narrowly skilled workman in a factory may find that his "short-order" or "lunch-counter" training has fitted him for only one job. He is then at the mercy of a rapidly changing and expanding technology.

It may be stated as a general principle that the higher the position in business or industry, the more general must be the background of the individual before he may safely specialize. This applies not only to executives and administrators, but to professionals and technical specialists also. It is not so much greater bookkeeping ability that distinguishes the chief accountant from his assistants as a broader background and experience that allows him to solve problems and make decisions not covered in the ordinary course of specialized training. The difference between the engineer who has completed a four-year college course and one who has passed a six-weeks correspondence course may only appear in greater ability of the former to overcome unusual difficulties or spot the source of trouble. The engineer with the broader training has the additional advantage of not having to backtrack so far before he can start in on a new specialty if that becomes necessary.

It is undoubtedly true that the type of education known as *general* or *liberal* has turned loose upon a hard-boiled business and industrial world a rather large number of graduates with no *special* abilities to offer except an exaggerated idea of their own importance. But it is also true that a complete swing to the highly practical type of instruction would turn loose upon an unsuspecting society a group of persons totally incompetent to face rapid changes in occupational requirements.

Since we do not fix adult occupations at birth, but wait for the socially valuable attributes and skills to appear, the question becomes one of drawing a line somewhere—the point at which general training is no longer profitable and specialization may begin. This point will presumably differ with each individual, or, for the sake of convenience, with different groups of individuals. When our training system, under whatever sponsorship, has been perfected to the degree that the line can be and is drawn at the appropriate place in every instance, our labor force will have achieved something like maximum employability, at least in the qualitative sense.

REFERENCES

AMIDON, BEULAH, "Manpower for Industry," *Survey Graphic*, 29: 602–605, December 1940.

BIDDLE, ERLE H., *Manpower, a Summary of British Experience*, Public Administration Service, Publication No. 84 (Chicago: 1942).

CARSON, DANIEL, "Accessions to and Separations from the Labor Force: Concepts for Analyzing Certain Types of Labor Problems," *Journal of Political Economy*, 49: 882–894, December 1941.

CLAGUE, EWAN, "The Problem of Unemployment and the Changing Structure of Industry," *Journal of the American Statistical Association*, 30: 209–214, March 1935.

CLARK, HAROLD F., *Economic Theory and Correct Occupational Distribution* (New York: Bureau of Publications, Teachers College, Columbia University, 1931), especially Chap. I, "Summary of Theses," and Chap. IX, "Objections and Obstacles to Correct Occupational Distribution."

COOKE, MORRIS LLEWELLYN, and PHILIP MURRAY, *Organized Labor and Production* (New York: Harper & Brothers, 1940), Chap. 18, "Adult Education for Management and Men."

CORSON, JOHN J., "The Labor Force: Its Recruitment and Training," *Law and Contemporary Problems*, 9 (3): 418–429, Summer 1942.

DAVIDSON, PERCY E., and H. DEWEY ANDERSON, *Occupational Mobility in an American Community* (Stanford University, Calif.: Stanford University Press, 1937).

DURAND, JOHN D., *The Labor Force in the United States, 1890–1960* (New York: Social Science Research Council, 1948).

HAGOOD, MARGARET JARMAN, and LOUIS J. DUCOFF, "Some Measurement and Research Problems Arising from Sociological Aspects of a Full

Employment Policy," *American Sociological Review*, 11: 560–567, October 1946.

HAUSER, PHILIP M., "The Labor Force and Gainful Workers—Concept, Measurement, and Comparability," *American Journal of Sociology*, 54: 338–355, January 1949.

KAHLER, ALFRED, and ERNEST HAMBURGER, *Education for an Industrial Age* (Ithaca: Cornell University Press, 1948).

KERR, CLARK, "Labor Markets: Their Character and Consequences," in Milton Derber, ed., *Proceedings of the Second Annual Meeting, Industrial Relations Research Association*, New York City, December 29–30, 1949 (Champaign, Ill.: 1950), pp. 69–84.

MYERS, HOWARD B., "Dynamics of Labor Supply," *Journal of the American Statistical Association*, 36: 175–184, June 1941.

NOLAND, EDWARD WILLIAM, and E. WIGHT BAKKE, *Workers Wanted* (New York: Harper & Brothers, 1949).

PANCOAST, OMAR, JR., *Occupational Mobility* (New York: Columbia University Press, 1941).

(Political and Economic Planning), *The Entrance to Industry* (London: PEP, 1935), Chap. I, "Introduction"; Chap. II, "The School-Leaving Age"; Chap. III, "Continued Education"; Chap. IV, "The Employment Situation."

REYNOLDS, LLOYD G., and JOSEPH SHISTER, *Job Horizons: A Study of Job Satisfaction and Labor Mobility* (New York: Harper & Brothers, 1949).

SIMONS, A. M., *Personnel Relations in Industry* (New York: The Ronald Press Company, 1921), Chap. IV, "Sources of Labor Supply," and Chap. IX, "Training."

SOROKIN, PITIRIM, *Social Mobility* (New York: Harper & Brothers, 1927), Chap. VIII, "The Channels of Vertical Circulation," and Chap. IX, "Mechanism of Social Testing, Selection, and Distribution of Individuals with Different Social Strata."

SPENGLER, JOSEPH J., "Some Effects of Changes in the Age Composition of the Labor Force," *The Southern Economic Journal*, 8 (11): 157–175, October 1941.

STEAD, WILLIAM H., CARROLL L. SHARTLE, and OTHERS, *Occupational Counseling Techniques* (New York: American Book Company, 1940).

UNITED STATES WAR MANPOWER COMMISSION, Bureau of Training, Training Within Industry Service, *The Training Within Industry Report, 1940–1945* (Washington: U. S. Government Printing Office, 1945).

VREELAND, F. M., and E. J. FITZGERALD, *Farm-City Migration and In-*

dustry's Labor Reserve, Works Project Administration, National Research Project, Report No. L–7 (Philadelphia, 1939). See entire series on Re-employment Opportunities and Recent Changes in Industrial Techniques, David Weintraub, Director.

WEBB, JOHN N., and ALBERT WESTFIELD, "Industrial Aspects of Labor Mobility," *Monthly Labor Review,* 48: 789–802, April 1939.

WOOFTER, T. J., JR., "The Future Working Population," *Rural Sociology,* 4: 275–282, September 1939.

WOYTINSKY, W. S., *Labor in the United States* (Washington: Committee on Social Security, Social Science Research Council, 1938), Chap. II, "Workers by Industry and Class of Work," and Chap. VII, "Economic Shifts of Workers."

——, *The Labor Supply in the United States,* rev. ed. (Washington: Committee on Social Security, Social Science Research Council. 1937).

ᴥঌ CHAPTER XX

WASTES OF LABOR RESOURCES

To SPEAK of "wastes of labor resources" is to tread on dangerous ground. Is the nonemployment of women and children a waste of manpower? Is the shortening of the work week and the extension of leisure a waste of valuable time? The answers to such questions are scarcely judgments of fact, but rather of sentiment, *unless a common value or goal be assumed*. Waste is an epithet that is applied to departures from "ideal" conditions of productivity or exploitation. If the ideal is not shared, or is shared subject to serious reservations, the epithet will be judged to be misapplied.

The term *waste* when applied to labor, then, implies a point of view that is rather common among older captains of industry: that labor is a commodity, or an expendable and exploitable resource. That point of view is momentarily adopted here simply as a mode of presentation of *one* aspect of the position of labor in an industrial society. The purpose of the present chapter is to formulate the conditions for the "maximum utilization of manpower," *as if* such a goal were in fact the sole significant value for consideration, and then to analyze the social issues involved in various types of departures from the "ideal" situation. The goal itself varies in its importance in relation to other societal goals from time to time (for example, in periods of war and of peace), and from one interest group to another at any given time (for example, in the attitudes of management and labor). Since a judgment of "waste" is a value judgment and not an assertion of fact unless the value is assumed, it may be well to bear in mind that for purposes of exposition we shall present the ideal and then indicate as nearly as possible why the departures from the ideal may or may not be considered wasteful in view of other considerations previously neglected.

MAXIMUM UTILIZATION OF MANPOWER

Under circumstances of heightened industrial production, particularly when coupled with large withdrawals of workers into armed forces, one hears a great deal about maximum utilization of manpower. In the preceding chapter the sources of supply were indicated, and we noted that the amount of labor available is at least partly related to the amount needed. We are now in a position to formulate what would be the maximum amount and quality of labor if there were no limits to exploitation, that is, if labor were considered simply as a utilizable resource.

Factors in Labor Utilization. We have previously observed that the number of workers is not the sole significant factor in labor supply: the workers must be at the right place and of the appropriate quality. In the dynamic utilization of labor supply, there are further important variables, namely, time and rate of work. In the concrete industrial situation, of course, there is a further highly relevant factor in productivity of labor: the availability of tools and the extent of mechanization. Under given conditions of industrial organization, mechanization, and availability of tools, therefore, *labor resources are used to the maximum when each of the following is at a maximum: the number of workers in the employed labor force; the correlation between usable skills and skills available; time spent at productive work; and speed or rate of work.*

The relevance of all these factors is fairly obvious, although the problem is rarely if ever formulated in precisely these terms. In the completely dynamic sense it might even be maintained that the factor of industrial organization and mechanization is an index of the extent of past utilization of skills. Thus labor resources are wasted if technological and organizational skills are not developed or used. It is certainly clear that an increase in mechanization or efficiency of organization can increase productivity without increasing the value or weight of any of the other factors.

The factor of "skill" seems to require a little further comment. To a large extent this is obviously a qualitative factor, although any given job may be done with more or less skill. The maximum utilization of skill of the entire labor force requires that the duties of every useful job be done with the greatest possible skill. This in turn requires that an appropriately skilled person be found for every job; in other words, "correct" occupational distribution. For any given or concretely possible condition of the productive organization of society, therefore, the available and *usable* skills will be fully exploited when all jobs are filled by the most competent persons.[1] To adopt a popular figure of speech, skills are maximally used when there are no square pegs in round holes (and no holes left without pegs).

The "time spent at productive work" has reference not only to the number of hours worked in any span of time (as the length of the work day or work week or the constancy of employment throughout the year), but also to the total duration of productive work in the worker's life span. The two may be reduced to the same thing by saying that the time factor consists in the total amount of time that workers devote to their employment throughout their lives. In practice, it is convenient to separate the short-time from the long-time utilization of the worker's time, since the problems and "wastes" in the two cases are of a different order.

The number of workers and rate of work seem self-explanatory, although subsequent discussion will reveal the necessary conditions for the attainment of these maxima, and the limitations that in fact prevail.

Relations between the Factors. The factors of number N, skill S, time T, and rate R are independent but interdependent variables. That is, a change in the value of one will not automatically pro-

---

[1] It is of course concretely possible either that the potential skills have not been developed (trained) and therefore that some jobs must be filled by persons of less ability than ideally possible, or that the skills available will be higher than the existing productive system can absorb, so that some persons are working at jobs considerably below their ability. From the strictly limited point of view here presented, either situation would represent a waste—the former through inadequate utilization of potential ability, the latter through the time and effort given to needless training. In the latter case, however, the "fault" may lie with the organization of production.

duce a determinate change in any other,[2] yet if the four are made into a functional equation equalling productivity P, as

$$P = N \times S \times T \times R$$

a change in the value of one *will* produce a determinate change in any other, under conditions of constancy in the values of the other factors. Thus, a given level of production may be maintained even if the number of workers is halved, provided one of the other factors is doubled.

Since the factor of skill is less subject to easy quantification, we may consider it momentarily as a qualitative condition (along with availability of tools, extent of mechanization, and the adequacy of organization, and direct our attention to the relations of the other three variables in labor utilization. Our equation then becomes

$$P = N \times T \times R$$

or algebraically,

$$P = NTR$$

In theory, this is a perfect functional relationship so that variations in the value of any variable must be reflected by a corresponding (direct or inverse) change in the value of one or more of the others. If we express the amount of the change in value by the symbol n, the following relationships hold by definition:

$$P = \frac{N}{n}(nR)T = (nN)R\frac{T}{n}\text{ etc.}$$

The productivity of the labor force may also be changed by varying the value of the factors in labor utilization. Thus,

$$nP = n(NRT)$$

or

$$= (nN)RT = N(nR)T = NR(nT)$$

Put in linguistic terms, the theoretical relationship of these factors is such that productivity may be expanded without limit provided

[2] It should be noted that the factors of time, skill, and rate are here being used as amounts *per worker*. Otherwise, it is apparent that these would all be dependent upon number, since a reduction of workers totally removes those persons' working time, skill, and speed from the field of utilization.

that a corresponding change can be introduced in the number of workers, the length of employment, or the rate of work. Any one of these factors may be subject to control, so that demands for increased productivity may be answered by selection of the number of workers or hours of labor as the "strategic factor" and changing that factor in the desired direction. In practice, there are limitations in any productive system on the increase of any one element or combination of them. Some of these limitations are intrinsic to the nature of the variables, and are thus in addition to the restrictions arising from the failure of our assumption of "ideal" conditions to hold in fact.

Limits to Maximization. We have just noted that at least three of the important variables in the utilization of labor stand in a mathematically functional relationship to one another when linked by an equation to productivity. But this theoretical relationship will hold only under certain conditions (which we have so far largely neglected), and subject to certain limitations. Thus, the value of N, or the *number* of workers, has an upper limit determined by the size of the population. Or, more significantly, the number is limited by the size of that segment of the population which has *any* capacity or utilizable skill under a given system of production. This upper limit of numbers is rarely if ever reached by any modern society because of other restrictions on labor utilization.

The factor of *skill* is also one that in actual situations is not capable of limitless expansion. The expansion of skills is limited by the character of the human organism, and also depends upon effective organization of training. Although the adaptability of the human individual is great, and the period of training represents a considerable portion of the total life span, the "weaknesses of the flesh" (including those of the mind) seem to provide barriers to further and further demands upon human ingenuity. However, this limitation may be partially circumvented by cooperative action— that is, by organization. An additional problem with reference to skills is that of their distribution in the working population. In so far as differences in usable skills represent differences in innate ability, their proportional distribution in the population is likely to approximate a "normal curve of distribution." That is, there seem to be relatively few individuals with markedly superior native capacity, and few markedly inferior. There is no evidence that the inherent ability of modern man is appreciably greater than that of his ancestors. If more skills are demanded, the difference would seem to depend on longer and more effective training, plus the advantages of division of labor. This is not to say that any modern society utilizes available skills to the maximum degree, but only that there is no reason to believe that the abilities of human beings are limitless.

Time is a notoriously scarce commodity, and few persons would argue against the point that the amount of it available for productive labor is limited. Without regard to restrictions on the working day, week, or career which have been made in view of other values, the goal of maximum productivity limits the length of the working period. If we simply take the view of efficient utilization (or exploitation) of labor resources, we must still recognize the limits of human endurance, both in the short run and in the long run. Just what those limits are will vary, of course, with the individual and the job. The longest working day is not necessarily the most productive one. The evidence concerning the duration of employability (under given industrial conditions) is extremely scanty, but there can be little doubt that a person can be literally "worked to death," and thus possibly his total time at work may be less than if he worked shorter hours or under more favorable conditions over a longer period of time. Since, unlike some other resources, the labor force tends to replenish itself, a deliberate or unconscious policy of exploitation might neglect the long-term employability of labor for greater short-term production. In view of the dependence of population reproduction upon a variety of social circumstances, however, it is doubtful if such a policy or practice could long operate in any area.[3]

The final factor we have considered, the *speed* or *rate* of work,

[3] Under the special circumstance of wartime demands, it is possible to view the labor force, like the armed forces, as "expendable." What this means is that the sacrifice of manpower is recognized as necessary for the accomplishment of war aims.

is again not capable of infinite increase. Although closely dependent upon organization and the extent of mechanization, the speed of laborers is also subject to independent variation. This factor is sometimes a "strategic" one in the sense that it may be pushed toward its maximum value by positive or negative inducement (reward or punishment), yet the limits set by the human organism are real, and the dependence upon training and differences in individual capacity are just as certain as with the more general factor of skill.

In addition to the absolute limits to the increase of numbers, skills, time, or rate, there are various practical limits determined by the circumstances pertaining to particular cases. Thus we have taken a general or over-all view of utilization of labor resources. A single industrial unit may attempt to increase production by considering any one of these factors as the strategic factor and pushing that variable toward its maximum. But how far any factor can be pushed will depend upon the state of the organization, the character of the local or regional labor market, and so on. Thus the size of the plant will place at least temporary limitations upon the expansion of the working force. The maximum utilization of skills will be largely conditional upon the nature of the activity involved; whether time or rate of work is the strategic factor has to be determined in individual cases. We might, therefore, distinguish maximum utilization of labor resources and *optimum* utilization, meaning by the latter the "most satisfactory" relationship between the variables under conditions not readily subject to control.

In our treatment of the use of labor resources we have consistently overlooked the obvious and important fact that labor is a social as well as a "natural" affair; our discussion has assumed a state of affairs that does not exist and probably could not exist in any complete way. Among the conditions assumed has been that of the complete irrelevance of considerations other than exploitation. The control necessary for such a policy would either have to be that of slavery, or that of such a complete agreement upon the goal of production taking precedence over all other interests that the value system of the society would support the view that the highest or possibly sole virtue was to be found in productive labor. Neither condition prevails or could prevail in the modern world.

It will be recalled that we have adopted this highly unrealistic position because "waste" is an evaluative term and requires a standard of reference. By this view, *a waste of labor resources is represented by any departure, however small, from utilization of the maximum number of workers at their highest usable skills, for the longest possible time and at their maximum rate of work.* We can now review the wastes occasioned by failure to achieve each of these four conditions, and note why those wastes exist.

WASTES OF NUMBERS

By general consent of all parties concerned, unemployment, or underemployment, represents an outstanding problem of the industrial history in the Western world. Our immediate concern is with this problem as a category of waste of labor resources. It may be repeated that the nonemployment of any person who has any ability, however small, that is productively usable represents a departure from maximum utilization of labor resources. But in actual social and industrial situations we must recognize different departures from that standard and different social values which would deny that all nonemployment represents "waste." Indeed, the ordinary discussions of manpower wastes do not so much as consider some of the restrictions on full employment.

Institutional Restrictions on Full Employment. One of the major sources of nonemployment of potential workers is to be found in the basic institutional structure of the society. In our discussion of the maximum utilization of labor resources we were speaking *as if* productivity were the sole aim of the society, to which all other values were secondary. Although in highly critical situations a country may temporarily approximate this state of affairs, in "normal" times the limits of employability are set more narrowly. Two great categories of our population have been employed in numbers far below their potential strength in the labor force. Those two groups are the women and children. It may be instructive to inquire briefly into this tremendous "waste" of manpower.

American popular speech is full of such expressions of senti-ment as "A woman's place is in the home." It is precisely the con-flict between the socially approved status of women as housewives and mothers of children on the one hand, and more directly pro-ductive workers on the other that accounts for the infrequency of their industrial employment. So strong did this restriction become in the first three decades of the present century that many persons were mistakenly led to believe that the traditional role of the Amer-ican woman had been that of the nonproductive and rather expensive luxury whose first business in life was to catch (and hold) a "good provider."

This mistaken impression has had a superficial validity because of the unquestionable fact that the occupational status of the American woman has been closely associated with her role as wife and mother. But it overlooks the equally unquestionable fact that production was formerly closely associated with the home and family, and that when production moved out of the home, women followed for only a brief period. With the growth of the industrial cities, the diminishing size of families, reduced size of living quar-ters for the housewife to take care of, aided and abetted by labor-saving conveniences, *women became America's outstanding leisure class.* The values attached to maintenance of some semblance of the traditional patterns of home and family outweighed the goal of continued productivity after the two could no longer be achieved together.[4]

The institutional restrictions on the employment of women be-cause of the incompatibility of familial duties and industrial work has until very recently been buttressed by the greater difficulty of

[4] It is interesting to note that the possessive treatment of women as luxuries was bitingly pointed out by Veblen in 1899. See Thorstein Veblen, *The Theory of the Leisure Class* (New York: B. W. Huebsch, 1918), first published in 1899. Since the nonemployment of women is dependent upon the ability of bread-winners to feed those who do not work, it has been true that the ideal and practice has spread from upper economic groups downward.

The special institutional character of the nonemployment of women is indi-cated not only by the historical change in American society, but by the wide-spread employment of women both in primitive and peasant societies on the one hand and in a large industrial society (the Soviet Union) on the other.

workers finding jobs than of employers finding workers. Thus, after the first years of factory development, during which women and children comprised the bulk of factory workers, productivity per worker increased so enormously that there were ample adult male workers for the available jobs. Women, indeed, became technologically unemployed, but few people seemed to notice, for the women seemed simply to return to their traditional roles as housewives. But this was only a seeming return; actually, they had come to occupy a new social status, for now .they were being supported.

It is true that during the first decades of the twentieth century, but especially after the first World War, women played a constantly increasing part in industrial production, as well as in business and the professions. But this increasing utilization of "womanpower" still proceeded slowly, and in the face of considerable opposition. Men, both employed and unemployed, resented the competition of the women, especially of married women. Many organizations, private and public, refused to hire married women if their husbands were employed. But the opposition did not stem simply from the conviction that the jobs ought to be given to those who most needed them. Performance, rather than need, has been the basis of selection in our competitive occupational order. But the employment of women meant the sacrifice, at least to some extent, of the major socially approved female "career": marriage and motherhood.

The institutional restrictions upon inclusion of women in the labor force have not operated as a complete and final barrier to use of their productive labor, but as a source of strong resistance which could only be overcome in "exceptional" cases. The barrier has been broken for some time in cases of relative poverty where the labor of all capable members of the household has been necessary for survival at the level which the family considers appropriate. In other cases, the desire for a "career" has prompted an ever-increasing number of women to overcome the extra obstacles thrown in their way. In times of national emergency, shortages of manpower provide the double incentive of lucrative jobs and patriotic service for large numbers of women to push back the customary restrictions.

According to the census of 1940, there were 50,549,176 women fourteen years of age and older in the American population. Of these 12,845,259 were part of the labor force (fully or partly employed or seeking work). This was only 25.4 per cent of the total number potentially available. According to a Bureau of the Census estimate relating to July, 1949, there were at that time some 55,748,-000 women 14 years of age and older in the United States, of whom 18,548,000 (33.3 per cent) were in the labor force.[5] Thus a favorable labor market accentuated a general trend toward increased employment of women.

We may repeat that the epithet "waste" when attached to the general nonemployment of women may be justified only under the assumption of exclusive preoccupation with labor utilization. There can be no doubt that the universal employment of adult females in full-time commercial and industrial jobs would have a major, and from certain points of view disastrous, effect upon the character of the American family. With an entirely different institutional system, there would remain a great amount of "domestic" work now largely done by housewives. Even under the narrow view of "wastes" here adopted, not all of the time of women who are not "gainfully occupied" is wasted. On the other hand, the character of the American family has already undergone considerable transformations in urban and other industrialized areas, and there seems to be no reason to expect this process to stop. On the contrary, it is apparent that the second World War has had an even more pronounced effect upon the size and composition of the labor force than did the previous world conflict. Yet the balance of social institutions is such that the addition of a large proportion of adult women to the work force must either come slowly or temporarily, or it will come disruptively.

The other major "institutionalized waste" of labor resources is that represented in the nonemployment of children. It is not true, of

[5] United States Department of Commerce, Bureau of the Census, *Current Population Reports: Population Estimates,* Series p-25, No. 39, May 5, 1950.

course, that barring children from productive labor constitutes a total waste even from the limited viewpoint here adopted. The early full-time employment of children would prevent their training for subsequent employment with greater productivity. But to the extent that abandonment of child labor is justified on other grounds—such as the protection of character and morals, or the "right" of children to be reasonably carefree—the restriction may be called wasteful.

The utilization of the labor of children, like that of women, is very old in human society, but attended by new problems in an industrialized society. Aside from the question of training, the chief objection seems to be to their employment by an outsider, rather than as part of a family group. Again, therefore, it is the traditional structure and function of the family that is usually at stake when the attempt is made to add children to the active labor force. To a certain extent, also, the formal but nonvocational education of the young provides a restriction on concentrated training for early industrial productivity. As we noted in the last section of the preceding chapter, there is some reasonable doubt about the length and type of training that society ought to provide for the young. Part of this doubt is due to the uncertainty of the child's present and future position in society. The arguments raised against child labor indicate pretty clearly that more is at issue than simply the future value of the resources if they are further trained. Even with wartime shortages of manpower the minimum ages of employability were pushed down only a little in some areas, not at all in others. The crisis was not great enough to force major institutional modification in this particular sphere.

Probably as a result of increasing restrictions on the employment of children, the census figures for 1940 do not reveal the number of employed children under fourteen years of age. In 1930 only 235,328 (2.4 per cent) of the 9,622,492 children aged ten to thirteen were "gainfully occupied," and only 157,660 (6.6 per cent) of the 2,382,385 aged fourteen. Neither the statistics nor the restrictions on employment apply to agricultural employment, or children working for their parents, so that there remains a considerable amount of at least seasonal or part-time child labor. The trend, even under wartime conditions, has been toward reduction rather than increase of this amount.[6]

Thus, with respect to at least two major groups in the population, the women and children, the organizational framework and values of our society have created "institutionalized wastes" of labor resources. We might add still a third group: those who are voluntarily unemployed, including not only those who, if not lazy, at least "do not feel like working," but also and more importantly those whose income is independent of gainful employment. Although the right to leisure is likely to be denied to those who have "no visible means of support," are able to work, and yet are unwilling to do so, it is generally upheld as a right of those whose income from investments makes work unnecessary. It is impossible to separate the two groups precisely from the statistical information available, and equally impossible to determine how many of the independently wealthy may be included in the labor force on the basis of essentially fictitious jobs. It may be noted that of the persons over fourteen years of age recorded in 1940 as "not in the labor force," 1,275,400 were not engaged in housework in their own homes, were not in school, in institutions, or listed as "unable to work," and must therefore be presumed to be "persons of leisure." [7]

Social institutions are of course subject to modification and realignment, and this has taken place to a considerable extent in the employment of housewives and the reduction of the "leisure class." Nevertheless, the institutionalized wastes are certainly the most difficult to overcome.

Quasi-Institutional Restrictions. There are other restrictions on full employment of available labor that are less official and much less

[6] See especially the summary prepared by the Industrial Division, Children's Bureau, "Trend of Child Labor 1937 to 1939," United States Department of Labor, Bureau of Labor Statistics, Serial No. R. 1058. It is interesting to note that the Bureau of the Census, in its releases on "labor reserves," makes no suggestion of any potential labor supply under fourteen years of age. See, for example, "Population: Potential Labor Supply in the United States," Sixteenth Census, Series P-9, No. 10; "Population: Labor Reserves in the United States by Household Relationship and Occupation," Sixteenth Census, Series P-14, No. 5.

[7] See Sixteenth Census, Series P-14, No. 5.

uniformly accepted as morally or ethically proper, yet bear some rather close similarities to truly institutional limitations. Outstanding examples of such semiofficial bars to employment are those excluding, or partially excluding, *noncitizens, convicts* and *ex-convicts,* and members of America's chief *racial caste,* the American Negro.

The white inhabitants of the Western hemisphere are either immigrants or the descendants of immigrants. The New World in general, and the United States in particular, have long been hailed as the land of opportunity for the oppressed peoples of the world. Yet in recent years immigration restrictions have been imposed, and the stream of migrants is reduced to a trickle. The "foreigner," always an object of some suspicion in any society, was increasingly made to feel the pressure for assimilation into the American social scheme. Yet it remained for the period of defense and subsequently war production, much of it on vital ordnance materials, to bring to a head the distinction between the citizen and alien. Even "resident aliens," that is, immigrants who have lived in the United States for twenty, thirty, or more years but had not considered it worth their while to become naturalized citizens, found many jobs, perhaps their own jobs, closed to them. It was difficult to tell to what extent this was a governmentally sponsored policy. Since it applied not only to the subjects of enemy and doubtfully neutral countries, but to friendly aliens as well, the policy seemed to be based on grounds other than those of danger to the national welfare.

The number of noncitizens in the population in the early 1940's was not large (approximately 3,850,000 over fifteen years of age by the 1940 census), but with the increasing shift of manpower to the armed forces and essential war production, many aliens either became unemployed or were forced to accept employment far below their full skill. Thus, the determination of employment policies on technically irrelevant grounds (however immediately practical they may have been) constituted a considerable waste of manpower. By the 1950's "loyalty," of citizen and alien alike, had become an increasingly important factor in many types of employment.

A comparable situation in many respects is the nonemployment or underemployment of jail and prison populations, and the prevalence of discrimination against ex-convicts. For the most part jails have few if any facilities for using the labor of inmates except in cus-todial duties, and even the largest and most modern prisons face many problems in attempting to establish labor systems. Among these problems may be mentioned the following: the opposition of manufacturers and laborers to direct or indirect competition from prison labor; the difficulty of combining close supervision to prevent escape with many types of work; the fact that prison populations tend to be a highly "select" group, and the basis of selection has nothing to do with the personnel requirements of the prison's in-dustries; and the problem of finding compromises between the labor requirements of prison industries and the fulfillment of the prison's avowed function of training the inmate for successful post-prison adjustment. The last problem calls attention to the fact that the partially understandable reluctance of employers to employ ex-convicts results in an extension of the waste of labor resources, fre-quently for the remainder of the potentially productive life of the man with a "record."

Perhaps a more outstanding, and certainly more persistent, waste is that represented in the nonemployment of Negroes, or employing them at jobs considerably beneath their capacity. Racial discrimina-tion in hiring and firing arises from what may be called a "caste division of labor." That is, a segment of the population, in this case the Negro, is marked off as inferior by definition and fit only for menial tasks. It is not necessary here to trace the fairly well-known history of Negro-white labor relations in the United States, but a few outstanding points should be noted.[8] American Negroes were

[8] The best single treatment of the role of the Negro worker in American industry is that of Sterling D. Spero and Abram L. Harris, *The Black Worker* (New York: Columbia University Press, 1931). These authors give available materials on proportional occupational distribution of Negroes and whites, and indicate the disproportionate unemployment of Negroes. For more recent dis-cussions of the role of the Negro in industry as affected by organized labor, see Horace R. Cayton and George S. Mitchell, *Black Workers and the New Unions* (Chapel Hill: University of North Carolina Press, 1939); Herbert R. Northrup, *Organized Labor and the Negro* (New York and London: Harper & Brothers, 1944).

predominantly concentrated in the rural south until the first World War. At that time heightened labor demand in the north started a mass migration to northern industrial centers. This migration has continued up to the present time. It was again given impetus, of course, by increased employment opportunities during the second World War. However advantageous the greater freedom of movement, and fewer obvious repressive symbols (such as "Jim Crow" cars) may have been, the industrial north has not exactly provided a land of golden opportunity for the American Negro. The Negro has usually been the last hired and first fired. Excluded from employment by employers, excluded from union membership by his fellow employees, and forced almost always to take the meanest jobs at the lowest pay, the Negro's time and talents have been a drug on the labor market.

Racial prejudice is not confined to any section or region in the United States, although some of its more blatant forms are largely confined to the Old South. Contrary to the culture of capitalism and of democracy alike, it still represents an almost official aspect of American institutional structure. It is not always possible even to fix responsibility for the nonemployment of Negroes in any given plant. Employers may blame the policy on labor unions, employees charge it to the employers, and both together throw the responsibility back on "public opinion." Labor unions may charge that Negroes have engaged in strike-breaking, and the charge is frequently true. On the other hand, Negroes were excluded from employment *before* they found employment opportunities at good wages in strike-breaking. They may and do reply, accordingly, that they have no reason to support unions that not only give them no advantages, but may actually prevent any advantages they may seek to gain "on their own." Employers and white employees alike may assert, with partial truth, that the Negro is not qualified for many types of industrial employment. But this is likely to leave, or actually seek to create, the mistaken impression that the lack of qualification is a racial trait rather than the result of past discrimination in opportunities for training and advancement.

Out of each period of increased labor demand, when the pressure for reducing discrimination is at its highest, the northern industrial Negro has gained some slight permanent advantage. Other factors have contributed to increased employment, or at least decreased discrimination in employment. Among these are: (1) the more recent policies of organized labor, particularly of the unions associated with the Congress of Industrial Organizations, in accepting or actively seeking Negro membership; (2) the activities of such organizations as the National Association for the Advancement of Colored People and the National Urban League; and (3) the reassertion of democratic principles growing out of the war against the fascist powers and exemplified in the Fair Employment Practices Committee and various state anti-discrimination statutes.

These recent changes have not solved the general "American Negro problem," or even the question of manpower utilization. They seem to have reduced somewhat the waste represented by the caste division of labor.

Unemployment of "Employables." The term *unemployment* is usually restricted to those persons who are not working and are seeking work. Such persons are included as part of the "labor force," whereas housewives, children under employment age, and coupon clippers are not. Those persons whose services are "wasted" because of quasi-institutional restrictions (the alien and the Negro) are therefore "unemployed" if they continue to seek employment, and excluded from the labor force if they bow to fate and seek other means for support. We must still distinguish other groups of the unemployed, whose services are from time to time, and for one reason or another, wasted. At least four additional groups deserve attention: (1) sub-marginal employables, (2) the seasonally unemployed, (3) the technologically and "frictionally" unemployed, and (4) the group most commonly thought of, which we may call the "business cycle unemployed." It may be noted in passing that wastes of numbers of the potentially useful labor resources are automatically wastes of time, speed, and skills. Since few persons in the various categories of the unemployed are permanently outside the employed labor force, these might with equal propriety be considered examples of loss of employable time. They are first discussed as wastes of numbers because in the immediate situation of unemployment that is the most obvious.

1. *Submarginal Employability.* The margin of employability, as was noted in the preceding chapter, is relative to the state of the labor market and the general characteristics of industrial production. With reference to the latter, it is clear that a person whose only skill is one not required by the existing state of industrial production is practically speaking not only unemployed but unemployable. He is, in other words, below the margin of employability. Taking the existing division of labor as given, this unemployability might be regarded as absolute, were it not for the additional considerations that (a) the unemployable may be trained in additional and usable skills and (b) the demand for labor may become so acute that production is reorganized to make a place for those formerly considered below the margin.

In addition to the long-term trends in changing productive organization, there is also a short-term variation in the categories employable and unemployable. Although there is some question whether such short-term variations would exist in a completely controlled economy, it is certainly true that when the supply far exceeds the demand in a competitive labor market, those workers who are physically or mentally handicapped, or whose skills are minimal, will be regarded as outside the active labor force.

The relativity of the margin of employability was most forcibly demonstrated by American experience during the second World War. Persons previously regarded as incapable of useful employment were brought into the labor force, partly through training programs, partly through a definite lowering of employment standards.[9] In some cases the lowering of employment standards was more apparent than real: it consisted in relaxation of *irrelevant* require-

[9] See John B. Knox, "Employment of Handicapped Persons," *The Conference Board Management Record,* December 1941; R. E. Thomas, "Vocational Rehabilitation," *Monthly Labor Review,* 53: 120–121, July 1941; United States House of Representatives, Select Committee Investigating National Defense Migration, *Hearings* (Washington: U. S. Government Printing Office, 1942), Part 27, Washington Hearings, "The Manpower of the Nation in War Production—Book One."

ments. Both the army and some industries came to the point of matching specific requirements with specific capabilities. The navy and other industries continued to require nearly perfect physical specimens for job assignments which required no such high standards.

The fact that standards of employability are capable of downward modification, and the capacities of individuals subject to some upward revision, justifies considering the nonemployment of so-called submarginal persons as a waste of labor resources.

2. *Seasonal Unemployment.* A waste that requires little explanation is that represented by the employment of persons only during certain seasons of the year. Although this type of unemployment is most marked among the migratory seasonal workers in agriculture,[10] other types of industry also are seasonal in character. This seasonality arises in part from the nature of the market demand (for coal and ice, for example), and in part from the direct limitations set by weather and climatic conditions on the organization of production (as in the oustanding example of the building trades). In a few industries seasonality, or at least off-and-on operation, seems to be dictated by the smallness of demand and the necessity, technological or economic, of operating at full capacity until the demand is met, then closing down until the supply is absorbed by the market. Whether seasonal unemployment is to be "blamed on" poor planning by individual employers, or simply on lack of over-all employment control and ease of transition from one job to another, it must be regarded as a waste from the point of view here adopted.

3. *Technological Unemployment.* Many books have been written on the question whether the introduction of labor-saving machinery is

[10] Large-scale agriculture in the Midwest and Far West has long depended at least partly on migratory seasonal workers. The waste of manpower, and especially the broader social problems involved, were publicly recognized when the previous supply of seasonal workers was augmented by refugees from drought-stricken areas. See Henry Hill Collins, Jr., *America's Own Refugees* (Princeton: Princeton University Press, 1941); Carey McWilliams, *Factories in the Field* (Boston: Little, Brown & Company, 1939); Paul S. Taylor, *Adrift on the Land,* Public Affairs Pamphlet No. 42 (New York: Public Affairs Committee, Inc., 1940); United States House of Representatives, Select Committee to Investigate the Interstate Migration of Destitute Citizens, *Hearings* (Washington: U. S. Government Printing Office, 1940–41), 10 vols.; *idem., Report,* 1941.

beneficial or harmful to labor in the long run. The argument on the one side runs, in bare outline, as follows. The introduction of labor-saving machinery, it is claimed, serves to increase the productivity per laborer, reduce labor and therefore production costs, and thus lower the market price of the goods produced. This results, it is further maintained, in a heightened demand, both for these and for other goods, which in turn creates new employment either in the same industry or in new industries. In general, it is claimed, the rise in the average level of living of the American workman is directly attributable to technological improvement.

On the other side it is argued that, although the over-all and long-term benefits of mechanization may be partially admitted, the short-term disadvantages may outweigh these benefits. Thus, it is pointed out that although mechanization may create new demands, this is a slow and uncertain process. Then too, there is no guarantee that the *same* workers who were technologically displaced will be hired in the new industries.

Technological change ordinarily increases the productivity of the labor unit, and may even create a net increase in productivity after taking account of the labor time lost through displacement. (This is, however, very difficult to compute.) But the *full benefits* of technological change in increasing production are only achieved under conditions of immediately utilizing the displaced labor for other productive work. Under present circumstances, technological change clearly displaces some workers permanently, forces others out of employment for considerable lengths of time, and requires others to accept employment considerably below their maximum skills. In any event, there is always enough loss of time between jobs to create what is called *frictional unemployment*. Some waste of this last type appears to be the minimum price of technological change.[11]

"Business Cycle Unemployment." The most outstanding example of the failure of our productive system to utilize labor resources to a

---

[11] For an extensive review of facts and interpretations relevant to the whole problem of the impact of technology on employment, see United States Congress, Temporary National Economic Committee, *Investigation of Concentration of Economic Power, Hearings* (Washington: U. S. Government Printing Office, 1940), Part 30, "Technology and Concentration of Economic Power."

maximum degree is provided by the apparently cyclical alternation of periods of "prosperity" and "depression." The whole problem of the causes of business cycles, or even whether the trend of business activities is more than superficially cyclical, cannot occupy us here. Neither are we here primarily concerned with the wider individual and social problems arising from loss of livelihood.[12] We must note, however, that in periods of seriously curtailed industrial activity the waste of unemployment may run as high as eighteen to twenty-nine per cent of the active labor force.[13] This is in addition to the waste

[12] The "wastefulness" of unemployment is so generally agreed upon that the norms or standards upon which judgment is based are frequently confused. The "waste" is most frequently stated in terms of such wider social reverberations as loss of public morale, increased poverty and crime, and of personal problems of adjustment. Now these indirect effects may be true, in view of the existing social situation, and still be condemned only in view of values other than loss of labor productivity. From the standpoint of maximum utilization of manpower, these other effects of unemployment may be indirect and incidental. Even if loss of employment had no untoward effects on family stability, the incidence of personality disorders, and so on, it would still represent a waste of human productive resources. As a practical matter, of course, the concern shown about the loss of values other than productivity facilitates increased manpower utilization. For this reason, the unemployed provide a more strategic source of manpower than the institutionally restricted nonemployed.

For treatment of the broader social problems of unemployment, see E. W. Bakke, *Citizens without Work* (New Haven: Yale University Press, 1940); Mirra Komarovsky, *The Unemployed Man and His Family* (New York: Dryden Press, 1940).

[13] Estimates, and even complete or sample censuses of unemployment, have varied widely. This represents not only the general inaccuracies of enumeration, but differences in definition as well. Thus, some estimators seeking to arrive at the number of unemployed in the middle 1930's excluded part-time workers and those working on public works projects or relief work; others included one or both of these groups. Part of the discrepancy in figures, ranging as high as three or four million, was also undoubtedly due to the neglect by some investigators of the tendency for the number of the "unemployed" to increase faster than the loss of gainful employment, and to decrease faster than the gain in employment. This tendency reflects the fact noted in the preceding chapter that, as the breadwinner falls out of employment, additional members of the family will register for employment and thus swell the ranks of the unemployed. Conversely, when the breadwinner is reemployed, he may remove from the unemployed category not only himself but several of his dependents as well.

The estimated percentages given in the text (eighteen to twenty-nine) are based on the following sources: Corrington Gill, *Wasted Manpower* (New York: W. W. Norton & Company, Inc., 1939), especially pp. 288–293. Gill's estimates are based on Works Progress Administration findings. Several estimates are given in a treatment of the problem by the editors of *Fortune* magazine, "The Dis-

of those institutionally barred from employment, the "submarginal" employables, and so on.

The over-all picture of the number of persons in the population who have some utilizable ability and who are not employed in productive occupations, therefore, leaves the definite impression that our industrial system has always operated far below capacity. This is not to say that all of these wastes are to be so regarded if other values are taken into account, or even that the social structure would long hang together if it were based on the value of "bread alone." We have rather indicated the major types of waste through nonemployment and noted something of the reasons for these wastes.

WASTES OF TIME

Wastes of numbers, that is, the nonemployment of those potentially employable, also automatically entail other wastes. This is most apparent in reference to time. It will be recalled that, by our abstract definition of waste, any departure from the maximum amount of usable time of each worker constitutes a waste. Thus, unemployment represents a loss of part of the usable time out of the total life span of the worker, or the work year, work month, and so on. Different varieties of time waste are partly the result of different units of comparison. This may range from the question of the maximum or "optimum" length of the work day or work week to the problem of the total duration of employment and the point at which the worker becomes "too old" (superannuated). For sake of convenience, we may divide this range into three units: (1) the work day and work week, (2) the work year, and (3) the work span.

The Work Day and Work Week. Since the first days of the factory system, the fairly steady trend of the work day and work week has been downward. The efforts of organized labor in this regard have been marked by such milestones as the twelve-hour day, the ten-hour day, the eight-hour day, the thirty- or forty-hour week.

---

possessed," *Fortune*, 21 (2): 94–96, 118, 120–121, 123–124, 126, February 1940. The peak of unemployment seems to have been in 1933 or 1934, with estimates ranging from eight million to thirteen million for those years.

At the same time, industrial productivity per man hour has enormously increased. Does this demonstrate that the shorter work period is automatically responsible for greater productivity, in other words, that the longer work period was beyond the maximum or optimum? The evidence for such a conclusion is by no means clear. The relationship is most obviously disturbed by the factor of increased mechanization. Yet, viewed either as a machine or as a biological organism, the laborer certainly has an optimum productive life, which may be shortened by overloading. Also, since the human individual *is* an organism, it is affected by the principles of bodily metabolism, so that over the short run there is certainly a maximum period of productive employability which is considerably shorter than the number of hours in the day or week.

The evidence concerning physiological, psychological, and social factors in fatigue has already been reviewed, but certain conclusions have immediate relevance here. In general, the maximum period of productive employment seems to be no greater than twelve hours a day, or seventy-two hours per week. Beyond this, not only proportional but total productivity may suffer. Even considerably short of this, the worker may have to be given much extra inducement to get him to maintain his effectiveness. The maximum in particular cases will depend not only on the nature of the work, the objective conditions of employment, and the physiological characteristics of the worker, but upon the worker's motivation, his definition of the situation, and so on. In view of the complexity of these factors, it is very difficult to determine the maximum even by our limited definition, and consequently difficult to judge the existence or extent of waste.

Nevertheless, it is clear that there is *some* waste as judged by our criteria, since the shorter work week or work day is sought on other grounds than increased "efficiency." Aside from questions of health, which might be regarded as an intrinsic factor, the values attached to leisure for other activities are clearly involved. Likewise, the assumption that there is a definite amount of work to be done (the "lump of labor theory") prompts workers, especially those organized in unions, to seek shorter work periods and more extensive employment. Without examining the economic validity of the theory, it should be noted that *either* nonemployment or unduly shortened employment represents a waste by our definition. "Spreading the work" amounts to the substitution of one waste for another, therefore, even if it works.

Two other wastes of working hours deserve brief mention: *voluntary absenteeism,* and *lost-time accidents and sickness.* Voluntary absenteeism refers, of course, to the practice of workers failing to report for work on some slight excuse or other, or none at all. It is understandably most prevalent when workers are most in demand and the absentee accordingly is in the least danger of losing his job because of his "vacation." Although it might be claimed that this practice constitutes a way of preventing a work week which is too long in terms of health and physiological fatigue (and therefore no waste), the evidence points rather to the inference that voluntary absenteeism follows from a work week which is "too long" *on other grounds.* Especially with a work week greatly lengthened with overtime work, paid for at an extra rate, the worker apparently stays away to spend his extra money, or because he feels he can afford to take a vacation.[14] This not only illustrates the falsity of the assumption that the laborer is exclusively interested in money for its own sake, but also suggests that efforts to approach the maximum utilization of the laborer's time are beset with considerable difficulty.

Sickness, whether occupationally caused or not, and lost-time accidents both on and off the job clearly represent wastes of laboring time. Industrial nursing and medical attention, safety devices, and educational campaigns may reduce this category of waste. On the other hand, as persons with less physical stamina and meager experience are added to the labor force, the increase in labor power

---

[14] The growth of voluntary absenteeism became a serious industrial problem during World War II with the increase of the work week for war production, compensated by extra overtime pay. Women were more frequent offenders than men, as might be expected because of the recency of their addition to the work force and the change from their traditional or customary roles as housewives and shoppers. In many instances there was no one else to perform essential services at home, such as caring for members of the family who were ill.

may be partially offset by greater frequency of sickness and accidents. Over two days of working time (around eighteen hours) out of every one thousand man hours is regularly lost through accidents in thirty manufacturing industries. The rate varies little from year to year and does not include accidents involving lost time of less than one day.[15]

It is clear that some reductions of time wastage would meet general approval, whereas other wastes arise from the "intrusion" of values other than maximum productivity, such as increased leisure or the expenditure and enjoyment of earnings. Thus increases in the work day or work week which are effected by other methods than reduction of sickness and accidents must in concrete circumstances be approached with understanding and caution.

The Work Year. The most convenient time unit for considering some varieties of time wastage is the longer one of the work year. This is evident in the seasonal, technological, frictional, and business-cycle unemployment already discussed. Because of the inadequacy of statistical records of employment and unemployment, it is virtually impossible to indicate the amount or proportion of available working time that is wasted by these departures from steady employment. That they represent major wastes is unquestionable.

Besides these varieties of "unemployment" we should briefly note some other departures from the full work year. These are, *strikes and layoffs, labor turnover, and serious accidents and disease.*

The "right to strike" is a major canon of organized labor, and now widely recognized in American law. Yet there can be no disputing the fact that strikes represent wastes of employable time. This is again a situation where the judgment of the significance of the "waste" will vary according to the values considered most important. Thus, union leaders will maintain that the waste is justifiable in

---

[15] The rate of days lost per one thousand man hours is computed by the Bureau of Labor Statistics of the United States Department of Labor. It is known as the "injury severity rate." See, for example, *Monthly Labor Review,* 44: 101, January 1936; National Safety Council, "Industrial Accidents in 1940," *National Safety News,* 43 (3): 9–11, March 1941; Ruth R. Puffer, "Industrial and Occupational Environment and Health," in Milbank Memorial Fund, *Backgrounds of Social Medicine* (New York: 1949), pp. 119–137.

terms of benefits received by labor, and will lay responsibility for forcing the strike on managerial groups. Employers' associations will attach considerable importance to this waste, and use it as an argument against organized labor. Here again values other than maximum productivity are concretely relevant.

Layoffs are less frequently spoken of as industrial wastes of employable time, but are as clearly in that category as are strikes. Whether the layoffs reflect market conditions, availability of raw materials, or simply poor organization and planning within the industrial plant, is not a matter of immediate concern. In any case the blame or responsibility may be hard to fix, and consequently the point of attack for reduction of waste is difficult to discover. There is little doubt that a "planned" or "controlled" economy would exhibit less of this variety of waste (as it would of wastes due to industrial disputes), but the "culture of capitalism" clearly places a greater value on the right of industry to make mistakes and take the consequences than on the possibility of eliminating layoffs through centralized control.

A widely discussed industrial problem, that of labor turnover, represents not only an important item of production cost, the usual point of discussion, but a loss of time as well. The time lost is the result of the lapse of time, however short, between jobs. Possibly also chargeable to labor turnover is the time required to train replacements. Because of the virtual impossibility of keeping records on each worker as he moves from one job to another, with temporary loss of work time between, there are no adequate figures for estimating the amount of this waste. Its reduction, of course, could be brought about by any device that stabilized employment. Yet in a society that places a value on freedom of occupational choice and an absence of formal barriers to mobility, this must be done by increasing "employee satisfaction" rather than direct forbiddance of movement. During the war, formal restrictions on free mobility were put into effect as a temporary measure, but a permanent measure without the justification of wartime production would have considerably less chance of success.

Little further comment need be made about accident and sickness as sources of waste, except to repeat that there is almost universal agreement concerning the desirability of reducing or eliminating this waste; of course, this is especially true of accidents and disease that take the worker out of employment for weeks or months rather than hours or days.

The Work Span. We need mention only a few further varieties of wastes of time, but these are highly significant ones for they represent a reduction of the worker's span of productivity. Most closely related to those previously discussed are wastes which permanently remove the individual from the potential work force through *death or physical incapacitation.* Most difficult to ascertain precisely, but certainly present in some degree, is the reduction of the worker's span of usefulness through long-continued employment at overtaxing assignments and under unfavorable working conditions. The closest approximation to a measure of this waste is afforded by statistics of total life expectancies of various occupational groups, but these differences reflect income differentials, adequacy of medical care, dietary habits, and other indirect effects of occupation as well as the direct effects of employment. It is nevertheless certainly true that some occupations are more healthful than others, and that one way to decrease labor waste would be to improve physical working conditions, adapt work assignments more closely to physiological capacity, and so on.

Other wastes are more directly chargeable to the nature and conditions of employment, especially incapacitating and fatal industrial diseases and accidents. Statistics are again not completely adequate, but indicate this as a major problem upon which there is common agreement.[16]

Less spectacular, yet probably greater in total loss, is the waste represented by "superannuation." Literally, superannuation refers

---

[16] The number of fatal and totally incapacitating accidents in 1940, for example, was estimated as 18,100. By standard methods of computing life expectancy, this represented 196,928,000 man days of irretrievably lost time. See Max D. Kossoris and Swen Kjaer, "Industrial Injuries in the United States During 1940," *Monthly Labor Review*, 53: 327–354, August 1941. See also Louis I. Dublin and Alfred J. Lotka, *The Money Value of a Man* (New York: The Ronald Press Company, 1946).

to getting "too old." But the difficulty (and consequently the waste) arises from a general failure to determine by objective standards when a man is too old to be useful. With the increasing mechanization of industry, and the constantly changing requirements for skills, there has been an understandable tendency on the part of American employers to seek younger workers. Both the untrained and the too highly specialized worker ran the risk of finding his experience counted as worthless, whereas the younger man with newer skills found employment opportunities. With more workers than jobs, the employment manager understandably sought the "best" man for the job, although his judgment of the superiority of the younger worker was likely to be colored by, if not exclusively based on, a sentiment favorable to youth, rather than a true appraisal of relative merit.

By our definition of waste, it is apparent that firing or retiring any worker before he has served out his full period of useful labor is a waste of labor time. The waste may be directly chargeable to management, as in the case of an older employee being dismissed to make way for a younger man whose advantage consists simply in the fact that he is younger, not that he is better qualified. It may be chargeable to inadequacy of the company's or the community's retraining program in keeping the worker's skills abreast of the times. It may in certain cases be chargeable even to the worker himself, who feels he has earned the right to quit after a long life of labor. In any case, an artificially early line of "superannuation" is likely to be a luxury of restricted production, with industries discovering that former employees thought too old to work can be advantageously employed when the pressure for increased manpower is acute.

It is impossible to estimate the numerical extent of the wastes of time represented in short-term and long-term work stoppages. The statistics collected are confined to only part of the wastes, and even in those cases do not sufficiently guard against the double danger of undercounting and overcounting (through overlapping wastes, as when an accident victim's period of disability extends into a layoff period at his place of employment). On the basis of figures available, plus the knowledge of additional wastes that are not so easily measurable, it is possible to make as a net judgment that our waste of time is tremendous.

WASTES OF SPEED OR RATE OF WORK

The mere fact that a single worker's maximum time is being used, or that the greatest possible number of workers is employed for the greatest possible time, does not mean that labor resources are not being wasted. It is also clearly necessary to ensure that the rate of work while the laborer is on the job will be at its maximum. The "time-server" is a notoriously wasteful worker.

It is impossible to find anything like a single numerical expression of maximum rate of work, or even to devise a formula for expressing the relations among the various factors involved. One of the factors is clearly that of the nature and extent of mechanization, or quality of the tools with which the laborer works. The character of the work itself and the physical characteristics and skill of the workman are equally involved, and equally difficult to generalize. But these factors are likely to be more important in the determination of maximum speeds than in explaining the *actual* rate of work. We are primarily concerned with the reasons for the difference between the *actual* and the *possible.*

Inefficient Organization and Supervision. A primary source of waste in the worker's rate of production is obviously the failure to give him enough to do. This may come about through improper planning or prediction of the time required, poor arrangement of tasks so that the worker is only occasionally required to operate at maximum speed, and so on. It is this aspect of labor waste that has been considered so extensively by "scientific managers," discussed in previous chapters. The worker who is not told the quickest way to do a certain job, or, knowing the quickest way, is not provided with sufficient materials to keep him busy, is falling short of maximum productivity through an error of managerial organization. Likewise, the worker who spends part of his time waiting for the machine, or the clerical worker who is slowed down by a rattletrap typewriter, is operating wastefully because of the shortcomings of engineering and maintenance personnel. These are but samples of the multitudinous ways in which potential speed may be lost through managerial failure. The variable factors are so numerous, indeed, that even in a highly "rationalized" organization the reduction of this type of waste is likely to consist in a series of "successive approximations" which have comparatively little chance of complete and final success.

Inadequate Incentive. The managerial responsibility for waste is enhanced by the very important fact that workers are not simply mechanistic units, and must be *induced* to perform at somewhere near their maximum capacity. We have previously noted that this has been a major stumbling block of scientific management. Simply to increase a worker's pay is frequently not enough. It may not even be necessary if other rewards or advantages are offered. This is the reason that managers resort to contests, public citations, and the like. Simply increasing the worker's pay without taking into account the extent or proportion of his increased productivity is likely to fail. The situation is even more complicated in view of the fact that the increased incentives may have to be *mcre* than proportional to the increase in rate of work demanded, since greater and greater sacrifices of other interests (such as informal organization and "horseplay") are required. Again, the practical maximum may be considerably below the "ideal" maximum, mechanistically considered, since all the worker's interests are not necessarily capable of direction toward the single goal of greater speed. In practical terms, in other words, the manager may have to be satisfied with considerably less speed than that of which the worker is physiologically capable, and the practically "irreducible waste" may be a matter only for theoretical consideration. Yet it is also certainly true that a recognition and utilization of the possible incentives would lead to much less waste of this type, whether in the behavior of executives and professional men or among the ranks of the lowly.

Voluntary Restriction of Output. Our emphasis on the necessity of providing adequate incentives illustrates the joint directional-operational (or, more specifically, management-labor) responsibility for waste of speed. On the one hand it may be asserted that management fails to take into account, and use, the worker's interests and motives for behavior. On the other hand, it may be claimed with equal validity that workers are concretely not primarily motivated by maximum productivity. If they were, the problem of incentive would be nonexistent; the question would simply be one of ways and means. But it is concretely true that *all* sane (and some insane) individuals in the population have certain ideas of their own worth, and of the proper reward for those services that are not directly or primarily for their own benefit (however defined). What scientific managers sometimes call "systematic soldiering" or what Veblen would call sabotage (conscientious withdrawal of efficiency) is so prevalent in every field of productive enterprise that it is commonly accepted and even verbally defended. The idea of a "fair reward," or a "fair day's work," is no more common among day laborers than among corporation executives or independent professionals.

The concrete motives for restricting output (in the broadest sense of the word) are as various as the range of individual interests that conflict with "living by bread alone." The day laborer may fear that he will work himself out of a job, the piece worker that the pay rate will be reduced, and the executive that his golf game will suffer. Partly because managerial and professional tasks are so difficult to assess and standardize, and partly because extra leisure and freedom of activity are widely accepted rewards for higher positions, the waste of speed or rate of work at these levels ordinarily goes unnoticed. Although it is possibly true that sustained effort is more difficult to maintain at work requiring a great deal of intelligence and reasoning, and involving frequent shifts of attention, it would be naïve in the extreme to assume that only the lower ranks of productive workers "soldier" on the job.

To repeat, the calculation of the quantity of waste of speed or rate of work in general is impossible, and extremely difficult even in very concrete cases. Yet it is possible to reduce the amount if the appropriate line of action is followed, *and if the goal of pro-*

*ductivity is considered, or made, sufficiently important to warrant the
sacrifice of pleasant wastefulness.*

WASTES OF SKILLS

A final set of departures from maximum utilization of labor resources merits brief consideration. Even though all available workers are employed, for the maximum amount of time, at the highest
speed of which the individual worker is capable, resources are still
being wasted if the occupational classification of the workers is
poor. Even an energetic cutoff saw operator is not likely to be an
effective corporation executive, and a really quick-moving chemist
may provide a sad picture as a fruit sorter in a cannery. If waste
is to be avoided, each worker must be doing that useful job that he
is best qualified to perform.

The qualification "useful" is necessary, since the judgment of
waste must always be in terms of the actual or concretely potential
productive organization. Thus, the failure to use some or all of the
special talents of an architectural engineer in a primitive society
like, let us say, the Trobriand Islands in the South Pacific, could
scarcely be regarded as a waste within the confines of that society.
On the other hand, the scarcity of jobs for men technically trained
in a complex industrialized society may represent either a waste of
past time in training, or a failure of productive organization to
change rapidly enough to capitalize on the skills available. The
sources of waste of skills may accordingly be classified as *inadequate training, and errors in classification.*

Inadequate Training. Not only does a complex industrial civilization
require diversified and very extensive training, but the ever-changing character of industrial organization and production necessitates
continual change in training, possibly even in the training of the
same individuals. Thus whenever the community through its formal
education program, the labor organization through its apprentice
program, or industry through its instructional facilities fail to develop potential skills, or provide opportunity to learn new and
more useful talents, there is waste. Where the responsibility lies is
not of immediate concern, although it would certainly be of pri-

mary importance to the one who would seek to reduce this waste. It is even difficult at any time to discover what reductions are possible, since ways of discovering potential abilities are poorly developed in most occupational fields, and the probable future utility of any very specialized training is hard to predict. Yet these questions, as we noted at the end of the preceding chapter, are fundamental in any consideration of the usefulness of labor in the modern world.

Errors in Classification. Even if the appropriate training has been provided, and the usable skills are at hand, there is no guarantee that the talents will be used. Any barriers to occupational mobility that prevent ready placement of the worker in the spot he can fill best (and that *he* best can fill) facilitates the waste of skills. Whether the barrier be the almost official ones barring women, Negroes, and other lowly valued persons from filling jobs for which they are qualified, or simply the result of inadequate methods of discovering and using the skill, the waste is apparent. An overrigid promotional system (such as seniority) is wasteful just as surely as whimsical promotion of friendly incompetents. The barrier may be self-created, as in the case of the individual who mistakenly believes he is qualified for expert salesmanship whereas his actual skills better fit him for managing the stock room. Both history and folklore are full of examples of wasted talents, and both are equally full of examples of incompetence in high places. So important, indeed, is the whole matter of maximum utilization of skills that not only may major departures waste the talents of the poorly placed individual, but his labor may be worse than useless: he can offset the work of others. Just as a large, well-trained, hard-fighting, and swift-moving army may go down in defeat because of the errors of the general staff, so a productive system may fail through insufficient attention to the exploitation of skills. Incompetence is, of course, always wasteful, but it becomes more so the higher the position and responsibility of the incompetent person. Although the wastes of numbers, of time, and of speed are usually more obvious, and certainly more capable of quantitative statement, the bottleneck to greater utilization of manpower may well consist in im-

TABLE 1 *Types of Waste of Labor Resources, and Some Social Values That Demand or Encourage Waste*

Major Types of Waste	Subtypes and Examples	Social Values at Issue

Number	Nonemployment:
	  Institutionally restricted: age, sex, financial independence
	  Quasi-institutionally restricted: caste, citizenship, criminal conviction
	Unemployment:
	  Marginal employability
	  Seasonal
	  Technological
	  Business Cycle
		Ascribed status and roles; stability and functions of the family
		In-group and upper group dominance; "free labor"
		
		"Right" (and obligation) to work
		Business and technological vs. "human" interests

Time	Work Days and Weeks
	  Legally or contractually restricted hours
	  Voluntary absenteeism
	  Lost-time accidents and sickness
	Work Year
	  Seasonal and other short-term unemployment
	  Strikes
	  Layoffs
	  Labor turnover
	  Serious accidents and diseases
	Work Span
	  Shortened life expectancy
	  Incapacitating and fatal accidents and diseases
	  "Superannuation"
		
		"Spread the work"
		
		Leisure
		Health
		
		Right to strike
		Business interests
		Free mobility
		
		Presumed superiority of youth

Speed or Rate of Work	Inefficient Organization and Supervision Inadequate Incentives Voluntary Restriction of Output	"Fair reward"; health (fatigue and monotony); "spread the work"

Skill	Inadequate Training
	  Erroneous prediction of requirements
	Errors in Classification
	  Failure to promote or "upgrade"
	  Irrelevant grounds for selection
		Free occupational choice
		
		Reward for ability; equality of opportunity

proper training and erroneous classification of personnel: a multitude of square pegs in an area predominantly characterized by smooth round holes.

A final summary of the major wastes of labor resources, and the chief interests and values that prevent maximum exploitation of labor, is presented in Table 1. This may serve as sort of "check list" of important wastes, as a basis for determining what may be the strategic factor in any concrete situation, as well as the relative ease or difficulty of attacking the problem at various points. We may repeat that wastes from a strictly technical point of view may not be regarded as such in view of other important social considerations, and that workers of all types and ranks provide considerable resistance to efficient exploitation.

REFERENCES

AMIDON, BEULAH, "Jobs after Forty," *Public Affairs Pamphlets No. 35* (New York: Public Affairs Committee, Inc., 1939).

——, "Negroes and Defense," *Survey Graphic*, 30: 321–326, 359–361, June 1941.

ANDERSON, H. DEWEY, and PERCY E. DAVIDSON, *Occupational Trends in the United States* (Stanford University, Calif.: Stanford University Press, 1940).

BAKKE, E. W., *Citizens Without Work* (New Haven: Yale University Press, 1940).

——, *The Unemployed Worker* (New Haven: Yale University Press, 1940).

BRIDGES, CLARK O., *Job Placement of the Physically Handicapped* (New York: McGraw-Hill Book Company, Inc., 1946).

BROUSE, HERMAN L., "State Laws Barring Aliens from Professions and Occupations," *Immigration and Naturalization Service Monthly Review*, 3: 281–284, March 1946.

CAYTON, HORACE R., and GEORGE S. MITCHELL, *Black Workers and the New Unions* (Chapel Hill: University of North Carolina Press, 1939).

CLARK, J. M., "The Attack on the Problem of Full Use," in National Resources Planning Board, *The Structure of American Economy* (Washington: U. S. Government Printing Office, 1940), Vol. II (Toward Full Use of Resources), pp. 20–26.

COLLINS, HENRY HILL, JR., *America's Own Refugees* (Princeton, N. J.: Princeton University Press, 1941).

DUBLIN, LOUIS I., and ALFRED J. LOTKA, *The Money Value of a Man*, rev. ed. (New York: The Ronald Press Company, 1946).

FLORENCE, P. SARGANT, *Economics of Fatigue and Unrest and the Efficiency of Labour in English and American Industry* (New York: Henry Holt and Company, Inc., 1924), Chap. VI, "The Loss by Labour Turnover"; Chap. VII, "The Loss by Absence"; Chap. VIII, "The Loss by Deficiency of Output"; Chap. IX, "The Loss by Defective Output"; Chap. V, "The Loss by Industrial Accidents"; Chap. XI, "The Loss by Industrial Ill-health."

GILL, CORRINGTON, *Wasted Manpower* (New York: W. W. Norton & Company, Inc., 1939).

GREAT BRITAIN, Ministry of Labour and National Service, *Hours of Work and Maximum Output* (London: The Ministry, 1940).

HAMMER, PHILIP G., and ROBERT K. BUCK, "Wasted Manpower in Agriculture," *Land Policy Review*, 5 (4): 9–18, April 1942.

HUMPHREY, DON D., "Alleged 'Additional Workers' in the Measurement of Unemployment," *Journal of Political Economy*, 48: 412–419, June 1940. See reply of Woytinsky, *Journal of Political Economy*, 48: 735–739, October 1940.

KNOX, JOHN B., "Employment of Handicapped Persons," *The Conference Board Management Record*, December 1941.

KOMAROVSKY, MIRRA, *The Unemployed Man and His Family* (New York: Dryden Press, 1940).

KUH, CLIFFORD, "Selective Placement of Older Workers," *Journal of Gerontology*, 1: 313–318, Summer 1946.

NICHOLS, FRANKLIN O., "Employment of the Colored Worker," *Personnel* 19: 409–417, July 1942.

NICKERSON, J. W., "Work Assignment," *Annals*, 184: 54–61, March 1936.

NOURSE, EDWIN G., and Associates, *America's Capacity to Produce* (Washington: The Brookings Institution, 1934), Chapter XIX, "The National Labor Force."

PARRISH, JOHN B., "Women in the Nation's Labor Market," *Quarterly Journal of Economics*, 54: 527–534, May 1940.

PATTERSON, S. HOWARD, *Social Aspects of Industry*, 3d ed. (New York: McGraw-Hill Book Company, Inc., 1943), Chap. XII, "The Problem of Unemployment: Quest for Security."

POLLACK, OTTO, "Discrimination Against Older Workers in Industry," *American Journal of Sociology*, 50: 99–106, September 1944.

PUFFER, RUTH R., "Industrial and Occupational Environment and Health," in Milbank Memorial Fund, *Backgrounds of Social Medicine* (New York: 1949), pp. 119–137.

RUBIN, ERNEST, "Unemployed Aliens in the United States, 1940," *Immigration and Naturalization Service Monthly Review,* 3: 308–312, May 1946.

SHOCK, N. W., "Older People and Their Potentialities for Gainful Employment," *Journal of Gerontology,* 2: 93–102, April 1947.

SIMONS, A. M., *Personnel Relations in Industry* (New York: The Ronald Press Company, 1921), Chap. XIII, "Labor Turnover."

SPERO, STERLING D., and ABRAM L. HARRIS, *The Black Worker* (New York: Columbia University Press, 1941).

STERN, BERNHARD J., *Medicine in Industry* (New York: The Commonwealth Fund, 1946), Chap. III, "The Extent of Industrial Disability," and Chap. IV, "The Handicapped Worker in Industry."

UNITED STATES DEPARTMENT OF LABOR, Bureau of Labor Statistics, "Standard Procedure for Computing Labor Turnover," *Monthly Labor Review,* 41: 1584–1586, December 1935; Same, 43: 1486–1488, December 1936.

UNITED STATES DEPARTMENT OF LABOR, Bureau of Labor Statistics, "Young and Old at the Employment Office," *Monthly Labor Review,* 46: 3–15, January 1938.

UNITED STATES DEPARTMENT OF LABOR, Division of Labor Standards, *Safeguarding Manpower for Greater Production,* Special Bulletin No. 1 (Washington: U. S. Government Printing Office, 1940).

UNITED STATES HOUSE OF REPRESENTATIVES, Select Committee Investigating National Defense Migration, *Hearings* (Washington: U. S. Government Printing Office, 1942), especially Part 27, Washington Hearings, "The Manpower of the Nation in War Production—Book One."

UNITED STATES SENATE, Committee on Education and Labor, *Investigation of Manpower Resources, Hearings before a Subcommittee* (Washington: U. S. Government Printing Office, 1942), especially Part 1.

VANCE, RUPERT B., and NADIA DANILEVSKI, "Population and the Pattern of Unemployment, 1930–1937," *Milbank Memorial Fund Quarterly,* 18: 27–43, January 1940.

VERNON, H. M., *The Health and Efficiency of Munition Workers* (London: Humphrey Milford, Oxford University Press, 1940), Chap. V, "Sickness and Absenteeism," and Chap. VI, "Accidents and Injuries."

WOYTINSKY, W. S., *Additional Workers and the Volume of Unemployment in the Depression,* Committee on Social Security, Social Science Research Council, Pamphlet Series No. 1 (Washington: The Council, 1940).

WOYTINSKY, W. S., *Labor in the United States* (Washington: Committee on Social Security, Social Science Research Council, 1938), Chap. III, "Workers by Sex"; Chap. IV, "Workers by Race"; Chap. V, "Workers by Age"; Note 12 (pp. 263–266), "Death Rates in Different Classes of Work."

CHAPTER XXI

THE AGED IN INDUSTRIAL SOCIETIES [1]

THE CONCERN of one generation or major age-group over the problems presented by another is no new thing. The young in all societies constitute a problem for adults, for they must be supported and socialized until they are ready to take an active part in the life of the community. And in rapidly changing societies adults have long bewailed the deteriorating manners and morals of their own or their neighbors' children. In such societies it is also quite likely that children approaching maturity will know more than their parents about many things, with consequent damage to time-honored principles of age-respect and consequent material for uncomfortable humor.

Over the last few decades in modern industrial societies an interesting and significant change has occurred in the pattern of expressed concern over particular age-groups. Adults have not ceased to worry about their troublesome offspring, but they have begun to worry also about their own and others' aged parents.

What gives rise to this recent concern for the aged in industrial societies? Three intricately interrelated explanations may be offered: (1) Old people form a larger proportion of the total population in "advanced" than in "undeveloped" areas, and the secular trend in this proportion is steadily upward. (2) In both obvious

[1] This chapter was originally prepared for and published in a symposium edited for the Industrial Relations Research Association by Clark Kerr, J. Douglas Brown, and Edwin E. Witte. See *The Aged and Society* (Champaign, Ill.: 1950). The editors kindly consented to the reprinting of the paper here.

The demographic data reported in the chapter are a product of the author's work with the Office of Population Research, Princeton University.

and subtle ways, the industrial economy places a peculiar emphasis on youth while the aged are subject to special hazards of obsolescence of skills. (3) The patterns of organization and social norms of modern industrial societies present peculiar problems with regard to the opportunities for security and satisfactory activities for the aged.

These points will be discussed in unequal detail. Together they permit a preliminary understanding of the connections between the social position of the aged on the one hand and the industrial mode of production and organization of society on the other.

RELATION BETWEEN INDUSTRIALISM AND AGING POPULATIONS

The aged are of special significance in industrial societies in part simply because they are numerous. In primitive and peasant societies life may not be nasty, brutish, and dull, but is very likely to be short. An important correlate of the increased levels of material production made possible by the industrial system is the increasing proportion of the aged in the population.

Table 2 shows the marked disparity in the proportion of old people in "advanced" and " undeveloped" societies. The "advanced" societies include the major industrial countries except the Soviet Union, where available statistics would seem to indicate a position about midway between the types indicated in the table. The "undeveloped" societies were selected in part for their direct or representative importance, in part in terms of availability of data. Column 1 of the table expresses the population aged 65 and over as a percentage of the total population for the country and year indicated. In this and the other columns of the table undue significance should not be attached to the exact rank order of countries, since the data derive from different census years and the age distribution in any population reflects vagaries in its own demographic history, including migrations and changes in birth rates as well as death rates. Considered as types, the two groups of countries exhibit sharp differences in the proportions of the aged. The variations internal to the groups appear to be roughly related to the time

TABLE 2 *Proportion of Population Aged 65 and Over and Ratio of Those Aged 15–64 to Young and Old Dependents in Certain "Advanced" and "Undeveloped" Countries* [a]

Country and Year	Population Aged 65 and Over as Per Cent of Total Population	Ratios of Population Aged 15–64	
		To Those Under 15 Years of Age	To Those 65 Years of Age and Over
Certain "Undeveloped" Countries			
India and Burma, 1931	2.2	1.4	26.3
Mozambique, 1940	2.2	1.2	24.3
Brazil, 1940	2.4	1.3	23.0
Colombia, 1938	2.9	1.3	19.2
Mexico, 1940	3.0	1.4	18.7
Chile, 1940	3.5	1.6	17.0
Philippines, 1939	3.5	1.2	15.5
Egypt, 1937	3.6	1.5	15.6
Turkey, 1935	3.9	1.3	14.0
Peru, 1940	4.3	1.3	12.5
Roumania, 1930	4.3	1.8	14.3
Palestine, 1931	4.4	1.4	12.7
Japan, 1930	4.8	1.6	12.3
Certain "Advanced" Countries			
Netherlands, 1930	6.2	2.1	10.2
Canada, 1941	6.7	2.4	9.8
United States, 1940	6.8	2.7	9.9
England and Wales, 1931	7.4	2.9	9.3
Belgium, 1930	7.6	3.0	9.2
Germany, 1939 [b]	7.9	3.3	8.9
Australia, 1947	8.0	2.6	8.3
Norway, 1930	8.3	2.2	7.6
Denmark, 1945	8.4	2.7	8.0
Switzerland, 1941	8.6	3.1	8.1
New Zealand, 1945	9.0	2.5	7.2
Sweden, 1940	9.4	3.4	7.5
France, 1936	9.8	2.6	6.6

[a] Based on official national statistical sources.
[b] Territory of 1939, including the Saar, Austria, and Sudetenland.

"modernization" has been going on and to the degree of its success.

Table 2 also indicates, in columns 2 and 3, the consequences of changing age distributions for the ratios of potential workers to probable dependents. In the "undeveloped" countries there are likely to be about one and one-half persons in the assumed working ages (15–64) to each person under 15,[2] whereas this ratio varies from two to three and one-half working-age adults to each person under 15 in economically advanced countries. In contrast, the aged constitute a much smaller burden of dependency in areas where industrialization is slight and recent.

The historical connection between industrial development and the increasing proportion of the aged is suggested by the comparisons given in Table 3, where the proportions of those over 65

TABLE 3   *Proportion of Population Aged 65 and Over in Certain Countries at Various Census Dates 1880–1901 and 1930–1947* [a]

Country	Population Aged 65 and Over as Per Cent of Total Population			
	Date	Per Cent	Date	Per Cent
Australia	1901	4.0	1947	8.0
Austria	1880	4.4	1934	7.9
Belgium	1900	6.1	1930	7.6
France	1891	8.3	1936	9.8
Switzerland	1900	5.8	1941	8.6
United States	1890	3.9	1940	6.8

[a] Based on official national statistical sources.

around the end of the last century and at the most recent census are shown for a limited group of economically developed countries. With the exception of France, which has the longest record of low fertility and its consequences for age distributions, there has been a pronounced increase in the proportion of old people over the periods represented.[3]

[2] The arbitrariness of the limits of working ages is indicated by the likelihood that in "undeveloped" countries many persons under 15 years of age will be at productive work, partly because production is labor-intensive and partly because of the extremely limited opportunities and demand for formal training in productive skills.

[3] In terms of the types of data presented in Table 2, the United States in 1890 would appear on that table in the approximate position of contemporary Egypt or Turkey, with 3.9 per cent of the population aged 65 and over, 1.7 per-

The demographic explanation of this changing age structure, although complex in ways of small importance here, is simple in its broad outlines. It may be stated briefly in terms of absolute and relative numbers of the aged.

With given fertility and barring the effects of migration, declining mortality will have the general effect of increasing the number of people living to an advanced age, the precise effect obviously depending on the differential impact of reduced mortality at various ages. Put simply, reduced mortality allows more people to die of "old age." [4]

An increase in the *relative* proportion of the aged will occur if, subsequent to a decline in death rates, birth rates also decline, with a consequently reduced proportion of young people in the population. The amount of the relative increase of the aged will obviously depend not only on the magnitude of the changes in deaths and births but also on the length of time elapsed since the changes occurred. For example, suppose a population has had stable birth and death rates for a considerable time. Should birth rates suddenly be cut in half and remain at the new level while death rates remain constant, the highest proportion of old people (65 and over) would occur just short of 65 years later.

Both the absolute and relative increase of the aged have accompanied the process of industrialization. Every industrial society still exhibits in some degree the effects of the relative increase of the aged. Persons are now reaching retirement age who would not have survived infancy had they been born a decade earlier, or might not have been born at all had their parents married a decade or so later.

This relative increase arising from the time gap between declin-

---

sons 15–64 to each person under 15, and 15.6 persons of potential working ages to each person 65 or older.

[4] By the latest available life tables, a male child born in one of the "advanced" countries listed in Table 2 has an average expectation of life of 56 to 66, depending on the country he chooses as birthplace. A male child born in one of those "undeveloped" countries for which mortality data are available has an average expectation of life of some 30 to 47 years, again depending on the area. (Females have a uniformly higher average expectation of life at birth.)

ing mortality and declining fertility may be regarded as "transitional," although not thereby unimportant. There remains the fundamental relationship between economic development and improved chances for living out something like a full "span" of life.

What accounts for this relationship between declining mortality and industrialization? One is tempted to jump immediately to an explanation in terms of individualistic values associated historically with capitalism but somewhat inherent in any industrial system through the requirement of competitive occupational distribution. This explanation has merit, but only when set in a somewhat less idealistic perspective.

The decline in mortality in the Western world, which started before the conventionally ascribed beginning of the Industrial Revolution, has been in large measure a by-product of political order, improved transportation from surplus to deficiency areas, control of epidemic diseases, and improved sanitation and nutrition. In later stages of industrial development the tremendous increases in production, of agricultural as well as manufactured products, have often resulted in greater disparities in income, but also in rising minimum levels of consumption.

All of these changes can be explained without *direct* recourse to the "value of human life" as a variable. The conditions necessary for an industrial mode of production with an urban population are conditions conducive to reduced mortality.

Industrial societies then provide and depend upon the conditions for making mortality reduction appropriate and feasible, and the means for improving material welfare and medical services. The canons of rational efficiency of production, when added to the universal valuation of preservation of life, might then be thought to constitute adequate bases for linking the available means to the ends of health and longevity. Although difficult to prove, it does additionally appear that the individualization of motives and rewards in industrial societies is related to an especially strong emphasis on health and preservation of life. No society encourages early death as a positive value in the ordinary course of affairs. But in industrial societies the greater means for preserving life are combined with the notion that life and health are fundamental values available to all within the limits of available services and technical knowledge.

Suppose that the rationale for mortality reduction were based solely on productive efficiency. The question would then immediately arise, Why not kill the aged on grounds that they are a drain on the social product? In view of the universal valuation of life-saving unless the community is obviously endangered by scarcity [5] —a condition difficult to imagine in peacetime in industrial societies—and in view of the values necessary to the system of individual motivation appropriate to industrial systems, such a policy if explicit would be impossible. The circumstances cannot be imagined that would make possible maximum devotion to productive efficiency during working life, followed by the certainty of death when no longer productive.

In sum, the relation between industrialism and increased longevity cannot be accounted for solely on the basis of increased supplies and improved medical techniques plus consideration of technical efficiency. It is necessary to add to the explanation the values attached to health and longevity for their own sake. Since these values are in some form universal, present knowledge lends only tentative support to the hypothesis that the motivational pattern typical of industrial societies places special emphasis on universal sharing of the benefits of vigor and long life. However, the nuances of the explanatory principles do not alter the basic association between industrialism and a high proportion of the aged in the population.

THE AGED AND THE INDUSTRIAL ORDER

Industrialization leads not only to an increased proportion of nonproductive old people but also to an increased proportion of pro-

[5] In many primitive societies the aged who require a great deal of care and those who would seriously impede or prevent movement of the group may be abandoned or even killed. It seems safe to say that life-preservation is a universal value, but that, like other social values, it is not maintained "at all costs" to the individual or the group. See Leo W. Simmons, *The Role of the Aged in Primitive Society* (New Haven: Yale University Press, 1945), especially Chap. VIII, "Reactions to Death."

ductive workers in the later years of life. Like the number of people beyond the ordinary retirement age, the proportion of older workers can be traced not only to declining death rates but also to later reductions in birth rates. The decline of birth rates leads to an increased relative number of persons who represent larger "baby crops" in earlier years.[6] The "bulge" in the age structure, representing the gap between declining birth rates and reduced death rates, must either move to steadily higher ages or else "move out" through increased mortality at the working ages. The latter is a highly improbable alternative in peacetime. Every industrial country provides evidence of this "bulge," although its dimensions vary with the demographic history of each area.

Several implications of this generalized phenomenon of an aging labor force are important for their bearing on productive organization in industrial societies. These implications may be appraised in terms of three ratios: workers and dependents, older and younger workers, and labor force entrances and retirements.

Although age is by no means the sole criterion of inclusion in the labor force, it is obviously an important one. For some purposes of examining the relation between age structure and a productive system, it is convenient to make the arbitrary assumption that persons aged 15–64 represent the potential labor force and that those under 15 and those 65 and over represent "dependents." This assumption was made in the discussion of Table 2, above, with regard to the increasing proportion of aged dependents in industrial societies. If now these two groups of "dependents" are treated as one, a significant feature of industrial societies emerges. Despite the number of old people in these societies, they enjoy a distinctly favorable ratio of potential workers to probable dependents. In the "undeveloped" countries listed in Table 2, there are only about 1.3 persons 15–64 to each person older or younger. In the "advanced" countries the ratio is about 2 to 1. This difference comes about because in industrial societies there is a smaller mortality

[6] For an exposition of this process and its projection into the future, see Frank W. Notestein and Others, *The Future Population of Europe and the Soviet Union* (Geneva: League of Nations, 1944), Chap. IV, "Changing Age Structures, 1940–1970," and Chap. V, "Manpower."

during working life (so that a person who reaches adulthood is more likely to be active 40 or 50 years later),[7] and more importantly because efficient human reproduction reduces the burden of supporting the young. The dependency of the young is a very serious drain on the productive arrangements in "undeveloped" countries. Were this simply a question of high birth rates, it might be argued that large accretions to the potential labor force are thereby assured. Actually, however, high birth rates are partially offset by high mortality in infancy and childhood. This means that many children are supported and educated formally or informally at very considerable social cost without living to contribute to their own and others' support. The waste involved in such circumstances is obvious and significant. Viewed solely in these terms, the industrial societies have clear advantages in age distribution, always assuming that economic arrangements permit effective utilization of potential manpower.[8]

The potential advantages to industrial societies in the ratio of workers to dependents may be offset by other characteristics of age distributions in industrial societies. One very important consideration is the ratio of older to younger workers. Durand shows that in the United States male workers 45 and over comprised only 26.0 per cent of the male labor force in 1890, 34.2 per cent in 1940, and systematic projection leads to an estimate of 36.9 per cent in 1960. Those under 25 comprised 27.7 per cent in 1890, only 19.0 per cent in 1940, and may fall to 15.3 per cent in 1960.[9] Thus the oldest workers were slightly outnumbered by the youngest in 1890, but by 1940 had become twice as numerous as the youthful members

---

[7] Seymour L. Wolfbein, "The Length of Working Life," *Population Studies*, 3:286–294, December 1949.

[8] Part of this advantage is a "transitional" phenomenon, since no industrial society has yet absorbed the full impact of the "bulge" in the age structure as it affects the number of persons over 65. The ratio of persons in the working ages to those over 65 is likely to be even lower, therefore, in the immediate future. Meanwhile, the upward swing in birth rates following World War II, even if temporary, will affect the ratios here discussed. It is virtually certain that the 1950 census will show that the United States now has a lower ratio of working ages to old and young dependents than in 1940.

[9] John D. Durand, *The Labor Force in the United States, 1890–1960* (New York: Social Science Research Council, 1948), p. 40.

of the labor force. Although increased educational exposure during this period had some effect on delaying entrance into the labor force, this change is mainly due to the factor of the changing age of the population.

It is not possible here to explore the full implications of this change in labor force composition. It may be appropriate, however, to mention some of the more obvious problems. One of these is the geographical and occupational *mobility* of workers. Family responsibilities, property ownership, community ties, and probable attitudinal changes combine to make the older worker less sensitive to geographical and occupational income differentials than is his younger and less encumbered colleague. In a very real sense, the longer a worker's experience in one place and occupation, the greater his "trained incapacity" for taking other jobs. A related problem deriving from the greater proportion of older workers is that of *efficiency* on the job. Here one must balance decreased physical stamina and mental ingenuity against accumulated knowledge and experience. Whether the net effect is positive or negative will depend in large measure upon the organization of productive work and upon the degree to which employers and labor unions are sensitive to the problem.

A further problem may be regarded as another dimension to the problems of mobility and efficiency: it is the *flexibility* of an aging industrial labor force with regard to the changing demand for skills. The industrial system of production depends upon and fosters rapid technical change. Now technology is often discussed as if it were a factor external to and impinging on labor, but it may also be viewed as the useful knowledge and skills represented in the productive sector of the population (including inventors and engineers as well as production workers). Technical innovation, fostered by one sector of the labor force, has two significant effects upon the demand for skills as related to age.

(1) Any technical change, whether an alteration of process alone or of both product and process, is likely to cause some degree of obsolescence of skills. This obsolescence may come about either through the demand for different skills of something like the same

relative order or through the dilution of skills through further mechanization and specialization. Specialization decreases the monopoly by the old and experienced of fairly complex but relatively static knowledge of social importance. This does not mean that all workers become unskilled, as is sometimes foolishly asserted, but only that any given command of skills is subject to fragmentation and obsolescence through technical changes.

(2) In any case, however, continued technical change requires a continued supply of new and high-order skills, whether as "operators" of the process or as designers, technical planners, and coordinators. A new occupation added to the repertoire of the labor force is likely to be filled by a new or recent entrant to the labor force. Conversely, the older an occupation, the greater the probable average age of its practitioners. This principle is commonly known and its implications commonly missed. The formal training programs for the young, whether at intermediate or advanced level and whether public or private, have been relied on to provide the ever-changing vocational skills. With a reduced proportion of younger workers, there is reduced adaptability to technical demands.

If the industrial system is to maintain anything like its historic dynamism, it would appear that adult retraining programs, designed to help supply the changing demand for skills, must be a definite part of social policy in the older industrial societies. This is a case where a change in social organization may serve both the interests of the individual worker whose skill has become obsolete and the interests of the economy as a whole.

This leads to a consideration of the third ratio mentioned above, that between labor force retirements and entrances. For the present and near future, severances may nearly equal additions, unlike the usual situation in populations recruited by high fertility and eroded by high mortality even in the middle years of life. The principal implication of the decreasing proportion of young workers has already been indicated. One or two other comments are in order. An increased number of retirements for "superannuation," whether voluntary or not, clearly poses problems of pensions or other support. Whether a large annual cohort of new workers is advantageous or not very much depends upon the state of the labor (including military) market. During the depression of the early 1930's the ranks of the unemployed were steadily swollen by new job aspirants without a correlative withdrawal of older workers by death or retirement. Aside from the problem of labor force flexibility discussed above no clear conclusion can be drawn from the probable decrease in the proportion of young labor force entrants in the near future.

It is possible, however, to conclude that the increasing age of the productive sector of the population in industrial societies presents clear challenges to public policy. It has been suggested that attention needs to be given to the organization of production for maximum adaptability to the characteristics of older workers, at the same time that the flexibility of the labor supply itself is fostered by adult retraining facilities. Changes in retirement age and employment policies will also affect the quantity and quality of labor. But even so the problem of the aged in industrial societies will not have been solved.

THE AGED AND THE INSTITUTIONS OF INDUSTRIAL SOCIETIES

Perhaps the fundamental problem of the aged in industrial societies is that they have no definite place in the social structure. That is, there are no regular, institutionally sanctioned responsibilities for their care and social participation which square with both traditional values and the requirements of an industrial system. To test these assertions, rather careful attention must be given to the place of the family in industrial societies.[10]

The family system of the modern Western world approaches one extreme along a range that extends from complete emphasis on extended biological kinship (the consanguine family) at one pole

---

[10] Although the exposition here differs sharply in emphasis, it follows the general theoretical position developed by Talcott Parsons in *Essays in Sociological Theory, Pure and Applied* (Glencoe, Ill.: The Free Press, 1949), Chap. X, "Age and Sex in the Social Structure of the United States," and Chap. XI, "The Kinship System of the Contemporary United States."

to complete emphasis on the marital relationship and its immature progeny (the conjugal family) at the other. Along this range the family in industrial societies is clearly nearer the conjugal type, and the degree of its approximation to the pure type stands in some proximate relation to the degree to which the various societies approach the pure type of urban industrialism as a mode of social organization. The most frequent appearance of the pure conjugal family appears to be in the United States.

The significance of this family type for the role of the aged may best be seen through comparison and contrast with other kinship systems. It is the universal function of the family to provide sanctioned sexual relations and legitimate reproduction, to educate the child in attitudes and at least partly in facts, and to establish the child as a member of society as a whole. A child is a member of society only by membership in an effective kinship unit, or in some substitute unit recognized as such.

In most societies, however, the immediate family of reproduction is part of an extended kinship system, so that the child is *structurally* related to siblings and parents but also to grandparents and collateral relatives descended from common ancestors (uncles and aunts, cousins of various degrees). *Structurally* related is emphasized because that form of kinship system sets definite patterns of social rights and responsibilities among kinsmen, varying with their relationship as defined in the structure. A most important attribute of the consanguine system in the present context is that it retains its forms of social relationships throughout the life of any member, shifting only by change of status from child to parent or grandparent (and their collateral equivalents) as a normal part of growing older. The important point is that the child remains a member of the same extended kinship group, with definite and continuing rights and responsibilities, even through marriage, parenthood, and old age. Neither adulthood nor marriage severs ties with the parental family and its broader kinship liaisons. The aged in such a system tend to acquire increasing power and responsibility, with correlative security, at least as long as they retain their normal faculties.

The extreme conjugal family stands in marked contrast to such a system. As in any system, the conjugal family is the nexus between the child and society. But the family into which a child is born and the family into which his children are born are two quite different units, only tenuously related through the single individual. In the conjugal system when an adult married person refers to "his" family he must perforce mean his wife and immature children and not his parents or brothers and sisters. In short, the conjugal family in the type case involves a radical separation of the generations, and of adult brothers and sisters. They are all members of different families. Each married adult male has a wife who also no longer belongs to the kinship unit into which she was born, although this separation is not uncommon in human societies.

The implications of this system for the role of the aged are clear and far-reaching. Old people have *no* definite claim upon an extended kinship group for support and social participation. The primary obligation of each brother and sister is to his or her *own* family, *and the same is true for married children.*

The increasing incidence of the conjugal family type in industrial societies is often interpreted in terms of "loss of functions" to more specialized agencies (government, factory, church, school, organized recreation). With this interpretation there are commonly explicit or implicit overtones of moral condemnation for those who have allowed timeless principles of kinship obligations and solidarity to fall into neglect. These interpretations usually rest upon a fundamental misapprehension of the structural requirements of modern industrial societies.

The conjugal family makes possible and indeed fosters the determination of adult status upon the basis of qualities and achievements of the individual as they are developed through childhood and maturity. This system of filling adult occupational and other positions is quite different from the determination of adult status at birth on the basis of criteria such as kinship group and birth order, over which the individual has no control. The efficiency of the industrial system rests upon the recruitment of individuals as individuals, for their technical competence and not for their membership in a kinship system. An adult can be assigned a status appropriate to the system and various rewards for his own performance in the occupational sphere only if he is not directly and completely dependent upon the success of his parents and siblings. This mode of occupational placement and reward requires also a substantial amount of movement from place to place and between occupations, and the necessary motivation to seek enhanced opportunities. Changes of this sort are most easily accomplished if the family is sufficiently small and free of entangling alliances with kinsmen.

The family universally prepares the child for adulthood, with or without the help of other agencies. It follows from the thesis presented here that the conjugal family supports the industrial system by preparing the child for adult independence of his parents and siblings.

Once this relationship between family and society becomes clear, considerable light is thrown on many contemporary problems associated with the aged. For example, the care of the aged is often discussed in terms of urbanization and urban housing. But urbanization simply gives a geographical dimension to the basic phenomenon of occupational change. And housing is merely a symptom and not a very reliable one at that. Comparisons of the ease of housing the aged in rural communities as contrasted with the cramped space in urban apartments are likely to involve unrecognized comparisons through time and across social strata. Not all rural families live in large, rambling dwellings where aged parents may be given a room and a corner in a spacious living room. The spacious dwelling unit is a rarity in rural as in urban communities; crowding is common in both.

The hidden comparison through time is that between the standards and expectations typical of the semi-isolated rural community at the turn of the century and those of urban dwellers (but also of many of their rural contemporaries) at the present time. Crowding is resented only when it is recognized as such, and it is increasingly alleged precisely because the basic structure of the modern family encourages spatial as well as social separation of the generations.

Married children have both the right and the duty to "lead their own lives."

The hidden comparison across social strata is that between low-income farm families, where more traditional types of kinship relations are likely to prevail, and white-collar and professional groups in the cities, which are precisely the most mobile as compared with parental occupations and status and as compared with the aspirations and expectations of other occupational strata. It is for the competitor in the urban occupational sphere that the separation of generations is most effective.

The unwillingness of the young married adult to make serious sacrifices for the benefit of his parents is then something different from a general attrition of morals. If he makes such sacrifices he not ony prejudices his own legitimate aspirations but also jeopardizes his responsibilities to his own children.

The foregoing structural analysis is, however, a little too neat. The conjugal family is *not* universally adhered to in industrial societies. In major sectors of the social systems of Western Europe, where change has been somewhat more gradual, and in older rural communities and among the very poor and families representing several generations of wealth in the United States, the generations and collateral kinsmen retain a variable but important range of social ties. These areas and sectors of the social order are precisely the least mobile in terms of generational change and of movement within a single career. It is therefore not accurate to refer to the pure conjugal family as *the* kinship system of industrial societies, but only as the kinship system best integrated with urban industrialism.

This lack of uniformity in practice is also reflected in the normative system. The conjugal family is *not* completely institutionalized, even in the United States. An adult married person may be criticized both for continuing to consider himself a member of his parental family and for failing to provide for his aged parents. Age-respect, honor to one's father and mother, and indeed intimate affectional bonds between generations are traditional values that do not mesh neatly with intergenerational mobility and achievement of social status. Parents are expected to provide maximum opportunities for their children, but without commensurate assurances for themselves.

Persons now in or approaching inactive old age were reared before the end of the last century, quite probably in a rural environment and certainly when urban industrialism was less firmly entrenched. They are likely to be kinship-oriented to a degree that disturbs their children and bewilders their grandchildren. Here the lack of clarity and uniformity as to the nature of the American family system may have acute consequences: the total incompatibility between the expectations of aged parents and their children as to their mutual obligations. Of the two, the children are the more likely to be ambivalent because of the inconsistency between the older expectations and the newer ones.

It is important to emphasize that this ambivalence is not one between moral obligation and crude self-interest. It is a moral obligation of the middle-class breadwinner to respect his primary responsibility to his own immediate family.

Only on the most superficial view can the sloppy sentimentality surrounding Mother's Day be attributed to clever commercialism. Its emotionalism is also cultivated and sanctified in urban churches. But the basic factor is surely the widespread prevalence of uneasy consciences about aged parents cut off from their adult offspring.

At the same time there are manifold signs of a sense of frustration among the aged. As Parsons suggests,[11] it is highly probable that the demand for pensions, especially as represented in pension clubs, is only partly a search for financial security. Emotional security is perhaps the acute need of the aged, and this can be assured only by stable and fairly intimate relationships that are regarded by participants as good in themselves and not as inferior substitutes.

There is a kind of deep tragedy in the vagaries of the normative patterns as they now stand. Parenthood, far from being "old age insurance," is a type of sacrificial duty. In the urban environment large families generally hamper both generations in competition for status. But even the small family does not assure the position of

[11] *Op. cit.,* pp. 231, 247.

the parents after their children reach adulthood. The parents' freedom from responsibilities is likely to be too late for effective utilization for enhancement of the parents' social status of the money, time, and effort formerly spent on the young. Even more important is the lack of satisfying social participation, as the available activities substituted for those centering around the family are likely not to provide the emotional sense of belonging and being needed. The aged are in effect members of no family except their own truncated one. If that is further severed by death of one member, the awkward question of living arrangements arises. And there are few definite and approved patterns for filling the gap.

The tragedy, however, does not consist primarily of the separation of the generations. Rather it arises from the differing expectations of the aged and their children as to rights and responsibilities. This in turn derives from the incomplete institutionalization of the conjugal family. Failure to recognize this situation accounts in large measure both for the lack of attention to the social participation of the aged and for the apparent feeling of the aged that available activities are inferior substitutes for kinship bonds.

The same complex process loosely called "urbanization" and "industrialization" has made it possible for more people to reach old age and has made it difficult or impossible for the aged to be used and supported in conformity with older patterns and values. It has been argued here that continued efficiency and technical innovation in the industrial system will require modifications in the organization of productive assignments and definite provisions for dealing with the obsolescence of skills of the older worker, probably through adult retraining. It has also been argued that the type of family system best fitted to the industrial order is incompletely supported by social norms. This fact has further implications not only for the expectations of the aged but also for the scant attention society has given to the emotional as well as financial security of old people and to the types of social participation which will be within the capacities and expectations of the aged.

The problems of the aged will be alleviated but not solved by pensions or other forms of financial security. The reintegration of the aged into an extended kinship system would entail tremendous sacrifices in the organization of industrial societies with their attendant norms—sacrifices of such degree and complexity as to result in a quite different form of productive organization. A solution consistent with the industrial order would require new activities and organizations *appropriate* for the aged, appropriate being defined not only in terms of their capacities and interests, but also in terms of ethical principles commonly held in the society at large.

REFERENCES

CLAGUE, EWAN, "The Working Life Span of American Workers," *Journal of Gerontology*, 4: 285–289, October 1949.

DURAND, JOHN D., *The Labor Force in the United States, 1890–1960* (New York: Social Science Research Council, 1948).

FRIED, EDRITA G., "Attitudes of Older Population Groups toward Activity and Inactivity," *Journal of Gerontology*, 4: 141–151, April 1949.

KERR, CLARK, J. DOUGLAS BROWN, and EDWIN E. WITTE, eds., *The Aged and Society* (Champaign, Ill.: Industrial Relations Research Association, 1950).

KISER, CLYDE V., "Significance of Our Aging Population," in New York State, Joint Committee on Problems of the Aging, *Birthdays Don't Count*, New York State Legislative Document (1948) No. 61 (Albany?: 1948), pp. 66–88.

NOTESTEIN, FRANK W., and OTHERS, *The Future Population of Europe and the Soviet Union* (Geneva: League of Nations, 1944), Chap. IV, "Changing Age Structures, 1940–1970," and Chap. V, "Manpower."

PARSONS, TALCOTT, *Essays in Sociological Theory, Pure and Applied* (Glencoe, Ill.: The Free Press, 1949), Chap. X, "Age and Sex in the Social Structure of the United States," and Chap. XI, "The Kinship System of the Contemporary United States."

POLLACK, OTTO, *Social Adjustment in Old Age: A Research Planning Report* (New York: Social Science Research Council, 1948).

SIMMONS, LEO W., *The Role of the Aged in Primitive Society* (New Haven: Yale University Press, 1945).

WERMEL, MICHAEL T., and SELMA GELBAUM, "Work and Retirement in Old Age," *American Journal of Sociology*, 51: 16–21, July 1945.

WOLFBEIN, SEYMOUR L., "The Length of Working Life," *Population Studies*, 3: 286–294, December 1949.

✒ CHAPTER XXII

THE INDUSTRIAL COMMUNITY

ALONG THE streets of an American town in the cool morning hours
the industrial army, dressed in uniforms roughly symbolic of occupational differences and armed with field rations in metal lunch
pails, hurries toward the gates of some local factory. Later a shrill
steam whistle indicates that another production day has begun, or
another "shift" of workers has manned the machines. A little later
the businessmen and clerks, the administrators, bankers, and professionals will walk or ride to office and administration buildings.
For the bulk of the gainfully occupied citizenry of the community,
a working day has begun. Although at other times of the day or the
week, or in a slack period in the so-called "business cycle," another
impression might be gained, the "normal" state of affairs we have
been briefly calling to mind leaves the unmistakable idea that the
life of the community revolves around the business of producing,
trading, and earning a living.

Certainly the most obvious, the most daily apparent, relation of
industry to society is to be found in the workaday life of an industrial community. It is here that the role of occupation and the
hierarchy of industrial organization has the most immediate effect
upon the life patterns of the individual. It is in the out-of-work life
on American Main Streets and suburbs that the distinctions between the social life of the administrative and professional people
and their families are most readily distinguishable from the associations and activities of the "working" population. Conversely, it is
in this small-scale impact of society upon industrial life that the
grouping of people in their nonoccupational life reflects itself in

538

the industrial organization. In our previous discussions of these matters, looking from the inside of the factory out upon the community, we have had occasion to observe the high relevance of religious, ethnic, and more intimately personal affiliations and differences upon the groupings and hostilities, the "efficient" or "inefficient" productivity of workers in the offices and shops.

It is our purpose in the present chapter to examine the interdependence of industry and the community, with some attention to the practical problems of industrial location on the one hand, and of the community's stake in economic production on the other. We shall then turn to some of the more immediate problems of conflicting interests, the powers and reciprocal rights and obligations that necessarily develop within the industrial community. Finally, we shall attempt to give point to these general considerations by a survey of various types of industrial communities, taking as our chief point of reference the relative dominance of industrial (and more particularly managerial) interests as compared with other aspects of communal life.

INTERDEPENDENCE OF INDUSTRY AND COMMUNITY

It is a perfectly obvious truism that an industry must locate somewhere, and that the personnel of a productive establishment must depend upon a community of some sort for their economic demands, to say nothing of other social activities. It is, of course, not equally true that a community is *directly* dependent upon locally established production, as long as trade facilities are available for securing necessary manufactured products. Yet short of completely self-sufficient agricultural production (a rarity in the modern world), the community must at least depend upon a trading center, and offer locally produced goods and services in exchange for those produced elsewhere.

If we limit the meaning of "industry" to mining, commercial agriculture, and manufacturing (and thus exclude finance and trade, and the marketing of services such as government and recreation), it cannot be said that every community must have one or more industries, although it remains true that every industry must depend upon a community. Of course, in most concrete cases such abstract questions of relative dependence are not likely to arise in this form; once an industrial activity has been located in an existing community or served as the attraction for the establishment of a residential and trading center, the dependence of that center upon the economic life of the industry may be absolute. These general considerations are perhaps best approached successively from the point of view of industrial managers concerned with the location of establishments and from the point of view of the community that is dependent for its existence or expansion upon the livelihood provided by industry.

The Location of Industry. As a business enterprise oriented toward the balance sheet of productive costs, any industrial establishment must weigh certain factors in choice of a location. Those factors that can be most easily assessed in monetary terms are, of course, raw materials and resources, sources of power, markets, transportation routes and costs, the availability of suitable sites at reasonable cost, and so on. These factors clearly bear no constant relationship to one another, since their importance varies with the type of establishment as well as with changes in market and other situations beyond the immediate control of industrial management. Thus the primary consideration for agricultural and extractive enterprises is clearly that of resources, although this is also clearly in the nature of a minimum condition. A virtually inaccessible deposit of high-grade iron ore cannot become the economic foundation of a thriving community until such time as transportation routes are established. So-called heavy industry must weigh transportation costs more heavily than manufacturers of small articles for a near-by market. The tremendous amounts of electrical energy required for the manufacture of aluminum prescribe location of plants near enough to the sources of that energy to make its use economically feasible. These and similar considerations indicate the complexity of the problems facing the technical experts who are asked to determine the location of industrial plants. The situation is, moreover, a dynamic rather than a static one, especially in view of an ever-changing technology which may make new raw materials available, open markets for new products, reduce transportation costs, or in many ways upset the previously existing relationship among the variables.

It is not meant to imply that all productive establishments are located with such care, and certainly not that plants can be moved about like checkers to take advantage of the latest developments. The necessity for careful planning clearly increases with the amount of risk involved, the stringency of price competition, and similar considerations. Then too, we noted in an earlier chapter that a characteristic of the "factory system" is that of fixed capital. What this means in the present context is that once a heavy investment in buildings and equipment has been made that situation may well be the overwhelmingly important factor in any future consideration of location. Although industrial establishments display both mortality and mobility, a fact to be discussed more fully below, it remains true that for the bulk of productive establishments the initial decision is a reasonably permanent one.

In so far as the factors that determine the location of industry can be expressed in monetary terms (which may imply extensive technical knowledge and predictability), the problem may be approached by the simple expedient of evaluating the relative advantages and disadvantages and reaching a conclusion. But such a procedure must either rest upon assumptions of "all other important things being equal," or else produce a partial rather than a final conclusion. And it is in the actual "inequality" of other important considerations that the significance of the dependence of industry upon an industrial community is most evident. Thus the economics of industrial location as we have briefly sketched it must assume the existence of an abundant, qualified, and "fluid" labor supply. Now although this assumption has been more or less correct throughout most of the development of industrialization, it is actually of highly unequal validity in time and space. The fluidity of labor supply is never complete with respect to either location or quality. "Economic opportunity," which presumably induces migration from less favored areas, must be at least sufficient to offset the expenses of movement, to say nothing of the familial and community ties, home ownership, and so on, which provide major barriers to mobility based solely on shrewd calculation of monetary advantage. Nor is the abundance of qualified labor always a safe assumption. The theory of course is that the unemployed and those seeking greater opportunity will together descend upon a new manufacturing location, at their own expense, and thus relieve the accountants from the necessity of considering labor supply or costs as a factor in location. However, barriers to mobility, labor shortages due to expanded production, local and regional wage differentials through unequal unionization, or a variety of other circumstances, belie the theory. Ample illustration of this has been provided during wartime with the location of plants in the open countryside under the naïve assumption that wartime labor shortages and the absence of housing and other community facilities would make no difference. The minimum penalty has been high rates of turnover and absenteeism.

With respect to houses, trade areas, schools, churches, professional services, and countless other aspects of normal community life required or expected by contemporary industrial workers, the company cannot be simply indifferent. In choosing a location it must either seek a community with services already established, or aid in their establishment in a new community. Indeed these considerations must figure at least as large as problems of industrial water supply, waste disposal, and police protection.

For the introduction of the factory system in countries or regions without industrial experience and traditions, the problem of labor supply in the qualitative and attitudinal sense is fully as important as considerations of raw materials, transportation, markets, and even the quantitative supply of able-bodied workers.[1] Even in older industrial areas there are sociological nuances in the patterns of social organization that may materially affect the economic as well as the social success of the enterprise. One important consideration is the social composition of the potential work force. If the labor supply is characterized by fundamental cleavages along ethnic, religious, or other lines the single company may find itself incapable

---

[1] See Wilbert E. Moore, *Industrialization and Labor: Social Aspects of Economic Development* (Ithaca: Cornell University Press, 1951).

of staffing its operations regardless of its desire to consider these distinctions as irrelevant to technical competence.

A consideration of a different order arises with respect to the characteristics of urban concentration and the ecology of the city. These pose problems of the proximity of residences to places of work and the correlative problem of rapid transportation and traffic control.[2] There is some evidence that voluntary absenteeism increases with the distance of workers' residences from their place of employment.[3] If zoning regulations prohibit manufacturing establishments in residential areas and the means of transportation to available manufacturing sites are already overburdened, other advantages offered by location in a particular city may be overbalanced by effective inability to get workers to the plant.

The extensive literature concerning industrial location—a subject to which economists and economic geographers have devoted considerable attention[4]—neglects in general the foregoing and other equally pertinent questions. The additional questions are chiefly those of a legal or normative character—ranging from attitudes of sympathy or hostility to the more formal expression of those attitudes in terms of organized interest groups or legislative enactments.

The community may provide various inducements to attract industrial location. Yet a community which is not completely dominated by industrial management may (and normally will) also establish various restrictions upon industrial location and activities in the protection of other interests. Thus most towns and cities

[2] See Gerald W. Breese, *The Daytime Population of the Central Business District of Chicago* (Chicago: University of Chicago Press, 1949); Kate K. Liepmann, *The Journey to Work* (New York: Oxford University Press, 1944).

[3] From an unpublished study carried out by the Industrial Relations Section at Princeton University.

[4] See, for example, Edgar Malone Hoover, *Location Theory and the Shoe and Leather Industries* (Cambridge: Harvard University Press, 1937), Part I (Chaps. I–VI), "The Theory of Location"; Hoover, *The Location of Economic Activity* (New York: McGraw-Hill Book Company, Inc., 1948); Alfred Weber, *The Theory of the Location of Industries,* tr. by Carl J. Friedrich (Chicago: University of Chicago Press, 1929). For other references see Douglas Moore McDonald, *A Select Bibliography on Location of Industry,* Social Research Bulletin No. 2 (Montreal: McGill University, 1937).

have "zoning" ordinances which may prevent the location of a plant in an otherwise desirable location in a residential area. Similarly, local governments are frequently pressed into restricting various industrial "nuisances," such as noise, odors, poisonous fumes, or stream pollution and other unhealthful practices in the disposal of wastes. Indeed, the local community may prevent industrial operation altogether, as in the prohibition upon brewing and distilling alcoholic beverages or the prohibition upon endangering home sites by mining operations. Labor unions, organized farmers' groups, or even religious groups in a particular community may have (from the industrialist's point of view) an unsavory reputation with respect to the policies of industrial enterprise. Since these are factors that vary widely from one community or area to another, the mere location of industry, to say nothing of its subsequent relations with the community, depends on considerations which are incapable of neat appraisal in a double-entry account book.

The Community's Stake in Industry. While the managers of a new plant attempt to find a "favorable" location, and the managers of established plants attempt to keep their position as favorable as possible, the community on its part may seek to attract or retain industrial establishments.

Clearly the chief stake a community has in local industry is in the payrolls of the company. The plant is not only a direct source of employment for the local citizens, but the trade and services required by the employees provide income for businessmen, insurance salesmen, physicians, lawyers, and a greater or smaller host of others. The clergyman's salary and the plumber's wage may come indirectly from the local mill. Although the intricacies of trade and exchange are difficult to trace, and it would be difficult to maintain that even in a one-industry community the industrial payroll is the sole source of "wealth," the disastrous effect upon such a community when the plant temporarily or permanently ceases operations illustrates clearly enough the community's stake in the payroll.

A secondary source of advantage to the community from a local industrial establishment is to be found in the collection of taxes for local government, education, municipal services, and the like. Again the advantages derive not only from the taxes collected directly from the company, but from the enhanced value of real estate and other taxable wealth throughout the community.

But the effect upon the community of the establishment of a factory or a near-by mining operation cannot all be put in monetary terms. Industrialization inevitably means a fairly extensive modification of previous community organization, to say nothing of familial relationships and personal behavior. Conservative elements in a rural community may view with considerable misgiving any imminent industrialization. It is undeniably true that industrialization is normally accompanied by urbanization, in the social if not in the strictly numerical sense. The commercialization of recreation, the introduction of larger varieties of manufactured products through a more extensive monetary exchange, and even the adoption of "urban" attitudes with respect to the independence of women, the practice of contraception, occupational and class distinctions, and the like—these are some of the results of industrialization that are either welcomed or despised by the local citizenry.

For the most part, however, the opposition to industrialization in the United States has arisen from a vociferous but definitely minority group. The economic advantages (real or imagined) of industrial payrolls and taxes, plus the welcome extension of urbanism, have combined to place communities in competition to attract industry, and so to order their local affairs that an existing plant will not close its doors. There is, of course, an even further factor in the imagined stake of the community in industry, and that is the generally accepted blessings of community size and volume of economic production, particularly if the latter is contributed by many small producers and thus avoids the stigma of Big Business. So oriented toward the ideology of commerce and industry is the ordinary American citizen that he takes considerable pride in belonging to a community that "has the largest volume of pork production in the state of Iowa," or "ships the most lumber to foreign markets," or is "the world center for the manufacture of four-holed pearl buttons." Although there is perhaps some occasional validity for the assumption that "what helps business helps you!" there is no evidence that the desire to advertise the advantages a community can offer to an enterprising industrialist rests upon any careful individual calculation of monetary returns. Just as the opposition to industrialization may be said to derive from nonrational sentiments, so there is every reason to suspect that its encouragement is also at least partly sentimental.

Methods of Attracting Industry. The community that seeks industrialization or additions to its industrial support need not rely solely on favorable position with respect to raw materials, power, markets, or transportation. Although the community that enjoys some advantages in these respects will not hesitate to point them out, chambers of commerce and similar organizations are sufficiently realistic to recognize the importance of other considerations. In the business and financial sections of metropolitan newspapers and in national magazines one may read advertisements on the order of the following:

LOCATE IN THE HEART OF INDUSTRIAL MARYLAND

If you are looking for an industrial site close to the Eastern markets and well situated for foreign trade, we recommend to your attention a number of unexcelled locations in progressive Marysville. Served by Eastern Shore and Transcontinental Railroads, close to Pennsylvania and West Virginia coal and to new hydroelectric developments, heavy and light industry will find many advantages. Low taxes, no restrictive or "business busting" legislation. Ample supply of skilled and unskilled laborers. No labor troubles in more than ten years.

Let us send you our illustrated brochure entitled "America's Most Progressive Industrial Community." Just write to

Industrial Bureau of Marysville
Marysville, Maryland

The foregoing hypothetical advertisement illustrates many of the more common inducements offered to industrialists. A favorable economic and legal situation is of course the most important factor. Especially in recent years the presumed advantages of an unorganized and "tractable" body of workers have figured prominently in industrial location. But the community may be in a position to offer added incentives. The most common of these is that of tax reduction or complete tax abatement for a period of years. Almost equally common is the offer of free sites, contributions to the building of railroad sidings, or similar directly financial inducements. In fact, if the bidding becomes spirited community political or business leaders may be tempted to offer more than sober reflection would justify in economic terms.[5]

Interdependence and Conflict. In the relations between an established industrial concern and its local community, many of the same problems are posed as appear in the question of industrial location. Traditionally the same power of giving or withholding employment, which ensured the dominance of the employer over the employee, also ensured his importance in the affairs of the community. Thus, the more nearly exclusive the economic dependence of the community upon the company, the heavier the weight of company policy in the affairs of schools, churches, fraternal organizations, and political groups in the town.

The traditional dominance in direct proportion to economic power remains the basic principle with respect to the relative position of management and the community today. The various types of industrial communities discussed in the latter part of this chapter are chiefly distinguishable in terms of relative degrees of subservience to industrial interests. But the principle is no longer unalloyed (if indeed it ever was). The fact that there are independent sources of power, particularly in the form of more strictly "political" control, suggests the possibility and explains the occurrence of communal opposition to company interests and policies.

It is, of course, true that a common pattern of management-community relationship is that of the extension of managerial

[5] For a review of common methods used to attract industry, see Chamber of Commerce of the United States, Department of Manufacture, *Special Inducements to Industries* (Washington: 1931). Some interesting case materials concerning the trials of certain New England communities in attracting and retaining manufacturing plants are given by Carle C. Zimmerman, *The Changing Community* (New York: Harper & Brothers, 1938), Chap. IX, "Lonely's Belligerency"; Chap. X, "Utopia's Belligerency"; Chaps. XX–XXI, "Zenith's Industrial Tolerance." Zimmerman's treatment heavily accents the advantages of tolerance and concessions to industries, and avoidance of challenges to industrial domination by labor unions or "agitators."

authority over most of the affairs of the economically dominated community. This domination becomes especially evident in some cases of industrial conflict, where control of the law enforcement agencies, as well as of the seemingly disinterested "Citizens' Committees," lends additional and possibly decisive force to the interests of the company.[6] The threat to close or move the plant is one of the most convincing arguments used by the company, and directly illustrates our discussion of the dependence of the community upon industrial payrolls. In fact the problem of migratory labor has been so much discussed in recent years that little attention has been given to the problems raised by migratory industry. Yet so common is the phenomenon of changing community economies that two extreme cases are commonly recognized as "boom towns" and "ghost towns," both of which are discussed below. Our present interest is in the fact that the stake of workers, and less directly of the community as a whole, in the continued operation of plants is so great that this very dependence serves as an effective instrument of managerial power in the community.

Again, however, it must be emphasized that organizational specialization is sufficiently developed in contemporary life that labor unions, political parties, religious organizations, and many other groups may raise a more or less effective dissenting voice in councils on local affairs. Part of the move for community independence is clearly a challenge to the primacy of narrowly economic interests, while part is based upon a challenge to the exclusive or universal character of the economic interests represented by management.

The "Community Obligations" of Management. The foregoing discussion provides some grasp on the slippery problem of the obligations of management to the community, and the reluctance of some

[6] Many of the indirect weapons of management in industrial conflict, as discussed in Chap. XVI, depend on gaining the support of that most important segment of the "public" represented by the local community and its political and legal structure. See Agnes Hannay, *A Chronicle of Industry on the Mill River*, Smith College Studies in History, Vol. 21, Nos. 1–4, October 1935–July 1936 (Northampton, Mass.: Smith College), especially Chap. VII, "Labor under Local Enterprise"; Liston Pope, *Millhands and Preachers: A Study of Gastonia* (New Haven: Yale University Press, 1942).

elements in the community to become recipients of such obligations. The issue at stake, of course, is the character and extent of the leadership and general "good works" expected of persons of wealth or high business position, and acceptable to the community.

The roots of the doctrine favorable to the extensive influence of "persons of property" are very deep in American tradition. The main transformation of English institutions with regard to social stratification in the northern American colonies was in the direction of substituting an *aristocracy of wealth* based on business acumen for a hereditary aristocracy of landed gentry. Thus the idea that political leadership (as well as the necessary economic control) should stem from the most "respectable" elements in the community. In this connection it is interesting to note that property qualifications for the suffrage were universal in the colonies comprising the original United States under the Constitution, even in those areas that had abolished religious and similar qualifications. The community leadership of high-ranking businessmen was throughout the nineteenth century rarely challenged in theory and even more rarely effectively challenged in fact.

But in the development of the factory system and the increased industrialization and urbanization of American society, the fairly intimate and traditionalistic form of local leadership gave way more and more to the specialized interests of big business. This development was all the more marked because of the increasingly corporate character of industrial enterprise, accompanied by what amounted to some form of "absentee ownership," with a more or less mobile staff of resident managers.

It is this turn of events that has disturbed many exponents of the values of community leadership by industry as a whole, or more particularly, by those qualified for community leadership by virtue of managerial ability demonstrated in the world of commerce and industry. The argument is somewhat as follows: In primitive society there is little specialization, and leadership tends to extend into many spheres and contribute to the unification of the whole social structure. Even in the history of Western civilization the kinship system localized in the village community, or, later, the extensive and pervasive influence of the church as the major social organization, gave integration to the life of the whole community. Now, it is argued, the organization and institutions of production and trade occupy a position in the daily lives of the population commensurate with earlier major organizations, but without a commensurate enrichment of social existence. In place of the personal, informal, unifying relationships, we have the phenomenon of individuation, the "poverty" of social existence. The moral that one is expected to draw is that this modern organizational equivalent of the medieval church should supply the moral (or at least "integrative") qualities lacking in modern life.[7]

The argument proceeds in its specific application to business to maintain that modern business leadership is a leadership of ability, and that high position in a powerful organization means not only the possibility of considerable extension of that power, but also exercise in administrative skill. Thus, it is claimed, the ethical responsibilities of business leadership should proceed beyond the protection of narrowly economic interests to one of genuine social leadership. More or less explicitly the doctrine is maintained that

---

[7] The general character of this argument, without however the uniform agreement upon the moral to be drawn with respect to business leadership, is to be found in an impressive quantity of literature. It has formed the basic assumption of more than one social theorist, of whom Ferdinand Tönnies may be taken as an outstanding example. His contrast is that between *Gemeinschaft* (community) and *Gesellschaft* (society), with the latter, of course, representing the present "unhappy" state of affairs. See his *Gemeinschaft und Gesellschaft,* translated as *Fundamental Concepts of Sociology* by Charles P. Loomis (New York: American Book Company, 1940). See also the "Foreword" by Pitirim A. Sorokin in *ibid.,* in which Professor Sorokin gives a brief account of the wide acceptance of the argument.

The application of this argument to the social responsibilities of industrial management, in more or less explicit form, is also very common. For example, see L. R. Boulware, "The Business Leader's Larger Job," in Marvin Bower, ed., *The Development of Executive Leadership* (Cambridge: Harvard University Press, 1949), pp. 49–69; William E. Mosher, "The Social and Civic Responsibilities of the Profession of Business Management," in Henry C. Metcalf, ed., *Business Management as a Profession* (Chicago: A. W. Shaw Company, 1927), pp. 202–214; Oliver Sheldon, *The Philosophy of Management* (London: Sir Isaac Pitman & Sons, Ltd., 1924), Chap. III, "The Social Responsibility of Management"; T. N. Whitehead, *Leadership in the Free Society* (Cambridge: Harvard University Press, 1937), Chap. XII, "The Organization of a Community," and pp. 253–259.

"the employer is the natural leader of his men," and, by very slight extension, that this is the pattern of leadership that the employer should exercise in the community.[8]

The foregoing line of reasoning seems to call for some analysis, both because it is a view widely expressed and because the implications of such a view are far-reaching. Thus, it is immediately pertinent to examine the "leadership principle" that would extend the authority and responsibility of the industrial manager to include the ordinary affairs of the community. So examined, it appears that the authority and leadership attributed to the business official are based on position in a highly structured organization. As such, he is a *responsible* individual. The argument summarized asks increased responsibility for community affairs on the part of industrial managers. But the argument neglects to specify: *responsibility to whom?* What is really being suggested is a moral conversion of industrial officials to accept a vague sentimental or ethical responsibility for those over whom they have the skill, and possibly the power, to exercise leadership.

Any leader, even a dictator, will and must attempt to claim that he is acting in the best interests of all. The suspicion with which managerial leadership over community affairs is viewed is that in an organizational sense there is no responsibility without *accountability*. And in a democratic political order, that accountability means the representative character of leadership and the following of democratic political institutions.

Put somewhat bluntly, but with essential adherence to fact, the

[8] As part of an excellent analysis of the policies and practices of American employers' associations in comparison with "big business" associations in several other countries, Robert A. Brady has pointed out the great weight placed by business interests on the ideology of leadership, trusteeship, and so on. See his *Business as a System of Power* (New York: Columbia University Press, 1943), Chap. VIII, "Social Policies: Status, Trusteeship, Harmony," especially pp. 259–274. See also Marshall E. Dimock and Howard K. Hyde, "Bureaucracy and Trusteeship in Large Corporations," United States Congress, Temporary National Economic Committee, *Investigation of Concentration of Economic Power*, Monograph No. 11 (Washington: U. S. Government Printing Office, 1940), Part IV, "The Implications of Trusteeship." The case for managerial control of government and society has been argued most forcibly (if not cogently) by James Burnham. See his *The Managerial Revolution* (New York: The John Day Company, 1941).

"community obligations of management" are either obligations within the system of power allocation in the community (that is, political organization), or they are no obligations at all.

It is somewhat pointless to argue that because business and industry are important in the life of the modern community, that the leadership of the former should *ipso facto* constitute the leadership of the latter. Viewed by the participant in the educational, religious, or similar organizations, *there is no effective guarantee that the leadership of businessmen will be disinterested.* In other words, the very fact that such officials represent an organization that is not only powerful but organized around very specialized and explicit goals justifies considerable doubt concerning the treatment of any interests that might conflict with those of the business organization. It must be repeated that the responsibility of an officeholder in a bureaucratic system is insured by accountability. Even the best intentioned industrial manager could scarcely be expected to weigh his fairly vague obligations to the community as heavily as he does the fairly clear-cut and organizationally sanctioned policies favorable to the financial and managerial interests of the company. Indeed, the officials of any powerful organization must wield their community influence in a way which preserves or enhances the power of the organization to which they are accountable.

It seems hard to avoid the conclusion that an extension of the community obligations of management will either be in the interest of the strictly organizational interests represented by management (and thus not community obligations at all), or else they will be asserted and enforced by an independent organization. Since the latter case must involve an effective exercise of power, the nature of its action must by definition be political; normally, of course, the existing political organization provides the medium for the control and adjudication of special interests, and it is through elections, law making, court decisions and the like that the leadership (or domination) of industrial officials over the affairs of the community is challenged.

It is with these fundamental issues and principles in mind that we can best approach the types of industrial communities, taking as our chief basis of distinction the relative extension or delimination of "company" interests in the organization of communal life.

TYPES OF INDUSTRIAL COMMUNITIES

It is apparent not only that communities differ widely, but that no single mode of classification would be equally satisfactory for all purposes. Thus, a classification according to size obscures differences in political units of approximately equal size: density of population, distance from other communities, occupational distribution, and so on. Yet it is also true that as size increases the specialization of community types tends to decrease, since the sheer fact of size tends to require the development of most aspects of communal living. Thus classifications of urban communities frequently refer to Chicago as a transportation center, Pittsburgh as an industrial center. Washington as a governmental center, New York as a commercial and financial center, and Atlantic City as a resort center. Although these distinctions have some merit in the statistical sense of the main single source of income, close examination will reveal that each of these cities has developed in some degree all of the other types of urban economies.

If we limit ourselves to communities directly dependent upon industry in the narrow sense of payrolls of manufacturing and extractive establishments, the problem of classification still remains. As previously indicated, the distinction most significant for the relation of industry to the community is precisely the degree of dependence or indepedence of the community in its relations with industrial organizations. Even so, it will be observed that there is at least a rough correlation between independence and size of the community, for reasons closely related to those just indicated with respect to the diversification of interests and activities in the urban community. Thus we may start our review of the types of industrial communities with the typically small and completely dependent community commonly known as the "company town."

Company Towns. Although industry of the modern type is in a real sense an urban phenomenon, or at least dependent upon an urban civilization, particular establishments may be located in very small communities, the bulk of whose residents have little contact with urbanism. Whenever the location of an industrial concern is decided on grounds exclusive of existing local labor supply, a "detached" industrial community grows up with the influx of workmen and managers and their families, as well as tradesmen and professionals supplying services to the industrial personnel. It is in such circumstances that the "company town" is likely to be established.

In the company town of "pure" type the company buys land encompassing the proposed site of factory, mine, or mill, and also sufficient area for the building of homes, necessary public buildings, roads or streets, and, possibly, even recreational areas. The company then builds homes and streets, a school, perhaps a church, provides water, light, and heating facilities, a general "company store," barracks, "bunk houses," or even a hotel for single men and any itinerants, and such other construction as may be indicated by managerial whim or local necessity. The workman lives in a company house, drinks company water, reads at night by company light, buys his food at the company store, and walks to the store on company streets. Frequently little money changes hands since subtractions for monthly accounts and other charges are made before the worker receives a check. Following a period of unemployment the laborer may work for months or even years without receiving any money, since all money due him above his current debts to the company is applied to the expenses incurred while the company was "carrying" him.[9]

The circumstances and motives inducing the establishment and maintenance of company towns are many and varied. Some such arrangement may be almost inevitable for the establishment of a new community. Individual resources are rarely adequate for establishing even the minimum essentials for the immediate operation of a

[9] Descriptions of the peculiar features of the company town, together with illustrations drawn from mining and textile communities, are given by Lois MacDonald, *Labor Problems and the American Scene* (New York: Harper & Brothers, 1938), Chap. V, "Company Towns: Coal Camps," and Chap. VI, "Company Towns: Textile Mill Villages." See also by the same author, *Southern Mill Hills* (New York: Alex L. Hillman, 1928); Jennings Rhyne, *Some Southern Cotton Mill Workers and Their Villages* (Chapel Hill: University of North Carolina Press, 1930).

completely new community. But unless the company has other reasons for maintaining its dominance, it may be able to sponsor the necessary developments without actual control, and at the most need retain this all-pervasive influence only temporarily. But the fact of the matter is that the operation of a company town is regarded by many concerns as a definite and permanent part of their activity.

The company town has, of course, many advantages to the company from a "strictly business" point of view. Thus the control of practically the entire economic life of the community provides an additional source of profit to the company. Indeed, the additional profit may be considerably larger than in a comparable "normal" community since monopoly conditions prevail. If that monopoly is at all threatened by near-by competing trade areas it can be enforced by making continued employment or residence in the community conditional upon acceptance of the company's goods and services at the rate charged. Such situations frequently prevail in the mining communities of Pennsylvania and West Virginia, the cotton mill towns of the South, and the lumber towns of the Pacific Northwest.

A somewhat different point of view apparently prevails in a minority of company towns, where management regards the supply of attractive houses, exceptional recreational and similar community services, model schools, and clean streets as "good business." The business motives are presumably the attraction of a labor supply of better than average quality, and the retention of that labor supply in an effort to reduce the cost represented by labor turnover. The managers of such companies (and therefore of such towns) may see advantages in minor withdrawals from some details of complete domination through the encouragement of purchase of homes from the company, allowing some semblance of competition in retail trade, withdrawing detailed scrutiny of primary school curricula and instructional personnel, and so on.

The company town that in some respects stands at the opposite extreme from the community whose economic life is completely and exploitatively dominated by the company is the town seemingly established and managed out of mainly philanthropic considerations. Houses may be furnished that are well above the quality and well below the rental of the living accommodations of workers of similar type elsewhere. Local taxes borne by the ordinary citizen may be negligible or nonexistent, despite exceptional community services supplied by the company. Artistic and other "cultural" interests may be fostered, and in all such respects a "model" community established.

Whatever the outward diversity of the company town, which in a single state like Pennsylvania may range from the unpainted and unsanitary rows of boxes of the typical "coal camp" to the highly advertised beauties of Hershey, the fact of company domination gives a good deal of similarity to the types as a whole. It is not meant to minimize the differences with which the domination is displayed, the possible diversity of motives which prompt the domination, and certainly not the quite apparent differences in results. But neither is there any gainsaying the fact that local political action, freedom of organizational affiliation (including especially independent labor unionism), unbiased secular and perhaps even religious instruction, and indeed the whole range of so-called "civil liberties" are either completely denied or effectively curtailed.[10] Whether the motives are mixed or unmixed, that is, whether paternalism or simple exploitation is most evident, the company town makes of the local citizenry the relatively fortunate or relatively unfortunate vassals of feudal overlords. If the managers have (for whatever reason) a high degree of the "community responsibility" previously discussed, the community may exhibit a high degree of stability and ordered prosperity, at least until such time as the "ungrateful" recipents of managerial bounty attempt some independent political or economic action. But whether the management of the company town is frankly in the interests of the company or nominally in the interests of all, this is planned economy without any but the most remote and indirect accountability of the planners to

[10] In 1947 a Connecticut worker was allowed unemployment compensation after he was discharged by his employer for violating a company rule against fraternization of male and female employees after working hours. See *New York Times*, Wednesday, June 25, 1947, p. 8.

the bulk of the population affected by the planning. The company town in fact provides ready evidence with respect to the leadership of the community by industrial managers, and that evidence indicates that, although the character of the leadership varies, the line between leadership and outright domination is self-imposed and therefore thin.

One-Industry Towns and Cities. We may distinguish a class of communities widely variable in size, with heavy stakes in local industry but with considerable independence of communal life. At the one extreme these communities—usually the smaller ones—are not greatly different from the company town, with the same variation between benevolent or exploitative domination by the local enterprise. But however great may be the direct power of the company to give or withhold employment either individually or collectively (through closing or abandoning the plant), and its indirect influence based largely on that power, the machinery for independent political action may be used for challenging company supremacy. Moreover, the fact that the company does not "own the whole town" means that other economic as well as political and similar interests may assert themselves. Although the examples of such communities are widely scattered and fairly common, perhaps the highest concentration is still to be found in the mill towns of New England.

At the other extreme is the city such as Pittsburgh, which, together with the group of towns and cities comprising the Pittsburgh area, tends to be poor or prosperous in relation to the market for steel. Similarly, the Detroit area largely depends in peacetime on the market for automobiles. In both of these areas, and others that are similarly dependent on a single type of production, the policies and decisions of the various top-ranking managers may affect the daily lives of millions. Even in such metropolitan districts there is some tendency for local areas, such as Aliquippa, Pennsylvania, and Dearborn, Michigan, to be developed as "closed" communities approximating the company town. In other cases the preeminence of a single company with scattered branch plants throughout an industrial area, such as the United States Steel Corporation and subsidiaries in and about Pittsburgh, ensures fairly heavy influence in community life through the sheer weight of economic control. In still other cases, as with the group of rubber companies centered in Akron, the common interests of the major companies with respect to labor policies, favorable political officials, and so on may provide the basis for a kind of joint domination. In any single-industry city, however, the difficulties of maintaining a control as complete as that possible in the small community are well-nigh insurmountable. The typical urban heterogeneity of interests, the virtual impossibility of a strict and detailed surveillance of private lives, the possibility of independent political action—all mean that the economic dependence of the community may be real, but may be kept within limits as far as the remainder of communal life is concerned.[11]

The Industrial Metropolis. The direct dependence of the community as a whole upon the whims, interests, and fancies of industrial managers is obviously least where industry is diversified, or where other special-interest groups are sufficiently well organized and powerful to assert their independence. It follows that the direct dependence of communal life upon local industry is at a minimum in the industrially diversified city.

Yet the indirect dependence of the modern city upon industrialization in the broad sense is clear. Industrialism in its full institutional development gives rise to and in turn depends upon concentrations of population. A great deal of attention has been devoted to the series of "social problems" brought in the train of urbanization. These problems include housing, sanitation and public health, social control (negatively, the problems of crime and conflict), congestion and transportation, and the like. An additional volume of literature

---

[11] For descriptions of industry-community relations in various one-industry towns and cities, see C. W. M. Hart, "Industrial Relations Research and Social Theory," *Canadian Journal of Economics and Political Science,* 15: 53–73, February 1949 (especially emphasizes the role of unions in Windsor, Ontario); Alfred Winslow Jones, *Life, Liberty, and Property* (Philadelphia: J. B. Lippincott Company, 1941), especially Chap. II, "Early Akron," Chap. III, "The Rubber Industry," and Chap. IV, "Present Akron"; Robert S. Lynd and Helen Merrell Lynd, *Middletown* (New York: Harcourt, Brace and Company, 1929), Part II (Chaps. IV–VIII), "Getting a Living"; Ruth McKenney, *Industrial Valley* (New York: Harcourt, Brace and Company, 1939); Zimmerman, *op. cit.*

has been devoted to the pattern of urban growth, the tendency for the various activities of the community to concentrate in "zones," and the social characteristics of urban living. All these studies may be said to constitute a commentary upon the communal effects of industrialization. But it is noteworthy that relatively little attention has been devoted to the direct relations of industry to the urban community, and very little more to the significance of the fact that the growth and organization of the modern city have been more influenced by business interests than by any other combination of interests. We are not here arguing the relative merits of the urban or the rural way of life, but merely emphasizing that at least until very recently urban concentrations have been the necessary and direct products of highly specialized and large-scale industrial production, commerce, and trade. Whatever the narrower relations between industry and the community, an industrial civilization is an urban civilization, and in the present circumstances there seems to be little point in nostalgic pinings for the homely virtues of the isolated rural community.

Decentralization. The foregoing discussion does not, however, necessarily lead to the conclusion that greater and greater densities of urban population may be expected in the future. Rather the increased productivity of agriculture and the development of manufactured and synthetic foods, on the one hand, and the tendency toward industrial and residential decentralization on the other hand, point to a more even dispersion of the urban industrial population. As already implied, the movement toward decentralization rests in part upon technological changes, including new methods, new products, and, especially, new developments in transportation and communication. Yet the new technology is partly in answer to demands for solution of the various "social problems" arising from urban concentration. It represents, in a sense, a declaration of independence from the factory as the literal center of the community. Thus in all large metropolitan districts there are to be found "bedroom suburbs," which are, in effect, communities without visible means of support. The various publicly and privately sponsored suburban housing projects have recently emphasized the divorce of communal activities from the mill, rather than the integration of life about the place of employment.[12] There are, indeed, enthusiasts for taking industry into the remoter hinterlands and combining industrial employment with the security of part-time farming, although the prospects for widespread decentralization of precisely this sort are not very great.[13]

The well-known development of "satellite communities" on the outskirts of established urban centers represents in a certain sense the older tendency toward concentration, yet many of these communities retain some semblance of the more isolated industrial communities of similar size. They do, however, inevitably share in at least part of the near-by urban organization, and this tends to make the local residents much less completely dependent on the local industrial and business establishments.[14]

The forms of industrial decentralization are so numerous, and its possible future forms so much more numerous, that it is difficult to characterize the communities resulting from this process by a single formula. Part of the movement of industrial plants from urban centers has been for the purpose of reestablishing managerial dominance over employees and the community, as we shall note below. On the other hand, considerable residential mobility has taken place to avoid at least the more visible domination of the community by factory smokestacks.

Migratory Industry: Boom Towns and Ghost Towns. The significance of industry for the economic life of the community, and the effects of fairly rapid changes in industrial activity upon the character of the population dependent upon that activity, are perhaps most startlingly

[12] See Earl E. Muntz, *Urban Sociology* (New York: The Macmillan Company, 1938), Chap. X, "Garden Suburbs, Villages, and Cities."

[13] See Carter Goodrich, *et. al.*, *Migration and Economic Opportunity* (Philadelphia: University of Pennsylvania Press, 1936), pp. 382–392, 618–659; United States National Resources Committee, *The Problems of a Changing Population* (Washington: U. S. Government Printing Office, 1938), Sec. II, "Regional Distribution of Economic Opportunity," especially pp. 71–73.

[14] See Leon Carroll Marshall [ed.], *Readings in Industrial Society* (Chicago: University of Chicago Press, 1918), Chap. X, "Concentration," especially pp. 668–682 ("C. The Modern Industrial and Commercial City"); Rhyne, *op. cit.*, Chap. VI, "A Suburban Mill Village."

illustrated by so-called "boom towns" and "ghost towns." So much attention has been paid to the problems of migratory labor that the transiency and mortality of industrial establishments have been somewhat neglected.

Migratory industries are likely to be those characterized by high labor costs and low capital investment and relatively minor transportation difficulties. Such establishments are relatively free to move about the country in quest of cheap and submissive labor. These conditions have been notably prevalent in the garment trades, where mobility was great until limited by collective bargaining agreements,[15] and to a lesser extent in the textile industry as a whole. Other factors that lead to the mobility or mortality of industries include: competition and technological change (for example, the loss of factories in New England supplying wooden body parts for automobiles with the introduction of all-steel bodies, and the closing of hand rolling mills in the steel industry with the introduction of continuous strip mills); the exhaustion of resources (especially notable in mining and lumbering); and activities that are by nature temporary (such as the boom towns that develop around public construction projects like the Grand Coulee dam and will become close to ghost towns after the project is completed).

Although boom towns are customarily associated with discovery of oil or gold, or some other spectacular event, the establishment of any industrial activity in an area without previous industrial employment or with a working population much smaller than that required by the new activities will create for at least a short time the conditions of a boom town. The boom town is typically characterized by underhousing; absence or inadequacy of water, sewage disposal, and similar public utilities; price inflation; and inability of law enforcement agencies to keep up with a growing and heterogeneous community, at least some of whose members have been attracted precisely by the profitable possibilities of crime.

The tremendous expansion of industrial production during the

---

[15] See "Notes: Legal Problems Raised by the Relocation of Industry: Runaway Shops," *Columbia Law Review*, 36: 776–794, May 1936; Dubinsky *v.* Blue Dale Dress Co., 292 N.Y.S. 898 (1936).

second World War resulted in turning previously stable industrial communities into suddenly overgrown beehives of activity and in the appearance of other boom towns where only farm lands existed before. Such rapid establishment or expansion of a community inevitably raises all of the problems noted, as well as that of preventing excessive population (and employment) turnover arising from the unsatisfactory conditions prevailing in the community.[16]

The establishment during the second World War of communities at Hanford, Washington, and Oak Ridge, Tennessee, for the manufacture of atomic bombs and subsequently for other aspects of atomic energy posed problems not only of the "boom town" but of the "company town" as well. Because of the high importance of secrecy of the processes involved in nuclear fission, the communities so established were not only subject to the "domination" of the employer (in effect, the government) to a marked degree, but were essentially closed communities. Even with the establishment of considerable community freedom, "security" considerations continued to affect community composition and social life.

The boom town has the possible advantage of widespread optimism—which may be partly unfounded—and certainly many of its problems are temporary: they exist until such time as the rate of business expansion subsides sufficiently to allow the machinery of the community to catch up. The plight of the town abandoned by its economic support is not so easy. If it seeks to avoid becoming a complete ghost town it must seek to attract new industry, take over the abandoned plants and operate them communally, or, possibly, settle back to a life dependent upon agricultural trade. The remaining residents of a community fast becoming a ghost town must face the prospect of an almost daily curtailment of community activities and services, and loss of familiar patterns of social relationships. These losses are of course in addition to losses of income, decline in property values, and similar economic disadvantages.

[16] See United States Senate, Special Committee Investigating the National Defense Program, *Investigation of the National Defense Program, Hearings* . . . (Washington: U. S. Government Printing Office, 1942), Part 12, pp. 5250–5281, 5373–5413.

Although some of the more famous ghost towns resulting from the abandonment of Western mining operations have been widely publicized in the popular magazines, few serious studies of the actual process of community collapse have been undertaken. Studies of the fairly long-range decline of industrial centers through shifts in markets and industrial location give some indication of the adjustments required in such communities,[17] but do not of course reveal the more drastic adjustments occasioned by the relatively sudden and complete abandonment of the community by industry.[18]

Migratory industry and communities resulting from industrial mobility illustrate two principles of the usual relations between industry and the community: (1) community and industrial interests are interdependent but by no means identical, and (2) although industrial location and activity tend to be determined on grounds independent of community interests, this is rarely completely possible, and in any event the structure and activity of the community are basically affected by industrial policies. The assertion of nonindustrial interests has been primarily local in character, and therefore highly unequal in strength or effectiveness. The modification of industrial privileges through state and national legislation, to be reviewed in a subsequent chapter, has certainly affected the position of industry in the community, but has so far reduced by very little the rather wide range of industrial community types discussed in this chapter.

REFERENCES

ARENSBERG, CONRAD M., "Industry and the Community," *American Journal of Sociology*, 48: 1–12, July 1942.

[17] See MacDonald, *Labor Problems and the American Scene*, Chap. IV, "Declining Towns and Cities."

[18] For a description of the situation in New Castle, Pa., a steel town virtually abandoned by industry through the closing of an old-style hand rolling mill, see Harold J. Ruttenberg and Stanley Ruttenberg, "War and the Steel Ghost Towns," *Harper's Magazine*, 180: 147–155, January 1940. See also United States Congress, Temporary National Economic Committee, *Investigation of Concentration of Economic Power, Hearings . . .* , Part 30, "Technology and Concentration of Economic Power" (Washington: U. S. Government Printing Office, 1940), pp. 16469–16474, 17332–17339. (The latter pages contain a reprint of part of the Ruttenbergs' article.)

BOULWARE, L. R., "The Business Leader's Larger Job," in Marvin Bower, ed., *The Development of Executive Leadership* (Cambridge: Harvard University Press, 1949), pp. 46–69.

BRADY, ROBERT A., *Business as a System of Power* (New York: Columbia University Press, 1943), Chap. VIII, "Social Policies: Status, Trusteeship, Harmony," especially pp. 259–274.

BREESE, GERALD W., *The Daytime Population of the Central Business District of Chicago* (Chicago: University of Chicago Press, 1949).

CHAMBER OF COMMERCE OF THE UNITED STATES, Department of Manufacture, *Special Inducements to Industries* (Washington, 1931).

DIMOCK, MARSHALL E., and HOWARD K. HYDE, "Bureaucracy and Trusteeship in Large Corporations," United States Congress, Temporary National Economic Committee, *Investigation of Concentration of Economic Power, Monograph No. 11* (Washington: U. S. Government Printing Office, 1940), Part IV, "The Implications of Trusteeship."

GILFILLAN, LAUREN, *I Went to Pit College* (New York: The Literary Guild, 1934). This book is an excellent description of small company towns in the coal region.

GOODRICH, CARTER, *et. al.*, *Migration and Economic Opportunity* (Philadelphia: University of Pennsylvania Press, 1936), Chap. VII, "The Changing Pattern of Industrial Location."

GREEN, CONSTANCE MCLAUGHLIN, *Holyoke, Massachusetts: A Case History of the Industrial Revolution in America* (New Haven: Yale University Press, 1939).

HANNAY, AGNES, *A Chronicle of Industry on the Mill River*, Smith College Studies in History, Vol. 21, Nos. 1–4, October 1935–July 1936 (Northampton, Mass.: Smith College). See especially Chap. VII, "Labor under Local Enterprise."

HART, C. W. M., "Industrial Relations Research and Social Theory," *Canadian Journal of Economics and Political Science*, 15: 53–73, February 1949.

HERRING, HARRIET L., *Passing of the Mill Village: Revolution in a Southern Institution* (Chapel Hill: University of North Carolina Press, 1949).

HOOVER, EDGAR M., *The Location of Economic Activity* (New York: McGraw-Hill Book Company, Inc., 1948).

——, *Location Theory and the Shoe and Leather Industries* (Cambridge: Harvard University Press, 1937), Part I (Chaps. I–VI), "The Theory of Location."

JONES, ALFRED WINSLOW, *Life, Liberty, and Property* (Philadelphia: J. B.

Lippincott Company, 1941). See especially Chap. II, "Early Akron"; Chap. III, "The Rubber Industry"; Chap. IV, "Present Akron."

LAHNE, HERBERT J., *The Cotton Mill Worker* (New York: Farrar and Rinehart, 1944), Chap. 3, "The New England Mill Village," and Chap. 4, "The Southern Mill Village."

LANDIS, PAUL, "The Life Cycle of the Iron Mining Town," *Social Forces,* 13: 245–256, December 1934.

LIEPMANN, KATE, K., *The Journey to Work* (New York: Oxford University Press, 1944).

LUMPKIN, KATHARINE DU PRE, and MABEL V. COMBS, *Shutdowns in the Connecticut Valley: A Study of Worker Displacement in the Small Industrial Community,* Smith College Studies in History, Vol. 19, Nos. 3–4, April–July 1934 (Northampton, Mass.: Smith College).

LUNDBERG, GEORGE A., *Marketing and Social Organization,* Charles Coolidge Parlin Memorial Lecture (Philadelphia: privately printed, 1945).

LYND, ROBERT S., and HELEN MERRELL LYND, *Middletown* (New York: Harcourt, Brace and Company, 1929), Part II (Chaps. IV–VIII), "Getting a Living."

LYND, ROBERT S., and HELEN MERRELL LYND, *Middletown in Transition* (New York: Harcourt, Brace and Company, 1937), Chap. II, "Getting a Living"; Chap. III, "The X Family: A Pattern of Business-Class Control."

MACDONALD, LOIS, *Labor Problems and the American Scene* (New York: Harper & Brothers, 1938), Chap. III, "Workers in Cities and Middletowns"; Chap. IV, "Declining Towns and Cities"; Chap. V, "Company Towns: Coal Camps"; Chap. VI, "Company Towns: Textile Mill Villages."

———, *Southern Mill Hills* (New York: Alex L. Hillman, 1928).

MARSHALL, LEON CARROLL, ed., *Readings in Industrial Society* (Chicago: University of Chicago Press, 1918), Chap. X, "Concentration," especially pp. 668–682 ("C. The Modern Industrial and Commercial City").

McKENNY, RUTH, *Industrial Valley* (New York: Harcourt, Brace and Company, 1939).

MILLS, C. WRIGHT, and MELVILLE J. ULMER, *Small Business and Civic Welfare,* Report of the Smaller War Plants Corporation to the Special Committee to Study Problems of American Small Business, United States Senate, 79th Congress, 2nd Session, Document No. 135 (Washington: U. S. Government Printing Office, 1946).

MOSHER, WILLIAM E., "The Social and Civic Responsibilities of the Profession of Business Management," in Henry C. Metcalf, ed., *Business*

Management as a Profession (Chicago: A. W. Shaw Company, 1927), pp. 202–214.

MUNTZ, EARL E., *Urban Sociology* (New York: The Macmillan Company, 1938), Chap. III, "Ground Plan and Physical Growth of Cities"; Chap. IV, "City Growth through Natural Increase and Rural Migration"; Chap. VII, "The Urban Housing Problem"; Chap. VIII, "Improved Housing under Private Auspicies"; Chap. X, "Garden Suburbs, Villages, and Cities."

PARKER, MARGARET TERRELL, *Lowell: A Study of Industrial Development* (New York: The Macmillan Company, 1940).

(Political and Economic Planning), *The Location of Industry* (London: PEP, 1939).

POPE, LISTON, *Millhands and Preachers: A Study of Gastonia* (New Haven: Yale University Press, 1942).

RHYNE, JENNINGS, *Some Southern Cotton Mill Workers and Their Villages* (Chapel Hill: University of North Carolina Press, 1930).

SHELDON, OLIVER, *The Philosophy of Management* (London: Sir Isaac Pitman & Sons, Inc., 1924), Chap. III, "The Social Responsibilities of Management."

SHEPPARD, MURIEL EARLEY, *Cloud by Day: The Story of Coal and Coke and People* (Chapel Hill: University of North Carolina Press, 1947).

SHLAKMAN, VERA, *Economic History of a Factory Town: A Study of Chicopee, Massachusetts,* Smith College Studies in History, Vol. 20, Nos. 1–4, October 1934–July 1935 (Northampton, Mass.: Smith College).

SLICHTER, SUMNER H., "The Problems of Business Leadership in a Laboristic Economy," in Marvin Bower, ed., *The Development of Executive Leadership* (Cambridge: Harvard University Press, 1949), pp. 3–27.

WARNER, W. LLOYD, and J. O. Low, *The Social System of the Modern Factory; The Strike: A Social Analysis* (New Haven: Yale University Press, 1947), Chap. IV, "From Clippers to Textiles to Shoes."

WEBER, ALFRED, *Theory of the Location of Industries,* tr. by Carl J. Friedrich (Chicago: University of Chicago Press, 1929).

WHITEHEAD, T. N., *Leadership in a Free Society* (Cambridge: Harvard University Press, 1937), Chap. XII, "The Organization of a Community," and pp. 253–259.

WOLFBEIN, SEYMOUR LOUIS, *The Decline of a Cotton Textile City: A Study of New Bedford* (New York: Columbia University Press, 1944).

ZIMMERMAN, CARLE C., *The Changing Community* (New York: Harper & Brothers, 1938). Chaps. VIII–XV and XVII–XXIV comprise a series of "case studies" of New England communities, in each of which the role of industry in community life is indicated. See especially Chap. IX, "Lonely's Belligerency"; Chap. X, "Utopia's Belligerency"; Chap. XIII, "Nudeal's Planned Life Organization"; Chap. XV, "Babbitt's Bourgeois Life Organization"; Chaps. XX–XXI, "Zenith's Industrial Tolerance."

CHAPTER XXIII

SOCIAL CLASSES AND THE INDUSTRIAL ORDER

THE PRECEDING chapter outlined various modes of relationship between industrial organizations and the communities in which they are located. The industrial community, it was pointed out, represents the relationship between industry and society in its most concrete and obvious form. A different range of problems arises with reference to the place of the productive order in the status system of society. In the most general terms, this may be phrased as the question: What significance does modern industrial organization have for social classes? We propose to answer that question in this chapter. More specifically, we are faced with three central issues: (1) the nature of social class, (2) the role of the industrial order in the class structure, and (3) the dynamic relations between classes in the sense of the factors determining harmony or conflict among the several social strata. As a whole, these issues have a direct bearing on contemporary discussion about industrial relations and social stability. Our examination should provide a groundwork of facts on a subject currently characterized by widely differing opinions.

THE NATURE OF SOCIAL CLASS

As a starting point for distinguishing this type of social differentiation from other methods of determining general social position, and as an introduction to the criteria of class membership, we may quote a satisfactory definition from a recent general text in sociology:

568

. . . classes are inclusive, loosely organized groupings whose members behave toward each other as social equals and toward outsiders as social superiors and inferiors, and who as individuals either stay in the group to which they are born, or rise or fall to different levels depending upon the way their social attributes correspond to the values around which the particular class system is organized.[1]

We may first consider the values that are used as the basis for determining class membership as a prelude to determining the lines of demarcation that separate one class from another.

Criteria of Class Membership. If one were to ask an American college student upon what distinctions one should place chief emphasis in determining higher or lower position in a community or the entire society, the first response would very likely be "wealth or income." This judgment is by no means insignificant, for it is upon the basis of many judgments of this sort that relative class position is to be determined. Wealth and income are certainly widely accepted indexes of general social position, not only among American college students, but as indicated by various official and unofficial studies and surveys which divide the population into income groups, or such categories as wealthy, well-to-do, comfortable, poor, and so on. But a little further questioning will reveal that wealth is by no means regarded as the sole criterion of class status. One must at least add how the wealth or income is acquired, and how it is used or spent. Thus low-paid school teachers rank above high-paid mechanics, or in an industrial plant, low-paid clerical workers often rank above high-paid "operatives" in the shops. Moreover, income is not necessarily spent for the appropriate symbols of social status, so that the well-paid lumberman or miner may spend his entire paycheck in riotous living every Saturday night and thus have nothing to "show" for his money.[2]

The significant variation of even such a thing as "property" is thus

---

[1] From Robert L. Sutherland and Julian L. Woodward, *Introductory Sociology*, 3d ed. (Philadelphia: J. B. Lippincott Company, 1948), p. 368. Italics in original omitted.

[2] The high importance of symbols of class status, particularly conspicuous consumption, leisure, and waste, has been noted in the classic work of Thorstein Veblen, *The Theory of the Leisure Class* (New York: B. W. Huebsch, 1918).

not limited to the quantitative range. In any society, and especially in ours, there is likely to be a difference between the quantitative variation in property values or cost, and the qualitative worth of valuable things as symbols of status. For example, a Cape of Good Hope triangular postage stamp may cost more than a new automobile, but gives its owner considerably less prestige among his neighbors who do not collect stamps.

But ranking does not stop even here. Especially in a relatively small community where many types of knowledge about one's neighbors are possible, one may also have to take into account one or more of the following: formal education; family respectability; relative authority; circle of acquaintances; and formal associational affiliations, including church, fraternal organizations, recreational clubs, and service groups.

In short, the criteria of class membership or general social position amount to any bases of differential valuation that are part of the value system of the society.[3] These do not, in an open-class society, constitute a homogeneous or completely interdependent system. In other words, each of these modes of valuation is to a marked degree an *independent* variable.[4] This makes it impossible to determine the individual's relative position in terms of any one of the variables and then predict with any degree of exactness his position with regard to the others. Given a certain income level, for example, all the other appropriate criteria of high or low class status do not necessarily follow. A person may earn a large income in an approved occupation, and spend it for furs, automobiles, and symphony tickets, yet be excluded from full membership in upper class circles by reason of nationality, religion, lack of appropriate man-

[3] The statement that any mode of differential valuation constitutes a criterion of class status is perhaps too broad. Notably, it neglects two important bases of distinction which partly coincide with, partly cut across class lines. Those two are age and sex, which are universally used for drawing lines within society. We shall note in a subsequent section of this chapter that age and sex qualifications tend to be assumed in class differentiation.

[4] The discussion here deals with the determinants of individual class affiliation. We shall note subsequently that for the community as a whole there is a significant grouping of variables around wealth and occupation as primary determinants in general class structure.

ners and etiquette, or other similar shortcomings. Thus the precision of the grouping decreases as more standards are taken into account. Only within a single organization, or with reference to a single value or interest, are very exact judgments possible. Thus it is very difficult to compare the social status of a leading university president and an outstanding entertainer. Usually a further question must be asked: upon what grounds of comparison? The judgment will certainly vary according to the values or symbols used.

Further difficulties in classification arise from the fact that, at least in reference to the more significant and widely accepted bases of social distinction, each scale is pretty much of a continuum, from bottom to top. Thus again drawing lines is likely to be arbitrary in "border-line" cases. For example, in what meaningful sense does a person without dependents who earns an annual salary of $2400 belong to a lower class than a person with several dependents who receives $2500 annually?

To determine an individual's generalized social status is thus likely to involve a quasi-statistical procedure. In this, two distinct types of information are necessary: (1) the individual's relative position on each of the several scales of differential valuation, and (2) the relative weight that the community or society attaches to each of these modes of valuation.

Thus, one might define an individual's (or family's) general social position as a weighted average of the scale values on each of the bases of differential valuation.

A number of difficulties arise from such an approach to the problem of social class:

1. It depends upon facts not easily obtainable. This is particularly true with regard to the weighting system, since the semiindependent character of the several modes of valuation means that they are usually treated separately, not comparatively.

2. Since comparison of social position is actually made by members of society at any one time only in reference to *part* of the various modes of valuation, the weighted average referred to is likely to be unduly abstract—that is, have no particular relevance for modes of behavior, attitudes, prestige, esteem, and so on.

It is not the observer who makes the valuations, or determines relative weights. The observer therefore has no authority to insist that the community ought to be consistent, or that the generalized social position arrived at by the inductive manipulation should correspond to the community's treatment of the individual so ranked.

The foregoing remarks concerning the difficulty of determining precisely the criteria of class membership indicate the wisdom of the tests indicated in the definition quoted above: the test of treating others as equals, superiors, or inferiors. Thus such highly important symbols of equality as marriage, and informal social relationships such as entertaining guests and acceptance into a particular circle of acquaintances, indicate common class membership. When such tests are lacking, resort to some more limited and more arbitrary criteria is necessary, but is likely to reduce the significance of the demarcations made.

Levels of Class Analysis. The problem of the "operational" definition of social class is considerably clarified if three distinct levels or contexts are recognized. (1) The first is stratification in the "mass society," that is, cutting across the social system as a whole. This is usually what is meant by social class, in the sense of "upper, middle, and lower," or "business and working." Now the fact that the categories must account for the entire population, and must presumably not be dependent upon all sorts of local judgment and variations in standards, means that criteria of membership must be few and closely interdependent. If the "operational" definition is built up upon the basis of judgments of prestige throughout the system, it appears that a more or less stratified order results, but not necessarily a *class* system. This is because occupation is of crucial importance in judgments that relate to the status of persons in the system as a whole, but occupations are more readily compared within fairly distinct "families" of jobs than between them.[5] If the criterion of class membership is essentially the behavioral one indicated at the beginning of the chapter, then obviously there are

[5] See Paul K. Hatt, "Occupation and Social Stratification," *American Journal of Sociology*, 55: 533–543, May 1950; Hatt, "Stratification in the Mass Society," *American Sociological Review*, 15: 216–222, April 1950.

few ways in which people not brought into contact by occupation or residence can behave in *any* way relevant to equality and inequality. In so far as strictly *class* phenomena exist in the society at large, therefore, they are likely to be represented in collective relations and oriented around symbols. Part of management-union relations and of national political behavior are of this sort. But it should be noted that where there is widespread freedom of association, cleavages do not necessarily follow a single line. The result is that "class" at this level may perhaps be identified by certain procedures without being a membership group or constituting the most significant segment of the society for all purposes.

(2) The second level is that of the neighborhood or community. This is the level of description that accounts for the greater part of the recent literature on American social stratification.[6] Here it is possible to build up a representation of a "class system" upon the basis of the statistical probability of various types of memberships and informal social relations and activities, and possibly simplify these by virtue of their intercorrelations. But since here contact does occur and more can be known about any individual or family, more criteria of valuation are typically taken into account. Thus the studies made in "typical" American communities lead to the identification of sectors of the population as "classes" only as a result of the particular procedures used. There is nothing methodologically wrong with this, as long as the partial populations are not then considered to be real membership groups with divisions more fundamental than would be yielded by some other procedure. Thus various studies have concluded that there are five, six, or nine "classes" in the community reported. Other procedures might yield a quite different number.

There are two further limitations on the legitimate inferences that

---

[6] See, for example, August B. Hollingshead, *Elmtown's Youth: The Impace of Social Classes on Adolescents* (New York: John P. Wiley and Sons, 1949); W. Lloyd Warner and Others, *Social Class in America* (Chicago: Science Research Associates, 1949). For criticisms of this approach, see Hatt, "Stratification in the Mass Society," previously cited; Harold W. Pfautz and Otis Dudley Duncan, "A Critical Evaluation of Warner's Work in Community Stratification," *American Sociological Review*, 15: 205–215, April 1950.

may be drawn from studies of stratification in the single community. The first limitation is that an increasing proportion of the population lives in large urban centers, which are not necessarily made up of neighborhoods that duplicate the small community. In the city, stratification phenomena approach those of the mass society, not those of "community reputation." The second limitation is akin to the first. Stratification in the society as a whole is not made up of community segments, like building blocks. As the context of inter-action and social valuation is more limited and oriented around such criteria as have a significance throughout the social system, stratification in the mass society is to a high degree in terms of rela-tively simple stereotypes as compared with the social system of the small community.

(3) Finally, many stratification phenomena relate to position within formally organized associations, and especially those associa-tions that constitute a livelihood for their members. Here more gradations may be taken into account than are commonly attributed to the class system even at the community level, but the formal criteria are rather clear and precise. Other elements of evaluation enter, but as variations of the established prestige scale in the or-ganization.

Occupational position accordingly may be of primary importance in all three levels of the phenomenon of stratification, but in dif-ferent ways and in different contexts.

The Number of Classes. The actual complexity of the criteria of class membership has a further significance, for it reveals the dif-ficulty of determining the number of classes in our society. Many people, it is true, are at no loss to tell how many classes exist in American society—there are three: upper, middle, and lower. It is, in fact, a common practice to divide any range of continuous varia-tion into the two extremes and the middle. But it must be empha-sized that this is a purely arbitrary division, and the lines are almost impossible to discover. Some authorities, finding that by any avail-able method of grouping a threefold classification yields groupings that are too heterogeneous to be at all significant, have distin-guished nine classes. That is, they proceed from "upper upper" and "middle upper" down to "middle lower" and "lower lower." Here again, however, the basis of distinction is likely to be either very thin, or not significantly related to other aspects of differential valuation.

The number of classes yielded by any method of demarcation will vary not only with how finely the distinctions are drawn, but also with the point of comparison chosen. Wealth, for example, yields any desired number of distinctions, whereas a division according to the possession of at least one college degree would yield only two groups. As in all scientific classifications, the first test ought to be pragmatic. The utility of any one method of classification is enhanced if it indicates other distinctions at the same time —that is, if it serves as an *index*. We shall examine one such index.

Occupation as a Basis for Class Distinctions. Among the various more limited and therefore more arbitrary criteria of class status, position in the economic productive order—"occupation" in the broadest sense—has been given the greatest attention by those attempting to deal with the subject.[7] The choice of this line of social cleavage is prompted by a number of considerations:

1. Occupation combines to a fairly high degree a number of the more important criteria of class membership. Thus gradations in wealth and income are ideally closely related to occupational position and achievement, and in fact the correspondence is rough but important. Although even less closely related, there is a notable tendency for the level and type of living, that is, what income is spent for, to follow occupational lines. The same correspondence is to be observed in regard to common interests (which are much more likely to follow occupational interests than merely common income levels) and social affiliations, including intermarriage.

2. As a partial explanation of the preceding general point, it may

---

[7] Much of the literature in the field stems directly or indirectly from the position taken by Marx and Marxians. Marx himself wrote very little on class analysis, and that little is widely scattered. (See references to Marx listed at the end of this chapter.) As developed by his followers, the Marxian analysis of class is not unimportant, but its extreme emphasis on a twofold division into owners and producers is of doubtful scientific utility in general, and certainly tangential to the issues raised in the present chapter.

be noted that to a large degree the primary criterion of social status in our society is the economic worth of the individual. This is most clearly seen, of course, in the idea that the impersonal market rewards the efficiency and industry of the individual enterpriser. It is to be observed in unconscious caricature in the not uncommon remark that "Businessman X must be worth close to $100,000." But the emphasis upon reward for useful labor is a basic part of our culture even in regard to occupations not so neatly rewarded by the operation of the market. In fact, one of our most frequent, and usually the first, method of placing a person in social space is to determine what he (or the breadwinner responsible for his support) does for a living.

3. In view of the two preceding considerations, it is understandable that shifting occupational position has been the chief avenue of class mobility. This is, as we shall see, significant in two respects: the factual possibility (or impossibility) of status mobility by means of occupational ladders, and the general conviction that the possibility is real and extensive, whatever the "facts."

4. A consideration of a different order, but none the less significant, is that data concerning occupational distribution and occupational mobility are available and more readily utilizable than are other types of information concerning class divisions.

OCCUPATIONAL DISTRIBUTION

Out of the immense variety of occupations in a society characterized by a minute division of labor, certain occupational groups stand out because of general similarity in type of work, level of skill demanded, and roughly equal social evaluation. Although again it must be emphasized that by reference to any specific component of social status there will be a good deal of overlapping between occupational groups, the principal categories are socially recognized as sufficiently distinct to imply general similarity within the group greater than similarities that include two or more groups.

Principal Occupational Categories. With these considerations in mind, we may note seven principal occupational categories that are of significance in general social status, and which therefore will provide a basis for determining the relationships between industry and the open-class system. The seven groups, roughly in order of their general status, are: (1) professionals, (2) proprietors and officials, (3) farmers (owners and tenants), (4) low-salaried workers, (5) wage earners, (6) servants, and (7) farm laborers. To repeat, such a classification is not meant to deny or completely to overlook the more or less definite gradations within each group, or the very real possibility of overlapping, so that in particular cases other criteria of social evaluation would have to be taken into account. Neither is it meant to imply that these groups represent a continuous gradation in the sense of possibly constituting stages in a single career. It is, on the contrary, evident that the divisions are to a certain extent *functional,* and thus represent different systems of gradation.[8] For example, one line of ascent might be that of farm laborer, to tenant, to owner. In the industrial hierarchy, strictly speaking, it is often convenient to divide wage earners into the unskilled, semiskilled, and skilled. The succeeding stages in this line would then be low-salaried worker and proprietor or official. It is interesting that, with reference to the professionals, there is no definite line of occupational ascent, but rather entrance is chiefly by means of special education and training. Nor is there any widely recognized step that follows domestic service. This probably indicates a lack of general cultural support for menial service as an

[8] The difficulty of ranking various occupational categories in order of general superiority and inferiority arises again from the problem of the criteria of social valuation. "Occupation" itself is not a simple criterion. Most lists, including the one here used, tend to confuse a number of points of comparison. These points of comparison which are "hidden variables" in occupational classification include ownership status, degree of skill required (which is about the same as saying "scarcity value"), the industry within which the occupation is found or character of the services rendered, and so on. Age distinctions may even be included, since the length of training necessary for some positions produces a higher average age of persons in those occupations. Sex distinctions are most certainly assumed, due to the minor occupational role of women, even at the present time. Since each of these occupational groups has its own internal gradations, and since the "hidden variables" will not operate equally in all cases, there will of course be some overlapping in general social position. However, the tendency for persons in the higher groups to remain occupationally active until a later age than the others introduces a time element into social valuation. Thus a low-ranking but young industrial official or professional will be judged not only on present position but on future promise.

avenue of social advancement. In general, both status comparisons and actual avenues of mobility are more appropriate within than between these categories.[9]

Granting the limitations noted, the classification here adopted represents a convenient division of our population according to approximate "rank order" in society. How these divisions compare in size and proportion of the total labor force may be seen from Table 4. This represents a considerable shift from the occupational distribution in 1880, as indicated in the same table. Notable in this shift has been the great reduction in the proportion of farmers of all types, indicating the well-known fact of increased urbanization and industrialization during this period, and the proportionally even greater increase of low-salaried workers. This latter movement is not so often recognized, but conforms with what we know concerning the tremendous growth of industrial bureaucracy, with the corresponding increase in the "white-collar" class of employees.

Aside from the significant increase of strictly industrial classes, however, a number of critical problems arise in reference to the selection of the membership of these classes and the chances, ideal and actual, for individual workers to "get ahead in the world." A consideration of occupational class mobility will therefore form the concluding section of this chapter.

OCCUPATIONAL MOBILITY AND THE OPEN–CLASS IDEOLOGY

If we now recall the definition of social classes previously quoted, we shall note the emphasis placed upon the three alternatives in regard to the stability of an individual's class position: he may stay in the class in which he is born, he may rise, or he may fall, according to the way he as an individual measures up to the general criteria of class membership and therefore of general social evalu-

---

[9] Hatt, in "Occupation and Social Stratification," previously cited, reports the following "families" of occupations, upon the basis of prestige ratings by a national sample of the American population: political, professional, business, recreation and aesthetics, agriculture, manual work, military service. The results of this study do not support a ranking of these families, but only of occupations within these categories.

TABLE 4 *Proportional Distribution of Occupational Classes in the Classified Employable Population, 1880 and 1940* [a]

Occupational Class	1880 (%)	1940 (%)
Professionals	4.2	7.1
Proprietors and Officials	5.1	7.9
Farmers (Owners and Tenants)	26.8	10.6
Low-Salaried Workers	3.3	16.6
Wage Earners	33.1	39.8
Servants	6.7	11.0
Farm Laborers	20.8	7.0

[a] Percentages for 1880 computed from census figures summarized in T. M. Sogge, "Industrial Classes in the United States in 1930," *Journal of the American Statistical Association,* 28: 199–203, June 1933. The 1940 percentages were computed from figures given in the Sixteenth Census, 1940, P-11 Series, Summary, June 9, 1942. In both cases the "Unclassified" employables were omitted from the computation.

ation. A class system, or open-class system, is chiefly differentiated from other methods of social stratification in that mobility, up or down, is possible and considered appropriate.[10] We may accordingly examine the general assumptions and ideals which underlie the American open-class system and then see how it works "in fact."

The Open-Class Ideology. Much of what may be called the ideology of the open-class system is included in the general features of the "culture of capitalism," with its emphasis on the role of the individual entrepreneur as the ideal, and presumably typical, example of individual initiative and achievement. Those who started in inferior positions might reasonably aspire to such independence, if they had the initial ability and played the game hard and fairly.

Primary among the assumptions of the open-class system is that

[10] The opposite extreme from the open-class system is the caste system, typified by the social stratification in India, but also approached to a significant degree in American Negro-white differentiation. For a schematic summary of the differences in the extreme types of stratification, together with the intermediate type of "estate" arrangement, see Max Weber, *Wirtschaft und Gesellschaft* (Tübingen: G. C. B. Mohr, 1925), pp. 177–180, 631–641. See also Kingsley Davis, "A Conceptual Analysis of Stratification," *American Sociological Review,* 7: 309–321, June 1942.

of *equality of opportunity.* The emphasis upon social judgment of the individual presupposes that no prejudice, that is, prejudgment, will stand in the way of his aspirations. Given equality of opportunity, the individual is expected to take part in an impersonal competition for social status within well-understood rules. In the most general terms, that social status is to be determined in accordance with *known* criteria of particular qualities and valued achievements, in addition to possessions and authority viewed as following from the first two.[11] It should be noted again that there is a general tendency to find a uniform measuring stick in terms of economic worth. It emphasizes the independent individual, and rewards those individuals who are frugal, industrious, and therefore virtuous. Negatively, the ideology of the open-class system assumes that no barriers will be placed on free mobility in the occupational structure according to ability. Positively, and as a consequence of the foregoing assumptions, *it assumes that every individual occupies that position in the occupational hierarchy which he of a right ought to occupy.* This accounts for the persistent "survival" from Puritanism of the close connection between poverty and sin. Not only is poverty in this system of ideas a cause of sin, or even a result of sin, but it comes close to *being* sin.[12]

We shall discuss below the importance of this system of values and basic conceptions concerning the nature of the social order. But in order to place this subsequent treatment in its proper setting, we must first examine certain "facts of the situation." Primarily we shall face the question: How accurately does the ideology of the open-class system reflect the actual situation in regard to equality of opportunity, impartiality of competition and judgment, and freedom of occupational mobility?

[11] See Talcott Parsons, "An Analytical Approach to the Theory of Social Stratification," *American Journal of Sociology,* 45: 841–862, May 1940.

[12] Perhaps the most elaborate and forceful exposition of the ideology of individualism and the open-class system is that of the early Yale sociologist, William Graham Sumner. See his *What Social Classes Owe to Each Other* (New Haven: Yale University Press, 1934, first published 1883). For the ideology as expressed by the residents of an American city in the 1930's, see Robert S. Lynd and Helen Merrell Lynd, *Middletown in Transition* (New York: Harcourt, Brace and Company, 1937), pp. 46, 406–410.

Facts of the Case. The first set of facts that strike one in regard to the assumptions of the open-class ideology is the notable *inequality* of opportunity that prevails in actual occupational competition and stratification. Nor can all of these inequalities be set aside as exceptional, or even as unethical departures from the ideal. Inequalities of this latter type would include such things as favoritism and nepotism, or the more indirect importance of family connections and "pull." But there are in addition more basic barriers to equality, which are structural and institutional in nature. Notable among the institutional forces that account for occupational rigidity are those associated with the economic position of the family, and its role in status-fixing and socialization. This includes (1) inequalities arising from inheritance of property, (2) differential access to the avenues of social welfare and occupational advantage through existing inequalities in family income, and (3) the general transferral to the children of the propensities, outlook, and culture of the father's occupation or occupational category.[13] There are also various structural limitations on opportunities, such as the restriction upon the number of available high-ranking positions in a highly bureaucratic system. This means, concretely, that, contrary to the popular adage, there is not always room at the top, but that able men often have to wait for an "opening." The increasingly large-scale nature of industrial enterprises also means that larger capital backing is necessary to compete successfully with established firms.[14] Thus there are even limitations on the industrial entrepreneur. These additional restrictions do not necessarily operate unequally, but do tend to enhance the inequalities noted above.

In view of these institutional and unofficial limitations to equality

[13] See Percy E. Davidson and H. Dewey Anderson, *Occupational Mobility in an American Community* (Stanford University, Calif.: Stanford University Press, 1937), p. 103.

[14] This is illustrated and documented by the findings of the Temporary National Economic Committee, *Investigation of Concentration of Economic Power* (Washington: U. S. Government Printing Office, 1939–1941). The two series of *Hearings* and *Monographs* run to over eighty volumes and provide a detailed commentary upon the rigidification of business enterprise. See particularly the testimony of Dr. Willard Thorp, in *Hearings*, Part 1, "Economic Prologue," pp. 81–156.

of opportunity, it is not surprising to learn that, despite the office-boy-to-president success pattern, there is relatively little occupational mobility between the distinct occupational categories.

Minor and major changes of occupational position may either occur within single careers, or between generations (that is, non-inheritance of occupation). With reference to the first, studies of various groups and in different areas show a good deal of job shifting, and comparatively little shifting in occupational level. In the San Jose, California, study made by Davidson and Anderson, somewhat less than half (forty-four per cent) of all occupational shifts involved no change in general level, whereas almost three-fourths of the shifts involved no more than one step up or down. This study includes six levels; in addition to professionals, proprietors, and clerks, the group we have called wage earners is divided into skilled, semiskilled, and unskilled. A good deal of the total occupational mobility has occurred among these three levels.[15] Sorokin has found similar occupational mobility without much shifting in occupational level.[16] The Lynds found in their study of "Middletown" in the mid-1920's that over a period of twenty-one months there was but one chance in four hundred twenty-four for wage earners to be promoted to foremen.[17] They found no reason to alter their conclusions in their second study in 1935. On the contrary, they found a marked development in the number of specialized technical and managerial jobs for which even the exceptional wage earner was unqualified.[18] All studies point to the unmistakable conclusion that anything like complete transversal of the occupational range within a single career is extremely rare.

It is often said that occupational mobility is simply slowing up, so that it takes more than a single generation to move a considerable distance up the stratification ladder. There is some evidence that this is true, although the available studies indicate that the son

[15] *Op. cit.*, pp. 84–102, 179–186.
[16] Pitirim Sorokin, *Social Mobility* (New York: Harper & Brothers, 1927), pp. 424–456.
[17] Robert S. Lynd and Helen Merrell Lynd, *Middletown* (New York: Harcourt, Brace and Company, 1929), pp. 65–66.
[18] Lynds, *Middletown in Transition*, pp. 67–73.

more frequently follows an occupation on the same level as that of his father than any other occupational level, and that the shifts in level from one generation to the next are chiefly confined to those occupational classes closest to the father's occupation.[19] For example, one study conducted in a growing Western community indicated that 41.7 per cent of the sons of unskilled would become unskilled workers and 71.9 per cent would remain among the ranks of wage earners.[20]

Thus, occupational class mobility is by no means a common phenomenon within one career, and even from one generation to the next the extent of shifting could be easily overrated. But does this mean that there is increasing likelihood of acute class consciousness or the necessary imminence of class struggle? The evidence supports no such conclusion. There are several additional considerations of high significance for the stability of American society.

Stabilizing Factors. The first of these additional facts that decreases the chances of a developing class consciousness as the result of the presumed rigidity in general class lines is to be found in the nature of occupational specialization and mobility itself. Competition and mobility are not limited to major shifts in general occupational status. Especially at lower occupational levels, and decreasing as one proceeds to positions requiring longer training and greater ability, there is a considerable "range of horizontal transferability." [21] Thus unskilled, semiskilled, and even some skilled laborers can make considerable shifts in specific occupations in an industrial

[19] See Davidson and Anderson, *op. cit.*, pp. 17–38, 162–167; Sorokin, *op. cit.*, pp. 428–457. The Davidson and Anderson study indicates considerably less occupational inheritance at the professional level than at others. This is probably related to the previously noted importance of specialized (ordinarily academic) training for professional status, rather than occupational climbing. This to be contrasted with a uniform indication in the various studies of considerable immobility in farming. In this regard, see also W. A. Anderson, *The Transmission of Farming as an Occupation,* Cornell University Agricultural Experiment Station, Bulletin 768 (Ithaca, N. Y.: October 1941).

[20] Davidson and Anderson, *op. cit.*, pp. 17–38.

[21] See William H. Stead, Carroll L. Shartle, and Others, *Occupational Counseling Techniques, Their Development and Application* (New York: American Book Company, 1940), pp. 203–205. See the discussion of occupational specialization in Chap. XVIII, above.

system characterized by a tremendous division of labor, without appreciably altering their general occupational rank. Since there is some range of vertical variation within one rank, these shifts may well appear to the worker as appropriate economic opportunity. Although the extent of occupational shifting is reduced to a minimum in higher occupational ranks, the range of variation within a particular occupation may be considerable. A professional man, for example, confines his competitive energies primarily to his own profession. The individual competition for general social status is likely to be less significant than competition within a single line of occupational differentiation.

This consideration is given added point if it is recognized that the translation of the occupational categories discussed here into "social classes" is an operation of doubtful validity. All occupations are not arranged on a single prestige scale, and certainly do not constitute possible steps in a single career. Even the relative rank of the major functional groups is doubtful, and since rank *within* these groups is usually the decisive question, failure to move from one "situs" [22] to another in the occupational career has no necessary implications for "class" conflict. The major difficulty with much of the argument and analysis in this area is the assumption that a single scale of occupational levels will produce classes that "really exist" and have concrete relevance for attitudes of identification with "class interests." Classes in the sense of strata cutting across the entire system may "exist" for certain purposes of collective relations or advancement of particular "interests" and yet not "exist" in many other contexts where a much more complex and differentiated social structure is relevant. There is no magic in the single number (or single scale) if it obscures the operation of a social system. Occupational position, we have noted, will have one sort of relevance within the concrete organization in which the individual is employed, a different relevance in the neighborhood or community or circle of acquaintances, and still another on national political issues or sympathies in cases of conflict between broad interests.

[22] Hatt, "Occupation and Social Stratification," previously cited.

A second major consideration with reference to occupational mobility and class consciousness is that much too little attention is customarily given to the increasing complexity of the occupational structure and the demand for *new* skills and the establishment of *new* organizations with their appropriate quota of leadership positions. This increasing complexity and appearance of new occupational opportunities is in turn related to the growing importance of the school as the avenue of occupational mobility. The increasing difficulty of traversing the entire range of positions in a single line of ascent is directly related to the fact that higher positions are increasingly filled directly from colleges and technical schools. Now access to higher education is by no means equal for persons of equivalent native ability, but the direction of change has been for greater educational opportunities, not smaller.

A third significant limitation to the appearance of class-conscious groups arising from major occupational distinctions derives from the degree of arbitrariness in fixing attention exclusively upon occupation as a mode of differential valuation. Failure to "get ahead in the world" by occupational advancement is no final barrier to "class" mobility. On the contrary, satisfactory social valuation on other grounds may compensate for considerable inadequacies in the productive order. Two typical examples are to be found in high status of Southern aristocrats living in respectable poverty, and in the assiduous "social climbing" of suburban clubwomen.

In addition to these "facts of the situation" there is another fact of considerable importance: the fact of belief in and support of the open-class system.

Functions of the Ideology. The Marxians have written and exhorted a great deal about class interests following from class position, as judged by relationships of production. While we must reject their reduction of social classes to a single dichotomy, and their claims that this necessarily leads to class opposition and class struggle, we have also noted that occupational affiliations form a primary, if complex, basis for social distinctions in our society. We have even indicated that a number of common interests are associated with occupational group membership. Indeed, because the child is socialized within the particular class position of his parents, it is possible on these grounds to maintain that divergent "class" attitudes follow from differing functional roles in the productive system.

But this differential participation in culture by no means automatically produces *conflict* in class interests, formulated in class ideologies. We should note the negative part played by such associations as the church and state which cut across class lines. Perhaps more important than these (or their values in religious ethics and national patriotism) as an integrative factor is the fact that differences of status, and even of "interest," are given an over-all justification in the ideology of the open-class system.

The integrative and stabilizing effect of the belief in the open-class organization, both as fact and ideal, is evident in a variety of circumstances. It is most generally recognized in a rather pervasive hope for better things. The absence of official barriers, and the emphasis upon rising in the social and economic world, give a stake in the future that may be illusory, but is real in its effects if it is thought to be real. A survey by the staff of the magazine *Fortune* indicates the generality of belief in personal chances for success.[23] Sometimes, especially among the middle-aged, hope for greater personal success may be lost, but this by no means ends the matter, or produces complete disillusionment. For the common tendency for parents to project their own unrealized desires upon their children simply postpones the realization of the hope for another generation.[24] Associated with this personal hope, or hope for one's children, is, of course, a general belief in continued opportunity. One frequently hears, for example, that the days of expansion and individual opportunity are not over, that the new frontiers are the new industrial opportunities. Amid some persistent doubt, and much occasional doubt, there is a widespread belief in industrial and economic "progress" which will challenge the best talent of the society.[25]

---

[23] See *Fortune*, "The Fortune Survey: XXVII. The People of the U. S. A.—a Self-Portrait," 21: (February 1940), pp. 134, 136.

[24] See for example the findings of the Lynds in *Middletown*, pp. 48–52.

[25] See the *Fortune* survey, *loc. cit.*, pp. 133–134; Lynds, *Middletown in*

To point up the previous observations, and to draw their logical conclusion, there is a widespread conviction that there is no intrinsic conflict between classes. Thus in the *Fortune* survey, in answer to the question, "Do you think that the interests of employers and employees are, by their very nature, opposed, or are they basically the same?" the following results were tabulated: [26]

	Percentages Answering		
	The Same	*Opposed*	*Don't Know*
Total	56.2	24.8	19.0
Prosperous	73.9	17.8	8.3
Lower middle class	58.8	25.4	15.8
Poor	44.4	29.0	26.6
Executives	80.2	15.3	4.5
White-collar workers	69.8	23.1	7.1
Factory labor	41.3	37.3	21.4
Unemployed	45.1	29.2	25.7

To be sure, this and other studies indicate some differences among various occupational and income groups. The Lynds, for example, found much incipient class consciousness, which was offset by hope in future opportunity.[27] Jones found evidence of very nearly polar reactions to the problem of corporate property rights as opposed to "human" rights, with industrial executives supporting property interests and industrial laborers giving preference to human rights. Yet he found no evidence of translating this difference into class ideologies, nor even of any widespread break-down of traditional adherence to the respect for property. He also noted the stabilizing function of hope for acquisition of property and higher status.[28]

The open-class ideology, then, is real in the double sense that it exists and that it works. That is, it works to preserve the existence of the prevailing system of social differentiation, and thus to inte-

---

Transition, pp. 454–461; William F. Ogburn and Meyer F. Nimkoff, *Sociology,* 2nd ed. (Boston: Houghton-Mifflin Company, 1950), Chap. 8.

[26] *Loc. cit.,* p. 133.

[27] *Middletown in Transition,* pp. 25–44, 450–454.

[28] *Op. cit.,* particularly Chap. XXIII. The managerial group showed the most consistent and extreme response. This may be evidence in support of Marx's generalization that the upper classes must always be "for themselves" (that is, have class consciousness) in order to remain in a position of dominance.

grate all groups about a common set of values and a common set of assumptions.

In summary, one might, in view of the notable gaps in equality of opportunity, speak of the "mythology" of the open-class system. But to call a particular belief a "myth" does not thereby dismiss its social importance. Scientific validity and social utility have no necessary relation to one another. And the mythology is "useful" for preserving a measure of social—and industrial—peace. It has of course by the same token a profound disutility for possible changes in the direction of increased economic opportunity or decreased differentials in economic welfare.

Whatever may be the numerical odds against advancement, it is *possible*. There are few official limitations, and the general equality of opportunity, though restricted, is nevertheless greater than in any other modern complex society. That may not be regarded as sufficient; it is, however, undeniably something.

The occupational categories we have discussed are to a large degree the product of an industrial civilization. They represent part of the wider ramifications of modern economic activity. But the interests represented by the several strata of society—the common levels of living, appropriate dress, speech, and general behavior, the social circles in which one moves and mates—are not simply "reflections" of industrial interests. Even in a society unusually preoccupied with getting ahead in the world, no single occupational group genuinely threatens to use extraordinary means for major transformations in the productive system.

REFERENCES

ANDERSON, H. DEWEY, and PERCY E. DAVIDSON, *Ballots and the Democratic Class Struggle* (Stanford University, Calif.: Stanford University Press, 1943).

ANDERSON, W. A., "The Transmission of Farming as an Occupation," *Cornell University Agricultural Experiment Station, Bulletin 768* (Ithaca, N. Y., October 1941).

BAKKE, E. WIGHT, *Citizens Without Work* (New Haven: Yale University Press for the Institute of Human Relations, 1940), Chap. V, "A Working Class."

CENTERS, RICHARD, *The Psychology of Social Classes* (Princeton: Princeton University Press, 1949).

DAVIDSON, PERCY E., and H. DEWEY ANDERSON, *Occupational Mobility in an American Community* (Stanford University, Calif.: Stanford University Press, 1937).

DAVIS, KINGSLEY, "A Conceptual Analysis of Stratification," *American Sociological Review*, 7: 309–321, June 1942.

DAVIS, KINGSLEY, and WILBERT E. MOORE, "Some Principles of Stratification," *American Sociological Review*, 10: 242–249, April 1945.

DOBB, MAURICE, "The Economic Basis of Class Conflict," in T. H. Marshall, ed., *Class Conflict and Social Stratification* (London: LePlay House Press, 1938), pp. 134–152.

ENGELS, FREDERICK, *Socialism, Utopian and Scientific* (Chicago: Charles H. Kerr and Co., 1907).

GINSBERG, MORRIS, "Class Consciousness," in *Encyclopaedia of the Social Sciences*, 3: 536–538.

HATT, PAUL K., "Occupation and Social Stratification," *American Journal of Sociology*, 55: 533–543, May 1950.

——, "Stratification in the Mass Society," *American Sociological Review*, 15: 216–222, April 1950.

HOLLINGSHEAD, AUGUST B., *Elmtown's Youth: The Impact of Social Classes on Adolescents* (New York: John Wiley and Sons, 1949).

HOOK, SIDNEY, *Towards an Understanding of Karl Marx* (New York: The John Day Company, 1933), Part II, "The Philosophy of Marx."

JONES, ALFRED WINSLOW, *Life, Liberty, and Property* (Philadelphia: J. B. Lippincott Company, 1941), Chap. XXIII, "Summary and Interpretation"; Chap. XXIV, "Conclusion—Class Consciousness and Property."

LORWIN, LEWIS L., "Class Struggle," in *Encyclopaedia of the Social Sciences*, 3: 538–542.

LYND, ROBERT S., and HELEN MERRELL LYND, *Middletown* (New York: Harcourt, Brace and Company, 1929), Chap. IV, "The Dominance of Getting a Living"; Chap. VI, "What Middletown Does to Get a Living"; Chap. VII, "The Long Arm of the Job"; Chap. VIII, "Why Do They Work So Hard?"

LYND, ROBERT S., and HELEN MERRELL LYND, *Middletown in Transition* (New York: Harcourt, Brace and Company, 1937), Chap. II, "Getting a Living" and pp. 406–410, 444–462.

MARSHALL, T. H., "The Nature of Class Conflict," in T. H. Marshall, ed., *Class Conflict and Social Stratification* (London: LePlay House Press, 1938), pp. 97–111.

MARX, KARL, *Capital* (Chicago: Charles H. Kerr and Co., 1906–09, 3 vols.), especially Vol. I, Chap. VII, "The Labour-Process and the

Process of Producing Surplus-Value," and Vol. III, Chap. LII, "The Classes."

MARX, KARL, *A Contribution to the Critique of Political Economy* (New York: International Library Publishing Co., 1904), "Author's Preface," and "Appendix."

——, *Revolution and Counter-Revolution, or Germany in 1848* (Chicago: Charles H. Kerr and Co., 1912).

——, *Value, Price and Profit* (Chicago: Charles H. Kerr and Co., n.d.).

MARX, KARL, and FREDERICK ENGLES, *Manifesto of the Communist Party* (Chicago: Charles H. Kerr and Co., 1906).

MCCONNELL, JOHN W., *The Evolution of Social Classes* (Washington: American Council on Public Affairs, 1942).

MEUSEL, ALFRED, "Middle Class," in *Encyclopaedia of the Social Sciences,* 10: 407–414.

MICHIGAN STATE COLLEGE, Social Research Service, *Youth and the World of Work* (East Lansing: 1949).

MILLER, DELBERT C., and WILLIAM H. FORM, "Measuring Patterns of Occupational Security," *Sociometry*, 10: 362–375, November 1947.

MILLS, C. WRIGHT, "The American Business Elite: A Collective Portrait," *The Tasks of Economic History,* Supplement V to *The Journal of Economic History,* December 1945, pp. 20–44.

——, "The Middle Classes in Middle-Sized Cities; The Stratification and Political Position of Small Business and White Collar Strata," *American Sociological Review,* 11: 520–529, October 1946.

MOMBERT, PAUL, "Class" in *Encyclopaedia of the Social Sciences,* 3: 531–536.

NORTH, CECIL CLARE, *Social Differentiation* (Chapel Hill: The University of North Carolina Press, 1926), Chap. III, "Differences of Rank"; Chap. X, "The Creation of Privileged Classes."

PAGE, CHARLES HUNT, *Class and American Sociology* (New York: The Dial Press, 1940).

PARSONS, TALCOTT, "An Analytical Approach to the Theory of Social Stratification," *American Journal of Sociology,* 45: 841–862, May 1940.

PATTERSON, S. HOWARD, *Social Aspects of Industry,* 3d ed. (New York: McGraw-Hill Book Company, Inc., 1943), Chap. VI, "The Ideal of Equality of Opportunity and the Facts of Economic Inequality: Division of National Wealth and Distribution of National Income."

PFAUTZ, HAROLD W., and OTIS DUDLEY DUNCAN, "A Critical Evaluation of Warner's Work in Community Stratification," *American Sociological Review,* 15: 205–215, April 1950.

ROBBINS, LIONEL, "The Economic Basis of Class Conflict," in T. H. Marshall, ed., *Class Conflict and Social Stratification* (London: LePlay House Press, 1938), pp. 112–123.

SOGGE, T. M., "Industrial Classes in the United States in 1940," *Journal of the American Statistical Association,* 39: 516–518, December 1944.

SOROKIN, PITIRIM, *Social Mobility* (New York: Harper & Brothers, 1927), Chap. II, "Social Stratification"; Chap. VI, "Occupational Stratification"; Chap XVII, "Vertical Mobility within Western Societies"; Chap. XVIII, "Vertical Mobility within Western Societies (Continued). Shifting on the Economic Ladder."

SUMNER, WILLIAM GRAHAM, *What Social Classes Owe to Each Other* (New Haven: Yale University Press, 1934).

THOMAS, BRINLEY, "The Problem of Bridges and Barriers," in T. H. Marshall, ed., *Class Conflict and Social Stratification* (London, LePlay House Press, 1938), pp. 73–96.

VEBLEN, THORSTEIN, *The Place of Science in Modern Civilisation* (New York: The Viking Press, 1932). See "The Socialist Economics of Karl Marx, I," pp. 409–430.

——, *The Vested Interests and the State of the Industrial Arts* (New York: B. W. Huebsch, 1919) Sec. VIII, "The Vested Interests and the Common Man."

——, *The Theory of the Leisure Class* (New York: B. W. Huebsch, 1918).

WANCE, WILLIAM, and RICHARD BUTLER, "The Effect of Industrial Changes on Occupational 'Inheritance' in Four Pennsylvania Communities," *Social Forces,* 27: 158–162, December 1948.

WARNER, W. LLOYD, and J. O. Low, *The Social System of the Modern Factory; The Strike: A Social Analysis* (New Haven: Yale University Press, 1947), Chap. V, "The Break in the Skill Hierarchy" Chap. IX, "The Workers Lose Status in the Community"; Chap. X, Blue Print of Tomorrow—General Conclusions"; Appendix 6, "Social Characteristics of the Shoe Workers."

WARNER, W. LLOYD, and OTHERS, *Democracy in Jonesville* (New York: Harper & Brothers, 1949).

WARNER, W. LLOYD, and OTHERS, *Social Class in America* (Chicago: Science Research Associates, 1949).

WARNER, W. LLOYD, and PAUL S. LUNT, *The Social Life of a Modern Community,* Yankee City Series Vol. I (New Haven: Yale University Press, 1941), Chap. V, "How the Several Classes were Discovered," and Chap. VI, "Class and Social Structure."

WARNER, W. LLOYD, and PAUL S. LUNT, *The Status System of a Modern*

Community, Yankee City Series Vol. II (New Haven: Yale University Press, 1942).

WOYTINSKY, W. S., *Labor in the United States* (Washington: Committee on Social Security, Social Science Research Council, 1938), Note 2 (pp. 236–239), "Rearrangement of Occupational Statistics"; Note 5 (pp. 249–251), "On Methods of Occupational Classification"; Note 14 (pp. 268–272), "Trends in the Socio-Economic Structure of the Working Population in the United States."

GOVERNMENTAL INTERVENTION

"LESS GOVERNMENT in business, more business in government"—so runs the slogan of the United States Chamber of Commerce, quoted frequently as an epigrammatic summary of the sentiments of all right-thinking persons. If added weight of authority be needed, Thomas Jefferson may be erroneously quoted to the effect that "That government is best which governs least." Yet despite these expressions of sentiment concerning the way in which political virtue lies, it is undeniably true that the visible social controls that limit freedom of action in economic affairs are steadily increasing.

Here we are concerned with the way the institutions of production, trade, property, etc., fit into the larger framework of the social order. Previous chapters have outlined the position of industry in the community, and the relation between occupational status and general social or class status. We must now examine how the vast and sprawling economic interests of our society are modified or controlled.

The social controls of industry are both numerous and varied. This is not surprising in view of the complexity of industrial organization and the diversity of interests which prompt some measure of control. The rules that guide the conduct of industrial affairs function not only to maintain order in an economy that is only nominally self-regulating, but also to ensure the consistency of economic organization with such values as individual health and familial stability.

The present chapter will first review briefly the traditional doctrines of a "free" economy and the controls actually hidden in the institutional structure comprised in the "culture of capitalism." We shall then note the ways in which the "automatic" (that is, unconscious) controls have been modified and supplemented as the economic system has become more complex and powerful; and the objectives served or goals sought by the additional controls.

MODIFICATION OF THE CULTURE OF CAPITALISM

Discussions of the role of government in economic affairs usually proceed rather quickly to theoretical comparisons of capitalized epithets like Capitalism, Socialism, Fascism, and Communism. In such discussions the scientific observer can take little part, since they tend to revolve around sentiments concerning the "good life" rather than fact, and, above all, because they are about the relative merit systems that do not in fact exist. That is, these grandiose systems of economic production and distribution do not exist in the "pure forms" usually taken as the basis of argument. The observer may, however, grant that the folklore or mythology that contains the blueprint of a system in theory has some effect upon the operation of that system in practice.

These remarks are prefatory to the commonplace observation that capitalism as pictured in the older learned treatises, and even as staunchly defended by corporate managers, no longer exists. We have already outlined the main principles of the traditional culture of capitalism (Chapter XVIII), and have had occasion at numerous junctures to point out how the conduct of contemporary industrial affairs departs from the true faith. We are not here concerned with a detailed review of the theory accompanied by an item by item contrast with the facts, however telling such a review might seem to be. We are not even primarily concerned with the fact that the theory could not work in the everyday affairs of the community, because it neglected the highly significant problems of harmony of interests. It is, however, important to note again that mere poking fun at the more ludicrous assumptions of an individualistic, *laissez-faire* economy does not remove the importance of the ideology. That ideology serves as a standard for approximation and as a convenient set of symbols for giving official sanction to the devices used in the production and distribution of economic goods. Thus if, as frequently happens, a vast public utilities empire of pyramided holding companies is treated in the rarified atmosphere of the courts as an individual whose private property must not be taken away "without due process of law," it is a little naïve to be either amused or angry. It is true that this is not capitalism of the textbook or Rotary Club variety, but neither is it a ritual that is entirely devoid of doctrinal significance. On the contrary, the strength of the doctrine of noninterference in "private" economic affairs is daily demonstrated in the resistance generated by any proposal for new controls.

Death of Homo Economicus. The "economic man," as a rational, self-interested, acquisitive individual, who competes with other economic men and thus serves the best interests of all, was of course always an abstraction. That is, it was possible and necessary to think of such a person as the active force in the economic theory of a competitive social order, but it was impossible to observe such an individual in fact. Difficulties, both theoretical and practical, continue to arise, however, when this abstraction is confused with actual manufacturers and traders, to say nothing of corporations. Without making untenable assumptions about a "natural identity of interests" it is impossible on such grounds to account either for the goals of competitive enterprise or for the rules that restrict the activities of competitors and keep them "fair."[1] It has been the merit of the so-called institutional economists to have pointed out some of the extensive legal and other controls required to make a competitive order work at all, as well as the ways in which those presumably limiting institutions may be manipulated to sanction practices and organizations not contemplated in the original doctrines.[2] We shall return below to a brief examination of the role of institutions in economic affairs.

[1] See Talcott Parsons, *The Structure of Social Action* (New York: McGraw-Hill Book Company, Inc., 1937), Chap. III, "Some Phases of the Historical Development of Individualistic Positivism in the Theory of Action."

[2] Much of the thinking in this field stems more or less directly from the work of Thorstein Veblen. See, for example, his *Absentee Ownership and Business Enterprise in Recent Times* (New York: B. W. Huebsch, 1923), and his *The Theory of Business Enterprise* (New York: Charles Scribner's Sons, 1936). See

The fact of the matter is that controls other than those exercised by the market have always been part of our social order, even in the days of "early" capitalism. This situation has been partly due to the fact that competition without rules is a contradiction in terms; and it will be noticed that in any critical case the rules must be regarded as referring to more fundamental values than the particular object of the competition. As a minimum statement of the situation, it is clear that the competitive system as such will be regarded as more important than an otherwise effective device (such as "cornering" the market) that threatens the system. Thus the rather efficient practices of force and fraud, which a pure specimen of economic man could scarcely be expected to overlook, would destroy the very bases of societal life.

The conception of an economic man has been lately under a great deal of attack, only part of it justified. Thus critics have discovered with ill-concealed glee that human beings, including businessmen, often act "irrationally," practice many rituals, apparently subscribe to quite inconsistent doctrines, and so on. Such criticism has been undoubtedly useful to the extent that it has served to call attention to the unreality and impossibility of a self-ordering society based upon shrewdly acquisitive behavior by self-interested individuals. It is scientifically unfortunate to the extent that it gives rise to the idea that human behavior is simply unpredictable: that is, that since people do not behave "rationally" as narrowly defined, there is simply no way to understand their motives or their behavior. Stated more positively, it is good to recognize that a society of economic men could not exist, but it is at least equally good to recognize *why* in terms of the whole fabric of social behavior. Especially is it necessary to recognize the fundamental significance of the controls of human behavior that make social life possible, and of the common values that those controls serve.

---

also Thurman W. Arnold, *The Folklore of Capitalism* (New Haven: Yale University Press, 1937); John R. Commons, *Legal Foundations of Capitalism* (New York: The Macmillan Company, 1934); Leverett S. Lyon, Myron W. Watkins, and Victor Abramson, *Government and Economic Life* (Washington: The Brookings Institution, 1939), Vol. I, Chap. II, "Conditioning Factors in America."

The "death" of economic man to which we have referred in the heading of this section is thus not a true demise. Rather, a ghost has been laid. But even this more limited homicide has been less attributable to the theoretical critics than to the course of events in the legislatures and courts. For the older and customary controls of economic behavior might be accepted and dismissed as part of the natural order of things. But as new controls have been introduced, for whatever reason, it has become increasingly clear—even, and especially, to the strongest adherents to the belief in the possibility and advisability of a *laissez-faire* economy—that the actions of the most self-reliant individual are circumscribed and hedged about by a host of regulations.

The Role of Institutions. The seeming absence of official administrative or legislative controls in the older "free" economy did not signify that there were no controls. Rather, the division of labor, the control of productive wealth, and the system of exchange and distribution were thought to be *self-regulating*. But such self-regulation could only exist within the framework of a fairly well-defined ideology and pretty rigid institutional system. As long as economic activities were carried on with reasonable conformity to the limits assumed in the ideology of liberal capitalism, the controls were not obvious. But a persistent and otherwise successful effort to violate the canons of "free enterprise" and individualism called forth definite legal controls, *presumably to make the self-regulation work according to theory.* Thus, we have noted that the doctrines of individual competition were *enforced* by the courts in the case of groups of workingmen. Similarly, every time a person who has entered an agreement with another person is forced by the courts to fulfill his contractual obligations, the so-called "sacredness of contract" is being made an objective of social control. And if the contract called for one party to surrender himself to enslavement by the other, the courts would refuse to uphold the obligation—no matter how valuable the consideration received by the prospective slave—because here the principle of freedom of contract violates the "public interest" in maintaining a free labor system.

We have purposely chosen examples of commonly recognized

legal principles, of sufficiently ancient vintage to escape any taint of new-fangled governmental interference with the free conduct of production and trade. The fact that the older structure of economic organization did allow a comparatively wide range of self-regulation (that is, regulation by unconscious controls of price competition, etc.) should not lead one to the mistaken conclusion that the social control of industry is a modern development. Indeed, it is simply impossible to maintain a society if a major part of social activity is unregulated.

If one were comparing a number of economic systems in relation to the societies in which they flourish, one would note at least three critical questions which every social order must answer in some well-understood way: *Who does what, Who controls what and whom, and Who gets what?* This rather commonplace way of asking the questions may be translated into the terminology of the social sciences: they are the spheres of the institutions of the division of labor, property, and distribution. The way these institutions define the situation with respect to economic affairs provides the major controls of the system.

As in all forms of social control, these controls will become obvious only to the extent that they are transgressed or are regarded as burdensome. In general, a *new* control is more obvious than one long familiar, partly because any new control affects some members of a society adversely.

This line of argument begs some questions, of course. Notably, it leaves unanswered the rather practical questions as to the mechanism of the control, and the ends toward which regulation is directed. We shall return to these problems in the latter part of this chapter. Rather than dealing with all of the controls in terms of the major institutional structures within which they fall, we may single out for special attention the rather fundamental modifications that have taken place in the realm of property.

New Property Conceptions. In Chapter III, in connection with the legal character of the modern corporation, the fundamental importance of property institutions as a source of control of economic activity was discussed, as well as the way in which the legal theory

of the corporation has gradually forced a modification in the traditional views of private property. Without a detailed analysis of
the system of private property,[3] we may nevertheless repeat the
assertion that a system of *completely* private property (that is,
with no limitations upon individual use of those types of wealth
which are "owned") is a social impossibility. There must always
be reservations and restrictions in the public interest, or to preserve
social order. If we add to this observation the further one, also
previously discussed, that property rights are divisible and capable
of considerable diffusion, we are in a position to understand the
ways in which the modification of property rules serves to provide
new social controls of industry.

Stemming partly from a slow but growing legal recognition that
corporate control of wealth is a far cry from traditional conceptions
of private property, there is in modern property conceptions an
*increased dichotomy between productive wealth and consumers'
goods.* Legal recognition has not been sharply defined, but is evident in increased restrictions on the uses of productive wealth in
view of the power inherent in concentration of economic control.
Popular recognition has been even less incisive, but may be observed in the attempt to distinguish property rights and human
rights. As ordinarily understood, the property rights in question
are those of capital ownership and not ordinary private ownership
of consumers' goods. Even though, as noted in the previous chapter,
the fairly widespread enjoyment of private ownership of consumption goods has tended to lend support to the system of nominally
private property as a whole, distinctions according to use are increasing. This is further illustrated by the sale of phonograph rec-

---

[3] For a statement of the elements in, and limitations on, a system of private
property, see Wilbert E. Moore, "The Emergence of New Property Conceptions
in America," *Journal of Legal and Political Sociology*, 1 (3–4): 34–58, April
1943. The following paragraphs of this section of the text are adapted from the
paper cited, by permission of the editors of the *Journal*. See also A. Irving Hal-
lowell, "The Nature and Function of Property as a Social Institution," *ibid.*, 1
(3–4): 115–138, April 1943; John R. Commons, *Legal Foundations of Capitalism* (New York: The Macmillan Company, 1924), Chap. II, "Property, Liberty,
and Value," and Chap. VII, "The Price Bargain–Capitalism and Exchange
Value"; R. T. Ely, *Property and Contract in Their Relation to the Distribution
of Wealth* (New York: The Macmillan Company, 1914), 2 vols.

ords or printed dramas for nonproductive use only, unless additional returns in the form of royalties are paid to the vendor.

Coupled with the distinction between productive wealth and consumers' goods is the radical departure from strictly private control of the former. There is every reason to expect even further development of the corporate principle of productive organization, with rights held either distributively or, possibly, publicly. The newer limitations on corporate action are especially significant in their recognition of the "trustee" character of corporate control. This is illustrated in the expansion of protection for the minority or unrepresented stockholder through Securities and Exchange Commission regulations. The possibility of increased public ownership is enhanced by the acceptance by the courts of such ventures as the Tennessee Valley Authority, even though so far the decisions have been in terms of such expansible generalities as "interstate commerce," "general welfare" (national defense), or the "police power."

In an increasingly complex society with an expanding technology, new uses—that is, new values—are found in familiar objects, ideas, and relationships. These call for new property regulations and illustrate a sort of "logic of growth" of property conceptions. Part of the change can be cushioned by reliance on general principles of relative worth or necessity. Thus, the natural rights doctrine of private property, particularly with reference to the principle of unlimited rights, has in the past consistently obscured the sociological fact that property institutions are societal creations. This has led to a general policy of attaching all new values accidentally or unpredictably accruing to some locus of value [4] to the recognized owner "as of right." For example, if a person buys a sheet of postage stamps presumably for the purpose of using them for postage and discovers that an error in their manufacture makes them far more valuable for sale to collectors, our ideas of property

---

[4] The term *locus of value*, although somewhat awkward, is suggested as a substitute for the common designation of property rights in "things." The limiting of property controls to controls of "things" not only is conducive to confusing values and rights in those values (as in the common and erroneous habit of speaking of objects as being property), but simply leaves out of consideration the vast number of property rights which do not refer to land or objects at all.

concede that the purchaser was lucky and has full claim to the extra value. Any restrictions on this principle have been viewed as requiring positive legislation unless particular cases clearly fall within the exercise of police power or the promotion of general welfare.

Nevertheless, the traditional principles are subject to considerable change, even if that change is chiefly in the form of slow accretions and slight modifications. The new uses of scarce objects or loci of value are numerous, and growing. Rather than attempting a complete catalogue of changes already apparent or which can be readily predicted, we may indicate three main categories of novel property controls: (1) controls of new uses of the natural environment, or new controls of old values; (2) controls of power relationships to prevent "exploitation," or to direct the benefits differently; (3) controls following from both of these, an ever-widening recognition of "intangibles."

1. With the constant development of scientific research, particularly that directed toward practical (technological) ends, new values are added to familiar aspects of the environment. This inevitably raises questions of allocation of rights, and the evidence points fairly uniformly to increasing public control of such new values. Two fairly recent situations will serve to illustrate this policy. Both involve new uses of "airspace" in the broadest sense: the control of navigable airspace and the control of radio wave lengths. Although the attempt was made in both instances to follow the traditional idea of allocation of additional rights to those already in "possession" (like the fortunate purchase of rare postage stamps), such a solution actually destroys the utility of the inventions that gave rise to the new uses of air. Thus, both have been placed under Federal jurisdiction as an extension of the "police power" and justified by the power of Congress to regulate interstate commerce.

Other cases of new controls are less clear-cut. Thus, the rate of exploitation of exhaustible natural resources has been a leading public issue for a generation, and only fairly recently have the traditional property rights of systematic and profitable destruction been placed under some modicum of public control. The fate of such controls at the hands of the courts has been variable. However, it may be safely predicted that legal devices to accomplish control "in the public interest" will be increasingly apparent in the future.

The situation with regard to patents is also in flux. As pointed out by Walton Hamilton and others,[5] the Constitutional purpose of granting patents "to promote the progress of science and useful arts" may be subverted by the possibility of maintaining the property right of advantageous nonuse. Either through positive legislation or through possible continuation of patent pools established in wartime, the private-property character of patents assigned to corporations will probably be modified in the future. It seems reasonably certain, for example, that the courts would prevent the withholding of a patented cancer cure in the unlikely event of such an attempt. The doctrines of "human rights" or "general welfare" are still capable of some expansion.

2. Property regulations, in defining the relation between persons and scarce values, necessarily also define social relations. To talk of property at all implies therefore an actual or potential power relation between the person holding property rights and the person excluded from their enjoyment. The ideology of private property, particularly as developed in a period of relatively "free enterprise," has consistently obscured this point. It is only in recent legislation and judicial decision that the effect of factory production, and especially of corporate enterprise, upon the bargaining power of the individual employee has been officially recognized and modified. The support of collective bargaining has the effect of extending to employees a virtually property interest in their jobs, as was pointed out in Chapter XVII.

The great power wielded by large concentrations of wealth has been recognized in other ways, of course. Much of the "trust-bust-

---

[5] Walton Hamilton, "Patents and Free Enterprise," United States Congress, Temporary National Economic Committee, *Investigation of Concentration of Economic Power, Monograph No. 31* (Washington: U. S. Government Printing Office, 1941). See also TNEC *Hearings,* Part 3, "Patents—Proposals for Changes in Law and Procedures" (1939); Part 30, "Technology and Concentration of Economic Power" (1940).

ing" of the present century has been vainly aimed at squaring traditional doctrine with contemporary economic organization by forcing the "facts" to change to satisfy the assumptions of the law. Yet even this antimonopoly legislation has served to indicate an awareness of the interdependence of modern economic life and to pave the way for even greater extensions of the "police power" in behalf of workers, investors, and consumers, as well as on behalf of actual or potential competitors. It is at the present time safe to say that we have so far departed from traditional morality with respect to private enterprise that any large and strategic corporation could not and would not be allowed completely to fail. The precedent is at hand in the governmental underwriting of banks. There is little doubt that a similarly critical situation in other fields would yield similar or comparable results. This amounts to increased *responsibility* to the public as some measure of compensation for the *power* for good or ill necessarily wielded by concentrations of wealth.

3. Much of what we have been saying about the emergence of new property conceptions and controls in America may be phrased in another way with partial accuracy: the ever-widening recognition of what the law calls "intangibles." Our social structure has become far too complex for property to be confused with real estate, or even with realty and objects of personal ownership. The division and multiplication of property rights points the way to further additions to an already impressive list: patents, trademarks, mining claims, franchises, company good will, stocks, bonds, insurance. Not all of the "intangibles" protected by law (such as a protected professional reputation) are called property rights by courts still considerably befuddled by the rapid development of new controls, and some rather important ones such as controls of the market (as in the phenomenon of "price leadership") have had an almost extralegal development.[6] It appears likely that the course of future development will be toward incorporating these controls into a more consistent body of property regulations.

[6] See Walton Hamilton, "Property Rights in the Market," *Journal of Legal and Political Sociology*, 1 (3–4): 10–33, April 1943.

Despite the fundamental character of these changes in property controls, they have frequently escaped the attention of laymen and even of those specialists whose implicit conception of society and its controls is far more simplified than the facts warrant. But some of the modifications of the culture of capitalism are too obvious to be overlooked, and may in fact be more apparent to the layman than to those lawyers and judges whose calling requires them to deal with abstractions and fictions as if they represented the actual state of affairs. We may conclude our survey of the changes in the old order of individual enterprise by brief attention to some characteristics of the modern social order that are not only significant but also fairly apparent to the casual observer.

Concentration of Economic Power. One of the outstanding modifications of the culture of capitalism, or rather a whole chain of modifications, has already received detailed examination in Chapter III. Those modifications are the ones stemming from the invention of the corporation and the concentration of economic power. It is true that the corporation did not immediately force any official modification of the ideology of individual enterprise; the corporation simply became a person within the meaning of the law. But it is also true that, whereas corporate enterprise might be treated as individual and private enterprise for some purposes, two considerations of ever-increasing importance make that position difficult to maintain: (1) the dispersion of stock ownership, the claims of bondholders, and so on have brought to the fore (even in the courts) the undeniably plural and even discordant character of the individual interests represented by the corporation; (2) the concentration of financial control through closely held minority blocks of stock and accentuated by pyramided holding companies has created organizations of such tremendous power that even the ablest and most imaginative myth-makers have been hard put to maintain the principle that the only restraints upon such enterprising "individuals" should be a few, simple rules.

Interest and Pressure Groups. In the face of the increasing size of industrial establishments, and the far-reaching effects of the activities and policies of these organizations, various "interest groups" have appeared to promote the common interests of their members in economic affairs. Such interest groups are of course made possible by the growing ease of communication and transportation in an increasingly urban civilization; they are made "necessary" by the threat to their interests represented by other special-interest associations, including those of big business.

It is apparent that such combinations of individuals for the purpose of gaining common objectives do not fulfill the strict expectations of "every man for himself." The fact of the matter is, of course, that the older principles of noninterference with private enterprise were themselves made a part of the law of the land by virtue of the fairly well-organized pressure of producers and traders. That a great number and variety of comparable associations have made their appearance has been partly due to the relative freedom of association allowed within our social order, and partly to the fact that in a political democracy with a widening suffrage the members of these groups have been provided with a relatively easy way of exerting influence in their own behalf.

Not only have special-interest groups become very numerous, but their methods of gaining their objectives have become so well known that they are frequently called "pressure groups." These groups are not, of course, mutually exclusive, since the very limited number of common interests among their members ensures realignments when other interests are at stake. We noted in the preceding chapter that this is one of the reasons a major class-conscious political or social movement has failed to appear in the United States. Yet on any given question of social policy, or even a closely related series of questions, those whose interests are affected in one way or another may be expected to make their views known and their influence felt through an organization.

Our immediate interest in pressure groups is not only in the fact that they represent in themselves a modification of the traditional theory of the self-reliant individual, but also in the fact that the specific forms of social control of industry are likely to represent the current "balance of pressures." The process of government is sometimes defined as a balancing of pressures, although it should be noted that it is not only at the time of voting, when "each counts for one," that pressure may be exerted. It is not even always true that counting noses provides the conclusive test of power in a democratic social order, since some account must be taken of existing principles as expressed in previous legislation, as well as the well-known fact that differences in wealth, general social position, official status, and the like circumvent the doctrine of equality. It is likewise true that not all special-interest groups are equally well organized to exert pressure, or equally vocal in their demands. But whatever may be the source of the real or implied power upon which pressure groups rest their claims to be heard, it is clearly true that they do affect, and even largely determine, both the amount and the direction of social controls upon industry.[7]

REGULATION IN THE "PUBLIC INTEREST"

Every major social activity, whether educational, religious, economic, political, recreational, or familial, must to a significant degree fit other aspects of social life. In a simple, homogeneous rural or peasant society this is not difficult. All tend to merge in what we might call the life of the community. But as these activities become larger and more complex, they tend to develop a certain autonomy —to have walls around them insulating and separating them from the rest of society. Then it becomes necessary to establish new rules for controlling their relations, to prevent the elaboration of one at the expense of the others. Viewed in this way, the problem of so-called social legislation is a problem of the same order as that of keeping the church, or the school, or the government in check. Just as the grant of religious freedom could not be extended to include a religiously sanctioned polygamy without endangering the customary structure of the family, so the principle of free competition for employment may be thought too extensive when it results in the widespread and economically advantageous employ-

[7] See Lois MacDonald, *Labor Problems and the American Scene* (New York: Harper & Brothers, 1938), Chap. XXXII, "The Process of Intervention by Government," especially pp. 623–628.

ment of ten-year-old children. The issue at stake may be called that of *institutional compatibility.*

The social controls of industry are thus at least partly aimed at maintaining a balance of major social activities. But control is a little more extensive than this: it involves the balance of interests *within* as well as outside of the major social organizations. This is especially apparent in the industrial sphere, where there is no necessary consistency in *economic* interests, apart from questions of interferences with health, familial life, political liberties, or other valued objectives.

Obviously, no social legislation (or any other social change) is in the immediate interests of everyone. It would be hard to imagine any change that would not affect some persons adversely. In such a situation it is clear that a governmental decision to exert control, and the direction and extent that control will take, depend on some standard of relative importance and worth. Because there is considerable debate both over the ideals and over the instrumentalities for achieving those aims, it is understandable that the social controls that now limit action in the industrial sphere represent compromises and occasional inconsistencies. That all are claimed to be "in the public interest" simply means that they also represent the more or less successful attempts of the legislatures and courts to maintain a distribution of powers and privileges somewhat in accordance with prevalent standards of judgment in such matters.

Protection of "Economic Opportunity." One class of social controls of industry is clearly aimed at preservation (or, in many cases, reestablishment) of private initiative and free enterprise. This is antimonopoly and antitrust legislation. Such legislation is not aimed at the corporate combinations *per se,* but at various devices to create intercorporate combinations or complete monopoly. The phrase "combinations in restraint of trade" (that is, in restraint of competitive trade) aptly summarizes the evil that the laws seek to prevent. The Sherman Antitrust Act of 1890 and the Clayton Act of 1914 are the two outstanding Federal enactments aimed at "trust-busting."

We are not here primarily concerned with a detailed account of the ups and downs in antitrust enforcement.[8] Rather, a few observations may be made about the general problems of control in this field. One fairly obvious limitation on the attempt to preserve individual economic opportunity in the field of industrial production and finance is that the corporation is already a "combination in restraint of trade": that is, its assets are so large and its advance competitive position so secure that if any new competitive enterprise is to offer an effective challenge, that enterprise must also be a corporation. Concerns already established may exercise economic power in a way to discourage competition: by control of basic patents, control of strategic raw materials, domination of markets, and so on. The total effect of these advantages is to limit new enterprises almost exclusively to new products or new markets. Even in pioneering, however, existing companies can usually branch out more easily than a new company can be established.

The preservation of economic opportunity in the modern organization of economic enterprise would seem to depend on one of two alternatives: (1) a wholesale splitting up and decentralization of capital, in an attempt to re-create a society of small enterprisers;

[8] For review of antitrust legislation and its enforcement, see Ford P. Hall, *Government and Business,* 2d ed. (New York: McGraw-Hill Book Company, Inc., 1939), Chap. XV, "Control of Business under the Antitrust Laws," and Chap. XVI, "The Control of Business by the Federal Trade Commission"; Leverett S. Lyon, Myron W. Watkins, and Victor Abramson, *Government and Economic Life* (Washington: The Brookings Institution, 1939), Vol. I, Chap. X, "The Maintenance of Competition in Business Enterprise," and Chap. XI, "The Plane of Competition in Business Enterprise"; George Matthews Modlin and Archibald MacDonald McIssac, *Social Control of Industry* (Boston: Little, Brown & Company, 1938), Chap. VII, "The Restriction of Competition," Chap. XIII, "Control of Industrial Monopoly," and Chap. IX, "Control of Trade Practices"; Myron W. Watkins, *et al., Public Regulation of Competitive Practices in Business Enterprise* (New York: National Industrial Conference Board, 1940).

For a statement of some of the difficulties involved in antitrust and similar legislation, see Thurman W. Arnold, *The Folklore of Capitalism* (New Haven: Yale University Press, 1937), Chap. IX, "The Effect of the Antitrust Laws in Encouraging Large Combinations." In this discussion the author notes that the attempt to make our economic system conform to the ideal of a collection of competitive individuals is virtually impossible in view of the necessity of organization. In a later book, written at a time when Professor Arnold was charged with the enforcement of these laws, he seems to have more faith in a return to small competitive enterprise. See his *Democracy and Free Enterprise* (Norman: University of Oklahoma Press, 1942).

(2) an admission of the advantages of size with extensive capitalization but with highly centralized control and increased responsibility to those whose interests are affected. In the latter case economic opportunity would have to take the form of occupational specialization, with possibly some choice in investments. Either alternative calls for extensive exercise of governmental controls: in the one case to break up the productive system into very small units and prevent new combinations under some new disguise, and in the other case to ensure responsibility and the protection of fairly equal opportunity. But true believers in economic opportunity should beware the preachments of those who would have their cake and eat it too—that is, who want to "keep government out of business" so that they can control other people's money as they see fit.

The emphasis on economic opportunity has been placed so exclusively in terms of independent business enterprise, which never occupied more than a minority of the working force, that the mistaken idea seems to prevail that only by competition among individual enterprisers in production and distribution can economic opportunity prevail. On the one hand, even were it possible to return to the simple days of individual competition among producers, there would be little incompatibility between that kind of "free enterprise" and the enslavement of the working population. In discussions of economic opportunity it is necessary to bear in mind two further questions: what kind of opportunity, and opportunity for whom? On the other hand, there is no question that a small establishment, granting competition and a free labor system, offers less danger to other establishments and other economic interests than does the large *and uncontrolled* enterprise. In view of the actuality and the necessity of large-scale organization in the contemporary conduct of industrial affairs, it seems reasonable to expect a gradual diminution of efforts to fight bigness as an evil in itself, and a turning of attention toward the control of powerful organizations. Above all, there is reason to expect an emphasis on opportunities other than those of the independent investor-manager-inventor who remains the (virtually nonexistent) stereotype of the free enterpriser.

Protection of Investors. Somewhat in line with the more recent developments in the attempted preservation of economic opportunity has been a possibly tardy official recognition that the bulk of investors are no longer capitalists or enterprisers, and stand to gain or lose on their investments through persons and circumstances quite beyond their effective control. This recognition was long retarded, as we have already noted, by the persistence of the legal fiction that corporate wealth is private property for which adequate guarantees are provided by the ordinary property laws. It is the exposed and frequently disadvantageous position of the minority stockholder or member of a dispersed majority of stockholders that has most forcibly given the lie to the comfortable practice of treating corporations like small enterprisers.

The incorporation laws of the several states provide a highly variable degree of control over the purposes of enterprises, the ratio between assets and liabilities, the availability of information for the investor, and so on. The obvious difficulty with such controls in a federal system of government is the inequality of control in the various states, coupled with the fact that a corporation may do business in a state other than the one where it has been incorporated. Thus a corporation with almost all its business located in Illinois may, for reasons best known to the original organizers, be chartered under the extremely "moderate" laws of Delaware. The registration of securities, licensing of agents and traders, and similar provisions in state laws are equally variable.

To offset some of this unevenness of control, as well as to provide some controls possible only as a national basis, the Federal government has since 1933 required the registration of securities with extensive information for the guidance of investors, and since 1934 has supplemented that mode of control by regulation of stock exchanges. Both of these controls are administered chiefly by the Securities and Exchange Commission.[9]

Both state and Federal laws attempt some measure of control over erroneous claims by promoters, issuance of stocks valued far in excess of the tangible assets of the company (sometimes called

[9] See Hall, *op. cit.*, Chap. XVIII, "Regulation of Securities."

"watered" stock), and various manipulative and speculative devices used in exchanges to alter the price of securities without regard to their value as long-term investments. However, these restrictions do not in any positive sense give governmental security to investments. They tend to reduce the margin of fraud by those in financial control or by the manipulative practices of traders. They do not guarantee an efficient (or even an honest) management of the affairs of the company, but they do provide information from which much of the company's past activity may be judged. They cannot prevent an investor from buying or selling stock because of his opinion of the United States President, the advice of his astrologer, or the state of his liver. They do provide a measure of protection against manufactured rises and declines in market prices through deliberate manipulation. Above all, the law still leaves many doubts concerning how far those in financial control can legally disregard the interests of unrepresented stockholders, although the tendency to increased "trusteeship" is quite apparent.

Protection of the Consumer. The equivalent of the older "hands-off" policy with respect to production and trade was the rule that the consumer should look out for his own interests. The traditional catchword for this policy was *caveat emptor,* "let the buyer beware." Under the assumptions of extensive knowledge and invariable rationality, such a policy was thought adequate safeguard for all concerned, even against most types of fraud. But the voidance of contracts by reason of fraud is a very old legal principle, and its extension to include the plain and fancy lying of shrewd traders marked the first major inroad into the freedom of the consumer to make his own mistakes.

As the preparation and manufacture of goods has become more complex and further removed from the direct knowledge of the ultimate purchaser, the simple provisions against fraud were widely held to be inadequate protection of the consumer. Thus, to take a simple example, the ordinary well-informed layman can scarcely be expected to know the nature and physiological effects of chemical preparations or the relative advantages of different methods of constructing automobile engines, or to detect the presence of charcoal in pepper, sawdust in whole wheat flour, and similar adulterations. To be perfectly sure of the nature and performance of the goods he buys, the consumer would have to set up an extensive laboratory with a complete research staff. Before buying any article he would have to check its weight and size against the public claims, analyze its composition, test its performance, to say nothing of taking all these facts into consideration with respect to comparable articles at the same or different prices. One hears a great deal these days about the "intelligent consumer." But no consumer could be reasonably expected to go to such lengths to protect his own welfare.

Yet the conditions prevailing before the first Federal Pure Food and Drug Act of 1906, and the number of prosecutions under the Act and the more extensive law passed in 1938, indicate that the buyer must "beware" of a great deal of chicanery if he is not to be duped, cheated, and possibly maimed or killed. These laws, and other Federal and state laws running along similar lines, operate chiefly to reduce the range of information which the consumer must secure to protect himself, and secondarily to remove some positively harmful products from the range of choice of the most willfully ignorant or "foolish" consumer.

The protection of the consumer through governmental control actually extends much further than protection of his health. Licensing, labeling, inspection of weights and measures, various devices for standardizing grades and their names, the reduction of false and misleading advertising, and many other interferences "in the public interest" gradually reduce freedom in manufacturing and marketing goods. Such controls, for example, may prevent or dissuade producers from calling the smallest size of peas "colossal," or the fourth grade of milk "Grade A." Inspectors may lead to the prosecution of butchers who weigh their thumbs, and the Federal Trade Commission may attempt to dissuade manufacturers from making extravagant claims for their products. Thus a fountain pen manufacturer was persuaded to cease guaranteeing the product "forever" (which is a long time), and the manufacturer now advertises that the *service* on the pen (at a fixed price) is guaranteed forever.

Federal and state laws do not seek to eliminate choice on the part of the consumer, but rather attempt to narrow the range of choice to those products that are not harmful or offered under false or misleading claims. Thus, as long as a moderately "free" market prevails, both price and quality competition may go on, subject only to the limits established by public control. In these circumstances, public control cannot guarantee that the choice of alternative but similar goods made by the consumer will be rational—that is, based on some narrowly defined self-interest. Certainly public authority intervenes only in extreme cases (such as charges of nonsupport) to insist that the consumer should buy one class of products and not another. At the risk of offense to a sensitive and highly articulate occupational group, it may be pointed out that the bulk of advertising copy appeals to anything else but the narrow calculation of prices and qualities for necessities. Courtship and class competition, appeals to bogus authority, the properly respectable (and costly) sentiments of and about mothers—these are grist for the advertisers' mill. And given certain values and symbols of proper conformity to those values, who is to say that the double prices charged for nationally advertised goods or the exclusive label of an eminently proper Fifth Avenue address are too high? Presumably the prices paid yield "satisfactions" of some sort.

Protection of Employment Standards. An impressive series of governmental controls limits the terms of the labor contract, and to a certain extent the relative powers of employers and employees in fixing upon labor conditions. We have already commented upon the role of government in attempting to equalize the power of employers and employees through collective bargaining (Chapter XIV), as well as the more limited attempts to procure agreements through mediation and arbitration (Chapter XVI). Collective bargaining legislation does not, in itself, directly affect employment standards except in so far as it protects union members from arbitrary dismissal for union activity. Its chief effect upon the terms of the labor contract is obviously indirect, although none the less real: by removing legal restrictions upon collective bargaining and actively intervening to prevent the employer from denying the right, the laws clearly add weight to the demands of labor for higher wages, shorter hours, and so on.

Many enthusiastic labor leaders claim that the only governmental control over the labor contract necessary is the assurance of the right of collective bargaining. Anything else, it is claimed, may be left to self-help by the unions. Yet for a variety of reasons, the state and Federal governments have gone much further than this in the matter of labor standards. Outstanding among the reasons for the more direct intervention of government is that labor standards are of considerably wider interest than simply the protection of organized labor. Add to this the fact that labor organization, and especially collective bargaining, have been looked upon with legal favor only recently, and the intervention of governmental control is readily understandable.

The regulation of the labor of women and children—who represented the bulk of early factory employees—got under way rather slowly in the last century, but during the present century has been extended fairly widely. Industrialization by no means introduced female and child labor, but rather introduced new circumstances and posed new problems. Even though factory hours might be no longer and the work no more difficult than was customary in rural areas, factory labor took place outside the home, under hours, wages, and working conditions determined by the employer. Under these circumstances, and the further highly important circumstance that ideas and values were also undergoing considerable changes, child labor came to be regarded as contrary to such values as health, the influence of the family, and extensive education. Similarly, the labor of women came to be regarded as either contrary to public policy, or at least as calling for special regulation to protect their health. It is true, of course, that adult male laborers were concerned over the fact that women and children, together with immigrants and other "substandard" workers, not only forced down wages through the sheer weight of numbers but could be employed for less money at the same type of work as the adult male. However, in view of the fairly weak political position of laboring groups until very recently, there seems to be no reason to lay all the opposition to child labor and the regulation of female labor to the competitive interests of other workers.

The laws regulating the employment of women and minors have not been welcomed by the courts. A fairly standard interpretation until recently was that such laws took away freedom of contract "without due process of law" (that is, the courts did not like it). Under the older constitutional interpretations, this was a matter for legislation by the individual states, if at all. But state legislation in this matter, as in all other matters having significance beyond state boundaries, was subject to great inequalities. Thus states that did not prohibit child labor gave to employers in the state an "unfair" (that is, unequal) competitive advantage over those employers not allowed to use such cheap labor. The Federal child labor law of 1916 was declared unconstitutional, as was the child labor tax law of 1919. Similarly the child labor provisions of the National Industrial Recovery Act of 1933 fell with the rest of the Act before the courts. An attempted amendment to the Constitution, started in 1924, failed of ratification by a sufficient number of states. Only with the Fair Labor Standards Act of 1938, which has been upheld, has the power of the Federal government in this field been allowed to stand. The Federal law applies only to those establishments engaged in interstate commerce by the new and expanded definitions, and so still leaves to state or no regulation a large number of factory and agricultural child laborers. The regulation of employment conditions for women has had an even more difficult history, the Supreme Court for a time having maneuvered itself into the position of denying both to the state and to the Federal government the right of interference. Recent decisions have again opened the way for state, but not for national, legislation.[10]

[10] See MacDonald, *op. cit.*, Chap. XXXIV, "Child Labor Legislation"; S. Howard Patterson, *Social Aspects of Industry*, 3d ed. (New York: McGraw-Hill Book Company, Inc., 1943), Chap. X, "Women and Children in Industry: Problems of Exploitation"; Emanuel Stein, "Government and the Terms of the Labor Contract," in Carl Raushenbush and Emanuel Stein, eds., *Labor Cases and Materials* (New York: F. S. Crofts & Co., 1941), Chap. 6, "Regulating the Supply of Labor." See also United States Department of Labor, Bureau of Labor Statistics, "Trend of Child Labor 1927 to 1936," and "Trend of Child Labor 1937 to 1939," Serial No. R. 677 (1938) and Serial No. R 1058 (1940).

As other examples of the gradually extending control over labor conditions, we should note the wages and hours provisions of the Fair Labor Standards Act, which narrows the range of collective bargaining for those workers in "interstate commerce" establishments covered by the Act. In popular speech this law is said to put a floor under wages and a ceiling over hours, thus effectively reducing the bargaining power of the employer on these matters. The regulation of what is currently called "industrial homework," which is the contemporary equivalent of the putting-out system, is also attempted by a number of states and by the Fair Labor Standards Act. Although the problems of low wages, long hours, night work, child labor, the transformation of the home into a factory, and so on, are commonly recognized, the substandard working conditions are chief among the reasons for the continuance of this mode of productive organization. Enforcement of special industrial homework laws is in other words difficult precisely for the reason that the evasion of factory standards and factory inspection accounts for much of this activity. Although the normal pattern of change is toward the gradual transfer of homework activities to the factories (especially where mechanization is possible or increased control necessary), the problem of bringing labor conditions in this type of work into line with those prevailing in larger establishments is likely to be present for some time.

In general the governmental controls aiming at the regulation of employment conditions seem to indicate several major tendencies: (1) modifications of freedom of contract and the "right to work" where those ideals markedly conflict with other values; (2) a standardization of employment conditions at equivalent levels in the division of labor; and (3) an attempted general raising of those standards, or at least a raising of the minimum standards.

Reduction of Risks. A final group of social controls of industry, both direct and indirect, are also aimed primarily at changing either the direct conditions of employment or the indirect results of a "free labor" system. Those controls are the laws designed to reduce the effect of the risks of the industrial employee. The risks of the employee are, of course, many, and our legislation does not provide for all of them equally. Indeed, compared with most European countries, our development of "social security" or "social insurance" is remarkably meager. That is, the slow development is remarkable unless one takes into account the pronounced institutional differences, which in our case have resulted in an emphasis on the self-reliant individual. As already noted, this emphasis made a positive virtue of getting on in the world without outside help, while tending to think that failure to get along (for whatever actual reasons) represented a moral judgment of inadequacy.

The risks of the employee revolve chiefly around his job and his capacity to earn. That the employee is frequently unable to underwrite those risks on his own account has been more or less recognized for a long time, although the older pattern of family assistance and neighborly mutual aid tended to cushion part of the changes in fortune. The oldest and most extensive modification of the doctrine of individual self-reliance and accountability is represented by workmen's compensation laws. Although the payment of benefits for industrial accidents causing injury and death—without regard to responsibility—is not compulsory in all states, and applies to different classes of workers in different areas, the principle is fairly commonly accepted.

Only very recently, chiefly since the passage of the Social Security Act in 1935 and its expanded coverage in 1950, have other industrial risks been considered a proper sphere for governmental intervention. With this Act both old age and unemployment insurance is made available to a major portion of industrial employees, the former directly by the Federal government, the latter through Federal-state cooperation. The application of the unemployment benefits is somewhat more limited than that of old-age payments, but the unemployment insurance has been extended in a number of states to cover additional workers.[11] Sickness insurance, apart from purely indus-

---

[11] See MacDonald, *op. cit.*, Chap. XXXVII, "Social Insurance Legislation," Chap. XXXVIII, "Federal Social Security Legislation," and Chap. XXXIX, "Unemployment Insurance"; Patterson, *op. cit.*, Chap XI, "Industrial Hazards and Social Insurance: Promotion of Safety"; Carl Raushenbush, "The State's Relation to Labor," in Emanuel Stein and Jerome Davis, eds., *Labor Problems in America* (New York: Farrar & Rinehart, Inc., 1940), Book V, especially Chap.

trial diseases, has made little headway in the United States. Some companies provide medical care for their employees, others for employees and their families. "Sick leaves" with pay and sometimes jointly sponsored insurance programs are occasionally written into collective labor agreements. For the most part, however, health and sickness—including maternity risks for employed women—remain highly individual matters in our society. There is no doubt that part of this is due to long-standing individualism, part to the definite and concerted opposition to anything remotely approximating "socialized medicine" by the medical profession.

Our major concern so far in this chapter has been with the principles and problems behind the exertion of public authority over the life and welfare of the individual citizen. Any specific measure, once adopted, raises a whole additional series of problems, partly administrative and technical in character, partly of a political character (that is, having to do with policy). The questions of policy seem bound to arise in some degree because of the difficulty of predicting all of the consequences of any given line of action. But they also arise because of the characteristically irregular and piecemeal manner with which "reforms" are introduced. So pronounced is the uneven and even inconsistent character of the controls that some critics have been led to advocate some form of "planned" economy. Just what such a social order might mean, and the relevant scientific considerations for either policy-forming or prediction, will constitute the major points of concern in the following section.

SOCIAL INTEGRATION AND PLANNING

A widely recognized characteristic of our economic organization is the fact of economic interdependence. But if the fact of economic interdependence is widely recognized, its significance is not. The classical theory of a nation of small producers did not deny interdependence, but rather placed reliance on "automatic" market adjust-

---

33, "Work-Injury Laws," Chap. 34, "Old-Age Legislation," Chap. 35, "Unemployment Insurance," and Chap. 36, "Health Insurance"; Stein, *loc. cit.*, Chap. 10, "Workmen's Compensation," Chap. 11, "Unemployment Compensation," and Chap. 12, "Old Age Assistance and Benefits."

ments and contractual agreements motivated by private gain to keep the productive and distributive systems in operation. The present organization of industry and trade has not only increased specialization (which inevitably spells dependence on others), but through concentration of economic power has placed a small number of individuals in such strategic positions that their decisions affect millions. If the president of the United States Steel Corporation were to order a shut-down of all of the company's plants, the entire metropolitan area of Pittsburgh would be faced with economic disaster. If the president of the United Mine Workers orders a strike in the coal fields, industrial power plants close down and householders shiver. And both of these actions may be dictated by the "state of the market," and in terms of traditional theory be perfectly sound.

Whether in wartime or in peacetime, these decisions would not be allowed to stand for an extended period of time. *The fact of interdependence produces the necessity of intervention in the public interest.*

Social Control and Economic Planning. Intervention in the public interest does not, however, constitute economic planning, strictly defined. It may be well to consider briefly the distinctions between the detailed social controls summarized in the preceding chapter and the characteristics of a planned economy.

In its broadest sense, social planning is simply organized and deliberate social control for the achievement of certain objectives. Whenever a pressure group secures the passages of legislation favorable to its interests, that group is sponsoring some measure of social planning. Indeed, in the same broad sense social planning is an integral part of any formal legal or political order. The law and the agencies of government constitute the structure responsible for the achievement of social objectives.

Economic planning differs from the more general social controls by a greater concentration on the control of the production and distribution of economic goods, and by a greater degree of integration. Our present concern, then, is with the deliberate and integrated control of the economic order for the achievement of certain objectives. It is perhaps unnecessary to add that we are primarily concerned here with the prospects and problems of a planned economy as a whole, and not with the otherwise important planning by industrial concerns, or even groups of industrial concerns. The controls characterizing a planned economy are exercised in behalf of, or at least in the name of, the entire society.

The integration of controls in a planned economy calls for a few words of comment. It is this feature which most disturbs those who see in planning a threat to traditional liberties. Most Americans are brought up in a tradition of distrust of politics and politicians in general, and in the political tradition of separation of powers, checks and balances, and the rest of the features of a federal system. The eternal vigilance that is supposed to be the price of liberty is thus directed toward spreading the evil of political authority as widely as possible, rather than concentrating power and responsibility in the hands of a few key officials. Thus a multitude of administrative agencies with conflicting jurisdictions have grown up in response to the pressure for increased control; the "planning" undertaken in these circumstances is haphazard and frequently self-defeating.

As critics of economic planning point out, there is scarcely any detail of our economic life that is not covered by some form of administrative supervision. The critics can also assert with some reason that this administrative supervision has neither resolved the issues in our economic order, nor uniformly attained even the limited objectives sought. But here our agreement with the critics must stop, since the latter customarily go on to the conclusion that the present difficulties in social control demonstrate the evils of "governmental interference."

Our previous discussion of the social controls of industry indicated the necessity of governmental intervention if anything like a stable economic order is to be maintained under present conditions of technology and economic organization. But our previous analysis also revealed something of the source and mechanisms of these controls in our political system as presently constituted. Some of them undoubtedly reflect very nearly a consensus, since they directly relate to the security of the society as a whole. For obvious reasons, these controls are most numerous and most apparent in wartime and in periods of marked international tension. Others, and these represent the majority at any time, reflect the opinions of particular segments of the population, whether or not those segments are organized as definite political pressure groups. This circumstance, coupled with the ideology that views *any* intervention as exceptional, has produced an immense number of controls, but it has produced practically no planning in the narrower sense of taking account of the facts of interdependence and functional relationships, and acting accordingly.

The difficulties of social controls that are haphazard and piecemeal thus partly derive from the neglect of economic interdependence. Any regulation or control of one phase of economic activity has repercussions not only in the whole structure of the national economy, but in general social organization. If the controls are minor or the activity unimportant, the repercussions may be of only academic interest (except, of course, to those most directly affected). But if, for example, wholesalers and retailers are obliged to observe wartime ceiling prices while producers are allowed to charge what they can get, a "black market" results. Moreover, the buying and law-abiding habits of numerous citizens are affected. If strikes are prohibited without provision of alternative methods for settling disputes, violence or political changes may ensue, and certainly the outlook and social status of workmen will be changed. If "industrial leaders" agree upon measures for price maintenance, production quotas, etc., as under the National Recovery Administration, the small producer may find himself "squeezed out" by lack of political power rather than lack of competitive ability in a free market. If collective bargaining is upheld by law, the authority of the industrial manager is reduced, and the property institutions of the society are modified. If minimum wage standards are enforced in plants employing pieceworkers, those workers who cannot meet the minimum earnings at the current rate may lose their employment rather than gain security.

The examples of the secondary consequences of social controls, many of them unforeseen and unfavorably regarded, could of course be extended almost indefinitely. They illustrate the absence of integrated economic planning rather than the inherent weakness of governmental control.

Enthusiasts for and opponents of a planned economy share in general at least one characteristic: their easy-going neglect of some of the more practical considerations involved in integrated social control. And although some of these practical considerations are "mere details," some of them are of such fundamental importance with respect to public policy that any discussion of planning without attention to them becomes meaningless. A review of some of the more fundamental problems posed by a planned economy may serve to throw more light on the possible future place of industry in society.

The Problem of Ends. It seems evident that any planning must be directed toward the achievement of certain objectives. Thus one of the very first questions which must be asked with respect to proposals for a planned society is, Planning for what and for whom? Were there perfect agreement in a society upon the objectives of social life, and a perfect community of interests, it would only be necessary to find the appropriate means for the universal ends. Such a state of affairs is approximated when the question at issue is the security of the society as a whole. Even traditional doctrine allowed to governments a wide scope of integrated control in obviously crucial cases, and in any event confined debate to the means rather than the objective. But when the problem concerns the internal distribution of rights and duties, no such uniformity of judgment prevails. The values prevailing in our society are highly diversified, and it becomes necessary to find some system for weighing their importance.

Given the requisite political power, it is of course possible to adopt almost any standard of judgment concerning relative worth. Thus, the objectives sought might be those of the farmers who do not have an "adequate" amount of land—the commonest aim of planning in prewar eastern Europe; or the objective may be to establish a society of workingmen—the professed goal of the Soviet Union; or the goal may be a society dominated by combinations of large industrial concerns—an early stage of the German and Italian fascist systems. Under the same assumption it would be equally possible to aim at the prosperity of all left-handed persons, or an assured social and economic position for all individuals whose family name begins with "R."

As we have seen, it is possible to develop a series of social controls which aim at all manner of objectives, and which conform to the wishes of various interest groups. But if integrated control toward definite and interrelated objectives be attempted, it is of primary importance to determine those objectives and their relative importance. Suppose, for example, that the principal aim of a planned economy were a higher minimum standard of living. Quite aside from questions about appropriate means, there remain some ticklish problems to be settled. Is the objective to be considered more important than existing property rights? What weight will be attached to effort, achievement, and need? Should relative as well as absolute levels be considered; that is, is any attention to be paid to great disparities in income?

Not all of the interests of individuals and groups within a society are concerned with material prosperity. This means that a planned economy would need to be concerned with matters such as health, education, recreation, and perhaps the preservation of various traditional rights and liberties. Even if planning were formally confined to the production and distribution of goods and services, the relative importance of those goods and services must be determined. As in an industrial organization, effective administration entails the prediction of sacrifices as well as incidental benefits deriving from a program of action.

The selection of goals for planning is facilitated by several characteristics of societal organization. Chief among these is the fact that any society already has a fairly clear hierarchy of values, so that in cases of conflict of objectives priorities can be determined. At the same time, although it is not the same thing, there exist within any society fairly common standards of relative worth of individuals, that is, bases for determining whose interests should be served. On the other hand, it would be a mistake to minimize the difficulties of choice of objectives in view of the tremendous weight of all manner of vested interests incorporated within existing ideals and controls. Thus the goal of equality of opportunity is widely approved, but usually not at the expense of inheritance of wealth, and certainly not at the expense of differential advantages provided by families of different social positions. Questions of this sort are not peculiar to social planning since they simply reflect the functional and interdependent character of social values and social controls, but they are likely to appear in more acute form in the event of formal planning and formal organization for the achievement of objectives.

Within the predictable future, the most likely over-all goals of economic planning in democratically disposed societies are those of economic security internally and military security externally. Security is of course an essentially negative goal; more positively, an assured minimum level of living and reasonably full employment (partly for external security) are likely to be emphasized.

The Problem of Responsibility. Even if the ends of social planning are readily agreed upon (for example, winning a war), there is an entire range of touchy questions concerning the agencies and techniques for achieving those objectives.

This problem frequently raises the horrible picture of a welter of agencies, bureaus, offices, and departments, issuing separate and contradictory statements of objectives and "directives" for their accomplishment. Such a state of affairs can happen; it has happened in various national political administrations, including that of the supposedly efficient Nazis. It is a product of (a) too little centralized control (not, as many "localists" seem to believe, of too much), which in turn arises from (b) uncertainty concerning immediate or ultimate objectives, and (c) the necessity of rapid expansion in time of crisis.

There is no question that a planned economy spells bureaucracy. But we earlier observed that bureaucracy is a general type of formal social organization, not limited to the agencies of government, and not necessarily "inefficient." Above all, it must be noted that a sprawling and disjointed administrative organization is not due to specialization, to detailed administration, or even to expansion *per se*. It is rather due to the absence of the necessary counterpart of specialization: coordination. It is true that expansion and adjustment to change (even if planning and control of change is the main business of the organization) places strains on a bureaucracy which can only be met by administrative attention to the main goals and the responsibility for achieving them. The administrative difficulties imposed by rapid change are not a special burden borne by political officials. If they are more noticeable in governmental circles, it is because industrial bureaucracies adhere to as rigid privacy as possible (so that even their own "public," the stockholders, are carefully shielded from any disturbing information). For this reason also, incompetence can be discovered and rectified at least as quickly in a public agency.

If the problem of objectives can be phrased with at least partial accuracy as the question, Planning for whom? the problem of responsibility may be expressed as, Planning *by* whom? This is partly, and secondarily, a question of the technical competence of administrators. It is more importantly a question of the *accountability* of administrators.

At first glance the essential question of responsibility for planning might seem to be whether the direction of social and economic activities will rest with the state or with "private" organizations. This question is not unimportant in so far as it relates to questions of administrative organization, but is meaningless with respect to final authority. By definition, the latter rests with the state. That is, the organization that effectively exercises the final authority *is* the state, whatever may be its particular name. Both on grounds of special interests and of special competence, it is reasonable to expect considerable decentralization and even latitude of judgment. But the decentralization is likely to be functional in character, with questions of more general policy necessarily decided by political organs.

The more significant question of responsibility for social planning is that of the responsibility of the officials of governmental planning agencies. That is, given certain objectives, how is the assurance maintained that those interests are being served? It is at precisely this point that various European experiments with planned economies diverge most radically from democratic doctrine. *The im-*

portant point is not that the ultimate control is exercised by the state, but that those who exercise the power are with respect to the bulk of the population not responsible for their actions. The experiences of the Italian "corporate state," of German "national socialism," and of the Russian "dictatorship of the proletariat" indicate a common pattern in at least one respect: however broad the claims to allegiance, and however great the opportunistic support of special-interest groups, the officials are ultimately responsible only to a very small power group—the inner circle of the "party." Other interests are served, at least to the extent necessary to avoid revolution and secure minimum allegiance to the program of the party. But through a virtual monopoly of armed power, authority remains with a relatively small group.

If the democratic way be followed, how are various interests to be represented? It is sometimes said that the role of government, whether the control be minimal or maximal, should at least be impartial. But impartiality in this sense cannot mean scientific objectivity, for the role of government is inevitably concerned with policy. The most that official impartiality can mean is a freedom from a highly specialized bias in view of other recognized interests and values—for example, a recognition and protection of interests beyond those of capital, or of labor, or even of capital *and* labor. This means, in terms of responsibility, that a planned economy that adhered to democratic doctrine would require a government that was representative (in the strict political sense of the term) of all interests consistent with the fundamental value system, and in approximate weight of their numerical or other importance.

Political representation in the United States is nominally on a territorial basis. However, it is increasingly evident that voting tends to follow economic interests, with the supplemental fostering of those interests by unofficial and extralegal pressure groups. As the direct participation of government in economic affairs increases, there is likely to be an increasing development of "guild" or "syndical" organizations representing common economic interests (including occupational interests). Short of a major political upheaval, it is, however, likely that such organizations will grow up gradually alongside more traditional forms of political representation. The wartime increases of such agencies of control as the War Labor Board—some of them with the familiar tripartite representation of management, labor, and the "public"—indicates one possible line of development. In testing the consistency of such organizations with democratic principle it is essential to inquire, not about their particular form, but especially about how the group holding the balance of power is chosen, and to whom it is responsible. It is frequently argued, with some merit, that representation and responsibility are more adequately secured through such means than through traditional political parties supplemented by more or less irresponsible "pressure" organizations and lobbies.[12]

The Problem of How Much Control. The problems of the objectives of social planning and the responsibility for accomplishing those objectives may be regarded as the most fundamental in future policy. The solutions to these problems do not, however, answer all the pertinent questions that may be asked. Notably, they only partially answer the question of how extensive and detailed the control is to be. This question is especially significant in a society with traditions of "freedom" and resistance to "regimentation."

A free economy, it has been noted, is not an uncontrolled one. We may go even further, since a "free" economy as commonly discussed meant simply freedom from market controls and from public interference with the use made of "private property." For large sections of the population, including both laborers and small investors, that kind of freedom has been illusory or nonexistent. Thus when the objection is raised that a planned economy takes away liberties, a legitimate question is always: Whose liberties? The control of a few for the benefit of many may or may not be sound policy; it is certainly a possible one.

It is possible to plan for and control an economic system in great

[12] See, for example, Georges Gurvitch, "Democracy as a Sociological Problem," *Journal of Legal and Political Sociology*, 1 (1–2): 46–71, October 1942; Lewis L. Lorwin, "Planning in a Democracy," *Publications of the American Sociological Society*, 29: 41–48, August 1935. The idea of occupational or similar representation is, of course, shared by the "Guild Socialists," the "pluralists" in political philosophy, and many other groups.

detail, with, however, a considerable margin of unpredictability and error.[13] On the other hand, it is possible to restrict the centralized controls to problems of general direction and policy and the setting of limits to variation and the results of activities not controlled in detail. In other words, planning may take such a form that fairly extensive competition (including occupational competition), relatively free choice of consumers' goods, relative freedom of association, and a variety of other customary "rights" and liberties are preserved. Planned economy of the latter type would seem to have more chance of success in the predictable future, not only because of the greater degree of support to be expected, but because a complex and heterogeneous economic order virtually requires considerable elasticity. Thus, to take but a single example, it would appear to be foolhardy to attempt such complete planning that the occupational structure, down to the last minute specialty, should be determined ten or twenty years in advance, and the prospective occupants of each little niche "earmarked" through some system of inheritance of occupation. Even the most enthusiastic supporters for planning must leave some things to competition and chance.

The preservation of liberties within a controlled economy is partly an administrative question. The opponents of detailed planning by centralized commissions are certainly correct in doubting both the ability and the interest of over-all policy makers in carrying out detailed programs in various fields. Thus, one of the most consistent objections by medical practitioners to "socialized medicine" is the presumed horrors of control by laymen. Similarly, businessmen look with no favor upon being told how to manage their concerns "by some Washington bureaucrat."

To the extent that the expressed fears are founded on fact, the opposition would appear to be justified in terms of expediency, with-

---

[13] The sources of unpredictability are of the same order as those previously discussed (in Chap. VIII) as applying to planning *within* an industrial organization. It is certain, however, that the margin of uncertainty is greater in planning an entire economy, simply because of greater size and complexity. On the other hand, this may be partially offset by the fact that a planned economy may rest upon a broader control of significant factors. See Robert K. Merton, "The Unanticipated Consequences of Purposive Social Action," *American Sociological Review*, 1: 894–904, December 1936.

out regard to questions of abstract rights. That is, a detailed directive by a layman on how to prescribe for a physiological complaint or perform an operation would scarcely aid the practice of medicine, either for the physician or for the patient. Similarly, the attempt of a governmental executive to oversee detailed manufacturing methods or the stocking of retail inventories would certainly result in disorganization rather than effective control. But the presumed disadvantages of centralized control are not inherent in that control. They simply indicate the necessity of functional specialization and decentralization.

Any large and specialized organization is faced with these same problems, and we have commented upon them in detail with reference to the managerial organization of industry. At that point we also noted, however, that *the development of "functional authority" with special spheres of competence, as well as decentralization with respect to administrative detail, are possible only within the framework of centralized responsibility for general policy.* Enthusiasts for a *complete* functional division of authority within industrial management are as mistaken as the pluralists in political theory who see no reason for political authority taking final precedence over other interests. Just as it is the specialized function of the industrial executive to be the final authority (at least within the organization) on questions of general policy and the adjudication of conflicts among special interests, so it is the function of political organization to be concerned with the achievement of ultimate societal objectives and the compatability of organizational interests. Just as it is unreasonable to assume that laymen should set rules for the diagnosis of disease, it is unreasonable to assume that a physician—as a physician—should determine the public policy with respect to the distribution of medical benefits. Just as it is unreasonable to expect an executive of a central planning board to be able competently to direct the manufacture of products from crude oil, it is unreasonable to assume that a manufacturer—as a manufacturer—has any special competence in determining policy with respect to the rate of efficiency of use of natural resources.

It is an old saw, but a true one, that freedom within a stable society implies and requires responsibility. To be truly effective, responsibility in turn always requires sanctions. How intimately the problems of a planned economy are interwoven can be seen from the simple fact that the question of how much control should be exercised is also partly a question of how to enforce responsibility for actions that affect the public interest. Traditional theory held stoutly that each individual was the best judge of his own interests. Even were this true—and it is patently not true with respect to matters of fact and policy beyond the individual's range of competence —this still leaves the question of the ability of the individual to *protect* as well as judge his interests. Certainly this calls for considerable decentralization to take account of detailed knowledge of local and special conditions. But it also requires the possibility of an appeal to sanctions of a more persuasive character when the stakes are high and the resources uneven.

The sanctions of the market (profit and loss, and even success or failure) are real, and their morality has been based upon the responsibility of the individual for his actions and his willingness to accept the consequences. According to this view, if an enterpriser failed, it served him right. The problem of policy that is posed for any program of economic control is whether the sanctions of competitive failure place the burden where it belongs. For example, the failure of a large corporation may "serve its president right," but does it also serve its investors, employees, and consuming public right?

The social controls of economic activity in the future may be expected to be as detailed as necessary to ensure the public interest, according to the definition of those interests that is then current. But if a planned economy is fitted to a democratic social order, the controls may also be *limited* in the public interest, since a fairly wide range of individual freedom and initiative (in the broadest sense) is certain to be regarded as one of the fundamental public interests.

Dichotomies and dilemmas in social affairs are likely to be false, since alternative courses of action are usually more numerous than the two extremes. It is noteworthy that almost every poser of dilemmas manages to find some "middle ground." The probable future course of economic planning is no exception to these rules. There seems to be no reason for maintaining that the choice lies between Fascism and Communism, or between a completely free economy and a completely controlled one. In the latter case at least, the extreme positions are considerably less likely than some middle ground, since both of the extremes are virtually impossible in modern society. The foregoing analysis seems to indicate that the future course of the social order presents many alternatives, in various possible combinations, and that any sound appraisal of the future must deal at least with the objectives of, the responsibility for, and the extent of social controls. These are matters of real concern to the ordinary citizen, who may not choose "wisely," and need not choose at all. But some choosing will be done by "ordinary citizens" within the framework of democracy, or by groups of "extraordinary citizens" within the framework of some narrower power structure.

REFERENCES

ANDREWS, JOHN B., *Labor Laws in Action* (New York: Harper & Brothers, 1938).

ANTHONY, ARTHUR BRUCE, *Economic and Social Problems of the Machine Age,* University of Southern California Social Science Series, No. 3 (Los Angeles: University of Southern California Press, 1930).

ARNOLD, THURMAN W., *Democracy and Free Enterprise* (Norman: University of Oklahoma Press, 1942).

——, *The Folklore of Capitalism* (New Haven: Yale University Press, 1937), Chap. II, "The Psychology of Social Institutions"; Chap. III, "The Folklore of 1937"; Chap. IX, "The Effect of the Antitrust Laws in Encouraging Large Combinations"; Chap. XI, "The Benevolence of Taxation by Private Organization"; Chap. XII, "The Malevolence of Taxation by the Government."

BERLE, ADOLF A., JR., and GARDINER C. MEANS, *The Modern Corporation and Private Property* (New York: The Macmillan Company, 1933), Book IV, Chap. I, "The Traditional Logic of Property"; Chap. II, "The Traditional Logic of Profits"; Chap. III, "The Inadequacy of Traditional Theory"; Chap. IV, "The New Concept of the Corporation."

BLAISDELL, DONALD C., "Economic Power and Political Pressures," United States Congress, Temporary National Economic Committee, *In-*

vestigation of Concentration of Economic Power, Monograph No. 26 (Washington: U. S. Government Printing Office, 1940).

BLUMER, HERBERT, "Group Tension and Interest Organization," in Milton Derber, ed., *Proceedings of the Second Annual Meeting, Industrial Relations Research Association,* New York City, December 29–30, 1949 (Champaign, Ill.: 1950), pp. 150–164.

BRADY, ROBERT A., *Business as a System of Power* (New York: Columbia University Press, 1934).

CLARK, JOHN M., *Social Control of Business,* 2d ed. (New York: McGraw-Hill Book Company, Inc., 1939), especially Chap. IV, "Purposes of Social Control," and Chap. XXVIII, "Economic Planning."

FISHER, THOMAS RUSSELL, *Industrial Disputes and Federal Legislation,* Studies in History, Economics and Public Law, No. 467 (New York: Columbia University Press, 1940), Chap. XI, "Contemporary and Future Need for Social Legislation."

GRAHAM, FRANK D., *Social Goals and Economic Institutions* (Princeton: Princeton University Press, 1942), Chap. III, "The Setting for Social Goals," and Chap. XII, "Implementation of the Program of Power-cum-Freedom."

GRAHAM, GEORGE A., and HENRY REINING, JR., *Regulatory Administration* (New York: John Wiley & Sons, Inc., 1943).

HALL, FORD P., *Government and Business,* 2d ed. (New York: McGraw-Hill Book Company, Inc., 1939).

HAMILTON, WALTON H., "Organization, Economic," in *Encyclopaedia of the Social Sciences* 11: 484–490.

LASKI, HAROLD J., *Trade Unions in the New Society* (New York: Viking Press, 1949).

LAUTERBACH, ALBERT, *Economic Security and Individual Freedom: Can We Have Both?* (Ithaca: Cornell University Press, 1949).

LYON, LEVERETT S., MYRON W. WATKINS, and VICTOR ABRAMSON, *Government and Economic Life* (Washington: The Brookings Institution, 1939), Vol I.

MACDONALD, LOIS, *Labor Problems and the American Scene* (New York: Harper & Brothers, 1938), Part Eight (Chaps. XXXII–XL), "Labor and the State: Protective Legislation."

MANNHEIM, KARL, *Man and Society in an Age of Reconstruction* (New York: Harcourt, Brace and Company, 1940), Part V, "Planning for Freedom," and Part IV, "Freedom at the Level of Planning."

MARSHALL, LEON CARROLL, ed., *Readings in Industrial Society* (Chicago: University of Chicago Press, 1918), Chap. XV, "Social Control."

MEANS, GARDINER C., "The Distribution of Control and Responsibility in a Modern Economy," in Benjamin E. Lippincott, ed., *Government*

Control of the Economic Order (Minneapolis: University of Minnesota Press, 1935), pp. 1–17.

MILLER, GLENN W., *American Labor and the Government* (New York: Prentice-Hall, 1948).

MOSSÉ, ROBERT, "Economic Planning and Freedom," *Journal of Legal and Political Sociology,* 3 (1–2): 122–133, Fall 1944.

NATIONAL ASSOCIATION OF MANUFACTURERS, Economic Principles Commission, *The American Individual Enterprise System: Its Nature, Evolution, and Future* (New York: McGraw-Hill Book Company, Inc., 1946, 2 vols.), Vol. II, Chap. XIV, "Government Regulation."

RAUSHENBUSH, CARL, "The State's Relation to Labor," in Emanuel Stein and Jerome Davis, eds., *Labor Problems in America* (New York: Farrar & Rinehart, Inc., 1940), Book V (Chaps. 27–36).

SCHUMPETER, JOSEPH A., *Capitalism, Socialism, and Democracy,* rev. ed. (New York: Harper & Brothers, 1947).

SHARP, MALCOM, and CHARLES O. GREGORY, *Social Change and Labor Law* (Chicago: University of Chicago Press, 1939), Part I, Chap. I, "Responsibility, Damages, and the Protection of Property"; Chap. II, "Contract and Constitution."

SPENGLER, JOSEPH J., "Power Blocs and the Formation and Content of Economic Decision," in Milton Derber, ed., *Proceedings of the Second Annual Meeting, Industrial Relations Research Association,* New York City, December 29–30, 1949 (Champaign, Ill.: 1950), pp. 174–191.

STEIN, EMANUEL, "Government and the Terms of the Labor Contract," in Carl Raushenbush and Emanuel Stein, eds. *Labor Cases and Materials* (New York: F. S. Crofts & Co., 1941), Part Two, including: Chap. 6, "Regulating the Supply of Labor"; Chap. 7, "Wage Laws"; Chap. 8, "Hours of Work Laws"; Chap. 9, "The Regulation of Working Conditions"; Chap. 10, "Workmen's Compensation"; Chap. 11, "Unemployment Compensation"; Chap. 12, "Old-Age Assistance and Benefits."

TELLER, LUDWIG, *A Labor Policy for America: A National Labor Code* (New York: Baker, Voorhis & Co., Inc., 1945).

WOLLETT, DONALD H., *Labor Relations and the Federal Law: An Analysis and Evaluation of Federal Labor Policy since 1947* (Seattle: University of Washington Press, 1949).

WOOTON, BARBARA, *Freedom under Planning* (Chapel Hill: University of North Carolina Press, 1945).

ZWEIG, FERDYNAND, *The Planning of Free Societies* (London: Secker and Warburg, 1942).

CHAPTER XXV

ON THE STABILITY OF THE INDUSTRIAL SYSTEM

Prophecy is a hazardous trade, as legend and recorded history amply testify. The attempt to predict the probable future of a world increasingly subject to industrial modes of productive organization is not a task to be undertaken lightly, or with supreme confidence in foresight. In view of the large range of ignorance about social processes on the grand scale, which is mainly ignorance of how a system of complex variables behaves through time, the soundest procedure for knowing the future state of the world is to stay alive and see. As this may be regarded as a counsel of perfection or despair, some attempt at foretelling the future may be thought to be as important as it is difficult.

This final chapter is not an essay in precise prediction, but rather represents an attempt to summarize some of the dynamic features implicit in the industrial system and to indicate some possible consequences for the future. After a brief review of the "success" of industrialism, attention is turned to some problems of internal stability in industrial societies and then to the relations between industrialism and the disorderly world.

THE SUCCESS OF INDUSTRIALISM [1]

Industrialization may be viewed with partial accuracy as a process involving an increasing range of resources exploited, an increasing amount and type of goods produced, and an increasing efficiency

---

[1] Several paragraphs in this section are quoted from the author's paper, "Utilization of Human Resources through Industrialization," *Milbank Memorial Fund Quarterly*, 28: 52–67, January 1950.

of capital and technique employed. From this point of view the process may be studied as a dynamic relationship among certain elements or "factors," which in their combination presumably determine both the pattern and rate of economic development.

The most general case for industrialization rests upon the range of goods and services made available for human consumption. As a productive system, it tends to free both supply and demand from traditional restraint, and to entail a dynamic rather than a static relation between man and nature.[2]

The particular case for industrialization as a mode of productive organization rests upon enhanced opportunities, through specialization, for utilizing special qualities and aptitudes of producers. Human beings both constitute necessary means and determine the ends of productive efforts. As means or as resources, human beings may be considered as coming within the general case for optimum utilization. The duality of the human role in this scheme complicates the issue, however. Inherent in the nature of human society are limitations to efficiency in the utilization of human resources for production, for in no society can production be the sole social function and in no human being can it be the sole motive. Within those limits, industrialism is that system of production which most effectively uses differences in aptitude and interest.[3]

---

[2] This abbreviated and therefore dogmatic formulation rests upon the abstract characteristics of the industrial mode of production and neglects many concrete problems and variations in experience. For example, differences in systems of control of production and allocation of products, and the problems of "balanced economies" as opposed to regional specialization are not irrelevant in the concrete instance but cannot be explored here. It may be maintained, however, that given certain characteristics of the industrial system—for example, utilization of advanced technology and of specialization of labor—other characteristics are inherent and in considerable measure independent of particular goals and procedures—for example, a reasonably elaborate system of exchange and of effective incentives to insure labor mobility and the development of skills. It follows that the case here does not assume or depend upon the institutional structure of liberal capitalism.

[3] Again, this formulation is abstracted from a host of concrete issues and problems: for example, the extent to which various categories of human laborers as means (or, in some economic formulations as "costs") of production share in determining the ends of production; the "dilution" of skill that accompanies some forms of specialization and the attendant problems of motivation; the multitudinous human problems of mobility and its accompanying uncertainty.

In terms of output, the industrial system has made possible tremendously increased levels of material production and the wide distribution of that production both at home and abroad. Even where production has been geared primarily to capital formation rather than immediate consumption, or has been diverted in considerable measure to armaments and the support of "nonproductive" armed forces, it is probable that the average level of consumption has increased if the minimum has not. This consequence is due to the importance of material rewards in incentive systems of industrial societies, with their great dependence on adequate numbers and performance of skilled workers, technicians, and administrators.

It is not just in production of material goods that the industrial system shows its superiority, however. By the tremendously greater efficiency of material production relative to workers directly involved, industrialism makes possible a wider diversion of time and talents to the production of services. Some of these services are indeed directly necessary to the industrial mode of production itself—for example, many administrative and professional activities, and the facilities for communication, transportation, and distribution essential to specialization of productive activities. Other services are also functionally related to the industrial system, although somewhat less directly—for example, medical care and public health in their connection with productive efficiency and the hazards of congestion fostered by the scale of industrial operations. Still other services or types of "material" production allow widespread participation at some level in recreational and aesthetic activities, although opinions differ as to the quality of these services and activities as compared with the spontaneous "folk" participation or the activities of a small élite in nonindustrial societies. In short, the industrial system lends itself to *mass* production and distribution of goods and services, including some not otherwise available at all. In the process, goods and services are torn from their traditional social context and subject to impersonal market transactions, and some items of "culture" are literally cheapened in the process.

The industrial system is rampant in the modern world. Its effects spread to the most isolated regions in some form or degree. Its system of communications and organization of world markets, and the political power that its productive system makes possible, have produced an interdependence of all peoples everywhere. The process is by no means complete, nor is its final fruition in any particular form determinate and inevitable. Even the results so far effected are not entirely clear or their implications commonly understood. Yet one elementary fact stands out: the isolated primitive or peasant community has everywhere lost part of its insularity. The true primitive represents a small and diminishing species. The self-sufficient peasant is shaken by forces beyond his control and perhaps even further beyond his understanding.

The impact of the industrial system on primitive and archaic cultures is a crude empirical phenomenon. It makes irrelevant or academic much of the well-meaning debate about interfering in other cultures. The question in most areas of the world is not whether change under external influence ought to be allowed, but rather the form and degree of chance, the interests taken into account, and the human as well as material costs of transition.

Ironically, the arguments in behalf of sealing off the effects of new productive organizations and processes, in order to preserve as much as possible of traditional values in the far places of the world, arrive approximately at the same policy as that of the most cynical "exploiter," who seeks to use native labor but to keep native societies otherwise outside the industrial system. If the effective utilization of human resources for the achievement of health, longevity, and heightened levels of material well-being be the goal, then education strictly "adapted" to *native* needs, wage labor as purely supplementary to primitive modes of production, and public health measures that do not change fertility patterns represent serious compromises in the short run and mixtures of doubtful stability in the long run.

The spread of the industrial system to primitive and archaic societies constantly poses anew problems not completely solved in the oldest industrial areas. Those problems differ widely in their details and specific incidence, but may be subsumed under the general category of maintenance of the integrative structures of society—

particularly those involving emotional and affective orientations and informal controls—in the face of the rationalized organization inherent in modern productive forms.

INTERNAL STABILITY OF INDUSTRIAL SOCIETIES

Viewed by the participant in a relatively stable nonindustrial social order, or, more accurately, one in which the impact of the industrial system is sufficiently small and recent that it may be regarded as a novelty, industrialism may not be regarded as an unmixed blessing. The industrialization process sets in motion transformations throughout a social system, many of which must be regarded as undesirable from the standpoint of any traditional set of norms and expectations. Were all of the costs of economic transformation to be viewed as purely transitional phenomena, viewers with alarm might be reassured. The continuance of tension and instability where the process of industrialization is far advanced removes any such comfortable rationalization.

Prophets of doom are never popular and, in company with all members of their trade, are not uncommonly wrong. Yet the tensions of the present and uncertainty of the future lend support to those who cry havoc. There are sources of tension and instability in industrial societies and between them. It is appropriate to examine those tensions, without, however, assuming that their existence makes disaster inevitable. The perfectly integrated society is a fiction, although for certain analytical purposes a useful one. The significance of existing sources of instability for prognosis of the future is an allowable scientific inquiry, although it may be difficult or impossible with available knowledge and technique. The appraisal of those tensions in terms of social values violated will sooner or later surpass the realm of objective inquiry and properly not be a part of discovery and generalization but rather of choice and policy.

The "Durkheim Dilemma." Before the end of the nineteenth century, Émile Durkheim, a French sociologist of lasting importance, arrived at a fundamental formulation concerning a major functional difficulty in industrial societies.[4] This formulation, which was quite at odds with the easy evolutionary optimism concerning atomistic self-regulation in social affairs characteristic of the period, may be summarized in the proposition that *interdependence is no guarantee of integration.* Durkheim distinguished two forms of social "solidarity" or integration, that based on likeness and common values and that based on specialization and interdependence. But the latter he observed very easily became a state of no solidarity at all, of *anomie*—rulelessness. He concluded that the division of labor characteristic of industrial societies was a viable basis of social stability only if "beliefs and sentiments held in common" remained of superordinate importance in the system. The "Durkheim dilemma" therefore is the fact that industrial societies depend upon a minute differentiation of social position and behavior, and therefore upon interdependence of specialized functions, but run the constant risk of collapsing into all sorts of specialized segments. Loyalties tend to follow narrow interests but therefore to shift with the context of social relations. "Interests," narrowly considered, will not keep a society operating; beliefs and sentiments are also necessary, and these must be in some measure unifying and not divisive.

Changed Significance of Membership Units. The dilemma discussed in the preceding paragraphs is made more acute by another feature of the "progress" of industrialization. That feature is the attrition of the scope of activities that come within the purview of concrete membership groups. This is a technical and somewhat more accurate way of summarizing the phenomena commonly called the "declining functions" of the family and neighborhood. The industrial system actually depends upon the small family, with its radical separation of generations and adult siblings. It also depends upon a considerable measure of residential mobility and formal group membership as opposed to informal neighborhood or community patterns and sanctions. But it is precisely these membership

---

[4] See Emile Durkheim, *On the Division of Labor in Society,* tr. by George Simpson (New York: The Macmillan Company, 1933). The first edition of this work was published in France in 1893, and the second edition, in which the diagnosis of relevance here was greatly sharpened, in 1902.

units, with their characteristic functional diffuseness, that form the "building blocks" of most societies.

The family in industrial societies is by no means without functions. Indeed, not only is the particular small-family structure functionally related to the industrial mode of productive organization, but the heightened specificity and formality of most social relations places a peculiar weight on the family as a group marked by legitimate affectional ties and broad obligations. The family, however, is subject to severe pressures because it is small and relatively isolated from broader kinship and community supports, and because it too is not immune from occupational competition and the emphasis on egoistic satisfactions.[5]

With the declining *scope* (which is not the same as declining *importance*) of membership units that encompass many aspects of personal interest and behavior, the industrial society produces a tremendous array of associations based on limited interests and characterized by highly specific forms of social relations. Some of these associations revolve around occupational interests, the outstanding example being the labor union. Despite the importance of the common interests represented, and despite the more or less conscious attempts of some leaders and members to broaden the scope of organizational activities, even labor unions are poorly equipped to provide *meaning* and social participation. Such tendencies are, at least in the United States, so meagerly supported by norms and expectations that wider participation is likely to be regarded by participants themselves as a substitute for more "normal" types of social relations.

These internal organizational features of industrial societies go far toward an explanation of the growing importance of the national state as a membership unit. The scope of state activities has increased steadily or by leaps and bounds in all industrialized economies. This trend is accounted for in part by the necessity of insuring order and maintaining interdependent relations in the face

---

[5] See Talcott Parsons, *Essays in Sociological Theory, Pure and Applied* (Glencoe, Ill.: The Free Press, 1949), Chap. XI, "The Kinship System of the Contemporary United States."

of powerful divisive forces stemming from group tensions and conflicting interests. But in all industrial societies there has been another trend scarcely noticed in most discussions. It is commonly observed that urban-industrial societies have undergone a pronounced attrition of older membership units with their extensive reciprocities, and also that established religious organizations and beliefs have been undermined by the process of "secularization." The trend usually not noticed in the same context has been the pronounced increase of emotional nationalism, of treating the national state as a sacred entity. Any definition of religion that will fit systems of organization and belief commonly recognized as religious will at the same time fit at least the more extreme types of ideological nationalism.

The heightened importance, both structurally and normatively, of the state in industrial societies is of course most readily observed in totalitarian systems. Whether of the fascist or communist variety, the totalitarian state has provided one kind of attempted solution of industrial instability. The solution has rested upon a combination of new forms of social organization and new ways of accentuating common or collective values and loyalties. The organizational innovation is the attempt to relate all groups—both those with broad and informal bonds and those with highly limited interests—in an orderly and definite way to the single, inclusive group, the state. Special occupational, territorial, and even recreational and "cultural" interests are all made subservient to an integrated system of policies and controls. A prescribed hierarchy of loyalties is actively fostered, with the pull-hauling upon the individual or small group typical of less tightly organized industrial societies reduced to a minimum. In case of doubt, the overriding loyalty to the party and state nominally settles the issue.

Viewed purely as a mode of societal organization, the modern totalitarian state is largely an outgrowth of tensions in industrial societies, and provides a sort of solution for those who maintain the ideal of the "perfectly integrated" society. Both direct and inferential evidence casts doubt on the actual achievement of integration in the full sense of emotional support. Not only is there a strong emphasis in such societies on coercion by the power holders, but also there is likely to be serious conflict within the leadership group itself. The struggle for power, the divisive force of special interests, may take less overt forms, but it is present. By virtue of the fact that the possibility of legitimate division is officially denied and that mechanisms for permitting disputes have been largely dissolved, conflicts are likely to be more fundamental and eventually disruptive of the system as a whole. Internal cohesion tends to be maintained in large measure by the device of a constant conflict orientation toward internal and external "enemies" as identified by the political authorities. The loyalty requirement is absolute and extends to all social behavior, rather than limited to national affairs or fundamental principles as such.

There is neither theoretical nor empirical basis for supposing that the totalitarian state provide a fundamental solution to the problem of stability, even if that is defined only with respect to internal order. The aggressive international policies that are apparently inherent in the ideology and structure of totalitarian systems cast further doubt on this form of solution to the tensions of industrial societies.

Competition, Mobility, Insecurity. The industrial mode of division of labor must rest in large measure upon merit judgments. Where many highly diversified skills are needed and small skill differences are important, recruitment must follow *universalistic* criteria. That is, the criteria of selection are those possible in any sector of the population and do not depend upon previously established social ties.[6] Within limits, the test of eligibility for a particular position is not lineage or regional background but technical competence. Internal to the productive and market systems, social relations are in high degree *functionally specific*. Interpersonal relations are nominally limited to those relevant to the transaction or the performance of technical duties in a complex organization. Both of these expectations are normatively sanctioned—they are regarded as *right*.

Functional specificity, which implies in most instances a tenuous,

---

[6] *Ibid.*, Chap. VIII, "The Professions and Social Structure," and Chap. IX, "The Motivation of Economic Activities."

impersonal form of social interaction, is subject to great pressure within complex organizations. As noted in an earlier chapter, the productive organization—the corporation or the local plant—constitutes a livelihood for its members, and they are in daily direct contact with small numbers of other members over considerable periods of time. The informal group, the development of ideas of "morale" and "loyalty," the sense of broad participation in a labor union—all these mark departures from strict canons of limited, segmental relations.

These same circumstances give rise to pressures on universalism. The "good fellow"—"our kind of man"—may be promoted and his more competent competitor passed by. In view of the expectation, which is ethically supported, that merit is specific and primary, inevitable tensions arise.

The tensions arising within the organization considered as an isolated entity are made more acute by "external" pressures on the productive system. Universalism and functional specificity are not and could not be the uniform norms for all social relations. Obligations that precisely depend upon established social ties and are not limited to "contractual" specifications are essential to the continuity of any social system. The most obvious case is that of the family and its functions. Children cannot be treated in terms of their economic merits, nor do the obligations of adults extend to all children indiscriminately. Affectional ties that relate only to particular persons and not to categories and types of persons are an important element of social behavior and the functioning of social systems. A major source of strain in any industrial system is the conflict between principles as they apply to concrete situations. Primary reliance on universalism and functional specificity alone would at most produce a temporary, atomistic interdependence of individuals and a system without loyalties or emotional allegiances—that is, no social system that could survive. Primary reliance on kinship ties or other particularistic relations would mean the collapse of any industrial system. But where one principle leaves off and another applies is neither uniformly clear nor uniformly observed. Thus the father who fails to provide for his children and give them the best

possible advantages for adult position is condemned, but if he secures his son's appointment to a position mainly on the basis of the
father-son relationship, he is almost equally condemned.

The strains deriving from the uncertain spheres in which particular norms are effective are further accentuated by competition
as the mode of placement and reward in the productive system.
Whether or not enterprises compete through an impersonal market,
allocation of position and reward on the basis of merit necessarily
involves competition. This elementary principle is often obscured by
a fallacious opposition of competition and cooperation. Competition
may be the effective mechanism for achievement of cooperative
goals.

Competition, however, entails hazards to social stability of at least
two kinds. The one hazard is that the several goals of competitors
supersede the common goals or functions of the activity, with resulting strain on the rules for limiting and directing competitive
activities. The second and related hazard is the frustration and insecurity fostered by competition. As Parsons has pointed out, such
insecurity is prevalent in varying degrees among different sectors
of industrial societies, but is most acute precisely where competitive
advancement is a primary orientation.[7]

The frustration and insecurity deriving from competition invites
group tensions and the diverting of aggression upon "scape-goats."
This process is certainly one of the explicit functions of the internal
"enemy" in totalitarian states, but also occurs in all industrial societies. Ethnic and "racial" groups are commonly the favorite target,
but any minority will serve if it appears in any way connected with
failure of the aggressors. Such group tensions, with their typical
emotionality, are also related to the loss of emotionally meaningful
participation in more socially recognized and regulated groups.

A final source of internal instability in industrial societies is that
of mobility, whether that of actual geographical migration or that
of occupational shifts even within the single plant or office. Mobility
is the mechanism that "frees" the individual from meaningful mem-

---

[7] *Ibid.*, Chap. XII, "Certain Primary Sources and Patterns of Aggression in
the Social Structure of the Western World."

bership groups and from participation in constituted patterns. Patterns of social conformity are of course especially effective when controls are informal, that is, the result of the opinions and suasion of those who matter to the individual. The greater the degree of occupational and residential movement in an industrial society, the less are individuals controlled through the constant reinforcement of learned behavior by the expectations of associates, neighbors, and friends. Moral judgments are typically formed early, but may be found not to fit exactly the changing situation of the mobile individual, and probably undergo attrition in any society in the absence of constant reinforcement by the expectations of persons bound to the actor by many bonds and reciprocities. The industrial society produces the phenomenon of the virtually isolated or atomistic individual—not usually as the typical case but as a representative of a significant fraction of the population. Without "roots" or clear responsibilities, such an individual is in a very real sense encouraged to pure instrumentalism in social relations, or else to grudging conformity and willingness to join movements subversive or otherwise where he really "belongs."

In sum, the impressive productive efficiency of the industrial system is secured at considerable cost to most traditional forms of social participation and allegiance. The actual experience of industrial societies raises the possibility that considerable instability is inherent, not only because change as such is institutionalized but because principles of efficiency and limited social relations are in almost constant tension with other necessary demands of the social order. New structures may appear or be deliberately created to add a measure of regularity and control of strains, but the nature of those structures is by no means clear nor is their appearance certain.

INDUSTRIALISM AND WORLD DISORDER

Industrialism has had a rough relation to nationalism at least in the sense of concomitant growth. We have noted some reasons for believing that this relation is not pure coincidence, but derives in part from social transformations inherent in the industrialization process. Numerous cases can be cited to disprove a perfect correlation between industrialization and aggressive nationalism, but the state as a political organ and as a focus of loyalties is important in all industrial societies. The sheer importance of internal political order for industrial operations provides a partial key to the functional connection. The connection is heightened by the economic bases of imperialism and the function of the state as a membership group where other groups are undermined or transformed by the industrial system.

The industrial system has increased the interdependence of all peoples everywhere, but at this level interdependence is even less of a guarantee of solidarity than within societies. Industry only assures that most of the world's peoples will be involved in national conflicts and provides the means for exceptional devastation.

Ideological imperialism, especially in the rise of the totalitarian fascist or communist state, adds a new dimension to world disorder, and the conflicting ideologies relate precisely to the organization of the industrial system. Appeals are thus made across geographical boundaries to disaffected elements in other societies. These tendencies give added support to pressures for "integration" and "order" within each social system, for loyalty becomes crucial in conflict situations.

Toleration of disputes, of voluntary associations, and of the privilege of protest, is regarded as a sign of "bourgeois decadence" in totalitarian states. Their own drive for power may seemingly confirm the allegation by making loyalty and integration the condition for survival of democratic states. This produces the paradox that "liberal" societies in order to survive may adopt repressive measures that undermine the very structural supports of those societies. The hackneyed character of the paradox does not change its importance.

It is not clear that toleration of disputes and protest is inherently a source of military weakness, as long as the form and degree of dissent do not constitute a "clear and present danger." But the near hysteria created by cases of proved and alleged treason would appear to be partially a product of internal tensions and in any event give a dim prognosis for the survival of liberalism.

Some students would suggest that in view of the growing interdependence of all societies, the essential solution to the pressing problem of world disorder is to be found in perfection of the "techniques of cooperation." [8] However, attention to techniques or mechanisms solves problems only if the ends are not in question. Cooperation is no more the solution of international issues than it is of disputes within industrial plants. The first requirement for genuine social cohesion, a requirement now of burning importance in a disorderly world, is a common set of values by which men live. Failing this requirement, and it is in all honesty not in sight, the industrial system may yet provide the means for its own destruction.

REFERENCES

DRUCKER, PETER F., *The Society: The Anatomy of the Industrial Order* (New York: Harper & Brothers, 1950).

DURKHEIM, ÉMILE, *On the Division of Labor in Society,* tr. by George Simpson (New York: The Macmillan Company, 1933).

MANNHEIM, KARL, *Power, Freedom, and Democratic Planning* (New York: Oxford University Press), especially Chap. 1, "Main Symptoms of the Crisis," and Chap. 2, "Alternative Responses to the Situation."

MAYO, ELTON, *The Social Problems of an Industrial Civilization* (Boston: Division of Research, Harvard Graduate School of Business Administration, 1945), Chaps. II and VI.

MEADOWS, PAUL, *The Culture of Industrial Man* (Lincoln: University of Nebraska Press, 1950).

PARSONS, TALCOTT, *Essays in Sociological Theory, Pure and Applied* (Glencoe, Ill.: The Free Press, 1949), Chap. XII, "Certain Primary Sources and Patterns of Aggression in the Social Structure of the Western World."

——, "Introduction," in Max Weber, *The Theory of Social and Economic Organization,* tr. by A. M. Henderson and Talcott Parsons (New York: Oxford University Press, 1947), especially V, "The Modern Western Institutional System."

——, "The Sociology of Modern Anti-Semitism," in J. Graeber and Steuart Henderson Britt, eds., *Jews in a Gentile World* (New York: The Macmillan Company, 1942), pp. 101–122.

——, "Some Sociological Aspects of the Fascist Movements," *Social Forces,* 21: 138–147, November 1942.

[8] See especially Elton Mayo, *The Social Problems of an Industrial Civilization* (Boston: Division of Research, Harvard Graduate School of Business Administration, 1945), Chaps. II and VI.

SOROKIN, PITIRIM A., *Social and Cultural Dynamics,* Vol. Three, *Fluctuations of Social Relationships, War and Revolution* (New York: American Book Company, 1937).

WARNER, W. LLOYD, and J. O. Low, *The Social System of the Modern Factory. The Strike: A Social Analysis* (New Haven: Yale University Press, 1947), Chap. X, "Blue Print of Tomorrow: General Conclusions."

Ogburn, William F., 431, **587**

Page, Charles Hunt, 590
Page, Kirby, 453
Pancoast, Omar, Jr., 467, 479
Pareto, Vilfredo, 158
Parker, Margaret Terrell, 566
Parmelee, Rexford C., 47, 48, 49, 53–54, 55, 56, 65
Parrish, John B., 516
Parsons, Talcott, 64, 186, 256, 271, 418, 424, 430, 434, 453, 454, 530, 535, 537, 580, 590, 595, 640, 642, 644, 647
Paschal, Elizabeth, 409, 414
Patterson, S. Howard, 226, 376, 386, 388, 390, 516, 590, 615, 617
Perazich, George, 132
Person, H. S., 170, 201
Petersen, Elmore, 99, 126, 153, 201
Peterson, Florence, 318, 414
Petrill, Jack, 251
Pfautz, Harold W., 573, 590
Pierson, Frank C., 318, 353
Pirenne, Henri, 39
Plowman, E. Grosvenor, 99, 126, 153, 201
Polanyi, Karl, 271, 453
Political and Economic Planning, 479, 566
Pollack, Otto, 516, 537
Pope, Liston, 548, 566
Porter, Robert W., 99
Princeton University, Industrial Relations Section, 543
Puffer, Ruth R., 505, 516

Queen, Stuart Alfred, 36

Raushenbush, Carl, 615, 617–618, 633
Reining, Henry, Jr., 632
Reynolds, Lloyd G., 257, 271, 465, 479
Rhyne, Jennings, 554, 560, 566
Rich, J. N., 251
Riegel, John W., 238, 247, 249, 251, 414
Robbins, Lionel, 591
Robie, Edward A., 353, 390
Robinson, A., 99
Rodnick, David, 294

Roe, Wellington, 308, 318
Roethlisberger, F. J., 96–97, 101–102, 103, 108, 115, 126–127, 133–134, 154, 158, 178–179, 180, 198, 201, 218, 220, 221, 223–224, 226, 261, 265, 266–267, 271, 276, 278, 279, 287, 288, 290–291, 294
Rose, Caroline Baer, 318
Rosen, Laura, 23, 39, 251
Rosen, S. McKee, 23, 39, 251
Ross, Arthur M., 353
Ross, Thurston H., 154
Rowland, James P., 409
Rubin, Ernest, 517
Ruttenberg, Harold J., 563
Ruttenberg, Stanley, 563

Saltz, Arthur, 453
Saposs, David J., 39, 317
Sargent, Noel, 66
Schlesinger, A. M., 39
Schneider, Eugene V., 202
Schulte, K. O., 268
Schumpeter, Joseph A., 633
Schurr, Sam H., 250
Schweinitz Dorothea de, 343, 352
Schwenning, G. T., 80, 81, 86, 95, 98, 409
Scoville, John, 66
Sée, Henri Eugène, 453
Seidman, Harold, 390
Selekman, Benjamin M., 307, 318, 340, 344, 353
Selznick, Philip, 99
Sharp, Malcolm, 66, 318, 393, 633
Shartle, Carroll L., 445–446, 447, 454, 479, 583
Sheldon, Oliver, 66, 99, 154, 201, 550, 566
Shepard, Herbert A., 318
Sheppard, Harold L., 197, 199, 202
Sheppard, Muriel Earley, 566
Shister, Joseph, 257, 271, 312, 318, 330, 335, 343, 346, 350, 353, 389–390, 414, 465, 479
Shlakman, Vera, 566
Shock, N. W., 517
Siegel, Irvin H., 237, 251
Sievers, Allen Morris, 453
Simmons, Leo W., 525, 537
Simons, A. M., 251, 479, 517
Simpson, George, 450, 452, 639, 647